Indicators
of Trends
in the Status
of
American Women

ABBOTT L. FERRISS

RUSSELL SAGE FOUNDATION

230 Park Avenue, New York, N.Y. 10017

1971

D1532586

© 1971 Russell Sage Foundation
Printed in the United States of America
Library of Congress Catalog Card Number: 76–153996
Standard Book Number 87154–252–8

To Ruth Sparks Ferriss

Foreword

In this volume, fourth in the Foundation's series on social indicators, Abbott L. Ferriss addresses the question of the changing status of women in the United States. Observing the recent upsurge of activities aimed at women's "liberation," Ferriss asks whether changes in the objective status of women might account for the rise of protest movements and related feminist endeavors.

The time-series data presented, which compare the relative status of men and women, do not provide sufficient evidence for explaining the new feminist activities. Though Dr. Ferriss hastens to point out the normative basis for the selection of many of his measures, the vast array of trend data presented cover a variety of life situations in which women are involved: education; marital status and fertility; labor force status; employment and income; health and recreation. In the data themselves he finds little cause for the reemergence of feminists' activities and refers to other plausible hypotheses.

An overview of the Foundation's continuing efforts to monitor the changing structure of American society was presented in the first volume of this series, *Indicators of Social Change* (1968) edited by Eleanor Bernert Sheldon and Wilbert E. Moore. Building on that general framework, Abbott

L. Ferriss has now completed three additional volumes, each collating, analyzing, and assessing data bearing on social trends: *Indicators of Trends in American Education* (1969); *Indicators of Change in the American Family* (1970); and this volume, *Indicators of Change in the Status of American Women*.

The undertaking of this series of social trend reports on the part of the Foundation was initiated in recognition of the rapid-paced change in American society and of the relative inadequacy of data and research for monitoring such changes. In the five or more years since the initiation of the Foundation's program in social indicators, the concept itself and research in the area have spiraled to national and international prominence. Our own federal statistical agencies are now planning periodic release of data on social trends. Thus, with the publication of this volume and another now in preparation, *Indicators of Change in American Health Status,* the Foundation will cease publications of basic time-series data and model indicators analyzing change.

Abbott L. Ferriss has made a seminal contribution to the nation's work in this area, providing a firm basis for continuing efforts in the analytical examination of social change.

ELEANOR BERNERT SHELDON
New York, New York
December 1970

Acknowledgments

In assembling data that originate primarily from federal government sources I have relied heavily for advice and assistance upon the individual agencies that collect, process, and interpret the data. Generous in contributing their time in response to my inquiries, and in many instances providing recent statistics prior to their publication, have been the responsible and knowledgeable civil servants of the Population Division of the U.S. Bureau of the Census; the Division of Health Interview Statistics and the Division of Vital Statistics of the National Center for Health Statistics; the Women's Bureau and the Bureau of Labor Statistics of the U.S. Department of Labor; the Bureau of Outdoor Recreation of the U.S. Department of the Interior; and the National Center for Educational Statistics of the U.S. Office of Education.

A number of librarians assisted in locating sources; particularly helpful were the staffs of the library of The Brookings Institution, the Population Reference Bureau, the Sociology Division of the Public Library of the District of Columbia, and the Library of the Business and Professional Women's Foundation.

I am particularly grateful to Ann Carmel, who assisted me in preparing the volume. Her experience in developing statistical information contributed greatly to the speed with which the volume was assembled. I wish to thank her for her attention to many statistical details, for her development of bibliographic sources, and for her untiring attention to accuracy. To Mary Ann Ferguson I am especially grateful for her patience, neatness, skill, and speed in preparing the drafts and the final text of the manuscript, as it is here reproduced.

For stimulating ideas that led to the formulation of the volume, her critical review of the manuscript and helpful suggestions for both content and presentation, I am grateful to Eleanor Bernert Sheldon of the Foundation staff. For their generosity in making the study possible, my thanks to the Trustees of the Russell Sage Foundation.

A.L.F.

Table of Contents

List of Tables

List of Figures

Notes to the Series and Data Sources

1.

Introduction

The status of women has become a topic of national interest, activated by the organizations women have formed and by the protests, confrontations and legal actions that groups of women have taken to alter their status.

As this flare of action has come somewhat unannounced upon the public, the question should be asked: Has women's status abruptly become worse? Relative to men's, is the status of women improving, declining, or standing still? Is the income of women who work improving relative to men's income? Is she better educated today than formerly? Is she more subject to some of the ills of society or less? -- the victim of attacks, or health hazards, or unwanted births out of wedlock, or being forced to be the sole breadwinner of a household? Out of despondency and alienation are women committing suicide more now than formerly? Are they breaking up their marriages more now than formerly?

What are the facts? The primary purpose of this volume is to bring together statistical evidence of trends in the status of women relative to the status of men.

From the close perspective of 1970, events of the past decade provide evidence of no compelling cause of the rise of the new feminist movement. A number of inciting forces may be mentioned but none of them appear primary. Historians of the future will have the task of sifting and sorting events to evaluate why women today have begun to be militant about changing their status. Perhaps they will find that it is not a unified movement but one that might be described as having its radical, middle, and conservative wings. Some women in the thick of the fray today are young college women, some are young housewives, some are older professional women who have been concerned over the status of women most of their lives. Certainly, historians will find that the numerous studies of women published during the Sixties had some influence upon the rational evaluation of women in the modern world, and, indeed, historians will find that the more polemic tracts of the latter part of the decade served to enlist recruits and commit them to the movement. Women who participated in the marches and confrontations for the rights of blacks undoubtedly were led to realize that the same tactics could also serve women's causes. Young college women who joined student protests against the ills and shortcomings of the establishment might have learned lessons that they could transfer to the service of the new feminist movement.

Certainly, in their discussions and rap sessions, educated young middle class women fed one
another's misgivings, one another's invidious comparisons of women's status vis-a-vis men's,
and other sources of discontent -- some undoubtedly being the same sources of discontent that
every young generation has felt and tried to resolve as part of its normal process of maturing --
and these rap sessions probably led to a few generalizations about the sources of women's unequal
status:

Many role ascriptions of the socio-cultural system impinge unnecessarily upon one's freedom
to become an individual with dignity, an individual in one's own right. Such role ascriptions
of the traditional culture, specifying what one might and might not do, prescribe women's place
in the household and family, circumscribing her with duties and obligations.

Mass culture and mass communication also have played their part, by stimulating women to
try to achieve the nearly impossible standards of pulchritude portrayed by fashion models.
Mass advertising has raised expectations of continuous rewards -- diamonds, travel, male adora-
tion, etc. -- that, in reality, could come to most women only occasionally in a lifetime.

Perhaps in their rap sessions young women also discovered -- or perhaps a future historian
will discover -- that the generation that matured after World War II, passing through high school
and college and into work or marriage, had missed something important in their learning, and
that they had not been assimilated into society as had previous generations. Imperfectly social-
ized in a fast-changing culture, the post-World War II generation may have grown up uncertain
about many things that prior generations had no reason to question.

The historian also may find that the larger size of the post-World War II generation -- some
two-fifths more numerous than ten years earlier -- both provided larger aggregates of peers for
the elaboration of a distinct culture of youth and posed a problem of socialization with which
society was ill prepared to cope.

Whether the new feminist movement arose from changed social conditions, from disenchantment
with women's role, from the prospects that protest would right their wrongs, from insufficient
socializing agencies in a fast-changing culture, or from a larger, more innovative peer group
capable of developing a "mod" culture of its own -- whatever may have been the causes, the new
feminist movement is gaining recruits, stimulating public interest, and, here and there, is
achieving a few modest gains. Civil suits are being won in women's favor; laws are being changed;
organizations are opening their doors to women; better jobs and promotions are coming to at least
some women. The historian of the future may find, however, that these gains did not satisfy or
placate members of the new feminist movement. I expect that he will find that the modest gains
in women's status coming as a consequence of women's protests will stimulate them to demand more
changes. The historian may find that the feminist movement did not quickly simmer down.

Without waiting for the historian of the future, however, we may compare the status of women
today with that of yesterday. We may compare the changing relation between women's status and

men's. Amidst the agitation for changes in the status of women, it is rationally desirable to array whatever objective evidence exists on trends in women's status: its direction of change, its rate of change, and its possible future direction.

Social indicators are gauges that tell us where we are in time on a given dimension. They are thermometers of our social temperature, so to speak. It is well to watch them, to monitor them, to sense the onset of change. They help to provide signals of the need for corrective action. In short, social indicators provide the basis for monitoring changes taking place in society.

Social scientists, however, do not agree which indicators are the most important ones to observe in order to monitor the changes of society. They have not yet reached the understanding that would enable the interpretation of a change in a statistical time series. While some labor economists may hold, for example, that an overall unemployment rate that goes much above five percent heralds a recession and calls for action, there is no such understanding about the infant mortality rate, nor the suicide rate, nor the rate of illegitimacy, nor the thousand and one statistical series that provide clues to what is happening in our society. Knowledge of the consequences of a change in an indicator within a functioning social system is the type of understanding required. Imbedded within a social system, an indicator may change as a result of other social forces, or it may signal future changes in its immediate subsystem or in the larger social system of which it is part. If the social system is understood well enough, a change in a measure in time series may then be interpreted for its import to the social system of which it is part. These critical changes are the ones to monitor.

Social norms play a part in the selection and evaluation of indicators. Maternal mortality, for example, may be viewed as an indicator of significance because death is evaluated negatively, especially death not dictated by age. Money is valued; the more income the better. Fair play and justice are norms that generally permeate our social life. Good health is desired and valued; a measure of health would provide a basis for comparing women's health with men's. If women are healthier than men, they are better off, and the quality of their lives is better. A secure family life, with supportive relatives and kin contributing to one another's welfare and well-being, is a desirable family situation. Do women enjoy a more stable family life than do men?

The preceding illustrate the role of norms in the selection of social indicators and explain the considerations that have entered into the selection of indicators to analyze the changing status of women in our society. However, the normative basis for selecting social indicators is not the only one. Consider, for example, the sex ratio. No normative consider-ations dictated that the sex ratio be chosen as a social indicator. Rather, it was chosen because it tersely summarizes a structural feature of society, a change which has implications for a number of life situations for women.

3

In sum, public interest in the status of women in American society gives rise to a need for objective information on their status. Statistical indicators provide a factual, objective basis for examining trends in the status of women on a variety of life situations in which women are involved. Ideally the social indicators that would be chosen would be those which sensitively index the significant changes affecting women. Our knowledge of the functioning of the social system being imperfect, we do not know the basis for social change well enough to select only those indicators that are crucial in determining women's status. Both the norms of society and our limited understanding of cause-effect sequences have guided the present selection of indicators on the status of women.

What can we say about the status of women in American society today? Is it or is it not improving in relation to the status of men? Here is a foretaste of some of the results of this study:

Numerically. Women are more numerous than men and their numbers, relative to men, will continue to increase, particularly in the ages above 40 years. However, they are less numerous than men in the younger ages. Immigration is now adding about one-fifth of the annual increase in the female population. Increases in widowhood and single status among older women may be expected in the future.

Education. Women do not remain in school as long as men do, but the average years of school they complete is increasing. In the future, younger women in their twenties will show a continuing increase in years of school completed. Attention to the school dropout years, 16-19 years of age, is particularly needed to improve women's educational status relative to men.

Marital Status. In the middle years of life nearly all women are married. Older women are increasingly divorced, separated, or widowed, and young women are increasingly remaining single. Young women today are not entering marriage in proportions as large as they did in the recent past. This decline in marriage among young women bears watching because of the consequences it holds for the family. Female heads of households, now about 5.4 million, have been increasing about 100,000 annually during the past decade.

Fertility. The birth rate has been declining since 1957. The birth rate for first births has declined only moderately, but higher-order birth rates, particularly the third, have declined considerably. These trends indicate that the family is likely to become smaller. While the legitimate birth rate has been declining, the illegitimate birth rate continues to increase.

Labor Force Status. Older women have been increasing in their participation in the labor force for some time, and now women in the middle years, 20-44 years of age, are doing so as well. Single women are working at about the same rates now as single men. Increasing proportions of women are expected to enter the labor force in the future. The work rates of women with children are increasing, but there is little or no evidence that the child's development is impeded because the mother works.

4

Employment Status. In most age groups women's unemployment rate is greater than men's, but there are many factors affecting the unemployment of women. It is affected adversely by some influences which do not affect men's employment -- greater part-time employment among women, a greater amount of shuttling in and out of the labor force than men, and a less consistent employment pattern through the life cycle. As women increasingly enter the more skilled and professional occupations, their unemployment rate may be expected to decline.

Income. Insofar as it is possible to equate men and women workers by education, occupation, and work experience, it appears that women are paid less than men. Furthermore, the trend is toward a more disadvantageous income position, rather than in the direction of improving women's earned income relative to men's. Many women work in women-only occupations. As they attain higher levels of education and enter occupations where they compete with men, rather than with women only, their income status is likely to improve.

Organizational Membership. Women appear to be abandoning sororal, ethnic and hereditary organizations, federated clubs, and rural life organizations. Their participation in religious-affiliated organizations is increasing, as it also is in social service clubs, public affairs groups, and the like. Organizations of women in the professions, education, recreation, and social welfare, also, are increasing in membership. These shifts in women's organizational affiliation indicates that women are discarding some of the features of the mother-homemaker role in favor of interests in the wider community. Voting is increasing among women, particularly among younger ones.

Recreation. Changes in outdoor recreation participation over the period 1960-1965 show improvements in this aspect of the quality of life. Women's average summer days participation in passive activities -- walking for pleasure and for viewing nature, sightseeing, picnicking, and the like -- increased approximately one-third in five years. Women's participation in water recreational activities also increased about as much as passive activities, but in recreation in the backwoods -- camping, hunting, hiking, and so forth -- women's participation has increased little, when compared with men's.

Health. Women are abed with illness nearly one-fifth more than men, but the average annual number of women's restricted activity days is declining. Women in low-income families are more restricted and are more likely to lose time from work than women in families with higher incomes. The incidence of acute conditions among both women and men is declining, but women still are subject to slightly more (some seven percent more) acute conditions on the average than men. The percent of women with one or more chronic conditions also is slightly greater than among men, when age is held constant. While the incidence of acute conditions is declining, the percent reporting chronic conditions is increasing. Men, however, are more subject to injuries than women.

5

Length of Life and Causes of Death. As a consequence either of the quality of their lives or of biological factors, women live considerably longer than men, on the average. Many of the illnesses which caused death in the past are becoming less and less important as hazards to life, but there are some causes of death that are not declining: arteriosclerotic heart disease, cancer of the respiratory system, suicides -- even though the increases among women are not as great as among men. As causes of death, hazards of social origin, also, are increasingly affecting women: cirrhosis of the liver, ulcers, homicides, motor vehicle accidents, and so forth.

Trends in statistical time series on these major topics, then, are the ones to be discussed in detail.

In addition to giving information on the status of women, this report presents some ideas for further analysis of the data. These suggestions, if implemented, would clarify some of the analytical difficulties which have been encountered in this study, would add to the available bases for interpreting social indicators depicting women's status and, more broadly, would increase our comprehension of the forces that generate change.

Some of the possibilities for further analysis are:

1. The assembling of information by household and/or family units, by types of families, in such a manner that probability distributions of significant social characteristics may be generated. These characteristics could be used to activate a model of the social system such that future states of the system could be forecast under various assumed rates of change of particular indicators.

2. A multivariate analysis of income, by sex, age, education, work experience, occupation, full- or part-time employment, color, and other variables, performed in successive years, to detect the changing influence of factors that contribute to income.

3. A multivariate analysis of factors contributing to health indicators, such as restricted activity days, bed disability days, hospital days, work-loss days, accidents, and so forth. The latter two suggestions could be carried out only if the assumptions of the method of multivariate analysis concerning the random selection of cases can be met.

The sources of data for most of the series presented herein are the Current Population Survey, the Health Interview Survey, The Vital Statistics of the United States, and estimates and projections of the U. S. Bureau of the Census. These surveys and records provide annual observations. Since its inception, the CPS has successively increased the refinement of its classification of data and of the tabulations it publishes and releases. Some of these series have been included, even when they covered only a short span of time. While the series extracted from these sources present much data under the status of women, the richness of detail of the Current Population Survey was not entirely utilized. Those interested in delving into the CPS for greater refinement of indices on the status of women will find the search rewarding for many topics.

The volume is organized around the major life activities or concerns of women, and the topics are arranged roughly according to these life experiences: education, marriage, fertility, work, employment, income, organizational activities, recreation, health and illness, and death. Within each chapter the major time series relevant to the topic are presented, discussed, and illustrated. References are made to the statistical data, which are presented at the end of the volume. At the end of each chapter there is a review of the social indicators discussed, with a limited number of suggestions on future monitorship of the series. Also at the end of each chapter there is a "key" to the series discussed in the chapter, placed there to assist the reader in locating the data.

In addition to the end-of-volume tables, Notes to the Series provide definitions applicable to the Series, footnotes to the tables, and other commentary on the data. The two major surveys from which much of the data are drawn, the Current Population Survey and the National Health Survey, are reviewed in two appendices. If the reader is interested in referring to the primary sources, the Notes to the Series, coupled with the Bibliography, provide references to the precise reports and page numbers where the original data may be found.

2.

Changes in the Female Population

The number of women relative to men in the population is a primary demographic factor, several important vital processes depending upon it. In assessing the trends in the status of women in American society, the magnitude of the population of women, its age distribution, the number of males in relation to females, and the volume of immigration, bear upon the underlying status of women. The number of males per 1,000 females, the sex ratio, affects the incidence of marriages, of births, and deaths. Over the recent history of the United States there have been important changes in the sex ratio, and still more significant ones can be foreseen in the future. These nationwide influences are important, but for particular ages and in particular states, cities and counties, the sex ratio may be even of greater significance, depending upon its magnitude. Similarly, the influx of female immigrants relative to men, bears upon factors that exert a moving influence upon the status of women.

The Female Population

The 1970 female population has been estimated at approximately 105 million, nearly three and one-half million more females than males. The sex ratio for the United States in 1970 is estimated at 966 males per 1,000 females.[1]/

Series A001-A060 present the male and female population by color, 1940 through 1969, in five-year age groups, as estimated by the U. S. Bureau of the Census. The Census also estimates the population by age and sex in single years of age. For illustrative purposes, the population of 18-year-old females is shown in Figure 2.1, as well as the 20-24 year old population of females by color.

The numbers in age cohorts change very slowly, usually moving in very small increments; only the births of 1946 and 1947 created a noticeable jump in the number in the annual cohort "under one year" in 1946 and 1947 (Census, 1965g). The number of 18-year-olds, for example, is affected by immigrants, as well as by age-differentiated mortality rates. The 1947 increase in births may be detected by the jump in the curve for 18-year-olds in 1965.

---

[1]/ The July 1, 1969 estimate was 103.4 million females, a sex ratio of 964 per 1,000. (Census, 1970b:12)

From 1940 to 1969, the female population has grown faster than the male population, 1.4 percent per year on the average for males as compared with 1.6 for females. The annual growth rates, however, were not uniform for all ages, as shown by the average annual rate of increase from July 1, 1940 to July 1, 1969 for total population (including armed forces overseas):[2]

	Male	Female
Under 15 years	2.0	2.0
15-25 years	1.3	1.2
25-44 years	0.6	0.7
45-64 years	1.3	1.8
65 years and over	2.2	3.1

The future average annual rate of population increase for the population as a whole, as projected by the Census Bureau, depends chiefly upon the fertility assumption one chooses. For the first five years of the decade, the varying assumptions produce annual average growth rates of 1.0 (Series D) to 1.8 (Series A), and for the second five years of the decade, annual average rates of growth of 1.1 (Series D) to 1.9 (Series A) (Census, 1967f: 4). The resulting projections for 1980 are as follows (thousands) (Census, 1967f: 58-59):

	Total	Male	Female
Series A	250,489	123,185	127,304
Series B	243,291	119,510	123,781
Series C	235,212	115,386	119,826
Series D	227,666	111,533	116,133

Whichever assumption proves correct, the population of females will continue to exceed the population of males, and the rate of growth will add 11 to 22 million females, net, to the population in the decade of the Seventies. At the moment the slower growth rate seems more probable.

The growth of the female population is shown in Table 2.1, projected to 1980.

Under the influence of changing fertility and declining mortality, the age distribution of the female population has been undergoing distinct changes. The percent of children under 15 years of age increased from 1940 to 1960, and, with the decline in fertility that began about 1957, the percent of girls in the population has been declining. It will continue to decline during the 1970s.

On the other hand, teen-age girls and younger women were a declining proportion of the female population to 1960. By 1969 they had increased to approximately 17 percent of the female population, at which level they are expected to remain until 1980.

_____

[2] Population for Alaska and Hawaii in 1940 was added to 1940 U. S. figures to make the geographic base for 1940 comparable with 1969.

Thousands of Persons
(Ratio Scale)

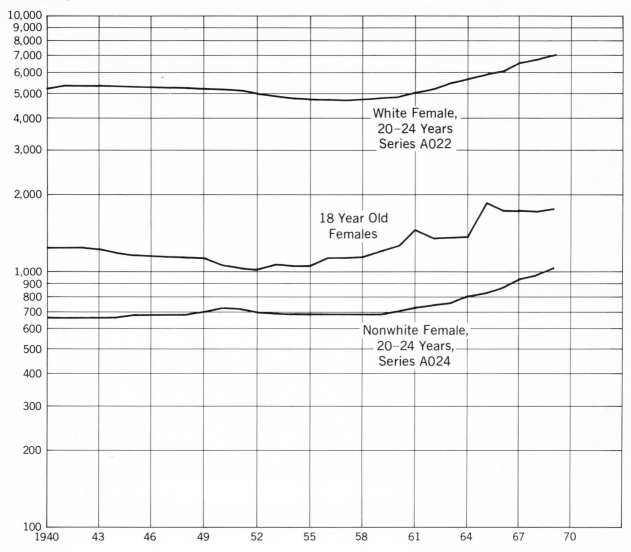

Figure 2.1 Number of Females 18 Years of Age (All Races) and 20–24 Years of Age (by Color), 1940–1969.

Table 2.1 - Age Distribution of the Total Female Population

	July 1, 1940	July 1, 1950	July 1, 1960	July 1, 1969	Projected 1975	Projected 1980
	Number (Thousands)					
All ages	65,771	76,422	91,352	103,445	111,743	119,826
Under 15 years	16,230	20,117	27,581	29,093	29,791	31,675
15-24 years	12,051	11,180	12,208	17,317	19,810	20,646
25-44 years	20,068	23,164	23,937	24,295	27,071	31,241
45-64 years	12,800	15,420	18,503	21,565	22,749	22,709
65 and over	4,623	6,541	9,121	11,175	12,323	13,557
	Percent Distribution					
All ages	100.0	100.0	100.0	100.0	100.0	100.0
Under 15 years	24.7	26.3	30.2	28.1	26.7	26.4
15-24 years	18.3	14.6	13.4	16.7	17.7	17.2
25-44 years	30.5	30.3	26.2	23.5	24.2	26.1
45-64 years	19.5	20.2	20.3	20.8	20.4	19.0
65 and over	7.0	8.6	10.0	10.8	11.0	11.3

Source: (Census, 1965g: 22-23, 42-43; 1965h: 11; 1970b: 12-13; 1967f: 59) Projections assume Series C.

Because of the decreased fertility of the 1930s, the working-age women and housekeepers -- currently 25-44 years of age -- have been declining as a percent of the female population. After 1970, however, this segment, also, is expected to begin to increase.

Older women, 45-64 years, remain a relatively constant proportion of the female population, while aged and retired women, 65 years and over, have been increasing and are projected into the Seventies as a small but increasing part of females in the population.

While in both absolute numbers and rate of growth, the female population has exceeded the male, changes are occurring in the balance between the sexes. The balance between the sexes has been shifting in two directions -- going in one direction among the younger ages, and in the opposite direction among the older age groups. This will next be discussed.

The Sex Ratio

The number of males per 1,000 females at various age levels is affected by the biological genesis of the sexes, by net migration, and by differential mortality between the sexes by age. Combined, these forces have vastly altered the sex ratio by age during the thirty years since 1940. Census Bureau projections anticipate present trends will continue for most of the age levels, at least until 1980. Figure 2.2 presents the sex ratio by age for 1940, 1969, and a projection to 1980.

12

Males per 1,000 Females

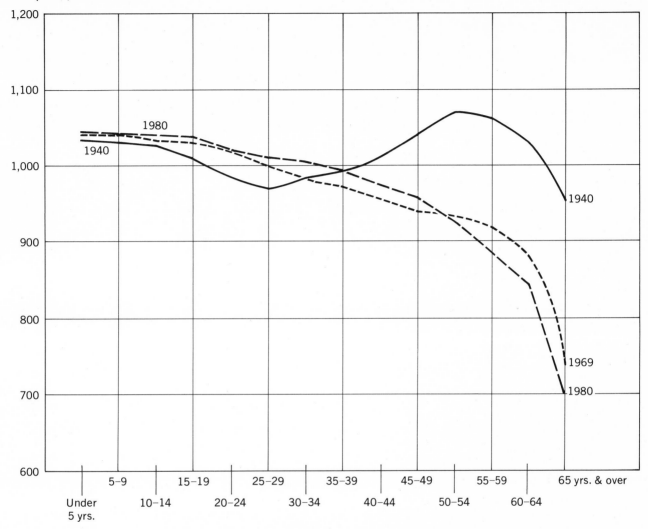

Figure 2.2 The Sex Ratio by 5-Year Age Groups, 1940, 1969, and Projected 1980, Series A062-A075.

The sex ratio of approximately 1,050 per 1,000 at birth decreases under the impact of infant mortality, which is always higher for males. In 1940 the sex ratio of the age group under five years of age was slightly more than 1,030. As infant mortality has improved (Series L033-L036) the sex ratio has increased, a trend likely to continue.

In their occupations and their leisure pursuits, men are subject to greater hazards than women. Their higher mortality rates in 1940 rendered them less numerous than females, by the time they were 20-24 years of age. By 1969, however, this differential had advanced to the 25-29 years of age group. Census Bureau projections to 1980 place it in the 35-39 year age bracket. This interesting consequence of the improving mortality rate, affected slightly by immigration, has produced and will continue to produce a surplus of men in relation to women under approximately 40 years of age. The trend in the approximate age when the number of females exceeds males, by single years of age, was 16 in 1946, 20 in 1957, and has increased eight years, to 28 years, during the dozen years following 1957.

In 1940 the number of men exceeded women in ages 40 through 65 years, the middle to late ages of life. While the mortality rates among men in these ages have declined, the mortality rates among women have declined even more, e.g., Series L057-L064. This, coupled with the persistent excess of female immigrants over males (Figure 2.3), has caused the sex ratio for these ages to decline. The decline in the sex ratio, shown in the graph for 1969, is expected, in Census Bureau projections, to reach its nadir about 1980.

These shifts in the balance between the sexes by age have produced and will continue to produce consequences of undeniable social importance, affecting marital status and marriage, birth, and death rates.

Marital Status. The median age of brides is about two years younger than the median age of grooms (NCHS, 1969g: 1-10). If this differential continues, one may expect widowhood or single status among older females to increase, leading to increasing proportions of females in the older ages who live alone and who must support themselves, live off of savings or social security. The following percentages of females were estimated to be single, divorced, or widowed in March 1969; see (Census, 1970d: 11) and Series C081-C160:

	Percent
35-39 years of age	12
40-44 years of age	14
45-64 years of age	24
65 years and over	65

Over the long term, these percentages have decreased slightly and over the short term they appear to be stable or are increasing very slightly. With the sex ratio decreasing among the older population, particularly those above 40 years of age, and with the traditional custom of a bride marrying a man older than herself, the consequence would appear to be a future increase in single status among older women.

14

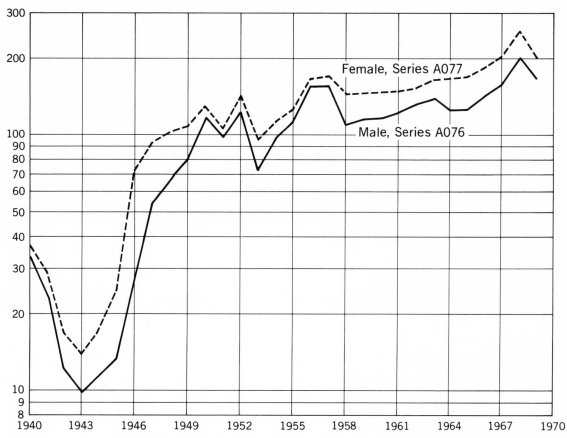

Figure 2.3 Immigrants Admitted into the United States, by Sex,
Year Ended June, 1940–1969.

However, there is some evidence that women are increasingly likely to marry men younger than themselves. The percent of women who marry younger men remained practically stable from 1951 to 1965, increasing only from 11.9 percent to 12.1 percent. Over this same period, on the other hand, the percent of women marrying younger men increased among all ages, except brides 26 to 29 years of age and those over 65. As shown below, the tendency to marry a younger man increases to about age 29 years, and then declines as the bride's age increases.[3/] The percent marrying a younger man reaches a high of about 30 percent among females 28 and 29 years of age:

Age of Bride	Percent marrying younger men	
	1951	1965
Total	11.9	12.1
18 years	1.0	1.9
19 years	3.7	6.5
20 years	6.6	8.4
21 years	8.1	10.1
22 years	13.8	15.1
23 years	17.9	20.4
24 years	21.8	23.1
25 years	24.4	24.6
26 years	27.4	26.4
27 years	29.5	28.5
28 years	30.6	28.1
29 years	31.0	30.5
30-34 years	23.5	23.8
35-44 years	17.9	18.2
45-54 years	15.5	20.0
55-64 years	14.6	17.7
65 years and over	20.7	17.7

Source: (VS, 1954b: 78), (NCHS, 1968d: 1-22).

The above-described trend, along with the decreasing sex ratio among the older ages, implies future increases in the coupling of brides with younger grooms. If this becomes an established marriage custom, the increase in the single state of older women, previously discussed, would be less likely to occur. Such a change, also, has economic and familial implications for housing, maintenance, and care of the aged, changes that could have extensive effects.

Female Immigrants

In a recent year, 1967, 1.7 million females were born (NCHS, 1969a: 1-18) and 0.8 million died (NCHS, 1999e: 1-46). Approximately 204,000 female immigrants arrived from foreign countries (Series A077). There were some U. S. females who emigrated with the intention of being away permanently or for an extended period of time, but the number is not known.[4/] The net addition to the 1967 population was thus approximately 1.1 million females.

3/ In each instance the data represent the Marriage Registration Area, 21 States in 1951 and 38 States plus the District of Columbia in 1965. In computing percentages, some cells had to be suppressed because the determination of the number of brides who were older within that cell could not be made. In removing these cells from both the numerator and denominator, however, the estimate of the percentages was not affected appreciably.

4/ Donald Bogue (1959: 359) has estimated that the annual number of emigrants now is approximately 7 percent of the immigrants. Upon this basis there are about 16,000 females emigrating annually.

The approximately 200,000 female immigrants who enter the population of United States in a year are no minor addition; in 1967, immigrants comprised about one-fifth of the net increase in the female population. Over the past ten years, the ages of these female immigrants have not been markedly different from the ages of the female immigrants, presented below. The distribution of the estimated total U. S. female population is shown for comparison:

	Female immigrants FY1969	U. S. female population Jan. 1, 1969
	Percent	Percent
Under 5 years	7.9	8.7
5-19 years	25.5	28.5
20-24 years	15.8	7.8
25-29 years	13.9	6.4
30-44 years	22.6	17.1
45-59 years	9.9	16.5
60 and over	4.4	15.0

Nearly half of the female immigrants were below 25 years of age, constituting an additional load on the educational system as well as a youthful and energetic addition to the population. About 45 percent of immigrant females, too, were single.

Compared with the host population of females, the immigrants are more heavily concentrated in ages 20 to 44. Immigrants are proportionately fewer in the younger ages and in the older ages than the resident female population.

The occupations of female immigrants are not published, but rough estimates suggest that approximately 30 percent are children or students under 20 years of age and that over one-third are housewives (37 percent in the year ended June 1969). The remainder, approximately one-third, or about 65,000 in 1969, then, probably seek to enter the labor force. This was approximately 5 percent of the increment in the female labor force from 1968 to 1969.

Prior to 1930, males comprised one-half to seven-tenths of immigrants almost every year. Since 1930, however, females have predominated (Census, 1960e: 62). Particularly during the years when World War II veterans returned to the United States, bringing foreign born wives, did female immigrants enter in larger numbers than males, comprising from two-thirds to three-fourths of those arriving at that time. In the year ended June 1969, 54 percent of the immigrants were female, a sex ratio of 857 males per 1,000 females.

In summary, female immigrants come in larger numbers than males, by approximately one-fourth, and they have been more numerous than male immigrants since 1930 (Census, 1960e: 62). They especially add to the young and the middle-aged female population, up to 40 years of age, and undoubtedly contribute to reducing the sex ratio in these ages. Occupationally, however, female immigrants are a small part of the annual female addition to the labor force. As approximately 200,000 foreign born females continue to enter the United States annually, they will become an increasing demographic influence in national life.

One-fourth more female immigrants come to the United States annually, than males. Approximately one-third of them come independent of family, that is, they are adults and choose the

United States over the country of their birth. This must imply a favorable evaluation of their prospective status in the United States vis-a-vis their home country. If the flow of female immigrants decreased, would it mean that their prospects were better elsewhere, than in this country?

The demographic aspects of immigration and the public policy issues involved have been extensively studied and discussed (e.g., Hutchinson (ed), 1966). The brief review of trends in immigration here indicates a sizeable in-flow of young adult females. They are now coming in numbers large enough to produce a cumulative effect upon the labor force and, perhaps, upon the annual number of births.

Female Aliens Naturalized

Not all immigrants become citizens, but, nearly 100,000 of them do annually, more than half of them females (Series A092-3). Immediately following World War II, more males were naturalized than females, but beginning in 1948 and continuously since then, naturalized females annually have exceeded males.

Most females who are naturalized are married, approximately three-fourths of them. About one-fifth are single. The percent of naturalized females who are single has increased since 1957, while the percent married and widowed has declined slightly.

The median ages of females who are naturalized are now about one year younger than newly-naturalized males, but the age of both naturalized males and females has been declining since 1960.

As a rough indicator of the naturalization process, the number of women naturalized is approximately one-third of the immigrants who entered the United States four or five years earlier. The marked increase in immigrants, beginning around 1965 and continuing to increase to 1968, is likely in time to increase the number naturalized. Series A092-A100 present these data, but they are not illustrated.

Summary of Indicators

An abrupt increase in the size of an annual population cohort over the preceding ones, such as occurred in 1946 and 1947, or any abrupt decrease in size, are significant demographic changes, with implications affecting other institutions, such as marriage, the labor force, etc., extending into the future.

The changing age distribution of the female population moves gradually and predictably. The decade of the Seventies will see increases in the population size of working age women (25-50 years) and in the population of females over 65 years, while the proportion of females under 15 years of age will decline.

The sex ratio is a useful measure of the net consequences of various demographic factors -- mortality, migration, etc. It will continue to decline for the population in the older ages and to increase for the working age population, 25 to 50 years. As a result of the interaction

18

between the male/female ratio, the age at first marriage, and the mortality rate, increases in widowhood or single status among older females may be expected. A critical indicator is the percent of brides who marry men younger than themselves. An increase in this indicator will diminish widowhood of that generation.

Female immigrants are adding a significant increment of young girls and women 20-40 years of age to the population, accounting for as much as one-fifth of the annual net population increase in females. The age distribution of female immigrants and of newly naturalized women are series of continuing importance, due to the increasing size of the annual quota entering the United States. The consequences of such an influx needs to be observed and its influence upon marriage, birth, and other vital processes assessed.

Key to Series Discussed in Chapter 2

Population, by age, color, sex	A001 - A060
Sex ratio, by age, projected to 1990	A061 - A075
The number of immigrants and their age distribution, by sex	A076 - A091
Naturalized aliens, by sex, their sex ratio, marital status and median age	A092 - A100

3.

Trends in the Educational Status of Women

In an open-class society such as ours, education has become the means of upward social mobility, the achievement of more prestigious occupational positions, higher income, and higher status. Measures of the level of education attained, then, are prime social indicators. An increase in the educational level may be expected to give rise to an increase in occupational status, income, and other desirable qualities.

To examine the status of women on this important social indicator, measures of attainment of the population of various ages are here reviewed, ages that reflect a particular educational level at the earliest possible point in the life cycle. Cumulative curves of educational level for selected years are next examined for a single age group, the 20-24 year olds. The output of the educational system -- graduates and degrees, by sex -- are then surveyed across time. Since the educational system consists of graded steps which typically the student passes through in sequence for delimited periods of time, the rates of movement through the system may be used to compare the status of women with the status of men. Before assessing educational attainment, however, school enrollment of females by school level is analyzed, paying particular attention to the transitional ages of 18 and 19 years.

. . . . .

School Enrollment by Level and Age

Enrollment by age and grade and enrollment rates are sensitive indicators of the state of the educational system. Details by single years of age and single years of school are regularly available only for decennial census years. As a surrogate, enrollment here is presented for groups of ages by sex and color (Series B001-B040). Age, color and sex are combined with school level in Series B041-B128.

There are two ways of examining enrollment. One is the enrollment rate during a time period, the approach of Series B001-B128. The other is the retention experience of successive age cohorts. The latter is most effectively pursued through the use of enrollment information

on successive single years of age, acquired each year. Even with data in groups of ages, however, the cohort approach can be quite successful (Duncan, B., 1968: 601-674).[1]

In assessing the magnitudes of student enrollment, both the rate of enrollment and the size
of the age cohort affect the aggregates. While nearly all youth from six years to 15 are
enrolled in school, the rates of enrollment decline for ages above 15. The historical record
shows an increasing rate of enrollment, however, for all ages. The school-age population by age
and sex is presented in (Ferriss, 1969: 412-417) and by single year of age, color and sex in the
Census Bureau sources cited.

The magnitude of the birth cohort also affects the enrollment. It reached a peak in 1961,
when 4,268,326 births were recorded, and has been declining since then. This demographic effect
may also be seen in the decline in the size of the "under 5" age group, Series A005-A008, and
Series B041-B052, showing the kindergarten and school enrollment for children 5-6 years of age.

The percents of the population of various ages enrolled in school, by color and sex, are
presented as Series B001-B040. Although not illustrated, the trend in these statistics show
that attendance rates have improved for all age groups, from 1954 to 1968.

Almost all the population six to 15 years of age are in school. In older ages, however,
enrollment rates begin to fall off. By the 18th and 19th year, white females are enrolled some
20 percentage points less than white males. As aging continues, enrollment rates decline, but
the differences become smaller between male and female in each of the color categories after the
age of 21. In particular, the nonwhite female rate in the older ages resembles the nonwhite
male rate more closely than is the case among whites.

In all cases there has been an improvement in enrollment rates, an increase particularly
marked among nonwhites up to 21 years during the 1960s.

Enrollment of 18 and 19 Year Olds

Trends in the percent of 18 and 19 year olds are presented in Figure 3.1, to illustrate
enrollment rates, Series B017-B020. These are the ages immediately following the completion of
high school -- the time of transition to work, to marriage or to college. Large numbers do not
continue in school. The percent dropoff in the enrollment rate for 18-19 year olds (as compared
with 14-15 year olds) is heavy, a reduction in 1968 of from 34 to nearly 54 percentage points
among these sex/color groups. An improvement in retention across this hiatus would do much to
increase the educational attainment of a cohort. What has been the trend?

Figure 3.1 presents a three-year moving average of the percent of persons 18 and 19 years
old enrolled in school, by color and sex. The CPS sample for these categories are numerically

---

[1] A partial analysis of enrollment trends, without reference to sex, has been made in another
     volume (Ferriss, 1969: 17-67, Series A27 to A37).

Percent

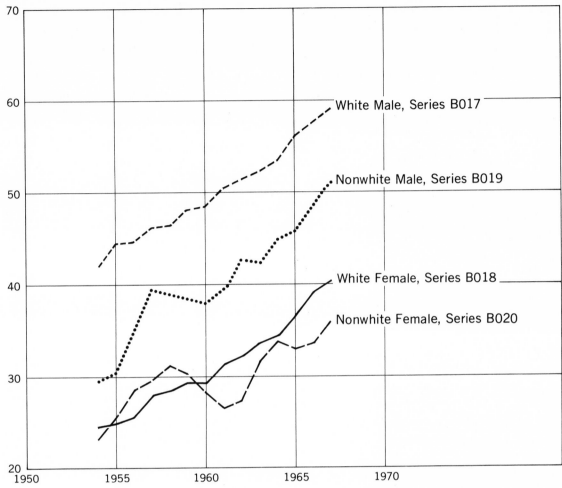

White Male, Series B017

Nonwhite Male, Series B019

White Female, Series B018

Nonwhite Female, Series B020

Figure 3.1 Percent of Persons 18–19 Years of Age Enrolled in School, by Color and Sex, 1954–1967. (Three-year moving average)

small, particularly the nonwhite, creating year-to-year distractions in the trend due to sampling error. The three-year moving average reduces this effect.[2/]

Across the span of the 13 years shown in Figure 3.1, enrollment rates for males, both white and nonwhite, have continuously increased. Since about 1955, the rates for females also have changed, the two color groups increasing in unison.

While the enrollment rate for nonwhite males is persistently below that of white males (approximately seven to 12 percentage points), the rates for nonwhite females have been approximately the same as the white female rates. Females, however, have considerably lower rates than males, reflecting both the traditional maxim that females do not need as much education as males, and the requirements of marriage and family life that keep females at home rather than in school or at work.

While the trend in enrollment of white females is the same as nonwhite females of these ages, the level of school at which they are enrolled is considerably different. Nonwhite females are much more likely to be enrolled below the college level than are white females. The same is true of male enrollment rates, as shown in Table 3.1.

Table 3.1 - Enrollment Rates by Level of School, for 18 and 19 Year Olds, by Sex and Color, October 1968

| | Percent enrolled | | |
	Total	Below college	In college
Male			
White	61.5	14.9	46.6
Nonwhite	53.5	31.0	22.5
Female			
White	41.3	7.1	34.3
Nonwhite	40.7	14.9	25.8

Source: (Census, 1969: 10-11).

Educational Attainment by Age

A change in the educational attainment of the population may first be detected when a change occurs in the rate of enrollment of an age group of the population. For example, an

_____

2/ The greater variation, year to year, in the nonwhite trends, as compared with the white, is a consequence of the smaller sample size and consequent larger sampling error in the non-white rates than in the white. The white rates, however, are subject to sampling errors of some magnitude, since the population base of the white age-sex group is only approximately 2 1/2 to 3 million over the 14-year period. In other words, the apparent annual fluctuations are not real, and the trend is better represented by a three-year moving average, shown in Figure 3.1. The sampling errors of 18-19 year old enrollment for October, 1968, are, as follows:

	Base (Total population) (000)	Percent enrolled	1 Standard error
Male			
White	2,710	61.5	1.08
Nonwhite	422	53.5	2.0
Female			
White	2,981	41.3	2.0
Nonwhite	473	40.7	1.08

Source: (Census, 1969m: 10-11).

24

increase in the percent of the 15-year-olds enrolled in school may foretell an increase three years later in high school graduates, and, eventually, an increase in the percent of an older age group who at least will have graduated from high school.

Similarly, another advance indicator of educational attainment is the percent completing a level of schooling in the age group immediately older than the modal age of enrollment for that educational level. For example, the modal age enrolled in the fourth year of high school is 17. The percent of the 18-year-olds completing four years or more of high school, then, is an indicator of the minimum educational attainment of this cohort at a future age and year. The modal year cannot always be used, because the Census data are not always classed in single years of age. The following provide advance indicators of changes in educational attainment:

> At least four years of high school: 18-19 year olds,
>
> Any college: 20-24 year olds,
>
> Four or more years of college: 25-29 year olds,
>
> Five or more years of college: 30-34 year olds.

Trends in these indicators will now be reviewed.

At Least Four Years of High School: 18-19 Year Olds. White females and nonwhite males have shown a slight improvement in this indicator since 1965 (Series B145-B156). White males and nonwhite females, however, have declined almost as much as they have advanced in recent years. The greater year-to-year variation exhibited by the curves for nonwhites in Figure 3.2 is partly explained by the larger sampling error in the data for nonwhites. The data show that educational attainment of this age group is affected more by color than by sex, but within color groups, females attain educational levels superior to males.

Any College, 20-24 Year Olds (Series B181-B188). In Figure 3.3 the marked increase among color-sex groups of these ages appears to have reached a plateau in 1968. This indicator should be monitored to determine whether the change in the rate of change implied in the figure continues or whether the upward drift of the long-term trend continues. The data exhibit more of a color difference than a sex difference in college attendance.

Four or More Years of College, 25-29 Year Olds (Series B217-B220). Figure 3.3 displays the generally increasing trend in the percent of 25-29 year olds, by sex and color, who have attended college four or more years. Dips in each of these curves at some time during the past five years by 1969 had recovered their former levels. The nonwhite male at present is increasing at a lower rate of increase than the other groups. However, the nonwhite female of 25-29 years shows the lowest standing, while the white male shows the highest percent of this age group receiving four or more years of college.

Five or More Years of College, 30-34 Year Olds (Series B253-B256). Representing graduate and professional educational levels beyond the customary four years of college, this indicator was less than 0.05 percent of each color-sex group prior to 1957 (Figure 3.3). Only after that date did the Census Current Population Survey sample begin to evidence differentiation among

25

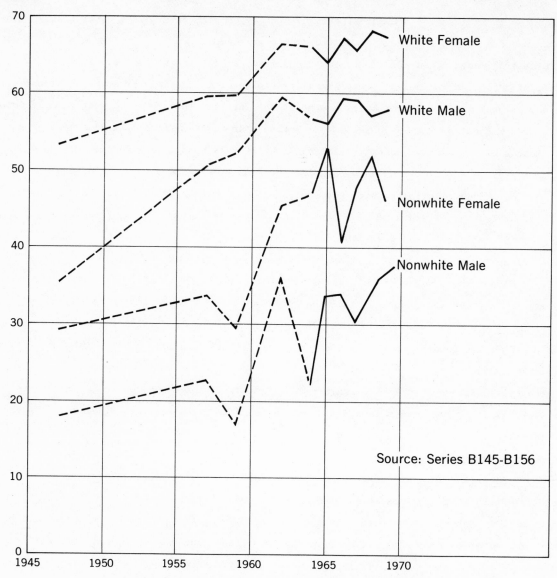

Figure 3.2 Percent of Persons Aged 18–19 Years having Four Years of High School or More, 1947, 1957, 1959, 1962, 1964–1969.

Percent

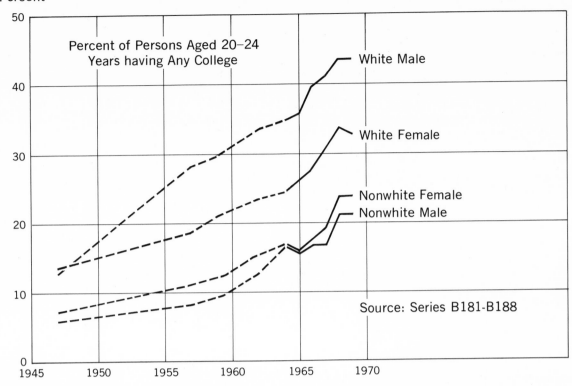

Percent of Persons Aged 20–24
Years having Any College

White Male

White Female

Nonwhite Female
Nonwhite Male

Source: Series B181-B188

Percent

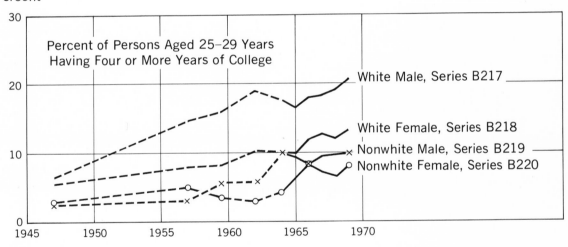

Percent of Persons Aged 25–29 Years
Having Four or More Years of College

White Male, Series B217

White Female, Series B218
Nonwhite Male, Series B219
Nonwhite Female, Series B220

Percent

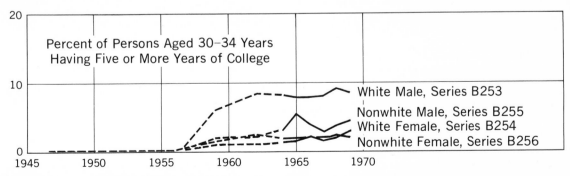

Percent of Persons Aged 30–34 Years
Having Five or More Years of College

White Male, Series B253

Nonwhite Male, Series B255
White Female, Series B254
Nonwhite Female, Series B256

Figure 3.3 Educational Attainment at Specified College Levels
by Three Age Groups, 1947, 1957, 1959, 1962, 1964–1969.

the four color-sex groups presented here. This indicator clearly presents the differences among the sexes in higher educational attainment, and illustrates their persistence. As revealed by other evidence on sex differences (See, for example Series B511-B513 on degrees), the lower percentages of women completing advanced college training and receiving advanced degrees indicates an even wider discrepancy between the sexes. According to these indicators, only the white male has made any notable advance since 1957 in higher levels of educational attainment.

The Lower End of the Educational Spectrum: Less Than Five Years Schooling, 18-19 Year Olds. Series B385-B388 (not illustrated) present the percent of 18-19 year olds who have completed less than five years of schooling, a level generally accepted as functionally illiterate. The most notable decline in this index has been among nonwhite males, who registered 19 percent on this measure in 1947 and now (1969), about four percent. The percentages of the other color/sex groups have dwindled to very near zero, considering the effect of the sampling error. Only among nonwhite males is there room for improvement.

To summarize the preceding sections, the indicators show the strong influence of color on educational attainment. When examined at the conclusion of high school, females both white and nonwhite hold the superior status within their color group. In the "any college" group, however, the nonwhite female is higher in educational attainment than the nonwhite male, but the white female is lower than the white male. In the remaining higher educational levels, larger proportions of males than females have achieved advantageous educational status.

Cumulative Curves of Educational Attainment, the 20-24 Year Old Group

Another approach to understanding the changing educational status of women consists of examining the change in a summary measure of educational attainment for each color/sex group in a single age category. The 20-24 year olds were chosen for this study. The median years of school completed is frequently used as a summary measure of educational attainment, but instead of it was used the proportion of the total area under a cumulative curve of the percent having attained the several levels of education. For further discussion of this procedure, see (Ferriss, 1969: 216-219) and (Folger and Nam, 1967: 147).[3]

Figures 3.4-3.7 illustrate the cumulative distributions for each color/sex group. The percentages, presented as Series B161-B192, were cumulated from the highest educational level to the lowest. Only four years (1947, 1957, 1962 and 1967) are presented in order to illustrate the major changes without imposing an unnecessarily confusing graph upon the reader.

Each figure illustrates the change in attainment of one color/sex group, the space between the lines being the gain, one period to the next, across two decades.

---

[3] The method of computing the area under the curve was the simple one of counting unit areas on graph paper. A computational formula, however, would simplify the calculations, if large numbers of them were required. The method for computing the annual rate of change was from (Census, 1966e: 115 ff.).

Cumulative Percent

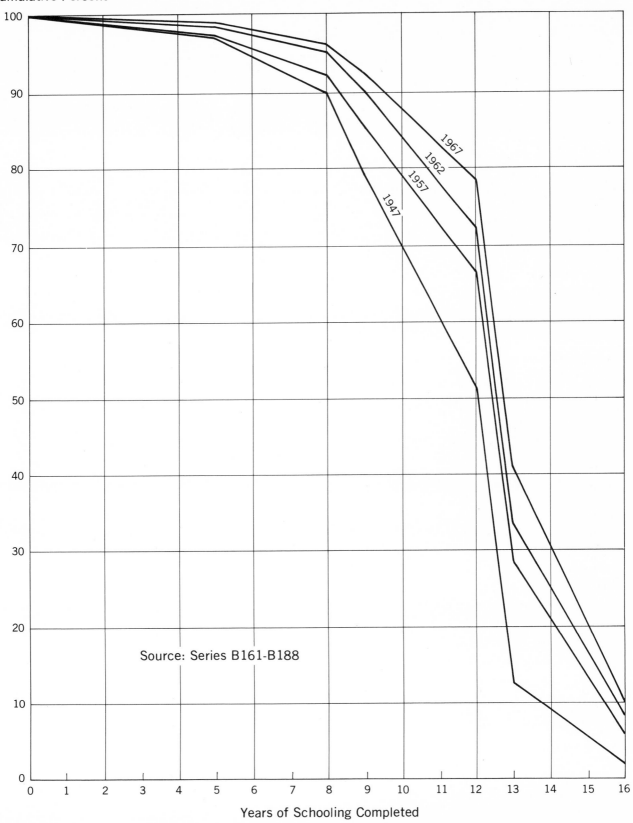

Years of Schooling Completed

Figure 3.4 Cumulative Percentage Curves of Educational Attainment of White Males 20 through 24 Years of Age, 1947, 1957, 1962, 1967.

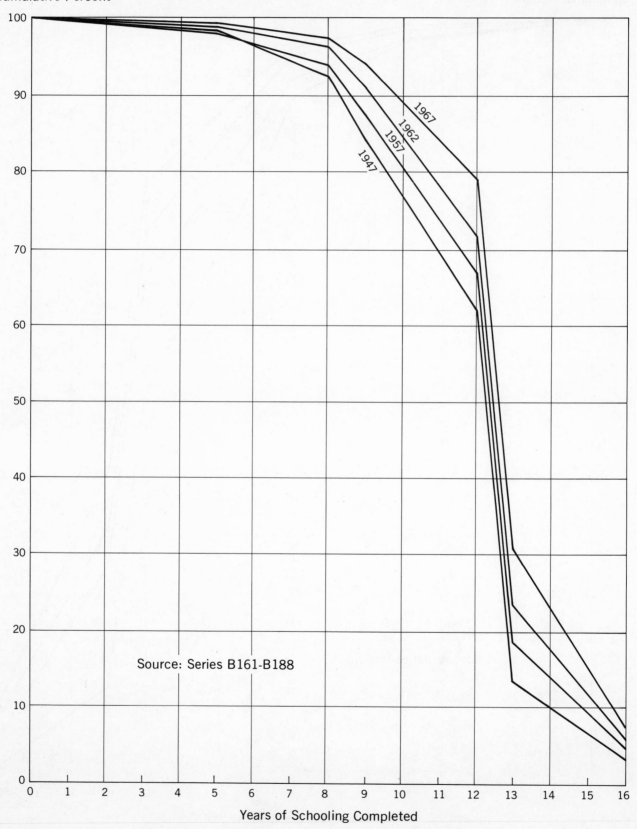

Cumulative Percent

Years of Schooling Completed

Source: Series B161-B188

Figure 3.5 Cumulative Percentage Curves of Educational Attainment
of White Females 20 through 24 Years of Age, 1947, 1957, 1962, 1967.

Cumulative Percent

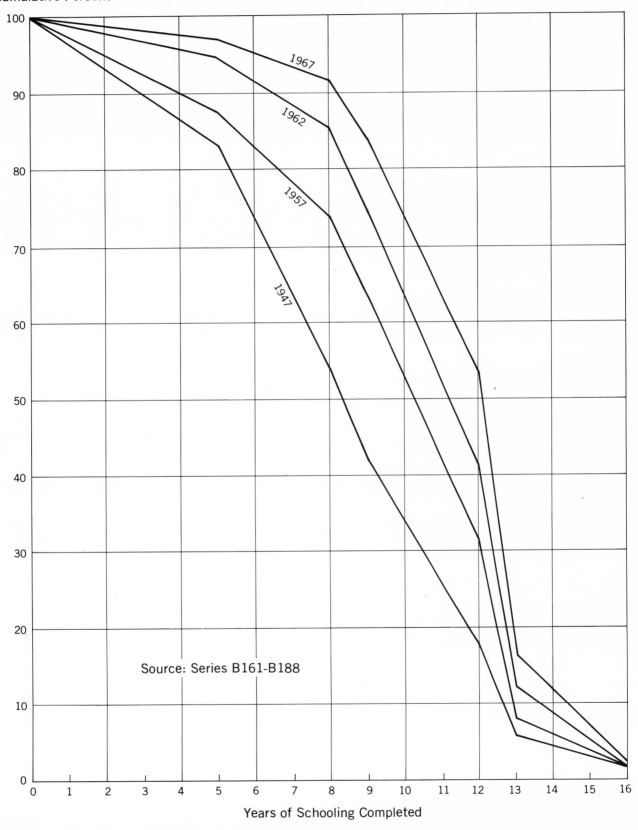

Years of Schooling Completed

Source: Series B161-B188

Figure 3.6   Cumulative Percentage Curves of Educational Attainment of Nonwhite Males 20 through 24 Years of Age, 1947, 1957, 1962, 1967.

Cumulative Percent

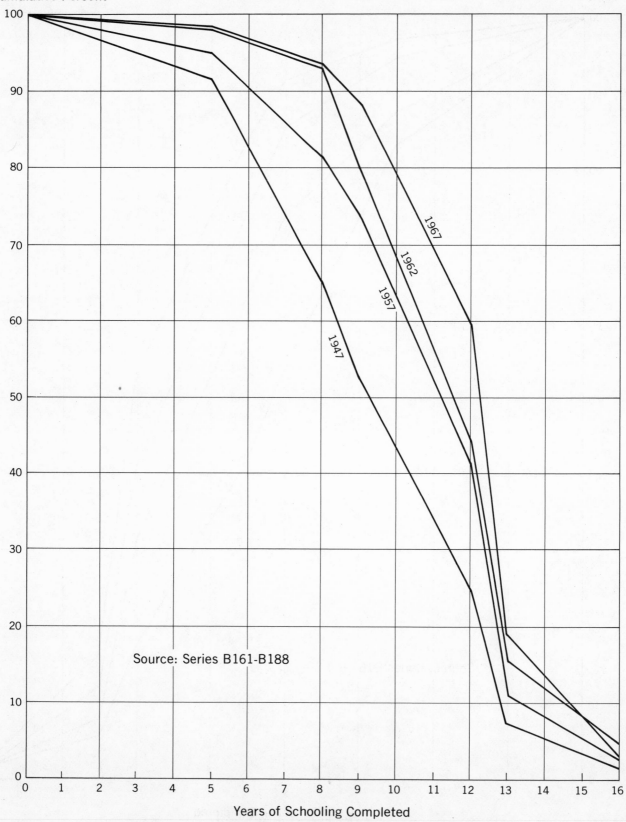

Years of Schooling Completed

Figure 3.7 Cumulative Percentage Curves of Educational Attainment of Nonwhite Females 20 through 24 Years of Age, 1947, 1957, 1962, 1967.

Summary statistics from the charts, however, present the actual change more precisely.
Table 3.2 shows that white females 20-24 years of age were better educated in 1947 than white
males of the same age, but that by 1957 white males had surpassed them and since then have maintained a slight superiority. Nonwhite females 20-24 years of age, on the other hand, have maintained educational levels superior to nonwhite males since 1947, but the difference between them
has been considerably reduced.

Table 3.2 - Areas Under Cumulative Curves of Educational Attainment and Their Rates of Change,
20-24 Year Old Population, by Sex and Color, 1947, 1957, 1962 and 1967

| | White | | Nonwhite | |
	Male	Female	Male	Female
Percent of area under cumulative curve:				
1947	69.1	72.1	51.2	57.2
1957	74.4	74.0	59.2	65.3
1962	77.4	76.1	66.3	68.9
1967	78.6	77.6	70.7	71.6
Annual rate of change in area under curve:				
1947 to 1957	+0.75	+0.25	+1.45	+1.43
1957 to 1962	+0.77	+0.60	+2.24	+1.07
1962 to 1967	+0.28	+0.37	+1.30	+0.80

Source: Figures 3.4-3.7.

The annual rate of change of the percent of the total area that is under the cumulative
curve gives further insight into trends in educational attainment. While the measure for nonwhite males moved ahead faster, 1947 to 1957, the rate of change in other years was also greater
among males than the corresponding female rates. In the most recent period shown, 1962 to 1967,
the rate of change has declined. For each period, however, the rate of change for the male group
was greater than that of the female. However, there was a lower rate of change for white males
to 1967 when compared with white females. As each of these measures approaches closer to a
maximum, the rate of change may be expected to proceed at a slower pace.

Earned Degrees

Earned degrees provide a continuing annual measure of the educational attainment of men and
women at three levels of degrees (Series B481-B488). Figure 3.8 presents the curves for each of
the three major degrees by sex. In each category, the number of males receiving degrees exceeds
the number of females. During this period the number of males per 100 females in the appropriate
ages for college graduation, 20-24 years, was changing from less than unity to more than unity
(See Chapter 2 on the Sex Ratio and Series A061-A075).

After World War II, the number of degrees granted greatly increased but by 1954 or 1955
the number returned to a normal level. Beginning at various times after 1960, it will be
noticed, degrees granted to females began to increase at a faster rate. This is illustrated by

Number (ratio scale)

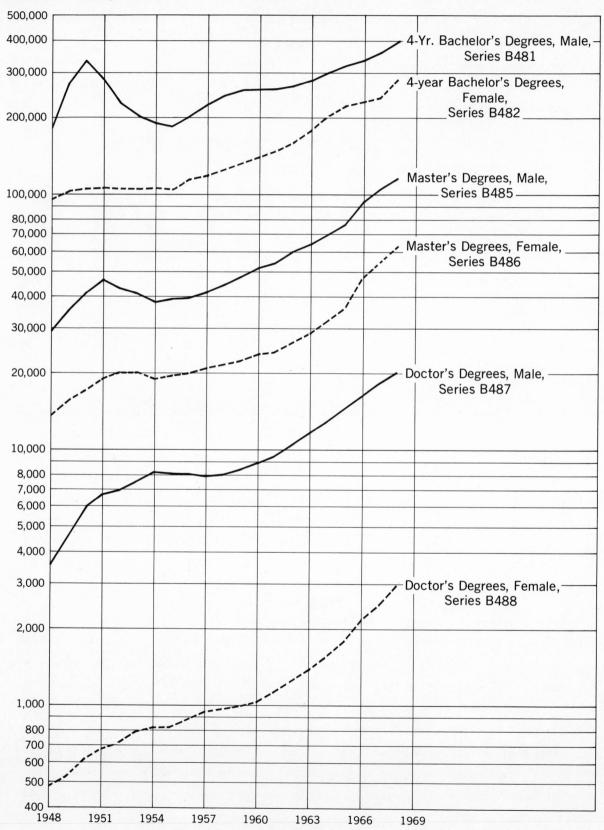

Figure 3.8 Earned Degrees Conferred, by Level of Degree and by Sex, 1948–1968

the steeper angle in the ratio curves for degrees granted to females when compared with those granted to males for the same type of degree. In spite of this upturn around 1965, the number of degrees granted to females will not soon equal the number granted to males. The trend in the "sex ratio" of the three levels of degrees since 1948 is presented in Figure 3.8, and Series B511-B513.

A sex ratio of 100 represents an even split between males and females. The value in excess of 100 represents the percent of additional degrees that would have to be granted to females to be equal to the number granted to males. For example, in 1968 the sex ratio of first level degrees (bachelor's and first professional degrees) was 140.9. If there had been 40.9 percent more degrees granted to females, the number granted to females would have been equal to the number granted to males, and the sex ratio would have been 100.

With this basis for interpretation, it is quite clear (Figure 3.9) that the number of bachelor's and first professional degrees granted to females has made rather rapid strides since 1958, but a two-fifths increase in degrees granted to females still is necessary to gain equality with males. In 1968 women received 42 percent of bachelor's and first professional degrees granted.

The status of women in attaining master's degrees had reached approximately the same point in 1968 that females had attained in bachelor's degrees eight years earlier. In 1968, 36 percent of master's degrees were granted to women.

While even more rapid changes have been made in doctor's degrees, particularly since 1964, the discrepancy, males to females, in doctor's degrees will not soon achieve equality. In 1968 females received 13 percent of doctor's degrees.

Grossly, the sex ratio of degrees by level appears to be a sensitive indicator of the progress of females toward equality with males. These indicators are particularly critical, since higher educational degrees represent credentials for occupational achievement. Such indicators as these may also be computed for each field of study.

While the ratio chart (Figure 3.8) illustrates the changes that have taken place in the rate of change in the number of degrees granted to males and females, Figures 3.10 and 3.11 present the actual percent change of one year over the preceding year (Series B489-B496).

Figure 3.10 shows the shifts in the rate of change of four-year bachelor's degrees. The rate of degrees granted to men after World War II veers widely. The rate of change in degrees granted to females was much steadier by comparison, and with considerable fluctuation, generally has been increasing since about 1955. Since 1959, the rate of change in bachelor's degrees granted to females has exceeded the rate of change of degrees granted to males, except for two years (1966 and 1967).

The rates of change of all first level degrees (including those requiring five and more years) are presented as Series B491-B492, but are not charted.

Number of Degrees to Males per 100 Degrees to Females

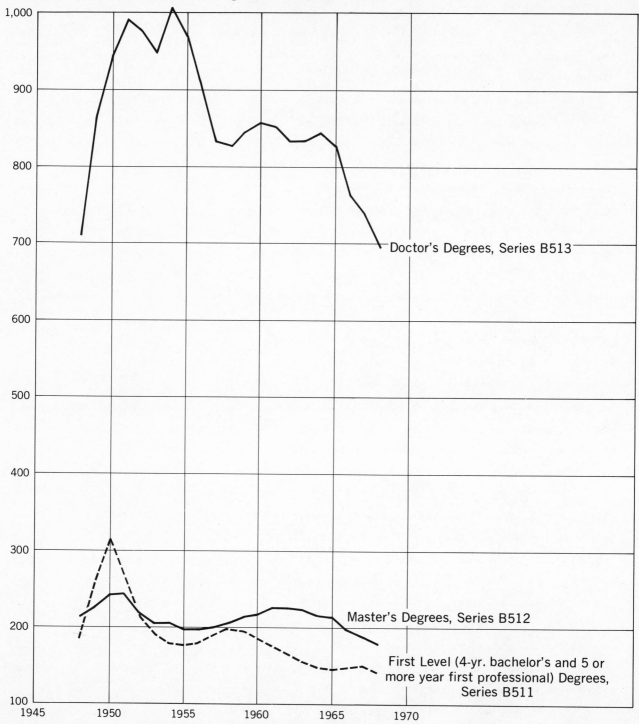

Figure 3.9 Sex Ratio: Degrees Granted to Males per 100 Degrees Granted to Females, by Level of Degree, 1948–1968.

Percent Change

Figure 3.10 Percent Change (as Compared with Previous Year) in Number of Four-Year Bachelor's Degrees Conferred, by Sex, 1949–1968.

Percent Change

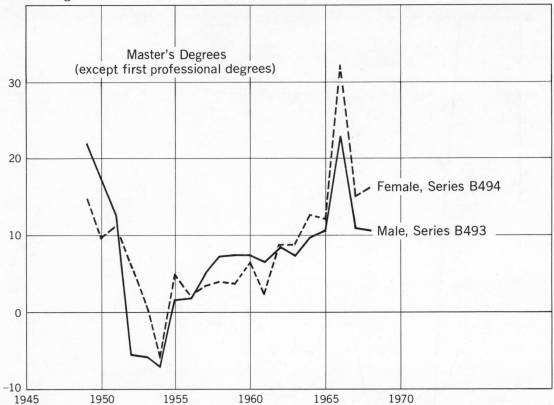

Master's Degrees
(except first professional degrees)

Female, Series B494

Male, Series B493

Percent Change

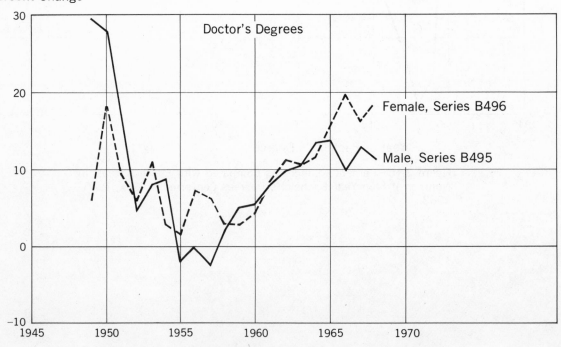

Doctor's Degrees

Female, Series B496

Male, Series B495

Figure 3.11 Percent Change (as Compared with Previous Year) in Number of Earned Master's and Doctor's Degrees Conferred, by Sex, 1949–1968.

The rate of change in master's degrees granted to females has followed approximately the same trend as those granted to males. The rate of change for females has been faster than for males since 1966.

The rate of change in the number of females receiving doctor's degrees has followed closely the rate of change of the number of males receiving doctorates. Since 1966, the rate of change for females has been notably higher than the rate for males. Only if this trend continues will the attainment of doctor's degrees by females approach parity with males.

While the trends presented here are irregular, the general drift in the rates of change since the early to mid-1950's has been increasing. There is some evidence, however, that the rate of change in graduate degrees (master's and doctor's) granted to males is slowing down. At present, the rate of change of females receiving higher degrees is slightly higher than the rate for males.

Rates of Progression through the Educational System

The educational system consists of graded steps of academic years through which pass successive age cohorts. The uniform quality of the system and the age-homogeneity of the students in it cause the system to behave with a high degree of regularity. This property makes measures of progression through the system relatively sensitive indicators, which, when calculated by sex, reveal the changing status of women in the system in relation to men.

The uniformity of behavior of the educational system, however, is not perfect. There are a number of logical, conceptual and definitional problems that cannot be easily solved. Consequently, in making the most of the available information, the analysis of the educational progression of women, which follows, still leaves something to be desired, for solutions to some of the problems were arbitrary.

The model for this analysis is based upon applying a ratio of attainment, first, to the population, and then, successively, to each attainment level. This could be done for each cohort for each year of educational attainment, but our purpose here will be served by examining the rates of transition from one major educational level to the next: high school graduation; first time enrollment in college; graduation from college with, successively, a bachelor's degree, a master's degree and a doctor's degree. The chief defect in such a model lies in the difference between the lag-times of the model and those actually obtaining in the population.

The rates are, as follows:

(1) $r_G = 100\ G/P$, where r_G = rate of high school graduation
    (Series B501-B502) G = high school graduates
                            P = .5 (17 year olds plus 18 year olds) July of graduation year

(2) $r_E = 100\ E/G$, where r_E = rate of entrance into college
    (Series B503-B504) E = first-time degree-credit fall college enrollment, same year as high school graduation

(3) $r_B = 100\ B/E$, where r_B = rate of baccalaureate graduation
      (Series B505-B506)   B = bachelor's degrees four years after entering

(4) $r_M = 100\ M/B$, where r_M = rate of master's graduation
      (Series B507-B508)   M = master's degrees two years after the bachelor's

(5) $r_D = 100\ D/B$, where r_D = rate of doctor's graduation
      (Series B509-B510)   D = doctor's degrees 10 years after the bachelor's degree

When these interlocking relationships are examined, the strengths and weaknesses in the status of women as they proceed through the educational system immediately becomes apparent. Larger proportions of females attain equal or higher status than men as they graduate from high school and, once in college, as they graduate from college. The weak points in women's continuation through the system are the step from high school graduation to first-time college enrollment and the step from graduation from college to graduation with higher-level degrees.

In Figure 3.12, the ratio of high school graduates to the average of the 17 and 18-year-olds at the time of graduation for males and females follow a very uniform trend after the effects of World War II upon the educational system subsided. The ratio for males has come closer to the ratio for females, particularly during the 1960s, but the female ratio was still about four points greater in 1968.

The ratio of first-time degree-credit college enrollments to high school graduates (Figure 3.13) presents greater irregularity. The aftermath of World War II distorted the number of males entering in relation to the high school graduates during the late 1940s. A second distorting influence was the rapid increase in the number of births in 1946 and 1947, creating a jump in high school graduates and entering college freshmen in 1965 and 1966. Since the numerator and denominator are not perfectly coordinated with the age groups actually entering during the period 1963-1966, the curves respond somewhat irregularly. Note that the consequence is similar in the ratios for both males and females. The upward trend in the female ratio actually represents a reduction of one-third of the difference that existed 10 years before. Some 16 points separated the male from the female in 1968. Closing this hiatus would accelerate the educational attainment of women. The focal point is continuation from high school graduation to college entrance.

Once in college, however, the completion ratio of females measures up satisfactorily with that of males (Figure 3.13, lower graph). It continued slightly lower than the male ratio until 1962, from which point on it has slightly exceeded the male ratio, but its long-term trend is relatively constant. The ratio for males, on the other hand, appears to be declining in the long term, the 1968 ratio being some eight points below the 1958 level. This decline may probably be attributed to the "wider" open-door policy of higher educational institutions in admitting persons of lower ability; to the increase in the enrollment of junior colleges, which provide technical training that may be translated immediately into a job without completing the additional two years necessary for a baccalaureate;[4] and, possibly, to military conscription.

4/   Data currently are being accumulated on two-year degrees by the Office of Education. This series will provide an additional step in the system of linkages set forth here.

Number of High School Graduates per 100 Population
Aged 17.5 Years

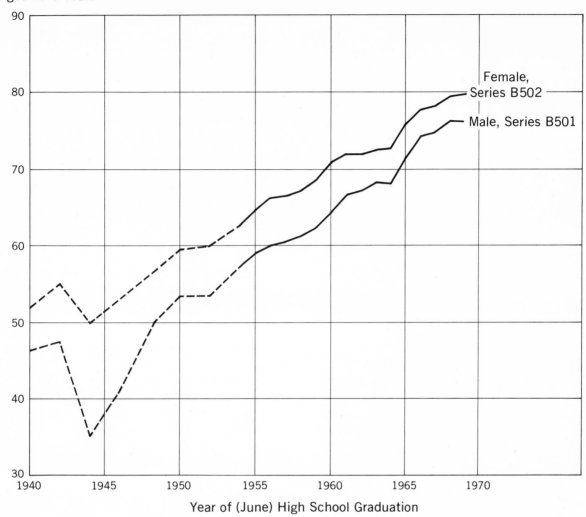

Figure 3.12 Ratio of High School Graduates to Population 17.5
Years of Age, by Sex, 1940–1969.

Number of First-Time Degree-Credit
Enrollments (Oct.) per 100 (June)
High School Graduates

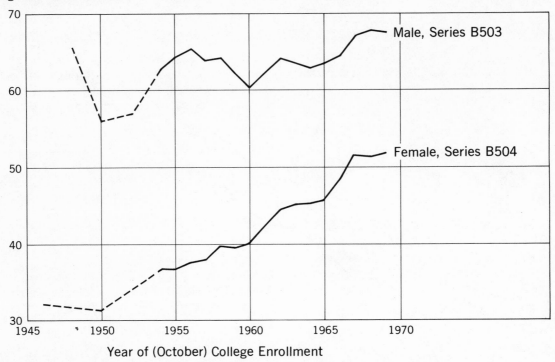

Year of (October) College Enrollment

Number of 4-Year Bachelor's Degrees
per 100 First-Time Degree-Credit
College Enrollments 4 Years Earlier

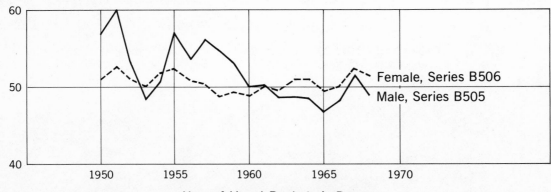

Year of (June) Bachelor's Degree

Figure 3.13 (Upper) Ratio of First-Time Degree-Credit College
Enrollments in October to June High School Graduates (Same Year),
by Sex, 1948–1969. (Lower) Ratio of Four-Year Bachelor's Degrees
to First-Time Degree-Credit College Enrollment Four Years Earlier,
by Sex, 1950–1968.

The rate at which females continued from the baccalaureate degree to the master's, relatively constant to 1965 at around 20 percent, began to increase, following an upward movement that the rate for males had begun four years earlier. There is a three year lag between them now (1968), the female master's recipients being, in 1968, approximately where the male ratio was in 1965. The rate of increase of the male ratio has been considerably stronger over most all of the period shown in Figure 3.14, upper. Approximately 10 points currently (1968), separate them.

Finally, the poorest showing of females is the ratio of doctor's degrees to four-year bachelor's degrees ten years earlier. This ratio has gradually increased, but, even so, it has gained only about one per 100, while the male ratio has increased steadily during the period 1960 to 1965, gaining five per 100. From 1965 to 1968, the ratio for males has remained relatively constant.

The variation in lapse time, bachelor's-to-doctor's, is great, the range being three to 23 years and it differs from one field to the next (Ferriss, 1969: 127-131, 390-393). Consequently, this indicator reflects only long-term changes and is not sensitive to short-term changes. The decrease in Federal fellowship support, for example, to be felt in academic year 1971-72, will undoubtedly prolong the lapse time but such a change is not likely to be immediately reflected in this indicator. The median lapse time, baccalaureate to doctorate, was some three years longer for women than men: 7.9 years for men and 11.2 years for women, among 1964-66 doctorates. Women doctorate recipients tend to be some four years older than men recipients, on the average, and they are more likely to enter or continue in teaching than men (NAS, Office of Scientific Personnel, 1967: 107-121).

In summary, the interlocking indicators of progression through the educational system, beginning with high school graduation, serve to identify the focal points for the improvement of the educational status of women. Primarily, if the percent of high school graduates who continue to college were increased, the probability is high that college graduates would increase. Two other steps should receive attention: the continuation from the bachelor's degree to the master's degree, which already is improving, and the step from bachelor's degree to doctorate, which has improved very little in the past. The development of programs aimed specifically at improving these continuation ratios would do much toward improving the educational status of women.

Unemployment and Years of School Completed

The beneficial effect of education on employment is clearly demonstrated by the rates of unemployment by educational attainment in Series B514-B529. The less schooling, the more likely is the worker to be unemployed. Females, even with the same amount of schooling as males, are more likely to be unemployed.

Number of Master's Degrees
per 100 Bachelor's Degrees 2 Years Earlier

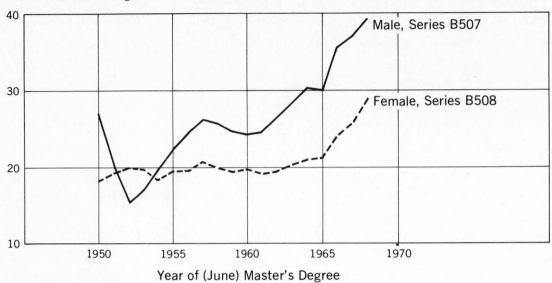

Year of (June) Master's Degree

Number of Earned Doctor's Degrees
per 100 Bachelor's Degrees 10 Years Earlier

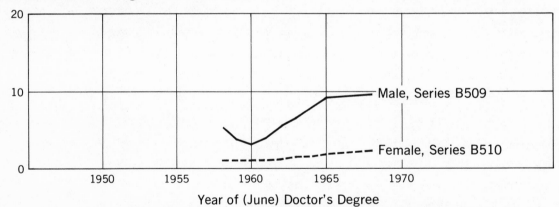

Year of (June) Doctor's Degree

Figure 3.14 (Upper) Ratio of Master's Degrees (Except First Professional) to Four-Year Bachelor's Degrees 2-Years Earlier, by Sex, 1950–1968. (Lower) Ratio of Earned Doctor's Degrees to Four-Year Bachelor's Degrees 10 Years Earlier, by Sex, 1957–1968.

The unemployment rate, of course, varies with the business cycle and is a sensitive indicator of the state of the economy. Those who have graduated from high school and who have completed higher levels of college, both male and female, are not as likely to be unemployed as those with less education. At various times in the past, those who have one to three years of high school but did not graduate, were more likely even than those with fewer years of schooling to be unemployed. This probably is a function of the marginal types of jobs held by high school dropouts.

Figure 3.15 illustrates only three of the levels of schooling, but the series present detail on seven categories of education. Unfortunately, the data are not available for every year.

Summary of Indicators

Available data provide three approaches to monitoring trends in the education of women: enrollment, years of education attained, and ratios of continuation through the system.

Enrollment of females begins to fall at ages 16-17 years and drops considerably more in the 18th and 19th years (Series B009-B012 and B017-B020). These are the ages to watch and these are the ages that should be retained in school if long-term improvement in the educational attainment of women is to be achieved.

Four age groups were singled out for special attention relative to educational attainment at four levels of education:

At least four years of high school, the 18-19 year olds, Series B145-B156;

Any College, the 20-24 year olds, Series B181-B188;

Four or more years of college, the 25-29 year olds, Series B217-B220; and,

Five or more years of college, 30-34 year olds, Series B253-B256.

These age groups and levels of education are suggested as the critical ones to monitor changes in the successive levels of educational attainment. In doing so, sampling variability must be taken into consideration, for some small error in the annual estimates of the attainment may be expected from this source.

Another statistical series has been suggested in addition to the percent of an age group attaining given levels of schooling. This is an overall summary measure of the attainment for an age group, not merely one level for an age group but all the levels (Series B161-B188 for the 20-24 year olds). The percent of the area under the cumulative curve of educational attainment, accumulated from the upper end of the years of educational attainment, provides a sensitive index to attainment of the entire age group. The rate of change of the area under the curve, also, is a useful summary measure of the state of progress in education (Table 3.2).

The number of degrees attained (Series B481-B488) have their uses, as also does the sex ratio of degree recipients (Series B511-B513). Such information, of course, is available by field for a more detailed study of the changing disciplinary preferences of men and women.

45

Unemployment Rate

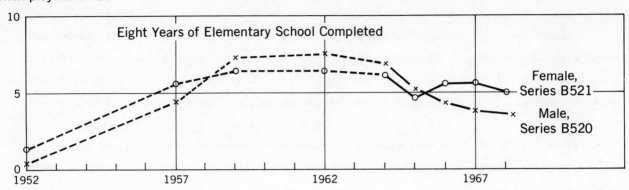

Unemployment Rate

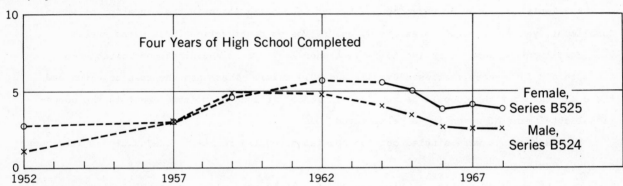

Unemployment Rate

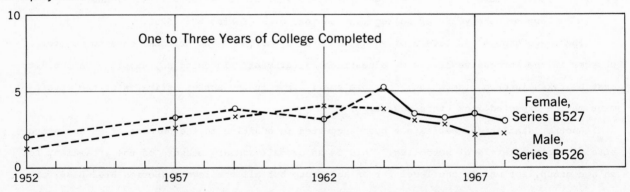

Figure 3.15 Unemployment Rates for Labor Force Members by Years of School Completed, by Sex, 1952, 1957, 1959, 1962, 1964–1968.

Those concerned with the higher education of women would do well to watch the continuing decline in the sex ratio by degree level. Women may be said to be gaining so long as the sex ratio is declining.

The rate of continuation from one stage of education to the next, using either graduates, first-time enrollment or degrees, provides a basis for comparing the progress of women with that of men as they move through and out of the educational system. Girls do better than boys in their high school graduation rates (Series B501-B502). Women who enter college do slightly better than men in graduating four years later (Series B505-B506) but too few enter college (Series B503-B504). Men also exceed women in the continuation ratio from baccalaureate degree to the master's (Series B507-B508), and women make an even poorer showing in the continuation ratio from the baccalaureate to the doctorate (Series B509-B510). These are interesting indicators to observe. The measure of women's attainment is improving in each of them except first-time college enrollment to college graduation, but even in this the female ratio exceeds the male.

Finally, this chapter has pointed up the sharp relationship between years of school completed and unemployment, unemployment being lower among the better educated (Series B514-B529). Years of school completed is associated with the occupation and the industry where employed; these, in turn, are affected by the business cycle,which gives rise to unemployment. The tendency of women to be unemployed more than men is discussed in Chapter 8.

Key to Series Discussed in Chapter 3

Percent enrolled in school,by age, color and sex	B001 - B040
Enrollment by school level, by age, color and sex	B041 - B128
Educational attainment: years of school completed,by age, color and sex	B129 - B384
Percent with specified levels of educational attainment,by age, color and sex	B385 - B480
Earned degrees conferred,by level of degree and sex	B481 - B488
Annual rate of change in degrees granted, by level of degree and sex	B489 - B496
High school graduates,by sex	B497 - B498
First-time degree-credit enrollment,by sex	B499 - B500
Continuation ratios of successive stages from high school through graduate education	B501 - B510
Sex ratio of degrees, by level of degree	B511 - B513
Unemployment rates,by years of school completed and sex	B514 - B529

4.

Indicators of Women's Marital Status

Whether she is married or single is one of the most pervasive influences in the life of a woman. Symbolized by the ring, the household and by offspring, woman's status in the institution of marriage and the family is intimately intertwined with her status in other institutions, and it affects the functioning of other institutions. The decision women make to change from single status to that of wife -- family formation -- bears upon the demand for goods and services and upon her labor force participation. Changes in her status as a mother, indexed by the birth rate, have ramifications for the subsequent demand for education, and, some twenty years later, for the formation of families and households. Marital status and the presence of children serve to motivate both men and women: for example, single men participate less in the labor force than married ones. Broken families are less secure than husband-wife families, and women whose status is divorced or widowed, particularly depending upon her age, affect the need for private or public intervention to assist the needy. This chapter reviews important changes that are taking place in the characteristics of households, in the marital status of women of various age and color groups, and in the proportion of households that have a women as head.

. . . . .

Households

As the population has expanded, the number of households has increased. There were nearly 63 million households in March, 1970. During the five years ended March, 1970, for example, there has been an average annual net increase of about 1.5 million households. However, husband-wife households have not increased commensurately. As Figure 4.1 illustrates, the percentage of husband-wife households is declining gradually and now approximates 70 percent of households of all types.

The proportion of other types of households are either increasing or holding constant. Primary individual households -- "a household head living alone or with nonrelatives only" -- are gradually increasing among both males and females. Primary families with a female head and "other" primary families with a male head, that is, families with a male head other than husband-wife families, have been holding relatively constant as a proportion of the total.

Percent

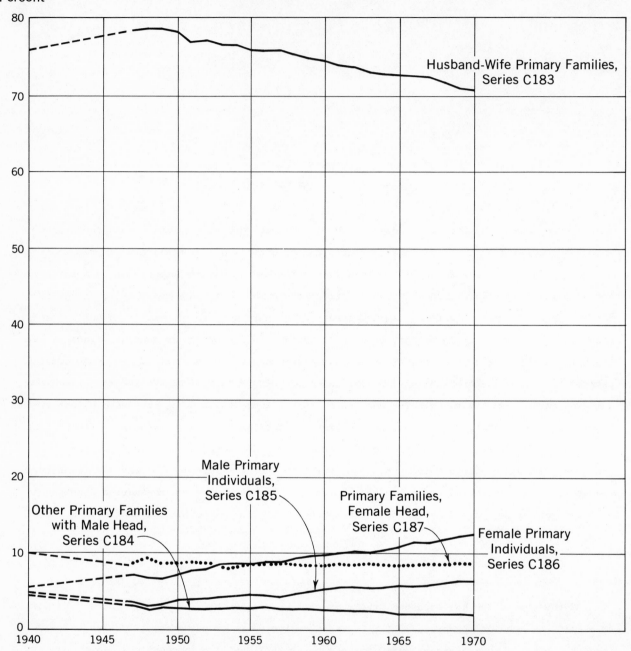

Figure 4.1 Percent Distribution of Households by Sex of Head, Families and Primary Individuals, 1940–1970.

During the five years ending 1968, the marriage rate has been relatively constant (near 145 per 1,000 unmarried females, 15-44 years of age), the rate of divorce has been increasing and the proportion of females remaining divorced has increased slowly. At the same time, the percent of females who are single has increased, and the percent who are widowed has remained relatively constant. These, then, are the vital, demographic changes that are bringing about changes in the characteristics of households and the sex of household heads. These indicators might be said to be coincident with the indicators of the marital status of women. No abrupt changes in them are to be expected (Ferriss, 1970: 98, 101, 123).

Changes in the Marital Status of Women

The percent of the female population married is declining among females of younger and of older ages. Women in their middle years, 30 to 44 ages, have increased in percent married over the long term, since 1940, but during the Sixties the percent married has been fairly constant. The latter group is illustrated, in Figure 4.2, by the percent married of the 30-34 age group, these ages representing the trend among the 35-39 and the 40-44 year groups.[1]

Figure 4.2 also illustrates the shifting marital status of females across the life cycle. Those most likely to be married are 25-34 years of age. Those least likely to be married are under 20 years of age. Females 20-24 years of age have varied the most, since 1940, in the percent married: from approximately 52 percent to nearly 70 percent and then to approximately 62 percent. Not illustrated on the graph are two age groups between 35 and 44 years of age. These ages are similar to the trend in the 30-34 year age groups. Both 35-39 and 40-44 aged females have increased in the percent married over the long term.

Series C001-C160 include 160 series that disaggregate the preceding rates by age and color and also present comparable series for men. Rather than trace each of these trends, only illustrative series will be discussed. The following summarizes some of the principal trends in the marital status of women:

Over both the long and the short term, intact marriages of white and nonwhite females (14 years of age and over) have declined slightly (expressed as a percent of all married females of the specified color group) (Ferriss, 1970: 46-47). The percent of intact marriages have declined among females 14-19 years of age, 18-19 years of age, 20-24 years of age, 25-29 years of age, and 30-34 years of age, although the decrease is slight in the older ages, particularly among white females (Ferriss, 1970: 48-49).

The decline in the percent of the female population married is partly a consequence of the changing age distribution of the female population (see Chapter 2). The percent unstandardized for age has declined much more than the percent standardized for age, but the latter, particularly since 1959, has declined nearly 3 percentage points (Ferriss, 1970: 11).

---

[1] Series C001-C160 present the percent in each marital status for each age, color and sex group. The totals for selected age groups of women, shown in Figure 4.2, are Series 5-8, 11 and 12 of Indicators of Change in the American Family (Ferriss, 1970: 99), supplemented by data from (Census, 1970d: 11). These series are not reproduced in this volume.

Percent Married

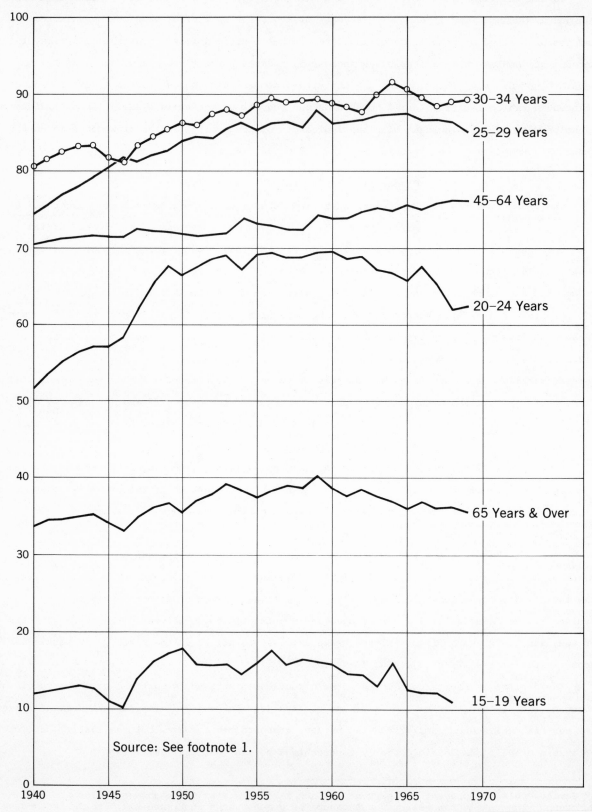

Figure 4.2 Percent of Females Married, within Specified Age Groups, 1940–1969.

As the percent of white and nonwhite females married has declined, the percent single has increased (Ferriss, 1970: 18-19). The percent of white females widowed has increased slightly while the percent among nonwhite females has declined. On the other hand, the percent of both white and nonwhite females who are divorced has increased (Ferriss, 1970: 20 and Series 3-60 and 101-126).

Series C001-C160, herein, verify the results presented above and lead to the following general conclusions concerning trends in the marital status of females:

The younger aged females are increasingly single. Older ages are less likely to be single and the trend among some older age groups is declining (in percent single). Divorced females are increasing among females of the middle and older ages.

These changes are gradual and are manifested in data that are subject to sampling error, particularly for nonwhite females. The trends, however, especially among those under 30 years of age, suggest an approaching decline of the marriage institution. For example, in the ten years ending 1969, the percent of white women 18 and 19 years of age who are single has increased 12 percentage points, and the percent among nonwhite females has increased almost as much, while the percent married among both color groups has declined correspondingly. Among the 20-24 year olds, single status has increased some six percentage points (white female) over the Sixties while the percent married has declined (by 7 percent and 14 percent, respectively) among white and nonwhite females. Among the 25-29 age group of women the percent married has declined some two percentage points during the 1960s and the percent divorced has increased slightly. Figure 4.3 presents illustrative trends of the percent single, married, widowed and divorced among white females and Figure 4.4, among nonwhite females.

These data should be monitored to detect a continuation of the upward trend in single status among the younger ages, a decline in the percent married among the younger ages, and an increase in the percent divorced among the older ages. If these trends continue, the consequences to the family and other institutions of society should be examined. Some of these consequences might be: a decreased legitimate birth rate, an increase in the illegitimate birth rate, an increase in primary individual households and single-person families, a decline in sales of industries serving family and household formation, an increase in the percent of females in the labor force, and longer-term effects upon the educational agencies, religious institutions, and others.

The norm of our society favors family formation, marriage, and a monogamous, connubial existence. The family primary group can counteract and minimize some of the harsh and unsympathetic social relationships that may be encountered outside the family. The incidence of certain types of pathological behavior is greater among single persons and those in broken homes than is the case among intact marriages -- indices such as suicide, nervous breakdown, alcoholism, and the like. Even so, the evidence does not completely condemn the single life nor does it entirely sanction a conjugal existence. Consequently, evaluative studies are needed

53

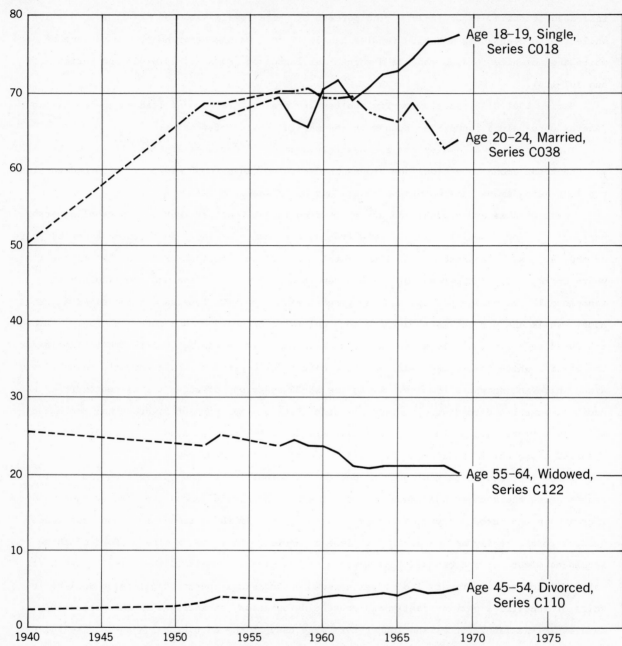

Figure 4.3 Percent Single (18–19 Year Olds), Married (20–24 Year Olds), Widowed (55–64 Year Olds), and Divorced (45–54 Year Olds) White Females, 1940–1969.

Percent

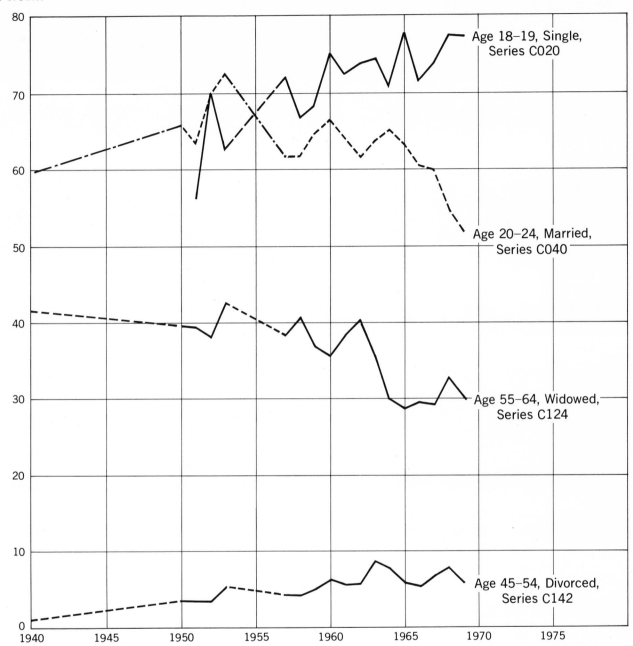

Figure 4.4 Percent Single (18-19 Year Olds), Married (20-24 Year Olds), Widowed (55-64 Year Olds), and Divorced (45-54 Year Olds) Nonwhite Females, 1940-1969.

that would set forth the personal-social conditions wherein the married or single state is more appropriate. Such studies would provide an empirical basis for delineating social policies respecting marriage and the family.

A final note on Figure 4.4, illustrating the nonwhite trends: The trends among nonwhite females resemble the trends among the white. The nonwhite trend is more accentuated and irregular than the white. The accentuation -- for example, the greater decrease in the percent married of 20-24 year olds among nonwhite than white females -- reflects the wider extremes in marital status of nonwhites. But the irregularity of the statistical series is to a great extent a consequence of the greater sampling variability of the nonwhite series, being based upon a smaller number of sample cases, and should not be interpreted as real variation.

Broken Families

The preceding discussion of the marital status of females omitted a review of social indicators of married females who are separated, for one reason or another, from their spouses. These indicators have been relatively constant for the past 15 years. A distinct increase in the percent of married females separated from their husbands would herald an increase in family dissolution. See(Ferriss, 1970: 76-77).

The two categories, husband in the armed forces and husband absent for other reasons (other than separation), appear primarily to reflect the necessity of the husband's being in another location because of his work. The chief exception to this is the absence of the husband in order to be institutionalized for reasons of health, imprisonment, and so forth. A significant increase in the percent absent for these reasons could lead to marriage dissolution, as the experience of World War II demonstrated. However, the series of primary interest is the "separated" category. The percent of married women separated from their husbands (under conditions of a legal separation, or with the intention of getting a divorce, or being separated for other reasons arising from marital discord) has drifted slightly higher in the 16 years presented in Series C162 and C166.

As has been shown in the Family Study (Ferriss, 1970: 76-77), the absolute number of women separated in one year predicts the number of divorces the following year. The stability of the former series, then, is partly a function of the fact that those separated in one year appear the following year, either in the divorced "column" or in the married "column", this time with a new spouse. Almost any increase in the percent separated, then, should be interpreted as a harbinger of marriage dissolution.

Distinct differences in the status of white and nonwhite married females are also revealed by these data. Proportionately, approximately seven times more nonwhite than white females are separated from their husbands. In addition,separations related to the work status of the husband are about twice as frequent, proportionately, as among white women. The absence of the husband from nonwhite marriages, then, is evidence of the greater instability of the nonwhite family.

56

Percent of Female Heads of Families

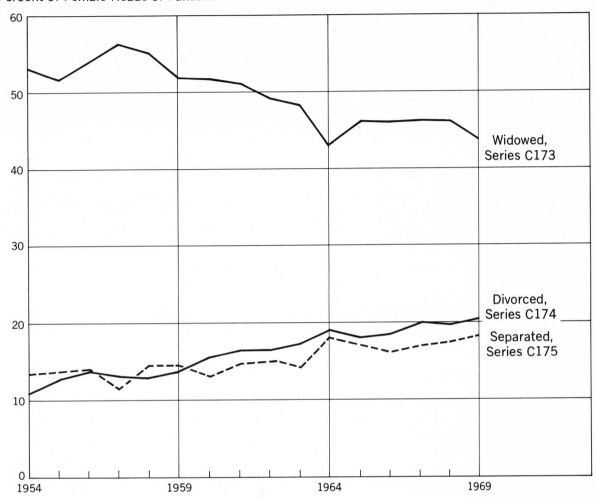

Percent of Married Women

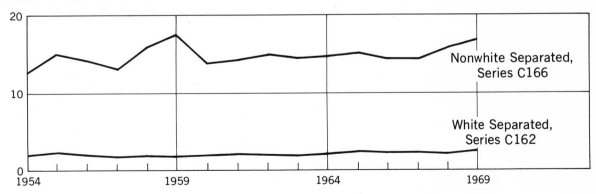

Figure 4.5 Upper: Female Heads of Families: Percent Who Are Separated, Widowed, or Divorced, 1954–1969. Lower: Married Women: Percent Who Are Separated, by Color, 1954–1969.

While the trends in the nonwhite series are more volatile than in the white series, trends over time show only slight increases. Consequently, any marked change in the rate of change should be viewed as an indicator of disturbance in the marital institution. This has occurred in 1968 and 1969 among nonwhite female marriages, and probably will be reflected in divorce statistics in 1969 and 1970, when available.

Females with Sole Responsibility for the Family

Some females who are not married have assumed responsibility for a family, such as a daughter who cares for a parent. Also, females become the only parent in the home when their marriage is dissolved because of death, discord, or other reasons. In March, 1969, there were some 5.4 million females who were heads of families, while there were 1.2 million males (other than heads of husband-wife families) who were heads of families.

The number of female heads of families increased about two-fifth during the past 15 years (April 1954-March 1969) and they represent a fairly constant proportion of all families, approximately 10 to 11 percent (Series C169 and C176).

The number of males who have parallel responsibilities for their families, on the other hand, is relatively constant in absolute numbers, now about 1.2 million, and is a declining proportion of all families.

The difference between the number of male (other than in husband-wife families) and female heads apparently rests with the greater initiative of males in remarrying, thereby removing themselves from the responsibility of being the head of a family without a wife, a difference arising from traditional roles of male and female.

The largest category of female head of family, among both males and females, is widowhood. However, the percent so allocated is declining slightly among males and more noticeably among females. Family heads who became family heads because of divorce, however, are increasing among both males and females. Females who are married, though separated, have also increased. The percentage separated has increased about one-third over the fifteen year period, 1954-1969, and males in the "separated" category have likewise increased (Series C170-C174, C177-C180).

While about one-third of the males who are heads of families (other than husband-wife families) still are single, that is, they have never been married, only about 10 percent of female heads of families are single. Neither the single male nor the single female series present a consistent trend, each varying considerably without an apparent pattern (Series C175 and C181).

As social indicators these categories are insufficient. For example, consider the largest category, widowed. The important questions are: how adequate is the widow's income in relation to the family members for whom she is responsible, how adequate her health, how adequate the quality of her life, and so forth. These questions are not answered by available published data. The solution lies in approaching the phenomena from the standpoint of the family within the household as a unit. Characteristics of such units should be delineated so as to provide indices of the quality of life of the unit. At least some of this information already is available in the files of previous surveys (Current Population Survey, Health Interview Survey, etc.), and other characteristics might be added to the survey files in the years ahead, in order to definitively characterize family units. The measures that need to be generated are measures of the unit, rather than of the individuals composing the unit. The number of families of given types and the number of individuals in them would be the basic tabulation.

One might elaborate endlessly upon the characteristics that might compose such a typology of family units. Below is a suggested basis for beginning an index of the quality of life of American families. In general it should include a range of measures, such as adequacy of income, of health, of employment, of the correction of physical impairments, of recreation, of mental health, and so forth. Some of the measures might be, as follows:

Family stage and the number of adults and children

Male or female head

Income above poverty level (or meeting some other criterion)

Proportion of total family income derived from welfare payments

Days per person bed disability

Impairments, or serious impairments, per person

Number needing hospitalization or other health care, per person

School/work status of the members of the family: the number of persons not actively
     engaged in work or study, per person

An index of recreational participation: days of outdoor recreation per person per year

Incidence of suicide or attempted suicide during the past year

Incidence of hospitalization in a mental institution or being under the care of a doctor
     for mental reasons

Reason for absence of family members (divorce, separation, etc.).

Information is needed on the occurrence during a past period, such as a year, of selected events: a death in the household, a marriage, a birth, a promotion, a member who entered school, quit school, was graduated, entered the labor force, was sentenced by a court, bought a house, took a vacation, ran for political office, joined a golf club, and so forth. While much present social bookkeeping records the number of persons who do many of these things, the information often is an aggregate, unrelated to the social factors that give meaning to the event. The events must be enumerated so that the characteristics of the family unit generating them may be known in relation to the event. Upon the basis of such a typology of the family, the probability of events then would be known.

For example, four characteristics of a family typology might be: family stage, income, number of members present, and age of head. For each family type, there would be a probability of a death occurring, of a marriage, a birth, of receiving a promotion, and so forth. Such

59

probabilities would be changing across time at observable rates. With probabilities known, events could then be simulated. Forecasts could be prepared upon the basis of assumed changes in rates of change of the probabilities. A system such as this would be capable of assessing the consequences of a proposed social program under the assumption that the program would alter the rate of change of one of the probabilities. The model would be capable of generating aggregates of events from the primary decision-making units -- the family or the household. Such aggregates, arising from a classification of primary units into relatively homogeneous types, is much more likely to produce an accurate estimate of the aggregate than would a macro-approach to estimating it (Orcutt, et. al., 1961: 11).

Summary of Indicators

While trends in the percent of households and families by type change slowly, distinct trends have been developing that justify a continuing review. There is an increase in both male and female primary individual households and a concomitant decrease in husband-wife families. Behind this development is the percent of females married, by age and color. Continued decline in the percent married, particularly among the younger ages, will have extensive consequences for society. The marital status of the 18-19 year olds and the 20-24 year olds, particularly, should be closely scrutinized. If present trends continue, an assessment of the implications for family life should be made. In particular, several possible consequences suggested in this chapter should be evaluated. See page 53.

Among the older population, the percent widowed and divorced provide indices of special significance. The percent of female-headed households due to divorce and separation has been increasing while the percent widowed has been declining.

The percent of married women separated from their husbands, by color (Series C162 and C166) does not show a marked upward trend, but the number of women separated, husband absent, has been increasing and bears reasonable relationship to the number divorced the following year (Ferriss, 1970: 76-77). For this reason, a periodic assessment of the percent separated indicator is warranted.

The status of married nonwhite females requires special attention, as revealed by "separated, husband absent", by the series on nonwhite wives whose husbands are absent (Series C165-C168), and by the percent of households with female heads by color (Ferriss, 1970: 111, Series 100). These and various other indicators reflecting the status of the nonwhite family (BLS, 1969c, and 1969d) should receive continuing attention, particularly in relation to the various Federal and State programs that bear upon the family (e.g., Aid to Dependent Children, Old Age Assistance, etc.).

Finally, it was suggested that data on a variety of events occurring to the family/household be periodically assembled. A unified data system of this kind would make it possible to relate the event to the personal-social situation out of which the event arose. The system was proposed as a basis for generating characteristics of society over time. The changing probabilities of events might be assumed in order to anticipate the consequences of programs that are potentially capable of altering the family situation. A number of characteristics of families/households were suggested as part of this system.

Key to Series Discussed in Chapter 4

Percent single, married, widowed and divorced, by age, color and sex	C001 - C160
Total number and percent of civilian married women with husband absent, by reason for absence, by color	C161 - C168
Number and percent distribution of female heads of family, by marital status, and of male head of family (other than husband-wife families)	C169 - C181
Number of households and percent distribution, by type of family (husband-wife, male head, etc.)	C182 - C187

Series referred to herein that may be found in Indicators of Trends in the American Family

(Ferriss, 1970: 98-106, 112-113, 124):

Marital status of the female population 15 years of age and over, standardized and unstandardized for age,	Series 3, 4
Marital status of the female population, by age	Series 5-12
Marital status, by age, sex, and color	Series 13-60
Percent of intact marriages of female, by age and color	Series 101-126
Number of divorces and number of females reporting "separated, husband absent" the previous year	Series 195-196

5.

Trends in the Fertility of American Women

Procreation and nurture of the young traditionally have been the great contributions women have made to society. Changes in the fertility rate index certain social psychological assessments couples make of the future, a process as yet not clearly understood. An economic depression, for example, reduces the fertility rate, and so does a war, but after a war the birth rate increases. In addition to mirroring certainty or security respecting the future, fertility signifies that a mother is committing six months to a year in the prenatal and post-natal attention to the child, and often a much longer time than that. In fact, the responsi-bility of the mother for the child becomes one of the dominant motives of the mother's life. Whether she continues in a full-time job or maintains the household full-time, she is involved with the care and rearing of her child for ten, fifteen, or even twenty years after its birth. For this reason, this chapter examines the number of women at one point in time who have child care responsibilities, before looking at trends in birth rates by live birth order.

In addition to being an index to the size of families, birth rates by live birth order dissect fertility into its situational components relative to the mother. Cumulative live births by age of mother, on the other hand, compare the cumulative fertility trends of women of a given age and of women of the same age in the past. On an annual basis, age specific fertility rates, a period statistic, do somewhat the same thing but do not take into account past births. The chapter closes by examining illegitimate birth rates, comparing them with the rates for legitimate births, and examines the changing proportion of births delivered by physicians.

. . . . .

Responsibility for Children

The care of children consumes the time of a major segment of American women. In a survey made in March 1969, the U. S. Census Bureau found that almost two-fifths of females 14 years of age and over (approximately 29 million women) had responsibility for the care of their own children under 18 years of age. Some of these women (3.4 million) were heads of their families and also cared for children under 18 years of age. Estimates of the percent of all women having various levels of child care responsibilities are as follows (Census, 1970d: 15; 1970e: 22, 32, 64, 66):

	Percent
All females 14 years of age and over (75,793,000) March 1969	100.0
Not in families:	
In institutions	1.2
In primary- and secondary-individual households	11.3
In families:	
Children and other female family members	20.8
Wives and female heads of families:	
No children under 18 years	28.5
One child under 18 years	12.8
Two children under 18 years	11.5
Three children under 18 years	7.1
Four or more children under 18 years	6.9

The above distributes all women 14 years of age and over according to their responsibility for their own children under 18 years of age. "Responsibility" in this context is not accurately determined. It merely means that the children were her own children and that she lived in the house with them. For our purpose this is an adequate basis for estimating that nearly two-fifths of American women, 14 years of age and over, in addition to various other responsibilities, were looking after their offspring.

As part of the above cross-section picture of the home responsibilities of American women, at least 3.6 million women completed their pregnancies during the year, 3.5 million giving birth to babies born alive (NCHS, 1970c: 1). Thus, approximately 4.7 percent of women 14 years of age and over (or, 5.3 percent of women 18 years of age and over) were occupied during the year with pregnancy or by the complications of pregnancy. These, too, are minimum estimates for the following reasons: they include only pregnancies terminating during 1969; and, fetal deaths (here estimated at 82,000 annually) are known to be underregistered and to be registered under different periods of gestation among the States. There can be little doubt, however, that these 3.6 million women were quite fully occupied in caring for their recent offspring. Among women with children under 18 years, those with births during the year are one-eighth of the total.

In summary, fertility rates are an important element in population change and have implications for future socioeconomic projections, but fertility rates also constitute indicators of a commitment of considerable portions of women's lives to bearing, nurturing, and rearing children. Some two-fifths of American women have responsibility for rearing children who are under 18 years of age.

Birth Rates by Live Birth Order

Birth rates by parity for successive age groups of mothers (Series D001-D168) provide data that makes it possible to detect changes in decisions couples make that affect the size of their families. These indicators of fertility and family size show some very interesting developments concerning the size of families.

From the abnormally high birth rate for first child (Series D001-D003) that came in 1947, after World War II, the birth rate for first child declined and was relatively stable during the 1950's. It drifted somewhat lower during the 1960's, but the 1967 rate of 31 per thousand is approximately the average rate for the birth of the first child during all of the 1960's. In short, decisions to have the first child continue to occur at a relatively stable incidence.

Birth rates of the second child (Series D004-D006) reached a peak in 1952, and since have drifted lower. The rate of decline after about 1963 has been somewhat faster than before 1963. In the 16 years ending with 1967 the birth rate for the second child declined 10 births per thousand females or about one-third. This is a rather sharp decline and most of it came during the 1960's. The significance of the decline is that it portends a decline in the size of the American family.

The birth rate of the third child (Series D007-D009) reached a peak in 1957. By 1961 it began to fall rather rapidly and by 1967 it was two-fifths lower than it had been ten years earlier. The 1967 rate of 13.9 per 1,000 women is approximately the same rate that was observed in 1944.

Decisions to have a fourth child (Series D010-D012), also, have declined quite rapidly since about 1960-61. The birth rate for the fourth child approaches the low rate experienced during the early 1940's.

Decisions to have a fifth child (Series D013-D015) increased to 1961 and since has declined very rapidly. The 1967 rate is less than five per 1,000.

The preceding concerns rates for women 15-44 years of age, illustrated in Figure 5.1

The general picture of fertility by live birth order, then, is one of marked decline in all but the rate for first births. Table 5.1 summarizes the major rates of change by age of mother, showing the date of the peak in the rate in recent years, the 1967 rate, and the average annual rate of change in the rate.

The greatest average annual decline in any of the rates shown in the table is that for the third child born to women 20-24 years of age, declining more than 10 percent per year on the average over the seven years ending with 1967. A decline almost as large, eight percent per year over the six years ending 1967, was observed for the fourth child of women 25-29 years of age. Generally, the annual average rates of decline are greater for higher order births than for the first child.

Table 5.1 - Average Annual Rate of Change of the Live Birth Rate from Recent Peak Rate to 1967, by Selected Live Birth Orders and Age of Mother

Age of mother	Birth order	Date of peak of rate	Peak rate	1967 rate	Period (years)	Annual average rate of change
15-19	First	1957	68.7	51.1	10	-2.91
20-24	First	1957	92.9	75.3	10	-2.06
20-24	Second	1959	88.2	59.5	8	-4.76
20-24	Third	1960	49.9	25.0	7	-10.27
25-29	Second	1952	58.2	40.2	15	-2.44
25-29	Third	1959	51.3	34.4	8	-4.85
25-29	Fourth	1961	34.5	20.4	6	-8.42
30-34	Third	1954	29.0	17.1	13	-3.94
30-34	Fourth*	1959	22.6	15.3	8	-4.76
		1961	22.6	15.3	6	-6.28

* Two recent peaks

Source: Series D028, D043, D046, D049, D067, D070, D073, D091, D094.

From the above it is apparent that one-child families will hold their own, but that larger-sized families will become less prevalent in the future, assuming that these trends continue. These series, then, are useful indicators of the future size of the family as well as indicators of family responsibilities women are assuming.

Differentials between white and nonwhite women, also, are presented in Series D001-D021. Generally, the trends in nonwhite birth rates by parity is the same as the white. The nonwhite birth rates by live birth order during the Sixties were higher for each birth order than the corresponding white rate, and the differences between them becomes greater as the birth order increases, nonwhites tending toward larger numbers of offspring.

Figure 5.1 graphically displays, first, the increase and then the decline in birth rates by live birth order since 1940. The decline in the birth rates for fourth and higher order births began about the time that the contraceptive pill was introduced, about 1961. However this is not the case for the rate for the third child, which began to decline after 1957, nor for the second child, which began to decline after 1952, nor for the first child, which has decreased only gradually since 1951 (after the wild increase following the return of veterans from World War II).

The birth rate for first child has not decelerated as a result of the introduction of the pill following 1960. The general stability of the birth rate of the first baby is a continuing affirmation of American couples in procreation and family life. It also should be observed that the birth rates by live birth order, except the "6th and 7th" and "8th and over" orders, were all higher in 1967 than they were in 1940. The trend, however, suggests that all except the birth rates of the first and second order births will shortly be below the 1940 rate.

In the notes to the series a precaution is stated which is important enough to repeat here. Live birth order data are not probabilities that a female who has had, say, k babies, will have the (k + 1)st child. Rather, they are birth rates by live birth order for women of various ages.

Total Annual Live Births per 1,000 Women
Aged 15–44 Years

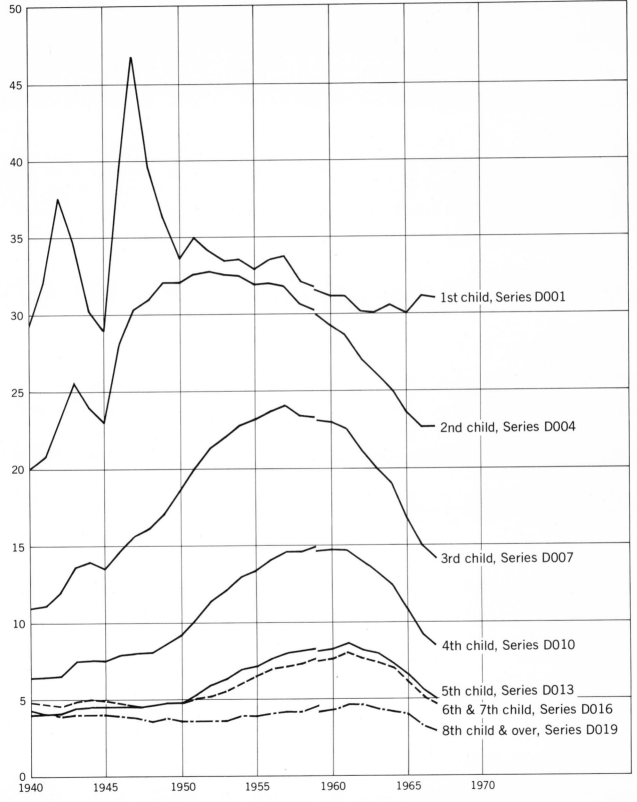

Figure 5.1 Annual Live Birth Rates, Women Aged 15–44, by Live
Birth Order, 1940-1967.

Consequently, the rates are subject to changes in the demographic composition of the female population, such as the age composition in relation to birth order. Even with this limitation the series provide significant indicators of changes in the responsibilities for child care that women are assuming and in the future composition of the family.[1]

Another factor affecting the birth rates for the total population of women 15 to 44 years of age is the increase in the birth rate in 1946 and 1947. This resulted in an increase in 15-year-old cohorts in 1961 and 1962. The fact that these young women had lower birth rates at ages 15, 16, etc., than slightly older women, created a synthetic decline in the birth rate for a few years. Of course, as these women enter ages when childbearing is more probable, the increase in the size of the cohort should increase the number of births. This caveat, however, does not apply to the age-specific rates.

Series D022-D168 present birth rates by live birth order and age of mother in five-year age groups.

Cumulative Live Births

A sensitive index to the changing fertility pattern of American women is the cumulative number of live births born to women of specified ages. Across time, as women mature from one age group to another, the effect of changes in the fertility pattern may be observed. The fertility level of an age group presages the state of fertility of the next higher age group in the next time period.

Figure 5.2 illustrates the trends in Series D169-D175. In addition to presenting the movement of this measure of fertility by five-year age groups, it shows estimates of cumulative live births per 1,000 women that are required to replace the population, based upon prevailing mortality experience (Ferriss, 1970: 52).

The graph illustrates the relatively stable birth rate of young women under 20 years of age, the declining rates for those in the middle childbearing years, and the continuing high fertility of women 35 years of age and older. The latter is a consequence of accretions in births that go back to the high fertility of the latter years of the 1940's and early 1950's, best observed in the cohort fertility graph, Figure 5.3.

In Figure 5.2 the group of women 35-39 years of age presents the highest fertility record in recent years, perhaps in our entire fertility history. As a consequence of its present level of fertility, the cumulative births of the 40-44 year old group in 1973 will increase to 3,100 or more.

The dots on the graph show the population replacement level. They indicate that the cumulative births of women 30-34 years of age in 1955 were sufficient to replace the population at that time, without additional births during their older years. Because of the increase in fertility, however, particularly among younger women, the cumulative births of women 25-29 years of age, in

---

[1] Birth probabilities by exact age and parity of mother are available: (NCHS, 1968h: 128-130).

Number of Births per 1,000 Women

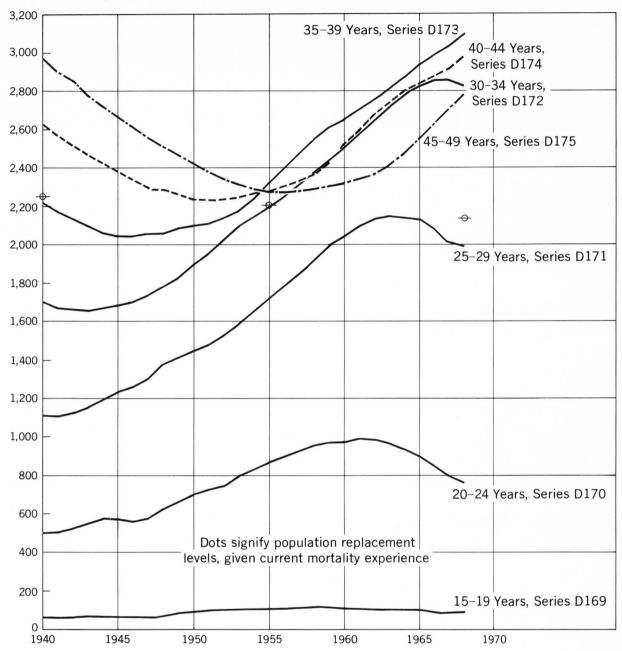

Figure 5.2 Cumulative Live Births per 1,000 Women, by Age of Mother, Selected Five-Year Age Groups, 1940–1968

Cumulative Live Births per 1,000 Women

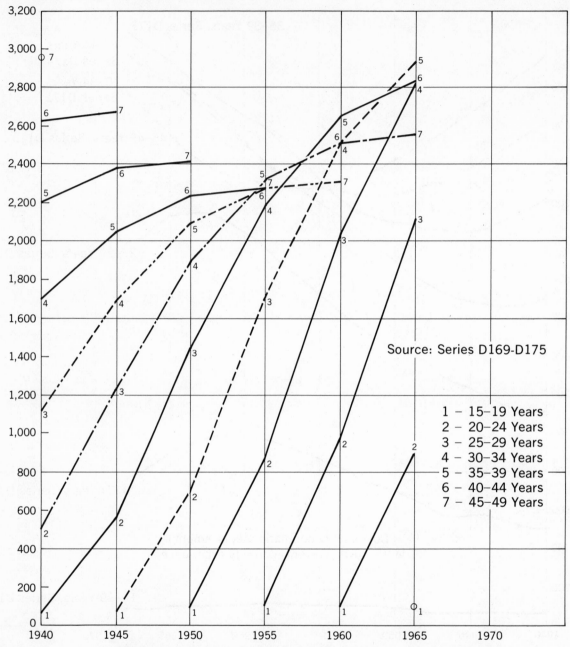

Figure 5.3 Cumulative Live Births per 1,000 Women, by Age of Mother, for 12 Age Cohorts, 1940–1965.

Source: Series D169-D175

1 – 15–19 Years
2 – 20–24 Years
3 – 25–29 Years
4 – 30–34 Years
5 – 35–39 Years
6 – 40–44 Years
7 – 45–49 Years

1963, had reached approximately the level necessary for population replacement. The birth experience of the 25-29 year olds, however, has since declined below the current replacement level. Note that replacement would be attained even though the 25-29 age group gave birth to no more offspring during the remainder of their childbearing period. The decline signifies that young couples are beginning to complete the desired size of their families early and are suspending further additions to their families.

The downturn of the cumulative live births of the 30-34 age group, observed in 1968, indicates that a decline may be expected in the 35-39 year age group, as the members of the 30-34 year age group mature and move into the 35-39 year group. The effect will probably show up in 1970 or 1971.

Figure 5.3 illustrates twelve cohorts of women, in five-year, non-overlapping age groups. Complete data cannot be presented for any of the cohorts since the period 1940-1965 is short of the thirty years' experience required for a cohort's complete fertility history.

The cohort that entered its childbearing period (the 15-19 year age group) in 1945 and the 1950 cohort most certainly will achieve fertility levels higher than any of the others illustrated. At the other extreme, the 1960 cohort, in its 20-24th year, is beginning to reflect the more recent decline in fertility. The ratio of the rates of successive age groups by their stability are predictable and make possible estimates of considerable reliability of the next stage for a cohort. For example, the 1955 cohort had reached 25-29 years of age by 1965. Upon the basis of the continuation of present rates of change in the ratio of 30-34 year rate to 25-29 year rate, one might predict the 1970 level of the 1955 cohort to be slightly above 2,700 births. This mechanical approach to prediction is a simple method for short-term estimates, its reliability resting entirely upon the continuation of the observed trend.

Age-Specific Fertility Rates

To complete the picture of trends in fertility of American women, Series D177-D194 present the number of live births per 1,000 women 15 to 44 years of age by color. The total for the color groups combined, also, is included (Series D176).

Figure 5.4 presents the trend of the total for white and nonwhite and the trend in the age group with the highest fertility, the 20-24 age group. Each age group follows roughly the same pattern of variation across time. The sharp increase in births in 1946 and 1947 was followed by a more gradual rise in fertility to about 1957, after which the rate began to decline. The present trend (1968) indicates a continued decrease in the birth rate for all age and color groups, even though the preliminary total fertility rate for 1969 was up nearly one percentage point over 1968.

The initial decline in the birth rate that began after 1957 cannot be attributed to the contraceptive pill. The pill was introduced in 1960 and did not gain wide acceptance immediately. The year 1962 was the first birth year actually subject to its effects. Widespread use of the contraceptive pill is recognized, there having been perhaps nearly four million users in 1965.

71

Live Births per 1,000 Women (ratio scale)

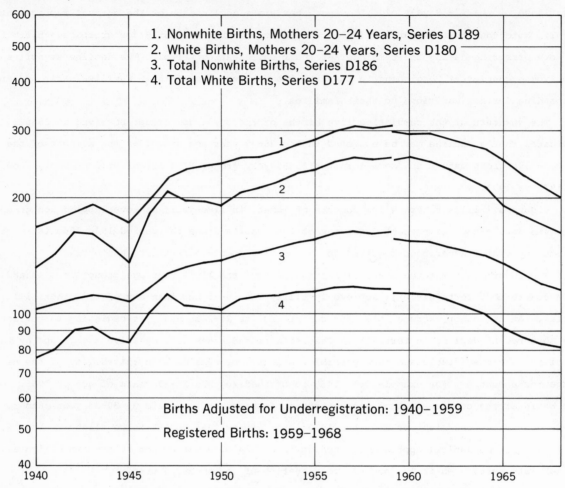

Figure 5.4 Live Births per 1,000 Women, by Color: Births to Women of All Ages per 1,000 Women Aged 15–44 Years, and Births to Women 20–24 Years per 1,000 Women Aged 20–24 Years.

Without the pill, however, other means of contraception would have been used, as, for example, the experience during the 1930's when the birth rate dropped to a low of 75.8 per 1,000 women 15-44 years in 1936 (NCHS, 1968h: 114). Other possible explanations of the decline in fertility are presented in (NCHS, 1967i) for 1964 and related analyses in monographs for 1963 and 1962.

In addition to the contraceptive pill, the intra-uterine device has also contributed to improve birth control practice. Movements afoot to legalize abortions in several States, when passed by State legislatures, are likely to lead to further reductions in fertility. The consequences of these measures on the growth of the population, however, are not likely to be effectively noticed for 20 to 30 years, when the birth cohorts of smaller aggregate size enter their childbearing period and adopt lower rates of birth.

Births Out of Wedlock

While the total and age-specific birth rates have been declining since 1957, no such change has taken place in the rate of illegitimate births. The rate for illegitimate births continues to increase, as Table 5.2 illustrates (Series D202-D204). While the nonwhite rate has always exceeded the white, the rate of change in the birth rates shows that the nonwhite rate is receding while the white continues to increase at a relatively constant pace. Although nonwhite illegitimate births account for 55 percent of all illegitimate births (1967), the illegitimate birth rate among nonwhite unmarried women declined during the 1960's.

Table 5.2 - Illegitimate Births per 1,000 Unmarried Women, 15-44 Years of Age, and Annual Average Rate of Change of the Rates, Selected Years, Total and by Color

	Illegitimate births per 1,000 unmarried women 15-44 years of age		
	Total	White	Nonwhite
1940	7.1	3.6	35.6
1950	14.1	6.1	71.2
1960	21.6	9.2	98.3
1967	23.9	12.5	89.5
	Annual average rate of change in the rate		
1940-50	7.1	5.4	7.2
1950-60	4.4	4.2	3.3
1960-67	1.5	4.5	-1.3

Source: (NCHS: 1968b) and unpublished NCHS data.

In recent years, age-specific illegitimate birth rates have declined for all except the youngest age group -- the age group most prolific of illegitimate births -- 15-19 year old women, both white and nonwhite, and among the 20-24 year old unmarried white women, Figure 5.6 (Series D205-D210). All other age groups have experienced a decline in the illegitimate birth rate. A decline now in the birth rate among teen-agers would produce a decline in the total rate.

The marked increase in the illegitimate rate among nonwhite unmarried women during the 1940's and 1950's may be partly attributed to the urbanization of the Negro that following World War II and continued at a rapid pace during the 1950's and 1960's.

Series D221-D244 present the illegitimacy ratio (illegitimate births per 1,000 live births). As the ratio has risen, illustrated in Figure 5.5, the percent of nonwhite births attended by a physician simultaneously has increased. While this is not proof, it is suggested that the recording of an illegitimate birth on the certificate is more likely when a physician delivers the child than would be the case if a midwife attended it.

At the same time that the illegitimate birth rate has increased, other observations suggest that many marriages are preceded by conception. The National Natality Survey showed that during 1964-66 approximately 22 percent of first births of married couples were recorded as taking place eight months or less after marriage (NCHS, 1970b: 1), suggesting a high incidence of premarital exposure to pregnancy. First births to couples married less than eight months comprised 42 percent of all births to married women 15 to 19 years of age.

While no adequate, comprehensive study of illegitimate births has been made (Vincent, 1968: 88), several characteristics may be cited, as follows:

a. In 1967 there were 175,800 illegitimate births to nonwhite women and 142,200 to white women. Nearly half of the women (48 percent) were under 20 years of age and 80 percent were under 25 years of age.

b. Illegitimate births per 1,000 unmarried women among nonwhites were more than seven times higher than the rate for whites in 1967 (89.5 and 12.5 per 1,000 respectively).

c. In 1964, 66 percent of illegitimate births to white women were first births. The corresponding figure for nonwhite women was 44 percent. Approximately 48 percent of illegitimate births are second, or higher order births. Of the 318,100 illegitimate births in 1967, 129,300 or 41 percent, were second or higher order births to unwed mothers, whose prior experience might have served as a signal (NCHS, 1969a: 1-23). The use of the first illegitimate birth as a "case finding" device would appear to be a practical means to identify potentially recidivistic unmarried mothers.

d. Illegitimate births are more likely than legitimate births to occur prematurely, the birth weight is likely to be lower, the birth is more likely to be attended by a midwife than is a legitimate birth, and fetal mortalities occur at a higher rate among unmarried mothers than among married women (NCHS, 1968b; and news releases from NCHS).

There is no clear explanation for the continued increase in illegitimacy. Those offered include: a decrease in the incidence of venereal disease, which may have improved fecundity and hence led to higher fertility rates; migration from farm to city, particularly by nonwhites, leading to residence under crowded conditions in urban places, where promiscuity becomes more "legally" noticeable and recordable than in rural areas (NCHS, 1968b: 16-17). Neither of these are satisfactory explanations. One could also mention the greater freedom in interpersonal relations among teen-agers, the greater permissiveness of parental control, and an assumed decline in mortality, but these are merely speculations.

Ratio Scale

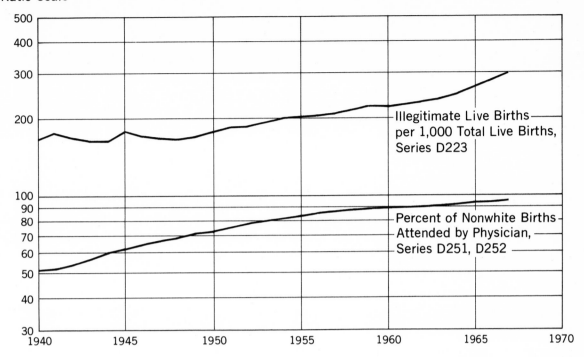

Figure 5.5 Nonwhite Illegitimacy Ratio and Percent of Nonwhite Births Attended by Physician, 1940–1967

The illegitimacy ratio -- illegitimate births per 1,000 live births for each category --
Series D221-D244, provides an indicator that is independent of changes in the birth rate.

The age-specific illegitimate birth rate by color is presented as Series D205-D220. By
contrast, the legitimate birth rate, Series D196-D201, for five-year age groups, shows the
changing trend in births to married women. As an illustration, trends in legitimate and illegitimate birth rates of the two most prolific age groups of women are presented in Figure 5.6.

For additional commentary on illegitimate birth rates, see (Ferriss, 1970: 54-64), but the
most comprehensive treatment is (NCHS, 1968b), a study by Alice J. Clague and Stephanie J.
Ventura.

Summary of Indicators

Birth rates by live birth order show that the birth rate of the first child is holding at
a relatively constant level (Series D001). Birth rates for higher birth orders, however, have
been falling since 1961 or before. These trends portend smaller families in the future.

Cumulative live births by age of mother (Series D169-D175) show the crescive fertility of
age groups now entering their most mature childbearing period. Cumulative births among younger
age groups (e.g., 25-29 years and 30-34 years) are lower than a few years ago, suggesting that
they will not achieve such high levels of reproduction. Even so, age groups now reaching 30-34
years already have produced one-third more offspring than are needed merely to replace the population (Series D172).

In addition to stating the number of cumulative births per 1,000 women by age group as a
period statistic, cumulative births may be arranged by cohort, the more easily to compare the
reproductive attainment of successive cohorts as they mature across the reproductive ages
(Figure 5.3). This is a most effective graphic technique for identifying the changing fertility
of oncoming generations.

Age-specific fertility rates (Series D176-D194), also, reveal the decline in the birth
rates that began about 1957 and continues to the present. With more effective birth control
technology available and with the prospect that legalized abortion will be more generally available, a continued decline in birth rates may be expected.

The contrast is striking between the decline in the legitimate birth rate and the continuing
increase in illegitimate fertility, due chiefly to the illegitimate birth rates of the 15-19 year
olds (Series D195-D220). While illegitimate births are more likely to require public assistance
than births in wedlock, the latter, when occurring within eight months of marriage, provide an
index to the nature of premarital relations.

There has been a marked improvement in the percent of nonwhite deliveries by physicians,
but in 1967, six percent of nonwhite births were still delivered by midwives (Series D253).

Each of these series contribute to our understanding the direction of the changing fertility
pattern of American women. To impose a standard upon fertility -- to set 2.11 births per woman,

Ratio Scale

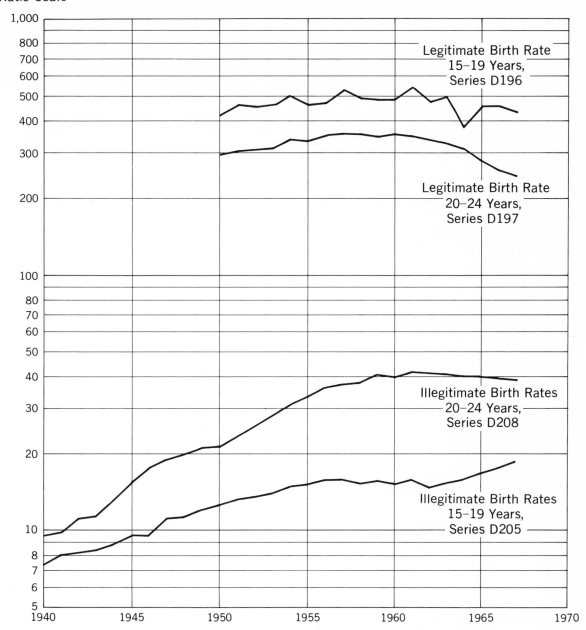

Figure 5.6 Legitimate and Illegitimate Births per 1,000 Women Aged 15–19 Years and 20–24 Years, 1951–1967 (Legitimate) and 1940–1967 (Illegitimate).

for example, as a desirable social goal for a stationary population (Census, 1970j: 1) -- may be requisite for social policy and in the best interests of the total society, but there are other considerations, other more important considerations insofar as women are concerned. These involve the fulfillment that women attain through motherhood. As social thinkers have pointed out (Alice Rossi, 1964: 628-634), women's fulfillment as mothers need not be purchased at the expense of denying the development of all of women's many other potentialities. For this reason, social policies should seek to provide agencies that facilitate child care and development and give the mother an opportunity to develop her capacities and achieve a satisfying life in addition to the contribution she makes to the nurture, growth, education and development of her children.

Key to Series Discussed in Chapter 5

Live birth rates, by age of mother, live birth order and color	D001 - D168
Cumulative birth rates, by age of mother	D169 - D175
Live birth rates, by age of mother and color	D176 - D194
Legitimate live birth rates, by age of mother	D195 - D201
Illegitimate live birth rates, by age and color of mother	D202 - D220
Illegitimacy ratios, by age and color of mother	D221 - D244
Distribution of births, by color, according to whether delivered in hospital and attended by physician	D245 - D253

6.

Women Migrants

Geographic movement usually is associated with a change in status -- educational status or employment status or marital status, etc. A change in the rate of migration of females, then, could connote a change in their status. The time series reflecting the migration of the population by sex, however, reveal only a few changes since 1948, when the series was initiated as part of the Census' Current Population Survey. In general, migration rates for most age groups have been fairly constant across this twenty-two year period.

Migration data is tabulated to provide classes roughly approximating the distance moved: within the same county, different county but within the same State, and movement between States. After examining mobility of women in relation to men in these terms, this chapter attempts to employ regression analysis to identify the effect of other influences over time on the rate of migration of 20-24 year old females -- a female age group that migrates more than any other. The relation of household and marital status to migration then is explored.

. . . . .

Migration through the Life Cycle and Distance

Since changes in status are more likely to occur at some ages than at others, one would expect the rate of migration to change with the life cycle. In the case of women in 1969, about 29 percent of the 18-19 year olds moved, while 44 percent of females 20-24 years of age moved (Series E006-E008, E014-E016, etc.). Thereafter, across the life cycle, smaller proportions moved as age advanced: 26 percent of the 25-34 age group, 14 percent of the 35-44 age group, nine percent of the 45-64 age group, and eight percent of females 65 years and older. The percent of males who migrate follows this same pattern, although the magnitudes of the percentages for males differ slightly, usually being somewhat higher.

The distance of the move, also, is associated with the life cycle. The older the person, the shorter the move. The percent of the female movers by distance are presented below in Table 6.1. They may be interpreted as probabilities.

79

Table 6.1 - Percent of Migrant Females Moving Different Distances*, by Age, 1969

Age	Same county	Different county, same State	Different State
18-19 years	63	18	17
20-24 years	59	18	21
25-34 years	61	16	20
35-44 years	62	16	18
45-64 years	67	17	14
65 years and over	73	14	12

* - The small residual percentages represent persons who moved from outside the United States.
Source: Series E005-E048.

Females in the young, industrious ages (20-24 and 25-34 years), if they move, are more likely than other ages to move from one State to another. With advancing age, this probability declines (from .21 among the 20-24 age group to .12 among females over 65 years). Conversely, among those who move, the probability that the move is within the county is lowest (.59) among those 20-24 years and increases to a maximum among females 65 years and older (.73). These probabilities are for 1969.

Given these uniformities, what trends over time does one observe? The answer: very few trends at all. For each age group there is very little change in the percent who migrate. The few changes that do appear actually are very small changes. There is, however, some sampling variation in the age-by-sex statistics that creates unsystematic variation in the time series. The 20-24 age group presents greater variation than any of the others, and younger ages show greater variation than older ones.

Migration of 20-24 Year Olds

Movement from one house to another within the same county may represent a distinct change of residential environment, but such a move undoubtedly has less meaning in terms of status adjustment problems than a longer move from one county to another or from one State to another. Consequently, the combined between-county and between-State migration of one age group, 20-24 year old females, will be examined. Migration of these women has increased from 12.8 percent of 20-24 year old females in 1948 to 17.2 percent in 1969, an increase of approximately one-third.

Figure 6.1 presents the trends in migratory movement of 20-24 year old males and females. Movement within the county varies more than other migratory moves. It increased to a peak in 1961-62 and another peak around 1965, and since has been declining. The net change in the 22-year time series has been an increase in the percent moving.

On a muter key, movement from one county to another in the same State also has increased, but the trend has varied much less than the within-county movement.

The percentage taking the longer move from one State to another has increased slightly for females, but, for males, the net trend since 1953 has been a declining percent moving across State lines.

80

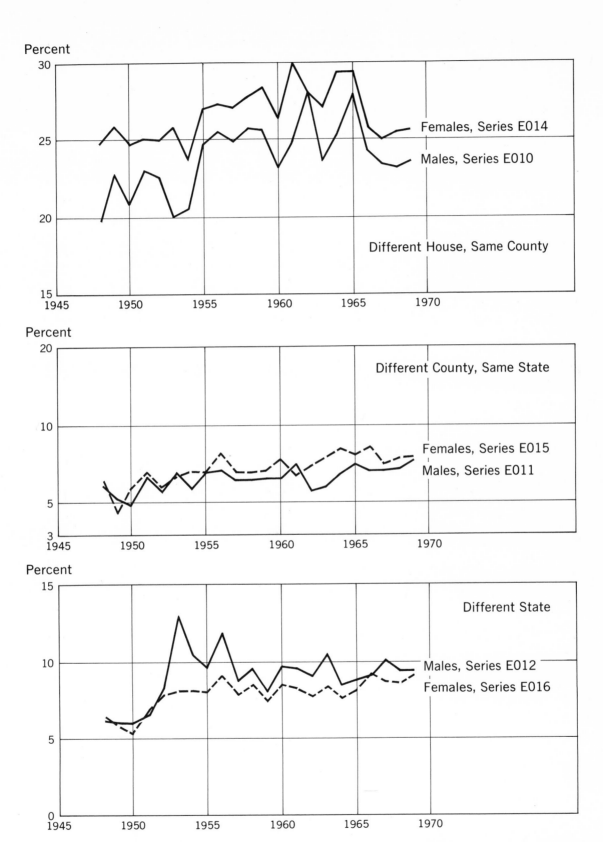

Figure 6.1 Mobility Status (Comparison of Place of Present Residence with Residence one Year Earlier), for 20–24 Year Old Males and Females, 1948–1969.

The sum of the percent moving from one county to another, same State, and the percent moving between States provides an aggregate measure of migration. This does not include within-county residential moves. This statistic for females 20-24 years of age increased 10 percentage points, 1949-1954, and in the next 15 years increased only two additional percentage points, net.

The percent of 20-24 year old females making inter-county and inter-State migratory moves is highly associated with time, the correlation coefficient being 0.77. Migration appears to be associated with a number of other factors, also, but when the effect of time upon the percent migrating is removed, the relation of the percent migrating to a number of other variables that one would expect to affect migration, vanishes. The correlation coefficients are presented below:

Table 6.2 - Correlation Between the Percent of 20-24 Year Old Females Migrating and
Other Factors

	Zero order correlation coefficient	Partial correlation coefficient, with time held constant
Time	0.77**	
Labor force participation rate, 20-24 year old females	0.57**	-0.20
Percent enrolled in school, 20-24 year old females	0.71**	-0.18
Unemployment rate of 20-24 year old females not enrolled in school	0.27	-0.41
Marriage rate, 20-24 year old females	-0.03	--
Birth rate, 20-24 year old females	0.69**	0.38

** - Indicates significant at .01 level.

In conclusion, there is a complex of forces that makes the migration of 20-24 year old females go slightly higher almost every year at an annual average rate of increase of 1.4%. When this complex, as expressed by a uniform annual linear increase, is removed, the remaining variance in the migration rate is not explained by the labor force participation rate, nor the unemployment rate of those not in school, nor the percent enrolled in school, the marriage rate, nor the birth rate (all based upon 20-24 year old females). A distinct change in the trend of one of these variables might demonstrate its impact upon migration. In the absence of such a "natural experiment", it is not possible to pin down a specific factor that seems to affect the migration of this group.

Household Status and Marital Status

The relationship of the person to the head of the household is associated with migratory status. When those holding similar household statuses are compared, however, males are more likely to move than females. Primary individuals, occupying a household alone or with nonrelatives, are most likely to have moved. The next most likely (excluding males whose wives are present) are persons who head primary families. Finally, the least likely to move are the heads of households with wife present, and the wife of the head, and the (male or female) relative of the head of the household. These data are presented in Series E115-E210.

Series E049-E114 present the percent moving, by age, sex, and marital status. The relationship between age, sex, and migration is the same as that discussed previously, and is illustrated by Table 6.3, below, for 1969, with the addition of marital status.

Table 6.3 - Percent Moving from One County to Another (Same or different State) by Age, Sex, and Marital Status, 1969

Age Group	Single		Married, spouse present		"Other" marital status	
	Male	Female	Male	Female	Male	Female
18-24 years	9.5	8.8	21.8	20.6		
25-34 years	11.4	7.6	10.6	9.1	20.7	12.4
35-44 years	5.5	4.5	5.5	4.7	14.9	5.5
45-64 years	5.0	2.7	2.9	2.8	8.1	3.3

To summarize the above, migration declines with age, for both males and females in each marital status group. Within each of these groups, the percent migrating is higher for males than for females -- considerably higher for "other" (i.e., separated, widowed and divorced) than for the single or married group. Finally, it is quite evident that, even with age and sex constant, marital status quite definitely is associated with migration. Single persons tend to be the least migratory. Married persons with spouse present are more likely to move than single persons in the younger ages (18-24 years), but in other ages, married persons are about as likely to move as single persons of those ages. Those who are separated, widowed, or divorced -- the "other" marital status -- are considerably more likely to have moved than either the married or single.

The trend across time for these categories is somewhat indistinct. One reason for this is the smaller sample size within each cell, which gives rise to a broader band of sampling error. Consequently, some of the variation across time is irregular, arising from the small sample base. Considering only females, the trend among the married (spouse present) group, generally, is constant. This is true, also, for the single females in the 18-24 age group and the 45-64 age group. The migration of the 25-34 age group of single females appears to be declining in recent years, and migration among the 35-44 age group is irregular, affected, again, by the small sample base. The trend among the "other" marital status females is generally irregular, presenting little overall change.

Summary of Indicators

Considering migration by age and sex, any marked change in the marital status of the population would undoubtedly lead to changes in the percent moving. Most migratory patterns over time, however, evidence considerable stability. In monitoring such trends, one should attempt

83

to identify any marked deviation and search for an explanation. Other than this, indicators of migration provide an index of general adjustment processes which demonstrate considerable stability over time.

<u>Key to Series Discussed in Chapter 6</u>

Percent, by mobility status, age and sex	E001-E048
Percent, by mobility status, single persons, by sex and age	E049-E072
Percent, by mobility status, married persons (spouse present), by sex and age	E073-E096
Percent, by mobility status, "other marital status", by sex and age	E097-E114
Percent, by mobility status, by relationship to head of household, and sex, 14-24 year olds	E115-E138
Percent, by mobility status, by relationship to head of household, and sex, 25-34 year olds	E139-E162
Percent, by mobility status, by relationship to head of household, and sex, 35-44 year olds	E163-E186
Percent, by mobility status, by relationship to head of household, and sex, 45-64 year olds	E187-E210

7.

Indicators of Women at Work

During the past twenty years or so, women have markedly increased their participation in
the labor force. As this increase has taken place, the rate of participation of males has
dropped.

Employment status and occupation, more than other factors (more than income or education
or family background, for example) contribute to the general social status of an individual
(Blau & Duncan, 1967). In the labor force, the occupation's position in the hierarchy, is
an important index to the status of the occupant, generally, in society.

In this chapter participation of women in the labor force is analyzed in relation to age,
color, educational attainment, husband's employment, marital status, and other factors. The
effect of the mother's employment upon the family is examined. The occupations women enter
are reviewed according to the distribution of all women who work and according to the prevalence
of women in each occupation. The extent of sexual segregation within occupations is reviewed.
Finally, the trend in the overall status of women in society, accorded by the occupations in
which they work, is presented and compared with that of men.

In addition to the data on women at work herein presented, an extensive supplementary discussion may be found in (Women's Bureau, 1969: 177-248), and information on the legal aspects
of the employment of women in the same publication (251-292).

. . . . .

An Overview

The overall trend of participation in the total labor force (including armed forces), by
sex, is presented in Figure 7.1 (Series F009-F010). Since 1947, the male participation rate
has declined nearly 6 percent, to 80.9 percent of males 16 years of age and over. The female
participation rate, on the other hand, has increased by 11 percent, and in 1969 stood at 42.7
percent of the female population 16 years of age and over. During the past 10 years the rate
of participation of females has inched up nearly one-half of a percentage point a year, on the
average. If this annual increment continues, one-half of the adult female population will be
in the labor force by about 1985. The Census Bureau projections, however, do not assume that

Participation Rate

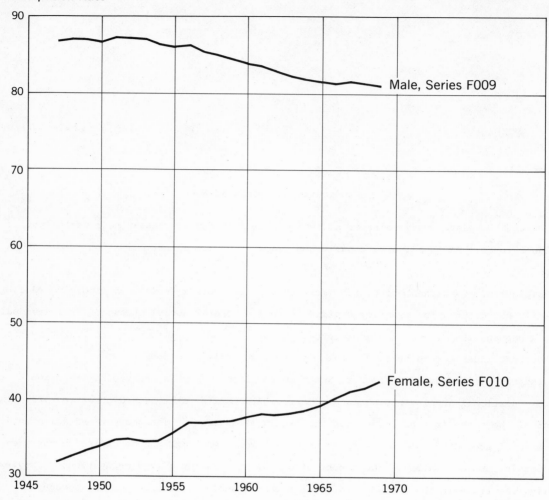

Unemployment Rate

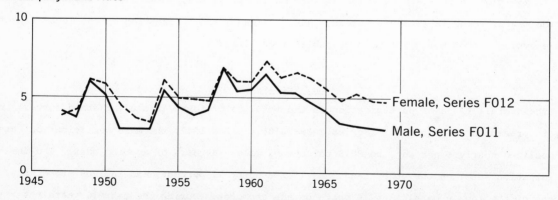

Figure 7.1 Total Labor Force Participation Rates (Including Armed Forces), and Unemployment Rates, Civilian Labor Force, Ages 16 Years and Over, by Sex, 1947–1969.

the present trend will continue. Instead, they assume a relatively constant rate for females to 1980 (Census, 1968d: 64). This assumption (Census Series B) seems unreasonable, for surely the present rate of change in the rate of women's participation in the labor force will continue for a few years, at least.

The increase in the participation of women in the labor force is a long-term trend of great significance, a number of influences bringing it about. Several of them may be mentioned: (1) The increased rate of industrial production, particularly since 1960, has created a greater demand for labor. The gross private domestic product increased at an annual average rate of 2.2 percent during 1955-60, but stepped up to an annual average rate of 4.8 percent during 1960-65 (Census, 1966e: Series A14). (2) The educational attainment of women has been increasing, thereby improving their employability (Series B001-B529). (3) Increasing numbers of families have attained the size they desire and the children have matured to ages that allow the mother to enter the labor force. Beginning with births in 1946 and 1947, birth cohorts have been larger, thereby introducing larger numbers of new workers annually into the labor force as they completed their education. In 1946 cohort became 20 years old in 1966, and, as Figure 7.2 illustrates, an increase in the labor force participation rate of the 20-24 year old females began at that time. (4) Women have become more dependent upon themselves, as evidenced by (a) an increase in the proportion of single women, (b) an increase in single nonwhite females, slightly greater than the white, and (c) a slight increase since 1960 in the percent of families and households with female heads (Series C186-C187).

In a comprehensive analysis of the long term supply and demand influences upon women's participation in the labor force, Valerie Kincade Oppenheimer found that the sex-labeling of jobs has affected the demand for women and the kinds of employment women train for and make themselves available for. She found this influence to be more pervasive than the much-touted augmentation of the supply of female labor through labor-saving devices in the home and related factors that have been thought to release women for employment (Oppenheimer, 1970: 62-63, 119-120).

The expansion of job opportunities for women resulting from industrial development and occupational changes -- all demand factors -- that took place, particularly, during the 1940s and 1950s, stimulated the supply of women for employment. Oppenheimer also found that demographic factors produced an impact upon the supply of female workers and, hence, upon their participation in the labor force. During the post-war period, she says, there was a decline in the population of young women and married women that was compensated for by an increase in the supply of older, married females. The latter demographic change generated growth in the labor force participation of older women and of the work rates of women as a whole (Oppenheimer, 1970: 187-189).

The male and female unemployment rate in the civilian labor force is presented in Figure 8.1 (Series F011-F012). Unemployment appears to be unrelated to the rate of participation in the labor force. Peaks and troughs in business activity in the pattern of unemployment of males and

87

females rise and fall in unison, each being affected by the same market influences. (In the next chapter, the tendency will be pointed out for wives to enter the labor force when unemployment is low.)

The unemployment rate of females, however, is persistently higher than that of males. Since 1958, when the unemployment rates of males and females during a recession in business activity were about equal, the two unemployment rates have spread wider and wider apart. In 1960 the difference was 0.5 percentage points. By 1969, the difference had increased to 1.9 percentage points. In actual numbers in 1969, there were approximately the same number unemployed, 1,428,000 females and 1,405,000 males, even though there were nearly 20 million more men than women in the civilian labor force at the time. These and other components of the labor force are presented as Series F001-F008.

Labor Force Participation and Age

Men in ages 25 to 44 years are nearly all in the labor force, less than three percent not participating. Women's heaviest participation, however, complements these ages. Women in the ages 20 to 24 years and 45 to 54 years participate most actively in the labor force. During the intervening years, many women are occupied with rearing children and housekeeping (Series F013-F030).

Since age is highly associated with participation in the labor force, especially among women, we shall consider age in some detail, identifying trends in participation of particular ages.

The 20-24 Year Age Group (Figure 7.2).(Series F019-F020). The increasing participation of the 20-24 year old males in the labor force during the last years of the 1940's and in the early 1950's, shown on Figure 7.2, resulted from their return to employment after their post-war attendance at technical training schools, colleges and universities. The labor force participation of women did not follow the same pattern. After 1953, the rate of participation of males 20-24 years of age began to decline and it has declined slowly but steadily since then. This decline is coincident with increases in school enrollment of males in these ages (Series B029 and B031).

Females in this age group began to participate more in the labor force beginning after 1959, increasing their rate of participation fairly rapidly.

The 25-34, 35-44 Ages (Figure 7.2) (Series F021-F024). Male participation rates among these ages have remained relatively constant for over 20 years. The participation of females in the labor force, on the other hand, decidedly has increased -- approximately 10 percentage points for the 25-34 year olds, and about 11 percentage points for the 35-44 year olds since 1950. Approximately half of the 35-44 year age group of females now are in the labor force.

The 45-54 Ages (Figure 7.3) (Series F025-F026). Male participation in the labor force has declined slightly, more than one percentage point, from its peak in 1953. Females in these ages

88

Participation Rate

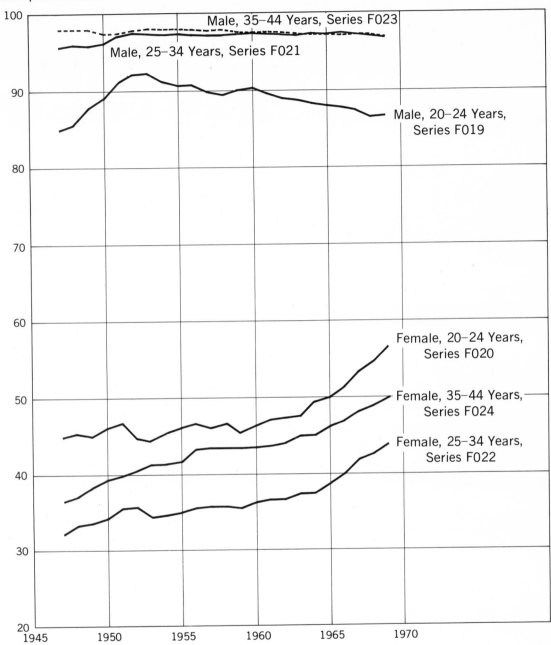

Figure 7.2 Total Labor Force Participation Rates (Including Armed Forces), Ages 20–24, 25–34 and 35–44 Years by Sex, 1947–1969

Participation Rate

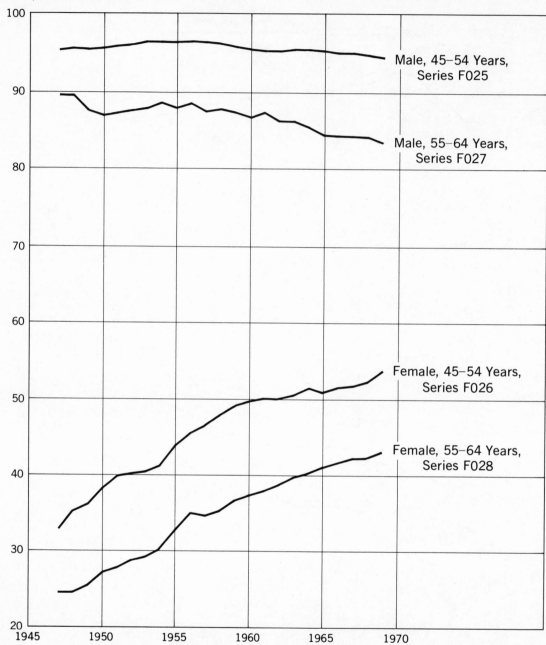

Figure 7.3 Total Labor Force Participation Rates (Including Armed Forces), Ages 45–54 and 55–64 Years, by Sex, 1947–1969

have increased participation more than any other female age group, from slightly over 32 percent to more than 53 percent, approximately 20 percentage points added in as many years. Females 45-54 years now have the highest participation rate of any age group among women.

The 55-64 Ages (Figure 7.3) (Series F027-F028). Participation of males of these ages in the labor force has declined six percentage points (1947-1969) while females of the same ages have increased in participation from 24 percent to 43 percent, or 19 percentage points.

Labor force participation rates for other age groups are presented as Series F013-F018 and F029-F030.

Differences in Labor Force Participation by Age and Color

The preceding review of labor force participation rates by age, will now be extended by illustrative series showing differences in trends by age and color. Not all series are illustrated; the Appendix presents additional data (Series F031-F070).

The basic trend, previously described, of decreasing participation of males in the labor force and increasing participation of women, is repeated for each of the color groups, white and nonwhite. There are, however, differences in level of participation and in the rate of change by color.

The trend in participation rates of nonwhite and white males is approximately the same (Figure 7.4, Series F031-F034), but the female rates by color differ considerably. Not only do nonwhite females participate more actively in the labor force than white females, but the trend, since about 1954, in the white female participation rate has been moving up much faster than the nonwhite female participation rate. The higher work rates of nonwhite females, than white females, is particularly noticeable in the middle and older ages. However, despite the increasing work rate of women, the differences between males and females are several times greater than the differences between the two groups of females.

The 20-24 Year Old Group (Figure 7.5) (Series F047-F050). In the young worker group, nonwhite males participate slightly more actively than white males, and the same is true of nonwhite females in relation to white females. However, the trend in the two measures is distinctly different. The males have been declining in participation, since about 1960, while females, both nonwhite and white, have been increasing in participation, roughly, since 1960. This increase in rate of labor force participation may have some bearing upon the marked increase in unemployment of nonwhite females, as evidenced by Series G16. The same is not true for white females; however, the participation rate for white females is somewhat less than that of nonwhite females.

The 35-44 Ages (Figure 7.6) (Series F055-F058). Figure 7.6 compares the active ages, 35 to 44 years, showing that white males have maintained a constant level of participation for twenty years, while the participation of nonwhite males has been declining slowly. The white participation rate now exceeds the nonwhite by approximately five percentage points. Nonwhite females, however, exceed white females in participation by more than 10 percentage points. The nonwhite

Participation Rate

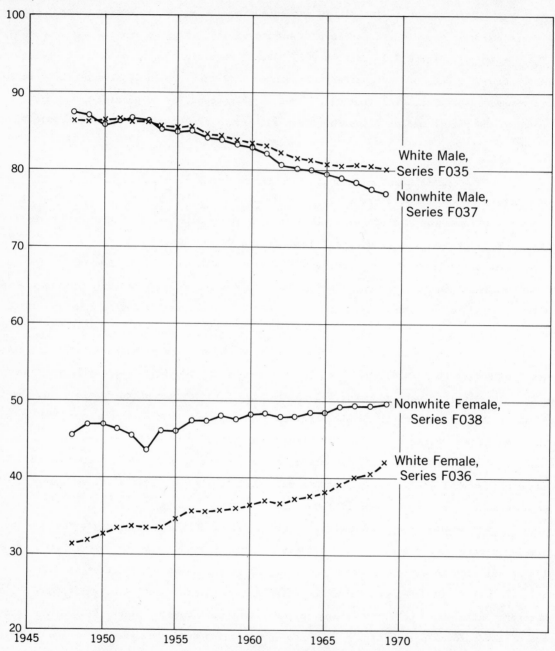

Figure 7.4 Civilian Labor Force Participation Rates, Ages 16 Years and Over, by Color and Sex, 1948–1969.

Participation Rate

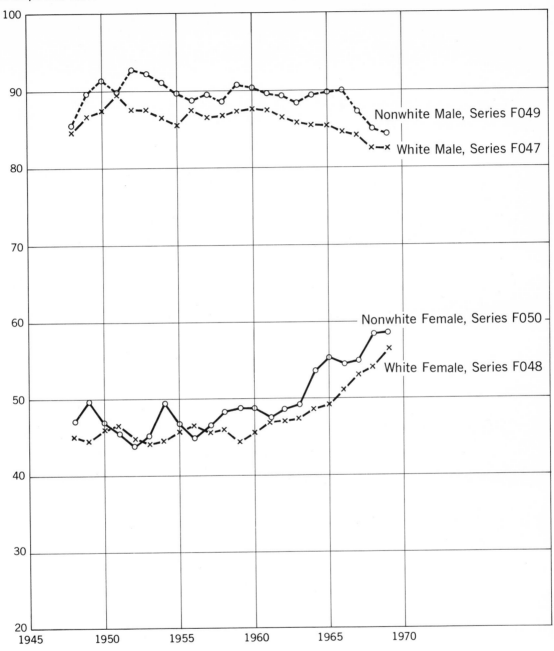

Figure 7.5 Civilian Labor Force Participation Rates, Ages 20–24 Years, by Color and Sex, 1948–1969

Participation Rate

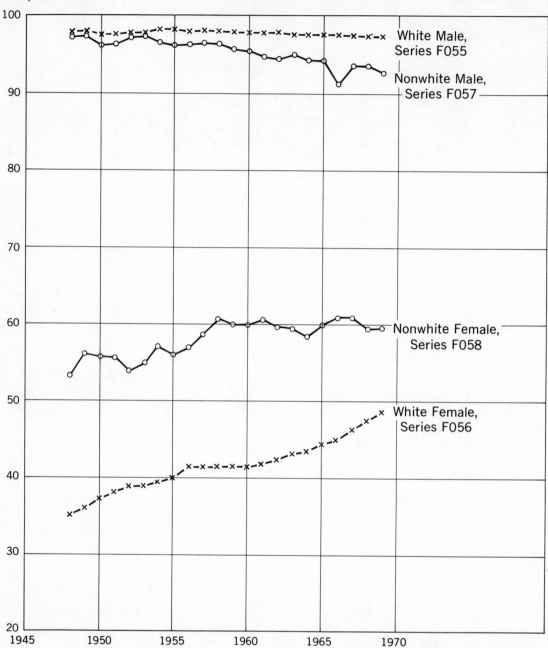

Figure 7.6 Civilian Labor Force Participation Rates, Ages 35–44 Years, by Color and Sex, 1948–1969

female rate has been relatively constant for the past 12 years, while the white participation rate, since about 1960, has been increasing fairly regularly.

The 55-64 Ages (Figure 7.7) (Series F064-F066). Figure 7.7 shows the changing pattern of labor force participation among the population of older workers. Since about 1954, the difference in participation rates of nonwhite and white males have been fairly constant, each declining slightly. On the other hand, the participation rates of both nonwhite and white females have been increasing over the long term. Participation of white females of these ages may be approaching the same level as nonwhite females.

Educational Attainment of the Labor Force, by Color and Sex

The civilian labor force has attained higher levels of education than the total population. Series F184-F211 present the distribution of the labor force by educational attainment for each sex/color group. The trend shows that each labor force sex and color group is attaining higher levels of education each year. The most general measure, the percent of the labor force attaining at least a high school education, shows white females to have attained higher levels of education than other sex/color groups in the labor force. White males are next, followed by nonwhite females, Series F208-F211 and Figure 7.8 (above).

A greater percentage of white males in the labor force have attained four years college or more than any other group, with white females following next (Series F204-F207).

In the lower levels of educational attainment, nonwhite males and nonwhite females register larger percentages than do white males and females (Series F184-F187).

Effect of Husband's Employment on the Work Rate of Wives

Series F125-F132 present the husband-wife families according to the employment status of the husband and the labor force status of the wife. In 1969, in more than half of these families, the husband was employed and the wife was not in the labor force. The trend in this percentage, however, has been decreasing since 1960. In approximately 42 percent of the husband-wife families in 1969, both the husband was employed and the wife was in the labor force. There were only a few families in which the husband was not employed.

The percent of wives in the labor force when the husband is not employed (Series F132) has always been greater than the percent of wives in the labor force when the husband is employed (Series F131) (Figure 7.8, below). By 1969, however, the difference between these two figures was only about two percentage points, for the percent of wives in the labor force with employed husbands has been increasing faster than the percent when the husband is not employed.

It appears, then, that the trend is for wives to be in the labor force whether or not the husband is unemployed. Formerly, ten years ago, it appeared to make a difference, but at present, 1969, the husband's unemployment has little effect on the wife's labor force status.

95

Participation Rate

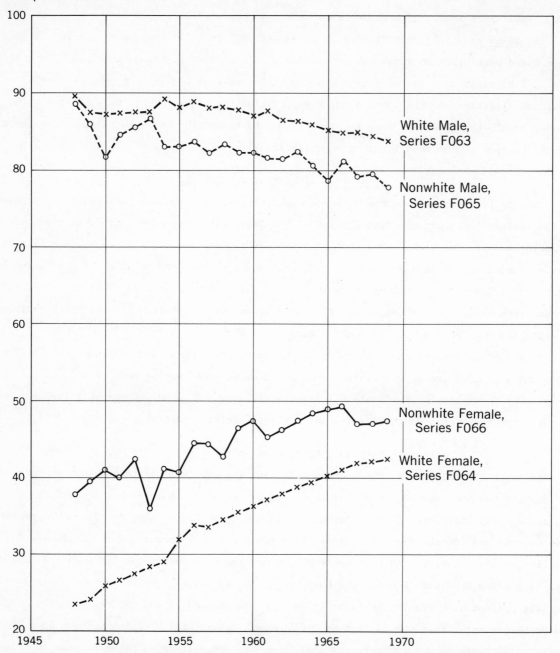

Figure 7.7 Civilian Labor Force Participation Rates, Ages 55–64 Years, by Color and Sex, 1948–1969

Percent of the Civilian Labor Force Having at Least 4 Years High School

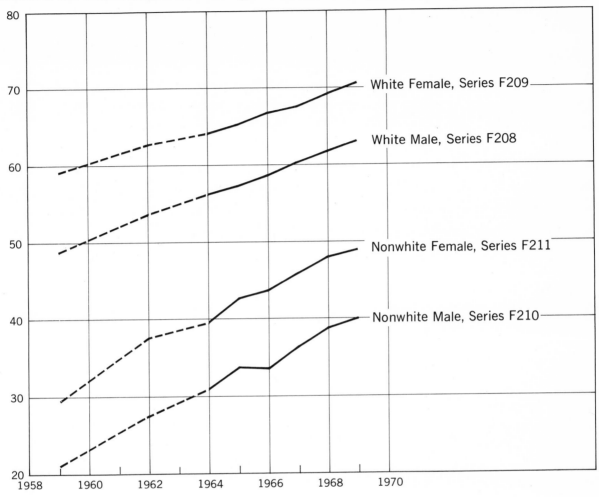

Percent of Wives in Labor Force

Figure 7.8 (Upper) Percent of Labor Force Attaining 4 Years of High School or More, by Color and Sex, 1959–1969; (Lower) Percent of Husband-Wife Families with Wife in Labor Force, by Employment Status of Husband, 1958–1969

Labor Force Participation by Marital Status and Age

Marital status is associated with participation in the labor force (Series F071-F118). Married men (wife present) have the highest work rates, single males the next highest, and widowed, divorced or separated males have the lowest participation rates. Among females, married women have the lowest work rates, single women have the highest, and widowed, divorced or separated women have rates that now are approximately the same as rates of married women.

The trends in these rates vary considerably by sex and marital status. All the work rates for males are declining. The rates among single females are declining, the rates among married women are increasing, while divorced, widowed, or separated women have rates that are relatively constant.

In the total civilian labor force, the (Series F071-F072) rates for single persons appears to increase in 1967, but actually this is due to the change in definition of the labor force, which eliminated the 14 and 15 year olds from the labor force. Up to that time the rates for single persons were declining. The data show that single persons in each age group, except the 14-17 year olds, declined in work rate, 1957-1969. The age-specific rates, rather than the total, for single persons should be examined.

Figure 7.9 presents the trend in the other marital status groups, showing the decline in the work rate among males, the stability of the rate among women who are widowed, divorced or separated, and the continuing increase among married women.

Trends by marital status, sex and age are illustrated by three graphs, Figures 7.10-7.12, showing the new entrants to the labor force, the 20-24 year olds, and the older population, 35-44 years and 45-64 years of age, respectively.

The 20-24 Year Olds (Series F077-F078, F085-F086, F093-F094). In Figure 7.10 this age group follows the general trend, previously described. Single females participate at about the same rates as single males and both trends are decreasing. Rates for both men and women who are widowed, divorced, or separated show greater sampling variability because of the smaller size of the samples. The work rate of married men, who are nearly all in the labor force, continues at a constant rate, while the work rate of married women is increasing, as it is among married women of all ages.

The 35-44 Year Olds (Series F097-F098, F105-F106, F113-F114). Married women in these ages are increasing their work rates while women of other marital statuses are either steady or declining slightly (Figure 7.11). Married men continue to present constant rates of participation, while single men and men of "other" marital status are declining slightly in their work rates.

The 45-64 year Olds (Series F099-F100, F107-F108, F115-F116). In this last phase of the work cycle, shown in Figure 7.12, the work rate of married women continued to increase, and women of "other" marital status also show a slight tendency to rise. Single female rates,

Participation Rate

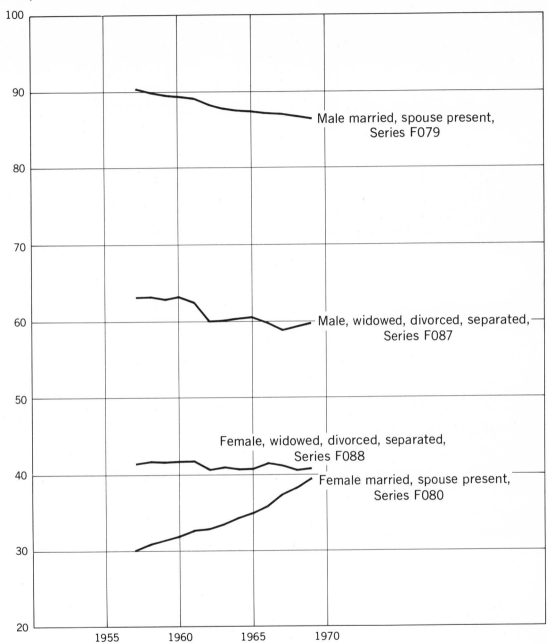

Figure 7.9 Civilian Labor Force Participation Rates, by Marital Status, Total Civilian Labor Force, by Sex, 1957–1969

Participation Rate

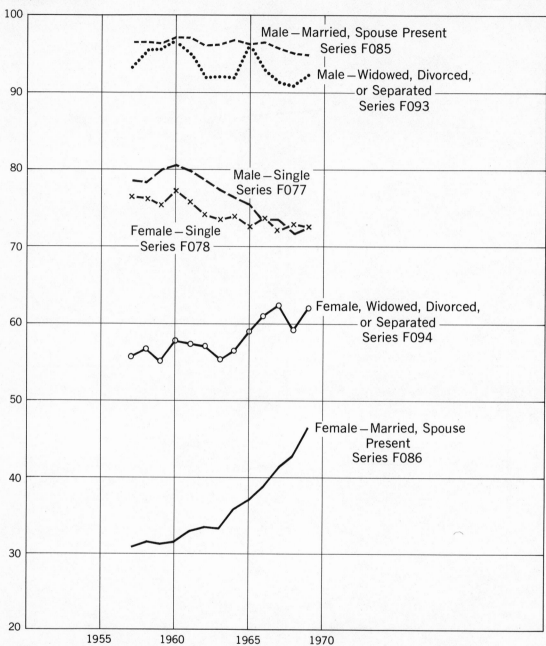

Figure 7.10 Civilian Labor Force Participation Rates, by Marital Status, Ages 20–24 Years, by Sex, 1957–1969

Participation Rate

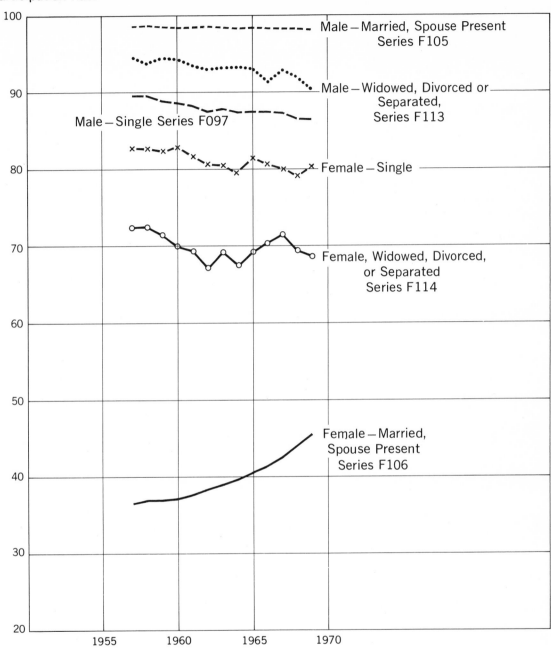

Figure 7.11 Civilian Labor Force Participation Rates, by Marital Status, Ages 35–44 Years, by Sex, 1957–1969

Participation Rate

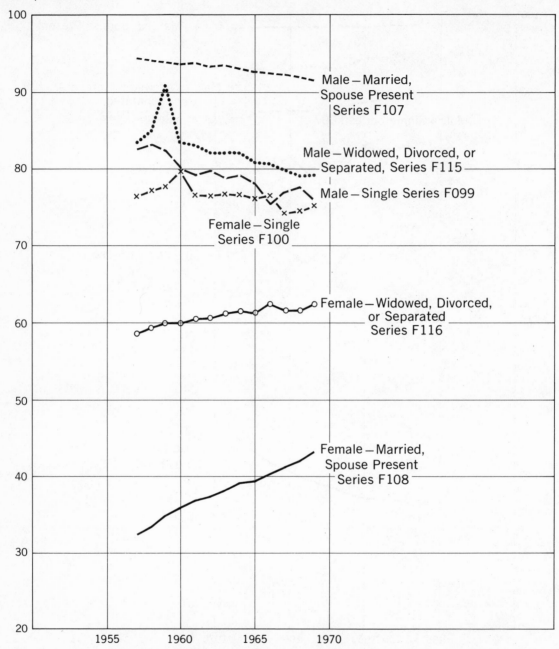

Figure 7.12 Civilian Labor Force Participation Rates, by Marital Status, Ages 45–64 Years, by Sex, 1957–1969

however, were lower in 1969 by some 4.6 percentage points than in 1960, and all rates for men in each marital status category are declining.

In summary, the trends in labor force participation by marital status, sex and age, show that married women of all ages are increasing their rates of labor force participation. The rates of participation of married men are relatively constant, while men in other marital status categories are participating at slightly lower rates. In general, women who are widowed, divorced or separated participate at relatively stable rates. The work rates among single women increasingly resemble the work rates of single men.

The Effect of the Presence of Children

Malcolm S. Cohen has analyzed in some detail the labor force participation rates of married women. He found that the labor force participation rates of married women decline with age. The more education she has, the more likely is she to be in the labor force. Married women with unemployed husbands, or husbands not in the labor force, are more likely to be in the labor force than women with employed husbands. However, Cohen found that the ages and number of children are the factors most highly associated with whether or not a married women is in the labor force. When all married women with the same number of children are considered, those who have completed college are more likely to be in the labor force than those with fewer years of education (Cohen, 1969: 31-35).

To examine the effect of children on the labor force participation of married women, Series F119-F124 present the trends.

Married women living with their husbands who have children 6 to 17 years of age at home, but no children under 6 years of age (Group II in Figure 7.13), participate in the labor force at higher rates than other married women with husband present. The next highest rate is among married women, husband present, who have no children at home under 18 years (Group I), a group including young women with no children in the home and older women whose children are 18 years of age or over.

Participating in the labor force at substantially lower levels are women having any children under six years of age. These wives are classified into two groups:

  II, those having children under six years of age and none older;

  IV, those having children under six years of age and also children 6-17 years of age.

There is no appreciable difference in labor force participation rates between these two groups. The key to lower labor force participation among these married women appears to be the presence of children under six years of age (Figure 7.13). These trends, then, bear out Cohen's findings for 1967.

For each of these groups of married women, the trend since 1948 has been one of increasing participation in the labor force. The rate of increase among women with no children under 18 years of age (Group I in Figure 7.13) is less than the rate of increase of the other groups, as evidenced by the slope of the trend lines.

103

Labor Force Participation Rate

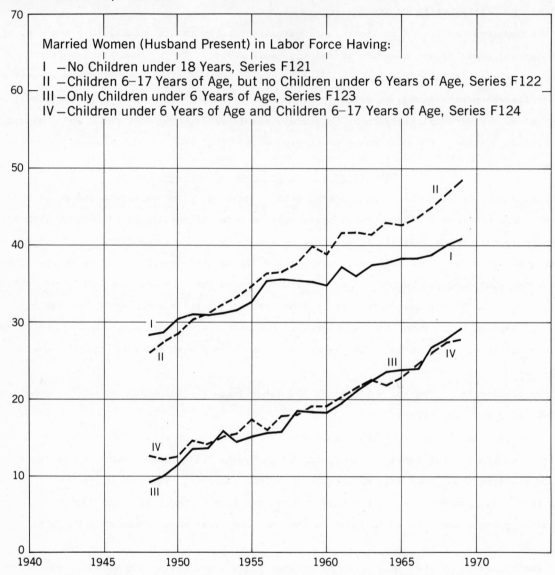

Figure 7.13 Labor Force Participation Rates of Married Women, Husband Present, by Ages of Children at Home, 1948–1969

While the trends for these four groups of women with different home responsibilities appear to follow the same pattern, the year-to-year variations do not appear to be associated with other influences.

White and Nonwhite Wives. Glen G. Cain finds, in his review of relevant data on married women in the labor force (1950 and 1960),two differences in the labor force behavior of white and nonwhite wives. These were: higher levels of labor force participation overall among non-white wives, and higher work rates for nonwhite mothers of young children than white mothers. In explaining these differences, he concluded that the labor force participation rate of non-white wives overstates their contribution to the economy. Their contribution is less than one would expect because their occupations are heavily represented in domestic service, involving part-time work, and other occupations which "reflect relatively low educational attainments, lesser training, and market discrimination" (Cain, 1966: 119). "Poorer housing conditions, smaller dwelling units, and more doubling up of families among nonwhites are all generally con-ducive to more market work and less homework by wives."

Cain thinks that the nonwhite wife continues to work because of the instability of the family and the ever-present possibility of her being the sole source of support for the children. He also feels that the nonwhite husband may be discriminated against more than the white husband, leading "to some substitution in market work between" husband and wife. These factors, Cain feels, lead to higher labor force participation among nonwhite wives, than white wives, and "lesser importance of children as a deterrent to work" among nonwhite wives (Cain, 1966: 119-120).

Three of Cain's major findings of particular interest to us: (1) as the educational status of women improves, their labor force participation increases; (2) low unemployment in the economy is associated with increases in labor force participation of wives; and (3) even though the work rates of mothers with young children has been increasing, the presence of young children in the home is negatively associated with wives' working (Cain, 1966: 118). Unfortunately, trends in these characteristics by color are not available.

Marital status, age of mother, color, and the presence and ages of children are associated with the participation of women in the labor force. From an obverse point of view, what is the effect of her participation upon the fertility rate, upon the stability of marriage and the family, upon the rate of juvenile delinquency experienced by the community? Should the public provide supervised recreational facilities or public child care centers, so that mothers may enter the labor force? If this is done, what effects will the absence of the mother have upon the development of the child?..upon the stability of the family? Decisions women make to enter the labor force may be viewed as affecting many sectors and problems of society. The following section explores some of the consequences of the mother of the family entering the labor force.

Effects of the Mother's Employment upon the Family

When the wife goes to work, what happens to the traditional role of wife and mother in her family? Does it affect the children's development? These questions are critical in assessing the consequences of the increasing work rate of married women and mothers. If the wife's entrance into the labor force adversely affects family life and disrupts the socialization of the young, should public policies encourage labor force participation of wives? Several studies bear upon these questions and lend guidance in interpreting the trends reviewed above.

Using a sample of working and non-working mothers, matched on other family characteristics, Alberta Siegel and her associates tested children for independent and dependent personality traits. She did not find differences related to the mother's employment (Siegel et. al., 1963: 80). Burchinal studied the personality and social development of a large sample of children during the first three, the second three, and the first six years of their lives, some having mothers who worked and others, mothers who did not work. He could not find important differences, and concluded that maternal employment had no apparent detrimental effect upon the development of children (Burchinal, 1963: 118-119). Parallel results have been reported by Burchinal (1961) using children's anxiety scores as a criterion, by Nolan and Tuttle, using the rated adjustment of children and their school grades, and by Hand, using personality adjustment scores (Burchinal, 1963: 119-120).

Studying the adolescent, Nye concluded, "School performance, psychosomatic symptoms, and affectional relationship to the mother appear unrelated to employment status of the mother. A small association appears to be present between employment status and delinquent behavior" (Nye, 1963a: 140).

If the mother's working does not adversely affect the development of children, does it have an impact upon the husband-wife relationship and the distribution of duties within the household? Evidence points to some redefinition of roles between husband and wife. Studying rural households, Francena Nolan found "a tendency toward a sharing" of housekeeping responsibilities by the husband in families where the mother worked, but she found no adverse effects of the mother's employment on the children, the housekeeping, nor participation in community affairs, and there was a general feeling of satisfaction and success among families of working mothers, in coping with problems of daily life (Nolan, 1963: 250). Heer (1958) also reports a difference in the role of the working wife: "...both in the working class and in the middle class the working wife exerts more influence in decision-making than the non-working wife" (Heer, 1958: 46-47). Blood reinforces this conclusion, finding that "the pressure for revising the division of labor results in conflict between husband and wife over marriage roles," and that the wife assumes a stronger voice in major economic decisions but "a lesser voice" in routine household decisions (Blood, 1963: 303-304). Nye's work supports the conclusion that the mother of a small family finds her role more engaging and interesting if she is employed under satisfactory conditions (Nye, 1963b: 362).

These studies, then, lend support to the general hypothesis that the employment of the wife and mother need not detrimentally affect the nurture and socialization of children, but may require realigning domestic roles, necessitating role adjustments by the husband and other members of the family. The advantages of improved personal and community adjustment of the family are marred only by the suggestion that juvenile delinquency may be a by-product of the mother's employment. Undoubtedly, continuing research on problems of family adjustment is required, but the potential for adjustment of roles within the family appear to be great, as are the capacities of women to adapt to multiple roles of wife, mother, housekeeper, and employee.

The Occupations of Employed Women

What occupational fields do women enter ? Are women shifting their areas of employment ? The long term trend of increasing participation of women in the labor force will be viewed here, not in absolute numbers nor in proportion to all females employed, but as a percentage of total employed in each occupational group (Series F167-F182). The orientation of this approach, is best illustrated by Table 7.1, below.

Table 7.1 - The Distribution of Employed Females by Major Occupational Group, the Percent of Females in Each Group in 1969 and the Rate of Change, 1947 to 1969

Occupation group	Employed females, ages 16 years and over, 1969		Females in each group as a per- cent of employed civilian workers, 1969	Average annual rate of change in females as percent of employed workers in each group		
	Number (000)	Percent distribution by occupat- ional group		1947 to 1958 (workers 14 yrs. & over)	1958 to 1969 (workers 16 yrs. & over)	1947 to 1969
Total	29,084	100.0	37.3	1.4	1.2	1.3
White-Collar	17,271	59.4	46.9	0.7	0.9	0.8
Blue-Collar	4,974	17.1	17.6	-0.4	1.4	0.5
Service	6,271	21.6	65.8	1.0	0.3	0.6
Farm	569	2.0	17.3	1.2	-0.3	0.4

Source: Series F136, F146, F154, F160, F167-F182 and (Labor, 1970: 226).

As the second column above shows, employed females are chiefly in the white-collar occupations, and service occupations are second. A somewhat different picture appears when employed females in these fields are expressed as a percent of all employed persons in each field, the third column. Females are seen dominating the service occupations and providing almost half of the workers in the white-collar fields. The last three columns show the average annual rate of change of the percent of females in each occupational group, 1947 to 1958, 1958 to 1969, and 1947 to 1969. In the total, females among employed workers have increased slightly more than one percent annually, on the average, 1947 to 1969. While the rate has become, in the last decade, a decreasing rate among farm workers, it is increasing most rapidly among blue-collar workers, an indicator that women are becoming increasingly numerous in factories. While the percents of females in farm and in blue-collar occupations are approximately equal, the percentage is increasing among blue-collar workers but declining among farm workers. The trend in the percent female of total employed civilians is presented in Figure 7.14. As a percent of all employed persons, females increased from 28.2 percent in 1947 to 37.3 percent in 1969. As a percentage of the workers in each occupational group, the increase in the white-collar group and among service workers has been approximately the same (about eight percentage points). The increase in blue-collar workers and farm workers has been slight. Details of these trends are next examined.

Prevalence of Women Employed by Occupation

Trends in the percent of female workers in white-collar occupations are shown in Figure 7.15 (Series F168-F182). The percent female among clerical workers has increased considerably since 1955. Sales workers and managers have increased slightly while the percent of females among professional and technical workers has actually declined slightly since 1947.

Women predominate in the occupations of service workers, approximating 65 percent of the total during the past decade (Figure 7.16). Females almost completely dominate the field of private household workers and are the majority among "other" service workers. In addition, women have recently increased as a percent of "other" service workers.

Among blue-collar occupations and crafts, females are a small minority (Figure 7.16). Recent increases in the percent of females employed in these occupations have occurred, particularly among blue-collar operatives.

The indicators of the employment of women by occupation show steady and fairly uniform change. Women are bowing out of farm work, probably gleefully. Except for this, the percent female in each occupational group is either steady or gradually increasing. With the increasing numbers of females attending college and universities, one would expect more pronounced increases in the percent of females employed in professional and technical occupations, but such has not been the case.

Occupational Distribution of Women

Women work primarily in white-collar occupations (Figure 7.17). The trend in their employment as white-collar workers has increased steadily, 1947 to 1969 (Series F135-F144). The percent of women in clerical and kindred occupations predominates among white-collar fields and increases over the 22-year period have been greatest among them. Women in professional, technical, and kindred workers also have increased during this period, but in the other categories among white-collar workers (managers, officials, and proprietors; and sales workers) each have declined slightly in the percent distribution of employed women.

The percent of employed women who are service workers has remained relatively stationary over the period since 1947. The percent of females in private household work has declined nearly half, while the percent of females in other service work has increased about half.

Percent

Figure 7.14 Employed Females, by Major Occupational Group, as
Percent of Total Employed Workers in their Occupational Group:
14 Years and Over, 1947–1958
16 Years and Over, 1958–1969

Percent

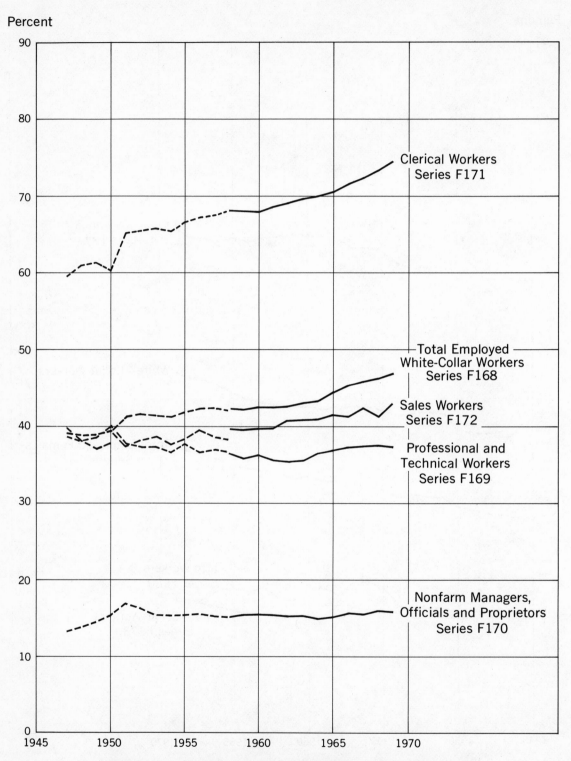

Figure 7.15 Employed Females in White-Collar Occupations as Percent of Total Employed White-Collar Workers, by Occupational Subgroup:

14 Years and Over, 1947–1958
16 Years and Over, 1958–1969

Percent

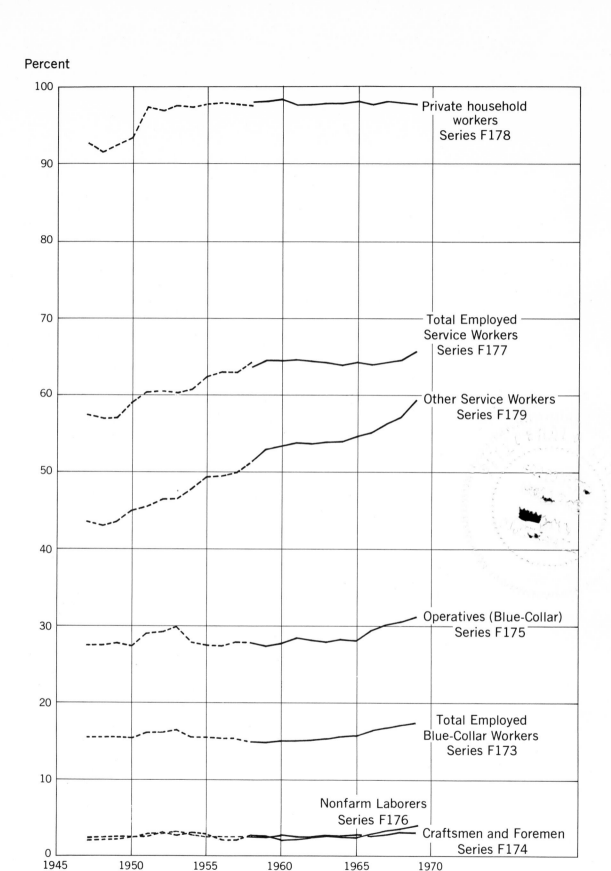

Figure 7.16 Employed Females in Blue-Collar Occupations as Percent of Total Employed Blue-Collar Workers, and Employed Females in Service Occupations as Percent of Total Employed Service Workers, by Occupational Subgroup:

14 Years and Over, 1947–1958
16 Years and Over, 1958–1969

111

Percent of All Employed Civilian Females

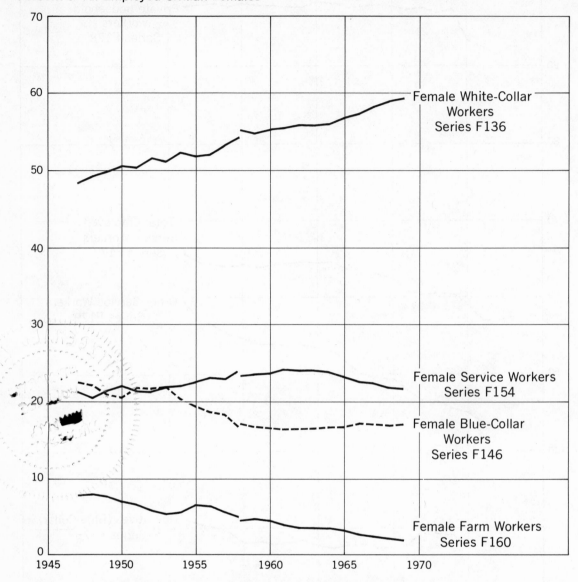

Figure 7.17 Percent Distribution of Employed Civilian Females, by Major Occupation Group:
14 Years and Over, 1947–1958
16 Years and Over, 1958–1969

Percent of All Employed Civilian Males

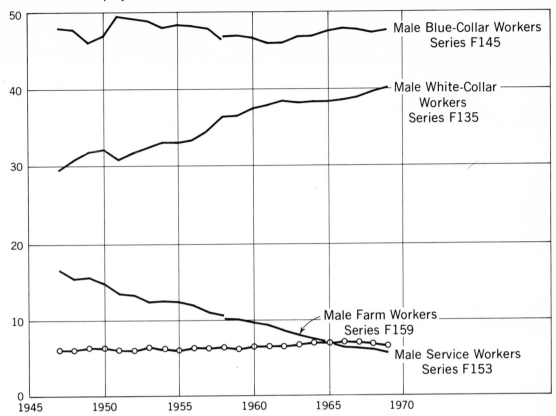

Figure 7.18 Percent Distribution of Employed Civilian Males, by Major Occupation Group:
14 Years and Over, 1947–1958
16 Years and Over, 1958–1969

The proportion of men in service occupations is approximately one-third the percent of females in them, and they have remained relatively constant as a percent of all employed men.

As a percent of all employed women, blue-collar workers and farm workers have declined. Blue-collar occupations attract nearly one-half of the employed males, but only about one-sixth of women workers. Operatives and kindred workers employed over 20 percent of all women in 1947, but by 1969 this had fallen to approximately 15 percent. Among men, each category of blue-collar work maintained a relatively constant proportion during this period.

Women have never entered farm work in large numbers. By 1969, only two percent worked on farms. But as the percent of women in farm work has declined, so has the percent of men in farm work, and by approximately the same factor, two-thirds to three-fourths less in 1969 than in 1947.

Figures 7.17 and 7.18 present these trends for the occupational groups, and Series F133-F164 give the data for these groups and for their major components.

Sexual Segregation in Occupations

Valerie Kincade Oppenheimer has shown that some occupations have come to be sex-linked or sex-specific (Oppenheimer, 1970: 65-120). Demand has created a requirement for _female_ labor in particular occupations. This, in turn, has influenced the supply. Women train themselves to go into jobs where there is a demand for their services. Consequently, a demand for men in some occupations does not exist, nor a demand for women in male-linked occupations. An employer would not readily be able to locate a male secretary, for example, if he wanted to hire one. Thus, occupations tend to be sex-linked (See, also, Hedges, 1970: 19-20, 28-29).

To measure the sexual segregation of occupations, Gross has contrived an Index of Segregation for each decade, 1900 to 1960. His results show practically no change over time in sexual segregation of occupations. His data, presented in Table 7.2, may be interpreted as the percentage of females (or males) who would have to change occupation in order that the distribution of sex by occupation should be the same (Gross, 1968: 201-202). In considering this result, Gross speculated that the relatively constant value of his Index of Segregation might be due to "structural differences" across time. For example, white-collar occupations are growing fast and these are heavy employers of women. Consequently, following a conceptualization developed by Jack P. Gibbs, Gross computed a Standardized Measure of Differentiation which treats all occupations as being of equal size. In interpreting this index, Gross states: "They (the figures) support the claim that there has been a reduction in sexual segregation in occupations but that reduction does not show up because those occupations that segregate more have been growing faster than those that segregate less" (Gross, 1968: 204). This index is also presented in Table 7.2.

Gross' Index of Sexual Segregation is based upon the full detail of the approximately 300 to 400 occupations listed by the Census. Series F183 presents a comparable measure based upon ll major occupational categories, Series Fl35-Fl64. This index, while different in magnitude from Gross' index because of (my) use of aggregate occupational categories, reveals the same constant trend as described by Gross' Index of Sexual Segregation.

Table 7.2 - Gross' Sexual Segregation in Occupations and Standardized Measure of Occupational Differentiation, 1900-1960

	Gross' Index of Segregation	Gross' standardized measure of occupational differentiation
1900	66.9	70.3
1910	69.0	68.1
1920	65.7	65.9
1930	68.4	66.6
1940	69.0	63.8
1950	65.6	59.3
1960	68.4	62.2

Source: (Gross, 1968: 202, 204).

Figure 7.19 presents the Index of Sexual Segregation of Occupations. It is to be interpreted as the percent of women that would need to change occupational categories in order for the male and female occupational distribution to be the same. This index shows very little trend. One may say that the degree of segregation has increased slightly since the 1947-1953 period, but that it is relatively constant. As Gross has shown, occupations that are sex-linked have grown faster than those that segregate less, and this has contributed to the stability of this index. As women have entered more primarily male-linked occupations, there has been a reduction in the sexual segregation of occupations (Gross, 1968: 204). Male occupations, 1900 to 1960, became more segregative, whereas typically-female occupations have become less segregative, according to Gross (205). While such conclusions reflect the broad occupations of employed civilians, they do not detect the differences between men and women employees that derive from position in the establishment, i.e., supervisor or supervisee, superordinate or subordinate positions.

The Status of Occupations

In evaluating these indices, it should be remembered that, while equality of occupational distribution between men and women is the standard for the index, equality of distribution would not necessarily be advantageous for women, nor, for that matter, for society as a whole. For example, seven percent of men and 34.3 percent of women are in clerical and kindred white-collar positions. To equalize the percent distribution (34.3-7.0)/2 = 27.3/2 = 13.6 percent, say, of women, would need to move. Movement would necessarily be into such occupations as the blue-collar, where nearly half the males find employment. To equalize the distribution, then, would not necessarily be advantageous to women, considering the skill, physical exertion, and related requirements of some typically male-linked occupations.

To evaluate the status factor in occupations, an Index of the Status of Occupations was constructed for each sex, presented as Series Fl65-Fl66. This Index was developed by applying

115

Index Number

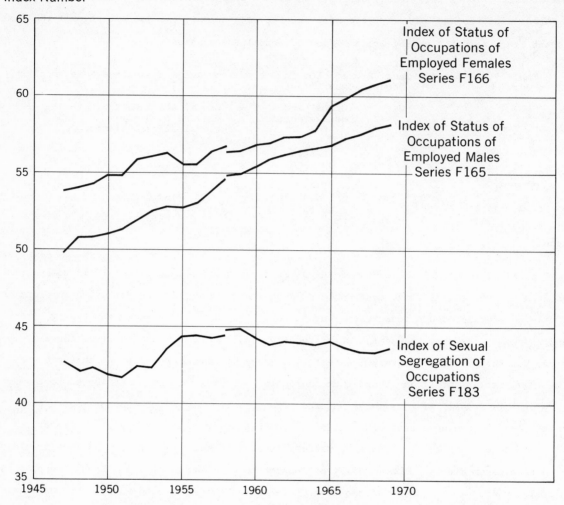

Index of Status of Occupations of Employed Females Series F166

Index of Status of Occupations of Employed Males Series F165

Index of Sexual Segregation of Occupations Series F183

Figure 7.19 Indices of Sexual Segregation and Status of Occupations, 1947–1969

weights employed by the U.S. Bureau of the Census on 1960 Census data. The weights were developed by the U.S. Bureau of the Census upon the basis of the 1950 education and income of the range of occupations. We multiplied these "scores" of weights for occupational groups by the percentage of the employed civilian population in each occupational group, by sex, and summed, to provide the indices for males and for females (Series F165 and F166). (For a description of the method, see Notes to Series F165-F166). Weights are constant across the time period presented in Figure 7.19.

These summary measures reflect the increases in the number of employees in white-collar occupations, the decline in workers in farm occupations, and other occupational changes. Women, it appears, have tended to work in occupations that, when indexed by education of the incumbents and income, are at levels higher than the occupations in which men have worked. The gap narrowed during 1957-1964 but, since 1964, the gap has begun to spread even wider. As the proportion of females in white-collar occupations continues to increase (Series F136), the index of the status of occupations of women undoubtedly will continue to rise gradually.

In a development similar to the above, Dale L. Hiestand (1964) employed median income as weights to detect trends in occupations of males and females by color. Following Gary S. Becker, Hiestand developed indices of the occupational position of women relative to men, by color, and of Negroes relative to whites, by sex. He weighted the numbers in each of seven occupational groups with constant weights, based upon median incomes of the occupational group from the 1950 Census, separately calculated for each color-sex group. His results show an improvement in the relative occupational position of Negro females relative to white females, an improvement slightly greater than that of Negro males relative to white males, 1910 to 1960. The position of females relative to males, by color, improved from 1910 to 1940, but since 1940, both have deteriorated, owing primarily to the entrance of women after 1940 into lower-paying positions.

The relative equality of women and men (the indices near 100) is due to the fact that women do not enter low paying occupations, such as farming and unskilled labor, as do men.

Hiestand's results are shown below:

	1910	1920	1930	1940	1950	1960
Occupational position of Negroes relative to whites:						
Male	78.0	78.1	78.2	77.5	81.4	82.1
Female	78.0	71.3	74.8	76.8	81.6	84.3
Occupational position of females relative to males:						
White	101.4	110.0	105.6	103.6	98.9	93.6
Negro	101.5	99.9	101.0	101.7	99.3	96.1

Source: (Hiestand, 1964).

117

Summary of Indicators

The participation rate of males in the labor force is declining; the participation rate of females is increasing (Series F009 and F010). A change in this trend will signal a change of a major influence on the status of women, but at present such a change does not seem likely.

Increases in the work rate of females are especially noticeable since 1964 in the younger, more vigorous ages -- 20-24 years, 25-34 years, and 35-44 years (Series F020, F022 and F024, respectively). These ages, the same as the principal childbearing ages, bear witness to changes in the mother's role within marriage and the family.

Longer-term changes in the labor force participation of older women -- 45-54 years and 55-64 years (Series F026 and F028) -- reflect increases of a more stable segment of the female labor force. Any change in these trends will warrant careful study to assess their consequences.

The labor force participation of white women is approaching that of nonwhite women for the 20-24 age group, the 55-64 age group, and others. While not a trend of great significance, the parallel of the two curves in several of the age groups suggests the converging influences that affect employment of both white and nonwhite women.

While the probability that a wife in husband-wife families is working is greater if the husband is not employed than if he is employed, these probabilities, also, are converging (Series F131, F132), indicating that wives today work less out of necessity than formerly. Married women living with their husbands are increasing in labor force participation, while the rate of participation of women who are widowed, divorced or separated maintains a relatively constant trend. The work rate of single women increasingly resembles the work rate of single men. Because of the varying effects of the life cycle, each of these trends also reflects the impact of age.

While all married women with children are increasing in labor force participation, women with no children or with children older than six years are more likely to be in the labor force than other women with children under 18 years. The mother's employment has not been shown to affect adversely the development of the child. While readjustments in family roles may be necessary if she works, these adaptations do not appear to be detrimental to the family. Continuing research on these problems, however, seems desirable.

Women are likely to be in service and white-collar occupations and they are increasing as a percent of the employees in these fields (Series F177 and F168). As a percent of the total in each occupation, they are increasing especially among clerical workers (Series F171) and "other service" occupations (Series F179), but they are not increasing proportionately in the more remunerative professional and technical occupations (Series F169). However, the status level of women's jobs, a rough measure of the desirability of the employment, has always been higher than the status of men's jobs and it continues to rise. Nearly sixty percent of all women employees are white-collar workers (Series F136), while the percents of all women

118

employees in service (Series F154), blue-collar (Series F146), and farm worker (Series F160) occupations continue to decline.

While the segregation of women in typically female-linked occupations continues, segregation today is but little more than it was some twenty years ago (Series F183), indeed, even seventy years ago. Type-of-work differences between men and women, thus, appear to be persistent.

Key to Series Discussed in Chapter 7

Population, labor force status and employment status, by sex	F001 - F008
Labor force participation rate and unemployment rate, by sex	F009 - F012
Labor force participation rates, by age and sex	F013 - F030
Civilian labor force participation rates, by age, color and sex	F031 - F070
Civilian labor force participation rates, by marital status, age and sex	F071 - F118
Labor force participation of married women, by ages of children	F119 - F124
Labor force participation of wives, by employment status of husband	F125 - F132
The number in the civilian labor force and the percent distribution, by major occupational group and sex	F133 - F164
Index of the status of occupations, by sex	F165 - F166
Percent female among employed civilians, by occupation group	F167 - F182
Index of the sexual segregation of occupations	F183
Percent of the civilian labor force attaining given levels of education, by color and sex	F184 - F211

Unemployment Indicators

The unemployed, according to the official statistical definition, are those who do not have a job and are looking for work. Women are more likely to be looking for work than men, and there are probably, in addition, many women who seek interesting employment from time to time and, not finding it, stop looking. If asked, these women would not be classified by a Census Bureau survey as unemployed. This suggests that larger proportions of women are available for employment than the official statistics portray as unemployed. Even so, these statistics provide the most general and reliable indicators of unemployment.

This chapter considers the series on the percent of women in the labor force who are unemployed, examining the trend in relation to the business cycle, to full- or part-time employment, to age and color of the unemployed person, and to marital status. Where appropriate, the unemployment rates of men are compared with those of women.

. . . . .

Two distinct differences between males and females in the labor force are illustrated by the trends presented in Table 8.1.

First, females in the labor force are much more likely to be employed part-time than are males. Almost all males are engaged full-time.

Second, females in the labor force are more likely to be unemployed than males.

The table shows a slight increase in the percent of females employed part-time and a slight decrease in full-time unemployed workers, but, otherwise the duration of the series is too short to indicate trends of any significance.

Table 8.1 - Percent of Males and of Females 20 Years of Age and Older in the Labor Force by Full-Time or Part-Time Work Status and by Employment Status

	Full-time				Part-time			
	Employed		Unemployed		Employed		Unemployed	
	Male	Female	Male	Female	Male	Female	Male	Female
1963	92.1	76.1	4.2	4.6	3.4	18.4	0.2	0.8
1964	92.6	76.4	3.6	4.3	3.5	18.4	0.2	0.9
1965	93.4	77.1	3.0	3.7	3.4	18.5	0.2	0.8
1966	94.0	77.4	2.3	3.0	3.5	18.5	0.2	0.8
1967	93.8	76.4	2.1	3.3	3.9	19.5	0.2	0.9
1968	93.8	76.2	2.0	2.9	4.1	20.1	0.2	0.8

Source: (BLS, 1969a: 57).

Unemployment in the Full-Time and Part-Time Labor Force

The employment status of men and women present contrasting pictures when the full-time and part-time labor forces are compared. This is significant because of the proportionately larger number of females in the part-time labor force, some 20 percent as compared with about four percent of males (Table 8.1).

The unemployment rate of females in the full-time labor force is typically higher than the unemployment rate of females in the part-time labor force (reversed, however, in 1967 and 1968). However, the opposite is true for males: males in the part-time labor force are more likely to be unemployed than males in the full-time labor force, sometimes by a factor of two (Table 8.2).

Within the full-time labor force, the unemployment rate of females is always higher than the unemployment rate of males. The opposite is true within the part-time labor force: males are more likely to be unemployed than females among part-time workers.

Table 8.2 - Unemployment Rates in the Full- and Part-Time Labor Forces, and Percent of the Labor Force Full-Time, by Sex

	Civilian labor force aged 20 years and over					
	Full-time labor force		Part-time labor force		Percent of labor force, full-time	
	Unemployment Rate		Unemployment Rate			
	Male	Female	Male	Female	Male	Female
1963	4.4	5.7	6.9	4.3	96.3	80.7
1964	3.7	5.3	6.5	4.5	96.2	80.7
1965	3.1	4.6	5.3	3.9	96.4	80.8
1966	2.4	3.8	4.8	3.7	96.3	80.4
1967	2.2	4.1	4.8	4.6	95.9	79.7
1968	2.0	3.7	4.9	4.0	95.7	79.1

Source: (BLS, 1969a: 57).

Women's unemployment rate responds to business conditions, as does the unemployment rate of men. The variation in the trend, across the twenty-year period for which we have data, follows the same pattern for each sex and color group. Figure 8.1 and Series G01-G36 present these rates for the labor force population 16 years of age and over by age, color and sex.[1]

Unemployment rates of nonwhites of both sexes are persistently higher than unemployment rates of whites. In fact, unemployment is clearly associated more closely with color than with sex.

However, there are sex differences. This is seen most clearly in the persistently higher unemployment rates of white females as compared with white males. Among nonwhites, this relationship is confused, nonwhite female unemployment sometimes being greater and sometimes being less than the nonwhite male rate. This may be due to characteristic occupational influences, but part of the variation certainly may be attributed to greater sampling variability in the nonwhite rates.

---

[1] Peaks and troughs in the business cycle, symbolized by "P" and "T" in Figure 8.1, are those estimated by the National Bureau of Economic Research (Census, 1966e: 66). The Federal Reserve Index of Total Industrial Production: 1940-1968 from (U.S. President, 1970: 217), and 1969 from (FR, 1970: 5a). The BLS Index of Output per Man-hour: 1940-1946 from (Census, 1966e: 188-189, Series A157), and 1947-1969 from (U.S. President, 1970: 216).

Index Number (1957–59 = 100)

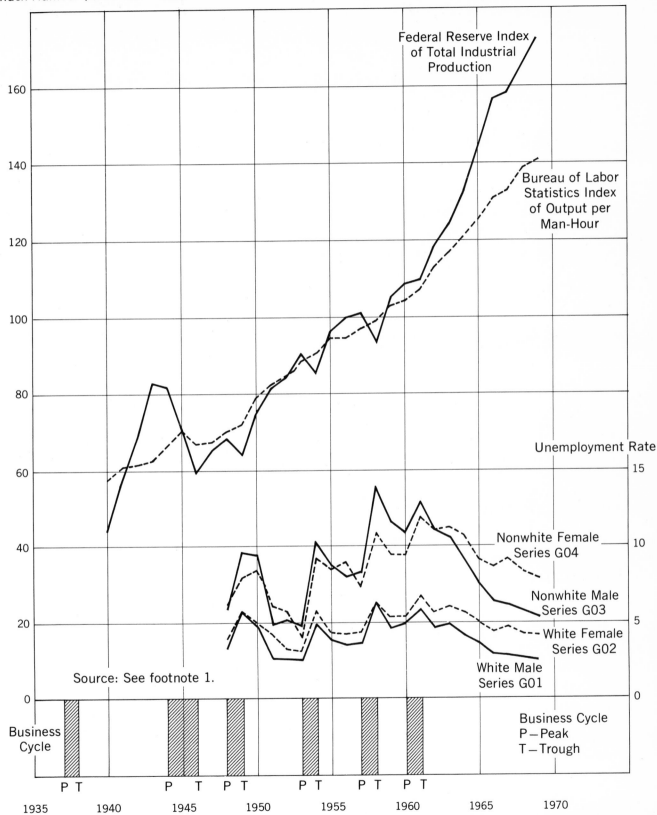

Figure 8.1 Unemployment Rates, by Color and Sex, 1947–1969; Indexes of Total Industrial Production and Output per Man-Hour, 1940–1969, and Peaks and Troughs of the Business Cycle, 1937–1969

The patterns of unemployment just described generally are repeated by each age group in the labor force. The few variations between the sexes by age will be indicated below.

Unemployment of each age and color-sex group varies according to activity of the business cycle. The few noticeable deviations from the business cycle pattern are the nonwhites among the 45 to 54 and the 55 to 64 year age groups. In these few instances, the unemployment rate merely precedes or follows by a year the corresponding point of inflection in the business cycle curve. Using annual data, as is done here, does not precisely pinpoint the real peaks and troughs in the cycle that would be revealed by monthly or even quarterly data.

Unemployment is greatest among the younger age groups, generally, 16 to 34 years, of both sexes. Among females it is most severe through age 24, particularly so since 1958.

Across time nonwhites' rates of unemployment vary considerably more than those of whites. Part of this is more apparent than real, because of the smaller sample size and great sampling variability of the nonwhite series, as has been mentioned. There remains, however, what appears to be less stability in the nonwhite unemployment rate than in the white. This is reflected in the series for each sex.

In the younger ages -- under 45 years -- nonwhite females experienced unemployment rates not greatly different from those of nonwhite males until about 1960. At that time, nonwhite female unemployment rates in these ages began to exceed those of nonwhite males. In the older ages above 55 years, unemployment rates of nonwhite females consistently are below those of nonwhite males.

Two factors probably influence this age-related unemployment pattern: the relation between age and employability in the occupations typical of nonwhite males and females, and the relation between age, sex and labor force participation.

Nonwhite females are largely employed as service workers (46 percent in 1968), whereas nonwhite males are more likely to be employed as laborers, semiskilled workers and operatives, on farms, etc. That their occupations are manual in character favors employment of younger over older nonwhite males.

Nonwhite females older than 55 years participate less in the labor force than do younger ages. Their unemployment rate declines as the unemployment rate of the older nonwhite male is increasing, even though his labor force participation, too, declines as he ages.

Among whites, the female unemployment rate typically exceeds the rate for the male, but the differences are not great for most age groups. The rates are particularly close for the 55 to 64 age group. For those 65 years of age and over, the male unemployment rate typically is slightly greater than that of the white female in these ages.

As the white female ages beyond 54 years, her rate of labor force participation drops off, as well as her rate of unemployment. Among white males, however, who also participate less in the labor force as they grow older, the unemployment rate increases with age. The female, more than the male, probably retires from the labor force when faced with unemployment.

Unemployment Rates by Age, Sex and Color

Young people, new to the labor force, are much more disadvantaged by unemployment than older persons. This is illustrated in the accompanying Figure 8.2, for 1969, showing unemployment rates for age groups through the life cycle by color and sex. While the young are more disadvantaged, young nonwhites are more disadvantaged than young whites, and, within each color group, females are more disadvantaged than males. Except for the ages beyond 55 years, nonwhite females are the most disadvantaged of all. However, the unemployment rates for those 35 years of age and over were below 5 percent for all age-sex-color groups in 1969, placing all these categories within a relatively narrow range. It is the younger ages, including those up to 25 years of age and some of those in the 25-34 years of age group, who are especially penalized by unemployment.

Trends in the unemployment rate of particular age groups now will be reviewed.

Unemployment, 16-17 and 18-19 Year Olds (Series G05-G12). In these transitional ages from school to work, unemployment rates are excessively high. Large numbers of the unemployed among the 16-17 year olds and fewer among the 18-19 year olds are enrolled in school, work being a part-time endeavor with them. This is shown in Table 8.3 for 1968. If the unemployment rates were based upon the total population in these ages, rather than only the labor force participants, the unemployment rates still would be excessively high, particularly among the nonwhites, but not as high as the rates that are based upon the standard labor force concept.

Table 8.3 - School Enrollment, Civilian Labor Force, and Employment Status of 16-17 and 18-19 Year Olds by Color and Sex, Civilian Noninstitutional Population, 1968

| | 16-17 year olds | | | | 18-19 year olds | | | |
| | White | | Nonwhite | | White | | Nonwhite | |
	Male	Female	Male	Female	Male	Female	Male	Female
Total	100.0	100.0	100.0	100.0	100.0	100.0	100.0	100.0
Enrolled in school:								
Not in labor force	54.3	62.8	64.1	67.8	34.6	28.2	33.6	27.5
In labor force:								
Employed	34.0	24.1	17.3	12.3	24.5	12.0	17.0	9.9
Unemployed	3.8	2.5	7.4	4.6	2.3	1.1	3.1	3.2
Not enrolled in school:								
Not in labor force	2.0	6.3	4.9	10.9	4.6	21.3	6.1	24.9
In labor force:								
Employed	5.2	3.4	3.9	2.2	31.4	33.3	32.2	25.6
Unemployed	0.7	1.0	2.3	2.2	2.6	4.1	8.0	8.9
Total, unemployed, age group	4.5	3.5	9.7	6.8	4.9	5.2	11.1	12.1
Total, unemployed, labor force	12.3	13.9	26.6	33.7	8.2	11.0	19.0	26.2

Source: (BLS, 1969b: A-6) and Series G05-G12.

Percent of the Labor Force Unemployed

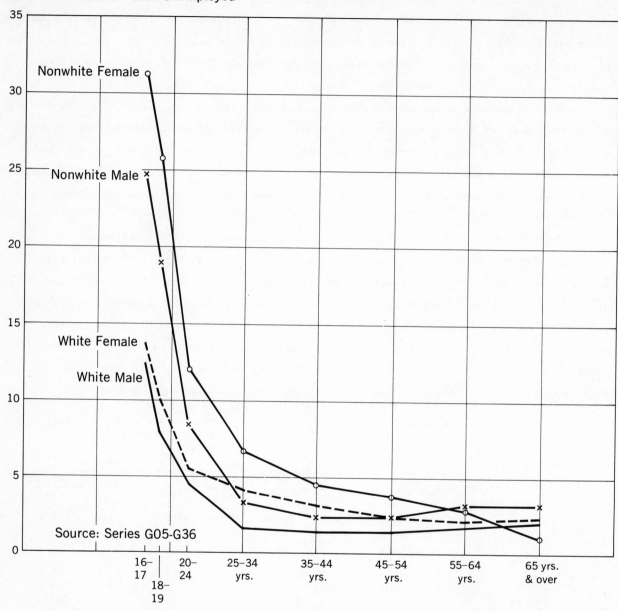

Age Group

Figure 8.2 Unemployment Rates Throughout the Life Cycle in 1969, by Sex and Color

Perhaps the critical question is, Are they occupied constructively? As Table 8.3 shows, among the sex/color groups of the 16-17 year olds, from over one-half to two-thirds are enrolled in school. Among the 18-19 year olds, from slightly more than one-fourth to one-third are enrolled in school. Unemployment among the 18-19 year olds, on the basis of the population in the age group, is higher than among the 16-17 year olds.

Even with this perspective, the present standard unemployment rates are much higher than they once were. The present disparity among the sex/color groups in these age categories is much more pronounced today than it was about 1953. Then the unemployment rate among the sex/color groups for these ages was relatively homogeneous (Figures 8.3 and 8.4). At that time the labor force participation rates were slightly higher for some of the age/sex categories, but some, also, were lower; consequently, the work rate does not appear to be a decisive factor in the increase in disparity in unemployment among the color/sex categories (See Series F039-F046). Another possible explanation would be the increased size of cohorts, due to the 1946 and 1947 increases in the birth rate. This wave in the fertility series would affect the 16 year old population in 1962; consequently, this would not have been influential during the 1955-1960 period. A third hypothesis, which cannot be tested because published data are not sufficiently detailed by age, sex, and color, is that the increase in unemployment accompanied the transition of nonwhites from rural to an urban environment, initially, and that the accumulation of non-whites of these ages in urban places continued to augment the available labor supply, which could not absorb it. There are some changes in the migration rate (Series E001-E008) but the available detail is insufficient to test this suggestion.

In these ages there is a gross disparity between white and nonwhite unemployment rates. While the nonwhite male and female unemployment rates among the 16-17 and 18-19 age groups have remained high, the unemployment rate for the total labor force during the period since 1961 was declining. The period as a whole is characterized as one of high employment and affluence. The high unemployment rates persisting among all youth of these ages, particularly among nonwhite youth, are indicators of grossly inadequate institutional arrangements for inducting new workers into the labor force, or of grossly inadequate means of retaining youth of these ages in school. Perhaps idleness during this period of life is sufficient to cause the much misunderstood "rebellion" of youth and one important basis for its criticism of the "establishment".

Unemployment, 20-24 Years (Series G13-G16) (Figure 8.5). Excessive unemployment characterizes this age group, the nonwhite being in an especially adverse position. Only the unemployment rate of the white male appears to have come within relatively modest bounds within the past five years. In the most recent period, both rates of white and nonwhite females exceed the corresponding rates for males, the nonwhite female rate being 43 percent greater than the nonwhite male rate in 1969.

Unemployment, 25-34 Years (Series G17-G20) (Figure 8.5). Male and female rates, both white and nonwhite, follow the same pattern of change, except for the independent course of nonwhite

Unemployment Rate

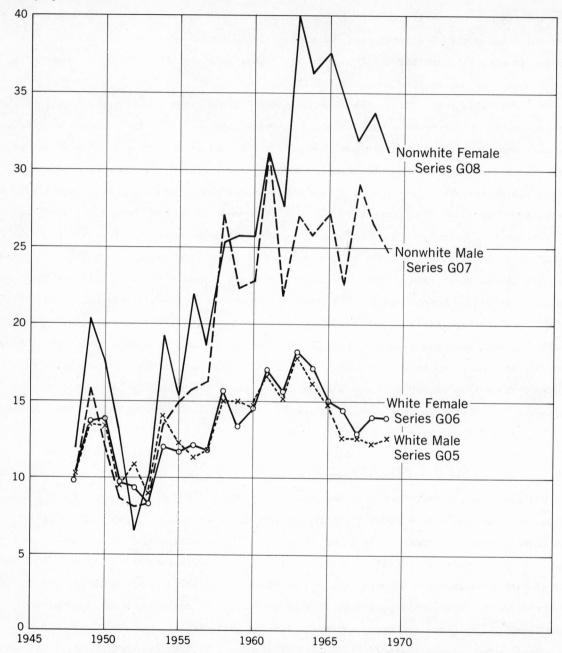

Figure 8.3 Unemployment Rates, Ages 16–17 Years, by Color and Sex, 1948–1969

Unemployment Rate

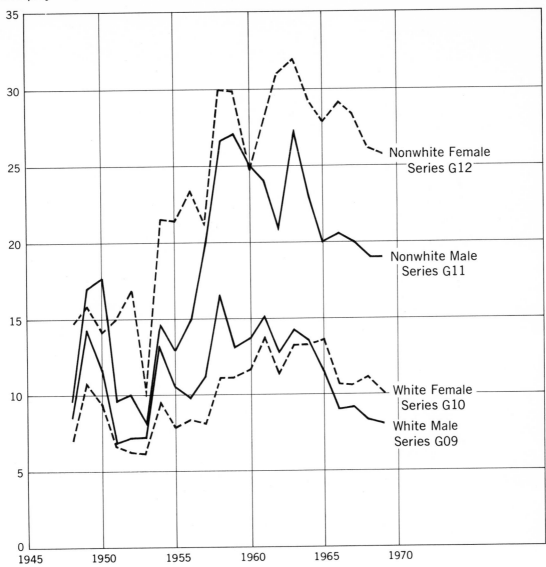

Figure 8.4 Unemployment Rates, Ages 18–19 Years, by Color and Sex, 1948–1969

Unemployment Rate

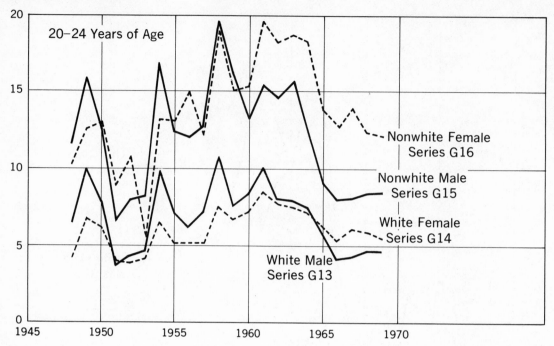

20–24 Years of Age

Nonwhite Female
Series G16

Nonwhite Male
Series G15

White Female
Series G14

White Male
Series G13

Unemployment Rate

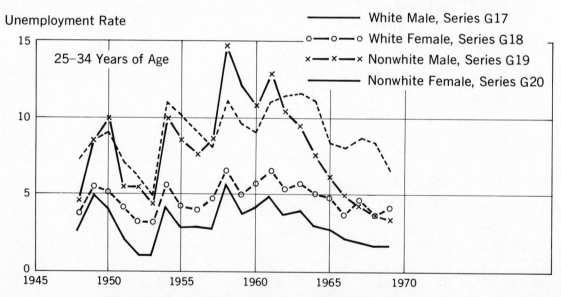

25–34 Years of Age

——— White Male, Series G17
o—o—o White Female, Series G18
×—×—× Nonwhite Male, Series G19
——— Nonwhite Female, Series G20

Figure 8.5 Unemployment Rates, Ages 20–24 and 25–34 Years, by Color and Sex, 1948–1969

female after 1961. The nonwhite male unemployment rate has approached the level of the white unemployment rates, while rates for nonwhite females have not.

Unemployment, 35-44 Years (Series G21-G24) (Figure 8.6). White male and female rates follow a uniform trend. At present nonwhite rates approximate white rates. Female rates, both white and nonwhite, are approximately double the corresponding male rates.

Unemployment, 45-54 Years (Series G25-G28) (Figure 8.6). In these ages, all the rates fall within a narrow margin, except for the nonwhite males, who appear to be quite adversely affected during periods of recession. Since 1964, all rates have been coming closer together (Figure 8.6). Female rates exceed corresponding male rates, for whites; for nonwhites the male rate was higher until 1966; slightly lower thereafter.

Unemployment, 55-64 Years (Series G29-G32) (Figure 8.7). All series in these ages follow the same pattern within a narrow range, except for the relatively high levels of unemployment of nonwhite males, particularly during recessions. Nonwhite females are not similarly affected. White female rates tend to exceed corresponding white male rates.

65 Years and Over (Series G33-G36) (Figure 8.7). All series, except nonwhite males, again, fall within a narrow range, especially since 1962. Nonwhite males have high unemployment rates during recessions. The subsequent recovery of their unemployment rate is not as complete as for other groups. Unemployment rates among these color/sex groups are more homogeneous, the rates for males, particularly nonwhite males, exceeding the rates for females.

Generally, among all ages of whites, the female unemployment rate has been higher than the male. Among nonwhites, from 1957 to 1962 the male unemployment rate was higher than the female, but since 1963 the unemployment rate of nonwhite females has been higher than the male rate.

Unemployment and Marital Status. Women in the labor force are more likely to be unemployed than men. This is true among nonwhite males and females as well as among white. It also is true for those married of both color groups. However, white single females are less likely to be unemployed than white single males, and this is generally true for nonwhite females in relation to nonwhite males, also (although it does not hold for 1967 and 1968). Among the widowed, divorced or separated, white men are more likely to be unemployed than white women, and this generally is true for nonwhites, also.

These trends are presented in a relatively short series (since 1962) for the population 20 years of age and over in the civilian labor force by color and sex, and in a longer series for the labor force by sex for all races combined. The latter series was interrupted in 1966 by a change in the ages included in the labor force, from "14 years and over" to "16 years and over." Figure 8.8 illustrates the trend by marital status.

Unemployment Rate

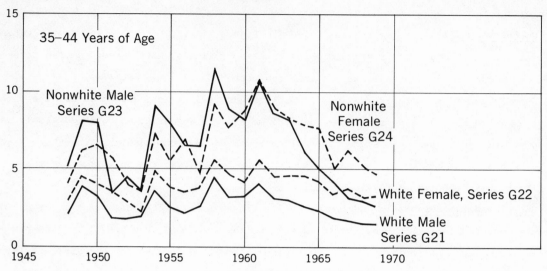

Unemployment Rate

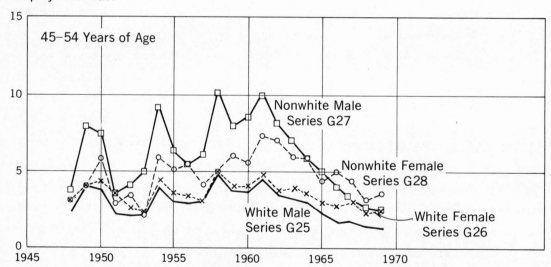

Figure 8.6 Unemployment Rates, Ages 35–44 and 45–54 Years, by Color and Sex, 1948–1969

Umemployment Rate

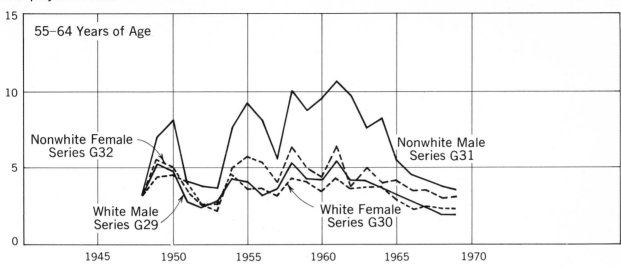

Unemployment Rate

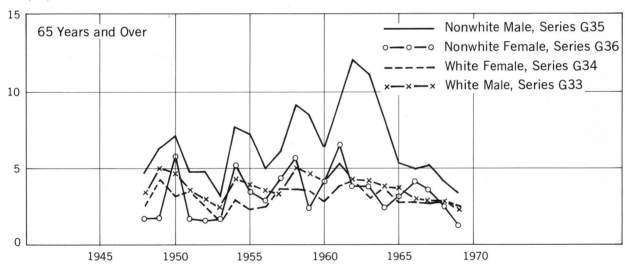

Figure 8.7 Unemployment Rates, Ages 55–64 Years and 65 Years and Over, by Color and Sex, 1948–1969

Unemployment Rate

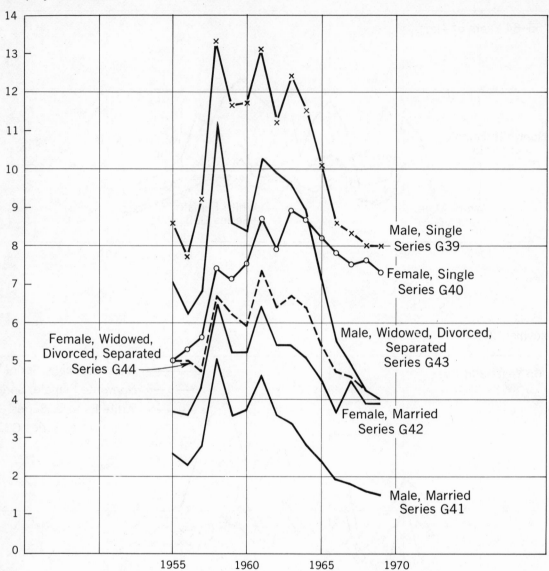

Figure 8.8 Unemployment Rates by Marital Status and Sex, 1955–1969

Additional Data on Unemployment

Numerous additional statistical series are available for a more comprehensive analysis of unemployment as it affects the status of women. Among them are the following: whether the unemployed person is in the full-time or part-time labor force, by age; whether the unemployed person is a household head, by age; unemployment rates by major occupational categories and by industry of last job; the unemployment level relative to last job (that is, whether lost last job or quit, is reentering the labor force, or is a new worker); information on the duration of unemployment, and others. The basic data for additional analyses of these factors are available in Employment and Earnings and the Monthly Report on the Labor Force issued monthly by the U. S. Bureau of Labor Statistics. Adequate analysis of many of these factors leads into an analysis of economic influences on employment and unemployment which is beyond the scope of this study of the status of women. Such an inquiry, however, would undoubtedly contribute to our understanding of the position of women in the world of work.

Summary of Indicators

This chapter has reviewed unemployment rates of persons in the labor force by age, color and sex, and by marital status. Observation of unemployment trends in these categories provides not only information on the economy but very meaningful information on the productive or unproductive activity of women in relation to their life situations. In the younger ages, say 16 to 20 years, the percent of the age group that is looking for work appears to be a more realistic basis for assessment than labor force unemployment statistics. These ages need to be "monitored," not merely for their standard employment and unemployment rates, but also for their rates of participation in the range of life activities: being enrolled in school, being married, having and caring for children, working, looking for work, being ill, traveling, and so forth.

While it is most important to monitor social indicators that reflect the activities of these youthful, formative ages, there also is a need to continually appraise the stages in the lives of women at the times when they (1) leave school, (2) enter employment, (3) leave the labor force to be married, or (4) to bear children, and (5) reenter the labor force after a period of child care or (6) marriage dissolution, or (7) enroll in school to gain or regain occupational competence, and (8) quit or retire from the labor force. Each step of life's stages is associated with a change in the life-cycle status of women, each represents a personal opportunity or setback, and each typically occurs at a different age. A more thorough knowledge of these stages, through the ordering of data on the labor force, educational, family, fertility, and other subjects, would provide a systematic basis for monitoring the status of women in society in all of its rich complexity. It would lead to identifying the needs for planned approaches to resolving the major impediments to a more orderly social life.

9.

The Income Status of Women

More than any other measure, the amount of income received by a person or family summarizes much information about status. An increase in income is an opportunity for greater discretion and liberty in conducting one's affairs, in making choices, in the use of leisure time, and in other refinements of life. These uses of income enhance the quality of life. An increase in income also may be used in other ways -- to increase savings, to improve one's earning capacity, conceivably, to engage in activities detrimental as well as beneficial to the quality of one's life. In this analysis of indicators of income we assume that an increase in income contributes to an improvement in the quality of life.[1]

The amount of income is associated with the level of education, one's health, one's occupation and industry, the length of work experience, full or part-time employment, geographic region of residence, and farm or nonfarm residential location. It also is associated with age, color and sex.

The extent of differences in income by sex when these other factors are held constant is not easily determined. For example, women typically are intermittently employed in the labor force, are frequently employed on a part-time basis by preference, and are engaged in occupations whose salary level is lower than other occupations (e.g., household service, sales workers). A valid comparison of income of women with the income of men would hold each such variable constant. It would compare the income of men and women who have the same level of education and training, are in the same occupation, are employed in the same industry, have approximately the same length of work experience, are employed full-time, are of the same age and color, and so forth. The interaction of some of these factors might make the use of one or more of the variables unnecessary. A multivariate analysis of this kind, however, performed for successive years, would describe the changing relation between income of men and women and would hold constant many of the annoying sources of variance that intrude upon an analysis based merely upon published statistical series classified by one or two variables.

_____

[1] Extensive analyses of income have been made, some with respect to income as a social indicator of welfare, consumption, etc. See: (Brady, 1965; Merriam, 1968; Miller, 1966; Miller, et. al., 1967; Moss, 1968).

In the absence of such a multivariate analysis -- a quite extensive undertaking in itself -- the more limited approach to be followed here will compare the income of men and women who are year-round full-time workers within the same occupation. In a separate analysis, income will be compared holding constant education of income recipients and age. The median annual money income of income recipients is compared for all persons; and for employed workers, the measure used is median annual money earnings.

After this, trends in the number of persons with no money income will be considered, this category being quite important among females as compared with males.

Next, data are presented that compare male and female heads of families and "unrelated individuals," persons living alone or with someone else not kin to them. In this comparison, also, the income of male heads of families whose wife is not in the labor force will be contrasted with the income of female heads of families.

Finally, the status of poverty, empirically defined for analytical purposes, is examined to reveal the trends for women in poverty in relation to trends for men in poverty.

. . . . .

No Income and Median Money Income: An Overview

Women, both white and nonwhite, are much more likely to be without income than men (Series H001-H008 and Figure 9.6). However, the percentage of females (14 years of age and over) with no income is declining, while the percentage of males with no income has remained relatively constant. From 1956 to 1968, the percent of white women with no money income declined 13 percentage points, while the percentage of nonwhite women in this status declined 8 percentage points.

Table 9.1 - Indices of Median Annual Money Income of Income Recipients, 14 Years
of Age and Over, in Constant 1968 Dollars

	White		Nonwhite	
	Male	Female	Male	Female
Median income, 1968	$6,267	$2,079	$3,829	$1,688
Increment, 1956-1968, in 1968 dollars	$1,368	$ 457	$1,269	$ 757
Annual average compound growth rate, 1956-1968	4.2	4.2	5.6	7.3
Percent increase, 1956-1968	28	28	50	81
1956 ratio to white males	1.0	.33	.52	.19
1968 ratio to white males	1.0	.33	.61	.27

Source: Series H005-H008 and (Census, 1970f: 10-11).

The median annual income of both male and female income recipients (measured in constant dollars) has increased since 1956. The increases, however, have meant an improvement for nonwhite males, relative to white males, and an improvement for nonwhite females, but no improvement for white females relative to white males (Figure 9.1). Indices of these changes, 1956 to 1968, are shown in Table 9.1.

Constant (1968) Dollars

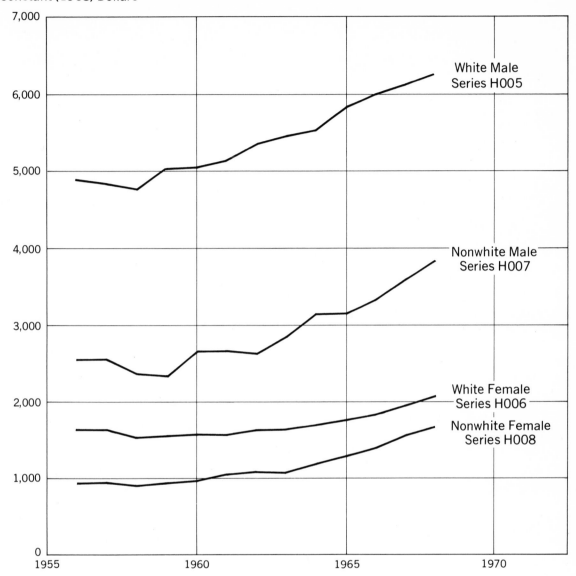

Figure 9.1 Median Annual Money Income of Income Recipients 14 Years Old and Over in Constant 1968 Dollars, by Color and Sex, 1956–1968

In summary, the income of nonwhite women has improved over the past dozen years (to 1968), but the overall income of white women has not improved when compared with the median income of white men.

Median Annual Earnings by Color and Sex

From 1956 to 1968 the median annual money earnings of year-round, full-time civilian male workers, in constant 1968 dollars, increased $1,948, a 34 percent increase in actual income. Comparable earnings of women workers increased only $838, a 23 percent increase. In 1956 there was a difference of $2,097 between earnings of men and women. By 1968, this difference had increased to $3,207, or a net increase in men's earnings over women's earnings of $1,110 in constant dollars. By these indices there can be no doubt that women's income status, in relation to men's, has declined (Series H009-H017).

Figure 9.2 presents the trends in the actual median annual earnings of white and nonwhite males and females, each based upon constant 1968 dollars. The trend in nonwhite earnings shows greater year-to-year variation because of the greater sampling error in the nonwhite statistics, not because of a markedly greater variation in the basic trend.

The differential between female and male earnings also is clearly shown by the ratio of their median earnings (Series H015-H017). Figure 9.2 presents these ratios for all civilian workers, and for white and nonwhite workers. While the ratio for whites follows quite closely the declining trend for all races, the ratio for nonwhites traces a more erratic course. The increase from 1963, however, appears to represent a genuine improvement in the income of nonwhite women relative to nonwhite men.

Occupation and Income

Women are concentrated in clerical occupations, while men are more likely to be craftsmen, foremen, and kindred workers, or operatives. Of secondary importance for women's employment are the professions, the operative occupations and the service (except household) occupations. These differences in the occupations of women and men affect the annual earnings women receive. Figure 9.3 shows the distribution of year-round full-time civilian workers by occupational group.

Within the same occupation women earn less than men, as shown in Table 9.2 for 1968. The ratio of the female median annual income to the male, shown in the last column, highlights the difference. In the totals for all occupations, women earned $4,457 annually, 58 percent of the median earnings of males. In the two occupations where more than one-half the women work, the clerical and salaried professional occupations, the median earnings women receive are 65 percent of the median earnings of men. Compared to men, women earn least as sales workers. The occupations in Table 9.2 are arranged from high to low median annual earnings of the male.

140

Constant (1968) Dollars

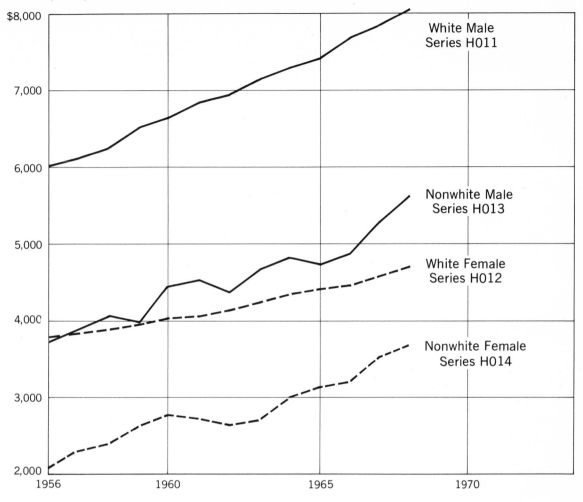

Ratio, Female to
Male (x 100)

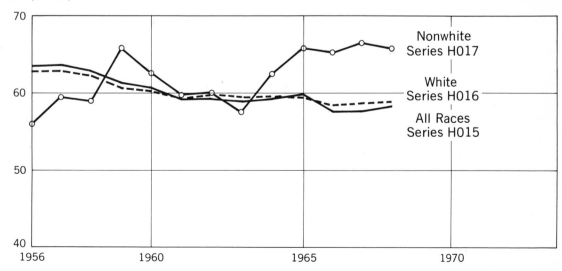

Figure 9.2 (Upper) Median Annual Money Earnings of Year-Round
Full-Time Civilian Workers, by Color and Sex, 1956–1968; (Lower)
Ratio, Female to Male, Median Annual Money Earnings of Year-Round
Full-Time Civilian Workers, by Color, 1956–1968.

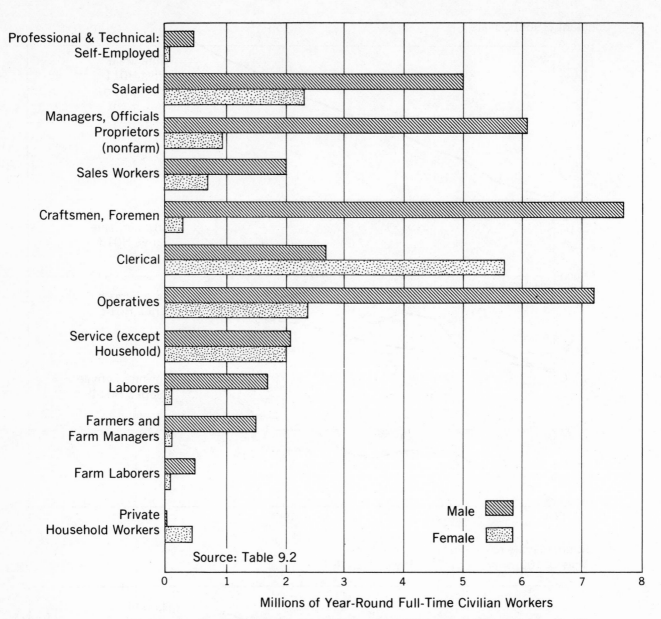

Figure 9.3 Number of Year-Round Full-Time Civilian Workers, by Occupation and Sex, 1968

Table 9.2 - Number and Median Earnings of Year-Round Full-Time Civilian Workers, by Occupation and Sex, and Female/Male Ratio of Earnings, 1968

	Full-Time year-round workers with earnings		Median earnings[a]/		Female/male ratio (x 100) of earnings
	Male (000)	Female (000)	Male	Female	
Total	37,068	15,013	$ 7,664	$4,457	58
Professional, technical:					
Self-employed	503	46	17,358	--	--
Salaried	5,043	2,333	10,243	6,634	65
Managers, officials, proprietors					
(except farm)	6,073	934	9,794	5,101	52
Sales Workers	1,995	702	8,292	3,388	41
Craftsmen, foremen	7,696	270	7,958	4,315	54
Clerical	2,694	5,716	7,324	4,778	65
Operatives	7,231	2,437	6,773	3,956	59
Service (except household)	2,132	1,991	5,898	3,159	53
Laborers	1,718	78	5,606	3,490	62
Farmers and farm managers	1,517	69	3,353	--	--
Farm laborers	446	34	2,870	--	--
Private household workers	20	403	--	1,464	--

Source: Series H018-H079 and (Census, 1969d: 103-105).

a/ - Not computed where base is less than 75,000.

Figure 9.3, which distributes full-time civilian workers by occupation, brings into relief the sex-specific nature of occupations, pointed up by Oppenheimer (1970: Ch. 3) and reviewed herein in Chapter 7. A comparison of earnings of women with those of men within occupational categories, then, is most appropriate.

In the several occupations where most women work, the trend in the median annual earnings has been favorable, even when the purchasing power of the dollar is held constant (1968 dollars). Figure 9.4 shows the continuous increase in women's actual earnings in most of the occupations from 1956 to 1969. Professional and technical is most generously rewarding, with clerical occupations following behind, with some $2,000 less annually. These trends bespeak an increase in women's income status. However, when women's earnings are compared with men's, as in Figure 9.5, the "earnings" status of women, relative to men, can only be interpreted as declining. In absolute dollars her status is improving but in relation to men's earnings, it is not.[2]/

In Figure 9.5 the median annual income for all year-round full-time civilian women workers declined from 63.3 percent of the income of all year-round, full-time civilian men workers in 1956 to 58.6 percent in 1969. In some of the occupations this ratio fluctuates, but the general trend in the income of women clerical and service workers is decreasing in relation to men's and the trend in the income of women workers in sales and professional and technical occupations generally is holding constant, in relation to the annual income of men in these occupations.

2/ Annual compound growth rates in total money income and wage or salary income for persons 14 years old and over, by current occupation and industry groups, race, and sex, are available in a recently released Census Bureau publication. Those interested in annual compound growth rates from one date to any other during the period 1939 to 1968 will find the publication useful (Census, 1970f).

Constant (1968) Dollars

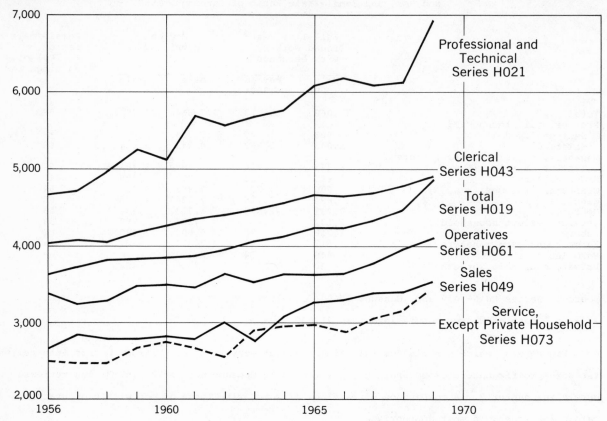

Figure 9.4 Median Annual Money Earnings (1968 Dollars) of Year-Round Full-Time Civilian Women Workers, Selected Occupations, 1956–1969

Ratio, Female/Male (x 100)

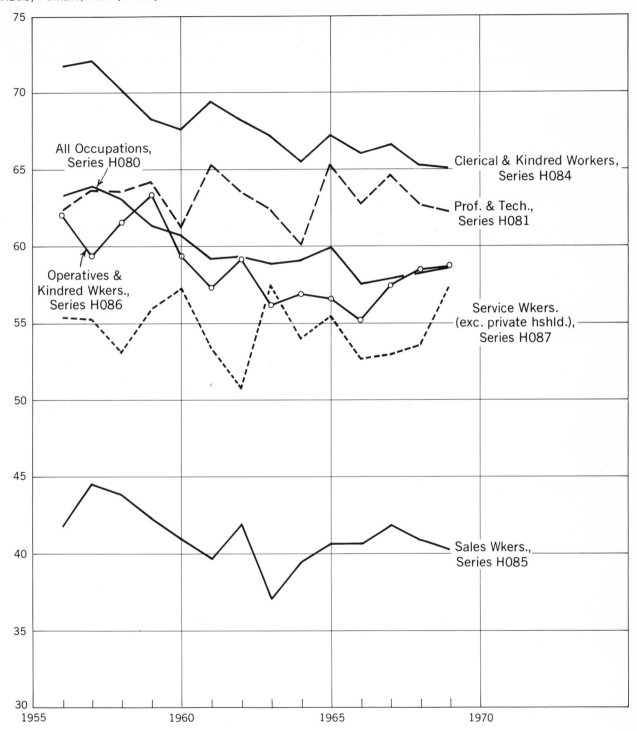

Figure 9.5 Ratio, Female/Male: Median Annual Income, Year-Round
Full-Time Workers, Selected Occupations, 1956–1969

It should be pointed out that the preceding compares money earnings of female with that of male year-round full-time workers. The distorting effect of the greater part-time employment of women, than men, and the distorting effect of occasional (not year-round) women workers has been eliminated. The above comparisons, also, are within occupational groups, thereby eliminating the effect upon earnings of women being in lower-paying occupations (except, of course, for the Total in Figure 9.4, which contains the effect of differential occupational distribution).

There remains the possibility that women are less qualified, by virtue of having less education than men. Series H104-H163 present earnings of men and women workers by age and education.

Income and Education

Over a short time-span, a series is available for the median annual money income by sex, age and education, 1963 to 1968 (Series H104-H163). This allows us to explore how the income women receive is affected by education.

Series H104-H163 illustrate the consistent relationship between education and income: income increases with an increase in education. This holds for each age group. Within an educational level, however, income generally increases with age up to a point, the point usually being either the 35-44 or the 45-54 age level. The next older group has slightly lower median income than women immediately younger.

No matter what educational level women achieve, all age groups of women have an annual median income less than the median income of men of the same age and educational level. The differential changes very little with age when education is constant, and it declines with increasing education when age is constant. This is illustrated by Table 9.3, for women in the ages 45-54 years, the largest age group of women in the labor force. Women's income improves in relation to men's as education increases, even though the relationship varies from year to year. This may suggest that one clue to an improved competitive position of women in the labor force, with respect to men, is through higher educational attainment.

Table 9.3 - Ratio of Income of Females to the Income of Males: Median Annual Total Money Income of Persons (income recipients), Age 45-54 Years, by Years of School Completed, 1963-1968 (Ratio x 100)

| Year | Years of School Completed | | | | | |
	Less than 8 years	8 years	1-3 years high school	4 years high school	1-3 years college	4 or more years college
1963	26.5	35.2	37.4	43.8	45.6	49.8
1964	35.2	37.4	40.7	40.6	39.7	46.4
1965	39.1	38.4	40.2	43.9	39.2	46.8
1966	37.0	39.6	36.8	42.7	39.3	48.3
1967	33.9	38.0	35.7	44.4	44.7	48.7
1968	37.5	40.8	38.7	43.0	40.5	49.6

Source: Computed from Series H140-H151.

Table 9.3 also illustrates some secular improvement in the ratio of women's income to men's. The ratio increases for the two lowest educational levels (through grammar school), but there is an absence of any consistent upward trend among the remaining educational levels. In general, within each educational level there has been some secular increase in the ratio of women's income to men's, 1963 to 1968, but the increase is less among the older than the younger ages. The income-by-education-by-age-and-sex comparison is affected by the relationship of education to occupation, which a more elaborate analytical design, than the present one, would be able to untangle.

Women with No Money Income

Women 14 years of age and over are more likely than men to have no income during a given year. This is true for both whites and nonwhites, as Figure 9.6 (Series H001-H004) shows.

While 84 percent of persons without money income in 1968 were women, most of the women without money income were the wives of family heads: 76 percent of white women with no money income and 49 percent of Negro women with no money income were the wife of the head of the family (Census, 1969d: 88-89). The large part of the remaining women with no money income were "other relatives" of the head of the family, meaning that they were young women below 20 years of age or older relatives or dependents. The lack of money income among females in families, consequently, does not signify destitution, but rather connotes the status of a young dependent, perhaps in school, or other relative or dependent whose family role places her in a position entitled to protective care.

The percent of males with no income, both white and nonwhite persons, remained relatively constant from 1956 through 1968. On the other hand, the percent of females with no money income has been declining over this period of time. White females with no income have declined approximately 13 percentage points, while nonwhite females have declined approximately seven percentage points since 1956. This reflects in part the increasing participation of women in the labor force. To the extent that income represents independence, the trend shows an increasing independence of women.

Table 9.4 - Percent of Persons with No Money Income, by Age, Sex, and Race, 1968

	White		Negro	
	Male	Female	Male	Female
All ages	7.1	36.2	11.5	26.3
14 and 15 years	63.9	70.4	63.9	81.2
16-19 years	25.0	38.5	34.7	46.4
20-24 years	4.6	24.7	7.5	20.4
25-34 years	0.8	43.3	2.0	18.2
35-44 years	0.5	41.5	1.6	18.1
45-54 years	0.8	37.2	1.4	23.4
55-64 years	1.0	34.8	1.3	24.1
65 years & over	0.6	17.8	2.0	7.6

Source: (Census, 1969d: 90-91).

Percent

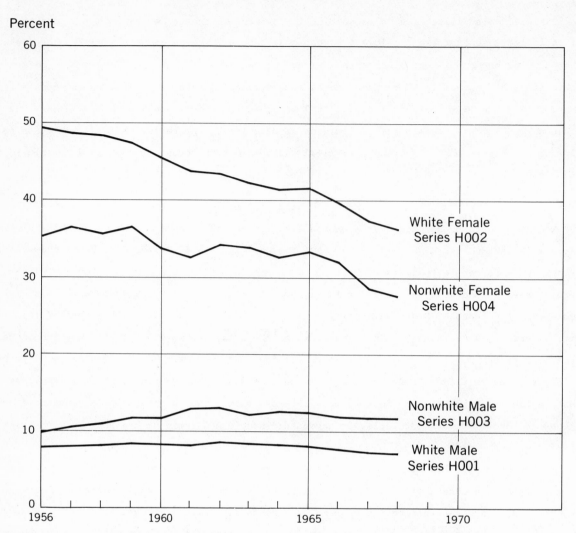

White Female
Series H002

Nonwhite Female
Series H004

Nonwhite Male
Series H003

White Male
Series H001

Figure 9.6 Percent of Persons 14 Years Old and Over With No
Money Income, by Color and Sex, 1956–1968

148

Table 9.4 serves to further identify persons with no money income. Negro males are more likely than white males to have no money income, but the opposite is true among females, white women being more likely to be without income. Young people (under 20 years of age) of both races are much more likely to be without money income than older persons. Furthermore, the percentage declines with age. In summary, the persons with no money income are young people and women, chiefly housewives. Females are much more likely to be without money income than males.

In addition to providing an index to the independence of women, the data on persons with no income in any given year provides a clue to the status the following year of those who make a transition to receiving an income (Series H164-H176). Figure 9.7 shows the relatively constant proportion of the population 14 years of age and over who had no income one year but were employed the following year. The percentage is approximately one percent for males and nearly three percent for females. Relatively constant, too, is the percent of males who had no money income one year and the next year were in the armed services or were not in the labor force (approximately five percent in 1968). Females in the latter category, however, present a trend of some significance. The percent with no money income one year who the following year were in the armed services or not in the labor force (women 14 years of age and over) has been continuously declining over the period shown (since 1956), and particularly since 1960. This decline has coincided with an increase in labor force participation rate of women (16 years of age and over), Series F014.

Nearly two million women who had no income in 1968 were employed in March, 1969. The transition to work status was to clerical occupations (28 percent), service work other than in private households (17 percent), farm work (13 percent), and private household employment (13 percent). Only about five percent went into professional and technical work and half that number entered nonfarm managerial positions. Most women making the transition from no income to employment of some kind, then, entered prevalent low-salaried positions. In March, 1969, 15 percent of women with no income the previous year were unemployed (this excludes women in the armed services or not in the labor force) (Census, 1969d: 102).

Women with no income one year who are employed the following year comprise a relatively stable influx into most occupational groups and a declining proportion of new workers in a few occupational categories. These indices, illustrated in Figure 9.8, show the following uniformities:

In each occupational group larger proportions of females than of males had no income the previous year.

These proportions are declining or are constant for females and are relatively constant for males in all occupational groups.

Female sales and service workers were without income the previous year in higher proportions than other occupational groups, while professional and technical workers are lowest in this respect. The percent with no money income the previous year among female professional and technical workers has been declining and approaches the percent of males in this category.

149

Percent of All Males or Females Age 14 Years and Over

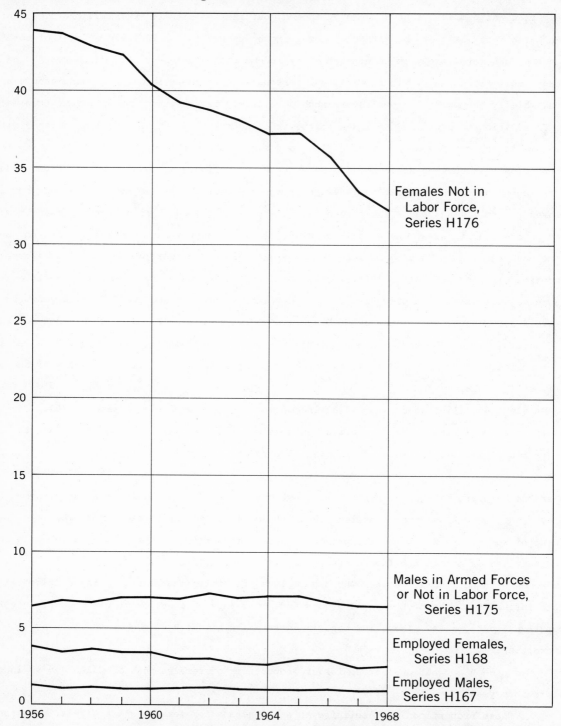

Figure 9.7 Persons 14 Years of Age and Over Having No Money Income in Current Year as Percent of Total Population 14 Years and Over, by Employment Status in March of Following Year, and by Sex, 1956–1968

Percent

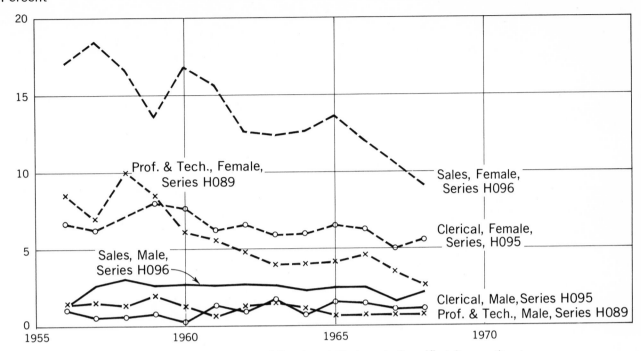

Figure 9.8 Percent of Employed Workers in Specified Occupational Groups and Subgroups Who had No Money Income in Previous Year, by Sex, 1956–1968

Income of Families and Unrelated Individuals

Figure 9.9 presents the median annual money income of families with male head (wife not working), with female head, and of unrelated male and female individuals, in constant dollars (Series H177-H206). The median income of families with female head has been increasing since 1959, but its rate of increase has been far less than the increase in the median income of families with male head, wife not in the paid labor force. Unrelated female individuals also have increased in median income, but the increase in income has not equaled the increase experienced by unrelated male individuals. The trend in income for each of these categories will now be separately examined and compared.

Each of the family categories in Figure 9.9 will next be separately presented in graphs in order to examine the trends in selected characteristics of each income distribution. Four statistics are presented on each figure. These statistics are:

a, the upper boundary of the fourth quintile, marking the lower boundary of the top twenty percent of families (or unrelated individuals);

b, the upper boundary of the first quintile, marking the highest income of the lowest twenty percent of families (or unrelated individuals);

c, the interquintile range, the difference in income between the top of the fourth and the top of the first quintiles;

d, a coefficient calculated by dividing the interquintile range by the median. This statistic is an easily calculated substitute for the coefficient of variation.

An increase in the first quintile means that the lower fifth of the income distribution is improving its earnings. An increase in the interquintile range in these charts means that the income of the upper fifth of the distribution is increasing more than the income of the lower fifth and that incomes are becoming less equitably distributed. If the interquintile range were constant across time, the incomes of the lower fifth would be keeping pace with the incomes of the upper fifth. If the interquintile range were decreasing, the two tails of the distribution would be coming closer together, indicating less difference between the upper and lower incomes.

The coefficient presented in these charts is the interquintile range divided by the median. If the median income increases while the interquintile range remains constant, the coefficient becomes smaller. If the interquintile range becomes smaller, bringing the high and low income groups closer together, and the median income remains constant, the coefficient becomes smaller. In short, a decrease in the coefficient means that income is improving in amount or in distribution.

Constant (1968) Dollars

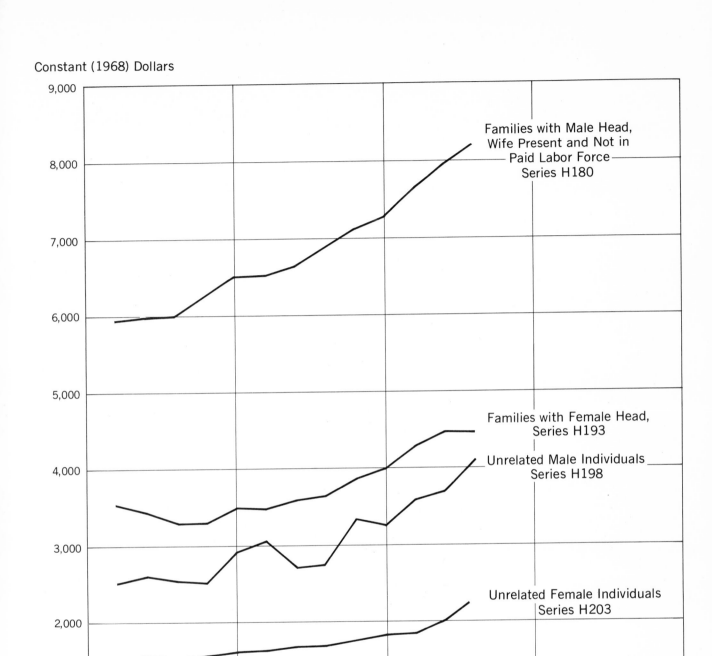

Figure 9.9 Median Annual Money Income for Families of Specified Types and for Male and Female Unrelated Individuals, in Constant (1968) Dollars, 1956–1968

Table 9.5 - Comparison of Income Measures of the Four Categories of Families, 1968

	Quintiles		Inter-quintile range	Median	Coefficient (range ÷ median)
	First	Fourth			
Families, male head, wife not in labor force	$4,500	$13,086	$8,586	$8,215	1.05
Families, female head	2,086	8,333	6,247	4,477	1.40
Unrelated individuals, male	1,500	8,128	6,628	4,086	1.62
Unrelated individuals, female	1,072	5,155	4,083	2,239	1.82

Source: Series H177-H206.

The above table enables a comparison of the statistics for one year. Income of families with a male head, wife not in the paid labor force, having a coefficient of 1.05, reflects the more favorable income distribution -- favorable in that the spread of income is less dispersed in relation to the median. At the other extreme, the coefficient of 1.82 for unrelated female individuals reflects a less favorable distribution.

The preceding suggests the following normative interpretation of trends in the interquintile range and the coefficient: a constant or a decreasing range may be interpreted as a favorable trend; a decrease in the coefficient may be interpreted as a favorable trend.

Families with Male or Female Heads

Figure 9.10 presents trends in these statistics for families with male head, wife present and not in the paid labor force (Series H187-H191). The slight rise in the coefficient suggests that the income distribution has become slightly less favorable. The inclination of the long-term trend in the interquintile range is an angle of approximately 30°. This is the least favorable of the four categories, reflecting an increasing difference in income between the top and bottom quintiles. For purposes of interpretation, an angle of 0°, that is, a horizontal trend, would mean that the difference between the upper and the lower quintiles was holding constant. Consequently, the lower the angle of inclination the more favorable the trend in income distribution. While the top of the fourth quintile has been steadily rising since 1957, the boundary of the first quintile has not similarly progressed. However, since 1965 the first quintile has improved more rapidly.

Families with female head, in Figure 9.11, are represented by the coefficient as having improved very little until after 1963 (Series H192-H196). Since then improvement has been rather rapid, except for an apparent setback in 1968. The interquintile range began to increase in 1958 and has followed an angle of approximately 18°. Since 1961 the fourth quintile has increased fairly rapidly, while about 1963 the first quintile began slowly to increase. The median income of families with a female head, in 1968, was $4,619 less than the median income of all families with a male head.

154

Constant (1968) Dollars

Coefficient

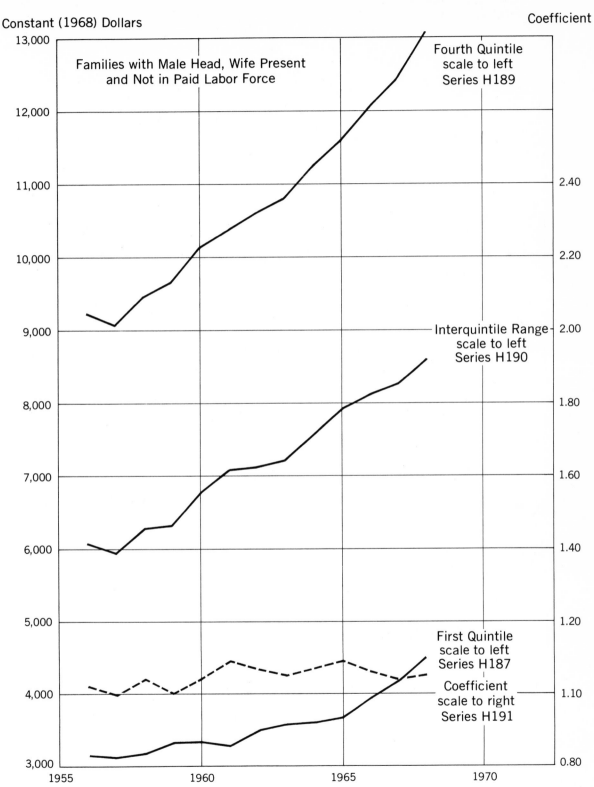

13,000

Families with Male Head, Wife Present
and Not in Paid Labor Force

Fourth Quintile
scale to left
Series H189

12,000

2.40

11,000

2.40

2.20

10,000

2.20

9,000

Interquintile Range
scale to left
Series H190

2.00

8,000

1.80

7,000

1.60

6,000

1.40

5,000

1.20

First Quintile
scale to left
Series H187

Coefficient
scale to right
Series H191

4,000

1.10

3,000

0.80

1955   1960   1965   1970

Figure 9-10 First and Fourth Quintiles of Annual Money Income
and Difference Between the Fourth and First Quintiles, in Constant
(1968) Dollars, 1956–1968

Constant (1968) Dollars   Coefficient

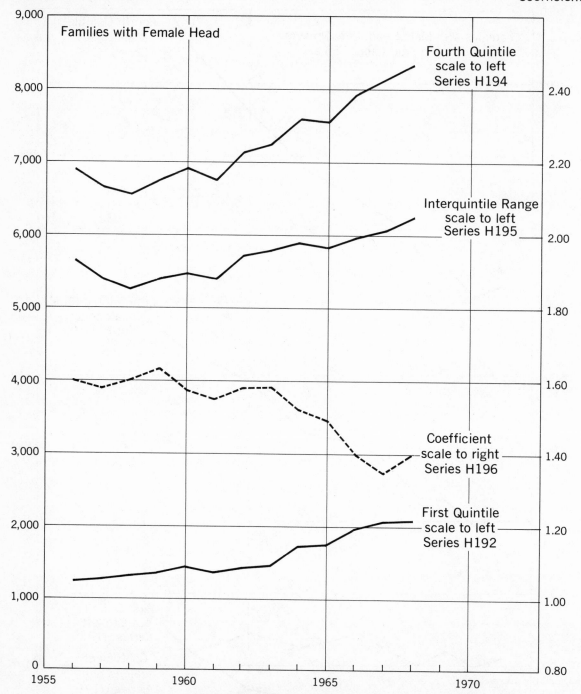

Figure 9.11   First and Fourth Quintiles of Annual Money Income and Difference between the Fourth and First Quintiles, in Constant (1968) Dollars, 1956–1968

Unrelated Individuals

Male unrelated individuals had a median income $1,847 greater than the median income of female unrelated individuals in 1968 (Figure 9.12 and Series H197-H201). While the lower fifth of the male distribution was increasing at a slightly faster rate than that of the female distribution (Figure 9.13 and Series H202-H206), neither of the lower quintiles has made notable improvement. The upper fifth of the male distribution, on the other hand, has increased much faster than the upper fifth of the female distribution. Because of this, the interquintile range of the female distribution (an angle of 20°) has increased less than the increase in the interquintile range of the male distribution (an angle of 24°). This indicates that there has been a slightly more effective realignment of income among female than among male unrelated individuals.

The coefficients of both distributions have declined since 1963, evidencing a general improvement in income in both distributions. The crucial trend in both distributions, slightly less advantaged among female unrelated individuals than among male, is the low income of the lower quintile, with its very gradual, almost creeping trend. The upper bound of the first quintile of both male and female distributions places both below the poverty level.

White and Negro Differences

The Bureau of the Census has made available information for recent years on Negro families. Table 9.6 presents summary statistics, by race, of the income distributions of the types of families discussed above.

Considering the median as a summary measure, Negro families occupy lower income positions than their counterpart white families. This is illustrated by the ratio of the median for Negro families to the median for white families, presented in Table 9.6.

Table 9.6 - Median Annual Money Income and First and Fourth Quintile of Annual Money Income for Families, by Type of Family, and for Male and Female Unrelated Individuals, by Race of Head of Family, 1968

Family type or unrelated individual	White			Negro			Median, ratio Negro/ white
	First quintile	Median income	Fourth quintile	First quintile	Median income	Fourth quintile	
Families with male head:							
All families with male head	$5,444	$ 9,297	$14,331	$3,510	$6,611	$10,928	.71
Families with male head, wife present:							
Wife in paid labor force	7,222	10,967	16,220	4,568	8,029	12,168	.73
Wife not in paid labor force	4,698	8,393	13,278	2,834	5,355	8,859	.64
Families with female head	2,316	5,160	9,000	1,687	3,140	5,620	.61
Unrelated individuals:							
Male	1,599	4,411	8,596	1,243	3,020	6,116	.68
Female	1,120	2,353	5,339	702	1,479	3,380	.63

Source: (Census, 1969d: 30-32).

Note: Upper boundaries of the quintiles are shown.

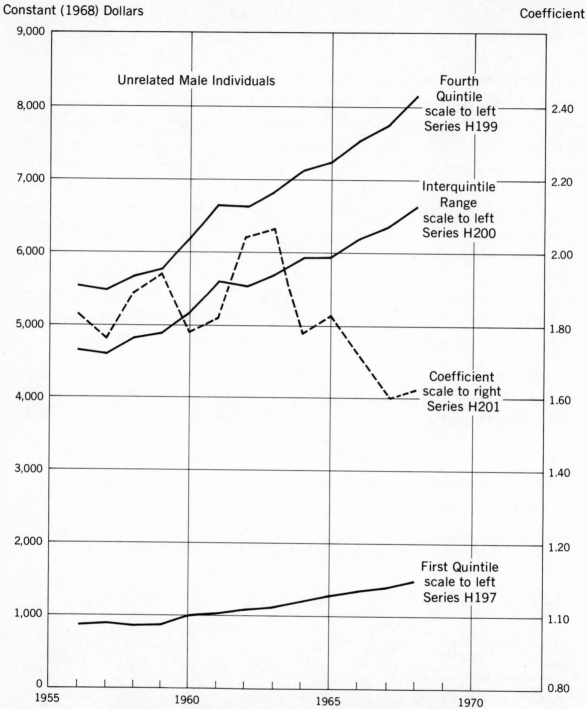

Figure 9.12 First and Fourth Quintiles of Annual Money Income and Difference between the Fourth and First Quintiles, in Constant (1968) Dollars, 1956–1968

Constant (1968) Dollars

Coefficient

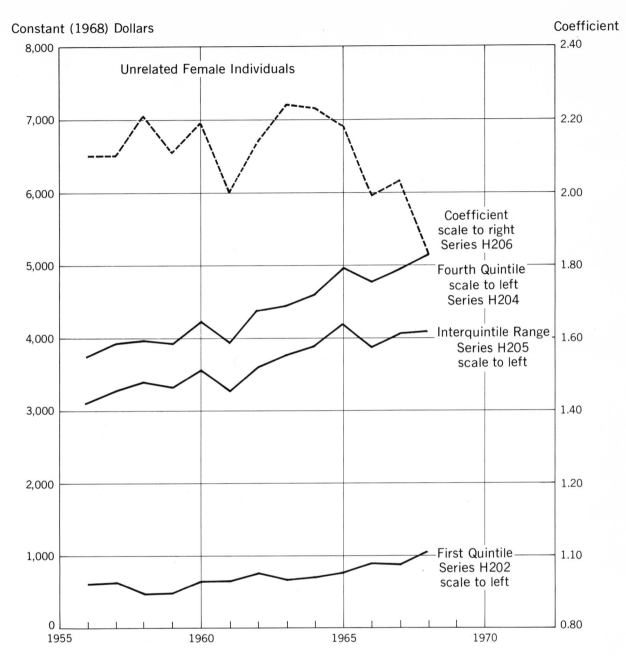

Unrelated Female Individuals

Coefficient
scale to right
Series H206

Fourth Quintile
scale to left
Series H204

Interquintile Range
Series H205
scale to left

First Quintile
Series H202
scale to left

Figure 9.13 First and Fourth Quintiles of Annual Money Income and Difference between the Fourth and First Quintiles, in Constant (1968) Dollars 1956–1968

The ratio of Negro to white families, male head, wife present but not in the paid labor force, is .64, and the ratio for families with a female head is .61.

Similarly, the ratio of Negro to white median incomes of male unrelated individuals is .68, while the comparable ratio for female unrelated individuals is .63. In each instance the Negro female is more disadvantaged in income than the comparable male family unit.

White and nonwhite (Negro) comparisons are listed at the end of this chapter. More information, of course, is to be found in the sources.

A comparison of earnings of income recipients, by color and years of school completed, is presented as Series H207-H226, but is not illustrated. At each educational level, the income of nonwhite females in relation to white females has increased 1964 to 1968 (considering only persons 25 years old or older). Except for one educational level (8 years) the same is true of the income of nonwhite males in relation to white males.

Families and Persons below the Poverty Level

A minimum income to provide "nutritionally adequate food...designed by the Department of Agriculture for 'emergency or temporary use when funds are low'" (Census, 1969k: 11) defines poverty. This income, approximately three times that required for food alone, was developed by the Social Security Administration in 1964 (Orshansky, 1965a and 1965b), and revised in 1967. The critical income levels vary according to the number in the family and according to the farm or nonfarm residence of the family. These poverty levels provide a criterion against which one aspect of the quality of life may be measured (Series H227-H242).

Families. Families by the sex and color of the head of the family, following the family types previously discussed, and unrelated individuals by sex and color, provide the basic types for studying poverty. The Series present both the number of persons and the percent of the population in poverty.

Figure 9.14 shows the trend in the number of persons in poverty. While the number of persons in poverty in nonwhite families with female head increased, 1959 to 1969, the number of persons in poverty in all other types of families has decreased. The graph, on the ratio scale, shows that in 1969 approximately the same number of persons, 3.6 and 3.4 million, were in white and nonwhite families, respectively, below the poverty level, with a female as the head of the family. Slightly fewer persons lived in poverty in nonwhite families with a male head in 1969. Some nine million persons, however, lived in poverty in 1969 in white families with a male as head of the family.

While the trend in the absolute number in poverty can be misleading, owing to the changing total size of the population, monitoring statistics such as these provides meaningful cues to the need for or the consequences of efforts to eliminate poverty. Insofar as families with a female head are concerned, the trends offer little encouragement that their condition is improving. Families with a male head, on the other hand, while numerically greater, have been decreasing in absolute number of persons in poverty.

160

Number of Persons (ratio scale)
(Thousands)

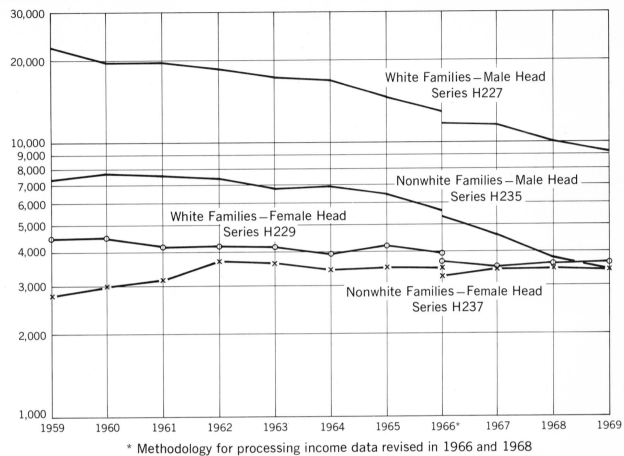

* Methodology for processing income data revised in 1966 and 1968

Figure 9.14 Number of Persons in Families in Poverty by Color and Sex of Family Head, 1959–1969

The percents of persons in poverty in these four types of families may be viewed as declining (Figure 9.15). The greatest percentage decline over the eleven year period was registered by the nonwhite families with male head, while the percentage for nonwhite families with female head also has declined considerably. White families with a female head and white families with a male head have lower percentages of their populations in poverty than corresponding nonwhite families, but the nonwhite percentages have declined much more than the white, since 1959. For programmatic concern, nonwhite families with female heads are nearly 60 percent in poverty and, with nearly 3.5 million persons in poverty, provide the most critical group for public concern (Series H237-H238).

Unrelated Individuals. The numbers of unrelated individuals in poverty, by sex and color, present an even more dismal picture (Figure 9.16). The number of white males and nonwhite males decreased somewhat from 1959 to 1967, rising very slightly thereafter, but the number of nonwhite females in poverty has actually increased over the period, 1959-1969, while the number of white females has remained approximately constant.

It should be pointed out that the individuals in these households are not necessarily the same across the ten-year span. There may have been exits to a better level of living and entrances from a better level of living into poverty status. The increase in the population over this period, also, must be taken into account by considering the percent of unrelated individuals in poverty.

Figure 9.17 shows the percent of persons in unrelated-individual households who are in poverty. The most notable decrease in percentage has been persons in nonwhite male unrelated-individual households (15%), followed closely by white female unrelated individuals (14%). Nonwhite females unrelated individuals, however, constitute the group with the highest percent in poverty. White males, again, represent the group experiencing the least poverty. The generally declining trend of all of the categories presented in the figure is evidence of the continually improving status of the population in poverty. However, the generally high percentages (ranging from 23 percent to 55 percent of the population in 1969 in each of the categories) leave no room for complacency. The percentage in poverty is higher in each color group for females than it is for males.

Women 65 Years of Age and Over with No Money Income

Another indicator of the income status of women is the proportion of those 65 years of age and over who have no money income, Series H246.

Both the absolute number and the percent of women 65 and older with no money income have been declining since 1956. The percents are presented in Figure 9.18. The absolute decline among females was from approximately 2.2 million in 1956 to approximately 1.8 million in 1968. While both the number and the percent of males aged 65 years and over having no money income has dwindled to very small magnitudes, both the number and percent of females 65 and older with no money income still remain at a level to warrant national concern.

162

Percent of Persons

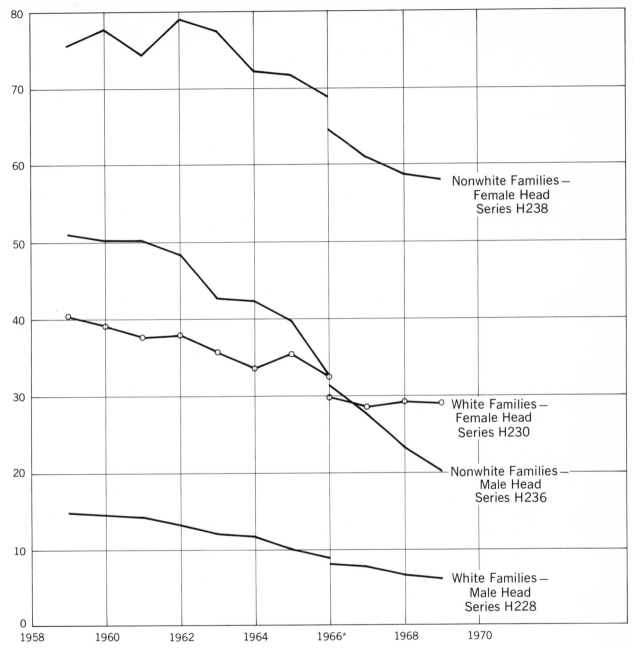

*Methodology for processing income data revised in 1966 and 1968.

Figure 9.15 Percent of Persons in Families in Poverty by Color and
Sex of Family Head, 1959–1969

Number (ratio scale)
(Thousands)

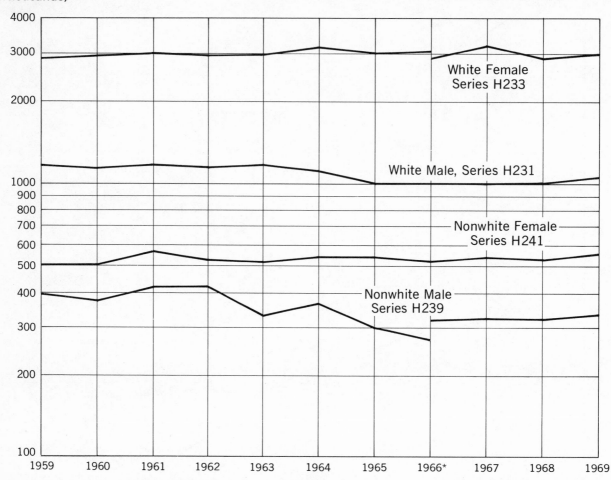

* Methodology for processing income data revised in 1966 and 1968

Figure 9.16 Number of Unrelated Individuals in Poverty by Color and Sex, 1959–1969

Percent

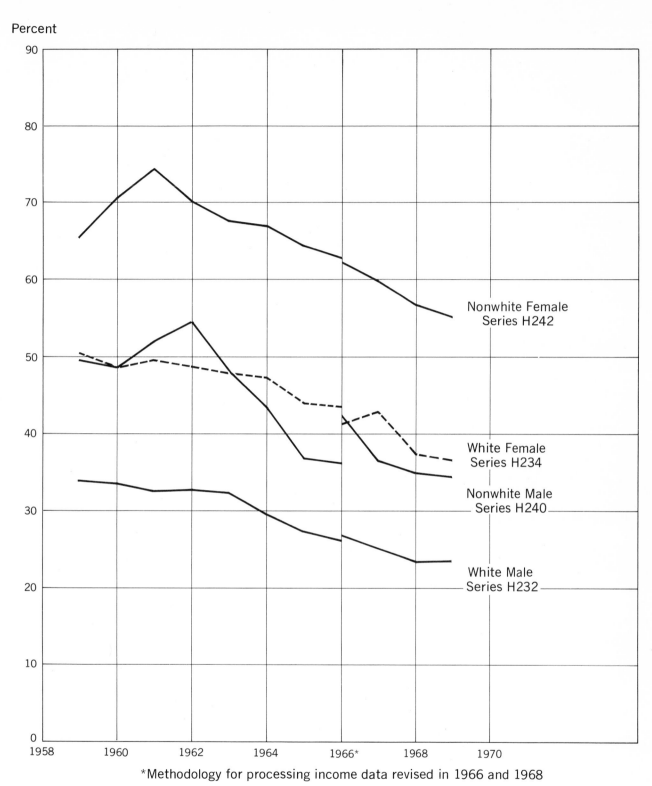

*Methodology for processing income data revised in 1966 and 1968

Figure 9.17 Percent of Unrelated Individuals in Poverty by Color and Sex, 1959–1969

Percent

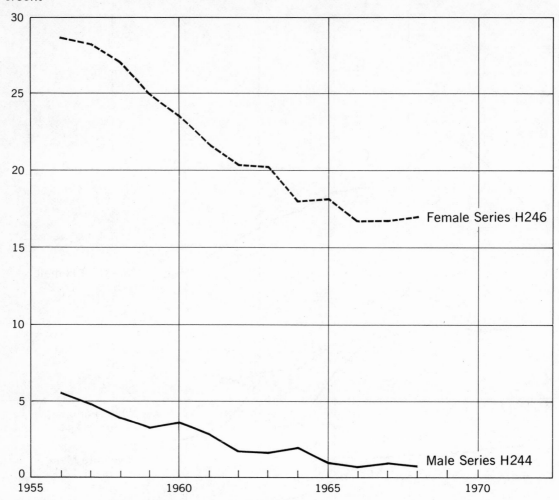

Figure 9.18 Percent of Persons Aged 65 Years and Over Without
Money Income by Sex, 1956–1968

Female unrelated individuals aged 65 and older are the largest single group in poverty, as Table 9.7, based upon the poverty criterion rather than the no-money-income criterion, illustrates.

Table 9.7 - Number and Percent of Family Heads and Unrelated Individuals 65 Years of Age and Over Below the Poverty Level, by Race and Sex, 1968

| | All races | | White | Negro and other races |
	Number (000)	Percent	Percent	Percent
All families	1,201	17.0	15.1	39.0
Families with male head	947	15.9	14.3	39.0
Families with female head	254	22.3	19.6	39.1
All unrelated individuals	2,584	48.8	46.7	70.2
Male unrelated individuals	575	43.5	41.1	59.7
Female unrelated individuals	2,009	50.6	48.5	76.5

Source: (Census, 1969k: 33-38).

Summary of Indicators

The increasing independence of women is inversely indicated by the percent of women with no money income. The continuing decline of this indicator will signify increasing independence (Series H001-H008).

The ratio of the median annual money income of white women relative to white men, has decreased slightly in the twelve years ending 1968 (Table 9.1), while the income of nonwhite women relative to white men improved considerably. These are general, easily interpreted summary indicators (Series H015-H017).

Similarly, the difference between the earnings of men and women, in constant dollars, for year-round full-time civilian workers, when compared with differences observed in the past, succinctly reveals the direction of changes in women's earnings (Series H009-H014).

A more precise contrast in earnings is the median earnings of men and women within the same occupation. Is the female to male ratio increasing? Series H018-H079 provide historical series as a basis for examining future experience. None of these ratios have increased and several have declined (Figure 9.5).

The income of women increases as their education increases, although the relationship is not entirely consistent. As women continue to increase in educational attainment, their income may be expected to increase relative to men's (Series H104-H163).

The percent of women employed, by occupational groups, who had no money income the previous year provides an index to the entry or reentry of women into the labor force. Continued entry into low-paying occupations will serve to keep women's income at their present low levels, relative to men's, while entry into the professions and other more remunerative occupations will tend to improve women's income status. These indices will provide significant metering points.

In monitoring the income of families of various types (male head, female head, etc.), two measures are suggested in addition to the median. If the interquintile range continues to increase, the income of the upper one-fifth will be improving faster than the income of the lower one-fifth. If the coefficient, as herein defined, decreases, the income will tend toward a more equitable distribution or will be increasing - both encouraging signs. The median income, of course, remains the most readily available summary measure for comparison among types of families. To monitor annual money income of families, then, Series H177-H206 provide the basic background data.

Nonwhite females, including Negro, comprise a special category for consideration. Data on money income of white and nonwhite women in relation to the corresponding income of men are presented as Series H207-H226. Distinct progress is evident. These series should be monitored to detect continuing elimination of differentials in income by sex and color.

Finally, in the clearest of terms, the number of white and nonwhite families with female heads in poverty has declined only modestly, particularly when compared with the decline in absolute numbers of male-headed families in poverty. The percent in poverty, however, is being reduced among all sex and color groups. The fact remains, however, that nearly 60 percent of the nonwhite families with female heads are below the poverty level and nearly 30 percent of white families with female heads are below poverty level. Such statistical series as these, reflecting as they do failure of sizeable segments of the population to achieve a minimum quality of life in terms of subsistence, with much of the burden devolving upon women, justify both the careful scrutiny of the analyst and the thoughtful attention of the public. The same can be said, only more loudly, of indices of both males and females 65 years of age and older living in poverty or having no money income (Series H243-H246).

Key to Series Discussed in Chapter 9

Percent of persons with no money income, by color and sex	H001-H004
Median annual money income, by color and sex	H005-H008
Annual earnings of year-round, full-time workers, by color and sex and ratio of female to male earnings by color	H009-H017
Annual earnings of year-round, full-time workers, by occupation and sex	H018-H079
Ratio, earnings of females to earnings of males, year-round, full-time workers, by occupation	H080-H087
Number employed, percent with no income, and median income, by occupation and sex	H088-H103
Annual income, by years of school completed, age and sex	H104-H163
Income status in current year, by employment and labor force status following year, by sex	H164-H176
Annual money income: median, first and fourth quintiles, interquintile range, and coefficient (range to median) for families, by type, and for unrelated individuals, by sex	H177-H206
Median income, by years of schooling, color and sex	H207-H226

10.

Trends in the Social Participation of Women

This chapter attempts to identify trends in women's participation in organizations devoted to serving various interests of women. It explores changing trends in their union membership, and it looks at the voting behavior of women. While the evidence on these linkages between women and society are not available in a form that makes it possible to draw conclusions about women's status, a look at the trends may be instructive.

. . . . .

Women's Participation in Associations

Participation in voluntary associations serves a number of individual and societal functions. To the individual woman, being a member provides sociable, convivial experiences with others. It gives her an opportunity to learn about many phases of social life and places her in communication with the larger society. These experiences serve to integrate women into the social fabric or segments of it. Being in an organization provides women with opportunities to learn and to exercise skills involving others: organizing skills, human relations skills, etc., which, in the long run, build competencies that facilitate the work of society.

Voluntary associations serve society by mediating between the several institutional sectors and integrating the activities of subgroups toward more general goals. Organizations, through ceremonial and through their command of allegiance, reaffirm old values and introduce new ones. Associations perform many regulatory functions in local communities and sometimes initiate (or restrain) social change. They also hold and distribute power (Sills, 1968: 372-376). Thus, a change in membership in organizations serving one of these functions will imply a change in that societal function as it affects women. Unfortunately for this purpose, the functions served by a particular organization do not uniquely contribute to a single social function but often serve several of them with different levels of effectiveness.

Women are less likely to belong to organizations than are men, but only slightly less so. For example, in a survey conducted in Denver by the National Opinion Research Center, 82 percent of men who were married and had children under 18 years of age were likely to belong to one or more voluntary association, while the comparable percentage for women was 56 percent (Wright and

171

Hyman, 1958: 292). Other national studies show about equal percentages of men and women belonging to organizations (Hausknecht, 1962: 37). Married women are more likely to belong to voluntary associations than unmarried ones. Other characteristics associated with membership are: home owners are more likely to belong than home renters; urban and city dwellers are more likely to belong than farm dwellers; those of higher socioeconomic status, than those of lower status; the better educated, than those with only elementary schooling. Members are more likely than nonmembers to be interested in public affairs, to vote, and to support local charities (Wright and Hyman, 1958: 293-294). Members are more likely than nonmembers to read magazines, and they spend more time reading books, and engage in voluntary public service work more than nonmembers (Hausknecht, 1962: 91-109).

In the absence of periodic assessments of the organizational affiliations of the population, we must resort to the aggregate membership of women in organizations of various types. Such a procedure enables only secondary inferences as to the significance of membership to the behavior of women or the function that the organizations play in society and in their lives, as suggested by the theoretical considerations mentioned above. To compound this problem, the statement of the functions and purposes of organizations, as set forth in such a reference volume as the Encyclopedia of Associations, does not enable a precise classification of membership in relation to activities, but merely provides a very general idea of the actual nature of participation. Even with these limitations, however, the data on women's membership in voluntary associations yield indices of the changes taking place in their organizational interests and affiliations.

Changes in Organizational Affiliation

Across the brief span of seven years for which the best information could be obtained, the number of memberships reported by women's organizations appears to be increasing. In 1961 there were 45.6 million members reported; in 1964 there were 48.9 million, and in 1968 there were 52.7 million reported (Series I003). As is explained in Notes to Series, these aggregates are minimum estimates, since organizations not reporting each year were excluded altogether. In relation to the female population, there were 76 memberships per 100 women 18 years old and over in 1961. This increased to 79 in 1964 and was constant at 79 per 100 in 1968. It appears, then, that women's organizations are holding their own in relation to the population and may even be widening their participation.

While the Notes to Series I003-I023 review the sources of the data on organizational membership, perhaps the reader should be reminded here that published records of the number of members in organizations and associations are not designed to be reliable sources of statistical information. The compendium accepts the organization's report and publishes it. When an organization reports the same number of members year after year, for example, one million or three million, one is led to question whether an accurate, up-to-date report is at hand. This type of unreliability is one fault of these data. However, the summary reported below reflects a constant set of organizations and the best estimates available of their membership.

172

Shifts in the organizational interests and affiliations of women can be observed. There is a decline in membership in rural life organizations, in hereditary organizations, and in fraternal and ethnic organizations. Membership in general women's clubs (federated clubs in our classification scheme) also is not growing. On the other hand, the expanding interests of women may be detected by pronounced increases in membership in organizations serving sports and recreation, business and professional groups, and religious-affiliated organizations. Recreation and work-oriented organizations are supplanting, in women's interests, the status-symbolic clubs (fraternal, ethnic, hereditary) and "cultural-social" clubs. The decline in rural-life organizations accompanies the general decline in the rural population. See Table 10.1.

Numerically, religious-affiliated organizations predominate among the memberships women hold. In the aggregate these groups are growing at an annual average rate of 3.1 percent -- considerably higher than the rate of female population growth (1.6 percent annually). In 1968, membership in religious groups encompassed almost one-half of all membership.

Table 10.1 - Distribution of Membership in Various Women's Organizations, 1968, and Annual Rate of Change, 1961-1968, by Major Type of Organization

	Percent of all women memberships 1968	Annual average rate of change 1961-1968
Organizations:		
Increasing at an accelerating rate-		
Religious-affiliated organizations	48.9	3.1
Social service	0.6	1.9
Public affairs	1.2	0.4
Female relatives of members of the armed services	2.8	0.1
Increasing at a decelerating rate-		
Sports and recreation	5.4	9.4
Business, industry and professional (except Education and Sports)	1.1	2.2
Girls' organizations	9.6	1.9
Social welfare (non-professional)	5.3	1.0
Education	2.6	0.5
Women veterans	0.2	0.2
Decreasing-		
Fraternal and ethnic	7.5	-0.1
Federated clubs	1.7	-0.1
Hereditary (except ethnic)	0.5	-0.2
Rural life, farm, and garden	12.6	-0.5

Source: Series I003-I017.

Rural life, farm, and garden clubs were the second largest in membership, but the membership was falling rather rapidly at an average decline of 0.5 percent per year. It appears that the decline in the rural population and the changing interests of the remaining rural people will contribute to a continued decrease in membership in rural, farm and garden clubs for women.

Numerically, girls' organizations comprise the third most numerous type of women's organization, making up 9.6 percent of all memberships in 1968. Their rate of growth of 1.9 percent per year is slightly above the rate of growth of the female population.

At the other extreme, several types of organizations are losing their proportionate share of memberships and, besides, are experiencing a declining rate of growth. In addition to rural clubs, membership is decreasing in women's hereditary organizations, women's fraternal and ethnic associations, and federated clubs -- organizations that serve numerous functions but ones that most certainly serve the status and prestige interests of their members.

Two types of organizations that are barely holding their own are organizations of women veterans (increasing at 0.2 percent per year) and organizations of women relatives of members of the armed services (increasing at 0.1 percent per year).

In Table 10.1, types of organizations identified as increasing at an accelerating rate were those whose annual average rate of increase during 1964-68 exceeded the average annual rate of increase during 1961-64. When the opposite prevailed, the type of organization was classified as increasing at a decelerating rate. Types losing members were classified as decreasing organizations. Within any class of organizations, of course, there may be both increasing and decreasing associations, Table 10.1 and Series I003-I017 giving only the net change. Series I003-I017 present the percentage distribution of membership for 1961, 1964 and 1968, as well as the rates of change. Series I018-I023 present membership information on types of organizations with principally female membership, but including men. Educational organizations predominate among these organizations with both men and women members.

In the search for trends in membership in organizations of various types (the types presented in Table 10.1), selected organizations have been identified and a special effort made to acquire a serial listing of their membership. These organizations may serve to indicate trends in membership over a longer span of time than that of Series I003-I023. Organizations were selected that had the more adequate records instead of those that might be considered more typical of a particular type of purpose and service. Series I024-I037 present membership trends in these organizations. Some types are not represented by these series because a representative organization could not be found to provide reliable membership information. Among the reasons for this unreliability is that some organizations keep inadequate records, some decline to reveal their membership, some national headquarters apparently do not have current information on membership in local units, and so forth.

Figure 10.1 illustrates the trends in membership of several national organizations. Membership began increasing about 1944 and increased fairly rapidly for several years. Home Economics Clubs reached their peak in 1954 and have now declined to below its membership in 1940. The American Legion Auxiliary increased immediately following World War II, remained relatively constant for 13 years; after 1960 it declined somewhat, but has shown an increase of 5,000 members from 1968 to 1969. Membership in the National Federation of Business and Professional Women's Clubs increased rapidly to 1949 and more slowly since then; membership declined slightly in 1962, apparently a consequence of a $1 increase in dues, but those losses have been recouped. The

174

Thousands of Members (ratio scale)

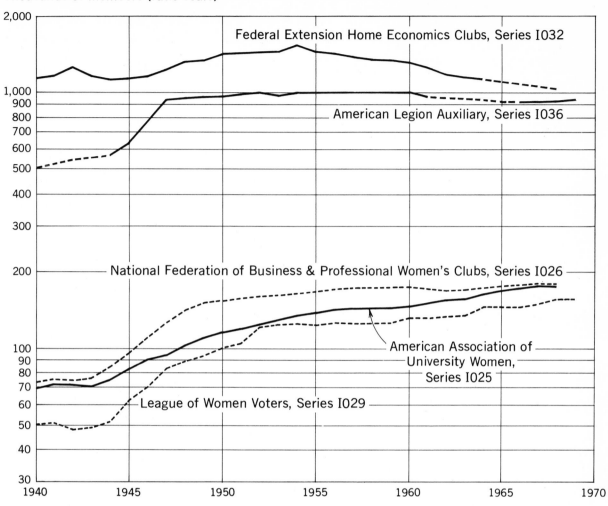

Figure 10.1 Membership of Five National Women's Organizations, 1940–1968/1969

American Association of University Women has maintained a fairly steady rate of growth since the end of World War II. Following the War, the League of Women Voters increased rapidly through the election year 1952, after which the rate of increase has been low but continuing.

Women in Labor Unions

Membership in unions is often not entirely voluntary. It is greatly influenced by the industry, occupation and place of work of the employee. As women have increasingly entered the labor force, many took jobs where union membership was not typical. Consequently, in 1968, only 12.5 percent of women in the civilian labor force belonged to a union. By way of contrast, union membership was more characteristic of the occupations and industries where men worked. Some 30.5 percent of men in the civilian labor force belonged to unions in 1968 (Figure 10.2).

The above are only rough estimates. Precise and comprehensive data are not available, for many unions do not release the number of their members to the U. S. Department of Labor in its biennial survey of unions. Similarly, a time series on membership in individual unions is subject to organizational amalgamations, separations, and changes of locals from one union to another. These changes render difficult any attempt to account systematically for the membership. As a result, the data cited in the preceding paragraph are based upon U.S. Bureau of Labor Statistics accounting, using the best available estimate, and are modified to remove a small number of women members of unions located chiefly in Canada.

The 1966 Bureau of Labor Statistics survey yielded responses from 190 unions and found that 140 of them had women members. None had exclusively female membership, but two -- the International Ladies' Garment Workers' Union and the Amalgamated Clothing Workers of America -- had over 364,000 and 286,000 women members, respectively (Women's Bureau, 1969: 82-83).

In a discussion of the status of women in American society, union membership connotes a work status that is significant primarily because unions are bargaining agencies through which salary, tenure, working conditions, and other rights of the worker are periodically assessed and established. If a member's income is inequitable for the job she performs, the union provides the means for obtaining justice. An increase in the percent of the female civilian labor force in unions, consequently, would suggest that women appreciate such benefits of membership as they enter industries and occupations that are "organized". The percent, however, has not been increasing. In 1954, an estimated 14.1 percent of women in the civilian labor force were members of unions. By 1968, the percent had declined to 12.5. On the other hand, 31.7 percent of men in the civilian labor force in 1954 were union members and this percent had declined to 30.5 by 1968. Such evidence, however, is merely suggestive, for only union membership by industry and occupation would give precise information of women's unionization compared with men's.

A 1967 Survey of Economic Opportunity provides some suggestive evidence on this last point. The salary advantage of women union members over women who were not members, for year-round, full-time private wage and salary workers, ranged from 12 percent to 50 percent, depending upon

occupation. The comparison (shown in Table 10.3), again, is not precise, for the problem, previously mentioned, of equating industry and occupation for men and women remains with us. The
data also show that the relation of women's wages to men's is more advantageous to women in
unions than is the relationship of women's and men's among nonunion members.

Table 10.2 - Estimated Number of U. S. Members of National and International Labor Unions
and Percent of Civilian Labor Force in Unions, by Sex, 1954-1968

Year	Estimate, U. S. women in national and international labor unions		Estimate, U. S. men in national and international labor unions	
	Number (000)	Percent of female civilian labor force 16 years and older	Number (000)	Percent of male civilian labor force 16 years and older
1954	2,775	14.1	13,943	31.7
1956	3,205	14.9	14,028	31.1
1958	3,055	13.8	13,731	30.2
1960	3,097	13.3	13,828	29.8
1962	3,058	12.7	13,384	28.7
1964	3,169	12.5	13,510	28.3
1966	3,430	12.6	14,340	29.6
1968	3,661	12.5	15,113	30.5

Source: (BLS, 1967b: 56; BLS, 1970).

Finally, Table 10.3 answers another question by showing the percent of women in unions in
the several census occupation categories. (The base for these percentages is year-round, full-
time private wage and salary workers, in contrast to the base for Table 10.2, which is the
civilian labor force,thus accounting for the small difference in the total percent belonging to
unions.) In all occupational categories except sales workers, men are more likely to be union
members than women. Women operatives are more likely to be in unions than women in any other
occupation, and this occupation also has large numbers of women in it. Women are more numerous
in the clerical occupations than any other, but here unionization plays a relatively minor role.

From these data for 1966, then, it is fairly clear that women are not organized into unions
as extensively as men, that women who do belong to unions have a salary advantage over their non-
unionized sisters in the same occupation, and that women's earnings in relation to men's are
higher for union than nonunion people.

Because of the large number of unions, trends in membership only for those with 10,000 or
more female members in 1968 are presented as Series I043-I093. Unions also are excluded if they
did not provide membership data for most of the years 1954-1968. Total female members in the
United States were estimated from the Bureau of Labor Statistics data, with an adjustment to
remove Canadian members reported by international unions. This total is a better indicator of
union membership and activity than the summation of incomplete reports of membership by the
unions themselves. Trends are illustrated for the number and percent of the labor force in
unions, by sex, in Figure 10.2. The individual union membership in the series may include a
relatively small number of members in Canada, Puerto Rico, or outlying U. S. possessions.

Millions of members (ratio scale)

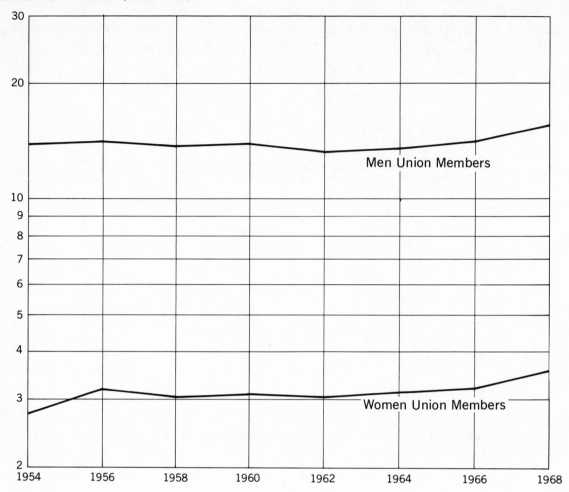

Percent

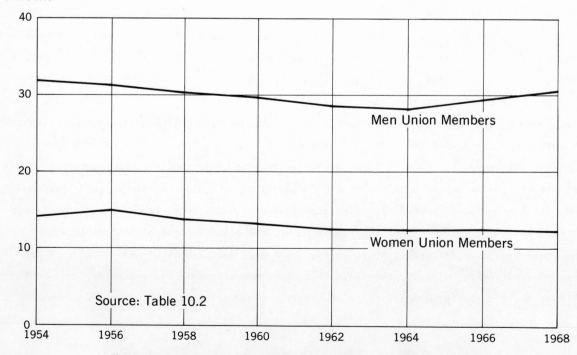

Source: Table 10.2

Figure 10.2 Number of U. S. Members of National and International Labor Unions and Percent of Civilian Labor Force in Unions, by Sex, 1954–1968

Table 10.3 - Union Membership and Income of Year-Round Full-Time Private Wage and Salary Workers, by Sex, United States, 1966

	Percent belonging to labor unions		Median annual earnings				Ratio, women's median salary to men's	
			Men		Women			
	Men	Women	In unions	Not in unions	In unions	Not in unions	In unions	Not in unions
Total, 16 years old and over	33.5	17.0	$7,419	$6,980	$4,382	$3,901	.59	.56
Professional, technical	11.7	4.4	8,824	9,514	c/	5,180	--	.54
Managers, officials, Proprietors (nonfarm)	9.0	3.0	9,322	9,590	c/	5,623	--	.59
Clerical and kindred workers	27.9	11.0	6,541	6,361	5,082	4,258	.78	.67
Sales workers	7.0	8.6	6,831	7,720	c/	2,778	--	.36
Craftsmen, foremen, & kindred workers	47.1	36.9	8,288	6,760	c/	b/	--	--
Operatives & kindred workers	53.6	43.0	6,916	5,539	4,164	3,631	b/	b/
Service workers, including private household	30.7	7.9	5,183	4,149	3,913 a/	2,603 a/	.75	.63
Nonfarm laborers	52.8	31.3	6,165	4,117	c/	c/	--	--
Farm workers	1.1	c/	c/	2,687	c/	c/	--	--

a/ - Private household workers excluded.

b/ - Women not comparable to men because of occupational differences.

c/ - Not computed because base was less than 100,000.

Source: (Census, 1970g: 5-6).

Voting

As one of the privileges and responsibilities of citizenship, voting for candidates for public office represents one of the cornerstones of the American political system. It provides the means for working through and even for changing the system. The evidence shows that women participate slightly less in this process than men, although the differences between the percents of men and of women voting have declined. In 1948 and in 1952, ten percent more men than women voted in the presidential election (Campbell, 1954: 70-73). At the time of the last presidential election (1968), only four percent more men voted than women (Census, 1969L: 10).

Evidence from surveys of voting experience in the 1968 presidential election shows that older persons, aged 45 through 74, are more likely to vote than younger ones. The age group 21 through 24 voted least frequently of all, but still more than one-half of the population in these ages voted. Furthermore, the difference between the percent of females voting and the percent of males voting increases with age, from practically no difference in the youngest voting age to as high as ten percent difference in the 65-74 age group, and over 17 percentage points among the population 75 years of age and over (Census, 1969L: 10). As the present young voters mature in age, the differential in the percent voting is likely to diminish.

The 1968 Census survey of the voting behavior of all persons 21 years of age and over (Table 10.4), also shows that the percent voting among both males and females increases with years of school completed. The disparity in voting rate between men and women decreases as education increases. The evidence for 1968 also shows that women in the labor force are more likely to vote than those not in the labor force. In the agricultural industries, self-employed women are more likely to vote than wage and salary workers, but female wage and salary workers vote at about the same rate as male wage and salary workers in agriculture. In the nonagricultural industries, women in various worker groups vote at only slightly lower rates than men in the same categories. Generally, it would appear that the voting behavior of women is only slightly lower than that of men of comparable employment status.

Unemployed women are slightly more likely to vote than unemployed men.

Table 10.4 - Percents of Persons 21 Years Old and Over, of Specified Classifications, Voting[a/] in 1968 Presidential Election, and Percent Not Registered, 1968, by Sex (Civilian noninstitutional population)

	Male	Female		Male	Female
Total, 21 years and older	100.0	100.0	Employed	73.3	72.4
			Agriculture	72.3	65.4
Total voting, 1968	71.9	67.6	Self-employed	82.6	73.0
			Wage & salary workers	47.7	45.5
White	73.0	68.7	Non-agricultural	73.3	72.6
Nonwhite	60.3	57.6	Private wage & salary		
Negro	61.7	59.1	workers	70.3	68.7
			Government workers	84.6	84.8
North and West	74.6	71.6	Self-employed workers	80.5	78.0
South	65.4	58.3			
			Unemployed	53.4	54.3
Completed elementary school:			Less than 5 weeks	56.2	53.9
0-4 years	46.3	33.3	5 weeks or more	49.8	54.9
5-7 years	54.4	48.0			
8 years	69.0	60.1	Not in labor force	66.5	64.5
Completed high school:			Total not registered, 1968	21.3	25.0
1-3 years	65.9	60.8	Reason for not registering:		
4 years	74.9	73.8	Not a citizen	2.0	2.6
			Residence requirement not		
Completed college:			satisfied	2.6	2.6
1-3 years	79.4	81.0	Not interested	11.3	13.4
4 years	85.4	83.8	Unable to register	2.6	3.5
5 years or more	86.1	89.0	Other reason	2.1	2.3
Civilian labor force	72.9	71.7			
White-collar workers	82.8	80.3			
Manual workers	66.0	57.9			
Service workers	72.4	61.9			
Farm workers	75.6	65.9			

Source: (Census, 1969L: 10-13, 17, 19, 23, 47).

a/ - Percents are based on those reporting on their voting or registration.

When examined in terms of the occupational grouping of workers, women vote at rates considerably less than men, except for women white-collar workers, who vote at a rate almost the same as men.

It would appear, then, that as women achieve higher levels of education and employment, their voting behavior equals or exceeds that of men. Greater involvement in activities of the larger society prompts women to greater involvement in governmental affairs.

Twenty-one percent of the men and 25 percent of women reported that they had not registered to vote for the 1968 election. The various reasons given for not registering were much the same among men and women. Only those saying, "Not interested", were slightly more numerous among women (2 percent more) than among men, and this was the most frequent "reason" given (13.3 percent of all women age 21 and over so answering).

Voting trends by sex can be derived only from the household survey. The Survey Research Center and the American Institute of Public Opinion have conducted some of these surveys periodically, but estimates of the population of voting age by sex is not always made available from these studies. Table 10.5 presents the meager evidence we were able to assemble on the percent voting of the voting-age population by sex. While the percent voting in 1952 exceeded that of 1948, the evidence otherwise does not show a marked increase in voting participation. In fact, it shows that the participation of men declined. Differences between proportions of men and women voting, however, are becoming smaller.

Table 10.5 - Percent of Voting-Age Population Voting in Presidential Elections, by Sex, 1948-1968

	Male	Female
1948	69	59
1952	79	69
1956		
1960		
1964	73	68
1968	72	68

Source: 1948, 1952: (Campbell, 1954: 70-73); 1964: (Census, 1965m: 9); 1968 (Census, 1969L: 10).

Table 10.6 shows voting in the two most recent presidential elections, by sex and age. The voting participation of women in the younger ages is almost the same as that of men, but with increasing age the difference between the percents of men and women who vote increases, women voting less frequently.

Table 10.6 - Percent of the Population Voting in Presidential Elections, by Age and Sex, 1964 and 1968

Age and Sex		1964	1968
21-24 years:	Male	52.8	53.4
	Female	51.7	52.7
25-34 years:	Male	65.9	64.3
	Female	64.5	63.3
35-44 years:	Male	74.9	73.8
	Female	71.9	71.5
45-54 years:	Male	78.9	78.4
	Female	74.6	76.0
55-64 years:	Male	79.6	79.3
	Female	73.5	74.1
65-74 years:	Male	78.2	79.3
	Female	67.2	69.1
75 years & over:	Male	66.8	68.2
	Female	49.7	51.1

Source: 1964: (Census, 1965m: 9-10); 1968: (Census, 1969L: 10).

Summary of Indicators

Since our statistical system does not provide periodic estimates of organizational participation, the series (I003-I017) give us a clue to the changing organizational interests of women.
The positions women hold in organizations and the roles they play in them are significant links
between the individual and the total society. The shifting pattern of women's affiliation with
organizations and particularly the rate of change in their membership pattern provide indications
of the sectors of social life in which women are involved.

Union membership must be interpreted in relation to women's work situation and compared with
the unionization of men in the same or comparable work settings. The total female membership of
unions has little meaning unless it can be so interpreted. Series I040-I093, then, are available
for the additional study that is needed to reveal the significance of the trends. Perhaps such
an analysis should be pursued on an industry-by-industry basis.

Voting behavior of women has been shown to be related to age, education, labor force participation, occupation and other factors. These provide clues to the forces underlying the
increasing voting participation of women. While the percent of women voting is available for
only a brief span of time, the new Bureau of the Census voting surveys eventually will give us
valuable indicators of voting behavior in detail, by age, sex, color, education, income, and so
forth.

Social, economic and governmental participation are interrelated in ways as yet inadequately
explored. The primitive indicators of these forces, examined in this chapter, demonstrate the
need for a unified data-collection system that periodically will assemble information from household members so that individual characteristics can be examined in relation to participation in
organizations, in governmental affairs, in other aspects of social life.

Key to Series Discussed in Chapter 10

Percent distribution of organizations with female members
  only, by type of organization   I001 - I017

Percent distribution of organizations with largely female
  membership, by type of organization   I018 - I023

Membership in selected organizations   I024 - I037

Female members of labor unions   I040 - I093

11.

Recent Changes in the Outdoor Recreation of Women

There is much information collected on indoor and outdoor recreation, sports, vacations, trips, and the like (Ennis, 1968), but most of the information in time series is not available by sex. To illustrate changes in participation in recreational activities of men and women, the data collected in 1960 and 1965 in similar surveys of outdoor recreation will be examined.

. . . . .

Patterns of Participation in Outdoor Activities

Participation in outdoor recreation is made possible by leisure time being available from work, by being interested in the activity, by having the vitality for it (if vitality is needed) and by the necessary outdoor resources being accessible. If an increase has occurred in days of participation per person during the summer months undoubtedly some of these factors have increased. The evidence consists only of 1960 and 1965 surveys of the population 12 years of age and over (Ferriss, 1962; and unpublished data from the Bureau of Outdoor Recreation, U. S. Department of the Interior).

Women participate in outdoor recreation approximately four-fifths as frequently as men (Series J01). This relationship seems to be relatively stable across time. Between 1960 and 1965, activity days per person during the summer months increased about the same for the two sex groups (44 percent for men and 41 percent for women). During this brief period, the activity days per person increased 12.4 days per person among women and 15.9 days among men.

The participation of women in passive outdoor activities exceeded that of men in both 1960 and 1965 (Series J02). Passive activities are those requiring relatively less activity -- automobile driving, nature walks and strolls, sightseeing, picnicking, and attending outdoor plays, concerts and sports events. These relatively mild recreational events and activities, as a group, play a more prominent role in the outdoor recreation of both men and women than any other type of recreation, constituting 45 percent of the summer activity days, on the average, of males and 59 percent of females in 1965.

In water-related activities, women participated approximately seven-tenths as frequently as men. The increase in days per person over the five-year period is only slightly greater for males than for females (an increase of 2.8 days per person for men and 2.09 days per person for women) (Series J10).

In backwoods activities neither men nor women participate to a very great extent, but women engage less than men (Series J19). The heaviest participants are younger persons, particularly boys and girls 12-17 years of age. The increase, 1960 to 1965, has been slightly greater for women than for men. One would not expect hunting to be much engaged in during the summer, and it is not.

Finally, in active outdoor pursuits, other than water and backwoods activities, women and girls participate only one-half as frequently as men and boys (Series J15). The increase in days participation per person for men was nearly double the increase for women. These are outdoor activities that appeal typically to younger persons.

These general trends in outdoor recreation participation are merely the initial observations on recreational indices of males and females. Women are participating more often in activities that are compatible with their interests. The more active participation of males than females in physically demanding recreation undoubtedly will continue.

Age. Women 25 to 44 years of age actually engage in outdoor recreation about as frequently as men, men exceeding them in 1965 by only 1.2 average days per person during the summer (Series J01). In these ages, men are almost altogether employed full-time, while women are predominately housewives and mothers. In all age groups except the very oldest, women engage in passive activities more than men. In all other activities, however, women in all age groups participate less than men.

In days participation per person, women 65 years of age and over increased more than men, 1960 to 1965 -- 4.8 days per person increase for women compared with 2.8 for men. Women increased their participation more than men, too, in passive activities, exceeding men in the 18-24 age group, the 25-44 age group, and the oldest age category. In water activities, young women 12 to 17 years of age increased 6.0 days per person more than boys of the same age. In backwoods activities, women increased more than men in all age groups except the 45-64 year-old group. Increases in backwoods activities, however, were less than one day's participation per person.

In summer 1965 women participated more in all outdoor activities than they did in summer 1960, except in driving for pleasure (Series J03). The decline in days participation per person in driving for pleasure was quite small (0.2 days per person decrease). Women increased their participation most in the simple leisure activity of walking for pleasure, averaging 8.1 days per person in summer, 1965, compared with 4.9 days in summer, 1960. Other recreational activities in which women increased at least one day per person during the summer were going on picnics, taking nature walks (including birdwatching and photographing wildlife and birds), swimming, playing outdoor games and sports, and bicycling. While increases occurred in other activities, such increases were less than one day per person, on the average.

Among females, the greatest increase in activity days per person was among those 12 to 17 years of age, this group increasing particularly in playing outdoor games and sports, bicycling and swimming (Series J16, J17 and J11).

These activities chiefly are pleasurable activities engaged in for relaxation, for release from the daily routine, and for the joy of engaging with others. As such, they represent gains in the quality of life for girls and women.

Summary of Indicators

Participation in recreational activities has been shown to be associated with education, income, color, degree of urbanization of residence, health and other factors (Ferriss, 1962). The trend of increasing participation of both men and women in relatively passive outdoor activities is in keeping with continuing urbanization, such passive recreational pursuits being more typical of urban people. Increases in participation were greater, too, among the younger population than the older, especially in active games and sports. Women in their middle years (25-44 years of age) are participating as much or more than men in many of these forms of outdoor recreation.

Trends such as these (Series J01-J22) reflect, as few other indices do, the quality of life in America. Dependent as most of them are upon the availability of recreational resources, the possession of equipment, the leisure time, etc., days of activity per person also are measures of a number of economic variables in addition to sociological ones.

Key to Series Discussed in Chapter 11

Days recreation activity per person (during summer), by age and sex: all activities	J01
Passive activities	J02 - J09
Water activities	J10 - J14
Other active recreation	J15 - J18
Backwoods activities	J19 - J22

12.

Trends in Women's Health and Illness

Health may be taken to be the absence of illness. Some object to this definition, however, saying health is more than that, "something positive, a joyful attitude toward life, and a cheerful acceptance of the responsibilities that life puts on the individual" /H. E. Siegerist, as cited by (Moriyama, 1968: 585)/. In describing trends, we are limited to an operational definition used to produce a time series on the incidence of health or non-health, even though such measures may fail to capture the number of those enraptured with life.

This chapter considers various indicators of health garnered by the Health Interview Survey and the next chapter reviews the causes of death, reflecting trends over time in the morbidity status and the mortality of women.

Days of restricted activity are days so below the level of "positive, joyful" living that the individual restrains from engaging in his or her usual activities. The incidence of the days restricted in this manner are examined in relation to family income, age, and sex. As part of restricted activity, bed disability days and loss-of-work days (among those in the labor force) also are studied in relation to income, age and sex. Actually, these restrictions could sometimes mean that the individual is better cared for, rather than that his (or her) health is deficient, but these are measurement faults we must tolerate if we are to compare women's status with men's status.

The causes of restrictions upon one's activities are various acute and chronic conditions or sometimes impairments that hamper one's normal activity. The broad spectrum of these disabilities is examined to determine which prove to be more disabling to men and women.

One basis for some illnesses, currently prominent, is cigarette smoking. This practice is examined to find out whether the percentages of men and women who smoke are declining and whether women are quitting smoking more than are men.

This chapter is primarily concerned with evidences of morbidity, while the chapter that follows (Chapter 13) concentrates on the causes of mortality.

. . . . .

Restricted Activity Days

Days per person per year of restricted activity provide a general index of illness in the population (Series K001-K032). Illness or injury that causes a person "to cut down on (his) usual activities for as much as a day," as the questionnaire is worded, are enumerated each week by the Health Interview Survey, a multistage probability sample of the civilian noninstitutional population of the United States. The survey also determines whether the restricted activity days involved bed rest or work loss.

Restricted activity days are associated with age, sex and income. Except for the younger ages (up to 10 years), females experience more restricted activity days per person than males. Differences between male and female are greater in the ages 25 to 44 years; thereafter, the difference between them in restricted activity decreases. Days of restricted activity increase among both male and female after the age of 24. Is the female population improving in health, as indexed by this measure?

Figure 12.1 presents restricted activity days per person per year. The apparent improvement in health from 1958 to 1959 is a transitory phenomenon, a consequence of the 1957-58 influenza epidemic. The rates for all females were 2.3 to 4.5 days per person per year greater than the rates for males. Since the rates for females have declined while the rates for males have remained relatively stable, the gap appears to be closing; the 3-year average for 1958-60 was 4.2 days (more than the rate for males) compared with 2.7 days difference for the three years ended 1967.

Restricted activity days for males and females 25 to 44 years of age differ even more than total restricted activity days of males and females (Series K005, K013). While the rate for males has increased since 1963 by approximately one day per person, the rate for females has declined by more than one day per person. One might suspect that this decline is associated with the decrease in the birth rate over the period shown in the graph. However, when disability days per person due to "deliveries and disorders of pregnancy and the puerperium" are removed from restricted activity days of females, the trend retains the same shape. Consequently, while the decline in the birth rate has tended to decrease female restricted activity days slightly, most of the decline may be attributed to other sources. As will be discussed later, these major sources are decreases in the incidence of infective and parasitic diseases, in upper respiratory infections, in diseases of the digestive system, and in "all other" acute conditions (Table 12.3).

In addition to age, restricted activity days vary with income; see Figure 12.2. Among females, the rates decline as family income increases. In 1967 females in the income group under $2,000 per year experienced approximately two times more restricted activity days per person than females in each of the two higher income classes. Similarly, the second lowest income group, $2,000 to $3,999, experienced approximately 50 percent more restricted activity days than the two higher income groups. The $2,000 to $3,999 income group, in fact, showed a long-term increase in

Restricted Activity Days

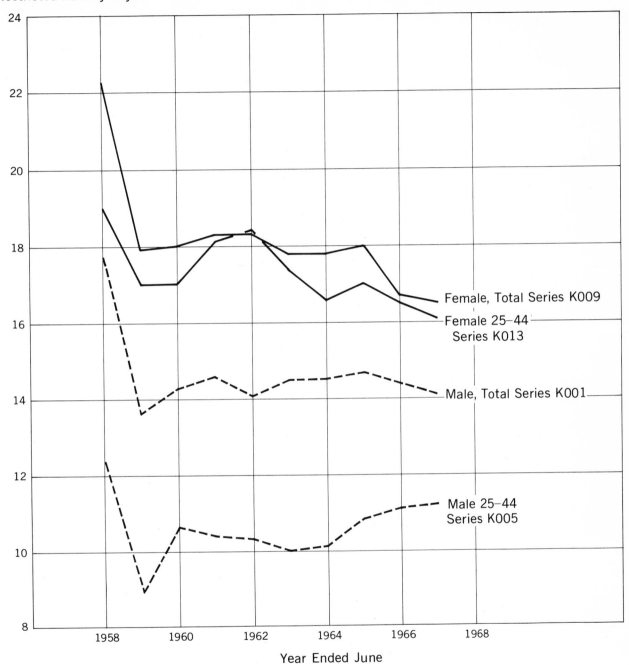

Figure 12.1 Restricted Activity Days per Person per Year, Total and 25–44 Years of Age, by Sex, 1958–1967

Restricted Activity Days

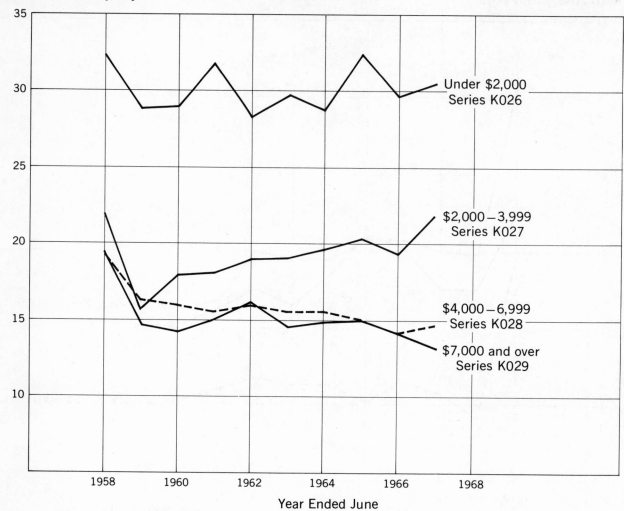

Year Ended June

Figure 12.2 Restricted Activity Days per Person per Year, by Family Income, Females, 1958–1967

restricted activity days per person per year.[1] Somewhat in contrast, the under-$2,000 income

group has varied from approximately 28 to approximately 32 days per person per year, but showed

no distinct tendency to increase or decrease over the long term. Females in the higher income

groups, if anything, are reducing the number of their restricted activity days. (All references

are to restricted activity days per person per year for females.) How does this compare with

males by income?

Table 12.1 - Differences in Restricted Activity Days of Females and Males, by Family Income,
1958-1967

Year ended June	Total	Under $2,000	$2,000- 3,999	$4,000- 6,999	$7,000 and over	$10,000 and over	Income not known
1958	4.5	0	2.8	5.4	5.3		6.0
1959	4.3	4.1	1.3	5.1	4.1		7.8
1960	3.7	2.3	2.1	4.7	2.8		4.9
1961	3.7	4.2	0.7	3.5	4.0		7.3
1962	4.2	3.4	2.3	4.0	4.8		6.2
1963	3.3	1.3	2.4	3.6	2.8		2.5
1964	3.3	2.5	1.3	2.8	3.5	2.8	5.1
1965	3.3	4.7	1.0	2.3	3.4	3.1	3.3
1966	2.3	0.8	-0.4	1.1	3.0	3.7	3.5
1967	2.4	1.3	2.2	1.0	2.1	1.4	4.1

Source: Series K017-K032.

Table 12.1 presents the differences between restricted activity days of females and males

by income class. Positive numbers indicate that females experienced a greater number of

restricted activity days than males. Over the entire ten-year period for all income categories,

the number of restricted activity days of females exceeded that of males, except in two instances.

Generally, the difference between the rates of males and of females is decreasing, a trend that

is most plainly evident among the two higher income groups.

Considered as a whole, the variation across time is not significant, whereas the variation

in the rate among income classes is quite significant and the variation between males and females

is significant (at the 0.5 level of confidence). This result is derived from an analysis of

variance of Series K017-K032.

---

[1] - A change in the income distribution (current dollars) of families may account for the
     increase in restricted activity days among the $2,000-$3,999 income group. During 1959-
     1967, persons in families with incomes up to $2,000, who experience a much higher incidence
     of restricted activity days per person, may have crossed the $2,000 income mark and entered
     the $2,000-$3,999 income class, thereby increasing the latter's rate of restricted activity
     days. The percent of families and primary individuals with total money income below $2,000
     for 1958 was 20.6 percent, and for each successive year thereafter: 19.5 percent, 19.0 per-
     cent, 19.3 percent, 18.0 percent, 17.2 percent, 16.0 percent, 15.5 percent, 14.2 percent,
     and 13.0 percent (1967). (Census, 1969c: 26).

Changes across time are slow, and occasionally fluctuate because of epidemics or other widespread disorders. However, differences due to sex, to income, and to age (not included in the analysis of variance) are much more persistent. Among these factors, the association of income with restricted activity days appears to be the relationship that is most subject to modification. Since differences between the two higher income groups are small, the population in income groups under $4,000 stand out as most adversely affected. Even among the low income groups, however, income itself is not the only variable of consequence. To quote the National Center for Health Statistics: "25 percent of the members of the group having under $2,000 income were 65 years and older, compared with 12 percent of the $2,000-$3,999 group, and four percent of each of the $4,000-$6,999 and $7,000 and over groups". (NCHS, 1963a: 9-10).

It is clear that age interacts with income, and even if costs of health care -- the apparent linkage between restricted activity days and income -- did not limit the availability of health care to the lower income groups, restricted activity days among lower income groups would still be greater because of age. To the extent that the Medicare program, launched in 1965, improves the health of the aged, it should, in the long-run, reduce the restricted activity days of the lower income groups. (In the short-run, restricted activity days of aged persons might be increased, as improved medical care occasions an increase in bed days of disability).

Summary of Trends in Restricted Activity Days

Table 12.2 summarizes relationships and trends in days of restricted activity. Omitting 1957-58 as atypical because of the influenza epidemic in that period, and smoothing the rates with a three-year moving average to eliminate minor variations, the table provides a comparison of 1959-61 with 1965-67, by age and sex, and by family income and sex.

Table 12.2 - Average Annual Restricted Activity Days for Two 3-Year Periods, by Age and Sex and by Income and Sex, 1959-61 and 1965-67

	Male			Female		
	1959-61	1965-67	Change (days)	1959-61	1965-67	Change (days)
Total	14.2	14.4	+0.2	18.1	17.1	-1.0
Under 5 years	11.2	11.1	-0.1	10.8	9.7	-1.1
5-14 years	11.4	10.5	-0.9	11.4	10.1	-1.3
15-24 years	7.7	8.5	-1.2	11.7	11.0	-0.7
25-44 years	10.0	10.0	0	17.3	16.5	-0.8
45-64 years	18.8	20.8	+2.0	23.4	22.3	-1.1
65-74 years	34.5	30.8	-3.7	34.3	33.2	-1.1
75+ years	42.4	38.0	-4.4	49.8	45.6	-4.2
Income						
Under $2,000	26.3	28.5	+2.2	29.8	30.8	+1.0
$2,000-$3,999	15.8	19.5	+3.7	17.2	20.4	+3.2
$4,000-$6,999	11.4	13.1	+1.7	15.8	14.6	-1.2
$7,000 and over	11.1	11.3	+0.2	15.2	14.1	-1.1

Source: Series K001-K032.

There has been some improvement among females of all age groups. Males have not improved as uniformly by age and have actually increased in the 45 through 64 years of age group. In the 3-year period centered on 1960, restricted activity days per person of females of all ages were 27 percent more than those of males; in the 3-year period centered on 1966, restricted activity days per person of females decreased to a point 19 percent greater than those of males.

The same basis for identifying trends is used in the lower segment of Table 12.2, comparing restricted activity days by income. Restricted activity days per person per year for females have increased among the two lower income groups, and have decreased among the two higher income groups. Among males, on the other hand, restricted activity days have increased among all income groups. Both of these trends -- by age and by income -- appear to be real gains of females.

It is not possible to pin down the precise sources of the differences between the restricted activity days of males and females. Not all illness conditions that contribute to restricted activity days are published, and the restricted activity days of persons with multiple conditions, such as a respiratory condition and an injury, are reported under both conditions. While a comparison can only be approximate, it nevertheless will identify a few of the sources of excess days of restricted activity of females over males.

Table 12.3 - Days of Restricted Activity per 100 Persons per Year Associated with Various Conditions, Calendar Year 1967

	Male	Female	Female minus male
Total days of restricted activity	1,390.8	1,653.7	262.9
Bed disability days	498.3	643.7	145.4
Other than bed disability	892.5	1,010.0	117.5
Associated with injury*	302.0	270.1	-31.9
Hospital days per 100 persons discharged per year (short-stay hospitals)	104.0	104.7	0.7
All chronic conditions and impairments (estimated)	706.2	838.3	132.1
All acute conditions	684.6	815.4	130.8
Infective and parasitic diseases	92.2	91.1	-1.1
Respiratory conditions	307.1	366.7	59.6
Digestive system conditions	33.5	36.6	3.1
Injuries*	182.2	162.0	-20.2
Genitourinary disorders	5.7	29.1	23.4
Deliveries and disorders of pregnancy and the puerperium	--	41.8	41.8
All other acute conditions	63.9	88.1	24.2

Source: (NCHS, 1969ᵃ: 11, 17, 19, 26).

Note: The categories in the table overlap. Although the acute conditions are independent of one another, a day of restricted activity may be counted more than once when a person has multiple conditions, injuries, or impairments.

* - Includes restricted activity days associated with impairments due to injury, as well as days associated with current injuries.

Only in restricted activity days associated with injuries do males register a greater number than females (Table 12.3). In all other categories, females are either approximately equal with males or exceed them. Higher rates for females are particularly noticeable for bed disability days, disability days not spent in bed, and both chronic and acute conditions. Among acute conditions, accounting for approximately half of the restricted activity days, females are restricted considerably more for respiratory conditions and genitourinary disorders. Deliveries and disorders of pregnancy account for approximately one-third of the excess in restricted activity of females due to acute conditions.

Bed Disability

About two-fifths of restricted activity days are spent in bed. Like restricted activity days, bed disability days are associated with sex, age, and income (Series K033-K064).

Females experience from one to two and one-half more bed disability days per person per year than males to about age 55, when the rate of bed disability days of females is approximately the same as that of males and continues so to the end of life. While there are year to year fluctuations in days of bed disability per person, a declining trend in bed disability days may be developing (Figure 12.3). Since 1963, bed disability days of females have declined approximately one day per person and of males, slightly less than one day per person. In general, bed disability days appear to fluctuate less than restricted activity days. Trends among males 45 to 64 years of age follow a pattern similar to those described above, but bed disability days among females of these ages do not.

Figures 12.4 and 12.5 illustrate the close relationship of bed disability days per person with age and show that no major decreases in bed disability days have taken place during the ten-year period, except for some decrease since 1962 among females over 65 years of age.

Bed disability days also vary with income, the pattern of variation resembling that of restricted activity days and income (Series K049-K064). The relation between income and bed disability days among females is quite similar to the relation of income and bed disability among males (Figures 12.6 and 12.7).

Bed disability has been relatively stable across time among those with incomes above $4,000, but it has been increasing within the $2,000 to $3,999 income group, and varying rather widely among those in the lowest income group. The epidemic of influenza and upper respiratory conditions during 1963 accounts for the steep increase in bed disability days of males and females in that year. Among older persons, influenza and upper respiratory infections account for over half of the acute conditions reported. Because older persons numerically dominate the lower income group, they exert a disproportionate influence on the trends in bed disability in it.

Work-Loss Days

While the series discussed above are based upon the total population in the several age-sex-income categories, the statistics on work loss due to disability are based upon the population of currently employed persons. Because of this, the trends and the differences between the sexes are dissimilar from those of restricted activity days, previously discussed.

Work-loss days per year per currently employed person vary much less by sex than restricted activity days. It appears that employed females lose little, if any, more time from work than males (Series K065-K074). Prior to 1964, as Figure 12.8 illustrates, females slightly exceeded males in days lost from work, while in 1964 and thereafter, males slightly exceeded females in days lost. In the age group 45 through 64 years of age, males have consistently experienced more work-loss days than females. One possible explanation is that because of their responsibilities, males remain employed under health conditions which females would consider grounds for leaving employment altogether, but this is merely conjecture. The 1963 peak is a consequence of an influenza epidemic.

The trend in work-loss days among females does not show a tendency to decline, even though a change in definition beginning with 1961-62 probably stimulated some decline, as interviewers cautioned females to exclude "work around the house" in reporting work loss. The trend for males, likewise, is relatively stable.

Another unusual characteristic of work-loss days is that work-loss days among males varys considerably more by income than do work-loss days among females (Series K075-K090). While there is evidence that females in the lower income groups lose more days from work than females in the upper income group, there is little evidence that work-loss days are declining for any income group. We have, then, the following results:

1. Work-loss days per currently employed person are strongly associated with age, the older age groups losing more days, except for employed females aged 65 years and over.

2. Work-loss days per currently employed person are more strongly associated with family income among males than among females.

3. Work-loss days per currently employed person are weakly associated with sex. When age is controlled, work-loss days are greater among females than males for ages below 45, but greater among males than females above 45 years of age.

4. There is no evidence that work-loss days of currently employed persons are declining.

A Suggested Analysis of Disability Days

The preceding has merely identified some of the major sources of differences in the population in restricted activity days. Published sources include various classifications for restricted activity days by region, size of place of residence, occupation, industry, employment status, by quarter of the year; for hospital days; for bed disability days due to injury; for restricted activity days due to various classes of accidents, and for other categories of information. The questionnaire used in collecting the health data includes even more variables. A model for analysis of these data might be set up with restricted activity days as the dependent

Bed Disability Days

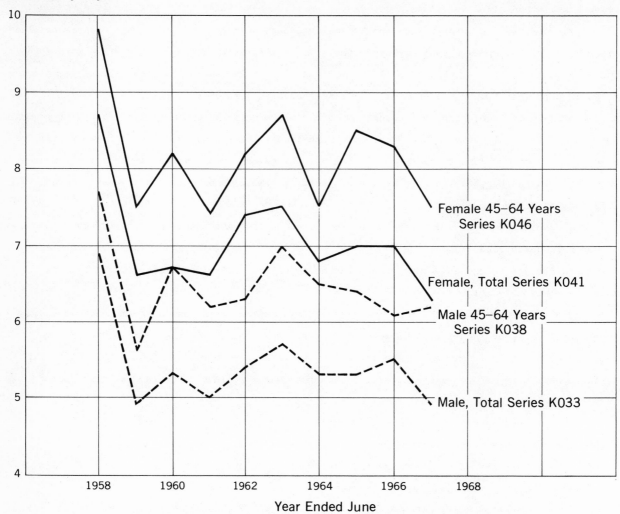

Figure 12.3 Bed Disability Days per Person per Year, Total and Age
45–64 Years, by Sex, 1958–1967

Bed Disability Days

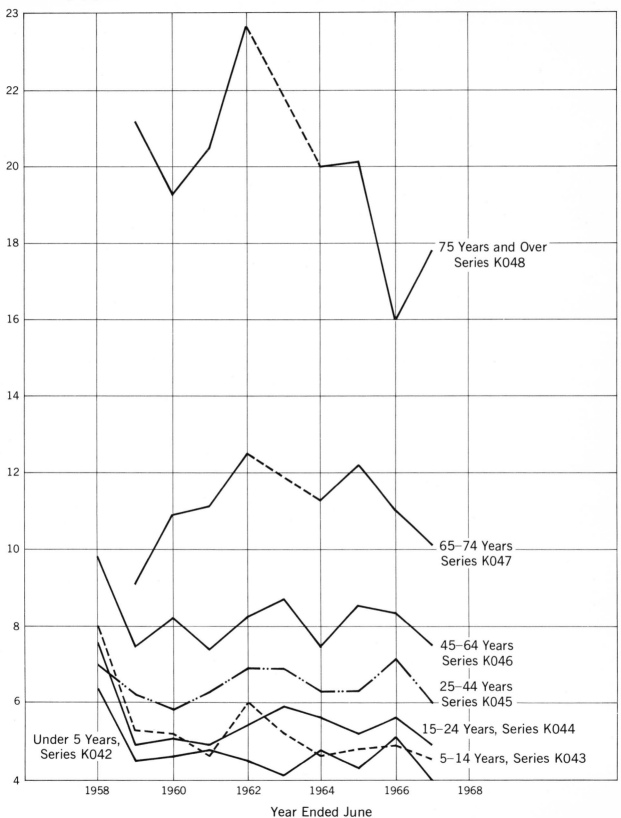

Figure 12.4 Bed Disability Days per Person per Year by Age, Females, 1958–1967

Bed Disability Days

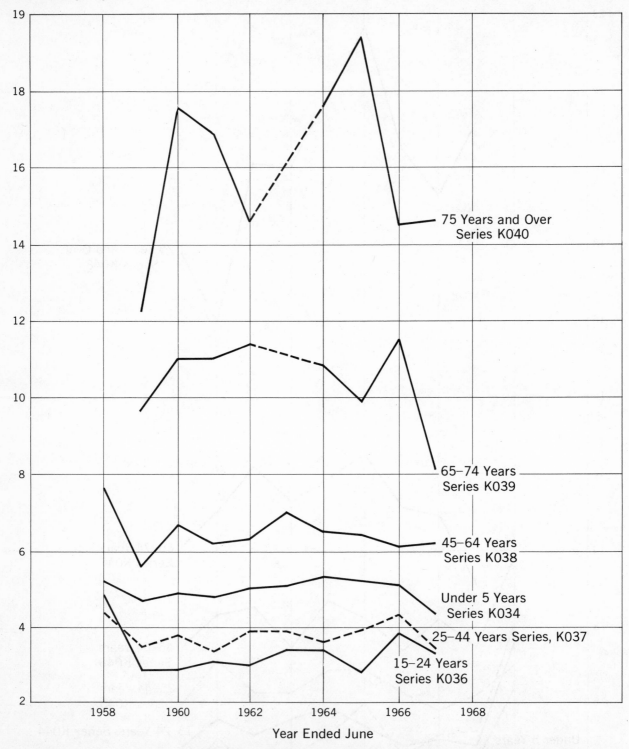

19

18

16

14

12

10

8

6

4

2

75 Years and Over
Series K040

65–74 Years
Series K039

45–64 Years
Series K038

Under 5 Years
Series K034

25–44 Years Series, K037

15–24 Years
Series K036

1958   1960   1962   1964   1966   1968

Year Ended June

Figure 12.5 Bed Disability Days per Person per Year by Age, Males,
1958–1967

Bed Disability Days

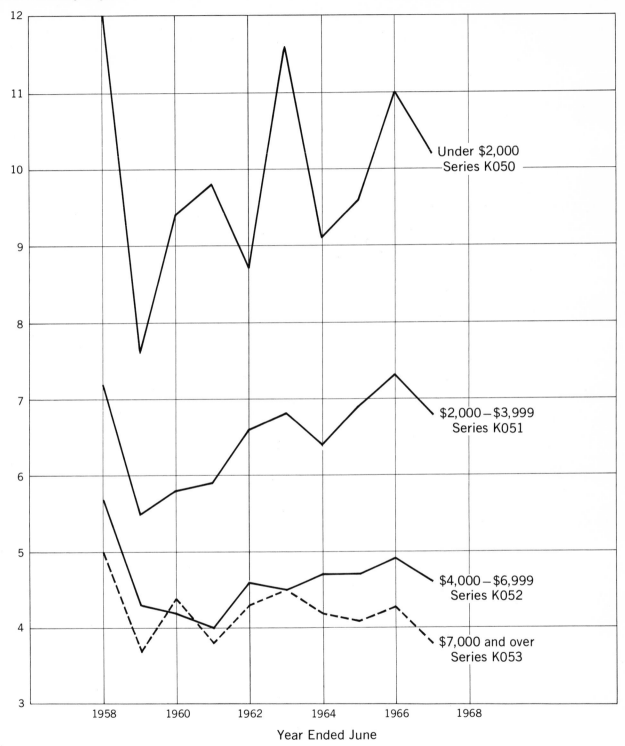

Under $2,000
Series K050

$2,000−$3,999
Series K051

$4,000−$6,999
Series K052

$7,000 and over
Series K053

Year Ended June

Figure 12.6 Bed Disability Days per Person per Year, by Family Income, Males, 1958−1967

Bed Disability Days

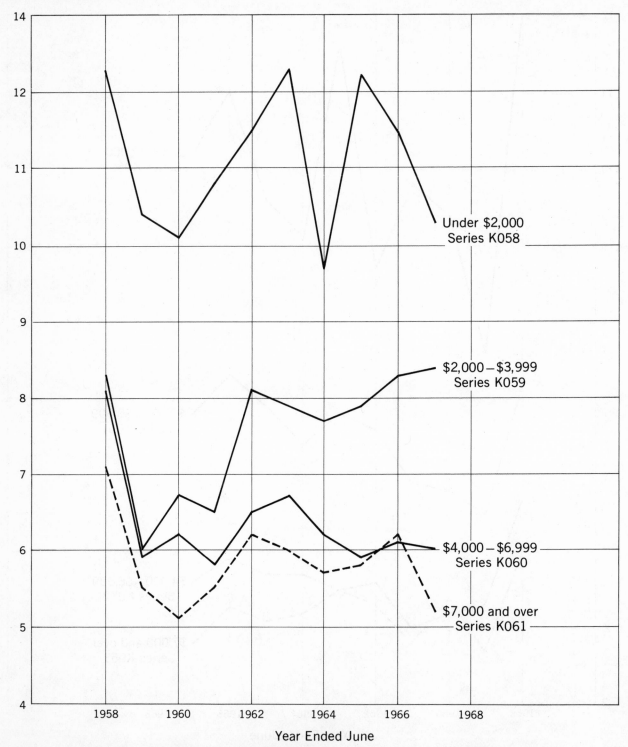

Figure 12.7 Bed Disability Days per Person per Year, by Family Income, Females, 1958–1967

Work-Loss Days

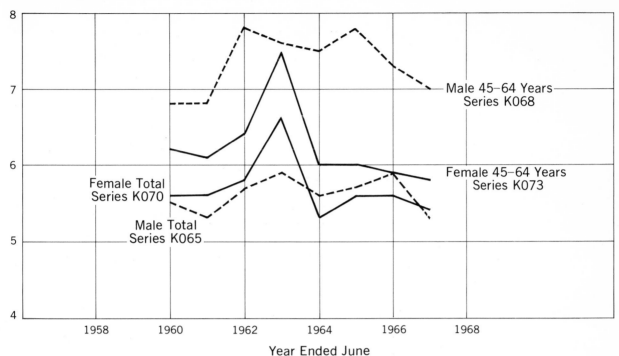

Figure 12.8 Work-Loss Days per Currently Employed Person per
Year, Total and 45–64 Years of Age, by Sex, 1960–1967

variable and a number of other factors as independent variables. The independent variables one might consider entering into the analysis are age, sex, education, family income, race, marital status, size of place of residence, region, occupation, employment status, quarter of the year, length of time since last visit to a physician, persons per room in domicile, and others. A multivariate analysis would show the contribution of each variable to the variance in days of restricted activity, with the contribution of the other variables held constant. The analysis could be performed separately for each sex in order to assess the varying influences on the illness behavior of men and women.

Such an analysis could be performed at several points in time over the dozen years of the life of the survey. Trends in the regression weights associated with each independent variable would show the changing consequence of that variable to health.

The same approach might be taken with bed disability, with hospital days, with accidents, and so forth, as the dependent variable.

While the analysis suggested above is not likely to produce any startlingly new results, it nevertheless would make it possible to identify with much greater assurance the changing influences upon health of the complex of variables on which information is available. It would provide much more information than the relatively crude approach of considering one, two, or at most three variables simultaneously in relation to the criterion of restricted activity days.

Trends in Acute and Chronic Conditions, Injuries and Hospitalizations

Reflecting a number of transitory illnesses that in some years reach epidemic proportions, acute conditions present an irregular annual trend (Figure 12.9). The rates for females are subject to the same annual influences as those for males, for the series seem to rise and fall in unison. Females, however, report that they are subject to a greater number of acute conditions per 100 persons than are males. In general, it appears that the annual incidence of acute conditions per 100 persons is declining over the long term, but, subject as it is to transitory factors, this indicator of health has, in the past, declined and subsequently increased, and it is likely to do so again. Series K091-K092 present these summary measures.

The percent of the population with one or more chronic condition is increasing at a relatively slow, steady rate. Whether this reflects poorer health or physicians' more meticulous attention to identifying these conditions cannot be said, but the trend shows a steady upward movement for both men and women (Figure 12.9). The percent reporting one or more chronic conditions is slightly higher, by about two percentage points, among females than males, a difference that could partly be accounted for by the data-gathering situation, wherein females are both interviewers and interviewees in larger proportions than is the case with males. However, the contribution of such a sex-linked interview factor probably is small. The differences in the percents of males and females reporting one or more chronic conditions appear to hold constant (Series K093-K094).

Number of Conditions

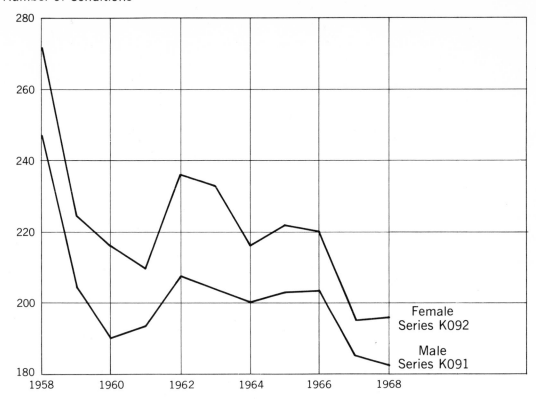

Percent

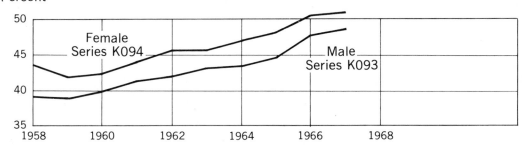

Number of Persons

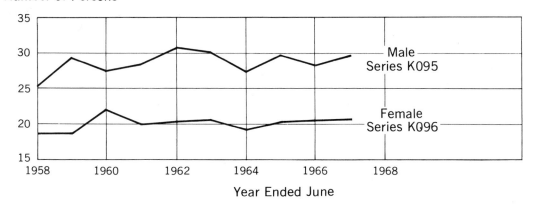

Year Ended June

Figure 12.9 Upper—Acute Conditions per 100 Persons per Year, by Sex, 1958–1968.
Middle—Percent of Persons with One or More Chronic Conditions, by Sex, 1958–1967
Lower—Number of Persons Injured per 100 Persons per Year, by Sex, 1958–1967

Females are less likely to be injured than males, nearly one-third less (Figure 12.9). This tendency, resulting from the more hazardous occupations and activities of males than females, is reflected not only in the annual rate of injuries but also in mortality rates from accidents (Series K095-K096, and L127-L130). The series for injuries appear to follow the same pattern among females as among males, but neither series evidences any marked trend. The rates of injuries appear to be relatively constant across the period covered by the data available.

The rates of discharge from short-stay hospitals are almost one-half greater for females than for males. This is because of women's higher incidence of acute conditions, among which childbirth is included. Women have a very much higher rate of occurrence of genitourinary disorders than do men (Table 11.3), and these two factors may be largely responsible for women's greater number of hospital stays. Once in the hospital, however, males stay longer than females. In 1968, women stayed an average of 7.9 days per episode while men remained an average of 10.5 days. These trends, not illustrated, are presented as Series K097-K100.

Cigarette Smoking

Cigarette smokers are less numerous among women than men. In 1968, 31 percent of women smoked cigarettes compared with 47 percent of men. Considering nonsmokers, 61 percent of women had never smoked cigarettes, compared with 33 percent of men (Series K101-K103, K121-K123).

Cigarette smoking is declining faster among men than among women, as Figure 12.10 shows. While larger proportions of men than women are eligible to stop smoking, men are more likely to have stopped smoking than women (Figure 12.10).[2] The rate of decline in the prevalence of smoking among both men and women, however, is quite slow.

The "quit ratio" of cigarette smokers is a measure of those who formerly smoked cigarettes and quit. It is based upon the ratio of former smokers to the sum of present and former cigarette smokers. As the measure increases, we may assume that cigarette smoking is declining. In Figure 12.10, the quit ratio shows that men are stopping smoking more than women. In 1968, for example, 21 of 100 women who had ever smoked cigarettes had stopped, as compared with 30 of 100 men.

Series K101-K140 present a number of refinements and variations of the above observations. Among both men and women, the 25-44 year age group smoke more heavily than other age groups. The percent smoking cigarettes declines with age beginning with the age group 25-44 years.

The average annual decline by age and sex also presents interesting variations. The decline in the percent smokers among women is greater for the younger than the older ages, but the maximum decrease, among the 17-24 year olds, is merely a decline of one percentage point per year. Among women above 65 years, the percent who smoke is increasing slightly, while it is declining among older men.

2/ - In Figure 12.10 annual data from the HIS are charted at the midpoint of the survey year (January 1st), while the CPS results are charted at approximately the month of the survey. The data, collected at irregular intervals, thus yield an irregular time series.

Percent

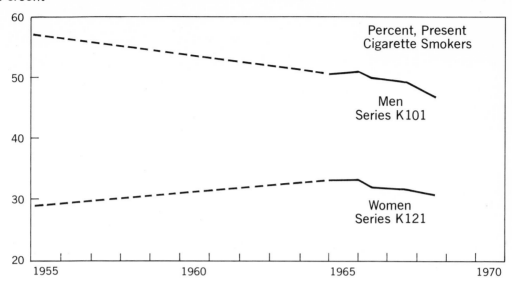

Quit Ratio

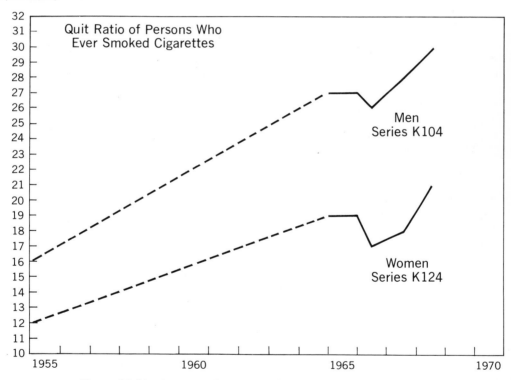

Figure 12.10 Percent of Present Cigarette Smokers and Quit Ratio of Persons Who Ever Smoked Cigarettes by Sex, 1955–1968

Differences in the effects of smoking upon the health of men and women is discussed else-where.[3] For example, the prevalence rate of persons with chronic conditions increased with the number of cigarettes consumed daily (NCHS, 1967f: 8). Cigarette smokers have more restricted activity days than nonsmokers, more work-loss days than nonsmokers, and more bed disability days than nonsmokers (NCHS, 1967F: 17). Specifically, smoking is associated with cardiovascular diseases, emphysema, cancer of the respiratory system and oral area, and has a deleterious effect upon pregnancy (PHS, 1969).

Summary of Indicators

Each of the indicators reviewed in this chapter provides valuable information on trends in women's health. Restricted activity days, despite some of the shortcomings identified, is per-haps the best of the general indicators here reviewed in sensing the state of the nation's health (Series K001-K032). Each age/sex group provides separate measures for observation. Restricted activity days by family income also give a running index to the consequences of one's income, but such a factor could more effectively be analyzed as an independent variable in a multivariate study of restricted activity days.

What has been said above applies also to bed disability days (Series K033-K064) and work-loss days (Series K065-K090).

The incidence of acute conditions might be more effectively monitored by quarter, for the Health Interview Survey generates such estimates (NCHS, 1969f: 7), acute conditions varying by season (Series K091-K092). Chronic conditions, on the other hand, are more stable as time series (Series K093-K094). They should be disaggregated to individual causes, which in turn should be observed annually by age, sex, and other relevant associated variables. Injuries (Series K095-K096) may be treated in similar manner, with the situation within which the injury occurs being the organizing principle for the analysis.

Discharges from hospitals may be a measure of the adequacy of health care, rather than an index of the state of the nation's health (Series K097-K100).

The percent of the population smoking, by age and sex, is an irregular time series. Con-tinued on an annual basis it will provide a historical record of the effects of a social experi-ment equal in importance to the Volstead Act. These measures must also be examined by age. The quit ratio is particularly useful in relation to age.

Additional indices reflecting health conditions are examined in the next chapter on mortality.

---

[3] - See, particularly, Smoking and Health and other reports of the Public Health Service: (PHS, 1964), (NCHS, 1967f), (NCHS, 1970e), and (National Clearinghouse for Smoking and Health, 1969).

Key to Series Discussed in Chapter 12

Restricted activity days per person per year, by age and sex	K001 - K016
Restricted activity days per person per year, by family income and sex	K017 - K032
Bed disability days per person per year, by age and sex	K033 - K048
Bed disability days per person per year, by family income and sex	K049 - K064
Work-loss days per currently employed person per year, by age and sex	K065 - K074
Work-loss days per currently employed person per year, by family income and sex	K075 - K090
Incidence of acute and chronic conditions, injuries, and discharges from short-stay hospitals, and average stay, by sex	K091 - K100
Cigarette smoking status and quit ratio by age and sex	K101 - K140

13.

Changes in the Mortality of Women

Just as statistics on disabilities and illness provide indicators of health, so mortality rates identify the consequences of some of life's conditions. If these conditions are improving, the mortality rate may decline; if they are worsening, the mortality rate may increase. The linkage is the problem, for the causes of a bodily condition more often than not are multiple rather than single. If stress causes heart disease and if cigarette smoking causes lung cancer, the relation between life's condition and the mortality rate is clear enough, but life's final hour can seldom be related to so simple an antecedent.

The expectation of life, as a statistic, is derived from death rates, and trends in it are clues to the vital state of the population. Death rates by cause for whites and nonwhites, males and females, are particularly meaningful social indicators when the etiology of death involves socio-cultural factors, and in many cases this is so. As social indicators, mortality rates thus provide an index to social forces operating on the population and clues to the status of population sub-groups -- e.g., men, women, whites, nonwhites, etc. -- respecting the underlying forces that bring about death.

. . . . .

Expectation of Life

The expectation of life for a given year is based upon the age-specific death rates for that year, and is stated for given ages (Series L001-L028). The expectation of life states the average years of life remaining for persons of a given age. It thus reflects the mortality experience for the year, and is not a forecast. The "expectation" is based upon the fiction that the mortality experience of the year will remain unchanged during the individual's lifetime. It is more logical to consider it a summary measure of mortality experience than a prediction of the actual average length of life of persons of given ages. As a summary of mortality experience, it is a meaningful indicator.

The expectation of life at birth by sex and color is shown in Figure 13.1. Both white and nonwhite females have longer expectation of life now than white or nonwhite males. From 1940 to 1967, the expectation of life was extended 5.7 years for white males, 9.6 years for nonwhite males, 8.5 years for white females and 13.3 years for nonwhite females. While these gains appear

Expectation of Life at Birth (years)

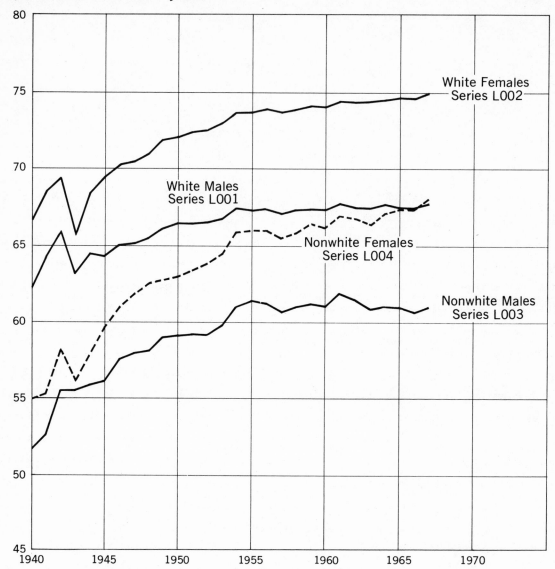

Figures 13.1 Expectation of Life at Birth by Color and Sex, 1940–1967

to be dramatic, they chiefly occurred before 1955, and since that time the expectation of life at birth has improved by slightly more than one year for white females and by just over two years for nonwhite females; it has remained practically stationary for males. In succeeding pages, mortality rates by specific cause will be examined as indicators for comparing rates of women with those of men.

Figure 13.2 presents two curves that generalize the years of life expected for white females for 1939-41 and 1967. The area between the two curves represents the gain in life expectancy. Obviously the greater gain has come from the improvement in life expectancy in the younger ages, and very little improvement has occurred after approximately age 70.

The superiority of the female expectation of life over the male probably rests upon a combination of factors, arising from biology and occupation. To the extent that females in the future enter occupations that provoke greater stress and other hazards to life, or expose themselves to risks in other ways, one may expect the female expectation of life to decline.

Age-Adjusted Mortality Rates, All Causes

Age, of course, is highly associated with mortality. Sex and color also have important consequences for some causes of death. In a comprehensive examination of trends in mortality by sex and color, age should be held constant, and, in such a comprehensive review, Moriyama has examined rates for each successive age group (NCHS, 1964e). In the relatively brief presentation which follows, age has been held constant (by employing rates standardized on the 1940 population) in order to examine trends from 1940 to the present. This approach provides the basis for identifying some of the differentials in these important mortality indicators, but it is not intended as a comprehensive study of the sources of mortality. For that, the work of Moriyama, Klebba (NCHS, 1966d), and others must be examined, and recourse to their work is necessary if one is to delve the analytical base for developing programs to reduce specific causes of mortality.

Figure 13.3 reveals a dramatic decline from 1940 to 1954 in the standardized mortality rate, all causes of death included. All age/color groups experienced decreases in the mortality rate, but nonwhite males declined the most. White females did not experience as great a decline in the standardized mortality rate as did nonwhite females, but white females already had lower rates than any other sex/color group. Over the 27-year span, the mortality of nonwhite females was reduced to a point below that of white males.

Since 1954 the experience has not been as encouraging. While both white and nonwhite females' rates have declined slightly, rates among males have remained relatively constant, and the rate for nonwhite males appears to have increased slightly since 1961.

The absence of any marked improvement in the standardized mortality rate since 1954 results from the fact that several of the more important causes of death -- causes that had been declining in response to medical advances -- appeared to reach a point, about 1954, where they ceased to decline or began decreasing at a much slower rate. These causes of death (to be

Years of Life Remaining

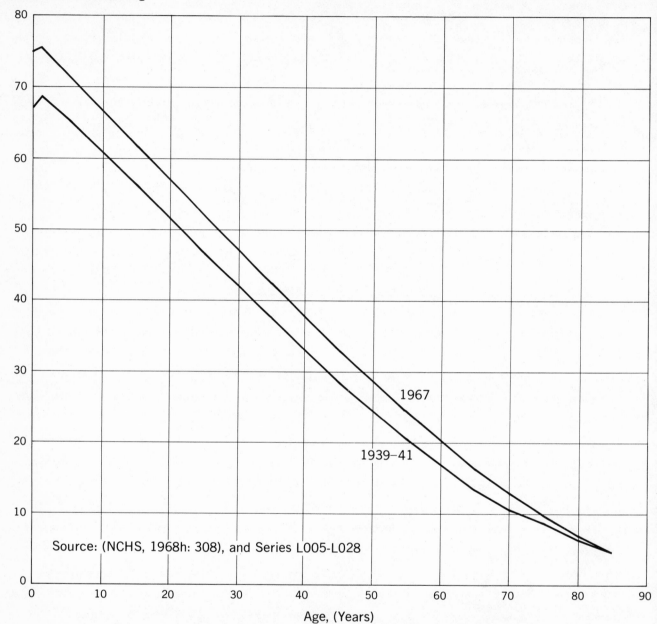

Figure 13.2 Expectation of Life by Age, White Females, 1939–41 and 1967

212

reviewed in greater detail subsequently) are: the major cardiovascular-renal diseases, influenza and pneumonia, and infant and maternal mortality. In addition, a few causes of death -- cancer, diabetes, cirrhosis of the liver -- have been increasing. The combined effect of these several sources of mortality, rather than any single cause, has prevented the overall mortality rate from making any concerted retreat. The same trend may be observed in the expectation of life, Figure 13.1. It shows only meager improvements in life expectancy since 1954.

On the basis of the evidence of Figure 13.3 and 13.1, what judgment would one make concerning the status of women in American society? One would first point out that the nonwhite female is considerably more disadvantaged than the white female. Both female groups, however, have lower mortality rates (all causes combined) than males and, consequently, longer expectation of life. While some might contend that this primarily connotes the biological superiority of the female, the evidence of the reduction in the nonwhite female mortality rate, the reduction in maternal mortality, and the reduction in infant mortality, suggests that the improvement in mortality of the female has resulted from a life-style related to the female role and from a concerted effort to reduce female mortalities.

Mortality Rates by Cause

The relative importance of various causes of death among males and females reveals some of the differences in life styles of the two groups and reflects differences in medical care accorded them. To make these comparisons accurately, the crude death rates by cause are not sufficient, for the differences in the age distributions of males and females must be accounted for. To do this, age-adjusted death rates by cause are used, based upon the 1940 age-distribution. They are presented as Series L077-L167.

While no one is liberated from death, at any given age females in the United States are less exposed to it than males, among both whites and nonwhites. At each age the death rate of females in 1967 was consistently lower than the death rate of males (Table 13.1). After the first year of life, the male death rate is at first only slightly higher than the female, but beyond the 15th year for nonwhites and the 35th year for whites, the differences begin to widen and are greatest for both races at 75-84 years of age. In 1967, the female death rate for all ages was 2.8 years per thousand less than the male for whites and 3.0 years per thousand less for nonwhites (Series L029-L032).

Table 13.1 summarizes the changes in death rates, 1940 to 1967. For each age group the female death rate has declined at a faster rate than the male, except two -- the rates for nonwhite males less than one year of age and those 85 years of age and over declined somewhat faster than the corresponding rates for nonwhite females. In general, the death rate declined faster in the younger ages, due largely to the improvement in health care of infectious and other diseases that affect children. But among females, the death rate also declined in the childbearing ages, reflecting improved maternal care.

213

Death Rate

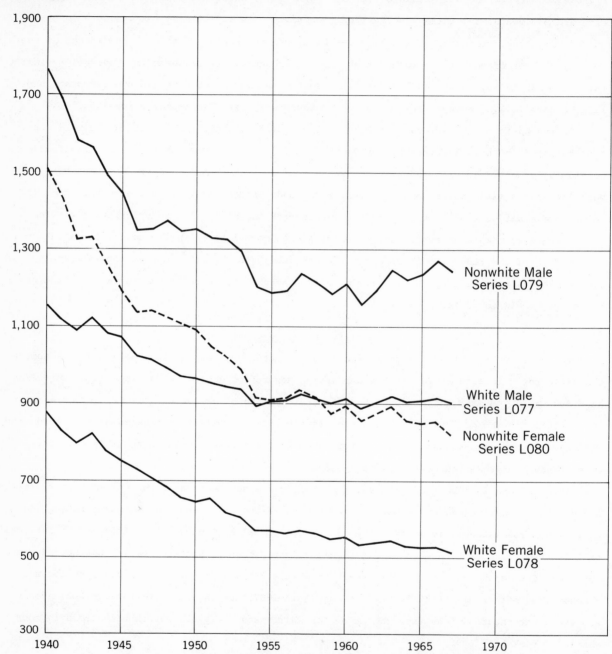

Figure 13.3 Age-Adjusted Death Rates, All Causes, by Color and Sex, 1940–1967

(Deaths per 100,000 population)

214

Table 13.1 - Difference Between Female and Male Death Rates, 1967, and the 27-Year Average Annual Rate of Change in Death Rates, by Color and Sex

| | 1967 | | 1940-1967 27-year average annual rate of change | | | |
| | Female minus male | | White | | Nonwhite | |
	White	Nonwhite	Male	Female	Male	Female
All ages	-2.8	-3.0	-0.3	-0.5	-1.2	-1.7
Under 1 year	-5.7	-6.8	-2.6	-3.5	-3.5	-3.2
1-4 years	-0.1	-0.3	-4.5	-4.5	-4.6	-4.7
5-14 years	-0.2	-0.3	-2.9	-3.6	-3.0	-4.5
15-24 years	-1.0	-1.5	-0.8	-3.1	-2.5	-5.8
25-34 years	-0.9	-2.4	-1.9	-3.7	-2.1	-3.9
35-44 years	-1.5	-3.4	-1.6	-2.4	-1.6	-3.0
45-54 years	-4.4	-6.0	-0.9	-1.8	-1.6	-2.7
55-64 years	-12.1	-10.3	-0.5	-1.9	-0.7	-1.8
65-74 years	-23.0	-20.9	-0.4	-1.8	0.1	-0.6
75-84 years	-30.0	-22.3	-0.8	-1.6	-1.2	-1.4
85 years & over	-18.1	-10.2	-0.6	-0.7	-2.1	-1.6

Source: Series L029-L076.

On the basis of the most recent mortality rates available, the three years ending 1967, the death rate is practically stationary for whites and is falling only slightly for nonwhites. Decreases in the nonwhite death rate are occurring chiefly in the infant death rate and in the advanced ages (75 years and over). There are a few countertrends, consisting of slight increases in some age groups.

A basis for assessing the shifting causes of death is provided by the percent distribution of age-adjusted death rates by cause. Infectious and communicable diseases have declined, proportionately, while disorders of middle and later life have increased. Table 13.2 compares the percent distribution for 1940 and 1965.

Influenza and pneumonia, tuberculosis of the respiratory system, syphilis, and diabetes have declined as causes of death nearly eight percentage points, altogether, among white males and females. On the other hand, heart disorders and cancer together have increased approximately 12 percentage points among white males and females. Proportionately, motor vehicle accidents and suicides have each increased slightly. Such changes as these have implications for the length of life, some of them being more likely to affect human beings early, rather than late, in life. Heart disease and cancer have increased proportionately, in part because individuals are less likely now to die earlier in life of the diseases (such as infective and parasitic diseases) that have come under more effective control.

Only those deaths occurring in the United States are registered. Deaths of United States citizens occurring overseas are not registered in the U. S. vital statistics system. The effect is to eliminate some of the mortality consequences of World War II, the Korean, and the Vietnam conflicts. In fact, the removal of men from exposure to death within the United States undoubtedly reduces the number of deaths that otherwise would have been recorded, thereby apparently accelerating the decrease in the rate during wartime; this is particularly noticeable during World War II, when so many men were overseas. However, the mortality rate for the most heavily exposed age group of males, those 15-24 years of age, increased after 1942 and did not return to its long-term trend until 1967 (NCHS, 1968h: 71).

Table 13.2 - Percent Distribution of Age-Adjusted Mortality Rates by Major Causes, 1940 and 1965

Causes increasing proportionately		White		Nonwhite	
		Male	Female	Male	Female
Major cardiovascular-renal	1940	46.3	45.8	39.2	43.0
	1965	52.7	51.3	46.0	51.7
All malignant neoplasms	1940	10.2	14.3	4.7	7.9
	1965	16.3	20.3	14.0	14.7
Motor vehicle accidents	1940	3.5	1.4	2.4	0.7
	1965	4.3	2.6	3.8	1.6
Suicide	1940	2.0	0.8	0.4	0.2
	1965	2.0	1.3	0.8	0.4
Causes decreasing proportionately					
Influenza and pneumonia	1940	6.1	6.3	8.7	8.1
	1965	3.0	3.0	4.2	3.8
Tuberculosis of the respiratory system	1940	3.6	2.9	7.7	7.1
	1965	0.5	0.2	1.2	0.6
Syphilis and its sequelae	1940	1.2	0.6	4.8	2.5
	1965	0.1	0.1	0.4	0.2
Diabetes mellitus	1940	1.8	3.7	0.8	2.1
	1965	1.3	2.4	1.5	3.4
All other causes					
Total enumerated above	1940	74.7	75.8	68.8	71.6
	1965	80.1	81.2	71.8	76.4
All other causes	1940	25.3	24.2	31.2	28.4
	1965	19.9	18.8	28.2	23.6

Source: Series L077-L167.

The source of the differences in the rates by sex and color will be identified in the discussion of specific causes that follows.

Infant Mortality

Ever since records have been adequately kept, the infant mortality rate in the United States has been declining. The decline prior to 1947 was more rapid than the decline since then (Series L033-L036). During the 1950's the decline slowed down in the United States. This slowdown in infant mortality "...was a worldwide phenomenon, and no one has satisfactorily explained why.

It cannot be explained in terms of medical care systems, because several countries had out-standingly good medical care systems at that time. It cannot be explained in terms of poor socioeconomic conditions, because the economy was booming all over the world". (Falkner, 1970: 19.)

Over the last 30 years, however, infant mortality rates for nonwhites have shown periods of retrogression as well as periods of rapid decline, while rates for whites have declined fairly consistently. The period 1961 to 1966 showed only nominal decreases for both races, but since approximately 1965, the nonwhite rate has declined fairly rapidly (Figure 13.4).

The rate for nonwhite males has always been higher than the rate for nonwhite females and the rate for white males has always been higher than the rate for white females. Nonwhites consistently present higher rates than whites, but the differential is closing fairly rapidly, owing primarily to the marked decreases in nonwhite rates since 1965.

Epidemiological studies have identified a large number of factors that appear to he associated with the infant mortality rates. The differences between rates for males and for females are greatest during the early days of life, and the difference between them narrows almost to equality at about nine months of age (NCHS, 1963b: 10). The medical causes of death do not show that the female is subject to markedly different causes than the male (NCHS, 1963b: 13). However, females have lower mortality rates than males, irrespective of birth weight (NCHS, 1965j: 21). Generally, female infants possess a markedly greater vital force than males, which sustains them through the trauma of early adaptation to life.

The reduction of infant deaths, however, is more than a problem of medical care. The means for reduction in the rates lie in altering the socioeconomic and cultural conditions that affect infant mortality (Falkner, 1970: 25).

Since infant mortality decreases as birthweight increases (Falkner, 1970: 19), the nutritional habits of the mother must be appropriately conditioned. This, of course, is associated with socioeconomic level, geographic area, ethnic group, and so forth.

An effect of culture is illustrated by the lower infant mortality rate of Orientals in the United States -- lower, even, than the white rates. Conversely, American Indians have a rate of preventable postnatal mortality greater than that of other races in the United States (Falkner, 1970: 26). The contrasting conditions of these two groups need to be examined to discover the basis for the differential.

Birth order, also, is associated with infant mortality, the fifth or higher birth running a greater risk of death. However, socioeconomic disadvantages affecting health accompany both higher birth orders and infant mortalities, thereby compounding the problem of identifying whether the more essential cause is improving socioeconomic status or introducing family planning. "... by helping couples avoid having unwanted children, family planning presumably reduces the number of unwanted children, who are less well cared for, and whose chances of healthy survival are therefore lower than those of wanted children" (Falkner, 1970: 31).

217

Deaths per 1,000 Population

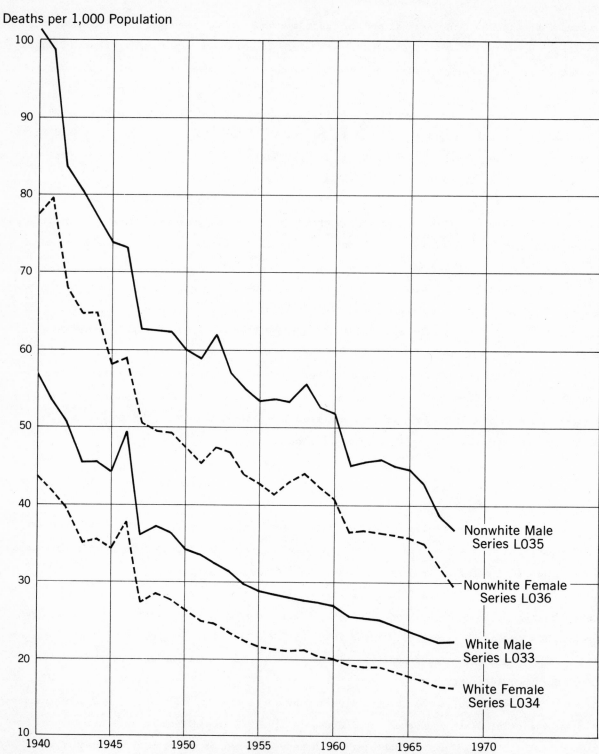

Figure 13.4 Infant Mortality Rate by Color and Sex, 1940–1968
(Deaths per 1,000 population under 1 year of age)

The Maternity and Infant Care project in New York City showed that the "neonatal death rate is 35 per 1,000 for deliveries occurring within one year after a preceding delivery. For births with an interval of one to two years, the neonatal death rate goes down to 17 per 1,000. If the interval is two to three years, the rate goes down to seven per 1,000" (Falkner, 1970: 32). Thus, the spacing of pregnancies affects the infant mortality rates.

The health of the mother prior to conception also affects the infant's condition. A study in New Orleans in 1964 showed that 75 percent of infant deaths and stillbirths were due to a serious medical condition of the mother before conception. Particularly women who have a serious medical condition prior to pregnancy run higher risks. Family planning would help avoid such deaths (Falkner, 1970: 32).

Infant mortality rates are also higher for very young mothers and for mothers in ages beyond the prime childbearing years. Mortalities also have been found higher among offspring of women whose first live birth is preceded by several abortions, the suction method of abortion apparently being the offending cause (Falkner, 1970: 34).

The complexity of the problem is further illustrated by a summary from Key Issues in Infant Mortality, cited above, as follows:

"Maternal and child health care, treatment and prevention, have been...related to immigration, cultural variability, rapid urbanization, control of infectious diseases, and control of environmental hazards, but we must look beyond these concerns to critical questions about the organization and delivery of services" (Falkner, 1970: 26).

A number of countries experience lower infant mortality rates than the United States and "the gap between the rate for the United States and figures for countries with the most favorable experience has widened" (Moriyama and Shapiro, 1963). There is evidence, too, that an infant mortality rate of approximately 12 is an irreducible minimum. This is some nine births per 1,000 lower than the 1969 rate in the United States (NCHS, 1970c: 1).

Whether the rate for males ever can be reduced to the lower rate characteristic of females also is questionable. But, comparisons of the United States rate with those of other nations, as well as intergroup comparisons (region, metropolitan area, ethnic, socioeconomic, etc.), demonstrate that the rate can be reduced. Such comparisons also lead to insights to the sociocultural factors affecting infant mortality.

The infant mortality rate, then, provides a summary social indicator of multiple influences affecting the well-being and status of women. While a change in the rate undoubtedly reflects the state of medical care of mother and child, it also mirrors changes in numerous other social indicators, some of them being: the rate of illegitimacy; the birth rate by birth order; the distribution of families by size; the socioeconomic status of families, particularly families in the childbearing period; the economic (income) status of the ethnic-racial groups, measures of urbanization, such as the percent of the population living in metropolitan places; cultural variability and integration within the country; immigration; and other indices. To adequately

219

evaluate any effort to reduce infant mortality, a rather comprehensive set of measures of social change, including many of those listed above, would be required.

Maternal Mortality

Maternal deaths have declined tremendously. In 1967, there were 987 deaths from maternal causes -- only 0.5 deaths per 100,000 population (NCHS, 1969e, Sec. 1: 39-40). The comparable figure for 1940 was 6.7 per 100,000 (NCHS, 1968h: 593).

The maternal mortality rate is usually expressed as deaths per 100,000 live births (Series L147-L167) (Figure 13.5).

Generally, the maternal mortality rate of the United States compares satisfactorily with rates in the Scandinavian countries, which exhibit the most favorable national experience. The U. S. rate among white women has decreased 16-fold since 1940, while among nonwhite women it has declined almost as much, approximately 11-fold. Although the rate of decline during 1958-1963 appeared to slow down, since 1964 the decline has been at a faster rate.

Toxemia is the most important cause of maternal deaths, accounting for about a third of them. Complications of delivery account for almost as many. The remainder are attributed to complications associated with abortions and with the puerperium.

At present, maternal mortalities among nonwhite women are almost four times greater than among white women. This differential is reflected, also, in higher rates in the Northeast and the South (NCHS, 1963b: 54-61).

Table 13.3 - Deaths from Maternal Causes, per 100,000 Live Births, and Nonwhite to White Ratio of Rates, 1967

Age of mother	Total	White	Nonwhite	Ratio, Nonwhite/ White
All ages: Number	987	571	416	0.73
Rate	28.0	19.5	69.5	3.6
Under 20 years	22.1	15.1	40.7	2.7
20-24 years	16.6	11.0	48.5	4.4
25-29 years	20.4	14.9	55.4	3.7
30-34 years	43.9	30.8	114.0	3.7
35-39 years	72.6	48.6	192.1	4.0
40-44 years	131.2	103.6	258.2	2.5

Maternal mortality rates increase with age, as Table 13.3, for 1967, illustrates. The 20-24 year old women exhibit the lowest rates, although the lowest rate among nonwhite women is the "under 20 years" group. Even in 1967, nonwhite females had 3.6 times higher mortality rates than white women. The differential between white and nonwhite maternal mortality rates is least among the under-20 and the 40-44 age groups. Between these extremes, the nonwhite rate is 3.7 to 4.4 times greater than the white rate. In 1967, nonwhite women accounted for 42 percent of maternal deaths, and women over 29 years of age accounted for 47 percent of the deaths. Consequently, the approach to reducing the rate might focus upon women over 30 years and nonwhite women.

Deaths per 100,000 Live Births (ratio scale)

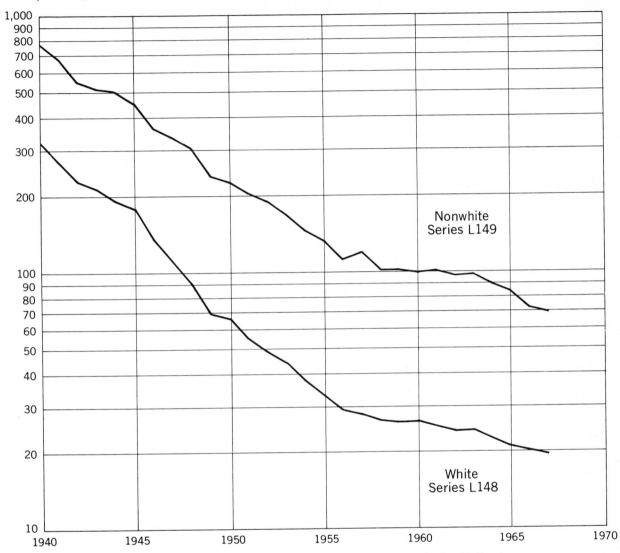

Figures 13.5 Maternal Mortality: Deaths per 100,000 Live Births, by Color, 1940–1967

Major Cardiovascular-Renal Diseases

These causes of death account for approximately half of all the total age-adjusted death rate. No other cause is as significant. The mortality rate from these conditions has been declining, particularly among females (Series L081-L084 and Figure 13.6). While the nonwhite female rate has declined more than any other age-sex group, a decline of more than 200 deaths per 100,000, the rate for white females remains the lowest and appears to be continuing to decline. Male rates, both white and nonwhite, are declining also, but each still is quite high when compared with the rate for the white female.

The lower mortality rate among females, than males, for these causes is often attributed not only to biological factors but also to the life style of women, usually involving less stress and tension than is the case for men (Lerner and Anderson, 1963: 60). A study in England and Wales, reviewed by Lerner and Anderson (1963: 61-62), shows the contrasting ways in which social class affects mortality from arteriosclerosis with respect to husbands and wives, and illustrates the difference in their life style. Among men, mortality from this cause increased with an increase in social class of the occupation. Among the wives of these men, however, exactly opposite mortality rates obtained. The wives in upper social class families apparently were disadvantaged by none of the occupational stresses to which the husband was subject, while simultaneously enjoying the advantages of better medical care and other amenities afforded by the remuneration of the high status occupation. At the other end of the continuum, the husbands in unskilled and semi-skilled occupations (which are generally considered relatively free of strain or pesssure) experienced low mortality rates from coronaries, while their wives, in the less advantaged situation of a lower socioeconomic family, showed higher rates than wives of higher social class families.

The white female rate might serve as a goal for the nation. The mortality rate, generally, would be greatly improved if the medical care afforded white females, and if the other socio-economic conditions surrounding her existence, were accorded the three other groups.

All Malignant Neoplasms

Mortality rates from cancer are presenting increasingly greater variance among sex/color groups (Series L097-L100). It is rather remarkable how the rates, since about 1950, have branched in four different directions, as Figure 13.7 illustrates. Female rates are either declining or holding constant, while mortality rates of males from this cause continue to increase. The rate for the nonwhite male has dramatically increased, while that of the nonwhite female increased only slightly from 1945 to 1950 and since has remained relatively constant. The rate for the white male has increased consistently across the time-span of 27 years shown in Figure 13.7, while the rate for the white female gradually has declined, especially since 1950. At present, both rates of the white and the nonwhite female appear to be resisting any improvement.

222

Death Rate

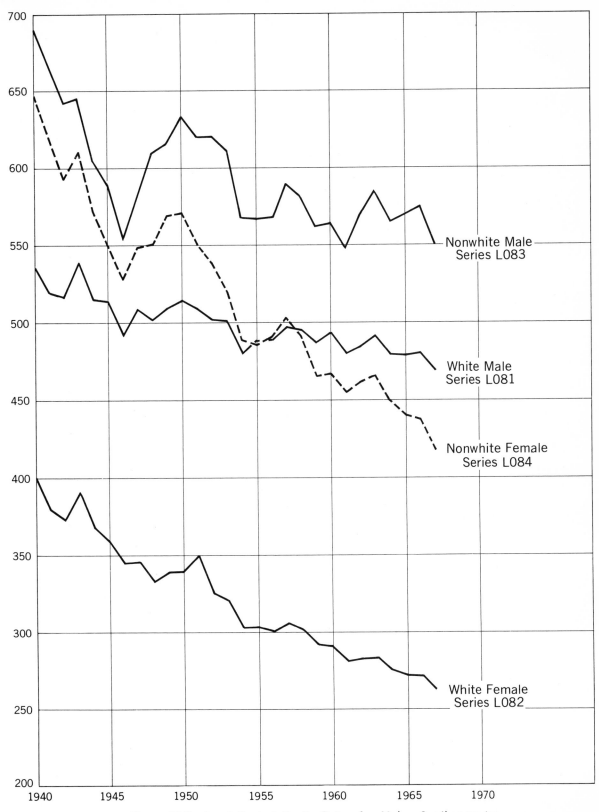

Figure 13.6 Age-Adjusted Death Rates for Major Cardiovascular-Renal Diseases by Color and Sex, 1940–1967 (Deaths per 100,000 population)

Death Rate

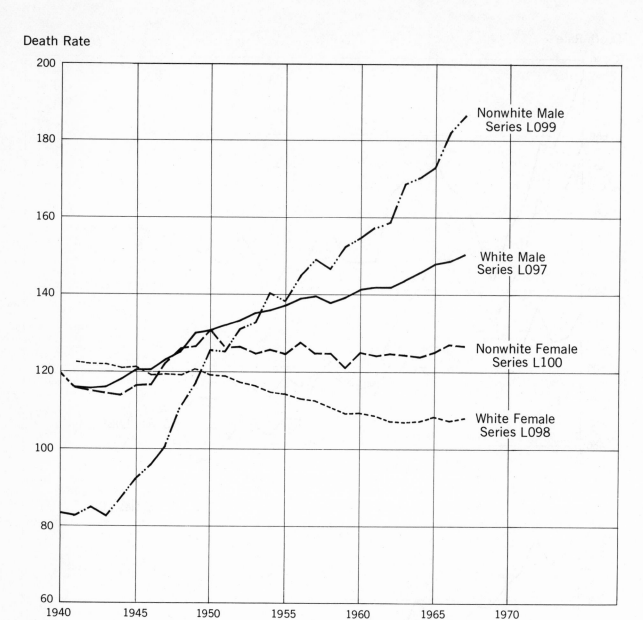

Figure 13.7 Age-Adjusted Death Rates for All Malignant Neoplasms by Color and Sex, 1940–1967
(Deaths per 100,000 population)

Again, a national goal respecting this cause of mortality might be stated in terms of the white female rate, for, since 1945, it has persisted as the lower rate.

Malignant Neoplasms of the Respiratory System

The trends in few sources of mortality are more distinctly associated with sex than are trends in mortality due to neoplasms of the respiratory system, and as little associated with color (Series L105-L108). While the trends for females, both white and nonwhite, have increased slightly during the 27 years pictured in Figure 13.8, the trends for males of both color groups have increased tremendously, in fact, by a multiple of nearly four for white males and over eight for nonwhite males.

Occupational hazards that affect the air men breathe and the greater incidence of smoking among men than women (cf. Series K101-K140) contribute to the greater mortality among males from malignancies of the respiratory system. While the percent of cigarette smokers among both males and females has recently declined (since 1965-66), 47 percent of men smoked cigarettes in 1968 compared with 31 percent of women. In addition, women do not smoke as frequently as men.

The mortality rate due to respiratory malignancies will not respond immediately to the decrease in smoking in the population; a prolonged lag in time may precede its reduction. Meanwhile, measures to identify and reduce dust, fumes, and other pollutants of the air in the hazardous work environments of men will eventually reduce this source of mortality.

Influenza-Pneumonia

Mortality from these conditions has declined greatly from 1940 to 1949 (Series L115-L118) (Figure 13.9). Since 1949, however, very little change in the rate for whites has occurred, while improvement has continued among nonwhites. The epidemic years are easily distinguished by the jagged peaks: 1957, 1960, and 1963. As the nonwhite female rate has improved, it has approached the rate for whites. The nonwhite male rate, however, must fall by 42 percent to approximate these rates.

The rate among white females does not respond markedly to epidemics, and it has resisted a major decrease since 1954. This may indicate that a minimum rate of approximately 12 per 100,000 population may be a reasonable goal to set for the population as a whole.

Diabetes

While the mortality rate from diabetes mellitus was once a sex-related cause of death, it is now more closely associated with color than with sex (Series L093-L096). During 1940-1949, the age-adjusted mortality rate due to this cause was almost the same for white as for nonwhite females, both being considerably higher than the rate for males. After 1948, however, the white female rate declined rapidly, and after 1960 began to approach the relatively low rate for white males. Meanwhile, after about 1955, the rates both for nonwhite males and females began to increase. By 1967, the rate for nonwhite females was almost two and one-half times the

225

Death Rates

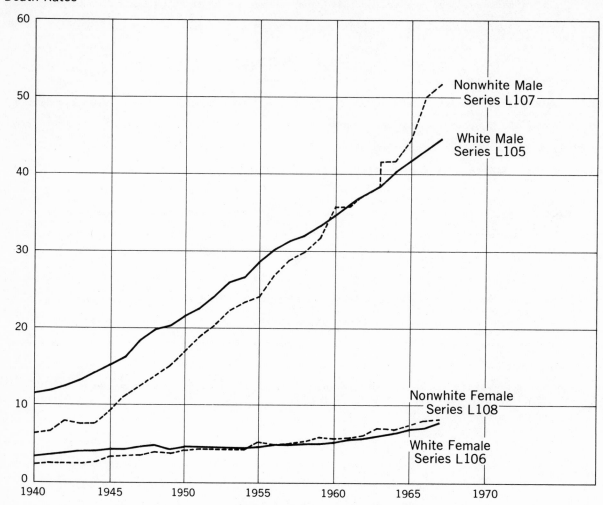

Figure 13.8 Age-Adjusted Death Rates for Malignant Neoplasms of the Respiratory System by Color and Sex, 1940–1967 (Deaths per 100,000 population)

Death Rate

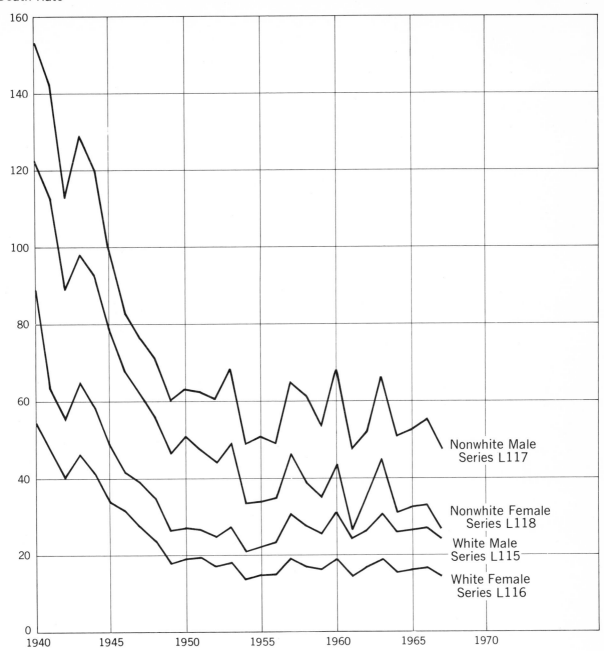

Figure 13.9 Age-Adjusted Death Rates for Influenza and Pneumonia
by Color and Sex, 1940–1967
(Deaths per 100,000 population)

white female rates and 60 percent greater than the rate for nonwhite males, but white male and female rates continued to be almost identical (Figure 13.10).

This surprising shift in the trend may not be attributed to a change in the etiology of the disease. Instead, it is much more logically attributed to improved care of the white patient while a corresponding improvement was not occurring among nonwhites. This, however, may only partly explain the difference.

Since neither white male nor female rates now appear to be declining, a rate of approximately 12 per 100,000 would seem to be a reasonable and an attainable goal for the reduction of diabetes mortality among nonwhites. To achieve it the trend in the rates for nonwhites must be reversed.

The disease follows the Mendelian laws of heredity, the offspring of two diabetics being quite likely to acquire the disease. The incidence is much greater with advancing age, and is particularly likely among married women after the menopause. Eighty of 100 new cases of diabetes are overweight (Schmitt, 1968: 4-6).

Ulcer of the Stomach and Duodenum

This source of mortality is sex-related, rather than color-related (Series L143-L146) (Figure 13.11). Females have a low rate of mortality from ulcer, approximately one-third the male rate. While the white female rate has remained relatively constant, the rate of nonwhite females declined somewhat during the 1940's. The rates among males, however, have declined considerably since 1940 and appear to be tending toward an even greater decline.

This disorder arises from stress, and the trend suggests that either the stress of modern society has declined or the capability of medical science to cope with the threat of death from ulcer has improved. The latter appears to be the more likely interpretation.

Cirrhosis of the Liver

Trends in the mortality from cirrhosis of the liver began to change about 1955 (Series L139-L142) (Figure 13.12). From 1940 until 1955 the most prominent movement in the trend had been a peak in mortalities for each sex-color group in 1948 -- probably a delayed consequence of World War II. Following this, the rate for males, both white and nonwhite, increased slightly to 1955. After 1955, however, a real division began to take place. While the rate among whites, male and female, began to increase only gradually, the rate for nonwhites of both sexes increased quite rapidly.

Rates of mortality from this disorder for females have always been lower than the rates for males, but the rate for nonwhite females now has begun to approach the rate of white males. As in many other indices of mortality, the rate of the white female is so low as to constitute a goal for the reduction of mortality from this cause for the other age-sex groups.

Evidence on the per capita consumption of alcohol -- considered to be the major cause of cirrhosis of the liver -- presents a gradual increase since about 1950, but no marked increases

Death Rate

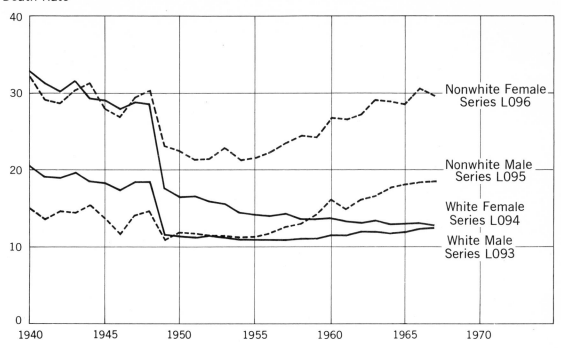

Figure 13.10 Age-Adjusted Death Rates for Diabetes by Color and Sex, 1940–1967

(Deaths per 100,000 population)

(Note: The decrease in 1949 is due to a revision in the International Statistical Classification Code.)

Death Rate

Figure 13.11 Age-Adjusted Death Rates for Ulcer of the Stomach
and Duodenum by Color and Sex, 1940–1967
(Deaths per 100,000 population)

Death Rate

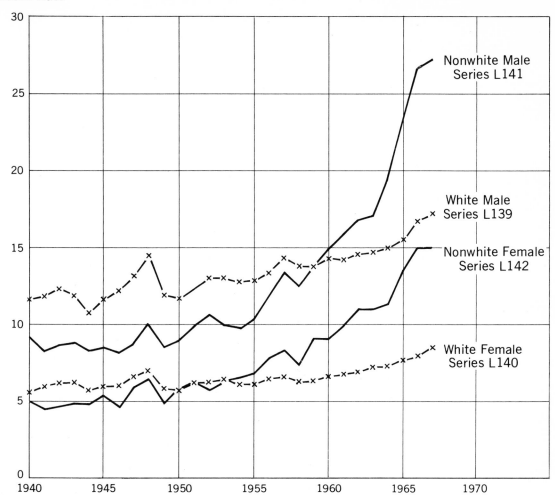

Figure 13.12 Age-Adjusted Death Rates for Cirrhosis of the Liver by Color and Sex, 1940–1967
(Deaths per 100,000 population)

in the period 1955-60 or thereafter that would explain the volatile reaction of the nonwhite trend. Such evidence is crude, however. To detect the connection between alcohol consumption and mortality from cirrhosis of the liver, evidence on the amount of individual consumption of alcohol over time would be required.

Motor Vehicle Accidents

Deaths of females follow the general trend in annual per capita miles of motor vehicle travel, but the death rate of males due to motor vehicle accidents does not.[1] The mortality rate of males from motor vehicle accidents is slightly greater than three times the rate of females, indicating that females are not exposed to accidents as much as males (Series L128-L130).

The decline in the rate during World War II undoubtedly was associated with the decrease in per capita motor vehicle miles traveled because of the limited sales of automobiles and gasoline (compare Figure 13.13 with Figure 13.14). Following the war, however, the miles traveled per capita increased and they have continued to increase since then. The rate of auto-mobile fatalities among females has increased correspondingly, although not as uniformly as per capita miles traveled.

The more widely-varying mortality rate among males cannot be easily explained, but Series L168-L219 provide suggestive evidence. In summary form, it is, as follows:

Approximately one-sixth of accidental deaths attributable to motor vehicles are pedestrian deaths (Series L194-L219). In each age group female mortalities for pedestrian accidents involving motor cars are fewer than males, in some age groups as much as one-fourth the male rates. Older males, 65 years of age and over, have pedestrian mortality rates much higher than other age groups. Older females also have higher rates than younger ones but the differences are not as great as among males.

When pedestrian deaths are excluded (Series L168-L193), the death rate among males exceeds by a factor of over three the death rate among females. Young men in their late teens and in their twenties have the highest mortality rates by far of all of the age groups. The mortality rates of females in these ages, also, is relatively high but it is only one-third to one-fourth the male rates.

---

[1] - Sources of data in Figure 13.14:

Percent of automobiles eight years old and over: (Census, 1969j: 552, and prior years, as indicated). The data originate from the Survey of Consumer Finances, conducted by the Survey Research Center, the University of Michigan, and are based upon household surveys.

Motor vehicle miles per capita: (Census, 1960e: 463, Series Q321; 1965i: 65; 1969j: 547). The population data used in the calculations were from (Census, 1960e: 7; 1969j: 5).

Percent of passenger cars exceeding 50 miles per hour, rural highways: (Public Roads, 1969: 56).

Death Rate

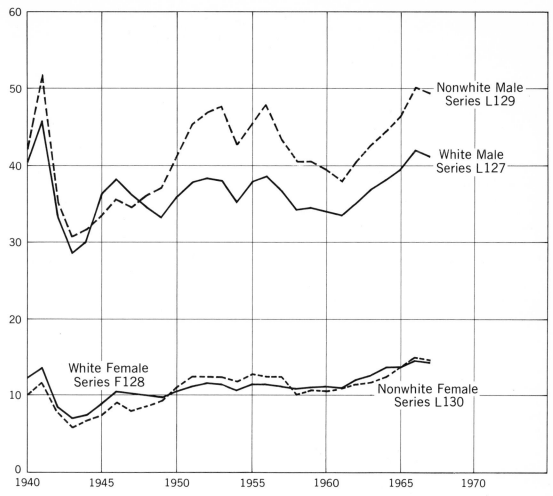

Figure 13.13 Age-Adjusted Death Rates for Motor Vehicle Accidents by Color and Sex, 1940–1967
(Deaths per 100,000 population)

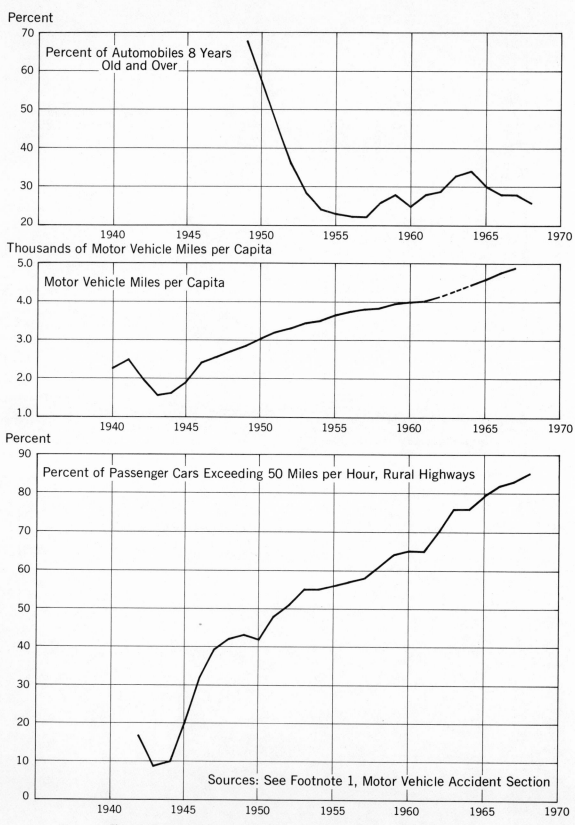

Figure 13.14 Three Factors Apparently Associated with Deaths from Automobile Accidents

In Figure 13.13 the long term trend in the rates of motor vehicle fatalities has been increasing since 1943. The rates were lower in 1949, 1954, 1958-1961 than at other times. Although there was a slight decrease in 1967, it was not large enough to give evidence of a real change in the long-term trend. While the rates for females evidence less variability over time than the rates for males, the female rates follow the same pattern, although muted, that the male rates exhibit, indicating that the same forces operate upon both rates.

While over 37,000 males and about 14,500 females lost their lives in motor traffic accidents in 1967 (NCHS, 1969e: 1-82), the number injured in a recent year far exceeded these numbers. In 1968 there were 1,770,000 males and 1,551,000 females injured in moving motor vehicle accidents (NCHS, 1970f: 2).

Homicide

Homicide in the United States is first a color-related cause of death, and second, a sex-related cause (Series L135-L138) (Figure 13.15). The rate for nonwhite males is about ten times greater than the rate for white males, and the rate for nonwhite females is about six times greater than the rate for white females. Although they were about 12 percent of the population, nonwhites were approximately 54 percent of the victims in homicides in 1968.

In murders, the offender and the victim usually are acquainted with one another. In the cases where a spouse kills a spouse or in romantic triangles and lovers' quarrels -- together accounting for approximately one-fifth of the victims -- the victim was a female in 54 percent of the cases of spouse killing spouse, and in 51 percent of the cases of lovers' quarrels. In the case of a romantic triangle, however, the victim is almost always a male (FBI, 1968: 7).

In offenses against nonwhites, other nonwhites are likely to be the offenders, while whites are more likely to be victimized by other whites. The rate for nonwhite males, which shows the greatest variation, appears to decline with the onset of a major war but begins to increase after war subsides. The rate among whites shows much less variation, but since about 1955 it seems to be increasing slightly.

Suicide

The suicide rates for females are always lower than the rate for males, within each color group, but since about 1950 the rates for females have been gaining slightly on the male rates (Series L131-L134) (Figure 13.16). Adjusted for age, the rate has increased very slowly since 1954 for white females and, since 1956 for nonwhite. In 1967, among whites the ratio of female to male rates was 0.39 and, among nonwhites, 0.33.

The aggregate suicide rate, historically, appears to be associated with various social and economic events. The rate declines during times of war. It increases with the onset of a major depression in economic conditions, but as the depression wears on, the rate falls, as happened during the 1930's. It fell even more during the war-time period of the 1940's.

235

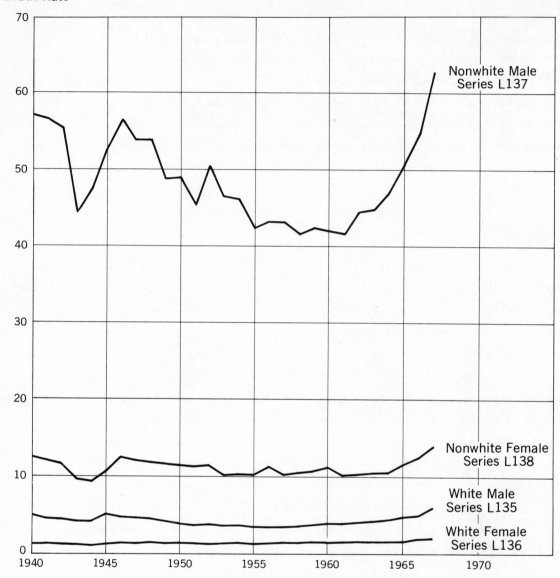

Figure 13.15 Age-Adjusted Death Rates for Homicide by Color and Sex, 1940–1967

(Deaths per 100,000 population)

For about two decades the age-adjusted suicide rate has varied between slightly under 10 to slightly over 11, and during this period of a fairly constant rate, the rate appears to have been unaffected by either the small recessions or the prosperity of the period. It may have been affected slightly by the Korean War. Aside from the small linear increase in the rate among females and among nonwhite males, the suicide rate has changed but little in recent years. Why, then, should it be of interest? Theoretically, the suicidal act is a "socially meaningful" event, taken by a person to communicate something to himself and to others (Douglas, 1968: 383). As a social indicator, suicide signifies the state of social relationships, the cultural and psycho-social conditions of society. The particular significance attached to a change in the rate of suicide rests upon the theoretical position one holds. If, following the French sociol- ogist Emile Durkheim, one posits that the critical relationship is the degree of integration of the individual in the group, then the state of anomie (normlessness), or egoism, or altruism, or fatalism -- whichever is the basic condition -- may be considered to be increasing if the rate of suicide increases. If so, the evidence in Figure 13.16 implies little if any change in these factors. Following this theory, then, the status of women in American society suffers less from the dysfunctional consequences of the basic causes of suicide than males, white or nonwhite. Even so, the trend for females is moving very slowly in an undesirable direction.

The communication function of suicide may predominate among females, for attempted suicide, as distinguished from accomplished suicides, occur among females in the ratio of approximately seven to one. As a cry for help, an act of aggression, the fixing of blame, or an expiation of one's own guilt -- whatever the meaning -- the would-be female suicide communicates effectively whether the attempt is successful or not.

Other characteristics of suicide may be noted, as follows: Across the age cycle, the rate for white females reaches a peak in the 45-54 year age group, and decreases thereafter. In con- trast, the rate for white males continually increases to the oldest ages (NCHS, 1967h: 16-17). From the Rocky Mountain States westward, the rate is higher than in the remainder of the nation. Consistent with the theory that the group relationship is the vital element in suicide, the rate is lower for married persons than for single, widowed, or divorced (NCHS, 1967h: 7). More highly integrated religious groups have lower suicide rates than more loosely organized ones.

As an indicator, the suicide rate has the defect of apparently being underreported. The circumstances of death may be interpreted as accidental when actually they were intentional, such as erroneously ingesting poison -- a means frequently (30 percent) used by females -- or the accidental discharge of firearms, or a motor vehicle accident. The slight increase in the rate in 1958 may partly be attributed to a change in the clerical practice of assigning "self- inflicted" injuries not designated either as suicide or accident to the category "suicide" (NCHS, 1967h: 10).

The preceding suggests that, while the long-term trend in suicides bears observation, the suicide rate disaggregated to meaningful socio-economic categories (age, sex, income, religion,

Death Rate

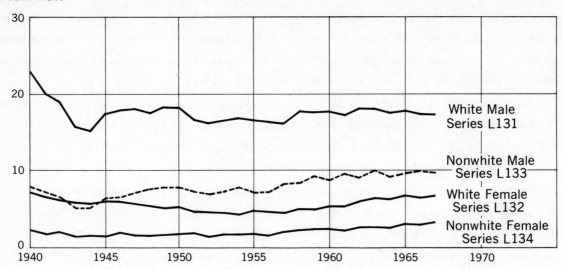

Figure 13.16 Age-Adjusted Death Rates for Suicide by Color and Sex, 1940–1967

(Deaths per 100,000 population)

color, etc.) would provide much more interpretable clues to changes in the socio-cultural situation.

Other Causes

The preceding graphs illustrate only some of the major causes of death. Trends in other specific major causes are presented in Series L001-L219 at the end of this volume. The differences among these in 1967 are presented in Table 13.4. Greater detail is available in Vital Statistics of the United States for the individual years.

Table 13.4 - Age-Adjusted Mortality Rates by Color and Sex, Total and Selected Causes, 1967

	Series number	Deaths per 100,000 population			
		White		Nonwhite	
		Male	Female	Male	Female
All Causes	L078-L080	900.9	518.1	1,243.3	820.7
Arteriosclerotic heart diseases, including coronary diseases	L085-L088	307.0	136.1	247.0	152.8
Hypertensive heart disease	L089-L092	14.7	14.2	58.1	55.0
Malignant neoplasms of digestive organs and peritoneum (not secondary)	L101-L104	44.0	30.3	62.4	36.5
Malignant neoplasms of breast	L109-L110		23.2		22.6
Malignant neoplasms of genital organs	L111-L114	13.2	17.8	24.3	29.5
Tuberculosis of the respiratory system	L119-L122	3.4	1.0	13.7	4.5
Syphilis and its sequelae	L123-L126	1.3	0.4	3.6	1.7

Summary of Indicators

The expectation of life (Series L001-L028) provides the most useful general index to the vital state of men and women. Expressed as the expected number of years of life remaining (Figure 13.1), as derived from the life table (e.g., NCHS, 1969e: 5-7), the indicator gives a continuing assessment of life chances by each single year of age by color and sex. Series L001-L028 give the expectation of life at birth, at age 15 and at ten-year intervals to age 65.

The individual causes of death (Series L077-L146), the infant mortality rate (Series L033-L036), and the maternal mortality rate (Series L147-L167) are each important indicators of aspects of the status of women. The interpretation of each, however, rests upon medical aspects of the causes of death and upon knowledge of the socio-cultural situation which gives rise to the mortality. To the extent that socio-cultural factors play a leading role in the etiology of mortality, the death rates provide valuable indices to women's status in society and to the forces that operate upon her life.

As has been seen in the foregoing discussion, mortality rates by specific causes tend, almost without exception, to be more favorable for females than for males.

Considering the changes in the rates for females only over the 27-year period, the following trends can be noted:

Mortality rates (with the age distribution of the population held constant) are declining among females for the following:

Infant mortality (Series L034, L036)

Maternal mortality (Series L147-L149)

Tuberculosis (Series L120, L122)

Syphilis (Series L124, L126)

Hypertensive heart disease (Series L090, L092)

Cancer of the digestive organs (Series L102, L104)

Cancer of the genital organs (Series L116, L118)

Influenza and pneumonia (Series L116, L118)

A few causes of death are holding relatively constant. Among them is the death rate due to ulcer of the stomach (Series L144, L146).

Some causes of death appear to be decreasing or holding constant among white but increasing among nonwhite women. These are:

All forms of cancer (Series L098, L100)

Diabetes (Series L094, L096)

Cancer of the breast (Series L109, L110)

The following causes of death are increasing, proportionately, among females:

Arteriosclerotic heart disease (Series L086, L088)

Cancer of the respiratory system (Series L106, L108)

Cirrhosis of the liver (Series L140, L142)

Motor vehicle accidents (Series L128, L130)

Suicide (Series L132, L134)

Homicide (Series L136, L138)

Trends in the causes of death reviewed in this volume are but a few of the major ones, (NCHS, 1969e) and other vital records provide the basis for monitoring others.

<u>Key to Series Discussed in Chapter 13</u>

Expectation of life at various ages, by color and sex	L001 - L028
Death rates, by age, color, and sex	L029 - L076
Age-adjusted death rates for selected causes, by color and sex	L077 - L146
Maternal mortality rates, by age and color	L147 - L167
Death rates for motor vehicle traffic accidents, excluding pedestrians, by age and sex	L168 - L193
Death rates for motor vehicle traffic accidents to pedestrians, by age and sex	L194 - L219

Appendix A

The Current Population Survey

Many of the series presented in this volume were compiled from Current Population Reports of the U. S. Bureau of the Census. These data are assembled through the Current Population Survey, a monthly area-probability sample. The definitions and concepts applicable to these series are introduced and discussed in the Notes to the Series.

This Appendix section presents general information about the CPS.

In 1969 the Current Population Survey consisted of designated interviews each month at approximately 50,000 households spread over 449 areas comprising 863 counties and independent cities, with coverage in each of the 50 States and the District of Columbia. Approximately 50,000 occupied housing units are designated for interview each month. Of this number, 2,250 occupied units, on the average, are visited but interviews are not obtained because the occupants are not found at home after repeated calls or are unavailable for some other reason. In addition to the 50,000 there are also about 8,500 sample units in an average month which are visited but are found to be vacant or otherwise not enumerated.

The estimating procedure used in this survey involved the inflation of weighted sample results to independent estimates of the civilian noninstitutional population of the United States by age, color, and sex. These independent estimates were based on statistics from the 1960 Census of Population; statistics of births, deaths, immigration, and emigration; and statistics on the strength of the Armed Forces. To these figures were added the members of the Armed Forces living off post or with their families on post and the institutional population. The estimated numbers of inmates of institutions shown in this report were obtained by assuming that the percent of population who were inmates in each age and sex group in 1969 was the same as in the 1960 census (Census, 1970d: 7).

While the basic principles of sampling have remained the same, there have been changes in the methodology of the Current Population Survey since it was transferred to the U. S. Bureau of the Census in August 1943. These are documented in a number of detailed descriptions of the survey (Steinberg, 1953; Census, 1963k; 1964e; and Census, 1967k). The last-named reference,

241

particularly, identifies the changes in detail. Improvements in the reliability of estimates have resulted mainly from changes in the number of primary sampling units and the number of households interviewed. Major improvements were instituted in October, 1943, February, 1954, May, 1956, and January, 1967. These changes are presented in the Table A.1, below.

Table A.1 - Major Revisions in Current Population Survey Sample

Date of Revision	Primary sampling units	Counties and independent cities	Households interviewed	Remarks
October 1943	68	125	25,000*	Sample converted to strictly probability basis
February 1954	230	453	21,000	25,000 households; sample expanded geographically
May 1956	330	638	35,000	40,000 households in sample; about 20 percent increase in reliability
January 1960	333	-	-	Alaska and Hawaii added
October 1961	357	-	-	About 5 percent gain in reliability
January 1967	449	863	52,500	60,000 households; about 20 percent increase in reliability.

* - Minus households not interviewed because not at home, vacant, etc.

Source: (Census, 1967k: 15-18).

A number of procedural and processing changes have been made from time to time to speed up the processing and make the data more accurate. These chiefly were:

a) August 1947: The method of selecting units within the sample area was changed so that each unit selected could be given the same weight in the tabulations.

b) July 1949: Coverage of the sample was extended to special dwelling places, such as hotels, trailer camps, etc.

c) February 1952: A document sensing card was introduced to speed the recording and transfer of data to IBM processing cards.

d) January 1953: 1950 Census data were first used to make ratio estimates from the sample data.

e) July 1953: A 4-8-4 rotation system replaced the system of keeping households in the sample for six consecutive months.

In the new system, a household was in the sample for four months, out for eight months, and back in the sample for four additional months before being retired.

f) September 1953: High speed electronic computers were first used to process the data.

g) July 1955: The timing of the survey was changed from the week containing the 8th of the month, to the week containing the 12th day of the month.

h) April 1962: Updated Population information based upon the 1960 Census was first used.

In addition to these, other changes in definition, coverage and so forth, affecting the data on the labor force were made (Census, 1967k). (Some of the preceding is quoted from (Ferriss, 1969: 300-302).)

Certain changes in some of the labor force concepts also have been made in the historical development of the survey. These have been described, as follows (Labor, 1970: 208):

"Beginning with data for 1967, the lower age limit for official statistics on persons in the labor force was raised from 14 to 16 years. At the same time, several definitions were sharpened to clear up ambiguities. The principal definitional changes were: (1) Counting as unemployed only persons who were currently available for work and who had engaged in some specific jobseeking activity within the past 4 weeks (an exception to the latter condition is made for persons waiting to start a new job in 30 days or waiting to be recalled from layoff). In the past the current availability test was not applied and the time period for jobseeking was ambiguous; (2) counting as employed persons who were absent from their jobs in the survey week (because of strikes, bad weather, etc.) and who were looking for other jobs. These persons had previously been classified as unemployed; (3) sharpening the questions on hours of work, duration of unemployment, and self-employment in order to increase their reliability.

"These changes did not affect the unemployment rate by more than one-fifth of a percentage point in either direction, although the distribution of unemployment by sex was affected. The number of employed was reduced about 1 million because of the exclusion of 14- and 15-year-olds. For persons 16 years and over, the only employment series appreciably affected were those relating to hours of work and class of worker. A detailed discussion of the changes and their effect on the various series is contained in the February 1967 issue of Employment and Earnings and Monthly Report on the Labor Force. ....

"Prior to the changes introduced in 1967, there were three earlier periods of noncomparability in the labor force data: (1) Beginning 1953, as a result of introducing data from the 1950 census into the estimation procedure, population levels were raised by about 600,000; labor force, total employment, and agricultural employment by about 350,000, primarily affecting the figures for totals and males; other categories were relatively unaffected; (2) beginning 1960, the inclusion of Alaska and Hawaii resulted in an increase of about 500,000 in the population and about 300,000 in the labor force, four-fifths of this in

243

nonagricultural employment; other labor force categories were not appreciably affected; (3) beginning 1962, the introduction of figures from the 1960 census reduced the population by about 50,000, labor force and employment by about 200,000; unemployment totals were virtually unchanged".

As is indicated in Table A.1, the reliability of estimates from the CPS has increased as result of improvements in the sample. To determine the reliability of an estimated percentage from the current sample, both the percentage and the population base of the percentage must be known. In most of the percentages presented in this volume, the population base is not given, only the percent is presented. As a consequence, it is not possible to estimate reliability from the data of this volume alone; the reader must refer to the primary sources. An example, however, will serve to indicate the general level of reliability of the data.

Consider Series C170, presenting the percent of families (other than husband-wife families) consisting of a female separated from her husband. Of the 5,439,000 households in March 1969 with a female head, 18.1 percent were wives separated from their husbands. According to the standard errors of percentages of households and families (Census, 1970d: 9), there are 68 chances out of 100 that the true population value of this percentage is plus or minus 0.5 of this percentage, or some value between 17.6 percent and 18.6 percent.

Two tables showing these sampling errors, applicable to the sampling design initiated in January 1967, are reproduced from one of the census reports, as follows (Census, 1970d: 8-9):

Census Table I - Standard Errors of Estimated Percentages of Persons
(68 chances out of 100)

Estimated percentage	Base of estimated percentage (thousands)							
	500	1,000	2,500	5,000	10,000	25,000	50,000	100,000
1 or 99	0.6	0.2	0.2	0.1	0.1	0.1	0.1	(Z)
2 or 98	0.7	0.4	0.3	0.2	0.1	0.1	0.1	0.1
5 or 95	1.0	0.7	0.5	0.3	0.2	0.1	0.1	0.1
10 or 90	1.4	1.0	0.8	0.4	0.3	0.2	0.1	0.1
15 or 85	1.6	1.1	0.9	0.5	0.3	0.3	0.2	0.1
20 or 80	1.8	1.3	0.9	0.6	0.4	0.3	0.2	0.1
25 or 75	2.0	1.4	1.0	0.6	0.4	0.3	0.2	0.1
35 or 65	2.1	1.5	1.1	0.7	0.5	0.3	0.2	0.1
50	2.3	1.6	1.3	0.7	0.5	0.3	0.2	0.1

Z - Less than 0.05.

Source: (Census, 1970d: 8).

Census Table J - Standard Errors of Estimated Percentages of Households and Families
(68 chances out of 100)

Estimate percentage	Base of estimated percentage (thousands)						
	500	1,000	2,500	5,000	10,000	25,000	50,000
1 or 99	0.4	0.2	0.1	0.1	0.1	0.1	(Z)
2 or 98	0.5	0.3	0.2	0.1	0.1	0.1	0.1
5 or 95	0.8	0.6	0.4	0.3	0.2	0.1	0.1
10 or 90	1.1	0.8	0.6	0.3	0.2	0.2	0.1
15 or 85	1.3	0.9	0.7	0.4	0.3	0.2	0.1
20 or 80	1.4	1.0	0.8	0.5	0.3	0.2	0.1
25 or 75	1.6	1.1	0.8	0.5	0.3	0.2	0.1
35 or 65	1.7	1.2	0.9	0.5	0.4	0.3	0.2
50	1.8	1.3	1.0	0.6	0.4	0.3	0.2

Z - Less than 0.05.

Source: (Census, 1970d: 9)

"Table I shows the standard errors of estimated percentages of persons for different sizes of the bases of the percentages. Table J shows the standard errors of estimated percentages of households or families. The guidelines used to decide whether Table G or Table H is appropriate for a particular item should also be used for deciding between the use of Table I and J". [1]

. . .

In March 1969 there were 3,065,000 married males, 2,855,000 or 93.1 percent of whom were living with their wives.

"Table I shows the standard error of 93.1 percent on a base of 3,065,000 to be approximately 0.6 percent. Consequently, chances are 68 out of 100 that the estimated 93.1 percent would be within 0.6 percent of a complete census figure, and chances are 95 out of 100 that the estimate would be within 1.2 percent of a census figure, i.e., this 95 percent confidence interval would be 91.9 to 94.3 percent" (Census, 1970d: 9).

_____

[1] - Tables G and H, (Census, 1970d: 8), present, respectively the "standard error of estimates of the number of persons in a given class", and "of the number of household or families in a given class". The "guideline" is simply to use Table I if the estimate is the percentage of persons and Table J if the percent is based upon an item of information that could appear only once in a household, such as married woman, or head of household, etc.

Appendix B

Health Interview Survey

The Congress authorized the Public Health Service to institute a National Health Survey. The survey was initiated in 1957 with the Bureau of the Census participating in most aspects of the work -- selecting the sample, interviewing, statistical processing, and so forth. The Health Interview Survey is based upon samples taken each week of a civilian, noninstitutional population of the United States living at the time of the interview. Members of the Armed Forces, U. S. citizens living in foreign countries, and crews of vessels are excluded from the population sample.

After several limited, experimental surveys, and after a period of on-the-job training for interviewers, the Survey began July 1, 1957 and has continued each week since then. The multi-stage probability design permits continuous sampling and is so structured that the weekly samples may be summed over various time periods to accumulate aggregates large enough to reflect health conditions that may be relatively rare. This procedure is also made possible by the high degree of stability of the questionnaire, the definitions, and other procedures used. These data-gathering procedures are described in the appendices to the publications of the Survey.

Table B.1 - Approximate Sample Size of Health Interview Survey, 1957-1968

Period	PSUs	Segments	Households	Persons
July 1, 1957-June 30, 1958	372	6,000	36,000	115,000
July 1, 1958-Dec. 31, 1958	372	6,200	37,000	120,000
Jan. 1, 1959-June 30, 1959	500			
Each 12-month period, ending June 30, to 1962	500	6,400	38,000	125,000
Each 12-month period, ending June 30, to 1968	357	6,700	42,000	134,000

Source: National Center for Health Statistics.

Table B.1 shows the changes in the magnitude of sampling units, segments, households and persons of the sample. The United States is divided into approximately 1,900 primary sampling units, which consist of a county, a group of counties, or a metropolitan statistical area. From this frame 357 PSU's are (1968) drawn, as the first stage of the sampling procedure. Primary sampling units are divided into segments, each consisting of ("an expected") nine households. A weekly sample of 90 segments, or approximately 800 households, is drawn and the household members are interviewed each week. Over a 12-month period the sample accumulates to the totals shown in Table B.1.

Estimates are developed through a two-stage ratio estimating procedure. "In the first of these, the control factor is the ratio of the 1960 decennial population count to the 1960 estimated population in the National Health Survey's first-stage sample of PSU's. These factors are applied for some 25 color-residence classes" (NCHS, 1965d: 34).

Second-stage factors are derived from ratios of population estimates produced by the sample to the Census Bureau estimates of the current population, applied in approximately 60 age-sex-color classes.

Nonresponse because of refusal and because, even after repeated attempts, the interviewer could not find the respondent at home, typically, is about five percent. The data, of course, are adjusted to compensate for such lack of information.

In the sample household, the interviewer questions each person 19 years of age and older, if available at the time of the interview. "Proxy respondents within the household were employed for children and for adults not available at the time of the interview, provided the respondent was closely related to the person about whom information was being obtained" (NCHS, 1965d: 35).

Statistics on the number of occurrences of health interest during a time period are based upon responses with reference to the last two weeks prior to the week of the interview, a procedure that reduces the loss of information through respondent error due to faulty memory. The average of these 2-week estimates over 13 successive samples, multiplied by 6.5, thereby produces a quarterly estimate. The sum of four quarters makes a year. "Thus, the experience of persons interviewed during a year -- experience which actually occurred for each person in a 2-calendar-week interval prior to week of interview -- is treated as though it measured the total of such experience during the year. Such interpretation leads to no significant bias" (NCHS, 1965d: 35).

Publications based on data from the National Health Survey usually contain, in the appendix, charts for use in estimating the sampling error of the estimates. (See, for example, NCHS, 1969c: 35-40).

Definitions of terms used in the Health Interview Survey relevant to data in this volume are presented in notes to the appropriate series. In addition, the following definitions apply:

Age - The age is the age at last birthday, recorded in single years.

Income of family or of unrelated individuals - All persons in the household who are related to each other by blood, marriage, or adoption, constitute a family. The total 12-month income of the family is attributed to each member of the family. Unrelated individuals are classified according to their own income. Wages, salaries, rents from property, pensions, and help from relatives, etc., are counted as income if received during the 12-month period preceding the week of the interview.

Labor Force Status - Persons 17 years of age or over are considered in the labor force if they were employed, or unemployed and looking for work, or were on layoff from work during the 2-week period prior to interview week. Since there are several differences in definitions and the concepts relative to labor force between NHS and CPS, the following explanation is quoted in detail:

"Currently employed persons - Currently employed persons are all persons 17 years of age or over who reported that at any time during the 2-week period covered by the interview they either worked at or had a job or business. Current employment includes paid work as an employee of someone else; self-employment in business, farming, or professional practice; and unpaid work in a family business or farm. Persons who were temporarily absent from their job or business because of a temporary illness, vacation, strike, or bad weather are considered as currently employed if they expected to work as soon as the particular event causing their absence no longer existed.

"Freelance workers are considered as having a job if they had a definite arrangement with one or more employers to work for pay according to a weekly or monthly schedule, either full time or part time. Excluded from the currently employed population are such persons who have no definite employment schedule but who work only when their services are needed.

"Also excluded from the currently employed population are (1) persons who were not working, even though having a job or business, but were on layoff or looking for work, (2) persons receiving revenue from an enterprise in whose operation they did not participate, (3) persons doing housework or charity work for which they received no pay, and (4) seasonal workers during the unemployment season.

"The number of currently employed persons estimated by the National Health Survey (NHS) will differ from the estimates prepared by the Current Population Survey (CPS), Bureau of the Census, for several reasons. In addition to sampling variability there are three primary conceptual differences, namely:

(1) NHS estimates are for persons 17 years of age or over and CPS estimates are for persons 14 years of age or over; (2) NHS uses a 2-week-reference period, while CPS uses a 1-week-reference period; (3) NHS is a continuing survey with separate samples taken weekly, while CPS is a monthly sample taken for the survey week which includes the 12th of the month" (NCHS, 1968f: 41).

Appendix C
Notes and Sources

Population: Series A001 - A060

The data are estimates of the total population of the States, the Armed Forces overseas included. Alaska and Hawaii are included beginning 1950. The data are estimates of the population for July 1 of each year and are by five or more year age groups. The sources present the population by age, sex, and color for single years of age (except the projections), but caution the user that single year of age estimates are subject to "considerable error". For developing single year of age rates and for developing age groupings for combination of years, however, the single year of age data are quite useful. For a detailed statement of the development of the estimates, see U. S. Bureau of the Census Current Population Reports, Series P-25, Nos. 98, 114 and 310, as well as the sources cited. For a critical review of the estimates, see (Ferriss, 1969: 269-275).

Sources: 1940-1959: (Census, 1965g: 4-43); 1960-1963: (Census, 1965h: 12-14); 1964-1966: (Census, 1968e: 11, 14-16); 1967-1969: (Census, 1970b: 12-15).

Sex Ratio: Series A061 - A075

The ratios were calculated from the corresponding population series, Series A001 - A060, and from projections, cited below.

Sources: See notes to Series A001 - A060. Sex ratio projections: (Census, 1967f: 58-59). The Census Bureau projection method is described (Census, 1967f: 1-46).

The following refers to the statistical series:

a/ - Population projection Series C was used.

Aliens Naturalized: Series A092 - A100

Included are total aliens naturalized under both general and special naturalization provisions, for the fiscal year ending June 30 of the year shown. The largest proportion of those naturalized under special provisions are persons married to U. S. citizens and the next largest category are children. However, approximately three-fourths of those naturalized entered under the general provisions of the naturalization laws.

251

Sources: 1940-1956: (Census, 1960e: Series C159, C160 and C161); 1957-1961: (Immigration, 1961: 84); 1962-1964: (Immigration, 1966: 110); 1965-1969: (Immigration, 1969: 112).

The following refers to the statistical series:

a/ - Marital status of the residual percentage is unknown.

Immigrants: Series A076 - A091

"An immigrant is an alien admitted for permanent residence". Aliens admitted for temporary residence are not included. "Returning resident aliens who have once been counted as immigrants are included with nonimmigrants". (Immigration, 1964: 22) The percentages by age sum to 100 for each sex.

Sources: 1940-1949: supplied by the Immigration and Naturalization Service, U. S. Department of Justice; 1950-1969: successive annual reports (Immigration, 1950-1969).

The following refers to the statistical series:

a/ - The "60 years and over" category includes a very small number for whom age was not reported.

Percent Enrolled in School: Series B001-B040

For a review of the Current Population Survey of the Census Bureau, see Appendix A. Definitions that apply to the survey are, as follows (Census, 1969m: 6):

"School enrollment -- The school enrollment statistics from the current surveys are based on replies to the enumerator's inquiry as to whether the person had been enrolled at any time during the current term or school year in any type of graded public, parochial, or other private school in the regular school system. Such schools include nursery schools, kindergartens, elementary schools, high schools, colleges, universities, and professional schools. Attendance may be on either a full-time or part-time basis and during the day or night. Thus, regular schooling is that which may advance a person toward an elementary or high school diploma, or a college, university, or professional school degree. Children enrolled in nursery schools and kindergarten are included in the enrollment figures for 'regular' schools, and are also shown separately.

"'Special' schools are those which are not in the regular school system, such as trade schools or business colleges. Persons attending 'special' schools are not included in the enrollment figures.

"Persons enrolled in classes which do not require physical presence in school, such as correspondence courses or other courses of independent study, and in training courses given directly on the job, are also excluded from the count of those enrolled in school, unless such courses are being counted for credit at a 'regular' school.

"School enrollment in year preceding current survey -- An inquiry on enrollment in regular school or college in October of the preceding year was asked in both the 1967 and 1968 surveys concerning persons 14 to 34 years old who were not currently attending regular school or who were enrolled in college.

"Level of school -- The statistics on level of school indicate the number of persons enrolled at each of five levels: Nursery, kindergarten, elementary school (first to eighth grades), high school (ninth to twelfth grades), and college or professional school. The last group includes graduate students in colleges or universities. Persons enrolled in junior high school through the eighth grade are classified as elementary school and the others as in high school.

"Nursery school -- A nursery school is defined as a group or class that is organized to provide educational experiences for children during the year or years preceding kindergarten. It includes instruction as an important and integral phase of its program of child care. Private homes in which essentially custodial care is provided are not considered nursery schools. Children attending nursery school are classified as attending during either part of the day or the full day. Part-day attendance refers to those who attend either in the morning or in the afternoon, but not both. Full-day attendance refers to those who attend both in the morning and afternoon. (See note a/ below).

"'Head Start' -- Children enrolled in 'Head Start' programs or similar programs sponsored by local agencies to provide pre-school education to young children are counted under 'Nursery' or 'Kindergarten' as appropriate.

"Public or private school -- In this report, a public school is defined as any educational institution operated by publicly elected or appointed school officials and supported by public funds. Private schools included educational institutions established and operated by religious bodies, as well as those which are under other private control. In cases where enrollment was in a school or college which was both publicly and privately controlled or supported, enrollment was counted according to whether it was primarily public or private.

"Full-time and part-time attendance -- College students were classified, in this report, according to whether they were attending school on a full-time or part-time basis. A student was regarded as attending college full-time if he was taking 12 or more hours of classes during the average school week, and part-time if he was taking less than 12 hours of classes during the average school week.

"Age -- The age classification is based on the age of the person at his last birthday.

"Race and Color -- The term 'race' refers to the division of population into three groups, white, Negro, and other races. The group designated as 'other races' consists of Indians, Japanese, Chinese, and other nonwhite races. The term 'color' refers to the twofold classification white and nonwhite".

Sources: Data are from the P-20 series of the Current Population Survey of the Bureau of the Census, as follows: 1954: (Census, 1955a: 8); 1955: (Census, 1956a: 9); 1956: (Census, 1957b: 9); 1957: (Census 1958a: 9); 1958: (Census, 1959a: 9); 1959: (Census, 1960b: 9); 1960: (Census 1961a: 11); 1961: (Census 1962a: 8); 1962: (Census, 1963d: 8); 1963: (Census, 1964a: 9); 1964: (Census, 1966b:10); 1965: (Census 1967a: 8); 1966: (Census, 1967b: 10-11); 1967 and 1968: (Census, 1969m: 10-11, 34-35); additional unpublished data for 1967 and 1968 from the Census Bureau.

The following refers to the statistical series:

a/ - Schools include kindergarten but not nursery school, elementary schools, high schools, colleges, universities, and professional schools. Attendance may be on either a full-time or part-time basis, and may be during the day or in the evening. "Special" schools such as trade schools or business colleges are not included. Correspondence and on-the-job training courses also are excluded unless such courses are being counted for credit at a "regular" school.

Number Enrolled by Level: Series B041 - B128

Definitions and sources are the same as those for Series B001-B040, above.

The numbers in kindergarten and elementary school in 1967 and 1968 are from unpublished data supplied by the U.S. Bureau of the Census. These enrollment figures do not include nursery school enrollment in order to make them comparable with earlier years. However, published Census enrollment figures starting for the year 1967 include nursery school enrollment.

Educational Attainment: Percent of Age Groups by Level, Color and Sex: Series B129 - B384

The data are from the Current Population Survey; see Appendix A. Pertinent definitions are, as follows (Census, 1970a: 4):

"Years of school completed -- Data on years of school completed in this report were derived from the combination of answers to two questions: (a) "What is the highest grade of school he has ever attended?" and (b) "Did he finish this grade?"

"The questions on educational attainment apply only to progress in 'regular' schools. Such schools include graded public, private, and parochial elementary and high schools (both junior and senior high), colleges, universities, and professional schools, whether day schools or night schools. Thus, regular schooling is that which may advance a person toward an elementary school certificate or high school diploma, or a college, university, or professional school degree. Schooling in other than regular schools was counted only if the credits obtained were regarded as transferable to a school in the regular school system.

"The median years of school completed is defined as the value which divides the population into two equal parts -- one-half having completed less schooling than the median. This median was computed after the statistics on years of school completed had been converted to a continuous series of numbers (e.g. completion of the first year of high school was treated as completion of the 9th year and the completion of the first year of college as completion of the 13th year). The persons completing a given school year were assumed to be distributed evenly within the interval from .0 to .9 of the year (for example, persons completing the 12th year were assumed to be distributed evenly between 12.0 and 12.9). In fact, at the time of the March survey, most of the enrolled persons had completed about three-fourths of a school year beyond the highest grade completed, whereas a large majority of persons who were not enrolled had not attended any part of a grade beyond the highest one completed. The effect of the assumption is to place the median for younger persons slightly below, and for older persons slightly above, the true median. Because of the inexact assumption as to the distribution within an interval, this median is more appropriately used for comparing groups and the same group at different dates than as an absolute measure of educational attainment.

255

"Assignment of educational attainment for those not reporting -- When information on either the highest grade attended or completion of the grade was not
reported in the 1969 survey, entries for the items were assigned using an edit
in the computer. The general procedure was to assign an entry for a person
that was consistent with entries for other persons with similar characteristics.
The specific technique used in the March 1969 survey was as follows:

"1. The computer stored reported data on highest grade attended by race
(white and all other) and age, and on completion of the grade by age and highest
grade attended, for persons 14 years old and over in the population.

"2. Each stored value was retained in the computer only until a succeeding
person having the same characteristics (e.g., same race and age, in the case of
assignments for highest grade attended) and having the item reported, was proces-
sed through the computer. Then the reported data for the succeeding person were
stored in the place of the one previously stored.

"3. When one or both of the education items for a person 14 years old and
over was not reported, the entry assigned to this person was that stored for the
last person who had the same characteristics". The percent of the population so
allocated, by age groups ranged from 0.6 percent of an age group to 0.9 percent.

Sources: Data are from the P-20 series of Current Population Reports on Educational Attain-
ment, as follows: 1947: (Census, 1948a: 9) and estimates; 1957: (Census, 1957a: 3, 9); 1959:
(Census, 1960a: 13-15); 1962: (Census, 1963c: 8,9); 1964: (Census, 1965a: 10, 11); 1965 and 1966:
(Census, 1966a: 8, 9, 18, 19); 1967: (Census, 1968a: 9, 10); 1968: (Census, 1969a: 10-12); 1969:
(Census, 1970a: 10-12).

The following refer to the statistical series:

a/ - (Census, 1948a: 9) for April 1947, gives the seventh and eighth grades combined. To
separate these two grades, percentages for each age-color-sex group were estimated on the basis
of the division between these two grades in the 1940 and 1950 decennial census.

b/ - Reports for 1947, 1957, and 1959 have a category, "not reported". The percentages
not reporting educational attainment were distributed proportionately throughout the grades-
completed categories within each age-sex-color group.

c/ - Less than 0.05 percent.

Percent of Age Groups with Specified Years of Schooling: Series B385 - B480
Definitions and sources are the same as those for Series B129-B384.
The following refers to the statistical series:
a/ - See footnote "b" to Series B129-B384, above.

256

Earned Degrees Conferred by Level and Sex: Series B481 - B488

The number of degrees conferred annually are reported to the U.S. Office of Education by the institution conferring the degrees, by field, level of degree and sex of recipient. However, first level degrees have not always been reported as four-year degrees. Only selected fields have a practice of giving degrees that require more than four years to complete. Four-year degrees were estimated by a procedure based upon a few years when four-year degrees were separately reported. For these years it was possible to obtain a percent four-year and the combined four-year and more first professional degrees (Series B483-B484) by field. Percentages thus derived were applied to other years to obtain the estimates. The procedure is described in detail in an (as yet) unpublished manuscript by the author, "Forecast of the Supply and Demand for Faculty in Higher Education to 1975-76," publication forthcoming in a volume of papers to be released by the U. S. Office of Education.

Sources: 1948-1964: (Education, 1966b: 12); 1965: (Education, 1966a: 4); 1966: (Education, 1968a: 10); 1967: (Education, 1968b: 5); 1968: (Education, 1969b: 4).

Percent Change in Earned Degrees: Series B489 - B496

These series were calculated from the corresponding Series B481-B488, by dividing the (current) year by the previous year, multiplying by 100, and subtracting 100.

High School Graduates, by Sex: Series B497 - B498

The data on public graduates are reported by state departments of education to the U. S. Office of Education. Except for occasional years, the data on graduates of private high schools are partly reported (the Catholic schools) and partly estimated by the Office. For additional notes, see (Ferriss, 1969: 291-292).

Sources: 1940-1952: (Education, 1963: 41); 1954-1957: from MS by D.S. Bridgman; 1958-67: (Education, 1969a: 30); 1969: unpublished data from the U.S. Office of Education.

First-Time Degree-Credit Enrollment: Series B499-B500

Enrollment is reported by the higher educational institutions to the U. S. Office of Education and published annually by institution in a series, Opening Fall Enrollment in Higher Education. "Degree-credit" signifies that the program of the enrollee includes courses acceptable for a baccalaureate or higher degree. A first-time student has not previously been enrolled in higher education. For 1966 and later years the "degree-credit" category is estimated, to adjust for a change in definition that year and used subsequently. For additional notes on this series, see (Ferriss, 1969: 315-317).

Sources: (Ferriss, 1969: 387).

Ratio, Graduates to Population: Series B501 - B502

The population by sex is estimated by the Census Bureau for July 1 of each year, by single years of age, including the armed forces overseas. The denominator is the average of the 17 and 18 year olds. The age of high school graduates has been estimated from the work of Donald Bridgman, as follows (based upon the years 1962, 1963 and 1964):

	Male	Female
16 or less	5.4	6.4
17	27.8	32.0
18	47.5	50.2
19	13.0	6.7
20 or more	6.4	4.6

Bridgman's method was to begin with the October school enrollment in the fourth year of high school by age and sex from the U. S. Bureau of the Census survey of school enrollment and to age that population according to estimates of their birth months from the vital statistics reports on births for years appropriate to the enrolled population. The average of the 17 and 18 year olds was accepted as an approximation of the population base of those eligible to graduate.

Sources: Population: 1940-1959: (Census, 1965g); 1960-1963: (Census, 1965); 1964-1966: (Census, 1968e); 1967-1969: (Census, 1970b). High school graduates: Series B497-B498.

Ratio, Enrollment to High School Graduates: Series B503 - B510

The ratios were calculated from Series B481-B488 and B497-B500, respectively. The selection of the ten-year lag time, baccalaureate to doctorate, is based upon the experience reported by the Office of Scientific Personnel, National Academy of Sciences (NAS, 1967). See, also (Ferriss, 1969: 330-331).

Sex Ratio, Degrees by Level: Series B511 - B513

Calculated from Series B483-B488, respectively.

Unemployment Rates by Years of School Completed: Series B514 - B529

For definitions of labor force and employment status concepts, see notes to Series F001-F012. Definitions affecting the educational attainment data are given as notes to Series B129-B384.

Sources: 1952: (Census, 1953h: 7); 1957: (Census, 1957e: 8); 1959: (BLS, 1960b: A6); 1962: (BLS, 1963c: A14); 1964: (BLS, 1965c: A14); 1965: (BLS, 1966b: A15); 1966: (BLS, 1967c: A15); 1967: (BLS, 1968b: A16); 1968: (BLS, 1969c: A15).

The following refer to the statistical series:

a/ - The unemployment rate is the percent of the civilian labor force that is unemployed.

b/ - For 1959 and earlier, persons not reporting years of school completed were distributed proportionally.

Marital Status: Series C001 - C160

These data are from the Census Current Population Survey made in March of each year for which data are shown (April in 1954 and 1955). See Appendix A for a description of the CPS, and refer to the Sources for additional definitions. The following is the explanation of marital status from (Census, 1969h: 7-8):

> "Marital Status -- The marital status classification identifies four major categories: single, married, widowed, and divorced. These terms refer to the marital status at the time of the enumeration.

> "The category 'married' is further divided into 'married, spouse present' 'separated', and 'other married, spouse absent'. A person is classified as 'married, spouse absent' if the husband or wife was reported as a member of the household, even though he or she may have been temporarily absent on business or on vacation, visiting, in a hospital, etc., at the time of the enumeration. Persons reported as separated included those with legal separations, those living apart with intentions of obtaining a divorce, and other persons permanently or temporarily separated because of marital discord. The group 'other married, spouse absent' includes married persons living apart because either the husband or wife was employed and living at a considerable distance from home, was serving away from home in the armed forces, was residing in an institution, had moved to another area, or had a different place of residence for any other reason except separation as defined above".

Sources: These data come from successive annual publications, "Marital Status and Family Status", of the March (or April) Census Current Population Survey. 1940 and 1950 are from the 1960 Census of Population (Census, 1963a: I-436-437); 1947: (Census, 1948c: 16-17); 1951: (Census, 1952b: 10-11); 1952: (Census, 1953e: 13); 1953: (Census, 1953f: 12); 1954: (Census, 1955d: 6); 1955: (Census, 1955e: 8); 1956: (Census, 1956b: 9); 1957: (Census, 1958d: 9); 1958: (Census, 1958e: 13); 1959: (Census, 1959b: 8-9); 1960: (Census, 1960d: 10); 1961: (Census, 1962d: 9); 1962: (Census, 1963e: 12); 1963 and 1964: (Census, 1965d: 15); 1965: (Census, 1965e: 13); 1966: (Census, 1967c: 9-10); 1967: (Census, 1968c: 11); 1968: (Census, 1969h: 12-13); 1969: (Census, 1970d: 11-12).

The following refer to the statistical series:

a/ - Data not available by age for the years 1954-1956; for ages 65-74 and 75 and over, not available for 1951-1956.

b/ - Not computed because of insufficient sample size.

c/ - Less than 0.05 percent

See notes to Series C001-C160.

Sources: 1954: (Census, 1955d; 8); 1955: (Census, 1955e: 10); 1956: (Census, 1956b: 11); 1957: (Census, 1958d: 9); 1958: (Census, 1958e: 13); 1959: (Census, 1959b: 9); 1960: (Census, 1960d: 10); 1961: (Census, 1962d: 9); 1962: (Census, 1963e: 12); 1963 and 1964: (Census, 1965d: 14-15); 1965: (Census, 1965e: 13); 1966: (Census, 1967c: 10); 1967: (Census, 1968c: 12); 1968: (Census, 1969h: 12-13); 1969: (Census, 1970d: 11-12).

Marital Status, Heads of Families: Series C169 - C181

Data are from the "Household and Family Characteristics" reports based upon the Current Population Survey. For details on the CPS, see Appendix A. The definitions are explained in the Census reports. For a definition of Marital Status, see the notes to Series C001-C160. Other pertinent definitions, from (Census, 1969i: 4-5), follow:

"Husband in Armed Forces -- When a woman was reported as married but her husband was not enumerated as a member of the same household, an additional question was asked to determine whether her husband was in the Armed Forces. Women who were reported as separated were not asked the additional question.

"Family -- The term 'family', as used here, refers to a group of two persons or more related by blood, marriage, or adoption and residing together; all such persons are considered as members of one family. A lodger and his wife who are not related to the head of the household, or a resident employee and his wife living in, are considered as a separate family and not as part of the head's family. Thus, a household may contain more than one family. However, if the son of the head of the household and the son's wife are members of the household, they are treated as part of the head's family. A household head living alone, or with unrelated persons only, is regarded as a household but not as a family. Thus, some households do not contain a family.

"Primary family -- A primary family is a family that includes among its members the head of a household.

"Secondary family -- A secondary family is a family that does not include among its members the head of a household. Members of secondary families may include persons such as guests, lodgers, or resident employees and their relatives living in a household.

"Persons living with relatives in group quarters were formerly considered as members of secondary families. However, the number of such families became so small (37,000 in 1967) that beginning with the current data for 1968 (and beginning with the census data for 1960) the Bureau of the Census includes persons in these families in the count of secondary individuals.

260

"Subfamily -- A subfamily is a married couple with or without children, or one parent with one or more own single children under 18 years old, living in a household and related to, but not including, the head of the household or his wife. The most common example of a subfamily is a young married couple sharing the home of the husband's or wife's parents. Members of a subfamily are also members of a primary family. The number of subfamilies, therefore, is not included in the number of families.

"Married couple -- A married couple, as defined for census purposes, is a husband and his wife enumerated as members of the same household. The married couple may or may not have children living with them. The expression 'husband-wife' before the term 'household', 'family', or 'subfamily' indicates that the head of the household, family or subfamily is a married man whose wife lives with him. For example, a husband-wife family is a family with a head who is 'married, wife present'.

"Head of household, family or subfamily -- One person in each household, family, or subfamily is designated as the 'head'. The number of heads, there-fore, is equal to the number of households, families or subfamilies. The head is usually the person regarded as the head by the members of the group. Married women are not classified as heads if their husbands are living with them at the time of the survey".

Sources: 1954 and 1955: (Census, 1956c: 13-14); 1956: (Census, 1957d: 12); 1957: (Census, 1958h: 15); 1958: (Census, 1958i: 10); 1959: (Census, 1960g: 11); 1960: (Census, 1961d: 14); 1961: (Census, 1962g: 12); 1962: (Census, 1963j: 12); 1963 and 1964: (Census, 1965k: 20-21); 1965: (Census, 1966g: 16); 1966: (Census, 1967h: 14); 1967: (Census, 1968g: 17); 1968: (Census, 1969i: 33, 66), and (Census, 1969h: 26); 1969: (Census, 1970e: 33, 66) and (Census, 1970d: 25).

The following refers to the statistical series:

a/ - "Families" include primary and secondary families. Secondary families comprise a very small percent of all families. In 1968, for example, secondary families with female head were 1.1 percent and those with a male head (other than husband-wife families) were 1.2 percent of all families. Because of the addition of secondary families to this table, the totals do not agree with those of Series C182 which is primary families and primary individuals.

Households by Type: Series C182-C187

Data are from the March or April Census Current Population Surveys, as indicated on the table. See Appendix A for description of CPS. See notes to Series C001-C160 and Series C160-C181 for additional relevant definitions. The following definitions also apply:

"Household -- A household consists of all the persons who occupy a housing unit. A house, an apartment or other group of rooms, or a single room is regarded as a housing unit when it is occupied or intended for occupancy as separate living quarters; that is, when the occupants do not live and eat with any other persons in the structure and there is either (1) direct access from the outside or through a common hall or (2) a kitchen or cooking equipment for the exclusive use of the occupants.

"A household includes the related family members and all the unrelated persons, if any, such as lodgers, foster children, wards, or employees who share the housing unit. A person living alone in a housing unit, or a group of unrelated persons sharing a housing unit as partners, is also counted as a household. The count of households excludes group quarters.

"Primary individual -- A primary individual is a household head living alone or with nonrelatives only.

"Secondary individual -- A secondary individual is a person in a household or group quarters such as a guest, lodger, or resident employee (excluding primary individuals and inmates of institutions) who is not related to any other person in the household or group quarters. (See section above on 'Secondary family' for slight change in coverage of secondary individuals in 1968.)"

Sources: 1940, 1947, 1950, 1955-1967: (Census, 1968f: 4); 1948, 1949, 1951-1955: (Census, 1963h: 4); 1968: (Census, 1969i: 78); 1969: (Census, 1970e: 84); 1970: (Census, 1970h: 14).

The following refers to the statistical series:

a/ - From (Census, 1963h: 3): "Through 1959, a household included all of the persons who occupied a house, an apartment, or other group of rooms, or a room which constituted a dwelling unit under the 1950 Census rules. Since 1960, a household has included all of the persons who occupy a house, an apartment, or other group of rooms, or a room, which constitutes a housing unit under 1960 Census rules...Housing units differ from dwelling units mainly in that separate living quarters consisting of one room with direct access but without cooking equipment always qualified as a housing unit in 1960, but qualified as a dwelling unit in 1950 only when located in a regular apartment house or when the room was the only living quarters in the structure."

Annual Live Birth Rates by Live Birth Order and Color: Series D001 - D021

In each color group, live births per 1,000 women 15-44 years of age, are shown. The numerator is the annual number of live births to women of all ages in a given birth order divided by the midyear population of women 15-44 years of age, multiplied by 1,000. The total file of birth records were used prior to 1951 and for 1955. A 50 percent sample of birth records was used for the years 1951-54 and 1956-66. Rates for 1967 are based upon a 20- to 50-percent sample of births. The sampling plan, sampling error, and related technical aspects are presented in (NCHS, 1969a: 3-8 to 3-11). Registration is initiated by physicians and midwives, the certificate is recorded in the vital statistics office of each State, and the records are transmitted to the Division of Vital Statistics, National Center for Health Statistics, Public Health Service, U. S. Department of Health, Education and Welfare. The population by age upon which these rates are based is estimated by the U. S. Bureau of the Census. For detailed published sources of these estimates, see (NCHS, 1969a: 3-11 to 3-12).

Source: (NCHS, 1969a: 1-9 to 1-10).

Births per 1,000 Women by Age of Mother, Live-Birth Order, and Color: Series D022 - D168

This annual birth rate by live birth order is the number of live births of a given birth order occurring during the year divided by the midyear population of women of the specified age group, multiplied by 1,000. It is not the probability that the population of women who have had one live birth, for example, will have a second. The rates to 1959 were adjusted for under-registration. See also notes to Series D001 - D021.

Sources: 1940-1957: (PHS, 1960: 41-45); 1958-1959: (VS, 1959: lxxviii; 1960: 3-21; 1961: 3-23); 1960-1962: (NVSD, 1962: 1-22; 1963: 1-23; 1964c: 1-11); 1963-1967: (NCHS, 1964a: 1-12; 1966a: 1-12; 1967c: 1-11; 1968a: 1-11; 1969a: 1-10).

Cumulative Birth Rates by Age of Mother: Series D169 - D175

"Rates are averages of single-year rates per 1,000 women for single-year cohorts; they are based on births adjusted for underregistration and number of women adjusted for underenumeration and misstatements of age in the censuses'."(NCHS, 1968a: 1-15). See, also, notes to Series D001-D021.

Sources: 1940-1958: (PHS, 1960: 46-51); 1959-1961: (NCHS, 1966a: 1-17); 1962-1968: (NCHS, 1969a: 1-15).

Live Birth Rates, by Age of Mother and Color: Series D176 - D194

The annual live births per 1,000 women of a specific age/color group are the quotients of the annual number of live births to mothers of specific age and color groups divided by the mid-year populations of females in the specific age/color groups. For notes on sampling procedures, population estimates, and the like, see notes to Series D001-D021, above.

Sources: 1940-1967: (NCHS, 1969a: 1-4, 1-7); 1968: (NCHS, 1970a).

Legitimate Live Births, by Age of Mother: Series D195 - D201

Legitimate births are estimated by the National Center for Health Statistics, Division of Vital Statistics, from data for registration areas in which legitimacy is reported. For infor- mation on sampling procedures, see notes to Series D001-D021. The female population married by age and color is estimated by the U. S. Bureau of the Census. The age group, 40-44 years, includes legitimate live births to all mothers 40 years and older.

Source: (NCHS, 1969a: 1-8).

Illegitimate Birth Rates, by Age and Color of Mother: Series D202 - D220

Estimates of illegitimate births are based upon data from States where legitimacy is reported. See notes to Series D001-D021 and D195-D201.

Sources: 1940-1965: (NCHS, 1968b: 4, 25, 26); 1966-1967: Data from U. S. National Center for Health Statistics.

The following refer to the statistical series:

a/ - Figures refer to births occurring within the United States. Alaska is included beginning 1959 and Hawaii, 1960. Mothers for whom age was not stated were distributed among the various age groups. The Census Bureau's March Current Population Survey was used in deriving estimates of the base population -- female population 14 years and over by age, color and marital status. Fluctuations caused by sampling error were smoothed by using three-term moving average estimates for the years 1955-1965.

b/ - Illegitimate births to mothers 40 years old and over per 1,000 unmarried women aged 40-44 years.

c/ - Illegitimate births to mothers 35 years old and over per 1,000 unmarried women aged 35-44 years.

Illegitimacy Ratios, by Age and Color of Mother: Series D221 - D244

The illegitimacy ratio is the quotient of the annual number of illegitimate live births divided by the annual number of live births, multiplied by 1,000. See notes to Series D001-D021 for additional information on the data, sampling, etc.

Sources: (NCHS, 1968b: 8, 36).

Percent of Births Delivered in Hospital and by Physicians: Series D245 - D253

This information comes from the birth certificate. The greater proportion of births in hospitals are attended by physicians.

Source: (NCHS, 1969a: 1-20).

Percent Distribution of Persons, by Mobility Status, Age and Sex: Series E001 - E048

Mobility status is determined by comparing the place of residence on the survey date, usually March of the year, with the place of residence one year earlier. Nonmovers, thus, are those who, at the time of the interview, were living in the same house they lived in one year earlier. All persons living in a different house are movers.

Movers are identified as having moved within the same county, or they are migrants -- persons living in a county different from the one they lived in a year earlier. The county may be in the same State or a different State, thereby producing intrastate migrants and interstate migrants. In addition to the foregoing categories, there is a very small remainder group: "persons abroad," consisting of persons, either U. S. citizens or aliens, whose residence one year earlier was in a foreign country or in an outlying area under the jurisdiction of the United States (Census, 1969g: 2). The remaining classifications used in these tables -- age, sex, relationship to head of household, etc. -- follow the usage of the Census Current Population Survey. For household and family definitions, see Notes to Series C001-C160, C169-C181, and C182-C187.

As concerns mobility, military personnel are especially important, because of their greater likelihood of having moved. In these reports members of the U. S. Armed Forces are included if they lived off the post, or if they lived with their families on the post. All other members of the armed services are excluded. As an example, the March 1969 survey included about 1,028,000 members of the armed services.

Sources: The data of Series E001-E048 are extracted from the P-20 series of the Current Population Reports on "Mobility of the Population of the United States," as follows: 1948: (Census, 1949: 7); 1949: (Census, 1950a: 8); 1950: (Census, 1951: 10); 1951: (Census, 1952a: 10); 1952: (Census, 1953c: 8); 1953: (Census, 1953d: 8); 1954: (Census, 1955b: 8); 1955: (Census, 1955c: 10); 1956: (Census, 1957c: 11); 1957: (Census, 1958b: 10); 1958: (Census, 1958c: 11); 1959: (Census, 1960c: 13); 1960: (Census, 1962b: 15); 1961: (Census, 1962c: 17); 1962: (Census, 1964b: 14); 1963: (Census, 1965b: 17); 1964: (Census, 1965c: 20); 1965: (Census, 1966c: 18); 1966: (Census, 1966d: 14); 1967: (Census, 1968b: 12); 1968: (Census, 1969f: 11); 1969: (Census, 1969g: 11).

Percent Distribution of Persons, by Mobility Status, Marital Status, Age and Sex: Series E049 - E114

The notes of the preceding series apply to these data also.

Sources: 1951: (Census, 1952a: 12-13); 1957: (Census, 1958b: 12-13); 1958: (Census, 1958c: 14); 1959: (Census, 1960c: 18); 1960: (Census, 1962b: 19-20); 1961: (Census, 1962c: 21-22); 1962: (Census, 1964b: 27-30); 1963: (Census, 1965b: 28-33); 1964: (Census, 1965c: 24); 1965: (Census, 1966c: 22-23); 1966: (Census, 1966d: 18-19); 1967: (Census, 1968b: 16-17); 1968: (Census, 1969f: 23-27); 1969: (Census, 1969g: 23-28).

The following refer to the statistical series:

a/ - Census reports on mobility status include members of the U. S. Armed Forces living off post or with their families on post; all other members of the Armed Forces are excluded. The 1969 survey included about 1,028,000 members of the Armed Forces. The "other marital status" category in Series E097-E114 comprises married, spouse absent; separated; widowed; and divorced.

b/ - Data not **shown** here for those who moved to a different house in the same county, nor for those who moved to their current residence from a location outside the United States. Therefore the percents will not add to 100.

c/ - In the 1957 report, the age groups 25-34 years and 35-44 years are grouped into a single category: 24-44 years.

d/ - Data for 1958 are for the category "45 years and older" and are therefore not comparable with other years.

Percent Distribution of Persons, by Mobility Status, Relationship to Head of Household, Age and Sex: Series E115 - E210

For definitions, see the references and explanations to Notes to Series E001-E048. In these series the percent who moved to a different house in the same county are not shown. By subtraction of the percents shown from 100 the percent of within-county movers plus the percent moving to the county from outside the United States may be obtained.

Sources: 1963: (Census, 1965b: 20-21); 1964: (Census, 1965c: 26-27); 1965: (Census, 1966c: 25-26); 1966: (Census, 1966d: 21-22); 1967: (Census, 1968b: 19-20); 1968: (Census, 1969f: 16-17); 1969: (Census, 1969g: 16-17).

The following refer to the statistical series:

a/ - Census reports on mobility status include members of the U. S. Armed Forces living off post or with their families on post; all other members of the Armed Forces are excluded. The 1969 survey included an estimate of about 1,028,000 members of the Armed Forces.

b/ - Percents were not computed by the Census Bureau where the base was less than the following numbers of persons: for the year ending March, 1967, and earlier years: 150,000 persons; for the year ending March, 1968, and later years: 75,000 persons.

c/ - Data not shown here for those who moved to a different house in the same county, nor for those who moved to their current residence from a location outside the United States. Because of this the percents do not add to 100.

Population, Labor Force, by Sex: Series F001 - F012

The principal labor force terms applicable to these series are presented below, from (Census, 1969d: 8):

>"Labor force and employment status -- The definitions of labor force and employment status in this report relate to the population 14 years old and over.

>"Employed -- Employed persons comprise (1) all civilians who, during the specified week, did any work at all as paid employees or in their own business or profession, or on their own farm, or who worked 15 hours or more as unpaid workers on a farm or in a business operated by a member of the family, and

(2) all those who were not working but who had jobs or businesses from which they were temporarily absent because of illness, bad weather, vacation, or labor-management dispute, or because they were taking time off for personal reasons, whether or not they were paid by their employers for time off, and whether or not they were seeking other jobs. Excluded from the employed group are persons whose only activity consisted of work around the house (such as own home housework, painting or repairing own home, etc.) or volunteer work for religious, charitable, and similar organizations.

"Unemployed -- Unemployed persons are those civilians who, during the survey week, had no employment but were available for work and (1) had engaged in any specific jobseeking activity within the past 4 weeks, such as registering at a public or private employment office, meeting with prospective employers, checking with friends or relatives, placing or answering advertisements, writing letters of application, or being on a union or professional register; (2) were waiting to be called back to a job from which they had been laid off; or (3) were waiting to report to a new wage or salary job within 30 days.

"Labor force -- Persons are classified as in the labor force if they were employed as civilians, unemployed, or in the Armed Forces during the survey week. The 'civilian labor force' is comprised of all civilians classified as employed or unemployed.

"Not in the labor force -- All civilians 14 years old and over who are not classified as employed or unemployed are defined as 'not in the labor force. This group who are neither employed nor seeking work includes persons engaged only in own home housework, attending school, or unable to work because of long-term physical or mental illness; persons who are retired or too old to work; seasonal workers for whom the survey week fell in an off season; and the voluntarily idle. Persons doing only unpaid family work (less than 15 hours) are also classified as not in the labor force.

"Paid labor force -- Persons are classified in the paid labor force if they were employed as wage and salary workers or self-employed workers during the survey week or were looking for work at the time and had last worked as wage and salary or self-employed workers."

Sources: Data are from the Manpower Report of the President, 1970 (Labor, 1970: 215-217).

Labor Force Participation Rates, by Age and Sex: Series F013 - F030

For definitions, see preceding Notes to Series F001 - F012.

Source: (Labor, 1970: 216-217).

The following refers to the statistical series:

a/ - Labor force participation rate is the percent of the noninstitutional population in the labor force.

Labor Force Participation Rates, by Age, Color, and Sex: Series F031 - F070

The definitions presented above, Series F001-F012, apply also to these series. For the definition of the classification by color, see Notes to Series H001-H008. Footnote is the same as footnote a/, above, Series F013-F030.

Source: (Labor, 1970: 219).

Labor Force Participation Rates, by Marital Status, Age, and Sex: Series F071 - F118

Definitions of labor force concepts referred to above apply (Series F001-F012). For definitions of marital status, see Notes to Series C001-C160.

Sources: 1957-1968: (BLS, 1969a: 32); 1969 from unpublished data provided by the Bureau of Labor Statistics.

The following refer to the statistical series:

a/ - Percent of civilian noninstitutional population in the civilian labor force.

b/ - Beginning with 1966, data revised to refer to persons 16 years of age and over and persons 16 to 17 years old (instead of 14 to 17) in accordance with changes introduced in January 1967. This change affects rates for "all ages" and for the 14-17 year group, especially in the "single" category.

c/ - Percent not shown where base is less than 50,000.

Labor Force Participation, Married Women (Husband Present), by Number and Age of Children: Series F119 - F124

For labor force definitions, see Notes to Series F001-F012, and Notes to Series C001-C160 for the definition of marital status. Footnote is the same as footnote a/ to Series F013-F030.

Sources: Series F119 from successive issues of "Marital Status and Family Status," P-20 series of Current Population Reports, as follows: 1948: (Census, 1949b: 10); 1949: (Census, 1950b: 10); 1950: (Census, 1951b: 10); 1951: (Census, 1952b: 10); 1952: (Census, 1953e: 10); 1953: (Census, 1953f: 9); 1954: (Census, 1955d: 6); 1955: (Census, 1955e: 8); 1956: (Census, 1956b: 9); 1957: (Census, 1958d: 8); 1958: (Census, 1958e: 9); 1959: (Census, 1959b: 7); 1960: (Census, 1960d: 8); 1961: (Census, 1962d: 7); 1962: (Census, 1963e: 9); 1963 and 1964: (Census, 1965d: 9, 10); 1965: (Census, 1965e: 10); 1966: (Census, 1967c: 7); 1967: (Census, 1968c: 9); 1968: (Census, 1969h: 12); 1969: (Census, 1970d: 11). Series F120-F124 from (Labor, 1970: 248).

Labor Force Participation of Wives, by Husband's Employment Status: Series F125 - F132

Definitions presented for Series F001-F012 and C001-C160 apply also to this series.

Source: (Labor, 1970: 247).

The following refers to the statistical series:

a/ - Includes members of Armed Forces living off post or with their families on post.

Employed Males and Females in Civilian Labor Force, by Occupation: Series F133 - F164

Employment status definitions are presented in Notes to Series F001-F012. Definitions of occupations are presented in Notes to Series H018-H079.

Sources: (Labor, 1967: 211-212; 1970: 225-226).

The following refers to the statistical series:

a/ - The change in age of population covered by the survey to exclude the 14 and 15 year olds is explained in footnote b/ in Notes to Series F071-F118.

Occupational Status Index: Series F165 - F166

The Status Index of Occupations, by sex, was developed by weighting the occupational distribution (Series F135-F164) with the weights developed by the Bureau of the Census in its report on socioeconomic status in the 1960 Census. The Socioeconomic Status report presents the "score" for 494 occupational categories (Census, 1967j: 264-267) and for the nine major categories (Census, 1967j: 268). The "scores" for occupations are a combination of the average levels of education and income in 1950 and are based upon data for males. In our occupational categories, household workers are separated from other service workers and sales workers are separated from clerical and kindred workers. The "scores" for each of these were computed from the Census Bureau scores by weighting the scores with the 1960 population in each occupation. The final weights used were, as follows:

Professional, technical and kindred	90
Managers, officials, and proprietors (except farm)	81
Clerical and kindred workers	74
Sales workers	68
Craftsmen, foremen and kindred workers	58
Operatives and kindred workers	45
Service workers (other than private household)	42
Laborers (except farm and mine)	20
Farmers and farm managers	16
Private household workers	10
Farm laborers and foremen	6

The above procedure could be improved upon. Weights could be developed using the data for males and females combined, and they could be developed for each decennial census in order that the possibility that changes in the assessment of an occupation (in terms of the education and the income of the incumbents) would be accounted for. In addition, a more comprehensive and precise study would be based upon the male and female population within each of the 494 occupational categories, rather than the eleven categories employed here.

Employed Females as Percent of Employed Persons, by Occupation: Series F167 - F182

Definitions, footnote, and sources are the same as for Series F133-F164, above.

Index of Sexual Segregation: Series F183

Data used to develop this index is Series F135-F164, the percent distribution of employed workers by sex. For each occupational category, the absolute difference between the percent male and the percent female is divided by 2. The index is the sum of these quotients. This method was used by Gross (1968: 201), and follows the original method developed by the Duncans (Duncan and Duncan, 1955).

Educational Attainment of Labor Force: Series F184 - F211

Labor force definitions are presented as Notes to Series F001-F012. The definition of years of school completed is presented as Notes to Series H104-H163.

Source: (Labor, 1970: 255).

The following refers to the statistical series:

a/ - Data for persons whose educational attainment was not reported were distributed proportionately among the reported categories.

Unemployment Rates, by Age, Color and Sex: Series G01 - G36

Labor force concepts and definitions are presented in the Notes to Series F001-F012.

Source: (Labor, 1970: 231).

Unemployment Rates, by Marital Status and Sex: Series G37 - G44

In addition to the labor force definitions specified above, marital status definitions are presented in the Notes to Series C001-C160.

The following refer to the statistical series:

a/ - The unemployment rate is the percent of the civilian labor force for the group.

b/ - Beginning with 1966, the data were revised to refer to persons 16 years of age and over, in accordance with change introduced in January, 1967.

c/ - Beginning with 1967, data may not be strictly comparable because of basic changes in concepts and definitions introduced in January, 1967.

Source: (Labor, 1970: 234).

Unemployment Rates for Persons 20 Years Old and Over, by Marital Status, Color and Sex:
Series G45 - G56

Definitions applicable to Series G37-G44, above, apply to this series also. Footnote a/ of those series also applies to Series G45-G56.

Sources: Unpublished data supplied by the U.S. Bureau of Labor Statistics. See, also (Ferriss, 1970: 84).

No Money Income, Median Income: Series H001 - H008

From the Consumer Income series of data collected each month through the Current Population Survey, the major definitions are, as follows (Census, 1969d: 4-12):

"Income -- For each person in the sample 14 years old and over, questions were asked on the amount of money income received in the preceding calendar year from each of the following sources: (1) Money wages or salary; (2) net income from nonfarm self-employment; (3) net income from farm self-employment; (4) Social Security; (5) dividends, interest (on savings or bonds), income from estates or trusts or net rental income; (6) public assistance or welfare payments; (7) unemployment compensation, government employee pensions, or veterans' payments; (8) private pensions, annuities, alimony, regular contributions from persons not living in this household, royalties, and other periodic income.

"The amounts received represent income before deductions for personal taxes, Social Security, bonds, etc. When an indefinite amount was reported by the respondent, a specific value was assigned during processing wherever possible. If the indefinite amount was reported in terms of a range, the midpoint of the range was assigned (i.e., $10,000 to $15,000 was coded as $12,500). Open-ended amounts were converted to designated specific amounts; e.g., over $10,000 was coded as $16,000.

"It should be noted that although the income statistics refer to receipts during the preceding year the characteristics of the person, such as age, labor force status, etc., and the composition of families refer to the time of the survey. The income of the family does not include amounts received by persons who were members of the family during all or part of the income year if these persons no longer resided with the family at the time of enumeration. On the other hand, family income includes amounts reported by related persons who did not reside with the family during the income year but who were members of the family at the time of enumeration.

"Data on consumer income collected by the Bureau of the Census cover money income (exclusive of certain money receipts such as capital gains) prior to deductions for taxes. The fact that many farm families receive part of their income in the form of rent-free housing and goods produced and consumed on the farm, rather than in money, should be taken into consideration in comparing the income of farm and nonfarm residents. It should be noted that nonmoney incomes are also received by some nonfarm residents. They often take the form of business expense accounts, use of business transportation and facilities, full or partial compensation by business for medical and educational expenses, etc. In analyzing size distributions

272

of income, it should be recognized that capital gains tend to be concentrated more among higher income units than among lower ones.

"The various sources for which income is reported are defined as follows:

"Money wages or salary is total money earnings received for work performed as an employee during the income year. It includes wages, salary, Armed Forces pay, commissions, tips, piece-rate payments, and cash bonuses earned, before deductions were made for taxes, bonds, pensions, union dues, etc.

"Net income from nonfarm self-employment is net money income (gross receipts minus expenses) from his own business, professional enterprise, or partnership. Gross receipts include the value of all goods sold and services rendered. Expenses include costs of goods purchased, rent, heat, light, power, depreciation charges, wages and salaries paid, business taxes (not personal income taxes), etc. The value of salable merchandise consumed by the proprietors of retail stores is not included as part of net income.

"Net income from farm self-employment is net money income (gross receipts minus operating expenses) from the operation of a farm by a person on his own account, as an owner, renter, or sharecropper. Gross receipts include the value of all products sold, government crop loans, money received from the rental of farm equipment to others, and incidental receipts from the sale of wood, sand, gravel, etc. Operating expenses include cost of feed, fertilizer, seed, and other farming supplies, cash wages paid to farmhands, depreciation charges, cash rent, interest on farm mortgages, farm building repairs, farm taxes (not State and Federal income taxes), etc. The value of fuel, food, or other farm products used for family living is not included as part of net income. In general, inventory changes were not considered in determining net income; however, replies based on income tax returns of other official records do reflect inventory changes.

"Social Security includes Social Security pensions and survivors' benefits, and permanent disability insurance payments made by the Social Security Administration prior to deductions for medical insurance and railroad retirement insurance checks from the U. S. Government.

"Dividends, interest (on savings or bonds), income from estates or trusts, or net rental income includes dividends from stockholdings or membership in associations, interest on savings or bonds, periodic receipts from estates or trust funds, net income from rental of a house, store, or other property to others, and receipts from boarders or lodgers.

"Public assistance or welfare payments include public assistance payments such as old-age assistance, aid to families with dependent children, and aid to the blind or totally disabled.

"Unemployment compensation, government employee pensions, or veterans' payments include: (1) Unemployment compensation received from government unemployment insurance agencies or private companies during periods of unemployment and any strike benefits received from union funds; (2) government employee pensions received from retirement pensions paid by Federal, State, county, or other governmental agencies to former employees (including members of the Armed Forces) or their survivors; (3) money paid periodically by the Veterans' Administration to disabled members of the Armed Forces and to survivors of deceased veterans, subsistence allowances paid to veterans for education and on-the-job training, as well as so-called "refunds" paid to ex-servicemen as GI insurance premiums; also includes (4) workmen's compensation received periodically from public or private insurance companies for injuries incurred at work. The cost of this insurance must have been paid by the employer and not by the person.

"Private pensions, annuities, alimony, regular contribution from persons not living in the household, royalties, and other periodic income include the following types of income: (1) Private pensions or retirement benefits paid to a retired person or his survivors by a former employer or by a union, either directly or through an insurance company; (2) periodic receipts from annuities or insurance; (3) alimony and child support; (4) contributions received periodically from persons not living in the household; (5) net royalties; and (6) other periodic income such as military family allotments, net gambling winnings, and other kinds of periodic income other than earnings.

"Receipts not counted as income -- Receipts from the following sources were not included as income: (1) Money received from the sale of property, such as stocks, bonds, a house, or a car (unless the person was engaged in the business of selling such property, in which case the net proceeds would be counted as income from self-employment); (2) withdrawals of bank deposits; (3) money borrowed; (4) tax refunds; (5) gifts; and (6) lump-sum inheritances or insurance payments.

"All sources of income may be combined into two major types:

"Total money earnings -- the algebraic sum of money wages or salary and net income from farm and nonfarm self-employment; and

"Income other than earnings - the algebraic sum of all sources of money income except wages and salaries and income from self-employment.

"Total money income -- The algebraic sum of money wages and salaries, net income from self-employment, and income other than earnings represents total money income. The total income of a family is the algebraic sum of the amounts received by all income recipients in the family.

"The income tables for families and unrelated individuals include in the lowest income group (under $1,000) those that were classified as having no income in the income year and those reporting a loss in net income from farm and nonfarm self-employment or in rental income. Many of these were living on income "in kind," savings, or gifts; or were newly constituted families, unrelated individuals who had recently left families, or families in which the sole breadwinner had recently died or had left the household. However, many of the families and unrelated individuals who reported no income probably had some money income which was not recorded in the survey.

"Median income -- The median income is the amount which divides the distribution into two equal groups, one having incomes above the median, and the other having incomes below the median. The medians for families and individuals are based on all families and individuals. The medians for persons are based on the distributions of persons with income. The medians for wage or salary income, income from nonfarm self-employment, income from farm self-employment, and income other than earnings are based on the distributions of persons or families and individuals having these types of income."

"Race -- The population is divided into three groups on the basis of race: white, Negro, and "other races." The last category includes Indians, Japanese, Chinese, and any other race except white and Negro. "Other races" are usually shown in combination with the Negro population."

Current dollars were converted to constant 1968 dollars by applying the following factors: 1956, 1.280; 1957, 1.237; 1958, 1.204; 1959, 1.194; 1960, 1.176; 1961, 1.163; 1962, 1.150; 1963, 1.136; 1964, 1.121; 1965, 1.103; 1966, 1.072; 1967, 1.042; 1968, 1.000; 1969, 0.949. These factors are quotients of the Bureau of Labor Statistics Consumer Price Index for 1968 divided by the BLS Consumer Price Index for each year. The BLS Consumer Price Index for All Items is based upon 1957-58 = 100 (BLS, 1970b: 112) and (Labor, 1970: 328).

Sources: The annual P-60, Consumer Income Reports of the U. S. Bureau of the Census, as follows: 1956: (Census, 1958f: 33); 1957: (Census, 1958g: 32); 1958: (Census, 1960f: 34); 1959: (Census 1961b: 37); 1960: (Census, 1962e: 39); 1961: (Census, 1963f: 29); 1962: (Census, 1963g: 37, 39); 1963: (Census, 1964c: 34); 1964: (Census, 1965f: 36); 1965 and 1966: (Census, 1967e: 20, 36); 1967: (Census, 1969c: 19); 1968: (Census, 1969d: 85).

The following refers to the statistical series:

a/ - These two medians are from unpublished data provided by the U. S. Bureau of the Census. The report giving 1968 data (Census, 1969d: 85) gives data for Negroes but not for 'nonwhite'.

Annual Earnings, Year-Round, Full-Time Workers by Color: Series H009 - H017

The ratios, multiplied by 100, presented as Series H015-H017, were calculated from Series H009-H014, respectively. For definitions, see notes to Series H001-H008.

Other applicable definitions follow (Census, 1969d: 8-9):

"Part-time or full-time jobs -- A person is classified as having worked at part-time jobs, during the preceding calendar year, if he worked at civilian jobs which provided less than 35 hours of work per week in a majority of the weeks in which he worked during the year. He is classified as having worked at full-time jobs if he worked 35 hours or more per week during a majority of the weeks in which he worked.

"Year-round full-time worker -- A year-round full-time worker is one who worked primarily at full-time civilian jobs (35 hours or more per week) for 50 weeks or more during the preceding calendar year.

"Nonworker -- A nonworker is one who did not do any civilian work in the calendar year preceding the survey."

Sources: The P-60, Consumer Income Series of the U. S. Bureau of the Census, as follows: 1956: (Census, 1958f: 46, 47); 1957: (Census, 1958g: 45, 46); 1958: (Census, 1960f: 50, 51); 1959: (Census, 1961b: 51, 52); 1960: (Census, 1962e: 47, 54); 1961 (Census, 1963f: 37, 44); 1962: (Census, 1963g: 45, 51); 1963: (Census, 1964c: 44, 50); 1964: (Census, 1965f: 45, 51); 1965: (Census, 1967d: 40, 46); 1966: (Census, 1967e: 45, 51); 1967: (Census, 1969c: 36, 57); 1968: (Census, 1969d: 103, 127).

Annual Earnings, Year-Round, Full-Time Workers by Occupation: Series H018 - H079

For applicable definitions, see notes to Series H001-H008. In the CPS, occupation is defined, as follows (Census, 1969d: 8):

"Occupation, industry, and class of worker -- The data on occupation, class of worker, and employment status....refer to the job held during the survey week. Persons employed at two or more jobs were reported in the job at which they worked the greatest number of hours during the week.

"The data on occupation and industry....refer to the job held longest during the income year.

"In several tables two or more of the major occupation groups are subdivided by class of worker into two groups: Wage and salary workers and self-employed workers. The former refers to persons working for wages, salaries, commissions, tips, paid 'in kind', or at piece rates for a private employer, or for any governmental unit. The latter refers to persons working in their own business, profession or trade, for profit or fees. Included in the self-employed groups in these tables are unpaid family workers, i.e., persons working without pay in a business operated by a member of the household to whom they are related by blood, marriage, or adoption.

"The occupation and industry groupings used here are mainly the major groups used in the 1960 Census of Population. The composition of these groups is shown in Volume I, Characteristics of the Population, Part 1, United States Summary, Chapter D.

Sources: The P-60, Consumer Income Reports of the U. S. Bureau of the Census, as follows: 1956: (Census, 1958f: 46, 47); 1957: (Census, 1958g: 45, 46); 1958: (Census, 1960f: 50, 51); 1959 (Census, 1961b: 51); 1960: (Census, 1962e: 47); 1961: (Census, 1963f: 37); 1962: (Census, 1963g: 45); 1963: (Census, 1964c: 44); 1964: (Census, 1965f: 45); 1965: (Census, 1967d: 40); 1966: (Census, 1967e: 45); 1967: (Census, 1969c: 36); 1968: (Census, 1969d: 103-105); 1969: (Census, 1970i: 6).

The following refers to the statistical series:

a/ - This table omits occupational categories with fewer than 75,000 full-time year-round female workers in 1968, except for the category, "professional, self-employed." Occupational categories omitted, however, are included in the totals.

Ratio, Female to Male Earnings: Series H080 - H087

These ratios, multiplied by 100, were computed from applicable data of the corresponding Series H018-H079.

Sources: See notes to the Series H018-H079.

Employed Civilians, Percent with No Income, and Income of Income Recipients, by Occupation: Series H088 - H103

For definitions of employment status, income, occupation, and other relevant usages, see notes to Series H001-H008 and to Series H018-H079. Median income is based upon income recipients only.

Sources: The P-60, Consumer Income Reports of the U. S. Bureau of the Census, as follows: 1956: (Census, 1958f: 38, 39); 1957: (Census, 1958g: 36, 37); 1958: (Census, 1960f: 40, 41); 1959: (Census, 1961b: 41, 42); 1960: (Census, 1962e: 43, 44); 1961: (Census, 1963f: 33, 34); 1962: (Census, 1963g: 41, 42); 1963: (Census, 1964c: 40, 41); 1964: (Census, 1965f: 41, 42); 1965: (Census, 1967d: 36, 37); 1966: (Census, 1967e: 41, 42); 1967: (Census, 1969c: 35); 1968: (Census, 1969d: 102).

The following refers to the statistical series:

a/ - 1958 and earlier: median not shown where there were fewer than 100 sample cases reporting "with income;" 1959-1964: median not shown where base is less than 200,000 population; 1965: median not shown where base is less than 150,000; 1966 and later: median not shown where base is less than 75,000.

For relevant definitions concerning income, see notes to Series H001-H008. Conversion of income to constant dollars is also explained in those notes. Years of school completed is based upon the following (Census, 1969d: 7):

> "Years of school completed -- Data on years of school completed in this report
> were derived from the combination of answers to questions concerning the highest
> grade of school attended by the person and whether or not that grade was finished.
> The questions on educational attainment apply only to progress in "regular"
> schools. Such schools include graded public, private and parochial elementary and
> high schools (both junior and senior high), colleges, universities, and profes-
> sional schools, whether day schools or night schools. Thus, regular schooling is
> that which may advance a person toward an elementary school certificate or a high
> school diploma, or a college, university, or professional school degree. Schooling
> in other than regular schools was counted only if the credits obtained were regarded
> as transferable to a school in the regular school system."

Sources: The P-60, Consumer Income Reports of the U. S. Bureau of the Census, as follows: 1963: (Census, 1964c: 39); 1964: (Census, 1965f: 39, 40); 1965: (Census, 1967d: 34, 35); 1966: (Census, 1967e: 39, 40); 1967: (Census, 1969c: 27-34); 1968: (Census, 1969d: 94-101).

The following refers to the statistical series:

* - Age is as of March of the year following the income year.

Percent With or Without Money Income in Current Year by Employment Status: Series H164 - H176

The income status (money income or no money income) refers to the year indicated in the stub, while the employment status is as of the time of the survey, i.e., March of the year following the "current year" in the stub. As in most of the personal characteristics reported in the Consumer Income surveys, characteristics are as of the time the data were collected. For definitions of the characteristics in this table, see notes to Series H001-H008.

Sources: See sources to Series H088-H103.

Median Income by Type of Family, 1st and 4th Quintiles, Interquintile Range and Coefficient: Series H177 - H206

Definitions of terms and concepts in the survey relative to income are given in notes to the Series H001-H008. Definitions relative to family status, unrelated individuals, etc., are presented with notes to Series C001-C187.

Quintiles were calculated from the percentage distributions presented in the sources. The first quintile was calculated from the lower end of the distribution and the upper limit of the fourth quintile was calculated from the upper end of the distribution. Medians are given in the source tables. The values were converted to 1968 dollars by use of the conversion factors reported in notes to Series H001-H008.

The Coefficient is a surrogate for the Coefficient of Variation. It is the interquintile range divided by the median.

Sources: The P-60, Consumer Income Reports of the U. S. Bureau of the Census, as follows: 1956: (Census, 1958f: 22); 1957: (Census, 1958g: 20); 1958: (Census, 1960f: 20); 1959: (Census, 1961b: 24); 1960: (Census, 1962e: 26); 1961: (Census, 1963f: 17); 1962: (Census, 1963g: 26); 1963: (Census, 1964c: 22); 1964: (Census, 1965f: 24); 1965: (Census, 1967d: 19); 1966: (Census, 1967e: 24); 1967: (Census, 1969b: 32); 1968: (Census, 1969d: 28).

The following refers to the statistical series:

a/ - Medians and quintiles of income are based on the distribution of all families and unrelated individuals in a given category, regardless of whether or not they had money income during the current year.

Median Earnings of Income Recipients, by Years of School Completed and by Color: Series H207 - H226

For definitions, see notes to Series H001-H008 and Series H104-H163.

Sources: The P-60, Consumer Income Reports of the U. S. Bureau of the Census, as follows: 1961: (Census, 1963f: 32); 1963: (Census, 1964c: 37, 38); 1964: (Census, 1965f: 39, 40); 1965: (Census, 1967d: 34, 35); 1966: (Census, 1967e: 39, 40); 1967: (Census, 1969c: 30, 34); 1968: (Census, 1969d: 97, 101).

The following refers to the statistical series:

a/ - Median income is based upon the income of income recipients only. Data for income by educational attainment was not published in the 1962 reports.

Persons below Poverty Level, by Color: Series H227 - H242

For standard definitions, see notes to Series H001-H008.

The concept of poverty is explained (Census, 1969k: 11) as follows:

"The Poverty Definition -- Poverty statistics published in previous Census Bureau reports were based on the poverty index developed by the Social Security Administration (SSA) in 1964.[1] This index provided a range of poverty income cutoffs adjusted by such factors as family size, the sex of the family head, the age of family members, and place of residence. At the core of this definition of poverty was a nutritionally adequate food plan ("economy" plan) designed by the Department of Agriculture for "emergency or temporary use when funds are low." Annual revisions of the poverty income cutoffs were based on price changes of the items in the economy food budget.

---

[1] For a detailed discussion of the SSA poverty standards, see Mollie Orshansky, "Counting the Poor: Another Look at the Poverty Profile," Social Security Bulletin, January 1965; and "Who's Who Among the Poor: A Demographic View of Poverty," Social Security Bulletin, July, 1965.

"In determining the proportion of total family income that should be consumed
by food requirements, the SSA observed that the percentage of income expended
for necessities, in particular food, reflects the relative well being of both
individuals and the society in which they live. In general, families that need
to use about the same proportion of their income for a given level of food
expenditure are considered to share the same level of living. For families of
three or more persons the poverty level was set at three times the cost of the
economy food plan. This was the average food cost-to-family income relationship reported by the Department of Agriculture on the basis of a 1955 survey of
food consumption.[2/] For smaller families and persons residing alone, the cost
of the economy food plan was multiplied by factors that were slightly larger to
compensate for the relatively higher fixed expenses of these smaller households.
The SSA poverty cutoffs also took account of differences in the cost of living
between farm and nonfarm families.

"As a result of the deliberations of a Federal Interagency Committee the
following two changes were incorporated into the definition of poverty employed
prior to 1969: (1) the SSA poverty thresholds were retained for the base year
1963, but annual adjustments in the poverty levels were based on the changes in
the Consumer Price Index (CPI) rather than on changes in the cost of food in
the economy food plans; and (2) farm poverty thresholds were raised from 70 to
85 percent of the corresponding nonfarm levels. The resulting poverty thresholds
for 1968 are presented in table I. The combined impact of these two modifications resulted in a net increase of 360,000 poor families and of 1.6 million poor
persons in 1967. The reasons for making these changes and the effect of each
revision on the poverty data are outlined below."

Table I. Weighted Average Thresholds at the Poverty Level in 1968 by Size of Family
and Sex of Head, by Farm-Nonfarm Residence

Number of family members	Total	Nonfarm			Farm		
		Total	Male head	Female head	Total	Male head	Female head
1 member	$1,742	$1,748	$1,827	$1,700	$1,487	$1,523	$1,441
2 members	2,242	2,262	2,272	2,202	1,904	1,910	1,812
3 members	2,754	2,774	2,788	2,678	2,352	2,359	2,258
4 members	3,531	3,553	3,555	3,536	3,034	3,031	3,018
5 members	4,158	4,188	4,191	4,142	3,577	3,578	3,565
6 members	4,664	4,706	4,709	4,670	4,021	4,021	4,020
7 or more members	5,722	5,789	5,804	5,638	4,916	4,919	4,847

2/ See U. S. Department of Agriculture, Food Consumption and Dietary Levels of Households in
the United States (ARS 626), August 1957.

(Census, 1969k: 11) also presents a table (Table J) showing the effects of the change in the cost of living adjustment, comparing 1959, 1963 and 1967. Compared with the original definitions, the revised definition for 1969 includes approximately 1.6 million more persons in poverty than would the original (1959) definition, had it been in use.

Sources: 1959-1968: (Census, 1969k: 21, 24); 1969 from unpublished data provided by the U. S. Bureau of the Census.

The following refer to the statistical series:

a/ - Definitions of poverty, presented above, were revised in 1966 and 1968. Data for 1967 not strictly comparable with 1966 and 1968.

b/ - Changes in the methodology relative to the poverty definition are elaborated upon in (Census, 1969k: 13, 15, 16).

Persons 65 Years of Age and Over with No Money Income: Series H243-- H246

For definitions, see notes to Series H001-H008. Age is based on the age at last birthday.

Sources: 1956: (Census, 1958f: 34); 1957: (Census, 1958g: 33); 1958: (Census, 1960f: 35); 1959: (Census, 1961b: 38); 1960: (Census, 1962e: 40); 1961: (Census, 1963f: 30); 1962: (Census, 1963g: 40); 1963: (Census, 1964c: 36); 1964: (Census, 1965f: 38); 1965: (Census, 1967d: 33); 1966: (Census, 1967e: 38); 1967: (Census, 1969c: 25); 1968: (Census, 1969d: 90).

Membership in Voluntary Organizations: Series I003 - I023

In assembling the membership information, the three sources (below) were recorded and compared. In some instances a selection had to be arbitrarily made of the membership figure that appeared to be most consistent in the time series. The membership for each year 1960-1969 was collected. However, since data for years other than 1961, 1964 and 1968 were not recorded for many of the organizations, only these three years are presented.

If the data were not available for each of the years, 1961, 1964, and 1968, the organization was excluded. This procedure leads to a reduced aggregate for 1968, but at the same time the year-to-year growth rate is more accurate.

Since our interest is to detect changes over time in the membership composition of various types of organizations, it was of primary importance that the organizations be included in each year in the series. An organization that went out of existence would not be included, and an organization that came into existence during the interval, 1961-1968, would not be included. This introduces errors in the aggregate number of members, but it makes possible a more accurate detection of shifts in the type of organizations to which women belong.

Organizations that predominately or exclusively serve women were identified through the sources, cited below. The purposes and objectives of these organizations were reviewed to identify the primary function. The 15 types of organizations were identified after several

attempts to develop a homogeneous classification scheme. The types of organizations are identified below, with a brief description and an identification of representative organizations in
each.

Girls' Organizations: Eight recreational and character-building organizations: Scouts,
homemakers, religious-oriented social clubs, and Y.W.C.A. Girl Scouts is the largest single
organization.

Educational: Thirteen organizations of college alumnae; educational workers, such as deans,
physical education directors, and educational administrators; fraternal honorary groups in
specialized fields; and the American Association of University Women. International Federation
of Catholic Alumnae is the largest organization.

Business, Industry and Professional (except Education and Sports): Professional includes
32 organizations and fraternal groups, each relatively small, and each centering upon a profession: ministers, chiropractors, physicians, accountants, dentists, architects, musicians,
home economists, journalists, and so forth. The largest organization is Sigma Alpha Iota, a
music sorority, with nearly 42,000 members in 1968.

Business or Industry: Twenty-one organizations of women, comprising workers in commercial
or industrial areas, no unions being included. Membership in most of these organizations is
small, the largest being Alpha Iota, an honorary business sorority, and the National Secretaries
Association. Types of businesses, industries, and occupations include: motion picture industry,
secretarial, fashions, radio and television, personnel, banks, insurance, construction, etc.

In addition, two federations of business and professional women's clubs are combined in
this category, the largest being the National Federation of Business and Professional Women's
Clubs with 178,300 members in 1968.

Service Organizations: Thirteen community service and consumer organizations, ranging in
size from 1,000 to 158,000 members in 1968, the largest being the P.E.O. Sisterhood. Included
are U. S. members of Altrusa, Venture Clubs, Toastmistress Clubs, Achievement Clubs, Pilot Club
International, Quota International, Soroptimist, and others.

Social Welfare: Six fairly large organizations of lay women devoted to welfare and social
service work, the largest being the Y.W.C.A. (except "Y" teens), consisting of 1,830,000 members in 1968. Other predominant groups are: National Women's Christian Temperance Union
(250,000), and American Women's Voluntary Services (605,000 in 1968). The Needlework Guild, with
1968 membership of one-half million members, was excluded because the 1961 data were unavailable.

Rural Life, Farm and Garden: Six organizations of women in farm bureau, agricultural
extension, homemakers organizations and the like. The largest is the Country Women's Council,
U.S.A., with three million women. Garden clubs likely to have men as members are excluded.

Sports and Recreation: Four organizations numerically dominated by the Women's International
Bowling Congress (over 2,800,000 in 1968). Three small organizations in curling, lacrosse, and
squash are omitted because the time series were incomplete.

Religious-affiliated Organizations: Twenty-five organizations that appear to be primarily religious in affiliation and function. Among the organizations with more than 200,000 members in 1968 are: Catholic Daughters of America, Hadassah, Lutheran Women's Missionary League, and National Women's League of the United Synagogue of America. Most of the large religious denominations are represented, but it was necessary to exclude three organizations because the time series were incomplete; these Baptist, Lutheran and Catholic organizations had an aggregate 1968 membership of 1,216,000. In addition, three national councils of churchwomen provided the predominant membership of this category, some 24 million: National Council of Catholic Women, National Council of Jewish Women, and Church Women United.

Fraternal and Ethnic Organizations: Twenty-six sororal organizations, women's auxiliaries to fraternal organizations, or organizations whose members share a common national origin. The largest, with approximately three million members, is the Order of the Eastern Star. Two organizations were excluded because of incomplete data, their membership totaling 63,000 in 1968.

Relatives of Members of the Armed Services: Nineteen organizations, primarily auxiliaries of servicemen's organizations, but also including widows, mothers, and wives of servicemen. The two largest organizations are the American Legion Auxiliary and the Ladies Auxiliary to the Veterans of Foreign Wars of the United States. Two organizations were excluded because of incomplete information, their 1968 membership being approximately 80,000.

Women Veterans: Five organizations of women veterans who had served as nurses, or in other capacities in the Army, Navy, etc. This category also includes women who served overseas with service organizations such as the Red Cross.

Public Affairs: Five organizations, with the National Federation of Republican Women and the League of Women Voters dominating, numerically.

Federated Clubs: Three organizations characterized by being aggregations of a number of local or national organizations, the purposes covering a wide range of interests. One large federation, numbering five million in 1968, was excluded because the data were not available for 1961. The General Federation of Women's Clubs (800,000 members in the U. S. in 1968) is the largest of these organizations.

Organizations with a Hereditary Basis: Eleven organizations whose members derive from kinship to persons in some historical context. These include membership in the Colonial Army, the Confederate or Federal Forces of the Civil War, the War of 1812, and others who were first settlers. The largest group, with 188,000 members, in 1968, is the National Society Daughters of the American Revolution.

Sources: Population data of Series I001 and I002 are from (Census, 1965g: 9), (Census, 1968c: 16), and (Census, 1970b: 14). Membership data: (Women's Bureau, 1960; 1965; 1969); (Encyclopedia of Associations, 1961; 1964; 1968); (World Almanac, each year 1960 through 1970); and information on membership from selected organizations by personal contact with their headquarters offices. Use of the library of the Business and Professional Women's Foundation facilitated the accumulation of these data.

Membership, Specific Girls' and Women's Associations: Series I024 - I037

Reports of membership were obtained from the national headquarters of the several organizations. The procedure was to assemble as much information as was available from published sources and then to ask the national headquarters of the organization to review, check, and complete the series.

Labor union data are from Series I042.

Column numbers I038-I039 were reserved for organizations that did not supply the information we requested.

Initial Sources: (Women's Bureau, 1948; 1950; 1952; 1954; 1956; 1960; 1965; 1969); (Encyclopedia of Associations, 1961; 1964; 1968); (World Almanac, annual issues, 1940-1970).

Women Members of Unions: Series I040 - I093

Series I042 is estimated by the Bureau of Labor Statistics on the basis of reports from unions and estimates of membership in unions that refused to report their membership. The total numbers of women members of national and international unions, including Canadian and "other," and the percentage that the women are of total union members, are from the BLS bulletins cited in the sources, below. The BLS also gives the number of union members of both sexes in the United States, but not the number of women members in the U. S. It was assumed that the percent of women union members in the United States was the same as the percentage of women are of total union membership (including Canadian and "other"), and the total was adjusted to exclude the Canadian and "other" women members.

Mergers and consolidations of unions and changes in affiliation of locals with nationals make accounting of membership difficult across time.

Sources: These data are assembled by the Bureau of Labor Statistics from the unions and published every other year, as follows: 1952: (BLS, 1953: 46); 1954: (BLS, 1955: 61); 1956: (BLS, 1957: 58-59); 1958: (BLS, 1959: 58-59); 1960: (BLS, 1961: 62-63); 1962: (BLS, 1963b: 66-67); 1964: (BLS, 1965b: 71-72, 53); 1966: (BLS, 1967b: 78-79); 1968: (BLS, 1970a).

The following refer to the statistical series:

a/ - BLS requested the union to give the "approximate percentage of membership who are women." BLS applied these percentages to the reported membership to obtain the estimate of female membership. A few unions submitted a range of percents and in these cases the midpoint of the range was used.

b/ - Data not reported.

c/ - Women members believed by the Bureau of Labor Statistics to account for at least five percent of membership.

Summer Recreation Activity Days per Person, by Age and Sex: Series J01 - J22

Activity days per person are the average number of days participation during June, July, and August for 1960 and 1965. Data were obtained through household interviews of national probability-samples of the population, carried out by the U. S. Bureau of the Census. Activities were listed on a card that was presented to the respondent, and were relative to week-end trips, one-day outings, and vacations, as well as any other outdoor recreation occasion that the respondent might report. All household members present at the time of interview were asked to respond concerning their individual recreational activities. The household respondent(s) gave information for persons not present. Consequently, some underreporting undoubtedly exists. Since the same interviewing procedures were employed in each survey, 1960 and 1965, the data are comparable. However the larger sample in 1965 renders those estimates slightly more relia-ble than the data for 1960. No special definitions are required; the meanings of the recrea-tional activities are straightforward. The grouping of activities was developed by Charles Proctor through use of factor analysis (Proctor, 1962: 77-94).

Sources: 1960: (Ferriss, 1962); 1965: unpublished data supplied by the Bureau of Outdoor Recreation, U. S. Department of the Interior, extracted from an unpublished report, Table C, and from Printout Table 1, the 1965 Survey of Outdoor Recreation Activities.

Restricted Activity Days, by Age and Sex: Series K001 - K016
and by Income and Sex: Series K017 - K032

The Health Interview Survey is the source of the information presented in Series K001 through K100; see Appendix B for detailed information on the survey. Terms relevant to these series K001-K032 are, as follows (NCHS, 1968k: 53):

"Disability -- Disability is a general term used to describe any temporary or long-term reduction of a person's activity as a result of an acute or chronic condition.

"Disability days are classified according to whether they are days of restricted activity, bed-days, hospital days, work-loss days, or school-loss days. All hospital days are, by definition, days of bed disability; all days of bed disability are, by definition, days of restricted activity. The con-verse form of these statements is, of course, not true. Days lost from work and days lost from school are special terms which apply to the working and

285

school-age populations only, but these too are days of restricted activity. Hence, 'days of restricted activity' is the most inclusive term used to describe disability days.

"Restricted-activity day -- A day of restricted activity is a day when a person cuts down on his usual activities for the whole of that day because of an illness or an injury. The term 'usual activities' for any day means the things that the person would ordinarily do on that day. For children under school age, 'usual activities' depend upon whatever the usual pattern is for the child's day which will, in turn, be affected by the age of the child, weather conditions, and so forth. For retired or elderly persons, 'usual activities' might consist of almost no activity, but cutting down on even a small amount for as much as a day would constitute restricted activity. On Sundays or holidays 'usual activities' are taken to be the things the person usually does on such days -- going to church, playing golf, visiting friends or relatives, or staying at home and listening to the radio, reading, looking at television, and so forth.

"Restricted activity does not imply complete inactivity, but it does imply only the minimum of 'usual activities.' A special nap for an hour after lunch does not constitute cutting down on usual activities, nor does the elimination of a heavy chore, such as cleaning ashes out of the furnace or hanging out the wash. If a farmer or housewife carries on only the minimum of the day's chores, however, this is a day of restricted activity.

"A day spent in bed or a day home from work or school because of illness or injury is, of course, a restricted-activity day."

Age is the age of the person as of his last birthday, determined in single years.

Family income is the total 12-month income of the family during the 12 months prior to the week of the interview. All persons in the household who are related to each other by blood, marriage, or adoption, constitute the family. Wages, salaries, rents from property, pensions, and help from relatives, etc., are counted as income.

In the lower right-hand corner of the page containing Series K017-K032 is the income classification as revised in 1966.

Sources: 1958 through 1961 (all data) and 1963, 1965 and 1967 (selected data): provided by courtesy of the National Center for Health Statistics; 1962: (NCHS, 1963a: 27); 1963: (NCHS, 1964b. 27); 1964: (NCHS, 1965i: 29); 1965: (NCHS, 1965e: 17); 1966: (NCHS, 1968k: 29); 1967: (NCHS, 1968f: 20).

Bed Disability Days, by Age and Sex: Series K033 - K048 and
by Income and Sex: Series K049 - K064

See Notes to Series K001-K032. Bed disability days per person per year are defined, as follows (NCHS, 1968k: 53):

"Bed-disability day -- A bed-disability day, sometimes for brevity referred to as a 'bed-day', is a day on which a person was kept in bed either all or most of the day because of an illness or an injury. 'All or most of the day' is defined as more than half of the daylight hours. All hospital days are included as bed-disability days even if the patient was not actually in bed at the hospital".

Sources: 1958 through 1961 (all data) and 1963, 1965 and 1967 (selected data): provided by courtesy of the National Center for Health Statistics. 1962: (NCHS, 1963a: 29); 1963: (NCHS, 1964b: 16); 1964: (NCHS, 1965i: 31); 1965: (NCHS, 1965e: 17); 1966: (NCHS, 1968k: 31); 1967: (NCHS, 1968f: 20).

Work-Loss Days per Currently Employed Person, by Age and Sex: Series K065 - K074
and by Income and Sex: Series K075 - K090

For general information on the Health Interview Survey, see Appendix B. For definitions relative to these series, see Notes to Series K001 - K032. Work-loss days are defined, as follows (NCHS, 1968k: 53):

"Work-loss day -- A day lost from work is a normal working day on which a person did not work at his job or business because of a specific illness or injury. If the person's regular work day is less than a whole day and the entire work day was lost, it would be counted as a whole work day lost. The number of days lost from work is determined only for persons 17 years of age or over who reported that at any time during the 2-week period covered by the interview they either worked at or had a job or business".

The Health Interview Survey concept of "currently employed persons" is presented in Appendix B.

Sources: 1960-1961 (all data) and 1963, 1965, and 1967 (selected data): provided by National Center for Health Statistics. 1962: (NCHS, 1963a: 30); 1963: (NCHS, 1964b: 16); 1964: (NCHS, 1965i: 32); 1965: (NCHS, 1965e: 17); 1966: (NCHS, 1968k: 32); 1967: (NCHS, 1968f: 20).

The following refers to the statistical series:

a/ - "Beginning with the survey year ended June 30, 1962, women were reminded to exclude 'work around the house' in reporting time lost from work. This reminder probably accounts for the reduction in work-loss days from this period (1962) on" (NCHS, 1965i: 53).

Incidence of Acute Conditions, by Sex: Series K091 - K092

Definitions relevant to these series are, as follows (NCHS, 1969f: 52):

"Condition -- A morbidity condition, or simply a condition, is any entry
on the questionnaire which describes a departure from a state of physical or
mental well-being. It results from a positive response to one of a series
of 'illness-recall' questions. In the coding and tabulating process, conditions are selected or classified according to a number of different criteria,
such as, whether they were medically attended; whether they resulted in disability; whether they were acute or chronic; or according to the type of
disease, injury, impairment, or symptom reported. For the purposes of each
published report or set of tables, only those conditions recorded on the
questionnaire which satisfy certain stated criteria are included.

Acute conditions are classified by type according to the International
Classification of Diseases, 1955 Revision, with certain modifications
adopted to make the code more suitable for a household-interview-type survey.

"Acute condition -- An acute condition is defined as a condition which
has lasted less than 3 months and which has involved either medical attention
or restricted activity. Because of the procedures used to estimate incidence,
the acute conditions included in this report are the conditions which had
their onset during the 2 weeks prior to the interview week and which involved
either medical attention or restricted activity during that 2-week period.
However, it excludes certain conditions which are always classified as
chronic (listed below) even though the onset occurred within 3 months.

"Conditions always classified as chronic: Asthma; hay fever; tuberculosis;
chronic bronchitis; repeated attacks of sinus trouble; rheumatic fever;
hardening of the arteries; high blood pressure; heart trouble; stroke; trouble
with varicose veins; stomach ulcer; any other chronic stomach trouble; kidney
stones or chronic kidney trouble; arthritis or rheumatism; mental illness;
diabetes; thyroid trouble or goiter; any allergy; epilepsy; chronic nervous
trouble; cancer; hemorrhoids or piles; tumor, cyst, or growth; chronic gall-
bladder or liver trouble; deafness or serious trouble with hearing; serious
trouble with seeing, even when wearing glasses; cleft palate; any speech
defect; missing fingers, hand, or arm - toes, foot, or leg; palsy; chronic
skin trouble; hernia or rupture; prostate trouble; paralysis of any kind;
repeated trouble with back or spine; club foot; permanent stiffness or any
deformity of the foot, leg, fingers, arm, or back; condition present since
birth".

288

Sources: 1958-1962: data supplied by the National Center for Health Statistics; 1963: (NCHS, 1964c: 15); 1964: (NCHS, 1965g: 12); 1965: (NCHS, 1965h: 15); 1966: (NCHS, 1967g: 17); 1967: (NCHS, 1968i: 16); 1968: (NCHS, 1969f: 15).

Percent of Persons Having Any Chronic Conditions, by Sex: Series K093 - K094

See Notes to Series K091-K092. Chronic conditions are further defined, as follows (NCHS, 1969b: 42):

"Chronic condition -- A condition is considered to be chronic if (1) it is described by the respondent in terms of one of the chronic diseases on the 'Check List of Chronic Conditions' or in terms of one of the types of impairments on the 'Check List of Impairments', or (2) the condition is described by the respondent as having been first noticed more than 3 months before the week of the interview.

"Impairment -- Impairments are chronic or permanent defects, resulting from disease, injury, or congenital malformation. They represent decrease or loss of ability to perform various functions, particularly those of the musculoskeletal system and the sense organs. All impairments are classi- fied by means of a special supplementary code for impairments. Hence, code numbers for impairments in the International Classification of Diseases are not used. In the Supplementary Code impairments are grouped according to the type of functional impairment and etiology. The impairment classifica- tion is shown in Health Statistics from the National Health Survey, Series B, No. 35.

"Persons with chronic conditions -- The estimated number of persons with chronic conditions is based on the number of persons who at the time of the interview were reported to have one or more chronic conditions".

Sources: 1958-1962: data supplied by the National Center for Health Statistics; 1963: (NCHS, 1964b: 11); 1964: (NCHS, 1964d: 12); 1965: (NCHS, 1965e: 13); 1966: (NCHS, 1967e: 12); 1967: (NCHS, 1968f: 15).

Injury Rates, by Sex: Series K095 - K096

See Appendix B on the Health Interview Survey. Definitions relative to injuries are, as follows: (NCHS, 1970d: 58);

"Injury condition -- An injury condition, or simply an injury, is a condition of the type that is classified to the nature of injury code numbers (N800-N999) in the International Classification of Diseases. In addition to fractures, lacerations, contusions, burns, and so forth, which are commonly thought of as injuries, this group of codes include: effects of exposure, such as sunburn;

adverse reactions to immunizations and other medical procedures, and poisonings. Unless otherwise specified, the term injury is used to cover all of these.

"Since a person may sustain more than one injury in a single accident, e.g. a broken leg and laceration of the scalp, the number of injury conditions may exceed the number of persons injured.

"Statistics of acute injury conditions include only those injuries which involved at least 1 full day of restricted activity or medical attendance.

"Person injured -- A person injured is one who has sustained one or more injuries in an accident or in some type of nonaccidental violence (see definition of 'Injury condition' above). Each time a person is involved in an accident or in nonaccidental violence causing injury that results in at least 1 full day of restricted activity or medical attention, he is included in the statistics as a separate 'person injured', hence, one person may be included more than once.

"The number of persons injured is not equivalent to the number of 'accidents' for several reasons: (1) the term 'accident' as commonly used may not involve injury at all; (2) more than one injured person may be involved in a single accident so that the number of accidents resulting in injury would be less than the number of persons injured in accidents; and (3) the term 'accident' ordinarily implies an accidental origin, whereas 'persons injured' as used in the National Health Survey includes persons whose injury resulted from certain nonaccidental violence.

"The number of persons injured in a specified time interval is always equal to or less than the incidence of injury conditions, since one person may incur more than one injury in a single accident."

Sources: 1960-1962 and 1968: data from the National Center for Health Statistics: 1963: (NCHS, 1964b: 12); 1964: (NCHS, 1964d: 13); 1965: (NCHS, 1965e: 12, 13); 1966: (NCHS, 1967e: 12, 13); 1967: (NCHS, 1968f: 15, 16).

Short-Stay Hospital Discharge Rates and Average Length of Stay, by Sex: Series K097 - K100

See Appendix B for information on the Health Interview Survey. Additional relevant definitions to this series are, as follows (NCHS, 1969c: 45):

"Hospital discharge -- A hospital discharge is the completion of any continuous period of stay of one or more nights in a hospital as an inpatient, except the period of stay of a well, newborn infant.
A hospital discharge is recorded whenever a present member of the household is reported to have been discharged from a hospital in the 12-month period

prior to the interview week. (Estimates were based on discharges which occurred during the 6-month period prior to the interview).

"Hospital episode -- A hospital episode is any continuous period of stay of one or more nights in a hospital as an inpatient, except the period of stay of a well, newborn infant. A hospital episode is recorded for a family member whenever any part of his hospital stay is included in the 12-month period prior to the interview week.

"Hospital -- For this survey a hospital is defined as any institution meeting one of the following criteria: (1) named in the listing of hospitals in the current Guide Issue of Hospitals, the Journal of the American Hospital Association; (2) named in the listing of hospitals in the Directories of the American Osteopathic Hospital Association: or (3) named in the annual inventory of hospitals and related facilities submitted by the States to the Division of Hospital and Medical Facilities of the U. S. Public Health Service in conjunction with the Hill-Burton program.

"Short-stay hospital -- A short-stay hospital is one for which the type of service is general; maternity; eye, ear, nose, and throat; children's; osteopathic hospital; or hospital department of institution.

"Hospital day -- A hospital day is a day on which a person is confined to a hospital. The day is counted as a hospital day only if the patient stays overnight. Thus, a patient who enters the hospital on Monday afternoon and leaves Wednesday noon is considered to have had two hospital days.

"Hospital days during the year -- The number of hospital days during the year is the total number for all hospital episodes in the 12-month period prior to the interview week. For the purposes of this estimate, episodes overlapping the beginning or end of the 12-month period are subdivided so that only those days falling within the period are included."

Sources: 1958-1962 and 1968: data supplied by the National Center for Health Statistics; 1963: (NCHS, 1964b: 15); 1964: (NCHS, 1964d: 16); 1965: (NCHS, 1965e: 16); 1966: (NCHS, 1967e: 16); 1967: (NCHS, 1968f: 19).

Cigarette Smoking Status of the Population, by Age and Sex: Series K101 - K140

The percentages presented have been adjusted to eliminate persons whose smoking status was not known to the interviewer.

The several sources are not all strictly comparable due to differences in methods of data collection, but these effects are thought to be minor. The data in the table reflecting a particular month were collected through the Current Population Survey (see Appendix A) and are

subject to the sampling errors of that survey. For example, the sampling error of the percent
of males who smoke (50.0 percent in June 1966), one standard error, is approximately 0.3 for
the June 1966 data and approximately 0.2 for the more recent years. The sampling error for the
percent of females who smoke is about the same order of magnitude.

Data shown over the two 12-month periods (ending June 1965 and 1966) were collected through
the Health Interview Survey in weekly samples so selected that they could be summed (see
Appendix B).

In the first and second segments of the table, the February 1955 survey did not include
the 17-year olds, while the remaining surveys did.

One reporting error has been identified (NCHS, 1969d: 4). The difference in the percent
derived from self-reporting by males is essentially the same as that derived from proxy-
reporting by males. But such is not the case for females. Self-reports on smoking by females
produced a percent present-smokers of 32.8 percent, while in the same surveys proxy reports
produced a percent of present-smokers of 25.9. The preceding is combined evidence from the
1966 and 1967 surveys; for separate evidence, see (NCHS, 1969c: 4). One would judge from this
that the true percent of smokers among females is slightly larger than represented by the data
of Series K121-K140.

Definitions used in the surveys, are as follows:

"Never smoked: A person was defined as having never smoked cigarettes if he reported that
he had not smoked 100 cigarettes during his entire life.

"Present smoker: A person is defined as presently smoking if he was smoking cigarettes at
the time of the interview.

"Former smoker: A person is defined as a former smoker if he had smoked at least 100
cigarettes during his entire life, but was not smoking cigarettes at the time of the interview".
(NCHS, 1969d: 46).

Sources: February 1955 data from (Haenszel et al, 1956: 72-73); July 1964-June 1965 from
(NCHS, 1967f: 23-24); July 1965-June 1966 from (NCHS, 1969c: 30-31); June 1966, August 1967
and August 1968 from (NCHS, 1969d). For additional data and interpretation, see (PHS, 1964);
(National Clearinghouse for Smoking and Health, 1969); and (NCHS, 1970e).

Expectation of Life, by Color and Sex: Series L001 - L028

Expectation of life at various ages is based upon age-specific mortality rates. The
accuracy of these rates rests upon the accuracy of the registration of deaths and upon estimates
of the population by age, sex, and color. No systematic periodic assessment is made of death
registration statistics, but evaluations are made from time to time. Generally, registration
is considered adequate. There is evidence, however, that not all fetal deaths are reported
(NCHS, 1969e:, Sec. 6:8). With regard to general mortality, a study of several counties in

Tennessee in 1949 and 1951 revealed some underregistration. In 1964, approximately 6,000 deaths failed to reach the NCHS file, thereby affecting results for the New England Division (NCHS, 1969e: Sec. 6:13). During the period included in the tables, all States and the District of Columbia were in the death registration area (Alaska was added in 1959, and Hawaii was added in 1960). At least ninety percent of deaths must be registered for a State to qualify for the death registration area. Only deaths occurring within these States are registered. The latter definition excludes deaths of U. S. citizens occurring in foreign countries, both military and civilian. This would affect the male rates, particularly during the time of foreign wars (NCHS, 1969e: 6-3).

Sources: Series L001-L004: (NCHS, 1969e: 5-8); Series L005-L028: 1939-41: (NCHS, 1969e: 5-7); 1945-1947: (VS, 1949: xlvii); 1948: (VS, 1951: lvi); 1949 and 1950: (VS, 1954a: 152); 1951: (VS, 1954b: xxxix); 1952 and 1953: (VS, 1955: xliv); 1954 and 1955: (VS, 1957: lxxxv); 1956: (VS, 1959: page c); 1957 and 1958: (VS, 1960: 5-5); 1959: (NVSD, 1963a: 2-11); 1960 and 1961: (NVSD, 1964a: 2-11); 1962: (NVSD, 1964b: 5-6); 1963: (NCHS, 1965a: 5-6); 1964: (NCHS, 1966b: 5-6); 1965: (NCHS, 1967b: 5-6); 1966: (NCHS, 1968c: 5-3); 1967: (NCHS, 1969e: 5-7).

Death Rates, by Age, Color, and Sex: Series L029 - L076

See Notes to Series L001-L028 and annual volumes of Vital Statistics of the United States, Volume II, Mortality, Part A.

Sources: 1940-1960: (NCHS, 1968h, 325-333); 1961-1967: (NCHS, 1969e, Sec. 1: 3-5).

The following refer to the statistical series:

a/ - Data for "Age not stated" are included in the total but not distributed among the age groups.

b/ - For 1962 and 1963, data exclude New Jersey, which did not keep records by color or race.

Age-Adjusted Death Rates, by Cause, Color and Sex: Series L077 - L146

The death certificate is completed by the attending physicians and filed with the State vital statistics office. The cause of death is coded according to the International Statistical Classification of Diseases, Injuries, and Causes of Death, which is published by the World Health Organization. The code numbers included in the categories of cause of death presented in these series are given at the head of the columns.

Sources: 1940-1960: (NCHS, 1968h: 366-373); 1961-1967: for All causes, Major cardiovascular-renal, diabetes, All malignant neoplasms, Influenza and pneumonia, Tuberculosis of the respiratory system; Motor vehicle accidents, and Cirrhosis of the liver: 1961: (NVSD, 1964a: 1-16); 1962: (NVSD, 1964b: 1-7); 1963: (NCHS, 1965a: 1-7); 1964: (NCHS, 1966b: 1-6); 1965: (NCHS, 1967b: 1-6); 1966: (NCHS, 1968c: 1-6); 1967: (NCHS, 1969e: 1-6). For all other causes in the series, data were supplied by the National Center for Health Statistics.

The following refer to the statistical series:

a/ - The U.S. National Center for Health Statistics computes the age-adjusted death rates by "using the distribution in 10-year age intervals of the enumerated population of the United States in 1940 as the standard population. Each figure represents the rate that would have existed if the age-specific rates of the particular year prevailed in a population whose age distribution was like that of the United States in 1940. The rates for the total population and for each color-sex group were adjusted separately, using the same standard population" (NCHS, 1969f, Sec. 6: 16).

b/ - The category "Major cardiovascular-renal diseases" is composed almost entirely of diseases of the cardiovascular system. In 1967, for example, only one percent of this category was accounted for by renal diseases.

c/ - Malignant neoplasm of breast not shown for males, as the figures are extremely small: 0.3 in 1940 and 0.2 in 1967.

d/ - "Age-adjusted rates based on age-specific rates of which more than half were for frequencies less than 20" (NCHS, 1968h: page x).

Maternal Mortality Rates: Series L147 - L167

See Notes to Series L001-L028 and to Series L077-L146. The rates are based upon live births, classified by age of mother. 1962 and 1963 exclude New Jersey, which did not classify their records by color or race.

Sources: 1940-1960: (NCHS, 1968h: 296-297); 1961: (NSVD, 1964a: 1-38); 1962-1963, courtesy of National Center for Health Statistics; 1964: (NCHS, 1966b: 1-40); 1965: (NCHS, 1967b: 1-40); 1966: (NCHS, 1968c: 1-40); 1967: (NCHS, 1969e: 1-41).

Death Rates for Motor Vehicle Traffic Accidents: Series L168 - L219

The deaths due to motor vehicle accidents, including pedestrians, are International List code numbers E810-E811, and E813-E825, and those of pedestrians are coded E812. For information on the vital statistics records, see Notes to Series L001-L028; for information on the International List, see Notes to Series L077-L146.

Sources: Mortality data: 1949: (VS, 1951: 148-149); 1950: (VS, 1954a: 114); 1955: (VS, 1957: 94-95); 1960: (NVSD, 1963a: 5-90); 1965: (NCHS, 1967b: 1-153); 1967: (NCHS, 1969e: 1-152; 153). Population data: 1949-1950: (VS, 1954a, 56-57); 1955: (NCHS, 1967c: 4-14); 1960: (NVSD, 1963b: 5-12, 13); 1965: (NCHS, 1967c: 4-13); 1967: (NCHS, 1969a: 3-15).

Appendix D

Statistical Series

Estimated Total Population of the United States (including Armed Forces Overseas), by Age
Group, Color, and Sex, as of July 1, 1940-1969 (Numbers in thousands)

As of July 1	All ages				Under 5 years				5-9 years			
	White		Nonwhite		White		Nonwhite		White		Nonwhite	
	Male	Female	Male	Female	Male	Female	Male	Female	Male	Female	Male	Female
	A001	A002	A003	A004	A005	A006	A007	A008	A009	A010	A011	A012
1940	59,718	58,911	6,634	6,860	4,717	4,544	656	662	4,727	4,566	675	681
1941	60,196	59,535	6,724	6,947	4,836	4,658	673	682	4,665	4,506	675	677
1942	60,775	60,217	6,822	7,046	5,043	4,845	704	709	4,604	4,465	669	675
1943	61,568	61,037	6,978	7,156	5,379	5,166	735	737	4,603	4,488	670	678
1944	62,250	61,759	7,128	7,260	5,611	5,389	763	761	4,713	4,552	674	683
1945	62,748	62,518	7,287	7,375	5,819	5,584	790	786	4,811	4,638	681	692
1946	63,287	63,277	7,344	7,480	5,943	5,702	801	798	4,933	4,755	697	711
1947	64,507	64,552	7,439	7,628	6,493	6,221	847	845	5,143	4,946	727	736
1948	65,582	65,726	7,548	7,776	6,712	6,429	890	887	5,489	5,276	754	761
1949	66,678	66,921	7,658	7,932	7,006	6,710	948	944	5,732	5,509	778	784
1950	67,848	68,135	8,001	8,287	7,328	7,020	1,034	1,028	5,980	5,730	831	833
1951	68,924	69,297	8,177	8,480	7,720	7,398	1,110	1,104	6,115	5,858	846	849
1952	70,023	70,503	8,349	8,677	7,671	7,351	1,147	1,144	6,654	6,373	891	893
1953	71,083	71,690	8,531	8,880	7,793	7,471	1,188	1,187	6,876	6,587	933	936
1954	72,242	72,951	8,731	9,102	7,963	7,635	1,229	1,231	7,176	6,874	990	992
1955	73,420	74,233	8,944	9,335	8,171	7,836	1,278	1,281	7,480	7,171	1,049	1,049
1956	74,616	75,547	9,163	9,577	8,349	8,008	1,322	1,324	7,857	7,538	1,128	1,128
1957	75,859	76,909	9,389	9,827	8,541	8,197	1,378	1,378	7,800	7,486	1,168	1,170
1958	76,996	78,203	9,609	10,073	8,694	8,347	1,423	1,423	7,912	7,600	1,214	1,215
1959	78,154	79,501	9,842	10,333	8,797	8,453	1,463	1,462	8,069	7,754	1,260	1,261
1960	79,266	80,767	10,066	10,585	8,863	8,522	1,489	1,490	8,259	7,941	1,312	1,313
1961	80,488	82,097	10,315	10,855	8,973	8,616	1,534	1,534	8,446	8,121	1,352	1,353
1962	81,624	83,358	10,557	11,117	8,991	8,620	1,571	1,565	8,631	8,305	1,399	1,400
1963	82,678	84,570	10,793	11,375	8,967	8,583	1,605	1,595	8,771	8,440	1,432	1,432
1964	83,704	85,743	11,035	11,638	8,915	8,509	1,632	1,615	8,877	8,542	1,464	1,464
1965	84,632	86,820	11,261	11,888	8,770	8,365	1,646	1,623	8,937	8,599	1,487	1,492
1966	85,469	87,833	11,480	12,138	8,486	8,097	1,626	1,602	9,050	8,694	1,533	1,535
1967	86,244	88,789	11,695	12,386	8,187	7,811	1,598	1,572	9,069	8,699	1,572	1,568
1968	86,943	89,682	11,900	12,627	7,874	7,514	1,572	1,547	9,043	8,660	1,606	1,599
1969	87,654	90,571	12,117	12,874	7,610	7,265	1,554	1,530	8,988	8,586	1,634	1,619
1970												

As of July 1	10-14 years				15-19 years				20-24 years			
	A013	A014	A015	A016	A017	A018	A019	A020	A021	A022	A023	A024
1940	5,243	5,077	694	700	5,534	5,441	664	704	5,203	5,237	580	669
1941	5,168	4,997	699	703	5,494	5,405	667	702	5,278	5,272	587	671
1942	5,099	4,903	704	705	5,413	5,358	666	701	5,386	5,298	598	673
1943	5,042	4,799	711	708	5,329	5,299	671	702	5,452	5,314	622	676
1944	4,843	4,685	713	710	5,329	5,228	678	702	5,426	5,321	637	678
1945	4,769	4,583	714	711	5,151	5,144	674	701	5,392	5,314	649	681
1946	4,773	4,554	7.5	707	4,976	5,037	667	698	5,368	5,315	638	684
1947	4,747	4,551	707	702	5,026	4,926	666	691	5,211	5,296	619	688
1948	4,793	4,605	709	703	4,920	4,815	655	681	5,215	5,264	622	693
1949	4,868	4,683	712	705	4,844	4,712	645	670	5,165	5,220	618	697
1950	4,968	4,774	739	732	4,730	4,616	652	678	5,161	5,168	634	718
1951	5,092	4,896	758	754	4,663	4,562	654	679	5,126	5,091	627	708
1952	5,301	5,090	789	782	4,646	4,554	654	681	5,035	4,988	623	704
1953	5,633	5,407	820	811	4,714	4,620	662	688	4,893	4,848	622	699
1954	5,869	5,637	847	838	4,811	4,712	673	697	4,786	4,731	621	695
1955	6,071	5,830	873	864	4,872	4,770	686	711	4,729	4,672	622	691
1956	6,199	5,955	886	878	5,008	4,898	705	730	4,676	4,629	623	688
1957	6,730	6,464	928	923	5,221	5,090	734	753	4,670	4,625	622	686
1958	6,941	6,671	969	965	5,552	5,407	763	779	4,744	4,695	627	690
1959	7,225	6,950	1,024	1,022	5,793	5,635	789	801	4,849	4,788	637	695
1960	7,516	7,236	1,080	1,078	6,002	5,829	813	823	4,913	4,851	647	706
1961	7,867	7,569	1,155	1,151	6,164	5,989	844	851	5,046	4,980	664	719
1962	7,816	7,514	1,191	1,188	6,688	6,491	898	905	5,263	5,191	694	741
1963	7,937	7,636	1,233	1,230	6,941	6,723	951	955	5,597	5,518	733	772
1964	8,100	7,794	1,272	1,272	7,267	7,027	1,016	1,020	5,836	5,749	770	799
1965	8,320	8,006	1,316	1,317	7,576	7,314	1,080	1,081	6,073	5,963	811	832
1966	8,510	8,191	1,356	1,358	7,938	7,650	1,155	1,155	6,242	6,119	842	860
1967	8,699	8,379	1,405	1,406	7,880	7,592	1,193	1,193	6,752	6,615	896	916
1968	8,843	8,514	1,438	1,440	7,993	7,710	1,234	1,236	6,992	6,841	947	968
1969	8,954	8,621	1,471	1,472	8,151	7,868	1,274	1,277	7,301	7,138	1,011	1,034
1970												

(continued)

Estimated Total Population of the United States (including Armed Forces Overseas), by Age Group, Color, and Sex, as of July 1, 1940-1969 (cont.) (Numbers in thousands)

As of July 1	25-29 years				30-34 years				35-39 years			
	White		Nonwhite		White		Nonwhite		White		Nonwhite	
	Male	Female	Male	Female	Male	Female	Male	Female	Male	Female	Male	Female
	A025	A026	A027	A028	A029	A030	A031	A032	A033	A034	A035	A036
1940	4,931	5,030	560	635	4,600	4,651	498	541	4,280	4,284	493	540
1941	4,981	5,092	565	640	4,643	4,722	501	547	4,331	4,361	500	547
1942	5,013	5,144	572	644	4,693	4,786	505	554	4,379	4,431	505	555
1943	5,084	5,190	587	649	4,761	4,847	516	560	4,433	4,499	515	563
1944	5,181	5,234	605	653	4,837	4,906	529	566	4,494	4,567	526	570
1945	5,215	5,280	644	658	4,854	4,967	543	573	4,556	4,640	539	578
1946	5,249	5,340	640	664	4,908	5,028	545	580	4,611	4,720	541	587
1947	5,322	5,408	637	672	4,967	5,093	547	590	4,701	4,813	546	597
1948	5,361	5,476	637	681	5,027	5,161	551	600	4,794	4,916	554	608
1949	5,394	5,537	632	689	5,087	5,229	551	609	4,897	5,023	559	619
1950	5,424	5,577	646	714	5,164	5,306	569	636	5,001	5,123	584	639
1951	5,404	5,535	643	713	5,257	5,401	585	652	5,050	5,175	593	644
1952	5,366	5,479	634	708	5,345	5,495	602	672	5,100	5,229	599	644
1953	5,360	5,447	624	701	5,369	5,528	618	693	5,141	5,277	603	643
1954	5,303	5,370	616	694	5,433	5,583	631	710	5,171	5,316	609	645
1955	5,247	5,286	611	691	5,471	5,615	639	722	5,218	5,371	615	652
1956	5,207	5,217	608	690	5,448	5,580	642	728	5,308	5,469	623	663
1957	5,119	5,120	609	692	5,406	5,527	641	730	5,394	5,565	631	678
1958	4,980	4,984	613	695	5,399	5,502	636	729	5,418	5,604	638	693
1959	4,867	4,866	616	697	5,333	5,426	634	729	5,473	5,661	640	704
1960	4,803	4,811	620	699	5,268	5,345	633	732	5,502	5,692	638	710
1961	4,777	4,772	618	694	5,190	5,248	630	729	5,502	5,680	640	719
1962	4,777	4,761	617	691	5,102	5,137	627	725	5,474	5,632	637	725
1963	4,830	4,817	623	696	5,002	5,030	623	717	5,423	5,557	632	728
1964	4,915	4,909	634	707	4,901	4,924	618	709	5,353	5,465	626	729
1965	4,988	4,984	644	716	4,849	4,869	615	704	5,271	5,369	621	728
1966	5,123	5,118	662	730	4,822	4,838	614	700	5,187	5,272	619	728
1967	5,333	5,327	693	755	4,822	4,840	616	700	5,098	5,173	619	726
1968	5,665	5,653	732	788	4,878	4,901	623	708	5,001	5,069	616	722
1969	5,898	5,878	768	817	4,968	4,998	634	719	4,905	4,968	611	715
1970												

As of July 1	40-44 years				45-49 years				50-54 years			
	A037	A038	A039	A040	A041	A042	A043	A044	A045	A046	A047	A048
1940	4,012	3,957	426	430	3,848	3,698	369	358	3,459	3,241	303	278
1941	4,058	4,024	433	438	3,876	3,751	377	368	3,493	3,299	310	286
1942	4,106	4,090	438	446	3,909	3,808	383	377	3,530	3,358	317	295
1943	4,162	4,154	447	454	3,944	3,866	391	386	3,567	3,416	324	304
1944	4,212	4,219	456	462	3,982	3,923	400	395	3,602	3,473	332	312
1945	4,254	4,286	464	470	4,020	3,977	408	405	3,640	3,532	339	321
1946	4,312	4,352	472	479	4,042	4,018	416	414	3,668	3,585	346	331
1947	4,377	4,418	479	489	4,058	4,043	424	425	3,692	3,636	353	340
1948	4,447	4,490	486	500	4,068	4,061	432	436	3,715	3,687	360	349
1949	4,524	4,563	493	510	4,082	4,081	440	447	3,742	3,743	367	358
1950	4,607	4,642	514	527	4,106	4,113	460	463	3,765	3,788	384	374
1951	4,671	4,721	520	539	4,182	4,203	461	467	3,775	3,808	395	386
1952	4,737	4,798	531	555	4,284	4,321	460	469	3,778	3,819	405	398
1953	4,796	4,871	542	573	4,374	4,432	459	470	3,811	3,855	416	411
1954	4,847	4,934	552	588	4,471	4,544	461	475	3,857	3,906	425	422
1955	4,900	4,997	559	599	4,562	4,647	467	485	3,903	3,959	432	431
1956	4,960	5,066	563	605	4,627	4,721	477	498	3,970	4,038	436	438
1957	5,021	5,136	563	608	4,693	4,793	491	517	4,062	4,144	438	443
1958	5,074	5,201	562	609	4,754	4,861	506	536	4,143	4,242	439	447
1959	5,112	5,258	562	613	4,804	4,919	520	554	4,228	4,340	443	455
1960	5,169	5,326	564	622	4,853	4,975	531	567	4,308	4,430	451	466
1961	5,238	5,415	574	635	4,904	5,041	534	576	4,384	4,524	458	480
1962	5,312	5,512	587	652	4,940	5,094	533	581	4,460	4,623	469	496
1963	5,382	5,601	601	669	4,969	5,145	531	585	4,534	4,719	479	513
1964	5,431	5,661	612	685	5,004	5,205	532	592	4,602	4,808	489	528
1965	5,450	5,683	618	697	5,052	5,279	537	602	4,657	4,885	494	540
1966	5,445	5,672	620	706	5,113	5,366	546	616	4,700	4,949	496	549
1967	5,419	5,630	618	715	5,190	5,466	559	633	4,735	5,005	495	556
1968	5,371	5,562	613	720	5,263	5,559	573	651	4,766	5,060	493	560
1969	5,307	5,477	608	723	5,317	5,624	583	668	4,805	5,122	493	568
1970												

(continued)

Estimated Total Population of the United States (including Armed Forces Overseas), by Age
Group, Color, and Sex, as of July 1, 1940-1969 (continued)
(Numbers in thousands)

As of July 1	55-59 years				60-64 years				65 years and over			
	White		Nonwhite		White		Nonwhite		White		Nonwhite	
	Male	Female	Male	Female	Male	Female	Male	Female	Male	Female	Male	Female
	A049	A050	A051	A052	A053	A054	A055	A056	A057	A058	A059	A060
1940	2,805	2,654	234	210	2,249	2,199	181	162	4,108	4,331	301	292
1941	2,858	2,720	242	217	2,306	2,261	187	168	4,211	4,466	310	300
1942	2,908	2,784	248	225	2,362	2,324	194	175	4,330	4,619	321	312
1943	2,955	2,846	255	233	2,414	2,386	200	182	4,442	4,767	333	327
1944	3,002	2,907	262	241	2,466	2,446	207	188	4,552	4,910	347	340
1945	3,053	2,973	268	249	2,523	2,513	214	195	4,693	5,087	360	354
1946	3,103	3,039	274	257	2,577	2,573	219	202	4,825	5,260	374	368
1947	3,163	3,114	279	265	2,640	2,638	222	207	4,968	5,451	386	383
1948	3,228	3,195	283	272	2,707	2,705	223	211	5,108	5,645	394	394
1949	3,330	3,282	287	280	2,780	2,774	226	216	5,258	5,855	402	406
1950	3,369	3,368	288	269	2,841	2,841	216	204	5,406	6,070	451	471
1951	3,422	3,448	297	282	2,887	2,913	223	214	5,561	6,287	464	489
1952	3,446	3,498	307	295	2,945	3,005	228	223	5,714	6,503	477	509
1953	3,449	3,524	318	309	3,001	3,098	234	234	5,872	6,726	492	528
1954	3,466	3,559	330	323	3,044	3,176	240	244	6,047	6,974	508	548
1955	3,499	3,609	342	338	3,082	3,249	248	255	6,214	7,219	524	568
1956	3,532	3,656	354	352	3,118	3,318	255	266	6,359	7,453	538	587
1957	3,558	3,694	367	367	3,126	3,359	263	276	6,518	7,709	554	608
1958	3,614	3,760	380	382	3,112	3,376	271	286	6,660	7,955	567	627
1959	3,682	3,839	391	396	3,113	3,402	281	297	6,811	8,210	583	647
1960	3,743	3,915	400	407	3,128	3,438	290	306	6,938	8,455	599	667
1961	3,800	3,987	404	413	3,160	3,481	298	314	7,038	8,675	611	689
1962	3,854	4,063	404	417	3,208	3,538	312	326	7,108	8,878	618	707
1963	3,904	4,138	402	419	3,261	3,601	326	341	7,159	9,062	622	722
1964	3,959	4,218	401	424	3,316	3,668	338	354	7,228	9,264	630	740
1965	4,018	4,303	404	433	3,365	3,736	346	363	7,295	9,465	640	761
1966	4,083	4,394	410	446	3,410	3,804	348	370	7,361	9,670	651	783
1967	4,157	4,490	419	463	3,455	3,878	348	375	7,448	9,885	665	807
1968	4,231	4,585	429	480	3,501	3,953	345	378	7,522	10,103	679	830
1969	4,298	4,673	439	495	3,551	4,031	344	384	7,602	10,321	693	854
1970												

Sex Ratios for Estimated and Projected Total Population (including Armed Forces overseas) as of July 1, by Age Group, United States, Five-Year Intervals, 1940-1990

Type of data and year	Number of males per 1,000 females, by age group									
	Total	Under 5 years	5-9 years	10-14 years	15-19 years	20-24 years	25-29 years	30-34 years	35-39 years	40-44 years
	A061	A062	A063	A064	A065	A066	A067	A068	A069	A070
Estimated										
1940	1,009	1,032	1,030	1,028	1,009	979	969	982	990	1,012
1945	1,002	1,028	1,030	1,036	997	1,008	987	974	976	992
1950	993	1,039	1,038	1,037	1,016	984	965	965	969	991
1955	986	1,036	1,038	1,037	1,014	998	980	964	969	976
1960	978	1,034	1,034	1,034	1,025	1,001	952	971	959	964
1965	971	1,043	1,033	1,034	1,031	1,013	988	980	967	951
1969 1970	964	1,042	1,041	1,033	1,031	1,017	996	980	971	954
Projected[a]/										
1975	963	1,044	1,043	1,041	1,030	1,019	1,008	995	980	968
1980	963	1,044	1,043	1,042	1,038	1,019	1,009	1,004	991	972
1985	964	1,045	1,043	1,042	1,039	1,027	1,008	1,005	999	983
1990	966	1,045	1,044	1,043	1,039	1,027	1,017	1,005	1,001	992

	45-49 years	50-54 years	55-59 years	60-64 years	65 yrs. & over
	A071	A072	A073	A074	A075
Estimated					
1940	1,039	1,069	1,061	1,029	954
1945	1,010	1,032	1,031	1,010	929
1950	998	997	1,005	1,004	895
1955	980	987	973	950	865
1960	972	972	959	913	826
1965	950	949	934	905	776
1969 1970	938	931	917	882	742
Projected[a]/					
1975	946	917	892	861	717
1980	955	924	882	842	701
1985	959	933	889	834	723
1990	971	938	898	841	773

Year ended June 30	Total number of immigrants admitted		Percent distribution of immigrants by age group							
	Male	Female	Male	Female	Male	Female	Male	Female	Male	Female
			Under 5 yrs. of age		5-19 years		20-24 years		25-29 years	
	A076	A077	A078	A079	A080	A081	A082	A083	A084	A085
1940	33,460	37,296								
1941	23,519	28,257								
1942	12,008	16,773								
1943	9,825	13,900								
1944	11,410	17,141								
1945	13,389	24,730								
1946	27,275	81,446								
1947	53,769	93,523								
1948	67,322	103,248								
1949	80,340	107,977								
1950	119,130	130,057	9.5	8.6	17.0	17.1	10.9	15.1	15.1	15.3
1951	99,327	106,390	10.5	9.2	16.9	17.1	8.7	13.9	14.0	15.1
1952	123,609	141,911								
1953	73,073	97,361	9.9	7.4	20.8	19.6	10.6	19.5	16.3	16.8
1954	95,594	112,583	9.1	7.3	20.1	20.9	10.8	19.7	16.2	16.6
1955	112,032	125,758	8.6	7.2	21.6	22.7	12.5	19.5	15.7	15.8
1956	156,410	165,215	9.0	8.3	22.0	23.1	13.1	18.7	15.2	15.0
1957	155,210	171,666	10.2	8.7	22.8	22.8	13.0	18.2	15.5	15.2
1958	109,121	144,144	11.0	7.8	23.8	22.4	12.6	20.3	16.0	15.4
1959	114,367	146,319	10.1	7.5	23.0	21.9	14.0	20.6	15.1	14.6
1960	116,687	148,711	10.5	7.9	22.5	22.0	13.6	21.4	15.2	14.6
1961	121,380	149,964	10.9	8.7	23.1	22.5	13.7	20.9	15.1	14.1
1962	131,575	152,188	10.8	8.1	22.0	22.5	14.9	21.0	16.2	14.1
1963	139,297	166,963	10.7	8.5	23.2	23.3	14.5	21.4	15.5	14.2
1964	126,214	166,034	11.5	8.1	24.9	22.8	14.3	22.2	15.0	14.4
1965	127,171	169,526	11.1	8.0	26.2	23.2	14.9	22.5	14.7	14.2
1966	141,456	181,584	11.0	8.3	29.4	25.6	10.7	18.0	13.5	13.3
1967	158,324	203,648	9.9	7.5	28.7	24.5	8.0	16.2	13.0	13.3
1968	199,732	254,716	8.3	6.3	27.0	23.4	8.9	16.0	13.4	13.3
1969	165,472	193,107	9.5	7.9	27.7	25.5	9.6	15.8	14.0	13.9
1970										

Year ended June 30	30-44 years		45-59 years		60 yrs. & over[a]	
	A086	A087	A088	A089	A090	A091
1950	29.6	24.6	14.4	14.1	3.4	5.2
1951	31.0	24.9	14.9	14.3	4.0	5.5
1952						
1953	29.5	23.2	10.3	10.3	2.5	3.3
1954	30.3	22.7	11.1	9.8	2.4	3.0
1955	29.1	22.2	10.6	9.5	2.0	3.0
1956	28.0	22.4	10.8	9.6	1.9	2.9
1957	27.0	22.9	9.4	9.2	2.2	3.1
1958	25.2	21.3	8.9	9.4	2.5	3.5
1959	24.0	21.2	10.4	10.1	3.5	4.0
1960	24.6	20.9	10.1	9.5	3.5	3.6
1961	24.0	20.5	9.8	9.3	3.5	3.9
1962	25.0	20.5	8.8	9.6	3.1	4.2
1963	24.8	20.4	8.5	8.6	2.8	3.6
1964	22.7	20.0	8.3	8.6	3.2	3.7
1965	21.6	19.7	8.1	8.7	3.3	3.8
1966	22.7	20.5	8.9	9.4	3.8	4.8
1967	25.1	22.4	10.6	10.8	4.6	5.3
1968	25.5	22.9	11.7	11.9	5.3	6.2
1969	26.0	22.6	9.9	9.9	3.5	4.4
1970						

Aliens Naturalized, by Sex, and Males per 1,000 Females, 1940-1968; Percent Distribution of
Females Naturalized, by Marital Status, and Median Age of Males and Females Naturalized,
United States, 1957-1968

Year ended June 30	Aliens naturalized		Males per 1,000 females	Percent distribution of females naturalized, by marital status[a]				Median age (years)	
	Male	Female		Single	Married	Widowed	Divorced	Males natural-ized	Females natural-ized
	A092	A093	A094	A095	A096	A097	A098	A099	A100
1940	132,406	102,854	1,287						
1941	136,348	140,946	967						
1942	112,040	158,324	708						
1943	157,663	161,270	978						
1944	202,698	239,281	847						
1945	116,691	114,711	1,017						
1946	76,296	73,766	1,034						
1947	52,998	40,906	1,296						
1948	33,147	37,003	896						
1949	27,865	38,729	719						
1950	25,745	40,601	634						
1951	18,711	36,005	520						
1952	28,597	60,058	476						
1953	34,657	57,394	604						
1954	54,477	63,354	860						
1955	95,850	113,676	843						
1956	64,962	80,923	803						
1957	60,289	77,754	775	14.0	76.5	7.2	2.2	39.9	36.9
1958	51,350	68,516	749	15.0	76.5	6.4	2.1	38.8	35.6
1959	43,719	60,212	726	15.5	75.9	6.4	2.1	38.4	35.7
1960	50,896	68,546	743	15.1	76.2	6.8	1.8	38.9	37.3
1961	58,795	73,655	798	16.5	74.3	7.3	1.9	38.8	37.7
1962	60,988	66,319	920	19.3	73.0	5.7	2.0	36.0	34.8
1963	58,303	65,875	885	19.7	73.8	4.5	2.0	34.4	33.3
1964	51,408	60,826	845	20.9	73.2	4.0	1.9	33.6	32.7
1965	48,495	55,804	869	21.0	72.5	4.3	2.1	34.6	33.7
1966	46,536	56,523	823	21.5	72.3	4.0	2.2	34.0	32.5
1967	46,014	58,888	781	20.6	73.4	3.8	2.2	34.8	32.8
1968	45,102	57,624	783	20.3	73.4	3.7	2.6	34.7	33.2
1969	45,177	53,532	844	20.0	73.5	3.6	2.9	33.7	32.7
1970									

	Percent of civilian noninstitutional population in specified age-color-sex groups enrolled in school[a]/ as of October											
	White		Nonwhite		White		Nonwhite		White		Nonwhite	
Year	Male	Female	Male	Female	Male	Female	Male	Female	Male	Female	Male	Female

	Total, 5-34 years of age				14-15 years				16-17 years			
	B001	B002	B003	B004	B005	B006	B007	B008	B009	B010	B011	B012
1954	54.3	46.4	52.0	45.6								
1955	54.9	46.9	54.4	47.4								
1956	56.5	48.6	54.3	49.0								
1957	57.7	49.8	55.9	51.3								
1958	58.8	51.1	58.0	50.3								
1959	59.2	52.0	58.0	52.4	98.1	97.7	95.8	92.0	85.9	81.6	76.3	76.4
1960	60.3	52.7	58.3	53.7	98.1	98.1	97.0	94.8	85.2	81.4	79.1	74.7
1961	60.4	53.4	60.0	53.8	98.3	97.7	96.6	93.5	85.5	83.5	78.6	75.1
1962	61.9	54.0	60.4	54.1	98.7	97.6	99.1	95.2	88.5	83.3	77.1	69.5
1963	62.3	54.7	61.9	56.0	98.8	98.2	98.2	96.9	89.8	85.7	85.9	78.2
1964	62.3	55.0	62.4	56.8	99.0	98.6	99.1	95.5	90.4	86.1	84.9	82.0
1965	63.5	55.8	63.3	57.1	99.1	98.9	98.7	97.7	88.6	87.0	83.3	85.9
1966	64.1	55.9	63.8	57.4	98.8	98.7	98.4	96.6	90.3	87.6	87.2	83.7
1967	64.0	56.2	64.4	58.3	98.5	98.5	96.7	96.1	91.4	87.4	88.0	82.0
1968	64.1	55.6	64.9	58.3	98.2	98.0	98.0	96.8	92.1	89.4	88.8	84.7
1969												
1970												

	14-17 years				18-19 years				20-21 years			
	B013	B014	B015	B016	B017	B018	B019	B020	B021	B022	B023	B024
1954	89.6	87.0	82.8	74.7	43.3	25.3	21.6	25.7				
1955	89.1	85.9	85.2	80.5	43.9	22.4	32.9	23.1				
1956	90.1	88.2	81.3	81.1	46.4	27.3	36.8	27.5				
1957	91.9	88.2	84.7	85.0	44.0	27.0	38.5	35.1				
1958	91.1	88.9	87.6	78.1	48.1	29.9	43.4	26.4				
1959	92.0	89.6	86.3	84.3	47.1	28.8	35.5	31.9	30.8	11.1	12.5	10.8
1960	91.7	89.8	88.5	85.2	49.5	29.7	36.9	32.2	29.2	13.5	13.7	10.4
1961	92.7	91.3	88.6	85.1	49.6	29.7	41.7	20.6	31.1	15.3	19.9	12.4
1962	94.2	91.3	89.4	83.8	52.7	34.6	40.3	27.3	33.7	16.3	15.0	14.9
1963	94.4	92.1	92.5	88.2	51.6	32.1	46.5	33.9	35.2	18.6	21.7	11.5
1964	94.7	92.2	92.3	89.0	52.4	33.7	40.6	34.0	36.6	20.3	18.0	14.0
1965	93.9	93.0	91.3	92.0	56.6	38.3	47.5	33.5	39.9	20.9	21.6	10.4
1966	94.7	93.3	92.9	90.3	59.0	38.6	49.1	31.9	44.9	22.3	17.4	11.6
1967	95.1	93.1	92.5	89.2	57.2	41.0	50.5	35.9	46.9	25.6	26.4	19.8
1968	95.2	93.8	93.7	91.0	61.5	41.3	53.5	40.7	47.8	22.3	25.7	16.0
1969												
1970												

(continued)

Percent of civilian noninstitutional population in specified age-color-sex
groups enrolled in school$^{a/}$ as of October (cont.)

Year	White		Nonwhite		White		Nonwhite		White		Nonwhite	
	Male	Female	Male	Female	Male	Female	Male	Female	Male	Female	Male	Female
	22-24 years				20-24 years				25-29 years			
	B025	B026	B027	B028	B029	B030	B031	B032	B033	B034	B035	B036
1954					20.5	6.4	10.1	2.9	6.5	1.7	7.9	2.3
1955					19.3	6.2	9.8	5.5	7.1	1.5	6.2	3.8
1956					21.8	7.0	12.5	5.7	9.3	1.8	5.3	1.3
1957					22.9	8.3	10.3	7.6	9.9	1.7	6.0	3.5
1958					22.3	7.5	11.8	6.0	9.9	2.2	6.3	1.9
1959	14.1	4.6	10.6	2.7	20.8	7.2	11.4	6.0	9.5	1.7	4.5	1.4
1960	16.3	3.5	6.3	2.8	21.5	7.6	9.4	5.9	8.9	1.8	3.9	2.1
1961	15.0	3.8	6.1	2.7	21.4	8.5	11.8	6.7	7.5	2.1	4.0	1.0
1962	18.8	4.1	10.1	3.0	25.0	9.3	12.2	8.0	8.9	1.8	5.8	2.2
1963	21.1	4.4	7.1	4.3	27.2	10.7	13.6	7.4	8.2	2.4	4.7	2.2
1964	17.7	4.5	4.2	3.8	25.6	11.3	10.0	8.3	8.3	2.6	6.6	2.5
1965	23.3	6.3	4.5	7.8	29.8	12.2	11.7	8.9	10.0	3.2	4.5	1.8
1966	23.0	6.6	8.6	6.5	31.6	12.9	12.3	8.6	10.3	3.9	4.4	2.1
1967	22.0	7.5	13.3	7.2	32.2	15.4	18.9	12.6	10.5	3.3	5.5	6.3
1968	21.9	8.2	9.4	9.1	32.5	14.6	16.3	12.1	11.4	3.7	6.5	2.0
1969												
1970												

Year	30-34 years			
	B037	B038	B039	B040
1954	1.9	1.1	1.9	0.9
1955	2.2	1.0	1.9	1.7
1956	2.9	1.3	0.9	0.6
1957	2.7	1.1	1.2	1.1
1958	3.0	1.6	2.4	0.4
1959	3.4	1.3	1.8	1.0
1960	4.0	1.2	1.0	1.0
1961	3.1	1.3	1.9	0.4
1962	4.2	1.4	1.7	1.3
1963	3.8	1.5	2.7	1.5
1964	3.6	1.6	3.9	1.8
1965	4.5	2.0	4.3	2.3
1966	3.8	1.7	4.2	1.7
1967	5.4	2.9	5.5	1.4
1968	5.0	2.8	4.9	3.2
1969				
1970				

	Fall school enrollment of civilian noninstitutional population 5-6 years of age (numbers in thousands)					
Year	Total enrolled	Kindergarten	Elementary school	Total enrolled	Kindergarten	Elementary school
	White male			White female		
	B041	B042	B043	B044	B045	B046
1954	2,442	709	1,733	2,360	561	1,709
1955	2,476	767	1,700	2,367	717	1,650
1956	2,485	790	1,695	2,383	754	1,629
1957	2,586	799	1,787	2,487	796	1,683
1958	2,730	944	1,786	2,591	825	1,766
1959	2,736	886	1,850	2,666	872	1,794
1960	2,867	991	1,876	2,707	858	1,849
1961	2,919	1,032	1,887	2,754	936	1,818
1962	2,963	1,066	1,897	2,798	959	1,839
1963	3,001	1,091	1,910	2,862	973	1,889
1964	3,001	1,104	1,897	2,887	1,053	1,834
1965	3,052	1,185	1,867	2,964	1,145	1,819
1966	3,096	1,186	1,909	3,010	1,168	1,843
1967	3,158	1,274	1,884	3,072	1,196	1,876
1968	3,096	1,260	1,836	2,994	1,142	1,852
1969						
1970						
	Nonwhite male			Nonwhite female		
	B047	B048	B049	B050	B051	B052
1954	304	63	241	338	84	254
1955	354	77	277	333	67	266
1956	354	106	248	375	108	267
1957	377	118	259	387	111	276
1958	393	105	288	386	117	269
1959	422	149	273	398	125	273
1960	425	124	301	439	119	320
1961	483	175	308	482	156	326
1962	436	143	293	454	151	303
1963	439	130	309	466	146	322
1964	477	164	313	477	148	329
1965	503	168	335	476	147	329
1966	523	180	343	527	174	352
1967	533	178	355	541	185	356
1968	545	193	352	528	184	344
1969						
1970						

	Fall school enrollment of civilian noninstitutional population 7-13 years of age (numbers in thousands)					
Year	Total enrolled	Elementary school (grades 1-8)	High school (grades 9-12)	Total enrolled	Elementary school (grades 1-8)	High school (grades 9-12)
	White male			White female		
	B053	B054	B055	B056	B057	B058
1953	8,293	8,117	176	7,999	7,792	207
1954	8,951	8,775	176	8,611	8,361	250
1955	9,451	9,297	154	9,034	8,772	262
1956	9,834	9,567	267	9,409	9,050	359
1957	10,151	9,918	233	9,698	9,393	305
1958	10,527	10,286	241	10,045	9,784	261
1959	10,936	10,757	179	10,463	10,237	226
1960	11,330	11,050	279	10,819	10,524	295
1961	11,378	11,182	196	10,856	10,571	284
1962	11,229	11,028	201	10,854	10,636	218
1963	11,465	11,234	230	11,086	10,841	245
1964	11,680	11,504	176	11,286	11,057	229
1965	11,998	11,829	169	11,584	11,325	258
1966	12,155	11,973	182	11,758	11,501	257
1967	12,320	12,126	194	11,904	11,700	204
1968	12,435	12,254	181	11,999	11,788	211
1969						
1970						
	Nonwhite male			Nonwhite female		
	B059	B060	B061	B062	B063	B064
1953	1,112	1,097	14	1,121	1,100	21
1954	1,188	1,158	29	1,202	1,180	21
1955	1,274	1,238	36	1,269	1,211	58
1956	1,345	1,312	33	1,358	1,329	29
1957	1,433	1,419	14	1,423	1,391	32
1958	1,533	1,512	20	1,519	1,496	23
1959	1,620	1,598	22	1,607	1,582	25
1960	1,744	1,729	15	1,728	1,692	36
1961	1,789	1,769	21	1,778	1,730	48
1962	1,774	1,758	16	1,777	1,752	25
1963	1,815	1,779	16	1,837	1,801	36
1964	1,869	1,847	22	1,891	1,855	36
1965	1,934	1,912	22	1,934	1,912	22
1966	1,984	1,968	16	1,997	1,963	34
1967	2,022	2,007	15	2,041	1,997	44
1968	2,078	2,043	35	2,107	2,065	42
1969						
1970						

Year	Fall school enrollment of civilian noninstitutional population 14-17 years of age (number in thousands)							
	Total enrolled	Elementary school (grades 1-8)	High school (grades 9-12)	College	Total enrolled	Elementary school (grades 1-8)	High school (grades 9-12)	College
	White male				White female			
	B065	B066	B067	B068	B069	B070	B071	B072
1953	3,405	439	2,888	77	3,216	283	2,840	92
1954	3,534	445	3,020	69	3,354	277	3,006	71
1955	3,606	455	3,104	47	3,401	302	3,021	78
1956	3,797	478	3,251	68	3,650	306	3,260	84
1957	4,133	508	3,557	68	3,893	304	3,496	93
1958	4,304	465	3,771	68	4,094	276	3,731	87
1959	4,481	460	3,933	88	4,243	290	3,848	105
1960	4,632	486	4,049	97	4,396	245	4,035	117
1961	5,037	560	4,397	79	4,811	273	4,413	125
1962	5,339	552	4,667	120	5,048	308	4,643	97
1963	5,632	509	5,030	94	5,367	304	4,986	77
1964	5,838	512	5,179	147	5,552	287	5,155	110
1965	5,770	547	5,118	104	5,557	278	5,151	129
1966	5,888	470	5,325	93	5,650	297	5,213	140
1967	6,068	531	5,449	88	5,770	284	5,353	133
1968	6,248	585	5,546	117	5,977	298	5,545	134
1969								
1970								
	Nonwhite male				Nonwhite female			
	B073	B074	B075	B076	B077	B078	B079	B080
1953	439	142	295	2	479	134	335	10
1954	468	160	304	5	428	118	304	7
1955	491	152	329	9	472	118	342	12
1956	478	153	316	9	488	113	369	6
1957	513	159	345	9	528	119	403	6
1958	549	152	393	5	498	78	413	7
1959	560	156	400	4	555	101	441	13
1960	615	149	465	2	598	119	472	6
1961	668	160	502	5	647	124	519	4
1962	693	170	518	5	660	99	550	11
1963	770	185	579	5	748	115	629	4
1964	821	157	646	18	803	129	658	16
1965	843	184	649	9	863	114	728	22
1966	884	159	713	12	873	107	757	9
1967	908	169	731	8	892	128	753	11
1968	951	186	748	17	942	131	798	13
1969								
1970								

	Fall school enrollment of civilian noninstitutional population 18-19 years of age (numbers in thousands)							
Year	Total enrolled	Elementary school (grades 1-8)	High school (grades 9-12)	College	Total enrolled	Elementary school (grades 1-8)	High school (grades 9-12)	College

	White male				White female			
	B081	B082	B083	B084	B085	B086	B087	B088
1953	568	--	183	384	481	--	147	334
1954	680	--	259	421	468	--	169	229
1955	674	--	256	418	417	5	115	297
1956	721	5	242	474	521	1	125	395
1957	686	--	176	570	528	2	115	411
1958	787	1	209	577	590	1	122	467
1959	824	2	202	620	588	--	107	481
1960	955	2	262	691	651	2	130	520
1961	1,045	--	259	786	714	--	112	602
1962	1,095	--	259	836	841	3	165	673
1963	1,041	5	290	746	764	2	116	645
1964	1,112	2	287	823	836	2	138	696
1965	1,520	--	367	1,152	1,108	2	185	922
1966	1,649	2	366	1,281	1,197	6	179	1,012
1967	1,436	--	209	1,097	1,227	1	217	1,009
1968	1,666	4	400	1,262	1,233	--	211	1,022
1969								
1970								

	Nonwhite male				Nonwhite female			
	B089	B090	B091	B092	B093	B094	B095	B096
1953	74	--	43	31	57	--	44	13
1954	50	4	35	12	69	--	43	27
1955	78	--	63	15	63	--	47	16
1956	88	4	46	38	77	3	47	27
1957	94	6	60	28	101	5	56	40
1958	111	3	64	44	77	5	45	26
1959	94	--	63	31	95	--	52	43
1960	107	2	62	43	102	--	57	45
1961	125	--	77	48	68	5	29	34
1962	117	2	60	55	91	--	43	48
1963	139	2	87	50	117	--	54	63
1964	127	2	82	43	122	--	68	54
1965	169	2	102	66	133	--	58	75
1966	193	2	117	74	139	--	66	73
1967	201	3	97	101	163	4	80	79
1968	226	4	127	95	192	--	70	122
1969								
1970								

Fall school enrollment of civilian noninstitutional population 20-24 years of age
(numbers in thousands)

Year	Total enrolled	Elementary school (grades 1-8)	High school (grades 9-12)	College	Total enrolled	Elementary school (grades 1-8)	High school (grades 1-8)	College
	White male				White female			
	B097	B098	B099	B100	B101	B102	B103	B104
1953	611	5	22	585	312	2	14	296
1954	633	5	23	605	303	3	20	281
1955	639	--	18	621	288	--	29	259
1956	766	3	30	733	324	1	31	292
1957	842	5	40	797	388	--	20	368
1958	848	7	38	802	353	1	18	334
1959	825	--	27	798	348	1	11	336
1960	877	--	18	859	371	--	21	350
1961	913	--	30	883	429	2	15	413
1962	1,102	4	32	1,066	488	--	37	451
1963	1,279	4	29	1,246	592	2	19	571
1964	1,264	--	38	1,226	650	--	26	624
1965	1,479	4	35	1,441	727	--	29	698
1966	1,582	--	41	1,541	805	6	26	772
1967	1,724	2	58	1,664	1,022	2	80	940
1968	1,746	2	57	1,687	1,002	2	42	958
1969								
1970								
	Nonwhite male				Nonwhite female			
	B105	B106	B107	B108	B109	B110	B111	B112
1953	74	--	43	31	57	--	44	13
1954	45	--	17	27	19	6	3	11
1955	47	6	15	25	36	3	7	26
1956	64	--	16	48	38	--	6	32
1957	55	2	23	30	51	--	10	41
1958	67	--	18	48	41	--	4	37
1959	67	--	9	58	43	--	7	36
1960	59	--	4	55	43	--	8	35
1961	76	--	12	64	50	2	9	39
1962	75	2	14	59	60	2	8	50
1963	86	2	22	62	57	--	7	50
1964	67	--	15	52	66	--	12	54
1965	80	--	17	62	74	2	7	65
1966	85	--	5	80	75	4	5	66
1967	139	3	16	120	116	--	27	89
1968	121	--	13	108	118	--	16	102
1969								
1970								

Fall school enrollment of civilian noninstitutional population 25-34 years of age
(numbers in thousands)

Year	Total enrolled	Elementary school (grades 1-8)	High school (grades 9-12)	College	Total enrolled	Elementary school (grades 1-8)	High school (grades 9-12)	College
	White male				White female			
	B113	B114	B115	B116	B117	B118	B119	B120
1954	409	--	17	392	150	2	31	117
1955	449	--	40	409	135	4	36	95
1956	586	2	51	533	165	3	54	108
1957	599	5	31	563	149	5	22	122
1958	600	5	44	552	193	1	49	143
1959	592	--	31	561	155	4	22	129
1960	593	--	26	567	150	1	7	142
1961	477	1	16	460	165	--	15	150
1962	587	--	23	564	157	5	25	127
1963	535	6	22	507	191	4	24	64
1964	537	2	11	524	207	2	18	187
1965	661	6	27	629	261	2	17	242
1966	649	2	26	624	279	2	29	248
1967	768	3	54	711	318	3	51	264
1968	828	5	46	777	346	3	46	297
1969								
1970								
	Nonwhite male				Nonwhite female			
	B121	B122	B123	B124	B125	B126	B127	B128
1954	23	--	5	50	22	--	--	22
1955	45	--	10	35	38	2	18	17
1956	34	--	5	29	13	--	6	7
1957	40	2	15	23	32	--	3	29
1958	48	--	15	33	16	1	3	12
1959	35	--	8	27	17	4	3	10
1960	28	--	3	25	21	1	4	16
1961	34	--	3	31	10	--	2	8
1962	42	--	5	37	24	8	7	9
1963	41	4	6	32	26	--	6	20
1964	58	1	3	54	29	2	13	14
1965	50	4	6	40	29	2	8	19
1966	49	2	--	47	27	2	8	17
1967	64	3	9	52	57	3	19	35
1968	69	1	6	62	38	2	7	29
1969								
1970								

Percent Distribution of Persons 18 and 19 Years of Age by Educational Attainment,
by Color and Sex, United States, 1947, 1957, 1959, 1962, 1964-1969

Period	White		Nonwhite		White		Nonwhite		White		Nonwhite	
	Male	Female	Male	Female	Male	Female	Male	Female	Male	Female	Male	Female
	Elementary school: 0-4 years completed				Elementary school: 5-7 years completed				Elementary school: 8 years completed			
	B129	B130	B131	B132	B133	B134	B135	B136	B137	B138	B139	B140
April 1947[a/][b/]	2.7	0.9	19.1	4.4	10.2	4.8	23.9	15.9	13.0	7.2	8.0	10.0
March 1957[b/]	1.6	1.9	10.8	2.8	5.5	2.3	16.1	12.7	5.3	4.5	8.3	9.9
March 1959[b/]	1.4	0.8	3.8	1.4	5.0	2.8	15.7	12.9	5.4	4.9	11.9	7.8
March 1962	0.6	0.5	4.4	2.4	3.2	1.6	13.2	9.1	3.3	2.7	7.8	3.3
March 1964	1.2	1.2	9.1	0.6	3.0	2.1	8.8	3.7	4.0	2.5	5.4	6.3
March 1965	0.9	0.4	3.2	2.1	2.8	2.0	4.4	3.7	2.7	3.1	9.7	6.6
March 1966	0.8	0.4	1.3	2.2	2.6	1.5	5.4	3.8	2.3	2.5	4.9	4.5
March 1967	0.6	0.3	1.2	0.4	2.0	1.7	5.8	5.6	2.4	2.1	6.3	3.4
March 1968	0.7	0.4	2.6	1.6	1.9	1.1	6.6	5.3	2.9	2.8	3.5	4.4
March 1969	0.9	0.9	3.8	1.3	1.9	1.1	5.3	3.3	3.0	1.6	3.7	5.5
	High school: 1-3 years completed				High school: 4 years completed							
	B141	B142	B143	B144	B145	B146	B147	B148				
April 1947[a/][b/]	38.8	33.8	31.0	40.5	29.3	44.7	13.2	23.7				
March 1957[b/]	37.3	31.5	41.7	41.0	39.6	50.5	19.8	29.0				
March 1959[b/]	36.0	31.7	51.7	48.6	42.1	48.4	14.9	25.2				
March 1962	33.4	29.0	39.0	39.7	44.9	54.9	31.5	34.8				
March 1964	35.1	28.44	54.6	42.9	43.2	53.4	19.2	40.0				
March 1965	37.4	30.5	49.6	35.1	43.4	52.9	28.0	46.3				
March 1966	35.1	28.6	54.9	48.9	45.0	55.1	29.2	31.7				
March 1967	36.1	30.3	56.4	43.0	44.5	52.0	26.0	39.1				
March 1968	37.4	27.8	52.1	37.2	43.4	54.5	29.4	41.1				
March 1969	36.7	29.1	50.1	44.0	43.8	54.2	29.4	38.5				
	College: 1-3 years completed				College: 4 or more years completed				College: 5 or more years completed			
	B149	B150	B151	B152	B153	B154	B155	B156	B157	B158	B159	B160
April 1947[a/][b/]	6.0	8.6	4.7	5.5	--	c/	--	--	c/	c/	c/	c/
March 1957[b/]	10.5	9.0	2.9	4.6	0.2	0.2	--	--	c/	c/	c/	c/
March 1959[b/]	10.0	11.3	1.9	4.1	--	--	--	--	--	--	--	--
March 1962	14.4	11.3	4.1	10.0	0.1	0.1	--	0.6	--	--	--	--
March 1964	13.4	12.4	2.8	6.9	--	0.1	--	--	--	--	--	--
March 1965	12.6	11.1	5.3	6.1	--	--	--	--	--	--	--	--
March 1966	14.2	11.9	4.4	8.6	--	--	--	--	--	--	--	--
March 1967	14.4	13.6	4.1	8.3	--	--	--	--	--	--	--	--
March 1968	13.5	13.5	6.0	10.4	--	c/	--	--	--	--	--	--
March 1969	13.7	13.0	7.8	7.4	--	0.1	--	--	--	--	--	--

Percent Distribution of Persons 20-24 Years of Age by Educational Attainment,
by Color and Sex, United States, 1947, 1957, 1959, 1962, 1964-1969

Period	White		Nonwhite		White		Nonwhite		White		Nonwhite	
	Male	Female	Male	Female	Male	Female	Male	Female	Male	Female	Male	Female
	Elementary school: 0-4 years completed				Elementary school: 5-7 years completed				Elementary school: 8 years completed			
	B161	B162	B163	B164	B165	B166	B167	B168	B169	B170	B171	B172
April 1947[a/][b/]	2.4	1.6	16.8	8.4	7.4	5.8	29.0	26.4	11.0	8.6	12.2	13.1
March 1957[b/]	2.5	1.8	12.3	4.8	5.4	4.4	14.1	14.0	6.9	6.4	9.9	7.7
March 1959[b/]	2.0	1.6	6.6	3.4	4.6	3.6	15.0	6.4	7.5	5.0	13.0	11.7
March 1962	1.4	1.1	5.2	1.7	3.4	2.7	9.2	8.2	5.4	5.3	11.4	10.3
March 1964	2.0	0.7	2.8	2.2	2.5	2.4	7.8	4.1	4.8	4.2	6.4	5.1
March 1965	1.4	0.9	5.1	1.7	2.8	1.4	7.0	4.2	4.3	4.0	5.7	5.3
March 1966	1.4	0.7	2.5	1.4	2.3	1.8	7.9	4.5	4.0	3.3	8.7	6.8
March 1967	0.8	0.7	2.7	1.4	3.0	2.0	5.6	5.1	3.8	3.2	7.6	5.1
March 1968	0.7	0.6	2.5	1.2	2.4	2.1	5.4	5.2	3.9	3.4	7.4	3.8
March 1969	1.0	1.0	2.3	2.1	2.5	1.8	6.2	5.4	3.2	2.6	5.9	3.1

Period	High school: 1-3 years completed				High school: 4 years completed			
	B173	B174	B175	B176	B177	B178	B179	B180
April 1947[a/][b/]	27.8	22.0	24.5	27.6	38.6	48.5	11.6	17.4
March 1957[b/]	18.6	20.5	32.4	31.9	38.6	48.3	23.3	30.6
March 1959[b/]	17.4	19.4	32.3	34.2	38.9	49.4	23.5	32.1
March 1962	17.8	19.5	32.9	35.5	38.7	48.1	29.0	28.8
March 1964	15.3	18.1	30.4	32.8	40.7	50.3	36.4	39.0
March 1965	15.9	16.8	30.9	39.7	39.9	51.1	36.1	33.6
March 1966	14.2	16.4	28.3	31.7	38.4	50.5	35.9	38.2
March 1967	13.7	15.4	31.0	29.0	37.7	48.1	36.3	40.3
March 1968	12.7	14.2	29.0	26.0	36.7	46.1	34.7	40.1
March 1969	11.6	14.1	33.7	25.2	38.3	47.8	31.0	40.7

Period	College: 1-3 years completed				College: 4 or more years completed				College: 5 or more years completed			
	B181	B182	B183	B184	B185	B186	B187	B188	B189	B190	B191	B192
April 1947[a/][b/]	10.6	10.4	4.6	5.6	2.0	3.2	1.2	1.5	c/	c/	c/	c/
March 1957[b/]	22.7	13.6	6.7	8.5	5.3	5.0	1.3	2.4	c/	c/	c/	c/
March 1959[b/]	22.1	15.7	8.5	9.8	7.6	5.3	1.2	2.5	1.8	0.7	--	--
March 1962	25.3	17.6	10.9	10.8	8.1	5.8	1.4	4.7	2.3	0.6	0.3	0.3
March 1964	27.3	17.4	13.0	14.2	7.4	6.9	3.4	2.6	2.2	0.6	0.5	0.3
March 1965	27.4	19.1	12.3	11.0	8.2	6.8	2.9	4.8	1.6	0.6	0.8	0.5
March 1966	29.6	19.5	15.0	14.8	10.1	7.9	1.7	2.6	3.1	0.9	0.3	0.4
March 1967	31.3	23.0	14.2	16.0	9.7	7.7	2.5	3.0	2.5	0.8	0.5	0.7
March 1968	33.9	25.5	16.7	17.6	9.6	8.1	4.2	6.0	3.2	1.0	0.6	0.1
March 1969	32.7	24.1	18.4	20.7	10.7	8.6	2.5	3.0	2.9	1.0	0.7	0.1

Percent Distribution of Persons 25-29 Years of Age by Educational Attainment, by Color and Sex, United States, 1947, 1957, 1959, 1962, 1964-1969

Period	White		Nonwhite		White		Nonwhite		White		Nonwhite	
	Male	Female	Male	Female	Male	Female	Male	Female	Male	Female	Male	Female
	Elementary school: 0-4 years completed				Elementary school: 5-7 years completed				Elementary school: 8 years completed			
	B193	B194	B195	B196	B197	B198	B199	B200	B201	B202	B203	B204
April 1947[a][b]	2.7	2.3	21.8	16.8	7.5	7.2	26.0	26.1	12.0	12.4	10.0	12.5
March 1957[b]	2.6	1.5	10.4	7.3	6.6	4.9	22.7	17.1	9.9	7.3	13.0	13.6
March 1959[b]	2.7	2.2	8.3	7.5	6.1	4.1	17.5	13.3	7.2	7.0	8.6	6.6
March 1962[b]	2.3	1.6	9.3	3.4	4.8	4.2	10.3	8.9	6.5	5.6	8.4	12.1
March 1964	1.7	1.6	6.9	3.7	4.1	3.6	10.8	6.7	6.3	4.8	8.5	12.9
March 1965	2.0	1.3	6.1	3.8	3.8	2.9	7.9	77.6	5.6	4.7	4.3	7.7
March 1966	1.5	1.3	3.9	2.6	3.8	2.8	6.1	8.1	4.8	4.4	8.1	6.8
March 1967	0.8	1.1	2.3	1.0	3.5	3.0	8.1	7.5	5.6	3.9	5.4	7.4
March 1968	0.9	0.9	3.7	2.0	3.3	2.9	5.8	5.1	5.2	3.9	5.4	7.4
March 1969	1.4	1.0	2.3	2.6	2.7	2.4	5.3	4.8	5.0	4.3	5.7	6.9

Period	White		Nonwhite		White		Nonwhite	
	High school: 1-3 years completed				High school: 4 years completed			
	B205	B206	B207	B208	B209	B210	B211	B212
April 1947[a][b]	24.9	21.3	22.6	19.9	35.7	42.2	13.6	18.2
March 1957[b]	19.6	20.2	26.5	26.9	34.7	48.5	18.4	25.0
March 1959[b]	17.1	19.3	25.0	34.1	37.6	49.0	27.2	28.2
March 1962[b]	17.2	19.3	33.0	31.8	36.4	47.7	23.6	32.9
March 1964	16.0	17.6	27.5	27.3	40.0	51.0	30.3	36.3
March 1965	15.8	18.3	28.3	29.6	42.0	51.0	34.6	36.5
March 1966	16.7	17.1	29.4	34.0	41.5	50.3	35.5	35.5
March 1967	15.8	16.3	26.0	29.2	40.2	48.5	37.7	38.8
March 1968	15.0	17.2	25.6	29.5	41.2	49.0	41.1	39.7
March 1969	13.5	15.7	25.3	31.5	39.7	49.7	41.5	37.7

Period	White		Nonwhite		White		Nonwhite		White		Nonwhite	
	College: 1-3 years completed				College: 4 or more years completed				College: 5 or more years completed			
	B213	B214	B215	B216	B217	B218	B219	B220	B221	B222	B223	B224
April 1947[a][b]	11.0	8.9	3.3	3.5	6.2	5.7	2.6	2.9	[c]	[c]	[c]	[c]
March 1957[b]	12.0	9.8	5.8	5.2	14.6	7.8	3.2	5.0	[c]	[c]	[c]	[c]
March 1959[b]	13.5	10.3	7.8	6.6	15.9	8.1	5.6	3.7	6.0	1.6	2.5	--
March 1962[b]	14.1	11.6	9.6	7.9	18.8	10.1	5.7	3.0	6.4	1.5	1.6	0.4
March 1964	14.4	11.5	6.0	8.8	17.5	10.0	10.0	4.4	7.4	2.1	3.7	1.3
March 1965	14.3	12.1	9.4	7.3	16.4	9.8	9.4	7.6	6.6	1.9	2.8	2.2
March 1966	13.9	12.3	8.7	4.8	17.9	11.8	8.3	8.3	7.2	2.4	3.6	2.1
March 1967	15.8	14.1	8.7	9.4	18.3	12.7	9.3	7.2	7.8	2.6	5.6	1.7
March 1968	15.2	13.7	9.1	9.6	19.1	12.2	9.5	6.6	7.9	2.6	4.3	0.6
March 1969	17.2	13.5	9.9	8.0	20.6	13.4	9.9	8.3	9.6	3.1	4.6	2.4

Percent Distribution of Persons 30-34 Years of Age by Educational Attainment,
by Color and Sex, United States, 1947, 1957, 1969, 1962, 1964-1969

Period	White		Nonwhite		White		Nonwhite		White		Nonwhite	
	Male	Female	Male	Female	Male	Female	Male	Female	Male	Female	Male	Female
	Elementary school: 0-4 years completed				Elementary school: 5-7 years completed				Elementary school: 8 years completed			
	B225	B226	B227	B228	B229	B230	B231	B232	B233	B234	B235	B236
April 1947a/b/	3.2	2.7	26.0	16.4	10.0	9.1	23.1	30.0	17.5	15.8	13.0	18.1
March 1957b/	2.9	2.6	15.8	8.5	6.7	5.0	23.7	20.9	10.1	9.4	11.9	14.7
March 1959b/	3.1	2.0	14.1	11.5	6.6	4.7	20.9	16.1	9.8	7.4	11.5	12.8
March 1962	2.4	2.2	8.7	6.2	5.7	4.2	19.5	12.3	9.4	7.2	11.9	10.1
March 1964	2.7	1.6	7.4	3.1	5.1	4.2	11.1	12.5	7.8	6.9	8.2	8.7
March 1965	3.0	2.0	7.7	4.0	5.2	4.7	16.3	8.6	6.8	6.6	8.8	13.3
March 1966	2.1	1.6	8.4	3.3	4.6	4.0	13.0	6.7	6.2	5.8	12.3	8.2
March 1967	1.6	1.5	6.4	1.2	4.7	4.1	12.9	8.8	6.8	6.2	7.9	5.9
March 1968	1.9	1.6	4.5	1.9	4.9	3.9	10.6	8.6	6.5	5.3	9.8	9.1
March 1969	1.7	1.2	4.4	2.7	4.7	3.4	10.4	4.3	5.8	4.7	7.4	6.5

Period	White		Nonwhite		White		Nonwhite	
	Male	Female	Male	Female	Male	Female	Male	Female
	High school: 1-3 years completed				High school: 4 years completed			
	B237	B238	B239	B240	B241	B242	B243	B244
April 1947a/b/	22.1	22.4	16.2	16.4	30.0	36.4	15.0	12.2
March 1957b/	23.1	20.3	22.9	27.0	31.2	47.0	20.2	21.2
March 1959b/	22.1	20.8	23.5	30.6	31.5	47.6	20.3	21.5
March 1962	17.5	18.9	25.2	33.6	35.4	46.7	21.4	26.8
March 1964	17.5	18.9	32.6	31.3	37.4	48.0	23.7	32.4
March 1965	15.6	18.5	23.4	32.3	38.7	47.5	24.6	27.2
March 1966	15.3	20.0	23.9	34.2	38.7	48.4	27.8	29.8
March 1967	15.5	19.2	22.7	28.9	37.5	49.0	32.9	37.7
March 1968	15.6	17.2	26.4	31.7	38.1	49.5	29.5	34.8
March 1969	15.2	18.0	28.2	31.7	39.8	49.8	32.1	39.8

Period	White		Nonwhite		White		Nonwhite		White		Nonwhite	
	Male	Female	Male	Female	Male	Female	Male	Female	Male	Female	Male	Female
	College: 1-3 years completed				College: 4 or more years completed				College: 5 or more years completed			
	B245	B246	B247	B248	B249	B250	B251	B252	B253	B254	B255	B256
April 1947a/b/	8.7	7.9	3.3	2.6	8.4	5.8	3.5	4.2	c/	c/	c/	c/
March 1957b/	10.3	9.5	4.0	4.3	15.6	6.2	1.5	3.3	c/	c/	c/	c/
March 1959b/	10.5	10.4	5.0	4.9	16.3	7.1	4.7	2.7	6.1	1.7	1.9	1.0
March 1962	11.3	11.6	7.7	4.4	18.4	9.1	5.5	6.5	8.3	2.2	2.1	1.0
March 1964	11.3	11.0	8.8	7.4	18.3	9.4	4.9	4.6	8.1	1.8	3.3	1.5
March 1965	11.2	11.0	8.2	7.2	19.4	9.6	10.9	7.3	7.9	2.0	5.4	1.7
March 1966	13.1	11.2	6.9	10.0	20.0	9.0	7.8	7.8	8.0	2.2	3.9	2.1
March 1967	13.3	11.2	9.7	10.5	20.6	8.7	7.5	7.2	8.2	1.7	3.0	2.0
March 1968	11.9	12.2	9.9	6.7	20.9	10.2	9.3	7.1	9.1	2.1	3.8	2.3
March 1969	13.2	11.6	7.5	7.4	19.7	11.2	10.0	7.6	8.7	3.2	4.5	2.0

313

Percent Distribution of Persons 35-44 Years of Age by Educational Attainment, by Color and Sex, United States, 1947, 1957, 1959, 1962, 1964-1969

Period	White		Nonwhite		White		Nonwhite		White		Nonwhite	
	Male	Female	Male	Female	Male	Female	Male	Female	Male	Female	Male	Female
	Elementary school: 0-4 years completed				Elementary school: 5-7 years completed				Elementary school: 8 years completed			
	B257	B258	B259	B260	B261	B262	B263	B264	B265	B266	B267	B268
April 1947[a/][b/]	4.9	4.1	29.4	19.8	14.2	12.0	31.5	35.2	24.4	22.6	14.7	16.6
March 1957[b/]	3.8	2.8	24.4	17.3	8.4	7.5	24.9	24.8	15.4	13.3	12.6	13.6
March 1959[b/]	3.6	2.1	22.9	12.3	7.3	7.2	26.4	26.7	12.5	11.5	13.2	13.7
March 1962	3.3	2.2	19.2	11.4	7.3	5.4	19.1	18.3	11.3	10.5	13.5	13.1
March 1964	3.1	2.2	14.0	7.1	6.9	5.5	18.9	19.0	10.6	9.3	12.9	10.0
March 1965	2.9	2.0	12.6	7.7	6.6	5.2	17.4	16.5	10.6	8.4	10.2	11.4
March 1966	2.9	2.4	13.5	4.8	6.2	5.0	16.3	18.3	10.4	8.1	13.5	10.4
March 1967	2.9	2.2	12.1	5.8	6.2	5.0	15.9	15.4	9.2	7.8	13.9	11.4
March 1968	2.5	1.6	12.5	7.5	5.8	5.0	16.3	13.9	9.5	7.8	10.6	11.7
March 1969	2.6	2.1	9.5	5.6	6.3	4.8	15.6	12.2	9.8	7.5	12.4	11.9

Period	White		Nonwhite		White		Nonwhite	
	Male	Female	Male	Female	Male	Female	Male	Female
	High school: 1-3 years completed				High school: 4 years completed			
	B269	B270	B271	B272	B273	B274	B275	B276
April 1947[a/][b/]	19.4	19.7	13.0	13.6	20.2	25.8	7.8	9.2
March 1957[b/]	20.8	21.2	18.4	21.4	32.5	40.3	11.2	16.2
March 1959[b/]	20.8	19.8	19.1	22.2	33.4	43.3	10.1	17.4
March 1962	20.0	19.1	19.6	25.3	32.4	44.0	18.9	21.5
March 1964	19.5	20.0	23.9	28.6	33.0	45.0	18.2	26.0
March 1965	19.1	19.4	25.1	30.1	33.9	46.6	20.3	24.5
March 1966	18.6	19.5	24.3	28.2	34.5	46.9	18.5	27.7
March 1967	18.5	19.5	26.1	26.8	34.7	46.3	19.8	27.8
March 1968	17.7	18.7	27.1	27.5	34.7	46.7	22.6	27.9
March 1969	16.5	18.3	23.6	28.2	34.5	47.3	25.1	28.4

Period	White		Nonwhite		White		Nonwhite		White		Nonwhite	
	Male	Female	Male	Female	Male	Female	Male	Female	Male	Female	Male	Female
	College: 1-3 years completed				College: 4 or more years completed				College: 5 or more years completed			
	B277	B278	B279	B280	B281	B282	B283	B284	B285	B286	B287	B288
April 1947[a/][b/]	8.1	9.2	1.7	2.8	8.8	6.5]	1.8	2.8	c/	c/	c/	c/
March 1957[b/]	8.4	7.9	3.2	3.7	10.6	7.0	5.2	2.9	c/	c/	c/	c/
March 1959[b/]	10.1	9.0	4.9	3.4	12.3	7.1	3.4	4.3	5.7	1.7	1.6	1.4
March 1962	10.7	11.2	5.0	5.1	15.1	7.5	4.8	5.1	6.5	1.8	1.6	1.2
March 1964	11.0	10.5	5.4	4.6	15.9	7.5	6.5	4.6	7.3	1.8	2.8	1.7
March 1965	10.6	10.6	7.1	4.9	16.4	7.9	7.3	4.8	7.2	2.1	3.3	1.1
March 1966	9.6	9.9	8.3	6.5	17.8	8.1	5.6	4.0	7.7	2.0	2.4	1.8
March 1967	11.0	10.6	6.5	6.9	17.7	8.6	5.6	5.6	7.3	2.2	2.3	2.4
March 1968	11.6	10.5	5.7	5.1	18.2	9.7	5.2	6.2	8.2	2.3	2.0	2.0
March 1969	11.9	10.3	5.8	7.4	18.4	9.6	7.8	6.2	8.4	2.9	3.2	2.6

Percent Distribution of Persons 45-54 Years of Age by Educational Attainment,
by Color and Sex, United States, 1947, 1957, 1959, 1962, 1964-1969

Period	White		Nonwhite		White		Nonwhite		White		Nonwhite	
	Male	Female	Male	Female	Male	Female	Male	Female	Male	Female	Male	Female
	Elementary school: 0-4 years completed				Elementary school: 5-7 years completed				Elementary school: 8 years completed			
	B289	B290	B291	B292	B293	B294	B295	B296	B297	B298	B299	B300
April 1947[a/b/]	9.3	8.7	39.8	39.2	18.4	16.8	30.5	31.0	30.3	28.7	13.6	11.1
March 1957[b/]	6.6	4.6	33.8	27.6	13.6	12.6	27.2	30.2	23.3	20.9	13.4	15.2
March 1959[b/]	4.8	3.9	34.2	21.1	12.0	11.6	28.4	31.9	21.2	19.8	13.2	15.9
March 1962	4.4	3.6	24.7	17.8	11.6	10.2	27.2	25.6	18.2	16.8	13.1	16.0
March 1964	4.3	2.8	23.0	11.8	9.5	8.7	23.2	31.6	17.5	15.7	14.4	17.4
March 1965	4.0	2.7	22.1	12.2	9.0	8.3	25.0	26.7	16.8	15.0	15.3	14.5
March 1966	3.9	2.6	23.4	13.5	9.5	8.6	18.9	24.2	15.3	14.4	15.6	13.5
March 1967	3.4	2.7	21.1	13.6	8.6	7.4	21.7	22.0	15.4	13.0	15.1	15.0
March 1968	3.3	2.6	18.1	14.2	8.4	7.0	20.6	21.9	13.9	12.3	13.6	14.9
March 1969	3.6	2.9	13.8	12.2	7.8	6.0	19.8	22.5	12.6	11.6	13.2	12.8

Period	White		Nonwhite		White		Nonwhite	
	Male	Female	Male	Female	Male	Female	Male	Female
	High school: 1-3 years completed				High school: 4 years completed			
	B301	B302	B303	B304	B305	B306	B307	B308
April 1947[a/b/]	16.6	16.0	5.5	9.7	13.7	17.8	5.5	4.4
March 1957[b/]	18.7	20.0	11.5	13.8	20.3	26.4	8.7	6.9
March 1959[b/]	21.2	19.9	10.8	15.6	22.5	29.0	6.9	9.2
March 1962	20.0	19.6	14.6	19.9	26.0	32.4	13.0	13.5
March 1964	19.3	20.4	19.8	18.3	29.3	35.9	11.3	13.0
March 1965	19.9	19.8	19.3	19.9	29.7	37.8	9.6	18.0
March 1966	20.5	19.9	19.6	22.9	30.9	37.8	12.8	16.8
March 1967	19.0	20.1	15.6	23.7	31.6	40.0	18.6	16.4
March 1968	18.1	19.4	20.4	19.5	33.1	41.9	17.2	18.6
March 1969	18.4	18.7	20.6	20.9	34.1	44.2	19.2	20.8

Period	White		Nonwhite		White		Nonwhite		White		Nonwhite	
	Male	Female	Male	Female	Male	Female	Male	Female	Male	Female	Male	Female
	College: 1-3 years completed				College: 4 or more years completed				College: 5 or more years completed			
	B309	B310	B311	B312	B313	B314	B315	B316	B317	B318	B319	B320
April 1947[a/b/]	5.7	7.6	1.5	2.1	5.9	4.3	3.5	2.5	c/	c/	c/	c/
March 1957[b/]	7.6	8.9	3.1	2.8	9.7	6.6	2.2	3.5	c/	c/	c/	c/
March 1959[b/]	8.0	9.2	3.1	3.4	10.3	6.6	3.3	2.7	4.9	1.8	1.5	0.9
March 1962	9.8	10.1	4.6	2.2	9.9	7.3	2.7	4.9	4.5	2.1	0.8	1.0
March 1964	9.7	9.0	4.6	4.2	10.2	7.5	3.8	3.6	4.6	2.7	1.4	0.5
March 1965	9.5	9.3	3.4	3.1	11.0	7.1	5.3	5.5	4.6	2.3	2.7	2.2
March 1966	9.0	9.3	4.3	5.3	11.0	7.3	5.3	3.9	4.4	2.3	2.8	1.5
March 1967	9.9	9.4	4.0	5.0	12.1	7.3	3.9	4.4	5.0	2.3	1.7	1.8
March 1968	10.7	9.7	4.9	5.2	12.6	7.1	5.2	5.7	6.0	2.1	2.3	2.2
March 1969	11.0	9.8	6.9	4.7	12.4	6.9	6.6	6.1	5.8	2.1	3.2	2.3

Percent Distribution of Persons 55-64 Years of Age by Educational Attainment,
by Color and Sex, United States, 1947, 1957, 1959, 1962, 1964-1969

Period	White		Nonwhite		White		Nonwhite		White		Nonwhite	
	Male	Female	Male	Female	Male	Female	Male	Female	Male	Female	Male	Female
	Elementary school: 0-4 years completed				Elementary school: 5-7 years completed				Elementary school: 8 years completed			
	B321	B322	B323	B324	B325	B326	B327	B328	B329	B330	B331	B332
April 1947[a/b]	16.0	13.5	51.1	42.6	21.0	19.0	22.4	30.7	31.5	31.4	11.4	13.1
March 1957[b]	11.3	9.6	49.6	41.6	18.4	16.9	25.9	27.5	28.4	26.1	9.2	13.4
March 1959[b]	9.6	8.5	43.2	32.0	17.0	15.6	29.8	33.0	29.2	25.6	11.5	16.5
March 1962	8.0	7.3	42.3	30.6	17.1	14.8	20.1	27.2	25.5	25.4	17.4	15.0
March 1964	7.4	5.9	35.4	25.7	15.4	13.8	26.8	27.7	25.4	23.8	16.7	18.1
March 1965	6.8	5.3	38.2	22.2	14.4	13.1	21.4	28.1	25.4	22.3	15.0	20.8
March 1966	6.7	4.9	36.2	21.3	14.6	12.7	23.6	27.6	24.5	22.0	15.5	17.7
March 1967	6.8	4.5	31.9	24.9	13.9	12.4	28.9	27.5	22.3	21.5	13.0	15.2
March 1968	5.3	4.4	35.8	24.7	14.1	11.9	27.1	28.3	21.5	19.7	9.7	16.5
March 1969	5.5	4.5	31.5	21.2	12.8	11.1	25.7	30.5	21.0	19.2	14.5	15.7

Period	High school: 1-3 years completed				High school: 4 years completed			
	B333	B334	B335	B336	B337	B338	B339	B340
April 1947[a/b]	9.7	12.7	9.1	7.6	11.9	14.5	3.1	4.1
March 1957[b]	14.2	15.6	9.3	9.2	14.5	19.1	4.1	4.8
March 1959[b]	16.0	16.5	6.2	8.6	14.9	19.6	5.1	6.5
March 1962	16.9	16.5	12.3	13.8	16.7	20.5	5.4	8.8
March 1964	17.2	17.0	9.4	13.6	18.8	24.4	5.3	9.1
March 1965	18.3	18.9	14.0	13.6	18.8	24.9	7.1	8.2
March 1966	18.1	18.5	13.1	15.7	19.1	25.2	7.7	11.3
March 1967	17.6	18.8	12.3	17.6	21.6	26.2	7.6	8.6
March 1968	18.7	19.2	10.9	14.7	22.0	27.7	8.9	9.2
March 1969	18.0	18.3	14.3	16.2	24.3	30.4	7.0	10.5

Period	College: 1-3 years completed				College: 4 or more years completed				College: 5 or more years completed			
	B341	B342	B343	B344	B345	B346	B347	B348	B349	B350	B351	B352
April 1947[a/b]	5.2	5.5	1.1	3.0	4.7	3.3	1.8	0.9	c/	c/	c/	c/
March 1957[b]	6.0	7.1	1.2	2.4	7.2	5.6	0.7	1.0	c/	c/	c/	c/
March 1959[b]	6.2	8.4	1.0	1.8	7.0	5.7	3.1	1.5	2.7	1.3	1.4	0.6
March 1962	6.6	9.2	1.1	2.7	9.2	6.2	1.5	1.8	3.6	1.7	0.6	0.4
March 1964	7.0	8.7	2.4	2.9	8.8	6.3	2.4	3.0	3.9	1.7	1.5	1.8
March 1965	6.7	8.5	1.2	3.8	9.5	7.0	3.1	3.2	4.6	2.5	1.3	1.1
March 1966	7.4	9.0	1.3	3.1	9.7	7.8	2.7	3.2	4.4	2.8	0.3	0.6
March 1967	8.0	9.1	2.0	3.5	9.8	7.5	4.3	2.5	4.7	2.2	1.3	0.6
March 1968	8.4	9.4	3.1	2.6	9.8	7.6	4.4	4.1	4.6	2.6	2.4	1.2
March 1969	8.1	8.8	3.5	2.6	10.3	7.7	3.3	3.2	4.9	2.5	1.1	0.7

316

Percent Distribution of Persons 65 Years and Older by Educational Attainment,
by Color and Sex, United States, 1947, 1957, 1959, 1962, 1964-1969

Period	White		Nonwhite		White		Nonwhite		White		Nonwhite	
	Male	Female	Male	Female	Male	Female	Male	Female	Male	Female	Male	Female

Elementary school: 0-4 years completed | Elementary school: 5-7 years completed | Elementary school: 8 years completed

Period	B353	B354	B355	B356	B357	B358	B359	B360	B361	B362	B363	B364
April 1947[a/b/]	22.4	16.8	67.3	58.5	22.3	21.5	16.2	23.2	31.2	33.4	6.8	6.2
March 1957[b/]	23.0	17.5	68.3	58.5	21.0	19.1	16.8	24.0	27.9	28.4	6.2	8.3
March 1959[b/]	21.2	16.0	61.2	46.0	21.9	19.8	18.4	26.5	26.9	28.2	8.0	13.3
March 1962	20.2	14.6	56.9	48.3	19.8	19.4	14.3	20.9	27.9	29.2	13.6	16.5
March 1964	19.4	14.7	51.3	49.2	20.2	18.3	24.3	22.0	27.2	28.1	9.7	10.1
March 1965	17.3	13.7	51.1	46.7	20.5	17.8	21.5	26.0	28.7	28.2	11.0	11.2
March 1966	16.1	12.9	52.3	44.7	19.4	17.2	18.7	27.7	28.9	27.5	11.3	11.3
March 1967	14.9	11.7	57.9	41.5	19.2	17.1	19.1	28.1	29.1	29.0	10.3	13.4
March 1968	14.8	11.9	51.2	40.2	18.8	16.2	20.4	25.6	27.8	27.6	12.4	14.6
March 1969	13.1	10.8	48.8	38.6	18.2	16.3	26.5	28.2	28.2	27.5	8.5	15.6

High school: 1-3 years completed | High school: 4 years completed

Period	B365	B366	B367	B368	B369	B370	B371	B372
April 1947[a/b/]	7.1	9.2	5.8	5.6	8.9	12.1	2.9	3.7
March 1957[b/]	9.9	12.4	2.9	4.6	8.7	14.3	3.3	2.4
March 1959[b/]	10.4	13.9	4.3	6.0	8.9	12.6	4.5	6.2
March 1962	10.1	11.5	6.9	6.4	11.3	14.9	3.0	4.8
March 1964	11.2	14.0	6.1	9.3	11.3	14.6	4.7	4.8
March 1965	10.6	14.2	6.5	8.3	11.8	15.1	6.3	4.5
March 1966	11.1	14.3	8.7	8.4	13.1	16.3	7.2	4.8
March 1967	12.1	13.7	8.0	7.5	13.2	16.7	2.7	6.0
March 1968	12.7	14.1	6.7	8.5	13.7	17.9	5.2	6.1
March 1969	13.1	14.3	4.7	8.3	14.6	18.6	6.9	5.1

College: 1-3 years completed | College: 4 or more years completed | College: 5 or more years completed

Period	B373	B374	B375	B376	B377	B378	B379	B380	B381	B382	B383	B384
April 1947[a/b/]	3.5	4.1	0.9	1.7	4.5	2.9	--	1.1	c/	c/	c/	c/
March 1957[b/]	3.5	4.8	0.4	1.0	6.0	3.3	2.0	1.2	c/	c/	c/	c/
March 1959[b/]	4.8	5.9	0.6	0.6	5.8	3.6	2.9	1.3	2.5	0.7	1.0	0.2
March 1962	5.4	6.5	1.4	1.9	5.3	3.9	3.9	1.1	2.0	0.9	1.3	--
March 1964	4.7	6.1	1.9	2.7	6.0	4.2	1.9	1.6	2.6	1.0	0.3	0.4
March 1965	5.2	6.2	1.2	1.3	5.9	4.8	2.2	1.7	2.5	1.1	0.3	0.3
March 1966	5.0	6.7	0.9	2.4	6.4	5.0	1.1	0.8	2.5	1.4	0.5	0.3
March 1967	4.9	6.7	0.6	2.0	6.6	5.2	1.2	1.6	2.8	1.3	0.6	0.5
March 1968	5.3	7.0	1.6	3.0	7.0	5.3	2.4	1.9	3.3	1.2	1.0	0.1
March 1969	5.5	7.1	2.3	3.0	7.3	5.4	2.0	1.4	3.2	1.5	1.3	0.5

Percent of Persons in Specified Age-Groups having less than Five Years Schooling,
by Color and Sex, United States, 1947, 1957, 1959, 1962, 1964-1969

Period	White		Nonwhite		White		Nonwhite		White		Nonwhite	
	Male	Female	Male	Female	Male	Female	Male	Female	Male	Female	Male	Female
	18-19 years				20-24 years				25-29 years			
	B385	B386	B387	B388	B389	B390	B391	B392	B393	B394	B395	B396
April 1947[a]	2.7	0.9	19.1	4.4	2.4	1.6	16.8	8.4	2.7	2.3	21.8	16.8
March 1957[a]	1.6	1.9	10.8	2.8	2.5	1.8	12.3	4.8	2.6	1.5	10.4	7.3
March 1959[a]	1.4	0.8	3.8	1.4	2.0	1.6	6.6	3.4	2.7	2.2	8.3	7.5
March 1962	0.6	0.5	4.4	2.4	1.4	1.1	5.2	1.7	2.3	1.6	9.3	3.4
March 1964	1.2	1.2	9.1	0.6	2.0	0.7	2.8	2.2	1.7	1.6	6.9	3.7
March 1965	0.9	0.4	3.2	2.1	1.4	0.9	5.1	1.7	2.0	1.3	6.1	3.8
March 1966	0.8	0.4	1.3	2.2	1.4	0.7	2.5	1.4	1.5	1.3	3.9	2.6
March 1967	0.6	0.3	1.2	0.4	0.8	0.7	2.7	1.4	0.8	1.1	2.3	1.0
March 1968	0.7	0.4	2.6	1.6	0.7	0.6	2.5	1.2	0.9	0.9	3.7	2.0
March 1969	0.9	0.9	3.8	1.3	1.0	1.0	2.3	2.1	1.4	1.0	2.3	2.6
	30-34 years				35-44 years				45-54 years			
	B397	B398	B399	B400	B401	B402	B403	B404	B405	B406	B407	B408
April 1947[a]	3.2	2.7	26.0	16.4	4.9	4.1	29.4	19.8	9.3	8.7	39.8	39.2
March 1957[a]	2.9	2.6	15.8	8.5	3.8	2.8	24.4	17.3	6.6	4.6	33.8	27.6
March 1959[a]	3.1	2.0	14.1	11.5	3.6	2.1	22.9	12.3	4.8	3.9	34.2	21.1
March 1962	2.4	2.2	8.7	6.2	3.3	2.2	19.2	11.4	4.4	3.6	24.7	17.8
March 1964	2.7	1.6	7.4	3.1	3.1	2.2	14.0	7.1	4.3	2.8	23.0	11.8
March 1965	3.0	2.0	7.7	4.0	2.9	2.0	12.6	7.7	4.0	2.7	22.1	12.2
March 1966	2.1	1.6	8.4	3.3	2.9	2.4	13.5	4.8	3.9	2.6	23.4	13.5
March 1967	1.6	1.5	6.4	1.2	2.9	2.2	12.1	5.8	3.4	2.7	21.1	13.6
March 1968	1.9	1.6	4.5	1.9	2.5	1.6	12.5	7.5	3.3	2.6	18.1	14.2
March 1969	1.7	1.2	4.4	2.7	2.6	2.1	9.5	5.6	3.6	2.9	13.8	12.2
	55-64 years				65 years and over							
	B409	B410	B411	B412	B413	B414	B415	B416				
April 1947[a]	16.0	13.5	51.1	40.6	22.4	16.8	67.3	58.5				
March 1957[a]	11.3	9.6	49.6	41.6	23.0	17.5	68.3	58.5				
March 1959[a]	9.6	8.5	43.2	32.0	21.2	16.0	61.2	46.0				
March 1962	8.0	7.3	42.3	30.6	20.2	14.6	56.9	48.3				
March 1964	7.4	5.9	35.4	25.7	19.4	14.7	51.3	49.2				
March 1965	6.8	5.3	38.2	22.2	17.3	13.7	51.1	46.7				
March 1966	6.7	4.9	36.2	21.3	16.1	12.9	52.3	44.7				
March 1967	6.8	4.5	31.9	24.9	14.9	11.7	57.9	41.5				
March 1968	5.3	4.4	35.8	24.7	14.8	11.9	51.2	40.2				
March 1969	5.5	4.5	31.5	21.2	13.1	10.8	48.8	38.6				

Percent of Persons in Specified Age-Groups having Four Years of High School or More,
by Color and Sex, United States, 1947, 1957, 1959, 1962, 1964-1969

Period	White		Nonwhite		White		Nonwhite		White		Nonwhite	
	Male	Female	Male	Female	Male	Female	Male	Female	Male	Female	Male	Female
	18-19 years				20-24 years				25-29 years			
	B417	B418	B419	B420	B421	B422	B423	B424	B425	B426	B427	B428
April 1947[a/]	35.3	53.3	17.9	29.2	51.2	62.1	17.4	24.5	52.9	56.8	19.5	24.6
March 1957[a/]	50.3	59.7	22.7	33.6	66.6	66.9	31.3	41.5	61.3	66.1	27.4	35.2
March 1959[a/]	52.1	59.7	16.8	29.3	68.6	70.4	33.2	44.4	67.0	67.4	40.6	38.5
March 1962	59.4	66.3	35.6	45.4	72.1	71.5	41.3	44.3	69.3	69.4	38.9	43.8
March 1964	56.6	65.9	22.0	46.9	75.4	74.6	52.8	55.8	71.9	72.5	46.3	49.5
March 1965	56.0	64.0	33.3	52.4	75.5	77.0	51.3	49.4	72.7	72.9	53.4	51.4
March 1966	59.2	67.0	33.6	40.3	78.1	77.9	52.6	55.6	73.3	74.4	52.5	48.6
March 1967	58.9	65.6	30.1	47.4	78.7	78.8	53.0	59.3	74.3	75.3	55.7	55.4
March 1968	56.9	68.0	35.4	51.5	80.2	79.7	55.6	63.7	75.5	74.9	59.7	55.9
March 1969	57.5	67.3	37.2	45.9	81.7	80.5	51.9	64.5	77.5	76.6	61.3	54.0
	30-34 years				35-44 years				45-54 years			
	B429	B430	B431	B432	B433	B434	B435	B436	B437	B438	B439	B440
April 1947[a/]	47.1	50.1	21.8	19.0	37.1	41.5	11.3	14.8	25.3	29.7	10.5	9.0
March 1957[a/]	57.1	62.7	25.7	28.8	51.5	55.2	19.6	22.8	37.6	41.9	14.0	13.2
March 1959[a/]	58.3	65.1	30.0	29.1	55.8	59.4	18.4	25.1	40.8	44.8	13.3	15.3
March 1962	65.1	67.4	34.6	37.7	58.2	62.7	28.7	31.7	45.7	49.8	20.3	20.6
March 1964	67.0	68.4	37.4	44.4	59.9	63.0	30.1	35.2	49.2	52.4	19.7	20.8
March 1965	69.3	68.1	43.7	41.7	60.9	65.1	34.7	34.2	50.2	54.2	18.3	26.6
March 1966	71.8	68.6	42.5	47.6	61.9	64.9	32.4	38.2	50.9	54.4	22.4	26.0
March 1967	71.4	68.9	50.1	55.4	63.4	65.5	31.9	40.3	53.6	56.7	26.5	25.8
March 1968	70.9	71.9	48.7	48.6	64.5	66.9	33.5	39.2	56.4	58.7	27.3	29.5
March 1969	72.7	72.6	49.6	54.8	64.8	67.2	38.7	42.0	57.5	60.9	32.7	31.6
	55-64 years				65 years and over							
	B441	B442	B443	B444	B445	B446	B447	B448				
April 1947[a/]	21.8	23.3	6.0	8.0	16.9	19.1	3.8	6.5				
March 1957[a/]	27.7	31.8	6.0	8.2	18.2	22.4	5.7	4.6				
March 1959[a/]	28.1	33.7	9.2	9.8	19.5	22.1	8.0	8.1				
March 1962	32.5	35.9	8.0	13.3	22.0	25.3	8.3	7.8				
March 1964	34.6	39.4	10.1	15.0	22.0	24.9	8.5	9.1				
March 1965	35.0	40.4	11.4	15.2	22.9	26.1	9.7	7.5				
March 1966	36.2	42.0	11.7	17.6	24.5	28.0	9.2	8.0				
March 1967	39.4	42.8	13.9	14.6	24.7	28.6	4.5	9.6				
March 1968	40.2	44.7	16.4	15.9	26.0	30.2	9.2	11.0				
March 1969	42.7	46.9	13.8	16.3	27.4	31.1	11.2	9.5				

Percent of Persons in Specified Age Groups having any College, by Color and Sex,
United States, 1947, 1957, 1959, 1962, 1964-1969

Period	White		Nonwhite		White		Nonwhite		White		Nonwhite	
	Male	Female	Male	Female	Male	Female	Male	Female	Male	Female	Male	Female
	18-19 years				20-24 years				25-29 years			
	B449	B450	B451	B452	B453	B454	B455	B456	B457	B458	B459	B460
April 1947	6.0	8.6	4.7	5.5	12.6	13.6	5.8	7.1	17.2	14.6	5.9	6.4
March 1957	10.7	9.2	2.9	4.6	28.0	18.6	8.0	10.9	26.6	17.6	9.0	10.2
March 1959	10.0	11.3	1.9	4.1	29.7	21.0	9.7	12.3	29.4	18.4	13.4	10.3
March 1962	14.5	11.4	4.1	10.6	33.4	23.4	12.3	15.5	32.9	21.7	15.3	10.9
March 1964	13.4	12.5	2.8	6.9	34.7	24.3	16.4	16.8	31.9	21.5	16.0	13.2
March 1965	12.6	11.1	5.3	6.1	35.6	25.9	15.2	15.8	30.7	21.9	18.8	14.9
March 1966	14.2	11.9	4.4	8.6	39.7	27.4	16.7	17.4	31.8	24.1	17.0	13.1
March 1967	14.4	13.6	4.1	8.3	41.0	30.7	16.7	19.0	34.1	26.8	18.0	16.6
March 1968	13.5	13.5	6.0	10.4	43.5	33.6	20.9	23.6	34.3	25.9	18.6	16.2
March 1969	13.7	13.1	7.8	7.4	43.4	32.7	20.9	23.7	37.8	26.9	19.8	16.3
	30-34 years				35-44 years				45-54 years			
	B461	B462	B463	B464	B465	B466	B467	B468	B469	B470	B471	B472
April 1947	17.1	13.7	6.8	6.8	16.9	15.7	3.5	5.6	11.6	11.9	5.0	4.6
March 1957	25.9	15.7	5.5	7.6	19.0	14.9	8.4	6.6	17.3	15.5	5.3	6.3
March 1959	26.8	17.5	9.7	7.6	22.4	16.1	8.3	7.7	18.3	15.8	6.4	6.1
March 1962	29.7	20.7	13.2	10.9	25.8	18.7	9.8	10.2	19.7	17.4	7.3	7.1
March 1964	29.6	20.4	13.7	12.0	26.9	18.0	11.9	9.2	19.9	16.5	8.4	7.8
March 1965	30.6	20.6	19.1	14.5	27.0	18.5	14.4	9.7	20.5	16.4	8.7	8.6
March 1966	33.1	20.2	14.7	17.8	27.4	18.0	13.9	10.5	20.0	16.6	9.6	9.2
March 1967	33.9	19.9	17.2	17.7	28.7	19.2	12.1	12.5	22.0	16.7	7.9	9.4
March 1968	32.8	22.4	19.2	13.8	29.8	20.2	10.9	11.3	23.3	16.8	10.1	10.9
March 1969	32.9	22.8	17.5	15.0	30.3	19.9	13.6	13.6	23.4	16.7	13.5	10.8
	55-64 years				65 years and over							
	B473	B474	B475	B476	B477	B478	B479	B480				
April 1947	9.9	8.8	2.9	3.9	8.0	7.0	0.9	2.8				
March 1957	13.2	12.7	1.9	3.4	9.5	8.1	2.4	2.2				
March 1959	13.2	14.1	4.1	3.3	10.6	9.5	3.5	1.9				
March 1962	15.8	15.4	2.6	4.5	10.7	10.4	5.3	3.0				
March 1964	15.8	15.0	4.8	5.9	10.7	10.3	3.8	4.3				
March 1965	16.2	15.5	4.3	7.0	11.1	11.0	3.4	3.0				
March 1966	17.1	16.8	4.0	6.3	11.4	11.7	2.0	3.2				
March 1967	17.8	16.6	6.3	6.0	11.5	11.9	1.8	3.6				
March 1968	18.2	17.0	7.5	6.7	12.3	12.3	4.0	4.9				
March 1969	18.4	16.5	6.8	5.8	12.8	12.5	4.3	4.4				

Earned degrees conferred by level of degree and sex

Academic year ending June –	Estimated 4-year bachelor's degrees		First level: 4-year bachelor's & 5-or-more year first professional degrees		Master's degrees (except first professional)		Doctor's degrees	
	Male (000)	Female (000)	Male (000)	Female (000)	Male (000)	Female (000)	Male	Female
	B481	B482	B483	B484	B485	B486	B487	B488
1948	151.5	92.9	176.2	96.2	28.9	13.5	3,496	493
1949	227.5	99.0	264.2	102.5	35.2	15.5	4,528	522
1950	284.3	100.5	329.8	103.9	41.2	17.0	5,804	616
1951	240.8	101.5	279.3	105.0	46.2	18.9	6,664	674
1952	195.9	101.5	227.0	104.9	43.6	20.0	6,969	714
1953	173.5	100.7	200.8	104.0	41.0	20.0	7,517	792
1954	162.2	102.1	187.5	105.4	38.2	18.7	8,181	815
1955	159.0	100.6	183.6	103.8	38.7	19.5	8,014	826
1956	173.3	108.3	199.6	111.7	39.4	19.9	8,018	885
1957	193.5	114.2	222.7	117.6	41.3	20.6	7,817	939
1958	211.4	119.2	243.0	122.8	44.2	21.4	7,978	964
1959	222.0	126.7	254.9	130.3	47.4	22.2	8,371	989
1960	222.8	135.5	255.5	139.4	50.9	23.6	8,801	1,028
1961	223.4	141.9	255.9	145.9	54.2	24.1	9,463	1,112
1962	228.4	154.4	262.0	158.5	58.7	26.2	10,377	1,245
1963	239.2	171.3	274.8	175.8	62.9	28.5	11,448	1,374
1964	263.1	197.4	299.8	202.3	69.0	32.1	12,955	1,535
1965	279.8	213.3	319.7	219.3	76.2	36.0	14,692	1,775
1966	289.3	218.6	331.1	224.5	93.2	47.6	16,121	2,118
1967	310.4	233.4	355.3	239.6	103.2	54.7	18,164	2,457
1968	343.2	271.5	392.8	278.8	113.8	63.4	20,185	2,906
1969								
1970								

Percent change (from previous year) in earned degrees

Academic year ending June –	Estimated 4-year bachelor's degrees		First level: 4-year bachelor's & 5-or-more year first professional degrees		Master's degrees (except first professional)		Doctor's degrees	
	Male	Female	Male	Female	Male	Female	Male	Female
	B489	B490	B491	B492	B493	B494	B495	B496
1948								
1949	50.2	6.6	49.9	6.5	21.8	14.8	29.5	5.9
1950	25.0	1.5	24.8	1.4	17.0	9.7	28.2	18.0
1951	-15.3	1.5	-15.3	1.0	12.1	11.2	14.8	9.4
1952	-18.6	0	-18.7	-0.1	-5.6	5.8	4.6	5.9
1953	-11.4	-0.8	-11.9	-0.8	-6.0	0	7.9	10.9
1954	-6.5	1.3	-6.6	1.3	-7.0	-6.5	8.8	2.9
1955	-2.0	-1.5	-2.1	-1.5	1.3	4.3	-2.0	1.3
1956	9.0	7.7	8.7	7.6	1.8	2.0	0.0	7.1
1957	11.7	5.4	11.6	5.3	4.8	3.5	-2.5	6.1
1958	9.3	4.4	9.1	4.4	7.0	3.9	2.0	2.7
1959	5.0	6.3	4.8	6.1	7.2	3.7	4.9	2.6
1960	0.4	6.9	0.2	7.0	7.3	6.3	5.1	3.9
1961	0.3	4.7	0.2	4.7	6.5	2.1	7.5	8.2
1962	2.2	8.8	2.4	8.6	8.3	8.7	9.6	11.1
1963	4.7	10.9	4.9	10.9	7.2	8.8	10.3	10.4
1964	10.0	15.2	9.1	15.1	9.7	12.6	13.2	11.7
1965	6.3	8.1	6.6	8.4	10.4	12.1	13.4	15.6
1966	3.4	2.5	3.8	2.4	22.3	32.2	9.7	19.3
1967	7.3	6.8	7.3	6.7	10.7	14.9	12.7	16.0
1968	10.6	16.3	10.6	16.4	10.3	15.9	11.1	18.3
1969								
1970								

Academic year ending June -	High school graduates (total of public lic & private schools)		First-time degree credit college enroll-ment (all institutions)		Ratio: high school graduates (June) per 100 total population (incl. Armed Forces overseas) aged 17.5 years July 1		Ratio: first-time degree credit college enrollment (Oct.) per 100 high school graduates (June)	
	Male (000)	Female (000)	Male (000)	Female (000)	Male	Female	Male	Female
	B497	B498	B499	B500	B501	B502	B503	B504
1940	579	643	--	--	46.4	51.9	--	--
1941	--	--	--	--	--	--	--	--
1942	577	666	--	--	47.5	54.9	--	--
1943	--	--	--	--	--	--	--	--
1944	424	595	--	--	35.3	49.9	--	--
1945	--	--	--	--	--	--	--	--
1946	467	613	500	197	41.3	53.1	--	32.1
1947	--	--	400	193	--	--	--	--
1948	563	627	370	199	49.6	56.1	65.7	31.7
1949	--	--	357	201	--	--	--	--
1950	571	629	320	197	53.3	59.6	56.0	31.3
1951	--	--	280	192	--	--	--	--
1952	569	627	324	213	53.5	59.9	56.9	34.0
1953	--	--	345	227	--	--	--	--
1954	615	667	386	244	57.3	62.7	62.8	36.6
1955	648	703	418	257	58.9	64.6	64.5	36.6
1956	682	739	446	277	59.9	66.1	65.4	37.5
1957	696	750	445	284	60.4	66.3	63.9	37.9
1958	729	784	469	312	61.2	67.0	64.3	39.8
1959	790	849	491	336	62.3	68.4	62.2	39.6
1960	898	966	543	387	64.1	70.6	60.5	40.1
1961	958	1,013	596	430	66.4	71.8	62.2	42.4
1962	941	984	602	437	67.0	71.8	64.0	44.4
1963	959	991	608	446	68.2	72.3	63.4	45.0
1964	1,123	1,167	706	528	68.1	72.7	62.9	45.2
1965	1,314	1,351	834	618	71.3	75.6	63.5	45.7
1966	1,326	1,346	857	652	74.0	77.5	64.6	48.4
1967	1,332	1,348	895	696	74.6	77.9	67.2	51.6
1968	1,373	1,386	931	713	76.0	79.2	67.8	51.4
1969	1,408	1,431	953	743	75.9	79.6	67.6	51.9
1970								

Academic year ending June –	Ratio: 4-year bachelor's degrees per 100 first time degree credit college enrollments four years earlier		Ratio: master's degrees (except first professional degree) per 100 bachelor's degrees two years earlier		Ratio: doctor's degrees per 100 bachelor's degrees ten years earlier		Ratio: degrees granted to males per 100 degrees granted to females		
							First level: 4-yr. bachelor's & 5-or-more year first professional degrees	Master's degrees	Doctor's degrees
	Male	Female	Male	Female	Male	Female			
	B505	B506	B507	B508	B509	B510	B511	B512	B513
1948							183.2	214.1	709.1
1949							257.8	227.1	867.4
1950	56.9	51.0	27.2	18.3			317.4	242.4	942.2
1951	60.2	52.6	20.3	19.1			266.0	244.4	988.7
1952	52.9	51.0	15.3	19.9			216.4	218.0	976.1
1953	48.6	50.1	17.0	19.7			193.1	205.0	949.1
1954	50.7	51.8	19.5	18.4			177.9	204.3	1,003.8
1955	56.8	52.4	22.3	19.4			176.9	198.5	970.2
1956	53.5	50.8	24.3	19.5			178.7	198.0	906.0
1957	56.1	50.3	26.0	20.5			189.4	200.5	832.5
1958	54.8	48.9	25.5	19.8	5.3	1.0	197.9	206.5	827.6
1959	53.1	49.3	24.5	19.4	3.7	1.0	195.6	213.5	846.4
1960	50.0	48.9	24.1	19.8	3.1	1.0	183.3	215.7	856.1
1961	50.2	50.0	24.4	19.0	3.9	1.1	175.4	224.9	851.0
1962	48.7	49.5	26.3	19.3	5.3	1.2	165.3	224.0	833.5
1963	48.7	51.0	28.2	20.1	6.6	1.4	156.3	220.7	833.2
1964	48.5	51.0	30.2	20.8	8.0	1.5	148.2	215.0	844.0
1965	46.9	49.6	31.9	21.0	9.2	1.8	145.6	211.7	827.7
1966	48.1	50.0	35.4	24.1	9.3	2.0	147.5	195.8	761.1
1967	51.1	52.3	36.9	25.6	9.4	2.2	148.3	188.7	739.3
1968	48.6	51.4	39.3	29.0	9.5	2.3	140.9	179.5	694.6
1969									
1970									

Date	Unemployment rates[a], by sex and by years of school completed							
	Male	Female	Male	Female	Male	Female	Male	Female
	Total civilian labor force aged 18 years and over		Elementary school: less than 5 years completed		Elementary school: 5-7 years completed		Elementary school: 8 years completed	
	B514	B515	B516	B517	B518	B519	B520	B521
Oct. 1952[b]	1.5	2.7	2.1	2.1	2.4	2.7	1.4	2.3
March 1957	4.1	4.1	8.0	6.7	6.2	5.3	4.4	5.6
March 1959	6.3	6.0	9.9	10.3	9.8	9.7	7.3	6.4
March 1962	6.0	6.0	10.4	7.5	8.5	7.7	7.5	6.4
March 1964	5.2	6.1	9.4	6.6	7.8	9.9	6.9	6.2
March 1965	4.4	5.3	7.1	8.9	6.5	6.6	5.2	4.7
March 1966	3.4	4.1	6.3	4.4	5.5	3.9	4.3	5.6
March 1967	3.1	4.5	5.7	5.8	4.7	5.0	4.0	5.7
March 1968	3.0	4.2	4.8	6.1	3.5	6.2	3.7	5.1
March 1969								
	High school: 1-3 years		High school: 4 years		College: 1-3 years		College: 4 years or more	
	B522	B523	B524	B525	B526	B527	B528	B529
Oct. 1952	1.6	4.0	1.1	2.8	1.2	2.0	0.4	1.4
March 1957	4.7	5.9	3.0	2.9	2.7	3.3	0.6	1.0
March 1959	8.1	9.3	4.9	4.6	3.3	3.8	1.4	1.3
March 1962	7.8	9.2	4.8	5.7	4.0	3.2	1.4	1.5
March 1964	6.6	8.5	4.1	5.6	3.8	5.2	1.5	1.6
March 1965	6.7	8.6	3.4	5.0	3.1	3.6	1.4	1.3
March 1966	4.8	6.1	2.6	3.8	2.8	3.3	1.0	1.3
March 1967	4.6	7.0	2.5	4.1	2.2	3.6	0.7	1.4
March 1968	4.8	6.6	2.5	3.8	2.3	3.0	0.7	1.6
March 1969								

Percent Distribution by Marital Status for the Civilian Population, 14 Years of Age and Over, by Color and Sex, United States, 1940, 1947, 1950-1969

Year	White		Nonwhite		White		Nonwhite	
	Male	Female	Male	Female	Male	Female	Male	Female
	Single				Married			
	C001	C002	C003	C004	C005	C006	C007	C008
1940	34.7	27.7	35.5	26.1	59.9	59.8	58.2	56.9
1947	27.8	22.0	32.3	22.5	66.7	64.7	61.5	60.2
1950	26.1	19.9	28.5	20.7	67.9	66.2	64.4	62.0
1951			25.7	19.9			66.3	62.0
1952	23.8	19.0	26.7	19.3	71.1	67.1	66.2	62.3
1953	23.4	18.5	26.5	16.7	71.0	67.5	66.1	62.4
1954	23.0	18.2	27.9	22.0	71.3	67.7	63.8	59.9
1955	23.5	17.9	30.4	20.5	70.7	67.5	62.6	62.1
1956	23.3	18.1	28.9	19.7	71.1	67.2	64.1	62.0
1957	23.2	18.3	30.3	21.3	71.2	67.2	63.6	61.0
1958	23.9	18.6	30.4	20.7	70.7	66.6	62.4	60.9
1959	24.2	18.5	31.5	20.8	70.6	66.8	60.9	61.2
1960	24.5	18.7	32.4	21.6	70.3	66.6	60.9	59.8
1961	25.3	19.2	31.6	21.0	69.6	65.8	62.0	60.9
1962	24.5	19.2	31.9	22.4	70.2	66.0	60.5	59.3
1963	25.2	19.7	32.0	22.8	69.7	65.6	61.0	58.9
1964	25.7	20.1	32.5	21.9	68.9	62.7	61.5	61.0
1965	25.9	20.4	32.5	23.1	68.8	64.4	60.8	59.8
1966	26.1	20.4	33.4	24.5	68.9	64.3	59.0	58.3
1967	25.9	20.5	33.0	24.5	68.9	63.9	59.8	58.1
1968	26.4	21.1	35.0	26.8	68.3	63.5	57.5	54.8
1969	26.4	21.1	35.8	27.8	68.4	63.3	56.3	54.6
1970								
	Widowed				Divorced			
	C009	C010	C011	C012	C013	C014	C015	C016
1940	4.1	10.8	5.3	15.4	1.3	1.6	1.0	1.7
1947	4.0	11.3	4.5	14.8	1.5	2.0	1.7	2.4
1950	4.0	11.5	5.2	14.6	2.0	2.4	1.9	2.7
1951			5.8	15.6			2.2	2.5
1952	3.8	11.6	5.3	15.5	1.4	2.2	1.7	2.8
1953	3.9	11.9	5.4	17.6	1.7	2.2	2.0	3.2
1954	3.8	11.9	5.4	15.1	1.8	2.2	2.9	3.0
1955	4.1	12.4	5.4	14.9	1.8	2.2	1.7	2.5
1956	4.0	12.4	5.5	15.2	1.6	2.4	1.6	3.2
1957	3.8	12.3	4.1	14.6	1.8	2.2	2.1	3.0
1958	3.8	12.5	4.7	15.7	1.7	2.3	2.5	2.8
1959	3.5	12.3	4.9	14.8	1.7	2.4	2.7	3.2
1960	3.4	12.3	4.8	14.3	1.8	2.4	2.0	4.3
1961	3.2	12.3	4.4	14.2	1.9	2.7	2.0	3.8
1962	3.2	12.3	5.1	14.5	2.0	2.5	2.5	3.8
1963	3.1	12.0	4.3	14.0	2.0	2.7	2.7	4.3
1964	3.3	12.2	3.8	13.0	2.1	2.9	2.3	4.0
1965	3.2	12.4	3.9	13.1	2.1	2.8	2.9	4.0
1966	2.9	12.2	4.1	13.5	2.1	3.0	3.6	3.8
1967	3.1	12.5	4.5	13.5	2.1	3.1	2.7	4.0
1968	3.0	12.3	4.7	14.1	2.3	3.1	2.7	4.3
1969	3.0	12.4	5.3	13.6	2.2	3.2	2.6	4.0
1970								

Percent Distribution by Marital Status for Persons 18-19 Years of Age, by Color and Sex, United States, 1951-1953, 1957-1969

Year[a]	White		Nonwhite		White		Nonwhite	
	Male	Female	Male	Female	Male	Female	Male	Female
	Single				Married			
	C017	C018	C019	C020	C021	C022	C023	C024
1951			92.3	56.6			7.7	42.6
1952	90.7	67.5	b/	70.2	9.1	31.3	b/	29.8
1953	92.3	66.7	86.4	62.7	7.7	33.1	13.6	35.8
1957	91.6	69.4	94.6	71.9	8.4	30.2	5.4	27.7
1958	91.6	66.3	91.6	66.7	8.4	33.5	8.4	33.3
1959	91.4	65.5	93.3	68.1	8.5	34.1	6.7	31.2
1960	90.3	70.3	95.8	74.8	9.5	28.7	4.2	24.0
1961	93.0	71.6	91.1	72.2	7.0	27.3	8.9	26.3
1962	90.4	69.0	93.2	73.6	9.3	30.3	6.8	25.2
1963	93.8	70.6	92.7	74.3	6.1	28.7	7.3	25.7
1964	92.9	72.3	94.3	70.5	7.0	27.2	5.7	29.0
1965	91.9	72.9	95.6	77.4	8.1	26.6	3.5	22.3
1966	92.0	74.5	92.6	71.3	7.9	25.0	7.4	28.0
1967	93.2	76.6	95.4	73.5	6.9	23.0	4.1	26.7
1968	91.4	76.7	94.9	77.2	8.6	22.9	5.1	22.8
1969	91.5	77.3	94.5	77.0	8.3	22.3	5.5	22.7
1970								
	Widowed				Divorced			
	C025	C026	C027	C028	C029	C030	C031	C032
1951			--	--			--	0.8
1952	0.3	0.2	b/	--	--	0.1	b/	--
1953	--	--	--	--	--	0.2	--	1.5
1957	--	0.1	--	0.4	--	0.3	--	--
1958	0.1	--	--	--	--	0.2	--	--
1959	--	--	--	0.7	0.1	0.4	--	--
1960	--	0.1	--	--	0.1	0.8	--	1.3
1961	--	0.1	--	--	--	1.0	--	1.5
1962	--	0.1	--	1.2	0.3	0.6	--	--
1963	--	--	--	--	c/	0.7	--	--
1964	--	0.1	--	--	0.1	0.5	--	0.6
1965	--	0.1	0.6	--	0.1	0.4	--	0.5
1966	--	0.1	--	--	0.1	0.5	--	0.7
1967	--	0.1	--	--	--	0.4	--	--
1968	--	0.1	--	--	0.1	0.3	--	--
1969	c/	c/	--	--	0.1	0.3	--	0.3
1970								

Percent Distribution by Marital Status for Persons 20-24 Years of Age,
by Color and Sex, United States, 1940, 1950-1969

Year[a]	White		Nonwhite		White		Nonwhite	
	Male	Female	Male	Female	Male	Female	Male	Female
	Single				Married			
	C033	C034	C035	C036	C037	C038	C039	C040
1940	73.5	48.4	60.4	37.2	26.1	50.3	38.7	59.6
1950	59.5	32.4	54.7	31.2	39.4	65.6	43.9	65.7
1951			41.5	33.6			56.3	63.3
1952	48.7	29.8	44.9	27.7	50.9	68.6	53.5	69.5
1953	49.4	30.3	43.8	24.9	50.3	68.5	55.8	72.4
1957	50.6	28.0	60.1	35.8	48.9	70.2	39.3	61.6
1958	50.5	28.1	63.2	35.3	48.5	70.1	36.1	61.6
1959	51.1	28.0	53.2	31.9	48.2	70.5	42.4	64.5
1960	53.0	28.7	65.7	30.4	46.5	69.7	34.3	66.3
1961	53.6	28.4	64.7	33.5	45.7	69.3	33.8	63.8
1962	51.5	27.9	58.4	37.8	47.8	69.5	41.3	61.4
1963	53.4	30.3	55.1	34.7	45.5	67.5	44.6	63.6
1964	55.6	30.7	58.5	33.4	43.3	66.7	41.3	64.9
1965	52.4	32.2	56.8	34.3	46.8	66.0	42.8	63.0
1966	50.6	29.1	60.9	38.0	48.7	68.6	39.1	60.3
1967	53.0	32.0	59.0	38.5	45.9	65.8	39.9	59.8
1968	54.1	34.9	61.5	43.1	45.2	62.7	37.6	54.3
1969	53.6	33.9	61.8	46.5	45.4	63.8	37.5	51.5
1970								
	Widowed				Divorced			
	C041	C042	C043	C044	C045	C046	C047	C048
1940	0.1	0.4	0.5	2.0	0.3	0.9	0.4	1.2
1950	0.1	0.3	0.5	1.1	0.9	1.6	0.9	1.9
1951			0.7	0.6			1.4	2.4
1952	--	0.1	0.5	0.6	0.4	1.4	1.1	2.1
1953	--	0.3	--	1.7	0.3	0.8	0.4	1.0
1957	--	0.1	--	0.8	0.5	1.6	0.5	1.8
1958	0.2	0.4	--	1.5	0.8	1.4	0.7	1.6
1959	0.1	0.1	0.3	1.7	0.6	1.4	4.0	1.9
1960	--	0.2	--	0.7	0.5	1.5	--	2.6
1961	0.1	0.4	0.7	0.3	0.6	1.9	0.7	2.4
1962	--	0.2	--	0.3	0.7	1.8	0.3	0.5
1963	0.2	0.2	--	0.3	0.9	2.0	0.3	1.4
1964	0.1	0.2	0.3	0.6	1.0	2.3	--	1.0
1965	--	0.2	0.4	0.7	0.8	1.6	--	1.8
1966	0.1	0.2	--	--	0.7	2.1	--	1.6
1967	--	0.3	0.1	0.3	1.0	1.9	0.9	1.3
1968	--	0.2	0.2	0.9	0.7	2.1	0.8	1.7
1969	c/	0.3	--	0.7	1.0	2.1	0.8	1.3
1970								

Percent Distribution by Marital Status for Persons 25-29 Years of Age,
by Color and Sex, United States, 1940, 1950-1953, 1957-1969

Year[a]	White		Nonwhite		White		Nonwhite	
	Male	Female	Male	Female	Male	Female	Male	Female
	Single				Married			
	C049	C050	C051	C052	C053	C054	C055	C056
1940	36.7	23.2	30.5	19.4	62.1	74.1	67.6	74.3
1950	23.6	13.2	25.2	14.1	74.4	83.7	72.4	80.2
1951			23.4	9.2			74.3	82.3
1952	21.9	12.6	24.8	10.5	76.5	84.4	71.9	84.9
1953	20.5	11.3	16.1	9.2	78.3	86.1	81.3	82.1
1957	21.6	10.4	36.1	16.8	77.3	87.4	61.7	78.3
1958	22.1	10.9	29.0	13.6	76.6	86.2	68.7	81.0
1959	22.9	8.9	38.4	12.3	75.8	88.4	60.1	83.4
1960	21.3	9.0	36.0	13.2	77.3	88.4	62.4	79.5
1961	21.8	10.8	26.3	10.0	76.4	86.6	72.9	84.0
1962	20.7	9.2	26.7	13.6	77.5	87.4	71.6	81.0
1963	20.0	9.0	31.1	14.0	77.5	88.2	67.3	79.5
1964	18.4	9.3	25.8	11.5	79.1	87.1	73.8	83.3
1965	15.9	8.0	27.3	11.6	82.2	88.0	72.2	81.8
1966	15.6	8.8	25.4	15.7	82.5	87.4	72.7	79.1
1967	14.5	9.2	21.2	14.8	83.7	87.3	77.1	80.0
1968	20.0	9.1	26.5	18.7	77.7	87.5	72.1	75.9
1969	16.5	9.8	30.5	19.5	81.4	86.4	66.7	74.1
1970								
	Widowed				Divorced			
	C057	C058	C059	C060	C061	C062	C063	C064
1940	0.3	0.9	1.1	4.2	0.9	1.7	0.8	2.1
1950	0.2	0.7	0.7	2.3	1.8	2.4	1.7	3.4
1951			0.4	4.1			1.9	4.4
1952	0.3	0.7	0.7	0.9	1.4	2.3	2.6	3.7
1953	0.2	0.7	--	4.8	1.0	1.9	2.6	3.9
1957	0.1	0.4	0.3	1.7	1.0	1.8	1.9	3.2
1958	0.1	0.3	0.3	1.6	1.2	2.6	2.0	3.8
1959	0.1	0.5	0.3	2.2	1.2	2.2	1.1	2.1
1960	0.1	0.4	--	2.6	1.3	2.2	1.6	4.7
1961	0.1	0.2	--	1.3	1.7	2.4	0.8	4.7
1962	0.1	0.6	0.5	0.7	1.7	2.8	1.2	4.6
1963	0.1	0.5	0.2	2.1	2.4	2.3	1.5	4.3
1964	0.1	0.5	--	1.0	2.2	3.0	0.5	4.2
1965	--	0.8	0.5	1.0	1.8	3.2	0.2	5.7
1966	--	0.3	--	0.4	1.8	3.5	1.9	4.7
1967	0.1	0.4	0.2	1.2	1.7	3.2	1.8	4.0
1968	0.1	0.4	0.3	1.5	2.2	2.9	1.2	3.7
1969	0.1	0.4	0.2	1.2	2.0	3.4	2.6	5.1
1970								

Percent Distribution by Marital Status for Persons 30-34 Years of Age,
by Color and Sex, United States, 1940, 1950-1953, 1957-1969

Year[a]	White		Nonwhite		White		Nonwhite	
	Male	Female	Male	Female	Male	Female	Male	Female
	Single				Married			
	C065	C066	C067	C068	C069	C070	C071	C072
1940	20.7	15.0	21.3	12.6	77.3	80.7	75.6	77.0
1950	13.1	9.3	14.4	8.9	84.6	86.5	82.2	83.1
1951			13.6	9.9			81.1	84.3
1952	12.9	8.8	11.9	8.8	85.5	87.8	86.4	82.8
1953	13.4	7.5	11.9	6.4	84.2	88.5	85.0	84.2
1957	12.5	7.4	16.4	6.3	85.2	89.3	80.5	85.6
1958	12.1	6.7	21.8	10.1	86.3	89.8	73.6	83.5
1959	11.6	6.7	21.8	9.8	86.7	90.0	72.2	82.5
1960	11.7	6.7	19.0	8.2	86.4	89.7	76.8	82.1
1961	13.3	7.0	17.3	5.9	84.6	89.0	80.7	84.7
1962	9.2	7.8	18.3	5.8	88.1	87.9	77.1	84.9
1963	9.2	5.7	19.5	7.7	88.9	90.6	79.0	84.1
1964	10.2	4.6	19.2	4.8	87.4	92.2	78.2	87.9
1965	10.8	5.0	15.2	7.1	86.8	90.9	81.2	87.3
1966	11.4	5.2	16.6	6.9	86.0	90.1	76.3	86.5
1967	10.8	4.7	18.8	4.7	86.7	90.0	76.8	86.0
1968	9.9	5.5	15.1	8.5	87.3	90.1	81.5	80.8
1969	10.2	5.5	13.2	9.8	86.8	90.3	83.2	80.4
1970								
	Widowed				Divorced			
	C073	C074	C075	C076	C077	C078	C079	C080
1940	0.6	1.9	1.9	7.7	1.4	2.4	1.2	2.7
1950	0.3	1.3	1.1	4.1	2.1	2.9	2.4	3.9
1951			2.9	3.6			2.5	2.1
1952	0.4	0.9	0.4	4.7	1.2	2.5	1.3	3.7
1953	0.6	1.0	0.3	4.5	1.8	2.9	2.7	4.8
1957	0.1	1.1	0.8	3.1	2.2	2.2	2.3	5.0
1958	0.2	0.9	1.6	2.1	1.5	2.5	3.0	4.3
1959	0.1	0.9	1.2	3.0	1.6	2.5	4.8	4.8
1960	0.2	0.8	1.2	3.9	1.7	2.7	3.0	5.7
1961	0.2	0.9	0.3	3.5	2.0	3.1	1.7	5.9
1962	0.2	1.1	0.8	2.6	2.4	3.2	3.8	6.6
1963	0.1	0.9	0.5	2.2	1.8	2.9	1.0	6.0
1964	0.1	0.4	0.7	2.2	2.4	2.8	2.0	5.0
1965	0.1	1.0	0.3	2.4	2.2	3.0	2.7	3.2
1966	0.2	1.2	1.3	1.6	2.4	3.5	5.7	5.0
1967	0.1	1.0	0.7	3.2	2.4	4.3	3.9	6.0
1968	0.1	1.1	1.0	3.2	2.7	3.3	2.3	7.5
1969	0.2	0.8	0.4	2.4	2.9	3.4	3.2	7.4
1970								

Percent Distribution by Marital Status for Persons 35-44 Years of Age,
by Color and Sex, United States, 1940, 1950-1953, 1957-1969

Year[a/]	White		Nonwhite		White		Nonwhite	
	Male	Female	Male	Female	Male	Female	Male	Female
	Single				Married			
	C081	C082	C083	C084	C085	C086	C087	C088
1940	13.8	10.7	15.5	8.0	82.8	81.8	79.1	74.3
1950	9.6	8.5	9.8	6.4	87.2	84.8	85.1	80.0
1951			11.1	5.6			84.3	79.4
1952	9.8	7.9	13.2	6.4	87.9	85.5	82.0	79.8
1953	10.4	6.8	13.8	7.4	87.2	86.7	78.7	75.6
1957	8.5	6.5	9.8	5.9	88.8	87.5	84.9	80.4
1958	9.6	6.4	10.4	5.3	87.9	87.5	85.0	80.0
1959	8.9	6.2	10.4	5.0	88.4	87.7	85.1	82.2
1960	9.3	5.9	8.2	5.6	88.1	88.0	87.7	81.7
1961	9.9	5.6	10.0	5.2	87.1	87.8	84.7	83.0
1962	7.7	5.3	14.4	5.5	89.7	88.9	80.9	82.4
1963	7.4	4.7	11.8	6.1	90.1	89.1	82.0	79.9
1964	7.4	4.6	11.1	4.0	89.7	88.6	82.4	83.3
1965	8.9	5.0	13.1	3.8	87.9	88.5	81.9	83.9
1966	8.4	5.3	10.8	3.2	88.4	89.1	83.7	84.8
1967	7.5	4.6	11.6	5.5	89.5	88.7	83.2	81.4
1968	7.3	4.6	14.2	7.7	89.3	88.3	79.6	78.8
1969	7.0	4.6	13.7	8.0	89.7	88.5	77.1	79.1
1970								
	Widowed				Divorced			
	C089	C090	C091	C092	C093	C094	C095	C096
1940	1.5	4.8	3.8	15.1	1.9	2.7	1.6	2.6
1950	0.7	3.1	2.4	9.4	2.5	3.5	2.8	4.2
1951			2.5	11.3			2.0	3.8
1952	0.8	3.1	2.7	9.9	1.4	3.5	2.1	3.9
1953	0.4	3.1	5.4	12.7	2.0	3.3	2.0	4.4
1957	0.4	2.8	1.9	8.6	2.3	3.2	3.4	5.2
1958	0.5	2.7	1.5	10.7	22.0	3.3	3.1	4.0
1959	0.5	2.6	1.7	7.5	2.2	3.5	2.8	5.2
1960	0.5	2.8	2.6	5.8	2.1	3.2	1.6	6.9
1961	0.4	2.6	1.4	6.4	2.5	4.0	3.8	5.4
1962	0.5	2.4	1.7	5.9	2.1	3.4	3.1	6.2
1963	0.4	2.4	1.7	6.6	2.0	3.7	4.5	7.4
1964	0.5	2.5	2.4	5.8	2.4	4.3	4.1	6.9
1965	0.5	2.4	0.9	4.8	2.7	4.2	4.2	7.5
1966	0.4	1.9	1.2	5.2	2.8	3.8	4.3	6.8
1967	0.4	2.2	0.9	6.1	2.6	4.4	4.2	6.9
1968	0.4	2.3	1.8	6.2	3.0	4.9	4.6	7.3
1969	0.4	2.2	4.2	7.2	2.9	4.7	5.0	5.8
1970								

Percent Distribution by Marital Status for Persons 45-54 Years of Age,
by Color and Sex, United States, 1940, 1950-1953, 1957-1969

Year[a]	White		Nonwhite		White		Nonwhite	
	Male	Female	Male	Female	Male	Female	Male	Female
	Single				Married			
	C097	C098	C099	C100	C101	C102	C103	C104
1940	11.1	9.0	10.8	5.2	83.1	76.9	79.5	65.6
1950	8.6	7.7	8.2	4.6	85.9	83.2	78.4	69.3
1951			7.8	5.0			82.0	65.6
1952	8.6	8.1	9.0	5.5	86.6	77.8	81.9	66.0
1953	9.2	7.6	7.0	3.7	85.9	79.6	85.5	64.8
1957	7.6	7.2	8.6	4.7	87.8	79.9	83.7	70.9
1958	7.0	8.1	8.1	3.9	88.3	79.5	83.6	71.1
1959	8.0	8.1	9.9	6.1	87.9	79.6	81.0	68.1
1960	8.6	7.3	9.2	6.5	87.0	80.1	80.8	68.6
1961	8.2	6.9	8.7	4.6	87.4	80.2	84.2	72.2
1962	7.5	6.4	9.6	6.8	87.2	81.4	81.5	71.5
1963	6.6	6.5	9.9	3.7	88.4	82.2	80.5	71.9
1964	7.5	6.9	8.1	3.0	87.7	81.2	86.1	74.7
1965	6.7	5.9	5.9	4.4	88.9	82.6	86.7	74.5
1966	6.5	5.6	5.9	6.9	89.7	82.4	85.5	70.8
1967	5.8	5.2	6.6	3.6	89.7	83.0	83.3	74.1
1968	6.7	4.9	9.7	4.9	88.4	83.7	81.9	70.7
1969	6.8	4.9	9.6	4.8	88.3	82.7	82.0	74.5
1970								
	Widowed				Divorced			
	C105	C106	C107	C108	C109	C110	C111	C112
1940	3.8	11.8	7.9	27.3	2.0	2.2	1.6	1.9
1950	2.5	6.3	9.9	22.8	3.0	2.7	3.5	3.4
1951		6.3		26.1			3.9	3.3
1952	2.1	10.9	6.8	25.1	2.7	3.2	2.3	3.3
1953	2.4	9.0	3.1	26.4	2.5	3.8	4.4	5.1
1957	1.9	9.5	4.0	20.4	2.7	3.4	3.7	4.0
1958	2.2	8.9	3.8	20.9	2.5	3.5	4.5	4.0
1959	1.5	8.9	5.2	21.0	2.6	3.4	3.9	4.8
1960	1.8	8.7	5.8	18.8	2.7	3.8	4.1	6.1
1961	1.4	8.9	4.1	17.7	2.9	4.0	3.1	5.4
1962	1.9	8.3	3.3	16.1	3.4	3.9	5.5	5.5
1963	1.6	7.2	3.1	15.9	3.4	4.1	6.5	8.5
1964	1.6	7.6	2.2	14.8	3.3	4.3	3.6	7.5
1965	1.3	7.4	2.3	15.8	3.1	4.1	4.9	5.5
1966	0.9	7.2	3.2	17.2	2.8	4.9	5.4	5.0
1967	1.5	7.4	4.6	16.0	3.0	4.4	5.8	6.4
1968	1.5	6.9	3.6	16.9	3.4	4.5	4.8	7.5
1969	1.2	7.5	4.3	15.1	3.7	5.0	4.2	5.7
1970								

Percent Distribution by Marital Status for Persons 55-64 Years of Age, by Color and Sex, United States, 1940, 1950-1953, 1957-1969

Year[a/]	White		Nonwhite		White		Nonwhite	
	Male	Female	Male	Female	Male	Female	Male	Female
	C113	C114	C115	C116	C117	C118	C119	C120
	Single				Married			
1940	10.8	9.3	8.8	4.4	78.7	63.8	76.0	52.6
1950	8.6	8.2	6.1	4.2	81.6	65.8	78.5	54.4
1951	--	--	6.7	2.9	---	--	76.9	55.7
1952	9.1	7.7	6.9	5.6	82.8	66.3	79.7	53.7
1953	10.2	8.4	5.0	2.2	79.9	64.8	82.7	53.3
1957	8.2	7.7	3.2	3.6	84.3	66.5	86.5	56.3
1958	9.4	8.2	6.3	3.9	82.3	65.2	80.6	53.5
1959	8.6	7.5	7.4	2.9	82.8	65.9	78.1	56.8
1960	8.0	6.8	6.7	3.5	82.9	66.6	77.5	56.8
1961	6.7	7.2	6.3	2.7	86.3	67.3	82.4	55.6
1962	7.6	6.8	8.5	6.4	85.4	69.0	76.6	49.5
1963	8.1	7.3	6.5	7.3	84.4	68.4	81.3	54.5
1964	7.6	7.5	9.9	5.1	85.1	67.8	79.5	61.4
1965	8.6	8.1	6.4	4.9	84.5	67.2	77.0	62.2
1966	7.6	7.4	7.4	5.1	85.2	67.5	74.9	60.8
1967	7.6	6.2	4.5	6.1	85.4	68.1	83.9	60.1
1968	5.9	6.1	5.7	3.7	86.9	68.6	80.2	58.8
1969	6.0	6.0	6.3	4.6	87.3	69.4	81.8	59.4
1970								
	Widowed				Divorced			
	C121	C122	C123	C124	C125	C126	C127	C128
1940	8.7	25.3	14.0	41.8	1.9	1.6	6.3	1.2
1950	7.1	23.6	12.9	39.5	2.7	2.4	2.5	2.2
1951	--	--	12.2	39.0	--	--	4.2	2.4
1952	6.4	23.5	11.8	37.7	1.7	2.5	1.6	3.0
1953	7.2	24.9	10.0	42.4	2.8	1.9	2.3	2.2
1957	5.0	23.5	8.8	38.0	2.5	2.4	1.5	2.1
1958	5.2	24.1	8.7	40.5	3.1	2.5	4.4	2.2
1959	5.8	23.5	11.7	36.6	2.8	3.1	2.9	3.8
1960	5.7	23.4	11.5	35.4	3.4	3.1	4.2	4.4
1961	4.2	22.6	7.7	37.9	2.8	2.9	3.6	3.8
1962	4.0	20.9	10.4	40.1	2.9	3.3	4.4	4.1
1963	4.6	20.7	9.2	35.3	2.9	3.7	3.1	2.9
1964	4.5	21.0	6.4	29.6	2.8	3.7	4.2	3.9
1965	3.9	21.0	9.1	28.2	3.1	3.7	7.4	4.6
1966	4.1	21.0	8.5	29.2	3.0	4.1	9.2	4.8
1967	4.1	21.1	8.1	28.9	2.9	4.7	3.1	5.2
1968	3.9	21.0	8.4	32.3	3.3	4.3	5.7	5.3
1969	3.8	20.1	9.3	30.0	2.9	4.5	2.7	6.0
1970								

Percent Distribution by Marital Status for Persons 65-74 Years of Age, by Color and Sex, United States, 1940, 1950, 1957-1969

Year[a/]	White		Nonwhite		White		Nonwhite	
	Male	Female	Male	Female	Male	Female	Male	Female
	Single				Married			
	C129	C130	C131	C132	C133	C134	C135	C136
1940	10.4	9.8	6.9	3.9	69.2	42.3	67.6	32.2
1950	8.9	9.1	5.3	3.9	71.7	44.7	68.6	34.4
1957	7.7	7.9	5.5	4.8	75.6	45.7	72.7	32.3
1958	7.3	7.7	2.4	2.2	76.1	45.9	76.4	33.7
1959	7.2	7.6	3.6	3.9	76.8	47.2	71.1	37.8
1960	6.7	8.7	7.5	4.0	79.3	46.6	73.3	31.9
1961	6.1	7.6	7.0	4.3	81.0	48.0	63.5	28.5
1962	5.7	7.6	9.0	3.3	80.9	49.3	64.8	36.5
1963	6.8	7.6	7.0	4.2	79.0	46.9	73.7	35.8
1964	6.6	7.9	2.4	3.1	78.8	47.7	78.1	37.6
1965	6.5	7.9	1.9	3.0	79.2	46.6	75.1	33.8
1966	7.6	7.9	6.0	3.7	78.4	47.8	72.9	34.8
1967	6.8	7.7	4.3	3.9	80.6	47.4	73.7	35.5
1968	6.8	8.1	--	3.8	80.5	47.5	75.9	35.1
1969	7.4	7.7	6.5	2.6	79.6	47.0	68.6	35.6
1970								
	Widowed				Divorced			
	C137	C138	C139	C140	C141	C142	C143	C144
1940	18.9	47.0	24.3	62.8	1.5	0.9]	1.2	0.9
1950	17.3	44.9	24.2	60.5	2.1	1.4	1.6	1.2
1957	14.7	44.7	19.3	62.4	1.9	1.6	2.5	0.6
1958	14.9	44.8	19.3	63.3	1.6	1.5	1.8	0.8
1959	14.0	43.5	22.0	57.2	2.0	1.6	3.3	1.0
1960	12.3	43.1	17.8	62.2	1.7	1.7	1.4	1.9
1961	11.6	42.6	28.4	66.0	1.3	1.8	1.1	1.3
1962	11.2	41.6	25.7	58.2	2.1	1.5	0.5	2.0
1963	11.7	43.5	16.8	58.3	2.5	2.0	2.5	1.7
1964	11.8	42.2	16.1	56.8	2.9	2.2	3.4	2.5
1965	11.2	43.1	18.4	60.2	3.2	2.4	4.4	3.2
1966	10.8	42.1	16.8	58.6	3.2	2.1	4.3	2.9
1967	10.1	42.7	19.6	58.5	2.6	2.2	2.2	2.7
1968	10.1	42.0	21.4	59.0	2.6	2.5	2.6	2.1
1969	10.6	42.6	21.5	58.3	2.4	2.7	3.5	3.4
1970								

Percent Distribution by Marital Status for Persons 75 Years of Age and Over, by
Color and Sex, United States, 1940, 1950, 1957-1969

Year[a]	White		Nonwhite		White		Nonwhite	
	Male	Female	Male	Female	Male	Female	Male	Female
	Single				Married			
	C145	C146	C147	C148	C149	C150	C151	C152
1940	9.2	9.3	6.5	3.5	50.2	18.0	50.7	14.0
1950	8.0	9.7	5.9	5.3	52.4	19.0	52.9	15.3
1957	6.7	9.0	8.6	1.8	53.7	21.2	55.3	23.0
1958	6.3	8.1	3.5	4.0	56.4	19.4	42.4	17.6
1959	7.7	8.2	3.1	2.3	58.9	21.4	55.6	12.3
1960	7.9	9.1	5.5	2.5	59.5	22.3	54.9	14.6
1961	5.8	7.9	2.9	5.2	57.6	21.6	59.1	20.4
1962	6.9	7.2	8.4	3.6	60.3	21.0	48.8	18.2
1963	7.9	8.1	6.4	7.0	61.7	23.3	46.8	18.9
1964	6.9	8.9	8.3	3.9	59.9	20.4	51.7	18.4
1965	7.6	8.4	8.7	4.2	57.3	20.3	55.4	18.9
1966	7.0	7.3	11.4	1.4	62.9	21.2	45.6	14.4
1967	6.1	7.5	3.6	2.6	59.7	20.0	50.2	17.9
1968	6.3	8.2	8.5	5.5	61.4	21.0	41.4	15.3
1969	5.7	8.5	4.4	4.9	61.0	19.8	41.9	14.1
1970								
	Widowed				Divorced			
	C153	C154	C155	C156	C157	C158	C159	C160
1940	39.7	72.3	41.6	82.3	0.9	0.4	1.3	c/
1950	38.3	70.7	40.3	78.6	1.3	0.6	0.8	0.8
1957	38.3	69.4	33.6	73.9	1.3	0.5	2.6	1.2
1958	36.6	72.0	54.1	76.7	0.7	0.5	--	1.7
1959	32.4	69.8	39.4	85.4	1.0	0.6	1.9	--
1960	31.0	67.3	39.0	82.3	1.6	1.3	0.6	0.5
1961	35.2	69.2	36.3	71.7	1.4	1.4	1.8	2.6
1962	31.6	71.1	42.4	77.7	1.3	0.7	0.5	0.4
1963	28.8	67.5	42.3	74.1	1.6	1.0	4.5	--
1964	31.9	69.5	37.9	76.5	1.3	1.2	2.1	1.2
1965	34.1	70.2	32.9	75.8	1.1	1.1	3.5	1.4
1966	28.9	70.0	39.7	83.6	1.2	1.5	3.4	0.7
1967	31.8	71.4	45.3	79.2	2.5	1.1	1.2	1.0
1968	29.9	69.3	47.4	78.3	2.4	1.5	2.8	0.9
1969	31.4	70.4	50.5	78.3	1.9	1.4	3.2	2.8
1970								

Period	White civilian married females				Nonwhite civilian married females			
	Total number (000)	Wives (husband absent) as percent of all married white females			Total number (000)	Wives (husband absent) as percent of all married nonwhite females		
		Separated	Husband in armed forces	Husband absent for other reason		Separated	Husband in armed forces	Husband absent for other reason
	C161	C162	C163	C164	C165	C166	C167	C168
April 1954	36,272	1.9	3.2		3,597	12.7	6.1	
April 1955	36,543	2.3	3.0		3,784	15.1	6.7	
March 1956	36,814	1.9	2.6		3,836	14.2	4.0	
March 1957	37,363	1.7	0.6	1.9	3,841	13.1	1.1	3.7
March 1958	37,562	1.9	0.5	1.6	3,895	16.0	0.8	3.0
March 1959	38,143	1.8	0.6	1.9	3,984	17.6	0.9	4.8
March 1960	38,545	1.9	0.5	1.7	4,038	13.8	0.8	4.8
March 1961	38,810	2.2	0.5	1.6	4,200	14.3	1.2	4.1
March 1962	39,617	2.0	0.6	1.8	4,229	14.9	1.1	4.5
March 1963	40,073	1.9	0.5	1.9	4,298	14.6	0.8	5.9
March 1964	40,199	2.2	0.5	1.7	4,556	14.8	0.8	4.9
March 1965	40,620	2.4	0.4	1.8	4,571	15.3	1.0	5.3
March 1966	41,189	2.3	0.7	1.8	4,554	14.5	0.9	5.5
March 1967	41,568	2.3	0.7	1.8	4,645	14.5	1.0	6.1
March 1968	42,100	2.2	0.7	1.2	4,510	15.9	1.3	3.2
March 1969	42,636	2.3	0.8	1.2	4,607	16.9	1.3	3.0

Marital Status of Heads of Families[a/] (other than husband-wife families), by Sex, United States, 1954-1969

Date	Total number (000)	Percent distribution			Widowed	Divorced	Single
		Married					
		Separated	Husband in armed forces	Other			

				Female head of family			
	C169	C170	C171	C172	C173	C174	C175
April 1954	3,825	13.5	2.6	9.2	53.0	10.8	10.7
April 1955	4,225	13.6	3.1	9.2	50.7	12.7	10.7
March 1956	4,239	13.9	2.1	6.4	54.0	13.7	10.0
March 1957	4,366	11.5	1.7	7.7	56.3	13.2	9.6
March 1958	4,310	14.4	1.5	5.9	55.2	12.8	10.3
March 1959	4,332	14.4	2.1	9.9	51.8	13.6	8.2
March 1960	4,494	13.2	2.3	9.0	51.7	15.4	8.4
March 1961	4,609	14.7	1.8	7.6	51.0	16.3	8.6
March 1962	4,643	15.0	2.6	9.3	49.2	16.3	7.6
March 1963	4,741	14.3	2.3	9.7	48.1	17.4	8.1
March 1964	4,882	16.2	2.1	7.8	47.3	18.0	8.7
March 1965	5,006	17.0	1.5	9.3	46.1	18.0	8.1
March 1966	4,992	16.2	2.8	9.0	46.0	18.5	7.5
March 1967	5,171	16.8	2.5	8.3	46.1	20.0	6.4
March 1968	5,333	17.4	2.5	4.3	46.0	19.7	10.1
March 1969	5,439	18.1	2.6	4.8	43.5	20.4	10.7

		Male head of family (other than husband-wife family)					
	C176	C177		C178	C179	C180	C181
April 1954	1,336	5.3		10.2	40.0	8.4	36.1
April 1955	1,314	4.5		8.4	42.4	7.3	37.4
March 1956	1,404	6.0		7.3	42.2	8.6	35.9
March 1957	1,230	5.6		9.8	42.0	6.0	36.6
March 1958	1,292	6.5		9.5	39.2	6.6	38.2
March 1959	1,285	6.5		8.2	39.3	7.6	38.4
March 1960	1,233	8.0		5.5	37.7	9.3	39.5
March 1961	1,202	8.8		5.0	36.9	8.0	41.3
March 1962	1,293	7.1		9.0	39.3	9.0	35.6
March 1963	1,334	7.0		14.1	37.3	10.1	31.6
March 1964	1,243	6.6		5.1	39.6	12.7	36.0
March 1965	1,182	8.0		7.9	37.9	10.1	36.2
March 1966	1,179	7.9		9.2	34.9	13.1	35.0
March 1967	1,197	7.2		10.3	37.6	13.5	31.6
March 1968	1,210	7.7		3.6	38.6	14.9	35.3
March 1969	1,229	10.0		6.4	36.4	13.6	33.6

Classification and date	All house- holds (pri- mary families and primary individuals) (000)	Percent distribution of households				
		Husband- wife pri- mary families	Other primary families with male head	Male pri- mary indi- viduals	Female primary individ- uals	Primary families with female head
	C182	C183	C184	C185	C186	C187

1950 definition[a]/

April 1940	34,949	76.0	4.3	4.6	5.3	9.8
April 1947	39,107	78.3	2.9	3.5	7.0	8.2
April 1948	40,532	78.7	2.5	3.0	6.7	9.2
April 1949	42,182	78.8	2.8	3.1	6.6.	8.6
March 1950	43,554	78.2	2.7	3.8	7.0	8.3
April 1951	44,656	77.0	2.6	3.9	7.7	8.9
April 1952	45,504	77.2	2.5	3.9	7.8	8.7
April 1953	46,334	76.7	2.6	4.1	8.5	8.1
April 1954	46,893	76.5	2.8	4.1	8.6	8.0
April 1955	47,874	75.7	2.8	4.3	8.5	8.7
March 1956	48,902	75.8	2.9	4.2	8.7	8.5
March 1957	49,673	75.9	2.5	4.1	8.8	8.7
March 1958	50,474	75.1	2.5	4.6	9.3	8.4
March 1959	51,435	74.7	2.5	4.8	9.8	8.3

1960 definition[a]/

March 1960	52,799	74.3	2.3	5.1	9.8	8.4
March 1961	53,464	73.9	2.3	5.3	10.0	8.5
March 1962	54,652	73.8	2.3	5.4	10.1	8.4
March 1963	55,189	74.0	2.3	5.2	10.0	8.5
March 1964	55,996	73.7	2.1	5.3	10.3	8.6
March 1965	57,251	72.6	2.0	5.7	10.9	8.7
March 1966	58,092	72.4	2.0	5.7	11.4	8.5
March 1967	58,845	72.2	2.0	5.8	11.3	8.7
March 1968	60,446	71.6	2.0	6.1	11.7	8.7
March 1969	61,805	70.9	2.0	6.3	12.1	8.7
March 1970	62,875	70.6	1.9	6.3	12.4	8.7

Type of data and year	Annual live births per 1,000 women aged 15-44 years											
	Total	White	Non-white	Total	White	Non-white	Total	White	Non-white	Total	White	Non-white
	First child			Second child			Third child			Fourth child		
	D001	D002	D003	D004	D005	D006	D007	D008	D009	D010	D011	D012
Births adjusted for under-registra-tion												
1940	29.3	29.4	28.6	20.0	20.0	19.6	10.9	10.5	14.1	6.4	5.9	10.5
1941	32.2	32.5	29.8	20.7	20.7	20.6	11.2	10.7	14.5	6.4	5.9	10.6
1942	37.5	38.3	31.0	22.9	23.1	21.1	11.9	11.5	14.9	6.6	6.1	10.8
1943	34.7	35.2	31.0	25.5	25.9	22.2	13.5	13.2	15.5	7.4	6.9	11.4
1944	30.2	30.4	28.7	23.8	24.2	21.1	13.8	13.6	15.6	7.6	7.1	11.7
1945	28.9	29.0	27.9	22.9	23.3	20.1	13.4	13.2	14.7	7.5	7.0	11.3
1946	38.5	39.5	31.1	27.9	28.5	23.4	14.5	14.4	16.0	7.8	7.3	11.8
1947	46.7	47.8	38.4	30.3	30.8	26.2	15.6	15.3	17.3	7.9	7.4	12.1
1948	39.6	39.9	37.3	30.9	31.1	29.5	16.1	15.7	19.4	8.0	7.4	12.9
1949	36.2	36.3	35.4	32.1	32.2	30.8	17.1	16.6	21.2	8.6	7.9	14.0
1950	33.3	33.3	33.8	32.1	32.3	30.3	18.4	17.9	22.9	9.2	8.4	15.3
1951	34.9	35.0	34.1	32.6	32.9	29.9	20.0	19.5	23.9	10.2	9.4	16.9
1952	34.0	34.1	33.1	32.7	33.1	29.2	21.3	21.0	24.0	11.3	10.4	18.1
1953	33.4	33.3	34.1	32.5	32.9	29.5	21.9	21.6	23.8	12.0	11.1	18.4
1954	33.6	33.3	35.6	32.4	32.8	29.7	22.7	22.6	24.4	12.8	12.0	19.1
1955	32.9	32.6	35.0	31.9	32.0	30.7	23.1	22.9	24.4	13.3	12.6	19.1
1956	33.5	33.2	35.9	31.9	31.9	31.7	23.6	23.4	25.2	13.9	13.1	19.7
1957	33.7	33.4	36.1	31.7	31.7	31.6	23.9	23.7	25.7	14.4	13.7	19.8
1958	32.2	31.9	34.7	30.6	30.6	31.0	23.3	23.1	25.4	14.4	13.8	19.5
1959	31.7	31.3	34.9	30.1	30.0	30.9	23.2	23.0	25.3	14.7	14.1	19.8
Registered births												
1959	31.5	31.2	33.9	29.9	29.9	29.8	23.0	22.9	24.4	14.5	13.9	19.1
1960	31.1	30.8	33.6	29.2	29.2	29.3	22.8	22.7	24.0	14.6	14.1	18.6
1961	31.1	30.7	33.6	28.4	28.3	28.8	22.4	22.2	23.7	14.6	14.0	18.8
1962	30.1	29.8	33.1	27.0	26.9	28.0	21.1	20.9	22.8	13.8	13.3	17.8
1963	29.9	29.4	33.8	26.1	25.9	27.6	19.9	19.6	21.8	13.1	12.6	16.9
1964	30.4	29.8	34.8	25.1	24.8	27.4	18.8	18.5	21.1	12.3	11.7	16.0
1965	29.8	28.9	35.8	23.4	23.0	26.6	16.6	16.2	19.6	10.7	10.2	14.6
1966	31.0	30.1	37.4	22.5	22.0	26.0	14.8	14.4	18.0	9.2	8.7	12.8
1967	30.8	29.7	38.4	22.6	22.1	25.9	13.9	13.5	16.8	8.3	7.9	11.5
1968												
1969												
1970												

(continued)

338

Type of data and year	Annual live births per 1,000 women aged 15-44 years (cont.)								
	Total	White	Non-white	Total	White	Non-white	Total	White	Non-white
	Fifth child			Sixth & seventh child			Eighth child & over		
	D013	D014	D015	D016	D017	D018	D019	D020	D021
Births adjusted for under-registration									
1940	4.1	3.6	7.8	4.8	4.1	10.4	4.3	3.5	11.3
1941	4.1	3.6	8.0	4.7	3.9	10.6	4.1	3.2	11.3
1942	4.1	3.6	8.1	4.6	3.8	10.5	3.9	3.1	11.1
1943	4.4	3.9	8.4	4.8	4.0	11.0	4.0	3.1	11.6
1944	4.5	4.0	8.6	4.9	4.1	11.3	4.0	3.1	11.6
1945	4.5	3.9	8.7	4.8	4.0	11.3	4.0	3.0	11.9
1946	4.5	4.0	8.7	4.7	3.9	11.3	3.8	2.8	11.7
1947	4.5	4.0	8.8	4.6	3.8	11.4	3.7	2.7	11.6
1948	4.5	3.9	9.2	4.6	3.7	11.7	3.6	2.6	11.6
1949	4.7	4.0	9.8	4.7	3.8	12.2	3.7	2.7	11.8
1950	4.8	4.1	10.4	4.7	3.7	12.6	3.6	2.5	12.0
1951	5.3	4.5	11.2	5.0	3.9	13.5	3.6	2.5	12.2
1952	5.8	5.0	12.4	5.2	4.0	14.2	3.6	2.5	12.4
1953	6.3	5.4	13.3	5.5	4.3	15.4	3.6	2.5	12.8
1954	6.8	5.9	14.2	6.0	4.6	16.5	3.8	2.5	13.5
1955	7.2	6.2	14.6	6.4	4.9	17.4	3.8	2.5	14.1
1956	7.6	6.6	15.0	6.8	5.2	18.7	4.0	2.6	15.0
1957	7.9	7.0	15.3	7.1	5.6	19.0	4.2	2.7	15.6
1958	8.1	7.2	14.9	7.3	5.7	19.1	4.2	2.7	15.9
1959	8.3	7.4	15.2	7.6	6.0	19.5	4.4	2.8	16.4
Registered births									
1959	8.2	7.3	14.5	7.4	5.9	18.7	4.2	2.8	15.6
1960	8.3	7.5	14.1	7.6	6.1	18.4	4.3	2.8	15.6
1961	8.5	7.7	14.1	7.8	6.4	18.4	4.5	2.9	16.0
1962	8.2	7.5	13.7	7.5	6.2	17.6	4.4	2.9	15.7
1963	7.8	7.1	13.1	7.3	6.1	16.6	4.3	2.9	15.1
1964	7.3	6.7	12.1	6.9	5.7	15.8	4.1	2.7	14.4
1965	6.4	5.8	10.8	6.0	5.0	13.8	3.7	2.4	12.6
1966	5.4	4.9	9.4	5.2	4.3	11.6	3.2	2.1	10.7
1967	4.8	4.3	8.1	4.5	3.7	10.1	2.7	1.8	9.0
1968									
1969									
1970									

Annual live births per 1,000 women of specified age-group

	Age 10-14 years						Age 15-19 years					
	First child			Second child			First child			Second child		
Year	Total	White	Non-white	Total	White	Non-white	Total	White	Non-white	Total	White	Non-white
	D022	D023	D024	D025	D026	D027	D028	D029	D030	D031	D032	D033
1940							38.7			11.2		
1941							41.1			11.4		
1942							44.8			11.5		
1943							44.2			11.9		
1944							38.6			10.7		
1945							37.1			9.7		
1946							43.6			10.7		
1947							60.6			12.6		
1948							59.8			15.7		
1949							57.7			18.0		
1950							56.1			18.5		
1951							61.3			19.3		
1952							60.4			19.6		
1953							62.4			20.4		
1954							64.2			20.6		
1955							63.4			21.4		
1956							67.0			22.7		
1957	0.9	0.4	4.8	0.0	0.0	0.0	68.7	62.9	99.7	23.1	18.6	49.0
1958	0.3	0.1	1.1	0.0	0.0	0.1	63.4	59.0	94.9	22.2	18.5	48.6
1959	0.8	0.4	4.1	0.0	0.0	0.2	62.7	58.0	95.9	22.0	18.3	48.2
1960	0.8	0.3	3.8	0.0	0.0	0.2	61.4	57.2	91.1	21.6	18.1	46.1
1961	0.8	0.4	3.8	0.0	0.0	0.2	61.4	57.4	90.1	21.2	17.9	44.4
1962	0.8	0.4	3.7	0.0	0.0	0.2	56.0	52.7	83.7	19.6	16.8	41.5
1963	0.8	0.3	3.8	0.0	0.0	0.2	53.7	50.0	82.9	17.7	14.8	39.3
1964	0.8	0.3	3.8	0.0	0.0	0.2	52.2	47.6	83.8	16.2	12.9	38.2
1965	0.8	0.3	3.8	0.0	0.0	0.2	51.5	46.7	84.0	14.8	11.6	36.5
1966	0.8	0.3	3.9	0.0	0.0	0.2	52.9	47.9	86.2	14.1	10.9	35.3
1967	0.8	0.3	4.0	0.0	0.0	0.2	51.1	45.3	88.2	13.6	10.3	34.1
1968												
1969												
1970												

	Age 15-19 years								
	Third child			Fourth child			Fifth child		
	D034	D035	D036	D037	D038	D039	D040	D041	D042
1940	2.2			0.3					
1941	2.3			0.4					
1942	2.2			0.3					
1943	2.3			0.4					
1944	2.2			0.4					
1945	1.9			0.3					
1946	2.0			0.3					
1947	2.3			0.4					
1948	2.6			0.4					
1949	3.4			0.5					
1950	3.7			0.6					
1951	4.1			0.7					
1952	4.3			0.8					
1953	4.4			0.7					
1954	4.7			0.8					
1955	4.7			0.8					
1956	5.0			0.8					
1957	5.2	3.3	16.5	0.9	0.4	4.0	0.1	0.1	0.8
1958	4.9	3.3	16.8	0.9	0.4	4.1	0.1	0.1	0.7
1959	5.2	3.5	17.0	0.9	0.4	4.2	0.1	0.1	0.7
1960	5.0	3.5	16.0	0.9	0.5	4.0	0.1	0.0	0.7
1961	5.0	3.5	15.9	0.9	0.5	4.1	0.1	0.1	0.6
1962	4.6	3.3	14.8	0.8	0.4	3.7	0.1	0.1	0.7
1963	4.2	2.9	13.5	0.8	0.4	3.4	0.1	0.0	0.7
1964	3.8	2.5	12.9	0.7	0.1	3.1	0.1	0.0	0.6
1965	3.3	2.0	12.0	0.6	0.3	3.0	0.1	0.0	0.5
1966	3.0	1.8	10.9	0.5	0.2	2.5	0.1	0.0	0.4
1967	2.7	1.5	10.1	0.5	0.2	2.3	0.1	0.0	0.4
1968									
1969									
1970									

Year	Annual live births per 1,000 women aged 20-24 years											
	Total	White	Non-white	Total	White	Non-white	Total	White	Non-white	Total	White	Non-white
	First child			Second child			Third child			Fourth child		
	D043	D044	D045	D046	D047	D048	D049	D050	D051	D052	D053	D054
1940	61.7			39.7			18.7			7.8		
1941	69.6			41.0			19.0			7.8		
1942	83.2			45.0			19.9			8.1		
1943	73.5			49.0			21.7			8.8		
1944	67.1			43.7			21.1			8.9		
1945	63.7			38.0			18.0			7.9		
1946	89.3			52.1			19.7			8.1		
1947	109.3			57.8			21.4			7.9		
1948	92.3			63.3			23.9			8.5		
1949	85.1			67.5			26.8			9.6		
1950	79.0			68.0			30.0			10.6		
1951	85.3			70.5			33.0			12.4		
1952	85.9			72.4			34.7			13.7		
1953	85.8			75.8			36.4			14.8		
1954	89.0			78.8			39.4			15.9		
1955	88.8			80.6			41.0			16.7		
1956	92.1			84.3			44.1			18.1		
1957	92.9	97.1	67.6	87.5	88.6	81.7	46.8	43.4	71.0	19.2	15.3	46.3
1958	89.9	93.6	63.7	87.4	88.6	79.7	47.3	43.9	70.6	19.7	15.8	48.6
1959	87.8	91.5	62.7	88.2	89.6	78.6	48.6	45.7	68.9	20.5	16.6	47.8
1960	87.9	91.5	63.5	87.9	89.6	76.3	49.9	47.3	68.0	21.0	17.4	45.7
1961	86.3	89.6	63.1	84.9	86.3	75.2	48.9	46.4	65.8	21.2	17.7	45.2
1962	83.5	86.0	63.4	81.5	82.7	73.3	47.1	44.9	64.7	20.4	17.2	43.9
1963	82.0	83.9	64.7	77.5	78.1	72.9	43.1	40.9	61.1	18.5	15.5	41.4
1964	81.2	83.4	65.6	73.2	73.5	71.5	39.4	36.8	57.9	16.6	13.6	38.8
1965	76.0	77.6	64.9	66.1	66.0	67.1	33.3	30.7	52.0	13.8	11.0	33.8
1966	77.7	79.4	65.4	62.2	62.0	63.6	28.5	26.0	46.7	11.4	8.9	28.9
1967	75.3	76.6	65.6	59.5	59.2	61.7	25.0	22.7	41.2	9.4	7.4	23.9
1968												
1969												
1970												

Year	Fifth child			Sixth & seventh child			Eighth child & over		
	D055	D056	D057	D058	D059	D060	D061	D062	D063
1940	2.8			1.2			0.1		
1941	2.9			1.2			0.1		
1942	2.9			1.2			0.1		
1943	3.1			1.3			0.1		
1944	3.2			1.3			0.1		
1945	3.0			1.2			0.1		
1946	3.0			1.3			0.1		
1947	2.9			1.3			0.2		
1948	3.0			1.3			0.1		
1949	3.5			1.4			0.2		
1950	3.6			1.4			0.2		
1951	4.1			1.6			0.2		
1952	4.8			1.8			0.2		
1953	5.5			2.0			0.2		
1954	5.9			2.5			0.2		
1955	6.3			2.6			0.3		
1956	6.7			2.9			0.3		
1957	7.2	4.5	25.0	3.1	1.5	14.2	0.3	0.1	1.7
1958	7.3	4.7	25.2	3.1	1.5	14.0	0.3	0.1	1.6
1959	7.5	4.9	25.3	3.3	1.6	15.0	0.3	0.1	1.7
1960	7.7	5.2	24.4	3.3	1.7	14.6	0.3	0.1	1.6
1961	7.7	5.3	24.3	3.3	1.7	14.5	0.3	0.1	1.6
1962	7.7	5.4	24.4	3.3	1.7	14.5	0.3	0.1	1.6
1963	6.9	4.8	22.9	3.0	1.6	13.5	0.3	0.1	1.6
1964	6.3	4.2	21.0	2.8	1.4	12.7	0.3	0.1	1.7
1965	5.2	3.4	18.1	2.3	1.1	10.4	0.2	0.1	0.1
1966	4.2	2.7	14.9	1.9	0.9	8.5	0.2	0.1	0.9
1967	3.4	2.1	12.1	1.4	0.7	7.0	0.1	0.1	0.7
1968									
1969									
1970									

	Total	White	Non-white	Total	White	Non-white	Total	White	Non-white	Total	White	Non-white
Year												
	Annual live births per 1,000 women aged 25-29 years											
	First child			Second child			Third child			Fourth child		
	D064	D065	D066	D067	D068	D069	D070	D071	D072	D073	D074	D075
1940	36.3			33.0			19.8			12.6		
1941	40.4			34.7			20.2			12.5		
1942	48.0			39.2			21.5			12.8		
1943	42.4			44.5			24.5			14.0		
1944	35.1			41.5			25.0			14.2		
1945	33.7			41.2			24.3			13.8		
1946	49.7			50.3			26.7			14.7		
1947	56.4			55.7			29.6			14.9		
1948	45.0			54.6			30.6			15.1		
1949	40.6			56.3			32.8			16.4		
1950	36.9			57.0			35.2			17.5		
1951	37.8			57.8			38.5			19.6		
1952	36.9			58.2			41.5			21.4		
1953	35.1			57.2			43.0			23.1		
1954	34.1			56.7			45.1			25.1		
1955	32.5			54.7			46.3			26.4		
1956	31.7			53.9			47.7			28.1		
1957	31.3	33.4	20.0	53.6	57.8	31.9	49.4	52.4	38.0	29.8	29.6	37.7
1958	29.7	31.0	19.6	52.3	55.2	31.1	50.4	52.3	36.9	31.8	31.0	38.2
1959	28.0	29.1	19.7	50.7	53.4	31.6	51.3	53.2	37.8	33.6	32.8	39.4
1960	26.6	27.7	18.8	48.8	51.6	29.7	51.0	53.3	35.3	33.8	33.5	35.8
1961	25.7	26.7	18.9	47.0	49.5	29.8	50.5	52.7	35.6	34.5	34.1	37.4
1962	24.8	25.4	18.2	44.9	46.8	28.9	48.7	50.6	34.6	33.9	33.7	36.3
1963	24.3	24.8	18.5	43.7	45.4	28.3	46.7	48.4	33.8	32.7	32.5	34.8
1964	25.2	26.3	18.1	42.7	44.8	28.1	44.6	46.3	32.7	30.8	30.5	32.8
1965	24.7	25.5	19.3	40.4	42.2	28.0	40.2	41.5	31.1	26.9	26.3	30.9
1966	25.9	26.7	19.8	39.6	41.3	27.9	36.2	37.2	28.9	22.7	22.1	26.9
1967	26.5	27.4	20.2	40.2	41.9	28.1	34.4	35.4	27.8	20.4	19.8	24.8
1968												
1969												
1970												

	Total	White	Non-white	Total	White	Non-white	Total	White	Non-white
	Fifth child			Sixth & seventh child			Eighth child & over		
	D076	D077	D078	D079	D080	D081	D082	D083	D084
1940	8.0			6.9			1.7		
1941	7.9			6.8			1.7		
1942	7.7			6.5			1.6		
1943	8.3			6.7			1.6		
1944	8.4			6.9			1.6		
1945	8.2			6.8			1.6		
1946	8.4			6.9			1.7		
1947	8.4			6.9			1.7		
1948	9.5			7.1			1.8		
1949	8.7			7.4			2.0		
1950	9.0			7.4			1.9		
1951	9.9			7.9			1.9		
1952	10.8			8.2			2.0		
1953	11.8			9.0			2.1		
1954	13.1			9.9			2.3		
1955	13.8			10.8			2.5		
1956	14.8			11.8			2.9		
1957	15.9	13.8	35.0	12.6	8.7	45.0	3.2	1.5	16.6
1958	17.2	14.8	34.9	13.8	9.3	46.4	3.7	1.7	18.1
1959	18.2	15.8	35.9	14.8	10.3	47.4	4.0	1.9	19.0
1960	18.4	16.3	33.1	14.9	10.6	44.5	3.9	1.9	17.4
1961	19.5	17.4	34.2	15.6	11.1	46.3	4.2	2.0	19.0
1962	19.3	17.4	33.9	15.6	11.5	45.4	4.2	2.1	19.4
1963	18.7	16.8	32.8	15.1	11.2	43.8	4.1	2.0	19.1
1964	17.5	15.7	30.3	14.1	10.2	41.1	3.9	1.9	17.7
1965	15.0	13.2	27.2	12.1	8.6	36.4	3.3	1.6	15.2
1966	12.5	10.9	23.4	9.9	7.0	30.2	2.6	1.2	12.1
1967	10.6	9.3	20.1	8.3	5.9	25.2	2.1	1.0	9.7
1968									
1969									
1970									

342

	Annual live births per 1,000 women aged 30-34 years											
Year	Total	White	Non-white	Total	White	Non-white	Total	White	Non-white	Total	White	Non-white
	First child			Second child			Third child			Fourth child		
	D085	D086	D087	D088	D089	D090	D091	D092	D093	D094	D095	D096
1940	14.4			18.0			13.0			9.2		
1941	15.9			19.2			13.5			9.3		
1942	18.7			21.9			14.7			9.7		
1943	17.9			25.0			17.4			10.9		
1944	15.4			24.5			18.4			11.4		
1945	14.9			26.1			19.4			11.5		
1946	19.5			28.2			20.7			12.1		
1947	21.5			28.6			21.5			12.3		
1948	17.1			26.5			20.9			12.2		
1949	15.5			26.4			21.5			12.9		
1950	14.2			26.9			23.0			13.8		
1951	14.3			27.4			25.0			15.3		
1952	14.0			27.8			27.4			17.1		
1953	13.0			26.6			28.3			18.3		
1954	12.6			26.2			29.0			19.8		
1955	11.4			24.0			28.7			20.3		
1956	10.8			22.8			28.6			21.1		
1957	10.4	10.8	8.0	21.5	22.7	14.3	28.5	30.1	17.9	21.8	22.4	19.0
1958	9.8	10.0	7.8	20.1	21.0	13.3	27.7	29.1	17.0	22.4	22.9	18.6
1959	9.3	9.5	7.7	18.8	19.6	12.7	26.7	28.0	16.8	22.6	23.2	18.0
1960	8.6	8.9	6.9	17.5	18.2	12.3	25.3	26.7	15.5	22.2	22.9	17.1
1961	8.2	8.4	6.7	16.8	17.4	11.8	25.0	26.3	15.6	22.6	23.4	17.3
1962	7.5	7.5	6.3	15.4	15.7	11.2	23.2	24.1	14.6	21.5	22.1	16.3
1963	7.2	7.2	6.2	14.5	14.8	11.2	22.2	23.0	14.5	21.0	21.7	16.0
1964	7.7	7.9	6.2	14.0	14.4	10.7	21.4	22.4	14.4	20.4	21.0	15.6
1965	7.3	7.4	6.3	13.3	13.7	10.9	19.8	20.6	13.9	18.5	19.0	15.0
1966	7.1	7.2	6.5	12.5	12.7	10.6	18.1	18.8	13.5	16.5	16.9	13.9
1967	6.6	6.7	6.0	12.3	12.5	10.7	17.1	17.7	12.8	15.3	15.6	13.2
1968												
1969												
1970												

	Fifth child			Sixth & seventh child			Eighth child & over		
Year	D097	D098	D099	D100	D101	D102	D103	D104	D105
1940	7.0			10.0			6.6		
1941	6.9			9.6			6.3		
1942	7.1			9.4			6.1		
1943	7.7			10.0			6.2		
1944	7.7			10.0			6.2		
1945	7.6			9.5			6.0		
1946	7.6			9.2			5.8		
1947	7.5			8.9			5.6		
1948	7.4			8.7			5.5		
1949	7.7			8.9			5.7		
1950	8.1			9.1			5.8		
1951	8.8			9.6			5.9		
1952	9.7			10.1			6.1		
1953	10.5			10.4			6.2		
1954	11.3			11.4			6.6		
1955	12.0			11.9			6.6		
1956	12.8			12.7			7.0		
1957	13.5	12.9	19.3	11.7	11.2	33.9	7.5	4.5	32.1
1958	14.0	13.4	18.1	14.3	11.8	34.1	8.0	4.7	33.5
1959	14.8	14.2	19.3	15.3	12.7	35.2	8.7	5.1	35.8
1960	14.8	14.5	17.4	15.3	13.0	32.2	8.8	5.3	34.2
1961	15.4	15.2	17.2	16.3	14.0	32.2	9.3	5.7	35.5
1962	15.3	15.1	16.7	16.3	14.3	31.6	9.6	6.1	35.6
1963	15.1	15.0	16.3	16.3	14.5	29.8	9.6	6.2	34.9
1964	14.6	14.4	16.0	16.1	14.1	29.9	9.4	5.9	34.1
1965	13.3	13.1	14.9	14.4	12.6	27.0	8.4	5.2	30.3
1966	11.7	11.5	13.6	12.6	11.0	23.5	7.3	4.6	26.2
1967	10.7	10.4	12.6	11.2	9.7	21.4	6.2	3.9	22.3
1968									
1969									
1970									

343

	Annual live births per 1,000 women aged 35-39 years											
Year	Total	White	Non-white	Total	White	Non-white	Total	White	Non-white	Total	White	Non-white
	First child			Second child			Third child			Fourth child		
	D106	D107	D108	D109	D110	D111	D112	D113	D114	D115	D116	D117
1940	4.3			6.0			5.8			5.0		
1941	4.7			6.4			6.0			5.1		
1942	5.6			7.1			6.6			5.3		
1943	6.0			8.4			7.8			6.0		
1944	5.9			9.2			8.4			6.4		
1945	6.1			9.9			9.3			6.8		
1946	7.3			10.7			9.9			7.0		
1947	8.0			10.8			10.2			7.3		
1948	6.7			10.1			9.7			7.1		
1949	6.1			9.7			9.6			7.1		
1950	5.6			9.5			9.8			7.3		
1951	5.4			9.4			10.2			7.9		
1952	5.2			9.4			11.0			8.5		
1953	4.9			9.1			11.2			9.1		
1954	4.8			9.0			11.8			9.8		
1955	4.5			8.8			11.8			10.2		
1956	4.2	8.4		8.4			11.8			10.4		
1957	4.0	4.2	3.5	8.0	8.4	5.7	11.7	12.4	7.7	10.9	11.3	8.6
1958	3.8	3.8	3.4	7.4	7.6	5.8	11.2	11.7	7.4	10.7	11.0	8.0
1959	3.5	3.5	3.3	6.8	7.0	5.0	10.7	11.1	7.2	10.7	11.0	7.9
1960	3.2	3.3	2.9	6.3	6.5	4.7	10.0	10.5	6.6	10.4	10.8	7.7
1961	3.0	3.1	2.7	6.0	6.1	4.7	9.6	10.0	6.7	10.0	10.3	7.8
1962	2.8	2.8	2.4	5.3	5.3	4.6	8.8	9.1	6.4	9.4	9.7	7.1
1963	2.6	2.6	2.5	5.1	5.1	4.3	8.2	8.5	5.7	9.0	9.3	6.6
1964	2.9	2.9	2.4	4.7	4.8	3.9	7.8	8.1	5.8	8.7	9.0	6.5
1965	2.8	2.8	2.3	4.3	4.4	4.0	7.2	7.4	5.5	8.0	8.3	6.2
1966	2.6	2.6	2.3	4.0	4.1	3.6	6.5	6.7	5.1	7.3	7.5	5.7
1967	2.2	2.2	2.0	3.8	3.8	3.7	6.1	6.3	4.9	6.7	6.9	5.4
1968												
1969												
1970												

Year	Fifth child			Sixth & seventh child			Eighth child & over		
	Total	White	Non-white	Total	White	Non-white	Total	White	Non-white
	D118	D119	D120	D121	D122	D123	D124	D125	D126
1940	4.6			7.7			11.3		
1941	4.4			7.4			10.6		
1942	4.4			7.2			10.2		
1943	4.8			7.5			10.2		
1944	4.9			7.5			10.0		
1945	5.1			7.4			9.8		
1946	5.0			7.2			9.3		
1947	5.1			7.0			9.0		
1948	4.9			6.7			8.5		
1949	4.9			6.7			8.7		
1950	5.0			6.6			8.3		
1951	5.3			6.8			8.1		
1952	5.7			6.8			7.9		
1953	6.1			7.1			7.6		
1954	6.6			7.6			7.9		
1955	7.0			8.0			8.0		
1956	7.4			8.5			8.2		
1957	7.8	7.8	8.8	8.9	8.2	17.2	8.5	6.0	31.2
1958	7.9	7.8	8.8	9.2	8.4	16.3	8.4	5.8	30.8
1959	8.2	8.1	8.6	9.7	8.8	17.3	8.9	6.2	31.8
1960	8.0	8.1	7.5	9.5	8.8	15.5	8.7	6.1	29.3
1961	8.1	8.2	7.9	9.9	9.2	15.4	8.9	6.3	29.8
1962	7.8	7.8	7.5	9.6	9.1	14.6	8.9	6.5	29.3
1963	7.6	7.7	7.2	9.6	9.1	14.0	9.0	6.6	28.7
1964	7.3	7.4	6.6	9.4	8.8	13.6	9.1	6.5	28.6
1965	6.8	6.9	6.6	8.7	8.2	12.9	8.5	6.1	26.3
1966	6.2	6.2	6.2	8.0	7.5	11.6	9.6	5.5	23.1
1967	5.6	5.6	5.5	7.3	6.8	10.7	6.8	4.9	20.0
1968									
1969									
1970									

	Annual live births per 1,000 women aged 40-44 years											
Year	Total	White	Non-white	Total	White	Non-white	Total	White	Non-white	Total	White	Non-white
	First child			Second child			Third child			Fourth child		
	D127	D128	D129	D130	D131	D132	D133	D134	D135	D136	D137	D138
1940	0.7			0.9			1.1			1.3		
1941	0.8			1.0			1.1			1.3		
1942	0.8			1.0			1.2			1.3		
1943	1.0			1.2			1.4			1.5		
1944	1.1			1.4			1.6			1.5		
1945	1.2			1.5			1.8			1.6		
1946	1.3			1.7			1.8			1.6		
1947	1.4			1.8			1.9			1.7		
1948	1.3			1.7			1.9			1.7		
1949	1.2			1.7			1.8			1.6		
1950	1.2			1.7			1.8			1.7		
1951	1.2			1.7			2.0			1.8		
1952	1.2			1.8			2.1			1.9		
1953	1.2			1.8			2.2			2.1		
1954	1.1			1.7			2.3			2.2		
1955	1.0			1.7			2.3			2.2		
1956	0.9			1.6			2.3			2.2		
1957	0.9	1.0	0.7	1.5	1.6	1.1	2.2	2.5	1.5	2.3	2.5	1.6
1958	0.8	0.9	0.7	1.5	1.5	1.1	2.2	2.3	1.3	2.4	2.5	1.7
1959	0.8	0.8	0.7	1.4	1.4	1.1	2.2	2.3	1.5	2.4	2.5	1.7
1960	0.8	0.8	0.7	1.3	1.4	0.9	2.1	2.2	1.4	2.4	2.5	1.7
1961	0.7	0.7	0.6	1.3	1.3	0.9	2.1	2.2	1.5	2.4	2.5	1.7
1962	0.7	0.7	0.6	1.2	1.2	0.9	1.9	2.0	1.3	2.3	2.4	1.7
1963	0.6	0.6	0.5	1.1	1.1	0.9	1.8	1.8	1.2	2.1	2.1	1.7
1964	0.7	0.7	0.6	1.0	1.0	0.9	1.7	1.7	1.4	2.0	2.1	1.6
1965	0.6	0.7	0.5	0.9	1.0	0.9	1.5	1.6	1.2	1.9	1.9	1.5
1966	0.6	0.6	0.5	0.8	0.8	0.8	1.4	1.4	1.2	1.7	1.7	1.5
1967	0.5	0.5	0.5	0.8	0.8	0.8	1.3	1.3	1.3	1.6	1.6	1.2
1968												
1969												
1970												

Year	Fifth child			Sixth & seventh child			Eighth child & over		
	D139	D140	D141	D142	D143	D144	D145	D146	D147
1940	1.3			2.6			6.8		
1941	1.3			2.5			6.4		
1942	1.3			2.4			6.1		
1943	1.4			2.5			6.2		
1944	1.4			2.5			6.0		
1945	1.5			2.6			5.8		
1946	1.5			2.4			5.4		
1947	1.5			2.3			5.2		
1948	1.4			2.3			4.7		
1949	1.4			2.1			4.7		
1950	1.4			2.2			4.4		
1951	1.4			2.2			4.5		
1952	1.6			2.2			4.2		
1953	1.7			2.4			4.2		
1954	1.8			2.5			4.1		
1955	1.9			2.5			3.8		
1956	1.9			2.5			3.9		
1957	1.9	2.0	1.8	2.7	2.7	3.6	3.9	3.0	12.2
1958	2.0	2.1	1.8	2.7	2.6	3.7	3.9	3.0	12.2
1959	2.0	2.0	2.0	2.9	2.8	3.8	4.0	3.0	12.1
1960	2.1	2.1	1.9	2.9	2.8	3.8	3.9	3.0	11.5
1961	2.1	2.2	1.7	3.0	2.8	4.0	3.9	3.0	11.7
1962	2.0	2.0	1.8	2.9	2.8	3.7	3.9	3.1	11.6
1963	2.0	2.0	1.9	2.8	2.8	3.7	3.8	3.0	11.1
1964	1.9	1.9	1.8	2.8	2.7	3.6	3.8	2.9	11.0
1965	1.8	1.8	1.7	2.6	2.5	3.5	3.5	2.7	9.9
1966	1.6	1.6	1.6	2.4	2.3	3.3	3.2	2.5	9.6
1967	1.4	1.4	1.3	2.1	2.0	3.1	2.9	2.2	8.7
1968									
1969									
1970									

	Annual live births per 1,000 women aged 45-49 years[a]/											
Year	Total	White	Non-white	Total	White	Non-white	Total	White	Non-white	Total	White	Non-white
	First child			Second child			Third child			Fourth child		
	D148	D149	D150	D151	D152	D153	D154	D155	D156	D157	D158	D159
1957	0.1	0.1	0.0	0.1	0.1	0.1	0.1	0.1	0.1	0.1	0.1	0.1
1958	0.1	0.0	0.1	0.1	0.1	0.1	0.1	0.1	0.1	0.1	0.1	0.1
1959	0.0	0.0	0.1	0.1	0.1	0.0	0.1	0.1	0.1	0.1	0.1	0.1
1960	0.0	0.0	0.1	0.1	0.1	0.0	0.1	0.1	0.1	0.1	0.1	0.1
1961	0.0	0.0	0.0	0.1	0.1	0.0	0.1	0.1	0.1	0.1	0.1	0.1
1962	0.0	0.0	0.0	0.1	0.1	0.0	0.1	0.1	0.1	0.1	0.1	0.1
1963	0.0	0.0	0.1	0.1	0.1	0.0	0.1	0.1	0.1	0.1	0.1	0.1
1964	0.0	0.0	0.0	0.0	0.0	0.0	0.1	0.1	0.1	0.1	0.1	0.1
1965	0.0	0.0	0.0	0.0	0.0	0.0	0.1	0.0	0.1	0.1	0.1	0.1
1966	0.0	0.0	0.0	0.0	0.0	0.0	0.1	0.1	0.1	0.1	0.1	0.1
1967	0.0	0.0	0.0	0.0	0.0	0.1	0.1	0.1	0.1	0.1	0.1	0.1
1968												
1969												
1970												

	Fifth child			Sixth & seventh child			Eighth child & over		
	D160	D161	D162	D163	D164	D165	D166	D167	D168
1957	0.1	0.1	0.1	0.2	0.2	0.3	0.4	0.3	1.4
1958	0.1	0.1	0.1	0.2	0.2	0.3	0.4	0.3	1.2
1959	0.1	0.1	0.1	0.2	0.2	0.3	0.4	0.3	1.2
1960	0.1	0.1	0.1	0.2	0.2	0.3	0.4	0.3	1.1
1961	0.1	0.1	0.1	0.2	0.2	0.2	0.3	0.3	1.0
1962	0.1	0.1	0.1	0.2	0.2	0.2	0.3	0.3	1.0
1963	0.1	0.1	0.1	0.2	0.2	0.3	0.3	0.3	0.9
1964	0.1	0.1	0.1	0.2	0.2	0.2	0.3	0.2	1.0
1965	0.1	0.1	0.1	0.2	0.1	0.2	0.3	0.2	0.9
1966	0.1	0.1	0.1	0.1	0.1	0.2	0.3	0.2	0.9
1967	0.1	0.1	0.1	0.1	0.1	0.1	0.3	0.2	0.7
1968									
1969									
1970									

Cumulative Birth Rates (cumulative live births per 1,000 women), by Age Group of Mother, United States, 1940-1968

As of January 1	15-19 years D169	20-24 years D170	25-29 years D171	30-34 years D172	35-39 years D173	40-44 years D174	45-49 years D175
1940	58.5	497.8	1,117.7	1,699.1	2,214.9	2,634.6	2,960.5
1941	57.8	509.2	1,116.7	1,674.7	2,170.1	2,576.3	2,908.2
1942	59.0	527.3	1,124.8	1,660.5	2,133.0	2,519.1	2,850.4
1943	62.3	557.9	1,150.4	1,658.5	2,097.7	2,472.6	2,787.2
1944	64.2	574.4	1,193.1	1,675.7	2,064.0	2,426.8	2,728.6
1945	60.7	569.1	1,233.0	1,686.9	2,046.1	2,379.8	2,672.8
1946	57.2	551.2	1,258.3	1,704.5	2,040.7	2,339.9	2,614.8
1947	59.5	570.0	1,308.4	1,735.4	2,046.7	2,310.1	2,558.1
1948	72.1	617.5	1,369.5	1,775.3	2,039.9	2,282.3	2,512.8
1949	81.3	655.0	1,409.1	1,824.2	2,080.3	2,250.8	2,467.1
1950	86.4	691.5	1,441.2	1,891.1	2,092.6	2,235.1	2,419.8
1951	89.5	720.2	1,478.9	1,953.1	2,110.5	2,230.2	2,378.9
1952	94.3	758.1	1,525.9	2,019.0	2,137.1	2,233.9	2,348.4
1953	95.1	792.5	1,584.3	2,085.1	2,173.5	2,243.3	2,319.0
1954	96.3	825.3	1,644.9	2,140.8	2,231.8	2,264.0	2,286.5
1955	98.1	857.1	1,711.5	2,188.8	2,316.9	2,277.6	2,271.5
1956	98.6	888.3	1,773.3	2,243.8	2,395.0	2,298.0	2,267.3
1957	102.3	919.6	1,841.6	2,300.5	2,472.8	2,326.3	2,271.5
1958	105.3	946.0	1,912.8	2,368.7	2,544.0	2,365.4	2,281.3
1959	104.2	959.1	1,979.8	2,434.6	2,602.0	2,426.6	2,302.2
1960	101.0	968.6	2,035.4	2,507.5	2,645.6	2,515.3	2,315.1
1961	96.8	976.0	2,088.9	2,573.7	2,697.2	2,594.2	2,335.3
1962	94.4	974.8	2,126.4	2,646.3	2,748.8	2,671.8	2,363.2
1963	93.2	956.7	2,140.4	2,714.1	2,808.8	2,739.4	2,401.9
1964	90.1	927.7	2,138.0	2,775.6	2,866.5	2,793.5	2,463.1
1965	86.1	888.5	2,121.1	2,817.4	2,931.0	2,831.4	2,552.3
1966	78.5	838.8	2,077.8	2,848.2	2,984.7	2,876.5	2,630.5
1967	79.4	789.9	2,010.0	2,849.7	3,038.3	2,918.5	2,706.2
1968	77.9	751.4	1,922.5	2,819.8	3,086.1	2,969.4	2,772.6
1969							
1970							

Live Births per 1,000 Women, by Color: Total and by Age Group of Mother,
United States, 1940-1968

Type of data and year	Total live births (to women of all ages) per 1,000 women 15-44 years old (all races)	Total live births to white women per 1,000 white women 15-44 years old	Live births per 1,000 white women of specified age group							
			Under 15 years	15-19 years	20-24 years	25-29 years	30-34 years	35-39 years	40-44 years	45-49 years
	D176	D177	D178	D179	D180	D181	D182	D183	D184	D185
Births adjusted for underregistration:										
1940	79.9	77.1	0.2	45.3	131.4	123.6	83.4	45.3	15.0	1.6
1941	83.4	80.7	0.2	47.6	141.6	120.1	85.2	45.1	14.3	1.4
1942	91.5	89.5	0.3	51.8	162.9	145.6	92.3	47.2	14.1	1.3
1943	94.3	92.3	0.3	52.1	161.1	150.7	100.2	52.2	15.0	1.3
1944	88.8	86.3	0.3	45.3	147.9	137.7	98.2	54.1	15.5	1.2
1945	85.9	83.4	0.3	42.1	134.7	133.1	100.5	56.3	16.0	1.4
1946	101.9	100.4	0.3	50.6	179.8	164.0	110.0	58.4	15.9	1.3
1947	113.3	111.8	0.4	69.8	207.9	179.1	113.0	58.4	16.1	1.2
1948	107.3	104.3	0.4	71.1	195.5	163.9	103.6	53.5	15.2	1.1
1949	107.1	103.6	0.4	72.1	194.6	165.2	101.5	52.2	14.6	1.1
1950	106.2	102.3	0.4	70.0	190.4	165.1	102.6	51.4	14.5	1.0
1951	111.5	107.7	0.4	75.9	206.0	174.2	106.5	52.6	14.6	1.0
1952	113.9	110.1	0.4	75.0	212.5	180.5	111.4	54.4	14.8	0.9
1953	115.2	111.0	0.4	77.2	219.6	181.5	111.9	55.1	15.0	0.9
1954	118.1	113.6	0.4	79.0	230.7	185.0	115.1	56.2	15.4	0.9
1955	118.5	113.8	0.3	79.2	236.0	186.8	114.1	56.7	15.4	0.9
1956	121.2	116.0	0.3	83.2	247.1	190.6	114.4	57.0	15.4	0.8
1957	122.9	117.7	0.5	85.2	253.8	195.8	115.9	57.4	15.4	0.8
1958	120.2	114.9	0.5	81.0	251.4	194.8	113.0	55.8	14.8	0.8
1959	120.2	114.6	0.4	79.8	253.3	196.7	112.0	55.7	14.8	0.8
Registered births:										
1959	118.8	113.9	0.4	79.2	251.7	195.5	111.3	55.1	14.7	0.9
1960	118.0	113.2	0.4	79.4	252.8	194.9	109.6	54.0	14.7	0.8
1961	117.2	112.2	0.4	78.8	247.9	194.4	110.1	53.2	14.8	0.9
1962	112.1	107.5	0.4	73.1	238.0	187.7	105.2	50.2	14.1	0.8
1963	108.5	103.7	0.3	68.1	224.7	181.5	102.6	48.9	13.4	0.8
1964	105.0	99.9	0.3	63.2	213.1	176.2	100.5	47.7	13.0	0.8
1965	96.6	91.4	0.3	60.7	189.8	158.8	91.7	44.1	12.0	0.7
1966	91.3	86.4	0.3	60.8	179.9	146.6	82.7	40.0	10.8	0.7
1967	87.6	83.1	0.3	57.3	168.8	140.7	76.5	36.6	9.8	0.6
1968	84.9	81.5	0.4	55.3	162.6	139.7	72.5	33.8	8.9	0.5
1969	85.8									
1970										

(continued)

Live Births per 1,000 Women, by Color: Total and by Age Group of Mother,
United States, 1940-1968 (cont.)

Type of data and year	Total live births to nonwhite women per 1,000 nonwhite women 15-44 years old	Live births per 1,000 nonwhite women of specified age group							
		Under 15 years	15-19 years	20-24 years	25-29 years	30-34 years	35-39 years	40-44 years	45-49 years
	D186	D187	D188	D189	D190	D191	D192	D193	D194
Births adjusted for underregistration:									
1940	102.4	3.7	121.7	168.5	116.3	83.5	53.7	21.5	5.2
1941	105.4	4.0	128.0	175.0	118.1	86.2	54.1	21.5	4.1
1942	107.6	3.9	131.8	182.3	119.6	88.1	54.0	20.8	4.0
1943	111.0	4.0	133.4	187.2	125.1	93.9	56.9	21.5	3.7
1944	108.5	3.9	121.5	182.4	126.8	97.3	58.4	21.5	3.2
1945	106.0	3.9	117.5	172.1	125.4	97.1	61.3	22.3	3.7
1946	113.9	3.7	121.9	197.3	139.2	99.3	61.0	21.8	3.5
1947	125.9	4.6	146.6	223.7	150.6	102.4	62.7	21.4	3.1
1948	131.6	4.9	157.3	237.0	159.6	104.1	62.5	20.4	2.8
1949	135.1	5.1	162.8	241.3	167.0	107.3	63.9	21.1	2.5
1950	137.3	5.1	163.5	242.6	173.8	112.6	64.3	21.2	2.6
1951	142.1	5.4	166.7	252.5	184.2	117.9	66.5	22.6	2.2
1952	143.3	5.2	162.9	254.0	194.2	122.0	66.6	21.9	2.2
1953	147.3	5.1	165.4	261.4	206.4	125.7	70.0	23.0	2.2
1954	153.2	4.9	170.3	274.7	215.7	131.3	72.9	22.5	2.1
1955	155.3	4.8	168.3	283.4	219.6	133.5	75.4	22.1	2.1
1956	160.9	4.7	172.5	299.1	225.9	139.4	78.8	23.6	2.0
1957	163.0	5.6	172.8	307.0	228.1	143.5	78.7	23.5	2.0
1958	160.5	4.3	167.3	305.2	224.2	142.3	78.4	21.8	1.9
1959	162.2	4.0	167.1	308.9	227.3	143.3	78.5	23.3	1.8
Registered births:									
1959	156.0	4.2	160.5	297.9	220.2	138.1	75.0	21.2	1.8
1960	153.6	4.0	158.2	294.2	214.6	135.6	74.2	22.0	1.7
1961	153.5	4.0	152.8	292.9	221.9	136.2	74.9	22.3	1.5
1962	148.8	3.9	144.6	285.7	217.4	132.4	72.0	21.7	1.5
1963	144.9	4.0	139.9	277.3	211.8	129.3	68.9	21.0	1.5
1964	141.7	4.0	138.7	268.6	202.0	127.5	67.5	20.9	1.5
1965	133.9	4.0	138.1	247.3	188.1	118.3	63.8	19.2	1.5
1966	125.9	4.0	135.5	228.9	169.3	107.9	57.7	18.4	1.4
1967	119.8	4.1	135.2	212.1	155.9	99.1	52.4	16.8	1.2
1968	114.9	4.4	133.3	200.8	144.8	91.2	48.6	15.0	1.2
1969									
1970									

Type of data and year	Total legitimate live births (regardless of age of mother) per 1,000 married women 15-44 years of age	Legitimate live births, by age group of mother, per 1,000 married women of mother's age group					
		15-19 years	20-24 years	25-29 years	30-34 years	35-39 years	40-44 years
	D195	D196	D197	D198	D199	D200	D201
Births adjusted for underregistration							
1950	143.9	421.5	287.9	195.0	118.0	60.7	17.9
1951	148.8	461.7	304.0	199.3	123.8	61.4	17.8
1952	151.4	451.9	306.4	209.4	127.3	63.9	18.0
1953	151.5	459.2	312.7	210.2	126.0	64.8	18.0
1954	155.8	501.5	335.4	213.3	130.6	66.1	18.2
1955	155.1	461.4	332.7	218.1	128.0	66.9	18.1
1956	158.8	468.6	344.9	221.3	127.3	68.6	18.6
1957	161.1	524.5	356.4	226.2	129.4	67.4	18.3
1958	158.5	48.51	352.8	226.1	127.1	64.7	17.7
1959	158.1	492.8	350.2	221.9	126.8	64.3	17.7
Registered births							
1959	156.2	485.1	346.5	219.6	125.3	63.3	17.5
1960	156.3	483.5	354.4	222.3	123.3	61.7	17.4
1961	156.5	538.1	349.1	221.2	124.6	60.9	17.1
1962	152.1	475.5	335.4	213.8	120.3	58.4	16.5
1963	146.3	490.1	325.5	205.7	114.2	55.5	15.4
1964	140.9	376.1	310.4	197.9	109.2	54.6	15.4
1965	131.1	452.9	279.7	178.9	101.1	50.1	14.1
1966	123.7	455.6	255.5	166.1	92.1	45.1	12.8
1967	119.0	432.6	246.6	158.5	85.1	41.5	11.6
1968							
1969							
1970							

Estimated Total Illegitimate Live Births per 1,000 Unmarried Women 15-44 Years of Age, by
Color, United States, 1940-1967, and Estimated Illegitimate Live Births, by Age Group and
Color of Mother, per 1,000 Unmarried Women of Mother's Color and Age Group,
United States, 1950 and 1955-1967[a]/

Year	Estimated total illegitimate live births (regardless of age of mother) per 1,000 unmarried women 15-44 years of age			Illegitimate live births, by age group and color of mother, per 1,000 unmarried women of mother's age group and color					
				15-19 years			20-24 years		
	Total	White	Nonwhite	Total	White	Nonwhite	Total	White	Nonwhite
	D202	D203	D204	D205	D206	D207	D208	D209	D210
1940	7.1	3.6	35.6	7.4	3.3	42.5	9.5	5.7	46.1
1941	7.7			8.0			9.8		
1942	8.0			8.2			11.0		
1943	8.3			8.4			11.4		
1944	9.0			8.8			13.1		
1945	10.1			9.5			15.3		
1946	10.9			9.5			17.3		
1947	12.1			11.0			18.9		
1948	12.5			11.4			19.8		
1949	13.3			12.0			21.0		
1950	14.1	6.1	71.2	12.6	5.1	68.5	21.3	10.0	105.4
1951	15.1			13.2			23.2		
1952	15.8			13.5			25.4		
1953	;6.9			13.9			28.0		
1954	18.7			14.9			31.4		
1955	19.3	7.9	87.2	15.1	6.0	77.6	33.5	15.0	133.0
1956	20.4	8.3	92.1	15.6	6.2	79.6	36.4	16.3	143.5
1957	21.0	8.6	95.3	15.8	6.4	81.4	37.3	16.6	147.7
1958	21.2	8.8	97.8	15.3	6.3	80.4	38.2	17.3	153.2
1959	21.9	9.2	100.8	15.5	6.5	80.8	40.2	18.3	167.8
	21.6								
1960	21.6	9.2	98.3	15.3	6.6	76.5	39.7	18.2	166.5
1961	22.7	10.0	100.8	15.9	7.0	77.6	41.7	19.7	169.6
1962	21.9	9.8	97.5	14.8	6.5	74.1	40.9	20.0	163.6
1963	22.5	10.5	97.1	15.2	7.0	73.8	40.3	20.8	161.8
1964	23.0	11.0	97.2	15.8	7.3	74.0	39.9	21.2	164.2
1965	23.5	11.6	97.6	16.7	7.9	75.8	39.9	22.1	152.6
1966	23.4	12.0	92.8	17.5	8.5	76.9	39.1	22.5	139.4
1967	23.9	12.5	89.5	18.6	9.0	80.2	38.3	23.1	128.2
1968									
1969									
1970									

(continued)

Estimated Total Illegitimate Live Births per 1,000 Unmarried Women 15-44 Years of Age, by
Color, United States, 1940-1967, and Estimated Illegitimate Live Births, by Age Group and
Color of Mother, per 1,000 Unmarried Women of Mother's Color and Age Group,
United States, 1950 and 1955-1967a/ (cont.)

Illegitimate live births, by age group and color of mother, per 1,000 unmarried women of
mother's age group and color

Year	25-29 years			30-34 years			35-39 years: Total	40-44 yearsb/ Total	35-44 yearsc/	
	Total	White	Nonwhite	Total	White	Nonwhite			White	Nonwhite
	D211	D212	D213	D214	D215	D216	D217	D218	D219	D220
1940	7.2	4.0	32.5	5.1	2.5	23.4	3.4	1.2	1.7	8.6
1941	7.8			6.0			3.7	1.4		
1942	8.4			6.3			3.8	1.2		
1943	8.8			6.7			3.8	1.3		
1944	10.1			7.0			4.0	1.3		
1945	12.1			7.1			4.1	1.6		
1946	15.6			7.3			4.4	1.8		
1947	15.7			9.2			5.6	1.8		
1948	16.4			10.0			5.8	1.6		
1949	18.0			11.4			6.8	1.9		
1950	19.9	8.7	94.2	13.3	5.9	63.5	7.2	2.0	2.1	20.0
1951	22.8			14.6			7.6	2.2		
1952	24.8			15.7			8.2	1.9		
1953	27.6			17.3			9.0	2.4		
1954	31.0			20.4			10.3	2.5		
1955	33.5	13.3	125.2	22.0	8.6	100.9	10.5	2.7	2.8	25.3
1956	35.6	14.0	132.7	24.6	9.2	113.7	11.1	2.8	3.0	27.0
1957	36.8	14.6	142.6	26.8	10.5	115.1	12.1	3.1	3.0	30.0
1958	40.5	15.8	161.2	27.5	10.8	110.5	13.3	3.2	3.4	32.5
1959	44.1	17.6	168.0	28.1	10.7	106.5	14.1	3.3	3.6	34.9
1960	45.1	18.2	171.8	27.8	10.8	104.0	14.1	3.6	3.9	35.6
1961	46.5	19.4	172.7	28.3	11.3	112.0	15.4	3.9	4.2	37.4
1962	46.7	19.8	172.7	29.7	12.6	115.2	15.6	4.0	4.3	35.5
1963	49.0	22.0	171.5	33.2	14.2	124.3	16.1	4.3	4.6	34.4
1964	50.2	24.1	168.7	37.2	15.9	132.3	16.3	4.4	4.8	34.5
1965	49.3	24.3	164.7	37.5	16.6	137.8	17.4	4.55	4.9	39.0
1966	45.6	23.5	143.8	33.0	15.7	119.4	16.4	4.1	4.9	33.8
1967	41.4	22.7	118.4	29.2	14.0	97.2	15.4	4.0	4.7	28.9
1968										
1969										
1970										

Estimated Illegitimacy Ratios: Estimated Number of Illegitimate Live Births, by Age Group and Color of Mother, per 1,000 Total Live Births to Mothers of the Same Age Group and Color, United States, 1940-1967 (All ages) and 1955-1967 (by age group of mother)

Illegitimacy ratio, by age group and color of mother

Year	Total	White	Non-white	Total	White	Non-white	Total	White	Non-white	Total	White	Non-white
	All ages			Under 15 years			15-19 years			20-24 years		
	D221	D222	D223	D224	D225	D226	D227	D228	D229	D230	D231	D232
1940	37.9	19.5	168.3									
1941	38.1	19.0	174.5									
1942	34.3	16.9	169.2									
1943	33.4	16.5	162.8									
1944	37.6	20.2	163.4									
1945	42.9	23.6	179.3									
1946	38.1	21.1	170.1									
1947	35.7	18.5	168.0									
1948	36.7	17.8	164.7									
1949	37.4	17.3	167.5									
1950	39.8	17.5	179.6									
1951	39.1	16.3	182.8									
1952	39.1	16.3	183.4									
1953	41.2	16.9	191.1									
1954	44.0	18.2	198.5									
1955	45.3	18.6	202.4	662.9	421.3	800.6	142.3	63.6	406.6	43.7	19.3	189.4
1956	46.5	19.0	204.0	660.8	425.9	798.4	139.9	62.6	404.8	44.4	19.6	189.7
1957	47.4	19.6	206.7	660.9	415.4	811.7	138.9	62.7	409.1	44.4	19.5	190.5
1958	49.6	20.9	212.3	661.9	453.2	825.0	143.3	65.9	419.0	45.9	20.6	194.2
1959	52.0	22.1	218.0	678.9	466.6	808.8	148.0	69.4	426.5	47.9	21.8	202.3
1960	52.7	22.9	215.8	678.5	475.4	822.4	148.4	71.6	421.5	47.7	21.9	199.6
1961	56.3	25.3	223.4	696.9	498.6	816.5	154.9	76.5	439.2	51.2	24.2	209.4
1962	58.8	27.0	227.8	694.8	480.1	842.0	157.3	78.2	439.3	53.6	26.2	212.5
1963	63.3	30.4	235.5	711.1	487.4	852.4	173.6	89.9	455.6	56.8	29.7	213.9
1964	68.5	33.9	245.0	742.1	523.2	856.0	190.2	101.7	468.3	61.1	33.1	220.4
1965	77.4	39.6	263.2	785.3	572.8	864.0	208.3	114.3	492.0	67.8	38.4	229.9
1966	83.9	44.4	276.5	762.8	525.1	878.8	218.5	123.6	500.9	71.3	41.6	237.2
1967	90.3	48.7	293.8	803.0	615.7	891.6	242.1	138.5	521.1	77.5	47.0	253.2
1968												
1969												
1970												

Year	25-29 years			30-34 years			35-39 years			40 years and older		
	D233	D234	D235	D236	D237	D238	D239	D240	D241	D242	D243	D244
1955	25.0	9.3	133.4	22.3	8.5	119.9	24.0	10.0	117.1	25.9	12.5	108.6
1956	26.0	9.6	136.0	23.4	8.5	123.4	24.8	10.4	116.7	26.4	13.5	111.6
1957	26.1	9.9	135.9	24.9	9.5	125.6	25.7	9.8	127.6	29.1	14.6	117.4
1958	27.8	10.4	141.6	26.3	9.9	130.9	27.6	11.3	127.1	28.8	13.7	119.7
1959	29.1	11.1	143.4	27.1	9.8	133.4	28.9	11.9	130.1	29.5	13.5	124.4
1960	29.4	11.4	141.3	27.5	10.2	129.9	29.5	12.7	127.7	31.0	15.8	116.8
1961	31.2	12.5	143.5	29.2	11.4	132.0	31.2	13.6	129.9	32.2	16.6	126.7
1962	32.5	13.3	147.2	31.0	12.9	134.6	33.2	14.5	136.6	34.2	17.1	120.7
1963	34.6	14.8	151.2	32.4	13.5	138.3	33.8	15.4	133.8	37.3	19.0	134.6
1964	36.1	16.5	155.0	33.3	13.7	140.7	35.8	16.9	136.2	39.0	20.7	125.2
1965	39.8	18.8	162.8	37.0	16.1	149.0	40.3	19.0	148.8	42.9	22.2	140.1
1966	40.7	19.9	167.5	38.8	18.3	147.7	41.6	21.4	145.9	43.1	23.1	137.2
1967	39.8	20.3	164.4	39.4	18.4	151.5	44.4	22.2	155.3	46.3	25.7	133.0
1968												
1969												
1970												

Year	Percent distribution of live births to women of all races			Percent distribution of live births to white women			Percent distribution of live births to nonwhite women		
	In hospi-tal	Not in hospital		In hospi-tal	Not in hospital		In hospi-tal	Not in hospital	
		By physi-cian	By mid-wife, other and not speci-fied		By physi-cian	By mid-wife, other and not speci-fied		By physi-cian	By mid-wife, other and not speci-fied
	D245	D246	D247	D248	D249	D250	D251	D252	D253
1940	55.8	35.0	9.3	59.9	36.5	3.6	26.7	24.1	49.2
1941	61.2	30.2	8.6	65.7	31.2	3.1	29.0	23.3	47.7
1942	67.9	24.7	7.4	72.7	24.8	2.5	30.6	24.0	45.3
1943	72.1	21.0	6.9	77.2	20.6	2.2	33.3	24.0	42.7
1944	75.6	17.7	6.7	81.0	16.9	2.1	37.0	23.1	39.9
1945	78.8	14.7	6.5	84.3	13.7	2.0	40.2	21.7	38.1
1946	82.4	12.2	5.4	87.1	11.2	1.6	45.2	20.0	34.8
1947	84.8	10.1	5.1	89.3	9.2	1.5	49.7	17.7	32.6
1948	85.6	9.1	5.3	90.4	8.1	1.5	52.9	16.6	30.6
1949	86.7	8.1	5.1	91.6	6.9	1.4	55.1	15.9	29.0
1950	88.0	7.1	5.0	92.8	5.9	1.3	57.9	14.3	27.8
1951	90.0	5.5	4.5	94.4	4.4	1.2	62.4	12.3	25.4
1952	91.7	4.2	4.1	95.7	3.2	1.1	66.4	10.6	23.0
1953	92.8	3.5	3.7	96.5	2.6	1.0	70.3	9.0	20.7
1954	93.6	2.9	3.5	97.0	2.1	0.9	73.1	7.8	19.1
1955	94.4	2.5	3.2	97.5	1.8	0.8	76.0	6.8	17.2
1956	95.1	2.1	2.8	98.0	1.4	0.6	78.7	5.8	15.4
1957	95.7	1.8	2.6	98.2	1.2	0.6	81.1	5.1	13.8
1958	96.0	1.5	2.4	98.4	1.0	0.6	82.5	4.5	13.1
1959	96.4	1.3	2.3	98.7	0.8	0.5	83.7	4.1	12.2
1960	96.6	1.2	2.2	98.8	0.7	0.5	85.0	3.5	11.5
1961	96.9	1.0	2.1	98.9	0.6	0.5	86.0	3.1	10.9
1962	97.2	0.9	2.0	99.0	0.5	0.4	86.9	2.7	10.4
1963	97.4	0.8	1.9	99.1	0.5	0.4	87.9	2.4	9.7
1964	97.5	0.7	1.9	99.1	0.4	0.5	89.0	2.0	9.0
1965	97.4	0.9	0.8	98.9	0.6	0.5	89.8	2.1	8.2
1966	98.0	0.5	1.5	99.3	0.3	0.4	91.6	1.4	7.1
1967	98.3	0.4	1.3	99.4	0.3	0.4	92.9	1.1	6.0
1968									
1969									
1970									

Percent Distribution of Individuals by Mobility Status, Age Group, and Sex,
United States, 1948-1969

Year ended	Male				Female			
	Non-movers (same house)	Movers[b]			Non-movers (same house)	Movers[b]		
		Different house, same county	Different county, same state	Different state		Different house, same county	Different county, same state	Different state

Age 18-19 years

Year ended	E001	E002	E003	E004	E005	E006	E007	E008
April 1948	75.8	12.7	2.8	6.2	67.6	22.6	5.4	3.8
April 1949	79.4	11.6	3.2	5.2	67.3	21.9	5.5	4.8
March 1950	82.5	9.1	3.5	3.8	70.4	21.0	3.8	4.8
April 1951	78.2	12.7	4.6	4.3	63.2	22.7	6.7	7.1
April 1952	76.3	13.6	4.5	5.2	67.1	20.2	6.6	6.0
April 1953	79.1	12.5	4.5	3.3	64.9	20.8	7.2	6.7
April 1954	81.9	11.7	2.8	3.4	67.5	17.9	7.6	6.7
April 1955	78.8	12.9	4.1	3.2	63.2	22.3	8.8	5.4
March 1956	77.8	12.2	5.6	3.6	63.9	24.1	5.9	5.8
April 1957	79.7	11.6	4.5	3.6	66.4	19.7	5.4	7.8
March 1958	76.3	13.3	4.7	5.0	66.1	21.2	6.3	6.0
April 1959	78.3	12.5	4.3	4.3	65.0	24.2	5.6	4.8
March 1960	77.8	13.2	3.9	4.0	64.7	21.5	7.5	5.6
March 1961	80.2	12.6	3.3	3.7	64.5	21.9	7.4	5.6
April 1962	76.7	15.2	3.3	4.0	64.4	23.2	5.3	6.5
March 1963	80.4	11.6	3.9	3.6	63.7	23.2	6.4	6.0
March 1964	77.4	13.7	4.4	4.0	66.0	19.8	8.1	5.6
March 1965	78.2	13.5	4.4	3.7	67.4	20.6	7.0	4.5
March 1966	80.3	12.5	3.4	3.4	68.1	20.6	5.2	5.5
March 1967	81.1	11.7	2.9	3.5	71.3	17.7	5.4	5.1
March 1968	80.2	11.6	3.6	4.0	68.3	19.3	5.8	5.6
March 1969	80.8	12.1	2.8	3.7	71.1	18.2	5.3	4.9

Age 20-24 years

Year ended	E009	E010	E011	E012	E013	E014	E015	E016
April 1948	65.4	19.7	6.1	6.2	62.1	24.7	6.4	6.4
April 1949	64.3	22.8	5.3	6.0	63.9	25.9	4.3	5.7
March 1950	67.0	20.9	4.8	6.0	63.8	24.7	6.0	5.3
April 1951	62.7	23.0	6.7	6.6	60.9	25.1	7.1	6.8
April 1952	61.0	22.6	5.7	8.3	60.9	25.0	6.0	7.8
April 1953	52.4	20.1	7.0	13.0	58.8	25.9	6.7	8.1
April 1954	54.2	20.5	6.0	10.4	59.9	23.7	7.1	8.2
April 1955	50.7	24.7	7.0	9.6	57.4	27.1	7.0	8.0
March 1956	49.4	25.5	7.2	11.7	54.8	27.4	8.2	9.1
April 1957	55.7	24.9	6.5	8.8	56.7	27.2	7.0	7.8
March 1958	53.7	25.8	6.5	9.6	55.7	27.8	7.0	8.5
April 1959	56.5	25.6	6.6	8.1	56.1	28.4	7.1	7.4
March 1960	57.2	23.3	6.6	9.7	56.3	26.5	7.7	8.5
March 1961	55.3	24.8	7.5	9.6	53.5	30.0	6.8	8.3
April 1962	54.4	28.1	5.8	9.1	55.7	28.2	7.4	7.7
March 1963	56.6	23.7	6.1	10.5	55.5	27.3	7.9	8.4
March 1964	56.6	25.4	6.9	8.5	53.3	29.5	8.5	7.6
March 1965	53.6	27.9	7.5	8.8	53.4	29.5	8.1	8.2
March 1966	57.1	24.4	7.2	9.2	55.5	25.8	8.6	9.3
March 1967	55.9	23.5	7.2	10.2	58.0	24.9	7.5	8.7
March 1968	55.0	23.4	7.3	9.4	56.6	26.1	7.9	8.6
March 1969	53.6	24.1	7.9	9.4	55.8	26.2	8.0	9.2

(continued)

Percent Distribution of Individuals by Mobility Status, Age Group, and Sex
United States, 1948-1969   (cont.)

Year ended	Male				Female			
	Non-movers (same house)	Movers[b]			Non-movers (same house)	Movers[b]		
		Different house, same county	Different county, same state	Different state		Different house, same county	Different county, same state	Different state

Age 25-34 years

Year ended	E017	E018	E019	E020	E021	E022	E023	E024
April 1948	69.8	20.3	4.1	5.3	74.3	17.5	3.6	4.3
April 1949	71.1	19.1	4.0	5.0	75.6	16.2	3.7	4.1
March 1950	71.3	18.7	4.5	4.6	75.6	16.1	4.0	3.8
April 1951	67.2	20.6	5.5	6.3	72.6	17.1	4.7	5.3
April 1952	68.8	19.2	4.9	5.9	73.4	16.4	4.2	5.4
April 1953	67.8	20.5	4.0	6.1	72.8	18.0	3.6	5.2
April 1954	69.1	18.8	4.8	5.5	75.5	15.6	3.9	4.6
April 1955	69.4	18.9	5.1	5.3	73.8	16.9	4.3	4.2
March 1956	68.5	19.8	5.4	5.1	72.5	17.9	4.8	4.0
April 1957	68.7	19.8	5.5	5.1	74.5	16.5	4.0	4.2
March 1958	67.3	19.8	5.7	5.9	73.2	17.4	4.4	4.3
April 1959	68.2	20.0	4.9	5.7	73.7	16.8	4.1	4.7
March 1960	68.8	10.9	5.3	5.6	75.4	15.8	4.3	4.0
March 1961	66.7	20.9	5.2	5.7	73.4	17.4	4.4	4.1
April 1962	68.5	19.9	4.7	5.6	74.4	16.7	4.0	4.4
March 1963	67.4	19.1	5.4	6.4	73.8	16.2	4.0	5.3
March 1964	66.5	20.1	5.9	6.1	72.2	16.8	4.9	5.3
March 1965	65.5	21.0	6.0	6.0	71.9	17.3	4.9	5.1
March 1966	65.8	21.3	6.1	5.5	72.5	17.3	4.6	4.8
March 1967	67.5	19.1	5.4	6.2	73.5	15.6	4.3	5.5
March 1968	67.5	18.7	5.9	6.2	72.8	15.6	5.1	5.8
March 1969	67.7	19.1	5.4	5.9	73.9	15.8	4.2	5.1

Age 35-44 years

Year ended	E025	E026	E027	E028	E029	E030	E031	E032
April 1948	80.0	13.1	3.3	3.4	84.3	10.8	2.5	2.3
April 1949	87.6	12.6	2.3	3.2	85.0	10.6	1.8	2.3
March 1950	81.9	12.9	2.7	2.2	84.6	11.1	2.1	1.9
April 1951	80.6	13.4	2.7	3.2	82.4	12.5	2.4	2.5
April 1952	80.7	12.8	2.9	3.1	84.0	11.2	2.3	2.2
April 1953	79.2	14.4	2.7	3.2	83.6	11.8	1.9	2.5
April 1954	82.5	11.4	2.8	2.7	85.7	9.3	2.4	2.4
April 1955	82.0	11.5	2.7	3.2	84.5	10.6	2.5	2.3
March 1956	80.9	11.9	3.7	2.6	83.7	11.0	2.4	2.4
April 1957	81.8	12.1	2.8	2.8	84.1	10.9	2.3	2.2
March 1958	81.2	11.9	3.2	3.2	84.8	10.1	2.3	2.6
April 1959	83.3	11.2	2.6	2.5	85.5	9.9	2.3	1.9
March 1960	81.5	11.6	3.2	2.9	84.5	10.4	2.1	2.7
March 1961	81.4	12.0	2.8	3.0	83.5	11.7	1.9	2.5
April 1962	82.2	11.1	2.9	3.1	84.8	10.6	2.3	2.1
March 1963	82.0	11.3	2.8	3.2	84.0	10.4	2.5	2.7
March 1964	82.3	11.6	2.7	3.1	85.0	10.5	1.8	2.4
March 1965	82.5	11.5	3.0	2.3	84.5	10.7	2.0	2.4
March 1966	82.2	11.4	3.0	2.7	84.7	10.4	2.3	2.2
March 1967	82.4	10.2	3.2	3.2	85.8	8.8	2.6	2.3
March 1968	82.0	10.7	2.9	3.4	85.1	9.2	2.4	2.9
March 1969	83.0	10.0	3.0	3.1	86.1	8.6	2.2	2.5

(continued)

356

Percent Distribution of Individuals by Mobility Status, Age Group, and Sex
United States, 1948-1969   (cont.)

| | Male | | | | Female | | | |
| | Non-movers (same house) | Movers_b/ | | | Non-movers (same house) | Movers_b/ | | |
Year ended		Different house, same county	Different county, same state	Different state		Different house, same county	Different county, same state	Different state

Age 45-64 years

	E033	E034	E035	E036	E037	E038	E039	E040
April 1948	87.3	9.4	1.8	1.4	88.4	8.1	1.7	1.6
April 1949	88.6	7.8	1.8	1.6	89.4	7.8	1.6	1.2
March 1950	88.3	7.9	2.0	1.6	89.9	7.6	1.1	1.3
April 1951	86.4	9.0	2.4	2.0	88.4	8.2	1.8	1.5
April 1952	87.9	8.3	1.5	2.1	89.0	8.2	1.5	1.1
April 1953	89.3	7.4	1.7	1.6	89.5	7.3	1.5	1.6
April 1954	88.0	8.2	1.8	1.7	88.9	7.7	1.6	1.6
April 1955	86.7	9.5	2.5	1.1	88.5	8.0	1.9	1.6
March 1956	87.0	8.7	2.5	1.5	88.4	8.4	1.9	1.1
April 1957	88.2	8.4	1.8	1.4	89.7	7.1	1.6	1.4
March 1968	87.9	8.1	2.3	1.6	88.8	7.9	1.7	1.4
April 1959	88.1	8.0	2.3	1.3	89.0	7.8	1.7	1.3
March 1960	87.7	8.9	1.9	1.3	88.9	8.0	1.7	1.3
March 1961	87.6	8.6	1.9	1.6	88.0	8.4	1.8	1.6
April 1962	88.2	8.1	2.1	1.5	88.7	7.9	1.7	1.5
March 1963	88.6	7.7	1.9	1.6	89.7	7.0	1.6	1.5
March 1964	88.7	7.8	1.9	1.3	89.2	7.5	1.9	1.3
March 1965	88.5	7.8	2.0	1.5	89.2	7.7	1.8	1.2
March 1966	88.8	7.6	1.9	1.6	90.0	6.9	1.5	1.4
March 1967	89.2	7.2	2.1	1.2	90.5	6.4	1.7	1.2
March 1968	89.7	6.9	1.8	1.2	90.2	6.8	1.6	1.3
March 1969	89.3	6.9	2.0	1.5	90.7	6.2	1.6	1.3

Age 65 years & over

	E041	E042	E043	E044	E045	E046	E047	E048
April 1948	88.5	7.7	2.0	1.7	88.3	7.9	2.1	1.6
April 1949	90.5	6.4	1.3	1.7	90.2	6.9	1.4	1.5
March 1950	90.9	7.2	1.2	0.7	90.4	7.2	1.4	1.0
April 1951	89.7	8.0	1.4	0.9	90.8	6.7	1.5	0.8
April 1952	91.6	6.4	1.4	0.5	90.5	7.4	0.9	1.1
April 1953	91.2	6.9	1.0	0.8	91.0	6.4	1.3	1.2
April 1954	90.6	6.5	1.8	1.1	90.1	6.1	2.0	1.6
April 1955	89.8	7.0	2.1	1.1	90.6	6.5	1.9	1.0
March 1956	90.3	6.9	1.9	1.0	89.7	7.5	1.7	1.1
April 1957	90.3	6.7	2.0	0.9	91.0	6.2	1.7	1.0
March 1968	90.4	6.9	1.5	1.2	90.1	7.2	1.4	1.3
April 1959	90.8	6.3	1.7	1.1	91.8	6.6	1.5	1.4
March 1960	91.2	6.4	1.3	1.0	89.8	6.8	1.8	1.4
March 1961	90.4	6.9	1.4	1.2	90.4	6.8	1.5	1.3
April 1962	90.4	6.8	1.5	1.2	91.3	5.5	1.8	1.2
March 1963	90.5	6.6	1.7	1.1	90.1	6.7	1.9	1.2
March 1964	91.4	6.1	1.6	0.9	90.9	6.2	1.6	1.2
March 1965	91.1	6.2	1.5	1.2	89.6	7.4	1.8	1.2
March 1966	90.8	6.7	1.3	1.2	91.1	6.3	1.3	1.3
March 1967	91.7	5.4	2.3	0.5	91.2	6.1	1.7	1.0
March 1968	92.3	5.0	1.7	0.9	91.7	6.0	1.4	0.9
March 1969	92.5	4.9	1.6	1.0	92.3	5.6	1.1	0.9

Percent Distribution, by Mobility Status, of Single Males and of Single Females, within
Specified Age Groups, United States, 1951, 1957, 1960-1969[a]

Year ended	Single males			Single females		
	Non-movers	Movers[b]		Non-movers	Movers[b]	
		Different county, same state	Different state		Different county, same state	Different state

Age 18-24 years

Year ended	E049	E050	E051	E052	E053	E054
April 1951	82.0	4.4	4.0	78.9	5.3	3.1
April 1957	78.5	3.6	5.0	79.8	3.1	4.6
March 1960	79.2	3.5	5.1	--	--	--
March 1961	78.6	4.2	5.8	--	--	--
April 1962	77.3	2.9	5.3	76.8	4.2	4.2
March 1963	78.2	3.5	6.7	76.0	5.6	4.4
March 1964	76.4	4.4	6.1	75.4	6.4	4.0
March 1965	77.5	4.2	6.1	77.0	5.4	4.1
March 1966	79.8	3.8	5.1	78.8	4.0	4.8
March 1967	78.2	3.8	6.2	81.7	4.3	4.1
March 1968	76.8	3.6	6.1	77.9	4.5	4.1
March 1969	76.1	3.9	5.6	77.8	4.4	4.4

Age 25-34 years

Year ended	E055	E056	E057	E058	E059	E060
April 1951	79.2	4.3	5.5	79.3	3.7	3.2
April 1957	[c]	[c]	[c]	[c]	[c]	[c]
March 1960	74.3	4.5	5.9	--	--	--
March 1961	70.7	4.6	7.3	--	--	--
April 1962	72.1	4.3	6.9	75.2	4.2	3.2
March 1963	72.1	4.9	8.1	78.1	3.8	3.8
March 1964	71.7	4.7	6.6	74.7	3.9	6.1
March 1965	73.8	3.7	4.5	76.5	3.1	4.4
March 1966	70.3	6.5	6.6	72.1	5.0	4.2
March 1967	69.8	6.0	6.6	73.0	5.2	5.2
March 1968	71.7	5.6	5.6	71.0	4.4	3.6
March 1969	69.9	5.2	6.2	70.8	3.6	4.0

(continued)

Percent Distribution, by Mobility Status, of Single Males and of Single Females, within
Specified Age Groups, United States, 1951, 1957, 1960-1969[a/] (cont.)

Year ended	Single males			Single females		
	Non-movers	Movers[b/]		Non-movers	Movers[b/]	
		Different county, same state	Different state		Different county, same state	Different state

			Age 35-44 years			
	E061	E062	E063	E064	E065	E066
April 1951	83.9	3.2	1.9	88.1	1.5	2.0
April 1957	c/	c/	c/	c/	c/	c/
March 1960	88.4	2.2	0.8	--	--	--
March 1961	83.2	2.7	3.2	--	--	--
April 1962	82.9	1.8	2.9	83.0	2.6	1.0
March 1963	80.6	3.6	2.6	88.7	1.6	0.8
March 1964	83.6	3.7	3.3	84.7	1.8	1.6
March 1965	82.6	3.3	1.3	81.2	2.3	1.8
March 1966	82.5	2.8	2.4	83.9	3.9	1.0
March 1967	78.8	4.3	4.4	81.8	5.2	2.4
March 1968	84.2	4.3	1.6	86.1	1.6	1.9
March 1969	83.4	3.4	2.1	86.5	3.2	1.3

			Age 45-64 years			
	E067	E068	E069	E070	E071	E072
April 1951	85.6	3.8	1.8	91.2	1.2	1.4
April 1957	85.7	3.6	0.8	91.1	1.4	1.2
March 1960	88.0	2.0	1.3	--	--	--
March 1961	86.7	2.3	2.3	--	--	--
April 1962	83.4	6.4	1.2	88.9	1.9	1.5
March 1963	89.5	1.9	1.5	91.9	1.5	1.1
March 1964	88.2	3.2	1.5	90.4	2.5	1.2
March 1965	90.2	1.5	0.3	88.7	2.3	1.1
March 1966	91.5	2.3	0.7	90.9	1.2	1.9
March 1967	85.9	1.9	1.5	90.6	1.9	1.0
March 1968	88.2	2.5	0.6	89.2	2.5	1.6
March 1969	87.3	2.5	2.5	90.7	2.0	0.7

Percent Distribution, by Mobility Status, of Married Men (wife present) and of Married Women (husband present), within Specified Age Groups, United States, 1951, 1957-1969[a]

Year ended	Husbands (wife present)			Wives (husband present)		
	Non-movers	Movers[b]		Non-movers	Movers[b]	
		Different county, same state	Different state		Different county, same state	Different state

			Age 18-24 years			
	E073	E074	E075	E076	E077	E078
April 1951	41.8	9.5	9.6	50.0	8.3	9.0
April 1957	34.9	9.7	11.2	44.9	9.0	9.8
March 1958	--	--	--	44.2	8.7	10.4
April 1959	38.9	9.1	7.8	--	--	--
March 1960	37.6	10.4	8.5	--	--	--
March 1961	35.0	9.4	8.9	--	--	--
April 1962	33.9	8.9	10.9	44.8	8.7	9.6
March 1963	35.8	8.7	11.4	45.1	8.7	9.9
March 1964	34.5	9.7	9.2	44.2	9.7	8.9
March 1965	31.3	10.6	9.0	41.6	9.7	9.4
March 1966	36.9	10.2	10.8	44.6	10.3	10.1
March 1967	35.6	9.9	11.6	45.4	9.4	10.3
March 1968	35.6	10.5	11.1	43.8	10.0	10.7
March 1969	34.6	10.7	11.1	44.3	9.8	10.8

			Age 25-34 years			
	E079	E080	E081	E082	E083	E084
April 1951	65.9	5.5	6.1	72.9	4.5	5.3
April 1957	c/	c/	c/	c/	c/	c/
March 1958	--	--	--	74.0	4.4	4.3
April 1959	68.5	5.1	4.7	--	--	--
March 1960	70.4	5.2	4.7	--	--	--
March 1961	68.5	4.8	4.4	--	--	--
April 1962	69.0	4.6	4.8	75.9	3.6	4.2
March 1963	67.9	4.7	6.1	75.3	3.6	5.2
March 1964	66.6	5.7	5.9	74.0	4.6	5.1
March 1965	65.1	6.1	6.1	73.0	4.9	5.0
March 1966	66.2	5.9	5.3	74.0	4.6	4.6
March 1967	68.4	5.1	5.8	75.1	4.0	5.5
March 1968	67.6	5.6	6.2	74.6	4.6	5.8
March 1969	68.8	5.1	5.5	75.6	4.2	4.9

(continued)

Percent Distribution, by Mobility Status, of Married Men (wife present) and of Married Women (husband present), within Specified Age Groups, United States, 1951, 1957-1969a/ (cont.)

Year ended	Husbands (wife present)			Wives (husband present)		
	Non-movers	Moversb/		Non-movers	Moversb/	
		Different county, same state	Different state		Different county, same state	Different state

Age 35-44 years

Year ended	E085	E086	E087	E088	E089	E090
April 1951	81.4	2.3	3.0	83.1	2.0	2.7
April 1957	c/	c/	c/	c/	c/	c/
March 1958	--	--	--	85.9	2.4	2.5
April 1959	85.4	2.2	1.9	--	--	--
March 1960	83.6	2.8	2.1	--	--	--
March 1961	83.6	2.2	2.2	--	--	--
April 1962	83.6	2.6	2.8	86.5	2.0	2.1
March 1963	83.4	2.3	3.1	85.6	2.1	2.6
March 1964	83.4	2.3	2.9	86.6	1.7	2.3
March 1965	84.2	2.6	2.4	86.8	1.9	2.2
March 1966	83.9	2.7	2.5	86.4	2.2	2.2
March 1967	84.1	2.7	3.0	87.3	2.3	2.2
March 1968	83.1	2.5	3.4	86.6	2.1	2.9
March 1969	84.9	2.6	2.9	87.6	2.1	2.6

Age 45-64 years

Year ended	E091	E092	E093	E094	E095	E096
April 1951	88.4	1.8	1.8	90.2	1.6	1.2
April 1957	89.6	1.5	1.2	91.1	1.8	1.2
March 1958	--	--	--	d/	d/	d/
April 1959	90.0	1.6	1.1	--	--	--
March 1960	89.7	1.5	1.1	--	--	--
March 1961	89.4	1.5	1.1	--	--	--
April 1962	90.0	1.5	1.3	90.4	1.4	1.4
March 1963	90.0	1.6	1.5	91.5	1.3	1.3
March 1964	90.6	1.5	1.0	91.0	1.7	1.0
March 1965	90.2	1.5	1.2	91.4	1.6	1.0
March 1966	90.5	1.5	1.3	91.9	1.2	1.2
March 1967	91.2	1.6	1.1	92.1	1.6	1.1
March 1968	91.5	1.3	1.2	92.5	1.2	1.1
March 1969	91.1	1.6	1.3	92.3	1.6	1.2

Percent Distribution, by Mobility Status, of Males and of Females of "Other Marital Status,"a/ within Specified Age Groups, United States, 1951, 1957, 1960-1969b/

Year ended	Male			Female		
	Non-movers (same house)	Moversc/		Non-movers (same house)	Moversc/	
		Different county, same state	Different state		Different county, same state	Different state

			Age 25-34 years			
	E097	E098	E099	E100	E101	E102
April 1951	51.7	10.4	13.7	65.1	7.3	7.7
April 1957	d/	d/	d/	d/	d/	d/
March 1960	46.3	6.6	9.9	--	--	--
March 1961	47.3	6.4	11.3	--	--	--
April 1962	47.5	7.7	15.3	60.0	6.4	6.0
March 1963	45.9	17.8	6.2	55.9	7.4	8.3
March 1964	48.1	12.0	9.0	64.7	7.8	7.1
March 1965	49.3	11.2	8.6	59.9	6.0	6.3
March 1966	47.4	8.2	6.0	61.0	4.4	7.0
March 1967	48.5	7.7	10.6	61.7	5.6	5.9
March 1968	52.8	11.9	8.9	58.8	9.5	7.8
March 1969	45.4	9.8	10.9	62.5	4.9	7.5

			Age 35-44 years			
	E103	E104	E105	E106	E107	E108
April 1951	65.1	7.0	8.3	75.3	5.7	1.7
April 1957	d/	d/	d/	d/	d/	d/
March 1960	61.5	6.8	5.9	--	--	--
March 1961	60.0	8.6	7.3	--	--	--
April 1962	58.3	10.8	8.7	73.6	3.7	2.7
March 1963	63.9	9.0	5.9	71.1	5.1	4.2
March 1964	65.5	7.4	5.3	74.3	2.6	3.6
March 1965	60.7	7.6	3.2	70.5	3.0	3.2
March 1966	60.6	7.5	5.7	73.8	2.2	3.0
March 1967	65.0	9.5	4.7	77.2	3.6	2.8
March 1968	64.8	7.1	5.6	75.0	4.3	3.3
March 1969	58.5	8.5	6.4	75.9	2.7	2.8

			Age 45-64 years			
	E109	E110	E111	E112	E113	E114
April 1951	72.6	6.1	4.0	83.0	2.5	2.4
April 1957	76.0	2.9	3.5	84.6	2.0	2.0
March 1960	75.1	2.9	3.2	--	--	--
March 1961	74.0	4.8	4.2	--	--	--
April 1962	74.2	5.0	3.1	83.5	2.5	1.8
March 1963	77.0	4.2	2.6	83.4	2.4	2.2
March 1964	74.0	4.3	3.7	83.0	2.3	2.4
March 1965	73.3	6.7	4.5	82.3	2.6	1.7
March 1966	71.9	4.9	5.4	83.7	2.3	1.8
March 1967	74.8	6.2	2.0	85.3	2.0	1.6
March 1968	74.1	5.8	2.1	83.1	2.6	1.9
March 1969	73.8	5.2	2.9	85.7	1.6	1.7

Percent Distribution, by Mobility Status, of Males and of Females Aged 14-24 Years, Having Specified Relationships to Head of Household, United States, 1963-1969[a]

Male head of household (wife present) / Wife of head of household

Year ended March-	Non-movers (same house)	Movers Different county, same state	Movers Different state	Non-movers (same house)	Movers Different county, same state	Movers Different state
	E115	E116	E117	E118	E119	E120
1963	34.6	9.1	11.6	44.0	8.9	9.7
1964	32.9	10.1	9.1	42.8	9.9	9.0
1965	30.3	10.8	9.0	40.0	9.8	9.4
1966	36.4	10.5	10.8	44.0	10.4	10.2
1967	34.2	10.3	11.0	44.1	9.5	10.0
1968	34.8	10.7	11.1	43.2	10.0	10.8
1969	34.2	10.7	11.0	43.7	10.0	10.7
1970						

Other male head of primary family[b] / Female head of primary family

Year ended March-	E121	E122	E123	E124	E125	E126
1963	--	--	--	36.7	4.2	8.9
1964	--	--	--	32.5	10.7	8.1
1965	--	--	--	33.2	11.8	8.1
1966	--	--	--	39.8	9.7	8.0
1967	--	--	--	38.3	5.5	8.9
1968	--	--	--	38.4	7.4	9.0
1969	--	--	--	37.4	7.8	8.8
1970						

Male primary individual / Female primary individual

Year ended March-	E127	E128	E129	E130	E131	E132
1963	27.3	14.3	19.2	29.2	13.9	15.3
1964	16.9	11.6	16.9	23.0	16.2	9.4
1965	15.3	10.7	25.1	20.9	20.5	12.1
1966	18.6	14.2	18.6	21.1	17.6	12.9
1967	23.7	13.3	21.2	27.9	12.5	18.0
1968	22.8	12.8	17.6	25.1	13.6	12.6
1969	18.0	13.6	18.6	26.8	13.5	16.1
1970						

Male relative of household head / Female relative of household head (except wife of head)

Year ended March-	E133	E134	E135	E136	E137	E138
1963	84.0	2.4	3.6	12.4	3.0	3.1
1964	83.6	2.7	3.5	84.0	2.7	2.5
1965	83.6	2.7	3.4	84.3	2.8	2.3
1966	85.0	2.2	3.0	84.4	2.4	2.9
1967	85.7	2.1	3.2	86.0	2.5	2.4
1968	83.9	2.3	3.7	85.1	2.2	2.7
1969	85.1	2.2	3.2	85.1	2.5	2.9
1970						

Percent Distribution, by Mobility Status, of Males and of Females Aged 25-34 Years, Having Specified Relationships to Head of Household, United States, 1963-1969[a]

| Year ended March- | Non-movers (same house) | Movers[c] | | Non-movers (same house) | Movers[c] | |
		Different county, same state	Different state		Different county, same state	Different state
	Male head of household (wife present)			Wife of head of household		
	E139	E140	E141	E142	E143	E144
1963	68.3	4.6	5.7	75.6	3.6	5.0
1964	66.9	5.7	5.8	74.1	4.6	5.0
1965	65.1	6.0	6.0	73.1	4.9	5.0
1966	66.5	5.9	5.1	74.1	4.6	4.5
1967	68.6	5.1	5.7	75.2	4.1	5.4
1968	67.8	5.5	6.1	74.7	4.6	5.7
1969	69.1	5.1	5.3	75.8	4.1	4.9
1970						
	Other male head of primary family[b]			Female head of primary family		
	E145	E146	E147	E148	E149	E150
1963	--	--	--	56.4	4.8	6.1
1964	--	--	--	56.2	4.6	5.3
1965	--	--	--	61.9	5.5	4.3
1966	--	--	--	58.5	4.3	5.3
1967	70.5	2.6	6.4	62.3	4.4	5.1
1968	61.5	8.9	8.2	61.7	5.3	5.0
1969	62.0	5.3	9.0	61.8	4.3	5.9
1970						
	Male primary individual			Female primary individual		
	E151	E152	E153	E154	E155	E156
1963	43.9	10.2	12.4	56.8	5.7	6.6
1964	39.8	7.7	9.4	53.5	8.0	8.4
1965	41.9	9.1	9.6	48.1	5.7	6.9
1966	37.6	10.4	9.1	52.4	10.3	6.9
1967	41.2	8.8	11.2	55.0	6.4	7.0
1968	48.9	9.0	10.1	53.2	8.4	6.0
1969	43.9	10.1	9.8	54.2	4.6	7.4
1970						
	Male relative of household head			Female relative of household head (except wife of head)		
	E157	E158	E159	E160	E161	E162
1963	75.7	3.4	7.8	77.8	3.4	5.1
1964	77.5	3.0	5.8	76.5	2.6	6.4
1965	79.5	2.7	3.9	78.5	3.7	4.5
1966	76.7	3.8	4.9	78.7	2.0	6.1
1967	77.2	3.3	5.6	77.6	3.4	5.4
1968	78.1	3.0	5.7	77.0	3.7	6.2
1969	77.8	2.6	6.3	78.0	3.6	5.6
1970						

Percent Distribution, by Mobility Status, of Males and of Females Aged 35-44 Years, Having Specified Relationships to Head of Household, United States, 1963-1969[a]

	Non-movers (same house)	Movers[c]		Non-movers (same house)	Movers[c]	
Year ended March-		Different county, same state	Different state		Different county, same state	Different state

	Male head of household (wife present)			Wife of head of household		
	E163	E164	E165	E166	E167	E168
1963	83.5	2.3	3.0	85.7	2.2	2.5
1964	83.4	2.3	2.9	86.8	1.7	2.2
1965	84.4	2.6	2.3	86.9	1.9	2.2
1966	84.0	2.7	2.5	86.4	2.1	2.2
1967	84.2	2.7	2.9	87.3	2.3	2.2
1968	82.0	2.9	3.4	86.6	2.1	3.0
1969	85.0	2.6	2.9	87.8	2.1	2.6
1970						

	Other male head of primary family[b]			Female head of primary family		
	E169	E170	E171	E172	E173	E174
1963	80.6	1.3	2.7	75.5	2.1	3.7
1964	83.9	1.4	2.3	76.0	2.7	3.0
1965	80.7	--	1.0	74.6	2.2	2.0
1966	75.6	2.3	4.1	74.7	2.0	1.8
1967	81.6	3.3	0.9	78.9	2.6	2.4
1968	83.1	2.5	3.4	76.7	3.1	3.0
1969	73.5	5.3	1.3	79.2	2.3	2.2
1970						

	Male primary individual			Female primary individual		
	E175	E176	E177	E178	E179	E180
1963	55.6	7.4	5.0	77.1	2.4	2.7
1964	65.0	5.8	4.5	73.0	4.1	2.0
1965	64.5	4.1	3.5	66.0	3.4	4.2
1966	63.2	5.8	6.3	73.5	2.6	2.4
1967	65.8	4.2	4.4	73.6	2.8	4.0
1968	70.7	2.8	2.8	74.4	4.0	2.3
1969	61.3	6.3	4.2	74.9	1.8	1.5
1970						

	Male relative of household head			Female relative of household head (except wife of head)		
	E181	E182	E183	E184	E185	E186
1963	82.1	2.8	2.2	83.3	2.4	2.8
1964	87.7	1.6	1.9	83.5	1.0	3.7
1965	84.9	2.7	1.6	81.7	2.3	3.9
1966	84.0	2.4	1.8	85.8	1.5	3.3
1967	82.5	3.3	4.5	86.9	4.3	2.6
1968	84.7	3.5	3.6	88.6	1.8	2.3
1969	85.2	2.8	3.7	85.6	3.5	2.6
1970						

Percent Distribution, by Mobility Status, of Males and of Females Aged 45-64 Years, Having Specified Relationships to Head of Household, United States, 1963-1969[a]

Year ended March-	Non-movers (same house)	Movers[c]		Non-movers (same house)	Movers[c]	
		Different county, same state	Different state		Different county, same state	Different state

	Male head of household (wife present)			Wife of head of household		
	E187	E188	E189	E190	E191	E192
1963	90.2	1.6	1.4	91.7	1.3	1.2
1964	90.7	1.5	0.9	91.0	1.7	1.0
1965	90.4	1.5	1.2	91.5	1.5	1.0
1966	90.7	1.4	1.2	92.1	1.2	1.2
1967	91.3	1.6	1.1	92.3	1.6	1.1
1968	91.6	1.3	1.2	92.6	1.2	1.0
1969	91.2	1.6	1.3	92.4	1.6	1.2
1970						

	Other male head of primary family[b]			Female head of primary family		
	E193	E194	E195	E196	E197	E198
1963	89.7	2.2	1.4	87.0	1.3	1.0
1964	90.9	1.1	1.6	87.7	1.6	1.2
1965	89.1	1.8	0.8	86.3	1.3	1.0
1966	91.0	1.9	0.9	86.8	1.1	1.1
1967	87.4	1.0	1.2	88.5	1.1	1.1
1968	91.0	1.1	0.3	86.5	1.7	0.9
1969	88.8	2.4	0.5	89.3	0.7	0.9
1970						

	Male primary individual			Female primary individual		
	E199	E200	E201	E202	E203	E204
1963	78.7	2.9	3.5	88.5	1.6	1.3
1964	77.4	2.5	2.3	86.0	2.0	1.7
1965	79.9	3.4	2.6	85.8	1.7	0.9
1966	73.0	4.6	4.4	88.0	1.8	1.1
1967	77.3	2.7	1.9	89.1	1.0	1.2
1968	78.5	3.6	1.5	86.2	1.3	1.7
1969	78.4	3.5	1.9	87.7	1.3	0.8
1970						

	Male relative of household head			Female relative of household head (except wife of head)		
	E205	E206	E207	E208	E209	E210
1963	85.0	2.3	2.6	82.7	2.2	4.3
1964	84.0	3.0	3.3	82.8	2.7	3.3
1965	90.4	1.5	1.2	84.2	2.4	2.8
1966	86.8	2.4	3.4	81.8	2.9	4.2
1967	83.0	2.1	2.2	83.7	2.5	2.3
1968	85.1	1.7	2.0	83.4	2.7	3.8
1969	85.3	2.8	2.4	82.9	2.2	3.8
1970						

Employment Status of the Noninstitutional Population 16 Years of Age and Over, by Sex,
United States, 1947-1969
(Numbers in thousands)

	Male				Female			
	Noninsti- tutional population 16 years and over	Civilian labor force		Not in labor force	Noninsti- tutional population 16 years and over	Civilian labor force		Not in labor force
Year		Employed	Unem- ployed			Employed	Unem- ployed	
	F001	F002	F003	F004	F005	F006	F007	F008
1947	50,968	40,994	1,692	6,710	52,450	16,045	619	35,767
1948	51,439	41,726	1,559	6,710	53,088	16,618	717	37,737
1949	51,922	40,926	2,572	6,825	53,689	16,723	1,065	35,883
1950	52,352	41,580	2,239	6,906	54,293	17,340	1,049	35,881
1951	52,788	41,780	1,221	6,725	54,933	18,182	834	35,879
1952	53,248	41,684	1,185	6,832	55,575	18,570	698	36,261
1953	54,248	42,431	1,202	7,117	56,353	18,750	632	36,924
1954	54,706	41,620	2,344	7,431	56,965	18,490	1,188	37,247
1955	55,122	42,621	1,854	7,634	57,610	19,550	998	37,026
1956	55,547	43,380	1,711	7,633	58,264	20,422	1,039	36,769
1957	56,082	43,357	1,841	8,118	58,983	20,714	1,018	37,218
1958	56,640	42,423	3,098	8,514	59,723	20,613	1,504	37,574
1959	57,312	43,466	2,420	8,907	60,569	21,164	1,320	38,053
1960	58,144	43,904	2,486	9,274	61,615	21,874	1,366	38,343
1961	58,826	43,656	2,997	9,633	62,517	22,090	1,717	38,679
1962	59,626	44,177	2,423	10,231	63,355	22,525	1,488	39,308
1963	60,627	44,657	2,472	10,792	64,527	23,105	1,598	39,791
1964	61,556	45,474	2,205	11,169	65,668	23,831	1,581	40,225
1965	62,473	46,340	1,914	11,527	66,763	24,748	1,452	40,531
1966	63,351	46,919	1,551	11,792	67,829	25,976	1,324	40,496
1967	64,316	47,479	1,508	11,919	69,003	26,893	1,468	40,608
1968	65,345	48,114	1,419	12,315	70,217	27,807	1,397	40,978
1969	66,365	48,818	1,403	12,677	71,476	29,084	1,428	40,924
1970								

	Labor force (including Armed Forces) as percent of total noninstitutional population (16 years and over)		Unemployed in civilian labor force as percent of total civilian labor force (16 years and over)	
Year	Male F009	Female F010	Male F011	Female F012
1947	86.8	31.8	4.0	3.7
1948	87.0	32.7	3.6	4.1
1949	86.9	33.2	5.9	6.0
1950	86.8	33.9	5.1	5.7
1951	87.3	34.7	2.8	4.4
1952	87.2	34.8	2.8	3.6
1953	86.9	34.5	2.8	3.3
1954	86.4	34.6	5.3	6.0
1955	86.2	35.7	4.2	4.9
1956	86.3	36.9	3.8	4.8
1957	85.5	36.9	4.1	4.7
1958	85.0	37.1	6.8	6.8
1959	84.5	37.2	5.3	5.9
1960	84.0	37.8	5.4	5.9
1961	83.6	38.1	6.4	7.2
1962	82.8	38.0	5.2	6.2
1963	82.2	38.3	5.2	6.5
1964	81.9	38.7	4.6	6.2
1965	81.5	39.3	4.0	5.5
1966	81.4	40.3	3.2	4.8
1967	81.5	41.1	3.1	5.2
1968	81.2	41.6	2.9	4.8
1969	80.9	42.7	2.8	4.7
1970				

Labor Force Participation Rates[a] (including Armed Forces) for Persons 16 Years and
Over, by Age and Sex, United States, 1947-1969

Year	Male	Female	Male	Female	Male	Female	Male	Female	Male	Female
	Total, 16 years of age & over		16-17 years		18-19 years		20-24 years		25-34 years	
	F013	F014	F015	F016	F017	F018	F019	F020	F021	F022
1947	86.8	31.8	52.2	29.5	80.5	52.3	84.9	44.9	95.8	32.0
1948	87.0	32.7	53.4	31.4	79.9	52.1	85.7	45.3	96.1	33.2
1949	86.9	33.2	52.3	31.2	79.5	53.0	87.8	45.0	95.9	33.5
1950	86.8	33.9	52.0	30.1	79.0	51.3	89.1	46.1	96.2	34.0
1951	87.3	34.7	54.5	32.2	80.3	52.7	91.1	46.6	97.1	35.4
1952	87.2	34.8	53.1	33.4	79.1	51.4	92.1	44.8	97.7	35.5
1953	86.9	34.5	51.7	31.0	78.5	50.8	92.2	44.5	97.6	34.1
1954	86.4	34.6	48.3	28.7	76.5	50.5	91.5	45.3	97.5	34.5
1955	86.2	35.7	49.5	28.9	77.1	51.0	90.8	46.0	97.7	34.9
1956	86.3	36.9	52.6	32.8	77.9	52.1	90.8	46.4	97.4	35.4
1957	85.5	36.9	51.1	31.1	77.7	51.5	89.8	46.0	97.3	35.6
1958	85.0	37.1	47.9	28.1	75.7	51.0	89.5	46.4	97.3	35.6
1959	84.5	37.2	46.0	28.8	75.5	49.1	90.1	45.2	97.5	35.4
1960	84.0	37.8	46.8	29.1	73.6	51.1	90.2	46.2	97.7	36.0
1961	83.6	38.1	45.4	28.5	71.3	51.1	89.8	47.1	97.6	36.4
1962	82.8	38.0	43.5	27.1	71.9	50.9	89.1	47.4	97.4	36.4
1963	82.2	38.3	42.7	27.1	73.1	50.6	88.8	47.6	97.3	37.2
1964	81.9	38.7	43.6	27.4	72.0	49.3	88.2	49.5	97.5	37.3
1965	81.5	39.3	44.6	27.7	70.0	49.4	88.0	50.0	97.4	38.6
1966	81.4	40.3	47.0	30.7	69.0	52.1	87.9	51.5	97.5	39.9
1967	81.5	41.1	47.5	31.0	70.9	52.3	87.5	53.4	97.4	41.9
1968	81.2	41.6	46.8	31.7	70.2	52.5	86.5	54.6	97.1	42.6
1969	80.9	42.7	47.7	33.7	69.6	53.5	86.6	56.8	96.9	43.8
1970										

Year	Male	Female	Male	Female	Male	Female	Male	Female
	35-44 years		45-54 years		55-64 years		65 years & over	
	F023	F024	F025	F026	F027	F028	F029	F030
1947	98.0	36.3	95.5	32.7	89.6	24.3	47.8	8.1
1948	98.0	36.9	95.8	35.0	89.5	24.3	46.8	9.1
1949	98.0	38.1	95.6	35.9	87.5	25.3	46.9	9.6
1950	97.6	39.1	95.8	38.0	86.9	27.0	45.8	9.7
1951	97.6	39.8	96.0	39.7	87.2	27.6	44.9	8.9
1952	97.9	40.5	96.2	40.1	87.5	28.7	42.6	9.1
1953	98.2	41.3	96.6	40.4	87.9	29.1	41.6	10.0
1954	98.1	41.3	96.5	41.2	88.7	30.1	40.5	9.3
1955	98.1	41.6	96.5	43.8	87.9	32.5	39.6	10.6
1956	98.0	43.1	96.6	45.5	88.5	34.9	40.0	10.9
1957	97.9	43.3	96.4	46.5	87.5	34.5	37.5	10.5
1958	98.0	43.4	96.3	47.9	87.8	35.2	35.6	10.3
1959	97.8	43.4	96.0	49.0	87.4	36.6	34.2	10.2
1960	97.7	43.5	95.8	49.8	86.8	37.2	33.1	10.8
1961	97.7	43.8	95.6	50.1	87.3	37.9	31.7	10.7
1962	97.7	44.1	95.6	50.0	86.2	38.7	30.3	9.9
1963	97.6	44.9	95.8	50.6	86.2	39.7	28.4	9.6
1964	97.4	45.0	95.8	51.4	85.6	40.2	28.0	10.1
1965	97.4	46.1	95.6	50.9	84.7	41.1	27.9	10.0
1966	97.3	46.9	95.3	51.7	84.5	41.8	27.0	9.6
1967	97.4	48.1	95.2	51.8	84.4	42.4	27.1	9.6
1968	97.2	48.9	94.9	52.3	84.3	42.4	27.3	9.6
1969	97.0	49.9	94.6	53.8	83.4	43.1	27.2	9.9
1970								

	Civilian labor force participation rates[a], by color, sex, and age										
Year	White		Nonwhite		White		Nonwhite		White		Nonwhite	
	Male	Female	Male	Female	Male	Female	Male	Female	Male	Female	Male	Female

	14-15 years				Total, 16 years & over				16-17 years			
	F031	F032	F033	F034	F035	F036	F037	F038	F039	F040	F041	F042
1948	26.1	11.1	39.3	21.0	86.5	31.3	87.3	45.6	51.2	31.7	59.8	29.1
1949	26.3	10.3	36.6	23.5	86.4	31.8	87.0	46.9	50.1	31.4	60.4	30.1
1950	27.6	11.5	37.7	22.0	86.4	32.6	85.9	46.9	50.5	30.1	57.4	30.2
1951	26.9	11.2	34.6	17.3	86.5	33.4	86.3	46.3	52.7	32.4	54.7	30.4
1952	25.3	10.2	30.5	18.5	86.2	33.6	86.8	45.5	51.9	34.1	52.3	27.4
1953	23.6	9.9	27.8	14.9	86.1	33.4	86.2	43.6	49.8	31.2	53.0	24.2
1954	24.5	10.5	27.2	16.2	85.6	33.3	85.2	46.1	47.1	29.3	46.7	24.5
1955	23.5	11.2	27.1	11.4	85.4	34.5	85.0	46.1	48.0	29.9	48.2	22.7
1956	26.7	12.7	25.5	14.4	85.6	35.7	85.1	47.3	51.3	33.5	49.6	28.3
1957	25.1	12.5	24.7	12.6	84.8	35.7	84.3	47.2	49.6	32.1	47.5	24.1
1958	24.1	12.2	21.3	11.6	84.3	35.8	84.0	48.0	46.8	28.8	45.1	23.2
1959	24.2	13.0	23.9	12.6	83.8	36.0	83.4	47.7	45.4	29.9	41.7	20.7
1960	22.2	12.5	23.3	13.2	83.4	36.5	83.0	48.2	46.0	30.0	45.6	22.1
1961	22.2	13.5	19.2	11.0	83.0	36.9	82.2	48.3	44.3	29.4	42.5	21.6
1962	22.3	13.7	16.5	9.7	82.1	36.7	80.8	48.0	42.9	27.9	40.2	21.0
1963	21.4	12.2	17.2	8.7	81.5	37.2	80.2	48.1	42.4	27.9	37.2	21.5
1964	21.2	12.7	18.7	8.0	81.1	37.5	80.0	48.5	43.5	28.5	37.3	19.5
1965	21.7	12.9	18.9	8.1	80.0	38.1	79.6	48.6	44.6	28.7	39.3	20.5
1966	22.3	14.5	17.3	7.5	80.6	39.2	79.0	49.3	47.1	31.8	41.1	23.6
1967	22.6	15.4	18.1	9.4	80.7	40.1	78.5	49.5	47.9	32.3	41.2	22.8
1968	22.7	16.0	18.3	7.2	80.4	40.7	77.6	49.3	47.7	33.0	37.9	23.3
1969	23.0	16.1	15.8	7.1	80.2	41.8	76.9	49.8	48.8	35.2	37.7	24.4

	18-19 years				20-24 years				25-34 years			
	F043	F044	F045	F046	F047	F048	F049	F050	F051	F052	F053	F054
1948	76.2	53.5	77.8	41.2	84.4	45.1	85.6	47.1	96.0	31.3	95.3	50.6
1949	74.8	54.0	80.8	44.8	86.5	44.4	89.7	49.8	95.9	31.7	94.1	50.9
1950	75.6	52.6	78.2	40.6	87.5	45.9	91.4	46.9	96.4	32.1	92.6	51.6
1951	74.2	54.1	80.8	40.2	88.4	46.7	88.7	45.4	97.0	33.6	95.7	51.1
1952	72.7	52.0	79.1	44.7	87.6	44.8	92.8	43.9	97.6	33.8	96.2	50.1
1953	72.8	51.9	76.7	37.8	87.4	44.1	92.3	45.1	97.5	31.7	96.7	48.1
1954	70.4	52.1	78.4	37.7	86.4	44.4	91.1	49.6	97.5	32.5	96.2	49.7
1955	71.7	52.0	75.7	43.2	85.6	45.8	89.7	46.7	97.8	32.8	95.8	51.3
1956	71.9	53.0	76.4	44.6	87.6	46.5	88.9	44.9	97.4	33.2	96.2	52.1
1957	71.6	52.6	72.0	42.8	86.7	45.8	89.6	46.6	97.2	33.6	96.1	50.4
1958	69.4	52.3	71.7	41.2	86.7	46.1	88.7	48.3	97.2	33.6	96.3	50.8
1959	70.3	50.8	72.0	36.1	87.3	44.5	90.8	48.8	97.5	33.4	96.3	50.0
1960	69.0	51.9	71.2	44.3	87.8	45.7	90.4	48.8	97.7	34.1	96.2	49.7
1961	66.2	51.9	70.5	44.6	87.6	46.9	89.7	47.7	97.7	34.3	95.9	51.2
1962	66.4	51.6	68.8	45.5	86.5	47.1	89.3	48.6	97.4	34.1	95.3	52.0
1963	67.8	51.3	69.1	44.9	85.8	47.3	88.6	49.2	97.4	34.8	94.9	53.3
1964	66.6	49.6	67.2	46.5	85.7	48.8	89.4	53.6	97.5	35.0	95.9	52.8
1965	65.8	50.6	66.7	40.0	85.3	49.2	89.8	55.2	97.4	36.3	95.7	54.0
1966	65.4	53.1	63.7	44.0	84.4	51.0	89.9	54.5	97.5	37.7	95.5	54.9
1967	66.1	52.7	62.7	48.7	84.0	53.1	87.2	54.9	97.5	39.7	95.5	57.5
1968	65.7	53.3	63.3	46.9	82.4	54.0	85.0	58.4	97.2	40.6	95.0	56.6
1969	66.3	54.6	63.2	45.4	82.6	56.4	84.4	58.6	97.0	41.7	94.4	57.8

(continued)

	Civilian labor force participation rates[a/], by color, sex, and age (cont.)											
Year	White		Nonwhite		White		Nonwhite		White		Nonwhite	
	Male	Female	Male	Female	Male	Female	Male	Female	Male	Female	Male	Female
	35-44 years				45-54 years				55-64 years			
	F055	F056	F057	F058	F059	F060	F061	F062	F063	F064	F065	F066
1948	98.0	35.1	97.2	53.3	95.9	33.3	94.7	51.1	89.6	23.3	88.6	37.6
1949	98.0	36.1	97.3	56.1	95.6	34.3	95.6	52.7	87.6	24.2	86.0	39.6
1950	97.7	37.2	96.2	55.7	95.9	36.3	95.1	54.3	87.3	26.0	81.9	40.9
1951	97.6	38.0	96.4	55.8	96.0	38.0	95.1	55.5	87.4	26.5	84.6	39.8
1952	97.9	38.9	97.2	54.0	96.3	38.8	95.0	52.7	87.7	27.6	85.7	42.3
1953	97.9	38.8	97.3	54.9	96.4	38.7	93.9	51.0	87.7	28.5	86.7	35.9
1954	98.2	39.4	96.6	57.5	96.8	39.8	93.2	53.4	89.2	29.1	83.0	41.2
1955	98.3	39.9	96.2	56.0	96.7	42.7	94.2	54.8	88.4	31.8	83.1	40.7
1956	98.1	41.5	96.2	57.0	96.8	44.4	94.4	55.3	88.9	34.0	83.9	44.5
1957	98.0	41.5	96.5	58.7	96.6	45.4	93.5	56.8	88.0	33.7	82.4	44.3
1958	98.0	41.4	96.4	60.8	96.6	46.5	93.9	59.8	88.2	34.5	83.3	42.8
1959	98.0	41.4	95.8	60.0	96.3	47.8	92.8	60.0	87.9	35.7	82.5	46.4
1960	97.9	41.5	95.5	59.8	96.1	48.6	92.3	60.5	87.2	36.2	82.5	47.3
1961	97.9	41.8	94.8	60.5	95.9	48.9	92.3	61.1	87.8	37.2	81.6	45.2
1962	97.9	42.2	94.5	59.7	96.0	48.9	92.2	60.5	86.7	38.0	81.5	46.1
1963	97.8	43.1	94.9	59.4	96.2	49.5	91.1	60.6	86.6	38.9	82.5	47.3
1964	97.6	43.3	94.4	58.4	96.1	50.2	91.6	62.3	86.1	39.4	80.6	48.4
1965	97.7	44.3	94.2	59.9	95.9	49.9	92.0	60.2	85.2	40.3	78.8	48.9
1966	97.6	45.0	91.1	60.9	95.8	50.6	90.7	61.0	84.9	41.1	81.1	49.1
1967	97.7	46.4	93.6	60.8	95.6	50.9	91.3	59.6	84.9	41.9	79.3	47.1
1968	97.6	47.5	93.4	59.3	95.4	51.5	90.1	59.8	84.7	42.0	79.6	47.0
1969	97.4	48.6	92.7	59.5	95.1	53.0	89.5	60.8	83.9	42.6	77.9	47.5

	65 years and over			
	F067	F068	F069	F070
1948	46.5	8.6	50.3	17.5
1949	46.6	9.1	51.4	15.6
	45.8	9.2	45.5	16.5
1950	45.8	9.2	45.5	16.5
1951	44.5	8.5	49.5	14.0
1952	42.5	8.7	43.3	14.3
1953	41.3	9.4	41.1	11.4
1954	40.4	9.1	41.2	12.2
1955	39.5	10.5	40.0	12.1
1956	40.0	10.6	39.8	14.5
1957	37.7	10.2	35.9	13.6
1958	35.7	10.1	34.5	13.3
1959	34.3	10.2	33.5	12.6
1960	33.3	10.6	31.2	12.8
1961	31.9	10.5	29.4	13.1
1962	30.6	9.8	27.2	12.2
1963	28.4	9.4	27.6	11.8
1964	27.9	9.9	29.6	12.7
1965	27.9	9.7	27.9	12.9
1966	27.2	9.4	25.6	13.0
1967	27.1	9.3	27.2	13.0
1968	27.3	9.4	26.6	11.9
1969	27.3	9.7	26.1	11.9

Civilian Labor Force Participation Rates[a]/, by Marital Status, Age, and Sex, United States, 1957-1968

Year	Total civilian labor force[b]/		14-17 years[b]/[c]/		18-19 years[c]/		20-24 years	
	Male	Female	Male	Female	Male	Female	Male	Female
				Single				
	F071	F072	F073	F074	F075	F076	F077	F078
1957	62.2	50.0	36.0	21.3	69.8	60.6	78.7	76.6
1958	60.7	48.5	34.1	19.7	67.6	60.6	78.4	76.5
1959	60.6	47.4	34.3	21.0	68.3	57.1	79.9	75.5
1960	60.2	48.0	33.9	20.9	67.1	58.6	80.3	77.2
1961	57.9	46.5	31.7	20.2	64.0	58.4	79.9	75.9
1962	56.3	44.8	30.5	19.3	64.2	57.4	78.6	74.1
1963	55.8	44.2	30.6	19.0	66.1	56.6	77.4	73.7
1964	55.6	44.2	31.7	19.8	64.5	54.9	76.6	74.0
1965	55.5	44.4	32.3	19.9	63.8	54.4	75.7	72.9
1966	55.0	45.6	33.5	21.9	62.8	56.3	73.5	73.8
1967	65.2	55.3	46.8	31.5	63.3	56.0	73.6	72.1
1968	64.6	55.6	46.2	32.1	63.2	55.5	71.9	73.1
1969	64.9	56.7	47.2	34.2	63.6	56.4	72.4	72.5
			Married,	spouse present				
	F079	F080	F081	F082	F083	F084	F085	F086
1957	90.3	30.1	--	17.0	96.1	29.8	96.6	30.9
1958	89.9	30.7	--	17.1	95.5	30.2	96.6	31.7
1959	89.6	31.2	--	16.8	97.2	30.1	96.4	31.4
1960	89.2	31.9	--	16.8	96.7	30.9	97.1	31.7
1961	89.0	32.5	--	18.4	96.7	31.1	97.1	33.0
1962	88.2	32.8	--	18.6	94.1	33.6	96.2	33.6
1963	87.8	33.4	--	19.8	92.5	33.8	96.3	33.3
1964	87.5	34.1	--	18.4	96.2	32.9	96.8	35.9
1965	87.4	34.9	--	18.6	92.9	34.1	96.4	37.1
1966	87.1	35.9	--	20.5	94.1	37.3	96.7	38.9
1967	87.0	37.3	--	21.8	96.2	38.6	95.9	41.5
1968	86.8	38.2	--	23.4	95.5	40.8	95.2	42.8
1969	86.5	39.5	--	22.0	93.7	41.7	95.2	46.4
			Widowed,	divorced,	or separated			
	F087	F088	F089	F090	F091	F092	F093	F094
1957	63.1	41.3	--	--	--	46.3	93.6	55.8
1958	63.1	41.6	--	--	--	44.0	95.6	56.9
1959	62.8	41.6	--	--	--	51.6	95.7	55.2
1960	63.1	41.6	--	--	--	47.9	96.9	58.0
1961	62.4	41.7	--	--	--	46.6	95.0	57.5
1962	59.9	40.6	--	--	--	45.0	92.0	57.1
1963	60.0	40.9	--	--	--	47.3	92.2	55.3
1964	60.3	40.6	--	--	--	43.1	92.0	56.6
1965	60.4	40.7	--	--	--	44.1	96.6	59.2
1966	59.7	41.3	--	--	--	54.4	93.2	61.1
1967	58.9	41.0	--	--	--	50.0	91.4	62.5
1968	59.4	40.4	--	--	--	50.9	90.8	59.3
1969	59.8	40.7	--	--	--	51.6	92.5	62.1
1970								

(continued)

371

Civilian Labor Force Participation Rates[a], by Marital Status, Age, and Sex,
United States, 1957-1968 (cont.)

Year	25-34 years		35-44 years		45-64 years		65 years and over	
	Male	Female	Male	Female	Male	Female	Male	Female

			Single					
	F095	F096	F097	F098	F099	F100	F101	F102
1957	89.8	84.4	89.6	82.9	82.6	76.4	31.0	23.7
1958	90.0	84.2	89.7	82.8	83.2	77.2	29.3	24.1
1959	91.0	82.9	88.9	82.3	82.3	77.8	30.0	22.3
1960	91.5	83.4	88.6	82.9	80.1	79.8	31.2	24.3
1961	90.1	84.1	88.3	81.7	79.4	76.7	28.5	23.0
1962	89.6	82.3	87.4	80.8	79.9	76.6	28.4	18.5
1963	89.2	81.9	87.9	80.6	78.9	76.8	25.1	19.3
1964	90.7	84.2	87.3	79.6	79.2	76.7	24.9	21.7
1965	90.0	82.9	87.5	81.8	78.1	76.1	23.2	22.4
1966	89.6	82.2	87.5	80.7	75.7	76.5	20.4	18.8
1967	90.1	82.2	87.3	80.0	77.0	74.2	22.1	19.4
1968	89.0	81.8	86.6	79.2	77.8	74.6	24.2	19.1
1969	87.8	82.4	86.5	80.5	75.9	75.2	24.8	20.2

			Married, spouse present					
	F103	F104	F105	F106	F107	F108	F109	F110
1957	98.7	27.6	98.7	26.5	94.2	32.4	42.3	6.6
1958	98.7	27.9	98.8	36.9	94.1	33.5	39.9	6.6
1959	98.7	28.2	98.7	36.9	93.9	35.0	38.2	6.3
1960	98.8	28.8	98.6	37.2	93.7	36.0	36.6	6.7
1961	98.9	29.1	98.6	37.8	93.8	36.9	35.3	6.8
1962	98.7	29.3	98.7	38.5	93.3	37.4	33.8	6.3
1963	98.7	30.1	98.5	39.0	93.4	38.2	31.4	6.3
1964	98.6	30.3	98.3	39.7	93.0	39.2	31.1	6.4
1965	98.5	31.5	98.4	40.5	92.6	39.5	31.0	6.7
1966	98.6	33.1	98.4	41.4	92.4	40.3	30.2	6.8
1967	98.5	35.5	98.3	42.7	92.2	41.3	30.1	6.9
1968	98.4	36.3	98.2	44.1	92.0	42.0	30.2	6.9
1969	98.3	37.3	98.1	45.5	91.5	43.2	29.9	7.1

			Widowed, divorced, or separated					
	F111	F112	F113	F114	F115	F116	F117	F118
1957	95.9	63.9	94.7	72.6	83.5	58.8	25.0	11.2
1958	94.7	64.1	93.9	72.6	85.2	59.5	24.4	10.8
1959	94.9	62.7	94.5	71.5	90.3	60.0	23.3	10.9
1960	95.2	63.1	94.4	70.0	83.2	60.0	22.7	11.4
1961	96.6	62.1	93.6	69.4	83.0	60.7	21.2	11.6
1962	94.4	60.3	92.9	67.3	82.1	60.8	20.2	11.2
1963	94.4	62.3	93.2	69.3	82.1	61.2	19.4	10.5
1964	94.5	61.5	93.3	67.8	82.0	61.7	18.7	10.9
1965	95.1	64.1	93.0	69.3	80.8	61.6	18.7	10.5
1966	94.6	63.2	91.6	70.4	80.7	62.5	17.7	10.4
1967	94.7	64.3	92.9	71.7	79.8	61.8	18.3	10.1
1968	94.4	63.6	92.1	69.7	79.0	61.8	17.7	10.1
1969	94.7	64.8	90.3	68.8	79.3	62.6	18.0	10.5

1970

Date	Married women (husband present)		Labor force participation rate a/ of married women (husband present) having -			
	Total number (000) F119	Labor force participation rate a/ F120	No children under 18 years of age F121	Children 6-17 years of age, but no children under 6 years F122	Children under 6 years only F123	Children under 6 years and children 6-17 years F124
April 1948	34,289	22.0	28.4	26.0	9.2	12.7
April 1949	35,323	22.5	28.7	27.3	10.0	12.2
March 1950	35,925	23.8	30.3	28.3	11.2	12.6
April 1951	35,998	25.2	31.0	30.3	13.6	14.6
April 1952	36,510	25.3	30.9	31.1	13.7	14.1
April 1953	37,106	26.3	31.2	32.2	15.8	15.2
April 1954	37,346	26.6	31.6	33.2	14.3	15.5
April 1955	37,570	27.7	32.7	34.7	15.1	17.3
March 1956	38,306	29.0	35.3	36.4	15.6	16.1
March 1957	38,940	29.6	35.6	36.6	15.9	17.9
March 1958	39,182	30.2	35.4	37.6	18.4	18.1
March 1959	39,529	30.9	35.2	39.8	18.3	19.0
March 1960	40,205	30.5	34.7	39.0	18.2	18.9
March 1961	40,524	32.7	37.3	41.7	19.6	20.3
March 1962	41,218	32.7	36.1	41.8	21.1	21.5
March 1963	41,705	33.7	37.4	41.5	22.4	22.5
March 1964	42,046	34.4	37.8	43.0	23.6	21.9
March 1965	42,371	34.7	38.3	42.7	23.8	22.8
March 1966	42,826	35.4	38.4	43.7	24.0	24.3
March 1967	43,226	36.8	38.9	45.0	26.9	26.2
March 1968	43,947	38.3	40.1	46.9	27.8	27.4
March 1969	44,440	39.6	41.0	48.6	29.3	27.8

Year	Husband-wife families in which husband is head of family and is in labor force a/						Percent of "husband-employed" families having wives in labor force	Percent of "husband-not-employed" families having wives in labor force
	Total number (000)	Total	Percent distribution					
			Husband employed		Husband not employed			
			Wife in labor force	Wife not in labor force	Wife in labor force	Wife not in labor force		
	F125	F126	F127	F128	F129	F130	F131	F132
1958	34,412	100.0	28.9	64.9	2.4	3.7	30.8	39.3
1959	34,625	100.0	30.4	65.3	1.7	2.6	31.8	39.7
1960	35,041	100.0	30.3	65.5	1.7	2.5	31.6	40.1
1961	35,453	100.0	32.0	62.3	2.3	3.4	33.9	40.6
1962	35,713	100.0	32.7	63.0	1.8	2.5	34.2	42.7
1963	36,079	100.0	34.0	61.8	1.7	2.4	35.5	41.3
1964	36,286	100.0	35.0	61.6	1.5	1.9	36.2	44.3
1965	36,545	100.0	35.7	61.5	1.3	1.6	36.7	44.4
1966	36,763	100.0	36.9	60.8	1.0	1.3	37.8	42.3
1967	37,060	100.0	38.5	59.5	0.9	1.1	39.3	45.8
1968	37,668	100.0	40.0	58.1	0.8	1.1	40.8	44.2
1969	38,144	100.0	41.6	56.8	0.7	0.9	42.3	44.5
1970								

Group a/ and year	Total number of employed persons in civilian labor force		Percent distribution of employed males and employed females by occupation group									
			White-collar workers									
			Total, white collar workers		Professional, technical, and kindred workers		Managers, officials, & proprietors (except farm)		Clerical & kindred workers		Sales workers	
	Male (000)	Female (000)	Male	Female	Male	Female	Male	Female	Male	Female	Male	Female
	F133	F134	F135	F136	F137	F138	F139	F140	F141	F142	F143	F144
Workers 14 yrs. & over												
1947	41,535	16,308	29.6	48.4	5.6	9.0	12.1	4.7	7.0	26.4	4.9	8.3
1948	42,457	16,851	30.8	49.3	5.8	9.0	12.9	5.2	6.9	26.9	5.3	8.2
1949	41,615	16,873	31.8	49.9	6.0	9.2	13.2	5.5	6.9	27.0	5.6	8.2
1950	42.156	17,493	32.1	50.4	6.4	10.3	12.9	5.7	7.2	26.3	5.6	8.2
1951	42,431	18,423	31.0	50.2	7.0	9.8	12.2	5.7	6.3	27.0	5.5	7.6
1952	42,334	18,655	31.8	51.6	7.5	10.2	12.2	5.4	6.6	28.5	5.4	7.5
1953	42,684	19,094	32.5	51.0	8.0	10.7	12.7	5.1	6.4	27.5	5.4	7.7
1954	42,420	18,740	33.2	52.4	8.4	10.9	12.4	5.1	6.7	28.5	5.8	7.9
1955	43,191	19,807	33.1	51.9	8.3	11.0	12.6	5.0	6.5	28.1	5.7	7.7
1956	44,157	20,771	33.5	52.1	8.7	10.8	12.5	4.9	6.6	28.6	5.6	7.8
1957	44,013	21,003	34.7	53.3	9.3	11.4	12.9	4.9	6.8	29.4	5.8	7.6
1958	43,042	20,924	36.4	54.4	10.3	12.1	13.4	4.9	6.8	29.7	6.0	7.6
Workers 16 yrs. & over												
1958	42,423	20,613	36.5	55.1	10.4	12.3	13.6	5.0	6.8	30.1	5.7	7.7
1959	43,466	21,164	36.7	54.9	10.5	12.1	13.5	5.1	6.8	29.9	5.8	7.9
1960	43,904	21,874	37.4	55.3	10.9	12.4	13.6	5.0	7.1	30.3	5.8	7.7
1961	43,656	22,090	38.0	55.6	11.4	12.4	13.8	5.1	7.1	30.5	5.8	7.6
1962	44,177	22,525	38.5	56.0	11.7	12.7	14.2	5.0	7.1	30.8	5.5	7.5
1963	44,657	23,105	38.2	55.8	11.9	12.8	13.8	4.8	7.0	30.9	5.5	7.3
1964	45,474	23,831	38.4	56.2	12.0	13.0	13.9	4.7	7.0	31.2	5.5	7.3
1965	46,340	24,748	38.3	57.0	12.1	13.3	13.4	4.5	7.1	31.8	5.7	7.5
1966	46,919	25,976	38.6	57.6	12.4	13.4	13.3	4.5	7.1	32.6	5.7	7.2
1967	47,479	26,893	39.0	58.4	13.0	13.7	13.3	4.4	7.2	33.2	5.5	7.1
1968	48,114	27,807	39.7	59.1	13.4	13.9	13.6	4.5	7.1	33.8	5.7	6.9
1969	48,818	29,084	40.1	59.4	13.8	13.8	13.8	4.3	7.0	34.3	5.5	6.9
1970												

(continued)

Group[a] and year	Blue-collar workers								Service workers	
	Total, blue-collar workers		Craftsmen, foreman & kindred workers		Operatives and kindred workers		Laborers (except farm and mine)		Total, service workers	
	Male	Female	Male	Female	Male	Female	Male	Female	Male	Female
	F145	F146	F147	F148	F149	F150	F151	F152	F153	F154
Workers 14 yrs. & over										
1947	47.9	22.5	18.2	1.2	21.4	20.8	8.3	0.5	6.1	21.2
1948	47.7	22.2	18.7	1.2	21.1	20.5	8.0	0.5	6.1	20.5
1949	46.2	21.0	17.9	1.0	20.4	19.5	7.9	0.5	6.4	21.3
1950	46.8	20.6	17.7	1.1	20.9	19.1	8.1	0.5	6.4	22.0
1951	49.5	21.8	19.3	1.3	21.1	19.9	9.1	0.6	6.1	21.4
1952	49.1	21.4	20.0	1.4	20.6	19.4	8.5	0.6	6.0	21.1
1953	48.8	21.9	19.5	1.4	20.9	19.9	8.3	0.6	6.5	21.9
1954	48.1	20.1	19.0	1.3	20.8	18.2	8.2	0.6	6.2	22.0
1955	48.4	19.4	18.8	1.1	21.3	17.8	8.3	0.5	6.1	22.5
1956	48.3	18.6	19.2	1.1	21.0	17.0	8.1	0.4	6.4	23.1
1957	47.9	18.2	19.2	1.1	20.5	16.6	8.2	0.4	6.4	22.9
1958	46.5	16.8	19.2	1.1	19.2	15.2	8.1	0.5	6.5	24.0
Workers 16 yrs. & over										
1958	46.8	17.0	19.4	1.1	19.3	15.4	8.0	0.5	6.4	23.3
1959	47.0	16.8	19.2	1.0	19.7	15.4	8.1	0.5	6.3	23.5
1960	46.6	16.6	19.0	1.0	19.6	15.2	7.9	0.4	6.5	23.7
1961	46.0	16.3	19.3	1.0	19.2	15.0	7.5	0.3	6.7	24.2
1962	46.1	16.3	19.1	1.0	19.5	15.0	7.5	0.4	6.7	24.0
1963	46.9	16.5	19.4	1.0	20.1	15.1	7.4	0.4	6.9	24.1
1964	47.0	16.7	19.2	1.0	20.3	15.3	7.5	0.4	7.0	23.9
1965	47.7	16.7	19.3	1.1	20.7	15.2	7.7	0.4	6.9	23.2
1966	48.0	17.1	19.9	1.0	20.8	15.7	7.3	0.4	7.1	22.7
1967	47.4	16.9	20.2	1.1	20.1	15.3	7.1	0.5	7.0	22.3
1968	47.7	17.1	20.2	1.2	20.2	15.4	7.2	0.5	6.9	21.8
1969									6.7	21.6

Percent distribution of employed males and employed females by occupation group (cont.)

Group[a] and year	Service workers (cont.)				Farm workers						Index status of occupations	
	Private household workers		Other service workers		Total, farm workers		Farmers and farm managers		Farm laborers and foreman			
	Male	Female	Male	Female	Male	Female	Male	Female	Male	Female	Male	Female
	F155	F156	F157	F158	F159	F160	F161	F162	F163	F164	F165	F166
Workers 14 yrs. & over												
1947	0.3	9.9	5.8	11.4	16.4	7.9	11.3	1.7	5.1	6.5	49.8	53.7
1948	0.3	9.5	5.7	11.0	15.4	8.0	10.4	1.6	5.0	6.5	50.7	54.0
1949	0.3	9.6	6.1	11.7	15.6	7.8	10.7	1.4	4.9	6.3	50.7	54.2
1950	0.3	10.0	6.1	12.0	14.7	6.9	9.9	1.4	4.8	5.6	51.1	54.8
1951	0.1	9.9	6.0	11.6	13.4	6.6	9.0	1.1	4.4	5.5	51.3	54.8
1952	0.1	9.4	5.9	11.7	13.1	5.9	8.9	1.0	4.2	4.9	51.9	55.7
1953	0.1	9.5	6.4	12.5	12.3	5.2	8.6	0.9	3.7	4.3	52.6	56.0
1954	0.1	9.2	6.1	12.8	12.5	5.6	8.8	0.7	3.7	4.9	52.7	56.2
1955	0.1	9.6	6.0	12.8	12.4	6.3	8.4	0.8	4.0	5.5	52.6	55.5
1956	0.1	10.0	6.3	13.1	11.9	6.2	7.9	0.8	4.0	5.4	53.0	55.5
1957	0.1	9.8	6.3	13.2	11.1	5.6	7.2	0.7	3.9	4.9	53.8	56.3
1958	0.1	10.3	6.4	13.7	10.6	4.8	6.9	0.6	3.8	4.2	54.7	56.7
Workers 16 yrs. & over												
1958	0.1	9.5	6.3	13.8	10.3	4.6	7.0	0.6	3.4	4.0	54.8	57.4
1959	0.1	9.1	6.2	14.4	10.0	4.7	6.7	0.6	3.3	4.2	54.9	57.4
1960	0.1	8.9	6.4	14.8	9.6	4.4	6.1	0.5	3.5	3.9	55.3	57.8
1961	0.1	9.0	6.6	15.2	9.3	3.9	5.9	0.6	3.4	3.3	55.9	58.0
1962	0.1	8.8	6.6	15.2	8.7	3.6	5.6	0.6	3.1	3.0	56.2	58.3
1963	0.1	8.6	6.8	15.5	8.0	3.5	5.1	0.6	2.9	3.0	56.4	58.3
1964	0.1	8.4	6.9	15.5	7.6	3.3	4.8	0.6	2.8	2.7	56.6	58.7
1965	0.1	7.7	6.8	15.5	7.1	3.1	4.6	0.5	2.6	2.5	56.7	59.3
1966	0.1	7.2	7.0	15.5	6.4	2.6	4.2	0.5	2.2	2.1	57.2	59.9
1967	0.1	6.5	7.0	15.8	6.2	2.3	3.9	0.4	2.2	1.9	58.0	60.9
1968	0.1	6.1	6.8	15.8	6.0	2.1	3.8	0.3	2.1	1.8	58.2	61.2
1969	0.1	5.5	6.6	16.1	5.6	2.0	3.6	0.3	2.0	1.7		
1970												

Percent distribution of employed males and employed females by occupation group (cont.)

Group[a] and year	All employed females in civilian labor force	Employed females as percent of employed civilian labor force in each occupation group				
		White-collar workers				
		Total white-collar workers	Professional, technical, & kindred workers	Managers, officials, and proprietors (except farm)	Clerical & kindred workers	Sales workers
	F167	F168	F169	F170	F171	F172
Workers 14 yrs. & over						
1947	28.2	39.1	38.8	13.2	59.7	39.8
1948	28.4	38.8	38.0	13.9	60.9	38.1
1949	28.8	38.9	38.4	14.5	61.3	37.1
1950	29.3	39.4	40.0	15.4	60.2	37.8
1951	30.3	41.3	37.8	16.9	65.1	37.4
1952	30.6	41.7	37.4	16.2	65.4	38.2
1953	30.9	41.3	37.4	15.4	65.8	38.7
1954	30.6	41.1	36.5	15.3	65.4	37.6
1955	31.4	41.8	37.7	15.4	66.7	38.4
1956	32.0	42.3	36.7	15.6	67.2	39.5
1957	32.3	42.3	36.9	15.3	67.5	38.7
1958	32.7	42.1	36.5	15.2	68.1	38.2
Workers 16 yrs. & over						
1958	32.7	42.3	36.5	15.2	68.2	39.7
1959	32.7	42.1	35.8	15.5	68.0	39.6
1960	33.3	42.5	36.2	15.6	67.8	39.8
1961	33.1	42.5	35.7	15.6	68.5	39.8
1962	33.8	42.6	35.6	15.3	69.0	40.8
1963	34.1	43.0	35.7	15.3	69.6	40.9
1964	34.4	43.4	36.4	14.9	69.9	40.9
1965	34.8	44.3	36.9	15.1	70.6	41.3
1966	35.6	45.3	37.3	15.8	71.6	41.2
1967	36.2	45.9	37.4	15.7	72.4	42.1
1968	36.6	46.2	37.5	16.0	73.4	41.4
1969	37.3	46.9	37.3	15.8	74.5	43.0
1970						

(continued)

Group[a] and year	Employed females as percent of employed civilian labor force in each occupation group (cont.)			
	Blue-collar workers			
	Total blue-collar workers	Craftsmen, foremen, & kindred workers	Operatives & kindred workers	Laborers (except farm and mine)
	F173	F174	F175	F176
Workers 14 yrs. & over				
1947	15.6	2.4	27.7	2.5
1948	15.6	2.4	27.8	2.6
1949	15.6	2.3	27.9	2.7
1950	15.5	2.5	27.5	2.4
1951	16.1	2.9	29.1	2.7
1952	16.1	3.0	29.3	3.1
1953	16.7	3.1	29.9	2.9
1954	15.6	2.9	27.9	3.1
1955	15.5	2.6	27.7	2.9
1956	15.3	2.7	27.6	2.4
1957	15.3	2.7	27.9	2.4
1958	14.9	2.7	27.9	2.8
Workers 16 yrs. & over				
1958	15.0	2.7	27.9	2.8
1959	14.8	2.5	27.6	2.7
1960	15.1	2.6	27.8	2.2
1961	15.2	2.5	28.3	2.3
1962	15.3	2.6	28.1	2.5
1963	15.4	2.7	28.0	2.6
1964	15.7	2.8	28.3	2.5
1965	15.8	2.9	28.2	2.4
1966	16.5	2.7	29.5	3.0
1967	16.8	2.9	30.1	3.3
1968	17.1	3.2	30.6	3.5
1969	17.6	3.3	31.2	4.0
1970				

(continued)

Group[a] and year	Service workers			Farm workers			Index of sexual segregation of occupations
	Total service workers	Private household workers	Other service workers	Total farm workers	Farmers & farm managers	Farm laborers & foremen	
	F177	F178	F179	F180	F181	F182	F183
Workers 14 yrs. & over							
1947	57.8	92.8	43.6	15.8	5.6	32.2	42.6
1948	57.2	91.6	43.1	17.2	5.7	33.9	42.1
1949	57.3	92.3	43.6	16.8	5.2	34.4	42.2
1950	58.9	93.4	45.0	16.4	5.4	32.3	41.8
1951	60.5	97.4	45.7	17.6	5.0	35.1	41.6
1952	60.6	96.9	46.6	16.6	4.8	34.1	42.4
1953	60.3	97.7	46.7	15.9	4.6	34.1	42.2
1954	60.9	97.6	48.0	16.5	3.2	37.1	43.4
1955	62.6	97.8	49.3	18.8	3.9	38.7	44.2
1956	63.1	97.9	49.6	19.7	4.8	38.6	44.4
1957	63.1	97.8	50.0	19.6	4.6	37.8	44.2
1958	64.3	97.6	51.2	18.0	4.0	35.2	44.4
Workers 16 yrs. & over							
1958	63.8	98.0	51.4	17.9	4.0	36.9	44.7
1959	64.5	98.2	53.0	18.8	3.9	38.1	44.8
1960	64.5	98.3	53.4	18.6	4.0	35.5	44.2
1961	64.8	97.7	54.0	17.3	4.8	32.8	43.8
1962	64.5	97.7	53.9	17.6	5.1	33.4	44.0
1963	64.3	97.8	54.1	18.7	5.5	34.7	43.9
1964	64.0	97.7	54.0	18.4	5.7	34.0	43.8
1965	64.3	98.0	54.8	18.7	5.9	34.6	44.0
1966	64.0	97.8	55.2	18.7	5.9	35.2	43.6
1967	64.7	97.9	57.2	16.9	4.3	32.8	43.4
1968	65.8	97.6	59.3	17.3	4.3	33.8	43.6
1969							

Employed females as percent of employed civilian labor force in each occupation group (cont.)

Percent of Civilian Labor Force 18 Years Old and Over Attaining Specified Levels of Schooling$^{\underline{a}/}$, by Color and Sex, United States, 1959, 1962, 1964-1969

As of March	White		Nonwhite		White		Nonwhite	
	Male	Female	Male	Female	Male	Female	Male	Female
	Elementary school: less than 5 years				Elementary school: 5-8 years			
	F184	F185	F186	F187	F188	F189	F190	F191
1959	4.3	2.2	21.5	12.2	25.7	19.2	34.6	33.9
1962	3.8	2.1	19.3	9.8	23.4	17.4	31.2	27.8
1964	3.2	1.8	14.8	7.0	21.7	16.2	29.9	28.2
1965	3.2	1.7	15.4	6.7	20.7	15.3	26.4	24.9
1966	2.8	1.3	14.1	7.0	19.8	14.4	28.0	24.9
1967	2.6	1.3	13.1	6.9	18.8	13.5	27.3	23.1
1968	2.4	1.3	12.2	5.9	17.9	12.8	24.0	22.7
1969	2.4	1.3	10.9	5.6	16.9	11.9	24.2	20.7
1970								
	High school: 1-3 years				High school: 4 years			
	F192	F193	F194	F195	F196	F197	F198	F199
1959	19.9	22.5	28.2	40.2	13.3	19.7	9.5	10.3
1962	19.3	17.9	22.2	24.8	29.9	40.8	18.3	24.9
1964	18.8	17.8	24.5	25.1	32.4	43.0	19.1	26.6
1965	18.8	17.7	24.4	25.7	33.2	43.9	21.4	28.6
1966	18.7	17.5	24.3	24.4	33.8	45.1	21.9	28.9
1967	18.3	17.6	23.3	24.2	33.9	44.7	24.4	31.6
1968	17.9	16.7	25.0	23.4	34.7	45.4	25.3	32.3
1969	17.4	16.2	24.7	24.7	35.4	46.9	25.6	31.9
1970								
	College: 1-3 years				College: 4 years or more			
	F200	F201	F202	F203	F204	F205	F206	F207
1959	9.5	10.3	4.1	5.0	11.0	8.5	3.5	4.6
1962	11.0	11.9	5.4	6.0	12.6	10.0	3.6	6.7
1964	11.1	11.0	5.7	7.8	12.7	10.1	6.1	5.3
1965	11.0	11.0	6.0	6.3	13.1	10.3	6.4	7.8
1966	11.1	11.4	6.6	7.9	13.7	10.3	5.1	6.9
1967	12.3	12.4	6.7	7.9	14.1	10.4	5.3	6.4
1968	12.7	12.9	7.6	7.9	14.4	10.9	6.0	7.8
1969	13.1	12.8	8.1	10.1	14.7	10.9	6.5	7.0
1970								
	4 years high school or more							
	F208	F209	F210	F211				
1959	48.7	59.0	20.9	29.3				
1962	53.5	62.7	27.3	37.6				
1964	56.2	64.1	30.9	39.7				
1965	57.3	65.2	33.8	42.7				
1966	58.6	66.8	33.6	43.7				
1967	60.3	67.5	36.4	45.9				
1968	61.8	69.2	38.9	48.0				
1969	63.2	70.6	40.2	49.0				
1970								

Note: Percentages for each color/sex group sum to 100.0 percent.

	Unemployment rate (number unemployed as a percent of civilian labor force in specified category)											
Year	White		Nonwhite		White		Nonwhite		White		Nonwhite	
	Male	Female	Male	Female	Male	Female	Male	Female	Male	Female	Male	Female
	Total, 16 years and over				16 and 17 years				18 and 19 years			
	G01	G02	G03	G04	G05	G06	G07	G08	G09	G10	G11	G12
1948	3.4	3.8	5.8	6.1	10.2	9.7	9.4	11.8	9.4	6.8	10.5	14.6
1949	5.6	5.7	9.6	7.9	13.4	13.6	15.8	20.3	14.2	10.7	17.1	15.9
1950	4.7	5.3	9.4	8.4	13.4	13.8	12.1	17.6	11.7	9.4	17.7	14.1
1951	2.6	4.2	4.9	6.1	9.5	9.6	8.7	13.0	6.7	6.5	9.6	15.1
1952	2.5	3.3	5.2	5.7	10.9	9.3	8.0	6.3	7.0	6.2	10.0	16.8
1953	2.5	3.1	4.8	4.1	8.9	8.3	8.3	10.3	7.1	6.0	8.1	9.9
1954	4.8	5.6	10.3	9.3	14.0	12.0	13.4	19.1	13.0	9.4	14.7	21.6
1955	3.7	4.3	8.8	8.4	12.2	11.6	14.8	15.4	10.4	7.7	12.9	21.4
1956	3.4	4.2	7.9	8.9	11.2	12.1	15.7	22.0	9.7	8.3	14.9	23.4
1957	3.6	4.3	8.3	7.3	11.9	11.9	16.3	18.3	11.2	7.9	20.0	21.3
1958	6.1	6.2	13.8	10.8	14.9	15.6	27.1	25.4	16.5	11.0	26.7	30.0
1959	4.6	5.3	11.5	9.4	15.0	13.3	22.3	25.8	13.0	11.1	27.2	29.9
1960	4.8	5.3	10.7	9.4	14.6	14.5	22.7	25.7	13.5	11.5	25.1	24.5
1961	5.7	6.5	12.8	11.8	16.5	17.0	31.0	31.1	15.1	13.6	23.9	28.2
1962	4.6	5.5	10.9	11.0	15.1	15.6	21.9	27.8	12.7	11.3	21.8	31.2
1963	4.7	5.8	10.5	11.2	17.8	18.1	27.0	40.1	14.2	13.2	27.4	31.9
1964	4.1	5.5	8.9	10.6	16.1	17.1	25.9	36.5	13.4	13.2	23.1	29.2
1965	3.6	5.0	7.4	9.2	14.7	15.0	27.1	37.8	11.4	13.4	20.2	27.8
1966	2.8	4.3	6.3	8.6	12.5	14.5	22.5	34.8	8.9	10.7	20.5	29.2
1967	2.7	4.6	6.0	9.1	12.7	12.9	28.9	32.0	9.0	10.6	20.1	28.3
1968	2.6	4.3	5.6	8.3	12.3	13.9	26.6	33.7	8.2	11.0	19.0	26.2
1969	2.5	4.2	5.3	7.8	12.5	13.8	24.7	31.2	7.9	10.0	19.0	25.7
1970												
	20-24 years				25-34 years				35-44 years			
	G13	G14	G15	G16	G17	G18	G19	G20	G21	G22	G23	G24
1948	6.4	4.2	11.7	10.2	2.6	3.8	4.7	7.3	2.1	2.9	5.2	4.0
1949	9.8	6.7	15.8	12.5	4.9	5.5	8.5	8.5	3.9	4.5	8.1	6.2
1950	7.7	6.1	12.6	13.0	3.9	5.2	10.0	9.1	3.2	4.0	7.9	6.6
1951	3.6	3.9	6.7	8.8	2.0	4.1	5.5	7.1	1.8	3.5	3.4	5.6
1952	4.3	3.8	7.9	10.7	1.9	3.2	5.5	6.2	1.7	2.8	4.4	4.0
1953	4.5	4.1	8.1	5.5	2.0	3.1	4.3	4.9	1.8	2.3	3.6	3.5
1954	9.8	6.4	16.9	13.2	4.2	5.7	10.1	10.9	3.6	4.9	9.0	7.3
1955	7.0	5.1	12.4	13.0	2.7	4.3	8.6	10.2	2.6	3.8	8.2	5.5
1956	6.1	5.1	12.0	14.8	2.8	4.0	7.6	9.1	2.2	3.5	6.6	6.8
1957	7.1	5.1	12.7	12.2	2.7	4.7	8.5	8.1	2.5	3.7	6.4	4.7
1958	11.7	7.4	19.5	18.9	5.6	6.6	14.7	11.1	4.4	5.6	11.4	9.2
1959	7.5	6.7	16.3	14.9	3.8	5.0	12.3	9.7	3.2	4.7	8.9	7.6
1960	8.3	7.2	13.1	15.3	4.1	5.7	10.7	9.1	3.3	4.2	8.2	8.6
1961	10.0	8.4	15.3	19.5	4.9	6.6	12.9	11.1	4.0	5.6	10.7	4.4
1962	8.0	7.7	14.6	18.2	3.8	5.4	10.5	11.5	3.1	4.5	8.6	8.9
1963	7.8	7.4	15.5	18.7	3.9	5.8	9.5	11.7	2.9	4.6	8.0	8.2
1964	7.4	7.1	12.6	18.3	3.0	5.2	7.7	11.2	2.5	4.5	6.2	7.8
1965	5.9	6.3	9.3	13.7	2.6	4.8	6.2	8.4	2.3	4.1	5.1	7.6
1966	4.1	5.3	7.9	12.6	2.1	3.7	4.9	8.1	1.7	3.3	4.2	5.0
1967	4.2	6.0	8.0	13.8	1.9	4.7	4.4	8.7	1.6	3.7	3.1	6.2
1968	4.6	5.9	8.3	12.3	1.7	3.9	3.8	8.4	1.4	3.1	2.9	5.0
1969	4.6	5.5	8.4	12.0	1.7	4.2	3.4	6.6	1.4	3.2	2.4	4.5
1970												

(continued)

Year	Unemployment rate (number unemployed as a percent of civilian labor force in specified category) (cont.)											
	White		Nonwhite		White		Nonwhite		White		Nonwhite	
	Male	Female	Male	Female	Male	Female	Male	Female	Male	Female	Male	Female
	G24	G26	G27	G28	G29	G30	G31	G32	G33	G34	G35	G36
	45-54 years				55-64 years				65 years and over			
1948	2.4	3.1	3.7	2.9	3.0	3.2	3.5	3.0	3.3	2.4	4.6	1.6
1949	4.0	4.0	7.9	4.0	5.3	4.3	7.0	5.4	5.0	4.1	6.2	1.6
1950	3.7	4.3	7.4	5.9	4.7	4.4	8.0	4.8	4.6	3.1	7.0	5.7
1951	2.2	3.6	3.6	2.8	2.7	4.0	4.1	3.4	3.4	3.3	4.7	1.6
1952	2.0	2.4	4.2	3.5	2.3	2.5	3.7	2.4	2.9	2.3	4.7	1.5
1953	2.0	2.3	5.1	2.1	2.7	2.5	3.6	2.1	2.3	1.4	3.1	1.6
1954	3.8	4.4	9.3	5.9	4.3	4.5	7.5	4.9	4.2	2.8	7.5	5.1
1955	2.9	3.4	6.4	5.2	3.9	3.6	9.0	5.5	3.8	2.2	7.1	3.3
1956	2.8	3.3	5.4	5.6	3.1	3.5	8.1	5.3	3.4	2.3	4.9	2.8
1957	3.0	3.0	6.2	4.2	3.4	3.0	5.5	4.0	3.2	3.5	5.9	4.3
1958	4.8	4.9	10.3	4.9	5.2	4.3	10.1	6.2	5.0	3.5	9.0	5.6
1959	3.7	4.0	7.9	6.1	4.2	4.0	8.7	5.0	4.5	3.4	8.4	2.3
1960	3.6	4.0	8.5	5.7	4.1	3.3	9.5	4.3	4.0	2.8	6.3	4.1
1961	4.4	4.8	10.2	7.4	5.3	4.3	10.5	6.3	5.2	3.7	9.4	6.5
1962	3.5	3.7	8.3	7.1	4.1	3.4	9.6	3.6	4.1	4.0	11.9	3.7
1963	3.3	3.9	7.1	6.1	4.0	3.5	7.4	4.8	4.1	3.0	10.1	3.6
1964	2.9	3.6	5.9	6.1	3.5	3.5	8.1	3.8	3.6	3.4	8.3	2.2
1965	2.3	3.0	5.1	4.4	3.1	2.7	5.4	3.9	3.4	2.7	5.2	3.1
1966	1.7	2.7	4.1	5.0	2.5	2.2	4.4	3.3	3.0	2.7	4.9	4.0
1967	1.8	2.9	3.4	4.4	2.2	2.3	4.1	3.4	2.7	2.6	5.1	3.4
1968	1.5	2.3	2.5	3.2	1.7	2.1	3.6	2.8	2.8	2.7	4.0	2.4
1969	1.4	2.4	2.4	3.7	1.7	2.1	3.2	2.9	2.1	2.4	3.2	1.1
1970												

Unemployment Rates$\underline{a}$/, by Marital Status and Sex, United States, 1955-1969

Group$\underline{b}$/ and year	Total civilian labor force		Single		Married, spouse present		Widowed, divorced, or separated	
	Male G37	Female G38	Male G39	Female G40	Male G41	Female G42	Male G43	Female G44
14 years of age and over								
1955	3.9	4.3	8.6	5.0	2.6	3.7	7.1	5.0
1956	3.5	4.3	7.7	5.3	2.3	3.6	6.2	5.0
1957	4.1	4.7	9.2	5.6	2.8	4.3	6.8	4.7
1958	6.8	6.8	13.3	7.4	5.1	6.5	11.2	6.7
1959	5.3	5.9	11.6	7.1	3.6	5.2	8.6	6.2
1960	5.4	5.9	11.7	7.5	3.7	5.2	8.4	5.9
1961	6.5	7.2	13.1	8.7	4.6	6.4	10.3	7.4
1962	5.3	6.2	11.2	7.9	3.6	5.4	9.9	6.4
1963	5.3	6.5	12.4	8.9	3.4	5.4	9.6	6.7
1964	4.7	6.2	11.5	8.7	2.8	5.1	8.9	6.4
1965	4.0	5.5	10.1	8.2	2.4	4.5	7.2	5.4
1966	3.3	4.9	8.6	7.8	1.9	3.7	5.6	4.7
16 years of age and over								
1966$\underline{b}$/	3.2	4.9	8.6	7.9	1.9	3.7	5.5	4.7
1967$\underline{c}$/	3.1	5.2	8.3	7.5	1.8	4.5	4.9	4.6
1968	2.9	4.8	8.0	7.6	1.6	3.9	4.2	4.2
1969	2.8	4.7	8.0	7.3	1.5	3.9	4.0	4.0
1970								

Unemployment Rates$\underline{a}$/ for Persons 20 Years Old and Over in the Civilian Labor Force, by Marital Status, Color, and Sex, United States, 1962-1968

Year	Single				Married, spouse present				Widowed, divorced, or separated			
	White		Nonwhite		White		Nonwhite		White		Nonwhite	
	Male G45	Female G46	Male G47	Female G48	Male G49	Female G50	Male G51	Female G52	Male G53	Female G54	Male G55	Female G56
1962	8.9	3.8	15.3	12.5	3.1	4.7	7.9	9.0	8.3	5.5	15.1	9.3
1963	9.1	4.1	16.3	12.4	3.0	4.7	6.8	8.6	8.2	5.6	14.5	9.4
1964	8.4	3.7	14.0	12.4	2.5	4.4	5.3	8.4	7.6	5.7	13.0	8.5
1965	6.9	3.6	11.9	8.9	2.1	3.9	4.3	6.8	6.7	4.5	8.7	7.9
1966	5.4	3.2	9.8	8.5	1.7	3.2	3.6	5.6	5.1	3.8	7.0	7.2
1967	4.9	3.2	8.6	9.2	1.6	3.9	3.2	7.0	4.6	3.9	5.9	6.5
1968	4.9	3.1	8.3	8.6	1.5	3.3	2.9	5.9	4.0	3.6	5.0	5.8
1969												
1970												

Percent of Persons 14 Years Old and Over with No Money Income, and Median Annual Money
Income of Income Recipients 14 Years Old and Over, in Constant (1968) Dollars, by
Color and Sex, United States, 1956-1968

Year	Percent of persons 14 years old and over with no money income				Median annual money income of income recipients 14 years old and over in constant (1968) dollars			
	White		Nonwhite		White		Nonwhite	
	Male	Female	Male	Female	Male	Female	Male	Female
	H001	H002	H003	H004	H005	H006	H007	H008
1956	7.9	49.6	9.9	35.2	$4,899	$1,622	$2,560	$ 931
1957	7.9	48.7	10.5	36.6	4,837	1,620	2,567	936
1958	8.0	48.4	11.0	35.8	4,787	1,540	2,385	903
1959	8.3	47.4	11.7	36.6	5,024	1,568	2,361	966
1960	8.2	45.2	11.7	33.8	5,053	1,586	2,655	983
1961	8.1	43.9	12.9	32.5	5,154	1,579	2,666	1,058
1962	8.5	43.3	13.0	34.2	5,359	1,627	2,635	1,092
1963	8.2	42.1	12.1	33.9	5,471	1,637	2,848	1,093
1964	8.1	41.2	12.4	32.7	5,533	1,696	3,135	1,195
1965	8.0	41.5	12.3	33.2	5,835	1,779	3,140	1,295
1966	7.6	39.8	11.8	32.0	5,995	1,838	3,320	1,399
1967	7.1	37.2	11.7	28.6	6,108	1,952	3,593	1,561
1968	7.1	36.2	11.7	27.4	6,267	2,079	3,829[a]/	1,688[a]/
1969								
1970								

Year	Median annual money earnings of year-round full-time civilian workers (aged 14 years and over) in constant (1968) dollars						Ratio (x 100) of earnings of females to earnings of males		
	All races		White		Nonwhite		All races	White	Non-white
	Male	Female	Male	Female	Male	Female			
	H009	H010	H011	H012	H013	H014	H015	H016	H017
1956	$5,716	$3,619	$6,029	$3,786	$3,727	$2,095	63.3	62.8	56.2
1957	5,830	3,721	6,123	3,843	3,880	2,308	63.8	62.8	59.5
1958	5,932	3,735	6,244	3,883	4,055	2,394	63.0	62.2	59.0
1959	6,220	3,812	6,514	3,947	3,987	2,622	61.3	60.6	65.8
1960	6,313	3,830	6,659	4,010	4,456	2,789	60.7	60.2	62.6
1961	6,507	3,855	6,838	4,047	4,516	2,704	59.2	59.2	59.9
1962	6,617	3,924	6,929	4,141	4,369	2,620	59.3	59.8	60.0
1963	6,793	4,004	7,131	4,229	4,662	2,690	58.9	59.3	57.7
1964	6,954	4,113	7,283	4,326	4,803	2,998	59.1	59.4	62.4
1965	7,046	4,222	7,395	4,402	4,718	3,106	59.9	59.5	65.8
1966	7,350	4,230	7,680	4,451	4,854	3,161	57.6	58.0	65.1
1967	7,484	4,324	7,828	4,579	5,282	3,504	57.8	58.5	66.3
1968	7,664	4,457	8,014	4,700	5,603	3,677	58.2	58.6	65.6
1969									
1970									

Median Total Annual Money Earnings, in Current Year, of Year-Round Full-Time Civilian Workers 14 Years Old and Over, by Occupation of Longest Job in Current Year and by Sex, United States, 1956-1969a/ (In constant 1968 dollars)

Year	All year-round full-time civilian workers with earnings		Professional, technical, and kindred workers					
			Total		Self-employed		Salaried, Total	
	Male	Female	Male	Female	Male	Female	Male	Female
	H018	H019	H020	H021	H022	H023	H024	H025
1956	$5,716	$3,619	$ 7,484	$4,672				
1957	5,830	3,721	7,410	4,713				
1958	5,932	3,735	7,777	4,950				
1959	6,220	3,812	8,161	5,236				
1960	6,313	3,830	8,367	5,125	$12,769		$ 8,178	$5,133
1961	6,507	3,855	8,685	5,670	10,564		8,583	5,701
1962	6,617	3,924	8,764	5,566	14,922		8,520	5,594
1963	6,793	4,004	9,073	5,658	13,385		8,889	5,678
1964	6,954	4,113	9,577	5,753	14,861		9,262	5,746
1965	7,046	4,222	9,330	6,082	13,014		9,121	6,116
1966	7,350	4,230	9,868	6,195	15,951		9,603	6,222
1967	7,484	4,324	10,193	6,590	15,246		9,971	6,594
1968	7,664	4,457	10,542	6,610	17,358		10,243	6,634
1969	8,226	4,818	11,151	6,935	19,245		10,844	6,939
1970								

Year	Professional, technical, and kindred workers (cont.)						Managers, officials, proprietors (except farm)	
	Salaried						Total	
	Medical & other health workers		Teachers, elementary and secondary		Other			
	Male	Female	Male	Female	Male	Female	Male	Female
	H026	H027	H028	H029	H030	H031	H032	H033
1956							$ 7,638	$4,512
1957							7,558	4,812
1958							7,679	4,503
1959							8,251	4,697
1960		$4,796	$ 7,130	$5,387	$ 7,812	$5,538	7,818	4,132
1961		5,278	7,571	6,078	8,160	5,637	8,114	3,967
1962		5,005	7,572	5,960	8,026	5,735	7,943	4,306
1963		5,032	7,895	5,996	8,494	5,953	8,337	4,282
1964		5,173	7,485	5,810	8,683	6,115	8,483	4,170
1965	8,149	5,602	7,806	6,235	8,691	6,434	8,708	4,635
1966	8,502	5,689	8,178	6,336	9,132	6,608	9,461	4,794
1967			8,195	6,645			9,691	5,182
1968			8,779	6,630			9,794	5,101
1969							10,453	5,549
1970								

(continued)

Median Total Annual Money Earnings, in Current Year, of Year-Round Full-Time Civilian Workers 14 Years Old and Over, by Occupation of Longest Job in Current Year and by Sex, United States, 1956-1969[a]/ (In constant 1968 dollars) ((cont.)

Year	Managers, officials, proprietors (except farm)							
	Self-employed						Salaried	
	Total		In retail trade		Other			
	Male	Female	Male	Female	Male	Female	Male	Female
	H034	H035	H036	H037	H038	H039	H040	H041
1956								
1957								
1958								
1959								
1960	$6,183	$2,117	$5,594		$6,997		$ 8,787	$4,963
1961	6,762	2,210	5,786	$2,260	7,582		8,941	4,931
1962	6,844	1,991	6,395		7,307		8,703	4,878
1963	6,568	2,196	5,998		7,234		9,219	5,017
1964	6,723	2,870	6,032		7,431		9,502	5,301
1965	7,462	2,395	6,599		8,181		9,410	5,134
1966	7,142	2,472	6,554	2,391	7,714		10,146	5,468
1967	7,584	3,234	6,611	2,685	8,345	$4,297	10,296	5,655
1968	7,409	3,384	6,801	3,291	8,250	3,731	10,661	5,466
1969	7,431	3,433					11,245	5,908
1970								

Year	Clerical and kindred workers						Sales workers total	
	Total		Secretaries, stenographers, typists		Other			
	Male	Female	Male	Female	Male	Female	Male	Female
	H042	H043	H044	H045	H046	H047	H048	H049
1956	$5,617	$4,026					$6,406	$2,675
1957	5,646	4,066					6,362	2,831
1958	5,778	4,045				6,366	6,366	2,786
1959	6,125	4,171					6,621	2,794
1960	6,222	4,204		$4,403	$6,215	$4,087	6,870	2,809
1961	6,228	4,325		4,511	6,246	4,194	7,002	2,781
1962	6,455	4,400		4,526	6,452	4,321	7,159	2,998
1963	6,662	4,469		4,638	6,654	4,361	7,426	2,758
1964	6,930	4,540		4,756	6,929	4,401	7,755	3,052
1965	6,927	4,658		4,893	6,940	4,516	7,970	3,232
1966	7,013	4,626		4,737	7,015	4,538	8,097	3,287
1967	7,037	4,688		4,931	7,037	4,522	8,080	3,380
1968	7,324	4,778		4,921	7,326	4,693	8,292	3,388
1969	7,537	4,898					8,762	3,519
1970								

(continued)

Median Total Annual Money Earnings, in Current Year, of Year-Round Full-Time Civilian Workers 14 Years Old and Over, by Occupation of Longest Job in Current Year and by Sex, United States, 1956-1969a/ (In constant 1968 dollars) (cont.)

Year	Sales workers				Craftsmen, foremen & kindred workers			
	In retail trade		Other		Total		Foremen	
	Male	Female	Male	Female	Male	Female	Male	Female
	H050	H051	H052	H053	H054	H055	H056	H057
1956					$6,376			
1957					6,452			
1958					6,406			
1959					6,751			
1960	$5,598	$2,738	$7,658		6,851		$7,992	
1961	5,903	2,719	7,924		6,984		7,900	
1962	5,699	2,959	8,208		7,186		8,452	
1963	6,373	2,704	8,035		7,176		7,995	
1964	6,441	2,869	8,436		7,323		8,135	
1965	6,703	3,109	8,516		7,446	$4,220	8,472	
1966	6,593	3,218	8,891	$4,452	7,677	4,516	8,687	$4,556
1967	6,527	3,277	9,017	4,532	7,771	3,918	9,087	4,440
1968	6,915	3,265	9,116	4,681	7,958	4,315	9,051	4,484
1969					8,295	4,704		
1970								

Year	Craftsmen, foremen and kindred workers		Operatives and kindred workers					
	Craftsmen		Total		Manufacturing			
					Total		Durable goods	
	Male	Female	Male	Female	Male	Female	Male	Female
	H058	H059	H060	H061	H062	H063	H064	H065
1956			$5,421	$3,369				
1957			5,439	3,230				
1958			5,325	3,278				
1959			5,501	3,482				
1960	$6,668		5,876	3,492			$6,129	$4,201
1961	6,845		5,989	3,432			6,174	4,221
1962	6,964		6,135	3,629			6,334	4,444
1963	7,013		6,297	3,539	$6,358	$3,643	6,509	4,205
1964	7,159		6,394	3,640	6,529	3,802	6,649	4,502
1965	7,261		6,378	3,610	6,582	3,706	6,769	4,298
1966	7,484	$4,461	6,577	3,631	6,667	3,706	6,913	4,219
1967	7,530	3,513	6,576	3,783	6,643	3,867	6,825	4,326
1968	7,759	4,155	6,773	3,956	6,884	4,073	7,113	4,518
1969			6,950	4,082				
1970								

(continued)

Median Total Annual Money Earnings, in Current Year, of Year-Round Full-Time Civilian Workers 14 Years Old and Over, by Occupation of Longest Job in Current Year and by Sex, United States, 1956-1969[a]/ (In constant 1968 dollars) (cont.)

| Year | Operatives and kindred workers (cont.) | | | | Private house-hold workers | | Service workers (except private household) Total | |
| | Manufacturing (cont.) Nondurable goods | | Other operatives and kindred workers | | | | | |
	Male H066	Female H067	Male H068	Female H069	Male H070	Female H071	Male H072	Female H073
1957						$1,125	$4,507	$2,496
1958						1,212	4,459	2,468
1959						1,386	4,654	2,475
						1,368	4,778	2,676
1960	$5,356	$3,222	$5,780	$2,922		1,359	4,807	2,752
1961	6,024	3,262	5,802	2,750		1,326	5,026	2,677
1962	5,987	3,474	5,998	2,875		1,309	5,044	2,556
1963	6,036	3,355	6,223	2,848		1,172	5,040	2,892
1964	6,275	3,563	6,189	2,874		1,288	5,252	2,839
1965	6,208	3,473	6,114	3,039		1,366	5,376	2,980
1966	6,140	3,512	6,441	3,227		1,430	5,485	2,889
1967	6,214	3,645	6,464	3,317		1,355	5,702	3,025
1968	6,349	3,843	6,627	3,331		1,464	5,898	3,159
1969						1,619	6,010	3,447
1970								

| Year | Service workers (except private household) (cont.) | | | | Laborers (except farm and mine) | |
| | Waiters, cooks, bartenders | | Other service workers | | | |
	Male H074	Female H075	Male H076	Female H077	Male H078	Female H079
1956					$4,365	
1957					4,589	
1958					4,384	
1959					4,692	
1960	$4,716	$2,621	$4,822	$2,831	4,724	
1961	4,943	2,507	5,043	2,783	4,943	
1962	4,715	2,239	5,098	2,669	5,034	
1963	4,638	2,707	5,109	2,965	5,163	
1964	4,840	2,531	5,384	3,029	4,842	
1965	5,383	2,538	5,369	3,174	5,130	
1966	4,814	2,669	5,585	3,033	5,503	
1967					5,555	$3,318
1968					5,606	3,490
1969					5,717	
1970						

Ratio (x 100) of Earnings of Female Workers to Earnings of Male Workers: Median Total Annual
Money Earnings of Year-Round Full-Time Civilian Workers 14 Years Old and Over, by
Occupation of Longest Job in Current Year, United States, 1956-1968

Year	All occupations	Professional, technical, and kindred workers		Managers, officials, proprietors (except farm)	Clerical and kindred workers	Sales workers	Operatives and kindred workers	Service workers (except private household)
		Total	Teachers (elementary and secondary)					
	H080	H081	H082	H083	H084	H085	H086	H087
1956	63.3	62.4	--	59.1	71.7	41.8	62.1	55.4
1957	63.8	63.6	--	63.7	72.0	44.5	59.4	55.3
1958	63.0	63.6	--	58.6	70.0	43.8	61.6	53.2
1959	61.3	64.2	--	56.9	68.1	42.2	63.3	56.0
1960	60.7	61.2	75.6	52.8	67.6	40.9	59.4	57.2
1961	59.2	65.3	80.3	48.9	69.4	39.7	57.3	53.3
1962	59.3	63.5	78.7	54.2	68.2	41.9	59.2	50.7
1963	58.9	62.4	75.9	51.4	67.1	37.1	56.2	57.4
1964	59.1	60.1	77.6	49.2	65.5	39.4	56.9	54.0
1965	59.9	65.2	79.9	53.2	67.2	40.6	56.6	55.4
1966	57.6	62.8	77.5	50.7	66.0	40.6	55.2	52.7
1967	57.8	64.6	81.1	53.5	66.6	41.8	57.5	53.0
1968	58.2	62.7	75.5	52.1	65.2	40.8	58.4	53.6
1969	58.6	62.2		53.1	65.0	40.2	58.7	57.4
1970								

Civilians Employed in Current Year, Percent with No Income in Previous Year and Median Annual
Money Income (of income recipients) in Previous Year, in Constant 1968 Dollars, by Sex and
by Occupational Class, Persons 14 Years Old and Over, United States, 1956-1968

Item	Total	White-collar workers							
		Professional, techni-cal & kindred workers			Nonfarm managers, officials & proprietors			Clerical and kindred workers	Sales workers
		Total	Self-em-ployed	Sal-aried	Total	Self-em-ployed	Sal-aried		
	H088	H089	H090	H091	H092	H093	H094	H095	H096
MALES (1956)									
Civilians employed, March 1957 (000)	43,273	4,141	632	3,509	5,598	2,935	2,663	2,988	8,413
Percent with no income in 1956	1.7	1.4	1.9	1.3	0.7	1.0	0.4	1.0	1.2
Median income, 1956 (in 1968 dollars)	$5,239	$7,388	$12,155	$7,246	$7,085	$6,220	$7,800	$5,457	$5,585
FEMALES (1956)									
Civilians employed, March 1957 (000)	20,592	2,436	135	2,301	1,080	633	447	6,161	1,507
Percent with no income in 1956	11.3	8.5	11.9	8.3	17.3	26.1	4.9	6.6	17.1
Median income, 1956 (in 1968 dollars)	$2,664	$4,010	a/	$4,068	$3,186	$2,341	$4,037	$3,530	$1,678
MALES (1957)									
Civilians employed, March 1958 (000)	41,767	4,314	650	3,664	5,608	2,784	2,824	2,886	2,580
Percent with no income in 1957	1.5	1.5	2.5	1.3	0.4	0.6	0.1	0.6	2.5
Median income, 1957 (in 1968 dollars)	$5,267	$7,369	$12,421	$7,112	$7,006	$5,731	$7,820	$5,421	$5,533
FEMALES (1957)									
Civilians employed, March 1958 (000)	20,544	2,618	109	2,509	1,037	554	483	6,160	1,496
Percent with no income in 1957	10.2	6.9	12.8	6.7	16.8	27.3	4.8	6.3	18.4
Median income, 1957 (in 1968 dollars)	$2,656	$4,182	a/	$4,266	$3,375	$2,048	$4,307	$3,556	$1,795
MALES (1958)									
Civilians employed, March 1959 (000)	42,842	4,471	676	3,795	5,695	2,871	2,824	2,919	2,745
Percent with no income in 1958	1.6	1.3	0.4	1.5	0.5	0.8	0.2	0.6	3.0
Median income, 1958 (in 1968 dollars)	$5,230	$7,697	$12,481	$7,438	$7,049	$6,105	$7,922	$5,484	$5,375
FEMALES (1958)									
Civilians employed, March 1959 (000)	20,985	2,721	164	2,557	1,112	562	550	6,134	1,582
Percent with no income in 1958	11.1	10.0	12.8	9.8	14.7	19.8	9.5	7.2	16.6
Median income, 1958 (in 1968 dollars)	$2,650	$4,248	a/	$4,325	$3,328	$1,746	$4,291	$3,647	$2,088
MALES (1959)									
Civilians employed, March 1960 (000)	43,048	4,791	702	4,089	5,963	2,968	2,995	3,116	2,640
Percent with no income in 1959	1.6	1.9	2.0	1.9	0.6	0.7	0.5	0.8	2.5
Median income, 1959 (in 1968 dollars)	$5,562	$8,030	$13,064	$7,796	$7,540	$6,327	$8,454	$5,855]	$5,841
FEMALES (1959)									
Civilians employed, March 1960) (000)	21,219	2,775	176	2,599	997	510	487	6,423	1,533
Percent with no income in 1959	10.2	8.4	4.0	8.7	11.9	15.7	8.0	8.0	13.6
Median income, 1959 (in 1968 dollars)	$2,732	$4,302	a/	$4,420	$3,718	$2,620	$4,359	$3,655	$1,918

(continued)

Civilians Employed in Current Year, Percent with No Income in Previous Year and Median Annual Money Income (of income recipients) in Previous Year, in Constant 1968 Dollars, by Sex and by Occupational Class, Persons 14 Years Old and Over, United States, 1956-1968 (cont.)

Item	Blue-collar workers			Service workers		Farm workers	
	Crafts-men, foremen, and kindred workers	Opera-tives and kindred workers	Laborers (except farm and mine)	Private house-hold workers	Service workers (except private house-hold)	Farmers and farm managers	Farm laborers and foremen
	H097	H098	H099	H100	H101	H102	H103
MALES (1956)							
Civilians employed, March 1957 (000)	8,413	8,953	3,477	49	2,708	3,064	1,403
Percent with no income in 1956	0.4	1.2	2.3	9.2	2.4	1.2	19.5
Median income, 1956 (in 1968 dollars)	$6,012	$5,084	$3,640	a/	$3,997	$1,933	$1,252
FEMALES (1956)							
Civilians employed, March 1957 (000)	215	3,438	117	2,174	2,700	139	625
Percent with no income in 1956	7.9	6.2	11.1	12.2	11.4	10.1	71.0
Median income, 1956 (in 1968 dollars)	a/	$2,862	a/	$ 765	$1,684	a/	a/
MALES (1957)							
Civilians employed, March 1958 (000)	8,096	8,185	3,117	52	2,690	2,938	1,301
Percent with no income in 1957	0.3	0.8	1.7	3.8	1.7	0.9	17.4
Median income, 1957 (in 1968 dollars)	$6,132	$5,115	$3,774	a/	$3,837	$2,074	$1,352
FEMALES (1957)							
Civilians employed, March 1958 (000)	224	3,175	96	2,223	2,915	115	485
Percent with no income in 1957	3.6	5.3	17.7	13.0	8.1	17.4	71.8
Median income, 1957 (in 1968 dollars)	a/	$2,750	a/	$ 732	$1,750	a/	a/
MALES (1958)							
Civilians employed, March 1959 (000)	8,158	8,324	3,394	43	2,754	2,922	1,417
Percent with no income in 1958	0.1	0.6	2.1	11.6	2.6	1.1	17.1
Median income, 1958 (in 1968 dollars)	$6,150	$4,916	$3,464	a/	$4,012	$2,292	$1,061
FEMALES (1958)							
Civilians employed, March 1959 (000)	199	3,167	90	2,163	3,151	108	558
Percent with no income in 1958	6.0	5.8	20.0	10.9	10.3	23.1	70.1
Median income, 1958 (in 1968 dollars)	a/	$2,644	a/	$ 733	$1,678	a/	a/
MALES (1959)							
Civilians employed, March 1960 (000)	8,154	8,631	3,085	47	2,861	2,632	1,128
Percent with no income in 1959	0.2	1.3	1.7	31.9	2.1	0.5	15.6
Median income, 1959 (in 1968 dollars)	$6,394	$5,112	$3,761	a/	$4,049	$2,270	$1,438
FEMALES (1959)							
Civilians employed, March 1960 (000)	189	3,392	66	2,081	3,240	90	433
Percent with no income in 1959	7.4	5.2	13.6	11.4	9.3	5.6	78.1
Median income, 1959 (in 1968 dollars)	a/	$2,815	a/	$ 768	$1,709	a/	a/

(continued)

Civilians Employed in Current Year, Percent with No Income in Previous Year and Median Annual
Money Income (of income recipients) in Previous Year, in Constant 1968 Dollars, by Sex and
by Occupational Class, Persons 14 Years Old and Over, United States, 1956-1968 (cont.)

Item	Total	White-collar workers (cont.)							
		Professional, techni-cal & kindred workers			Nonfarm managers, officials & proprietors			Clerical and kindred workers	Sales workers
		Total	Self-em-ployed	Sal-aried	Total	Self-em-ployed	Sal-aried		
	H088	H089	H090	H091	H092	H093	H094	H095	H096
MALES (1960)									
Civilians employed, March 1961 (000)	43,103	5,113	781	4,332	6,213	2,989	3,224	3,043	2,805
Percent with no income in 1960	1.5	1.2	1.3	1.2	0.7	0.9	0.4	0.3	2.6
Median income, 1960 (in 1968 dollars)	$5,671	$7,719	$11,225	$7,719	$7,666	$5,922	$8,927	$5,893	$5,868
FEMALES (1960)									
Civilians employed, March 1961 (000)	22,413	2,884	227	2,657	1,117	509	608	6,859	1,704
Percent with no income in 1960	9.8	6.0	4.4	6.2	12.0	15.7	8.9	7.6	16.7
Median income, 1960 (in 1968 dollars)	$2,761	$4,551	a/	$4,728	$3,467	$1,802	$4,384	$3,671	$1,770
MALES (1961)									
Civilians employed, March 1962 (000)	43,646	5,170	732	4,438	6,437	2,990	3,447	3,113	2,633
Percent with no income in 1961	1.7	0.5	1.4	0.4	0.5	0.7	0.3	1.3	2.5
Median income, 1961 (in 1968 dollars)	$5,855	$8,198	$10,046	$8,051	$7,832	$6,379	$8,848	$5,946	$6,001
FEMALES (1961)									
Civilians employed, March 1962 (000)	22,493	3,037	253	2,784	1,152	558	594	6,930	1,634
Percent with no income in 1961	8.8	5.5	6.5	5.7	9.3	10.0	8.6	6.2	15.6
Median income, 1961 (in 1968 dollars)	$2,744	$4,623	$1,811	$4,779	$3,166	$2,002	$3,996	$3,695	$2,009
MALES (1962)									
Civilians employed, March 1963 (000)	43,962	5,363	715	4,648	6,231	2,703	3,528	3,046	2,611
Percent with no income in 1962	1.7	1.2	0	1.4	0.6	0.8	0.4	0.9	2.6
Median income, 1961 (in 1968 dollars)	$6,026	$8,406	$13,805	$8,140	$7,844	$6,655	$8,710	$6,131	$6,174
FEMALES (1962)									
Civilians employed, March 1963 (000)	23,186	3,117	214	2,903	1,078	459	619	7,173	1,637
Percent with no income in 1962	8.9	4.8	8.4	4.5	12.2	21.4	5.3	6.6	12.6
Median income, 1962 (in 1968 dollars)	$2,814	$4,781	a/	$4,892	$3,497	$2,012	$4,340	$3,763	$2,065
MALES (1963)									
Civilians employed, March 1964 (000)	44,730	5,410	745	4,665	6,452	2,735	3,717	3,268	2,647
Percent with no income in 1963	1.6	1.4	0.8	1.5	0.5	0.4	0.7	1.6	2.5
Median income, 1963 (in 1968 dollars)	$6,170	$8,699	$12,983	$8,478	$8,242	$6,397	$9,312	$6,229	$6,622
FEMALES (1963)									
Civilians employed, March 1964 (000)	23,786	3,193	228	2,965	1,133	459	674	7,442	1,669
Percent with no income in 1963	7.8	3.9	3.9	3.9	7.6	9.4	6.4	5.9	12.3
Median income, 1963 (in 1968 dollars)	$2,854	$4,794	$2,130	$4,919	$3,427	$2,264	$4,179	$3,811	$1,935

(continued)

Civilians Employed in Current Year, Percent with No Income in Previous Year and Median Annual
Money Income (of income recipients) in Previous Year, in Constant 1968 Dollars, by Sex and
by Occupational Class, Persons 14 Years Old and Over, United States, 1956-1968 (cont.)

Item	Blue-collar workers (cont.)			Service workers (cont.)		Farm workers (cont.)	
	Crafts-men, foremen, and kindred workers	Opera-tives and kindred workers	Laborers (except farm and mine)	Private house-hold workers	Service workers (except private house-hold)	Farmers and farm managers	Farm laborers and foremen
	H097	H098	H099	H100	H101	H102	H103
MALES (1960)							
Civilians employed, March 1961 (000)	7,956	8,077	2,886	49	2,897	2,621	1,443
Percent with no income in 1960	0.01	0.9	2.6	8.2	1.7	1.2	16.4
Median income, 1960 (in 1968 dollars)	$6,564	$5,265	$3,373	a/	$4,013	$2,283	$1,297
FEMALES (1960)							
Civilians employed, March 1961 (000)	219	3,227	83	2,386	3,265	134	535
Percent with no income in 1960	7.8	4.8	12.0	10.0	9.7	14.2	60.7
Median income, 1960 (in 1968 dollars)	$3,675	$2,927	a/	$ 722	$1,924	a/	$ 485
MALES (1961)							
Civilians employed, March 1962 (000)	7,985	8,434	3,046	62	2,911	2,530	1,325
Percent with no income in 1961	0.3	1.4	3.7	6.5	2.5	1.3	17.4
Median income, 1961 (in 1968 dollars)	$6,559	$5,378	$3,651	a/	$4,064	$2,602	$1,358
FEMALES (1961)							
Civilians employed, March 1962 (000)	233	3,157	102	2,397	3,292	135	424
Percent with no income in 1961	6.9	4.9	10.8	9.0	9.1	15.6	68.9
Median income, 1961 (in 1968 dollars)	$3,475	$2,833	a/	$ 669	$1,778	a/	a/
MALES (1962)							
Civilians employed, March 1963 (000)	8,218	8,768	3,031	66	3,154	2,261	1,213
Percent with no income in 1962	0.5	1.9	3.6	4.5	1.7	0.4	12.4
Median income, 1962 (in 1968 dollars)	$6,752	$5,557	$3,682	a/	$4,237	$2,704	$1,556
FEMALES (1962)							
Civilians employed, March 1963 (000)	242	3,416	102	2,295	3,572	120	434
Percent with no income in 1962	9.5	4.6	14.7	11.1	10.4	12.5	63.8
Median income, 1962 (in 1968 dollars)	$3,622	$2,934	a/	$ 724	$1,760	a/	a/
MALES (1963)							
Civilians employed, March 1964 (000)	8,259	9,074	3,127	60	3,213	2,088	1,132
Percent with no income in 1963	0.4	1.0	2.7	10.0	2.6	1.5	14.8
Median income, 1963 (in 1968 dollars)	$6,831	$5,736	$3,541	a/	$4,355	$2,553	$1,321
FEMALES (1963)							
Civilians employed, March 1964 (000)	244	3,592	87	2,242	3,664	126	394
Percent with no income in 1963	2.9	4.8	21.8	10.6	8.0	10.3	65.2
Median income, 1963 (in 1968 dollars)	$3,488	$3,017	a/	$ 708	$1,744	a/	a/

(continued)

Civilians Employed in Current Year, Percent with No Income in Previous Year and Median Annual Money Income (of income recipients) in Previous Year, in Constant 1968 Dollars, by Sex and by Occupational Class, Persons 14 Years Old and Over, United States, 1956-1968 (cont.)

Item	Total	White-collar workers (cont.)							
		Professional, techni-cal & kindred workers			Nonfarm managers, officials & proprietors			Clerical and kindred workers	Sales workers
		Total	Self-em-ployed	Sal-aried	Total	Self-em-ployed	Sal-aried		
	H088	H089	H090	H091	H092	H093	H094	H095	H096
MALES (1964)									
Civilians employed, March 1965 (000)	45,675	5,586	774	4,812	6,381	2,569	3,812	3,255	2,780
Percent with no income in 1964	1.4	1.1	0.4	1.2	0.5	0.04	0.8	0.7	2.2
Median income, 1964 (in 1968 dollars)	$6,263	$8,912	$14,039	$8,656	$8,366	$6,571	$6,501	$6,461	$7,026
FEMALES (1964)									
Civilians employed, March 1965 (000)	24,494	3,448	252	3,196	1,102	441	661	7,707	1,767
Percent with no income in 1964	7.7	4.1	3.6	4.1	8.3	9.1	7.8	6.0	12.6
Median income, 1964 (in 1968 dollars)	$2,990	$4,951	$2,350	$5,101	$3,839	$2,902	$4,895	$3,931	$2,142
MALES (1965)									
Civilians employed, March 1965 (000)	46,393	5,774	7272	5,047	6,223	2,314	3,909	3,316	2,944
Percent with no income in 1965	1.4	0.6	0.7	0.6	0.2	0.4	0.1	1.5	2.4
Median income, 1965 (in 1968 dollars)	$6,361	$8,727	$12,025	$8,605	$8,666	$7,096	$9,537	$6,338	$6,572
FEMALES (1965)									
Civilians employed, March 1965 (000)	25,630	3,522	216	3,306	1,124	415	709	8,213	1,789
Percent with no income in 1965	8.1	4.1	5.1	4.0	9.4	11.6	8.2	6.5	13.6
Median income, 1965 (in 1968 dollars)	$3,138	$5,183	$2,711	$5,352	$3,861	$1,985	$4,633	$4,005	$2,363
MALES (1966)									
Civilians employed, March 1967 (000)	46,934	6,190	713	5,477	6,187	1,799	4,388	3,391	2,825
Percent with no income in 1966	1.5	0.6	0.3	0.7	0.4	0.6	0.3	1.4	2.4
Median income, 1966 (in 1968 dollars)	$6,740	$9,405	$14,307	$9,157	$9,302	$7,194	$10,060	$6,506	$7,008
FEMALES (1966)									
Civilians employed, March 1967 (000)	26,620	3,760	184	3,576	1,108	339	769	8,671	1,860
Percent with no income in 1966	7.9	4.7	6.5	4.6	8.7	12.1	7.2	6.2	11.9
Median income, 1966 (in 1968 dollars)	$3,160	$5,190	$2,579	$5,300	$4,207	$2,319	$4,750	$3,894	$2,310
MALES (1967)									
Civilians employed, March 1968 (000)	47,622	6,492	712	5,780	6,555	1,870	4,685	3,409	2,881
Percent with no income in 1967	1.3	0.6	0.8	0.5	0.4	0.7	0.2	1.1	1.5
Median income, 1967 (in 1968 dollars)	$6,888	$9,764	$14,729	$9,534	$9,656	$7,543	$10,339	$6,648	$7,100
FEMALES (1967)									
Civilians employed, March 1968 (000)	27,887	4,047	235	3,812	1,220	372	848	9,139	1,864
Percent with no income in 1967	6.0	3.4	5.1	3.3	4.1	8.1	2.4	5.0	10.4
Median income, 1967 (in 1968 dollars)	$3,290	$5,429	$2,155	$5,561	$4,662	$2,913	$5,267	$4,005	$2,205

(continued)

Civilians Employed in Current Year, Percent with No Income in Previous Year and Median Annual Money Income (of income recipients) in Previous Year, in Constant 1968 Dollars, by Sex and by Occupational Class, Persons 14 Years Old and Over, United States, 1954-1968 (cont.)

Item	Blue-collar workers (cont.)			Service workers (cont.)		Farm workers (cont.)	
	Crafts-men, foremen, and kindred workers	Opera-tives and kindred workers	Laborers (except farm and mine)	Private house-hold workers	Service workers (except private house-hold)	Farmers and farm managers	Farm laborers and foremen
	H097	H098	H099	H100	H101	H102	H103
MALES (1964)							
Civilians employed, March 1965 (000)	8,456	9,379	3,444	56	3,142	2,110	1,086
Percent with no income in 1964	0.4	1.1	2.8	16.1	2.4	0.6	14.3
Median income, 1964 (in 1968 dollars)	$7,026	$5,751	$3,653	a/	$4,557	$2,663	$1,457
FEMALES (1964)							
Civilians employed, March (1965 (000)	265	3,753	120	2,119	3,701	116	396
Percent with no income in 1964	1.5	4.9	12.5	11.4	7.4	9.5	63.1
Median income, 1964 (in 1968 dollars)	$3,521	$3,092	a/	$ 739	$1,823	a/	a/
MALES (1965)							
Civilians employed, March 1966 (000)	8,826	9,726	3,255	59	3,274	1,975	1,021
Percent with no income in 1965	0.4	0.9	4.0	15.3	3.1	0.4	10.7
Median income, 1965 (in 1968 dollars)	$7,135	$5,865	$3,687	a/	$4,487	$3,296	$1,602
FEMALES (1965)							
Civilians employed, March 1966 (000)	227	3,990	103	2,192	3,966	130	374
Percent with no income in 1965	6.2	5.2	11.7	10.6	8.2	17.7	63.4
Median income, 1965 (in 1968 dollars)	$3,803	$3,107	a/	$ 845	$2,042	a/	a/
MALES (1966)							
Civilians employed, March 1967 (000)	9,305	9,535	3,130	60	3,445	1,791	1,075
Percent with no income in 1966	0.3	1.2	3.4	15.0	3.2	0.4	14.0
Median income, 1966 (in 1968 dollars)	$7,409	$6,073	$3,773	a/	$4,432	$3,708	$1,859
FEMALES (1966)							
Civilians employed, March 1967 (000)	271	4,128	89	2,114	4,189	75	355
Percent with no income in 1966	7.0	5.5	11.2	11.4	8.0	18.7	61.1
Median income, 1966 (in 1968 dollars)	$3,736	$3,201	$2,900	$ 791	$2,015	a/	$ 649
MALES (1967)							
Civilians employed, March 1968 (000)	9,240	9,619	3,192	61	3,303	1,827	1,044
Percent with no income in 1967	0.4	1.0	3.2	11.5	2.5	0.3	12.2
Median income, 1967 (in 1968 dollars)	$7,527	$6,104	$4,146	a/	$4,722	$3,583	$1,767
FEMALES (1967)							
Civilians employed, March 1968 (000)	291	4,217	112	2,150	4,380	92	376
Percent with no income in 1967	3.4	4.0	11.6	8.7	7.3	15.2	59.8
Median income, 1967 (in 1968 dollars)	$3,987	$3,353	$2,738	$ 797	$2,163	$1,386	$ 611

(continued)

Civilians Employed in Current Year, Percent with No Income in Previous Year and Median Annual
Money Income (of income recipients) in Previous Year, in Constant 1968 Dollars, by Sex and
by Occupational Class, Persons 14 Years Old and Over, United States, 1956-1968 (cont.)

Item	Total	White-collar workers (cont.)							
		Professional, techni-cal & kindred workers			Nonfarm managers, officials & proprietors			Clerical and kindred workers	Sales workers
		Total	Self-em-ployed	Sal-aried	Total	Self-em-ployed	Sal-aried		
	H088	H089	H090	H091	H092	H093	H094	H095	H096

MALES (1968) Civilians employed, March 1969 (000)	48,538	6,797	677	6,120	6,657	1,879	4,778	3,329	2,818
Percent with no income in 1968	1.3	0.6	0.7	0.6	0.3	0.5	0.2	1.2	2.1
Median income, 1968	$7,080	$9,960	$16,356	$9,715	$9,765	$7,365	$10,717	$7,034	$7,367
FEMALES (1968) Civilians employed, March 1969 (000)	29,079	4,144	219	3,925	1,239	379	861	9,712	1,932
Percent with no income in 1968	6.6	2.6	5.0	2.4	4.4	8.2	2.7	5.5	9.0
Median income, 1968	$4,380	$5,598	$1,803	$5,733	$4,616	$2,902	$5,192	$4,002	$2,248

Item	Blue-collar workers (cont.)			Service workers (cont.)		Farm workers (cont.)	
	Crafts-men, foremen, and kindred workers	Opera-tives and kindred workers	Laborers (except farm and mine)	Private house-hold workers	Service workers (except private house-hold)	Farmers and farm managers	Farm laborers and foremen
	H097	H098	H099	H100	H101	H102	H103

MALES (1968) Civilians employed, March 1969 (000)	9,511	9,963	3,391	55	3,290	1,726	1,000
Percent with no income in 1968	0.3	1.3	2.6	7.3	2.8	0.1	12.6
Median income, 1968	$7,705	$6,209	$4,165	a/	$4,820	$3,734	$2,073
FEMALES (1968) Civilians employed, March 1969 (000)	318	4,321	123	2,015	4,833	68	374
Percent with no income in 1968	5.0	4.5	8.1	11.9	6.8	11.8	65.0
Median income, 1968	$4,145	$3,506	$2,984	$ 806	$2,226	a/	$ 795

Median Annual Total Money Income of Persons (income recipients) 25 Years Old and Over, by Years of School Completed, and by Age* Group and Sex, United States, 1963-1968
(In constant 1968 dollars)

Age group and year	Years of school completed											
	Less than 8 years		8 years		1-3 years high school		4-years high school		1-3 years college		4 or more years college	
	Male	Female	Male	Female	Male	Female	Male	Female	Male	Female	Male	Female
25 years and over	H104	H105	H106	H107	H108	H109	H110	H111	H112	H113	H114	H115
1963	$2,723	$ 967	$4,630	$1,347	$5,854	$1,797	$6,815	$2,599	$7,727	$2,643	$ 9,073	$4,583
1964	2,825	979	4,465	1,454	6,000	1,834	7,024	2,656	7,883	2,798	9,870	4,885
1965	2,841	1,000	4,644	1,531	6,104	2,013	7,123	2,806	7,966	2,952	9,980	5,144
1966	2,984	1,082	4,843	1,505	6,413	2,051	7,423	2,865	8,264	3,031	10,548	5,111
1967	3,116	1,133	4,979	1,437	6,416	2,126	7,548	3,031	8,498	3,212	10,998	5,390
1968	3,333	1,238	5,096	1,590	6,569	2,177	7,731	3,073	8,618	3,247	11,257	5,305
1969												
1970												
25-34 years	H116	H117	H118	H119	H120	H121	H122	H123	H124	H125	H126	H127
1963	3,339	1,227	4,927	1,551	5,570	1,595	6,375	2,465	6,901	2,661	7,892	3,720
1964	3,329	1,331	4,838	1,613	5,675	1,718	6,651	2,613	7,158	2,538	8,292	4,416
1965	3,399	1,073	4,936	1,903	5,795	1,894	6,785	2,739	7,430	3,446	8,244	5,039
1966	4,109	1,440	5,061	1,726	6,094	1,977	7,075	2,808	7,650	3,235	8,976	4,538
1967	3,953	1,719	5,367	1,730	6,171	2,250	7,171	2,893	7,720	3,295	9,130	5,014
1968	4,169	1,636	5,544	1,803	6,266	2,153	7,402	3,029	7,888	3,291	9,363	5,109
1969												
1970												
35-44 years	H128	H129	H130	H131	H132	H133	H134	H135	H136	H137	H138	H139
1963	3,976	1,330	5,735	1,997	6,509	2,212	7,423	2,758	8,638	3,119	10,369	3,923
1964	4,376	1,609	5,669	2,199	6,759	2,217	7,529	2,898	8,522	3,005	11,274	4,240
1965	4,266	1,581	5,757	2,206	6,748	2,459	7,765	3,155	8,984	3,455	11,537	4,837
1966	4,347	1,699	6,078	2,112	7,038	2,531	8,063	3,151	9,446	3,014	12,180	5,373
1967	4,582	1,706	6,174	2,307	6,895	2,581	8,156	3,308	9,543	3,660	12,855	5,407
1968	5,131	2,048	6,457	2,374	7,233	2,649	8,521	3,257	9,778	3,479	12,748	5,283
1969												
1970												
45-54 years	H140	H141	H142	H143	H144	H145	H146	H147	H148	H149	H150	H151
1963	4,014	1,064	5,820	2,048	6,409	2,400	7,344	3,218	8,439	3,846	11,822	5,886
1964	4,113	1,447	5,705	2,133	6,500	2,442	7,553	3,063	9,059	3,597	12,362	5,741
1965	4,033	1,576	5,989	2,299	6,740	2,707	7,674	3,366	9,623	3,770	13,054	6,106
1966	4,225	1,562	6,190	2,451	7,156	2,632	8,101	3,463	9,526	3,741	13,028	6,298
1967	4,511	1,527	6,366	2,416	7,236	2,585	8,221	3,650	9,620	4,300	13,553	6,594
1968	4,720	1,770	6,393	2,610	7,372	2,854	8,349	3,590	9,698	3,930	13,180	6,541
1969												
1970												
55-64 years	H152	H153	H154	H155	H156	H157	H158	H159	H160	H161	H162	H163
1963	3,244	1,038	5,194	1,765	5,741	2,027	6,725	3,069	7,952	2,740	11,983	5,721
1964	3,399	1,054	5,150	1,852	5,701	1,893	7,076	2,780	7,660	3,610	11,356	6,247
1965	3,309	1,051	5,397	2,000	6,102	2,109	7,308	3,087	7,505	3,075	10,581	6,060
1966	3,575	1,147	5,715	1,917	6,557	2,303	7,241	3,102	8,149	3,802	11,720	6,314
1967	3,784	1,240	5,700	1,861	6,623	2,367	7,324	3,211	8,793	3,688	12,333	6,635
1968	4,165	1,346	5,894	2,078	6,797	2,266	7,707	3,278	8,778	3,762	13,222	6,247
1969												
1970												

* - Age as of March of the year following the income year.

Percent Distribution of Persons 14 Years of Age and Over by Employment Status, March of Following Year and Money Income Status (current year), by Sex, United States, 1956-1968

Year (of income status) and sex	Total number of persons 14 years of age and over (000)	Percent distribution by employment status in March of following year							
		Employed				Unemployed			
		Having money income in current year		Without money income in current year		Having money income in current year		Without money income in current year	
		Male	Female	Male	Female	Male	Female	Male	Female
	H164	H165	H166	H167	H168	H169	H170	H171	H172
1956									
Male	56,591	75.1		1.3		3.1		0.3	
Female	61,304		29.8		3.8		1.2		0.3
1957									
Male	57,583	71.4		1.1		6.2		0.3	
Female	62,219		29.6		3.4		1.9		0.4
1958									
Male	58,378	72.2		1.2		4.7		0.4	
Female	62,995		29.6		3.7		1.7		0.5
1959									
Male	59,394	71.3		1.1		4.5		0.4	
Female	64,042		29.8		3.4		1.5		0.5
1960									
Male	60,359	70.3		1.1		5.7		0.5	
Female	65,282		31.0		3.4		2.1		0.4
1961									
Male	61,098	70.2		1.2		4.3		0.4	
Female	66,420		30.9		3.0		1.7		0.5
1962									
Male	62,189	69.5		1.2		4.3		0.5	
Female	67,628		31.2		3.1		1.6		0.6
1963									
Male	63,103	69.7		1.1		3.8		0.5	
Female	68,709		31.9		2.7		1.9		0.5
1964									
Male	64,012	70.3		1.0		3.2		0.4	
Female	69,871		32.3		2.7		1.6		0.4
1965									
Male	64,636	70.8		1.0		2.6		0.3	
Female	70,991		33.2		2.9		1.3		0.4
1966									
Male	65,335	70.8		1.1		2.3		0.3	
Female	72,224		34.0		2.9		1.4		0.4
1967									
Male	66,519	70.7		0.9		2.3		0.2	
Female	73,584		35.5		2.4		1.4		0.4
1968									
Male	67,611	70.9		0.9		2.0		0.2	
Female	74,889		36.3		2.6		1.4		0.4

(continued)

Percent Distribution of Persons 14 Years of Age and Over by Employment
Status, March of Following Year and Money Income Status (current
year), by Sex, United States, 1956-1968 (cont.)

Year (of income status) and sex	Percent distribution by employment status in March of following year			
	In armed forces or not in labor force			
	Having money income in current year		Without money income in current year	
	Male	Female	Male	Female
	H173	H174	H175	H176
1956				
Male	13.6		6.5	
Female		20.9		44.0
1957				
Male	14.2		6.8	
Female		21.0		43.7
1958				
Male	14.8		6.7	
Female		21.6		42.8
1959				
Male	15.6		7.0	
Female		22.4		42.4
1960				
Male	15.4		7.0	
Female		22.9		40.1
1961				
Male	16.9		6.9	
Female		24.7		39.2
1962				
Male	17.2		7.3	
Female		24.8		38.7
1963				
Male	17.9		7.0	
Female		25.0		38.1
1964				
Male	17.9		7.2	
Female		25.7		37.2
1965				
Male	18.2		7.2	
Female		25.0		37.2
1966				
Male	18.9		6.7	
Female		25.6		35.7
1967				
Male	19.4		6.5	
Female		26.9		33.4
1968				
Male	19.6		6.4	
Female		27.2		32.2

Median Annual Money Income, and First and Fourth Quintiles of Annual Money Income a/ for Families, by Type of Family, and for Male and Female Unrelated Individuals, United States, 1956-1968 (Income in constant 1968 dollars)

Year	First quintile of annual money income (1968 dollars)	Median annual money income (1968 dollars)	Fourth quintile of annual money income (1968 dollars)	Interquintile range (fourth quintile minus first quintile)	Coefficient (range divided by median)	First quintile of annual money income (1968 dollars)	Median annual money income (1968 dollars)	Fourth quintile of annual money income (1968 dollars)	Interquintile range (fourth quintile minus first quintile)	Coefficient (range divided by median)

	All families with male head					Families with male head and wife present and in paid labor force				
	H177	H178	H179	H180	H181	H182	H183	H184	H185	H186
1956	$3,480	$6,355	$10,124	$6,644	1.05	$4,623	$7,625	$11,360	$6,737	0.88
1957	3,481	6,380	10,010	6,529	1.02	4,600	7,596	11,272	6,672	0.88
1958	3,478	6,372	10,155	6,677	1.05	4,548	7,482	11,191	6,643	0.89
1959	3,651	6,720	10,502	6,851	1.02	4,855	8,006	11,572	6,717	0.84
1960	3,707	6,888	10,859	7,152	1.04	4,833	8,114	12,130	7,297	0.90
1961	3,717	7,000	11,090	7,373	1.05	4,961	8,360	12,688	7,727	0.92
1962	3,894	7,173	11,309	7,415	1.03	5,189	8,580	13,334	8,145	0.95
1963	4,033	7,453	11,696	7,663	1.03	5,447	8,848	12,975	7,528	0.85
1964	4,139	7,716	12,143	8,004	1.04	5,688	9,159	13,259	7,571	0.83
1965	4,234	7,980	12,473	8,239	1.03	5,935	9,482	13,832	7,897	0.83
1966	4,678	8,365	12,864	8,186	0.98	6,264	9,912	14,462	8,198	0.83
1967	4,967	8,753	13,754	8,787	1.00	6,574	10,374	15,061	8,487	0.82
1968	5,227	9,096	14,133	8,906	0.98	6,889	10,686	15,640	8,751	0.82
1969										
1970										

	Families with male head and wife present and not in paid labor force					Families with female head				
	H187	H188	H189	H190	H191	H192	H193	H194	H195	H196
1956	$3,151	$5,946	$9,225	$6,074	1.02	$1,244	$3,525	$6,899	$5,655	1.60
1957	3,120	5,978	9,063	5,943	0.99	1,274	3,418	6,670	5,396	1.58
1958	3,194	6,000	9,454	6,260	1.04	1,303	3,300	6,571	5,268	1.60
1959	3,336	6,348	9,657	6,321	1.00	1,356	3,300	6,751	5,395	1.63
1960	3,346	6,492	10,121	6,775	1.04	1,435	3,490	6,902	5,467	1.57
1961	3,299	6,503	10,376	7,077	1.09	1,361	3,481	6,758	5,397	1.55
1962	3,498	6,629	10,601	7,103	1.07	1,421	3,601	7,123	5,702	1.58
1963	3,585	6,860	10,792	7,207	1.05	1,465	3,648	7,247	5,782	1.58
1964	3,612	7,105	11,237	7,625	1.07	1,711	3,876	7,594	5,883	1.52
1965	3,694	7,271	11,595	7,901	1.09	1,738	3,896	7,546	5,808	1.49
1966	3,941	7,641	12,045	8,104	1.06	1,961	4,299	7,929	5,968	1.39
1967	4,184	7,931	12,427	8,243	1.04	2,076	4,474	8,128	6,052	1.35
1968	4,500	8,215	13,086	8,586	1.05	2,086	4,477	8,333	6,247	1.40
1969										
1970										

	Unrelated male individuals					Unrelated female individuals				
	H197	H198	H199	H200	H201	H202	H203	H204	H205	H206
1956	$ 878	$2,534	$5,522	$4,644	1.83	$ 622	$1,485	$3,741	$3,119	2.10
1957	891	2,600	5,480	4,589	1.76	632	1,564	3,916	3,284	2.10
1958	858	2,545	5,668	4,810	1.89	592	1,527	3,973	3,381	2.21
1959	874	2,529	5,772	4,898	1.94	597	1,574	3,925	3,328	2.11
1960	1,008	2,916	6,194	5,186	1.78	663	1,619	4,214	3,551	2.19
1961	1,027	3,068	6,626	5,589	1.82	665	1,636	3,941	3,276	2.00
1962	1,097	2,704	6,609	5,512	2.04	768	1,680	4,368	3,600	2.14
1963	1,130	2,754	6,816	5,686	2.06	683	1,677	4,445	3,762	2.24
1964	1,211	3,324	7,119	5,908	1.78	723	1,743	4,608	3,885	2.23
1965	1,297	3,248	7,208	5,911	1.82	788	1,916	4,964	4,176	2.18
1966	1,360	3,589	7,542	6,182	1.72	900	1,955	4,783	3,883	1.99
1967	1,381	3,693	7,730	6,349	1.60	891	2,004	4,950	4,059	2.03
1968	1,500	4,086	8,128	6,628	1.62	1,072	2,239	5,155	4,083	1.82
1969										
1970										

400

Median Annual Money Income (in constant /1968/ dollars) of Income Recipients who have Completed Specified Years of Schooling, by Color or Race and by Sex, United States, Persons 14 Years Old and Over, 1961 and 1963; Persons 25 Years and Over, 1964-1968

Age and year	White		Nonwhite (1961-66) Negro (1967-68)		White		Nonwhite (1961-66) Negro (1967-68)	
	Male	Female	Male	Female	Male	Female	Male	Female
	Less than 8 years schooling				8 years of schooling			
	H207	H208	H209	H210	H211	H212	H213	H214
14 years and over[a]								
1961	$2,678	$ 950	$1,807	$ 825	$4,207	$1,111	$2,913	$1,069
1963	2,735	994	1,966	820	4,259	1,196	3,113	1,091
25 years and over								
1964	3,015	1,022	2,238	862	4,532	1,493	3,873	1,121
1965	2,992	1,025	2,355	935	4,799	1,529	3,403	1,572
1966	3,157	1,131	2,547	999	4,943	1,518	3,946	1,397
1967	3,249	1,168	2,648	1,014	5,086	1,443	3,892	1,337
1968	3,526	1,284	2,716	1,085	5,184	1,607	4,261	1,456
1969								
1970								
	1-3 years high school				4 years high school			
	H215	H216	H217	H218	H219	H220	H221	H222
14 years and over[a]								
1961	4,757	1,158	2,823	1,149	5,995	2,285	3,932	1,821
1963	4,714	1,131	2,793	1,095	6,362	2,497	4,341	1,894
25 years and over								
1964	6,207	1,862	4,189	1,668	7,162	2,695	4,750	2,238
1965	6,363	2,089	4,273	1,618	7,252	2,841	5,012	2,505
1966	6,635	2,101	4,586	1,820	7,577	2,894	5,562	2,653
1967	6,677	2,129	4,622	2,080	7,688	3,047	5,564	2,826
1968	6,760	2,194	4,976	2,116	7,875	3,078	5,721	2,987
1969								
1970								
	Any college							
	H223	H224	H225	H226				
14 years and over[a]								
1961	7,419	2,785	4,938	2,803				
1963	7,758	2,874	4,624	3,299				
25 years and over								
1964	9,197	3,736	6,096	4,038				
1965	9,274	3,878	6,165	4,464				
1966	9,673	3,772	6,355	4,249				
1967	9,890	4,062	6,813	4,693				
1968	9,980	3,945	7,291	5,126				
1969								
1970								

Persons Below Poverty Level[a]/ by Sex and Color of Head of Family (or of Unrelated Individuals), United States, 1959-1969

| Color and year | Persons in families below poverty level having - | | | | Unrelated individuals (14 years of age and older) below poverty level | | | |
| | Male Head | | Female head | | Male | | Female | |
	Number of persons (000)	Percent of all persons in all families with male head	Number of persons (000)	Percent of all persons in all families with female head	Number (000)	Percent of all unrelated individuals	Number (000)	Percent of all unrelated individuals
	H227	H228	H229	H230	H231	H232	H233	H234
White								
1959	20,211	14.7	4,232	40.2	1,158	33.8	2,883	50.3
1960	19,966	14.4	4,296	39.0	1,136	33.3	2,911	48.6
1961	19,685	14.1	4,062	37.6	1,157	32.4	2,986	49.6
1962	18,524	13.0	4,089	37.9	1,133	32.5	2,926	48.7
1963	17,098	11.9	4,051	35.6	1,158	32.2	2,931	47.8
1964	16,805	11.6	3,911	33.4	1,106	29.4	3,135	47.1
1965	14,416	9.8	4,092	35.4	995	27.2	2,993	43.9
1966	12,840	8.7	3,892	32.4	997	26.1	3,022	43.4
(Revised method[b]/)								
1966	11,784	8.0	3,646	29.7	995	26.6	2,865	41.2
1967	11,398	7.7	3,453	28.5	985	24.9	3,147	42.8
1968	9,995	6.7	3,551	29.1	1,000	23.3	2,849	37.1
1969	9,108	6.1	3,601	28.9	1,048	23.4	2,914	36.4
Nonwhite	H235	H236	H237	H238	H239	H240	H241	H242
1959	7,337	51.0	2,782	75.6	394	49.6	493	65.6
1960	7,712	50.2	2,951	77.7	374	48.6	505	70.8
1961	7,572	50.2	3,190	74.7	416	51.9	560	74.4
1962	7,318	48.0	3,692	78.9	419	54.3	524	70.2
1963	6,754	42.6	3,595	77.2	329	48.1	520	67.3
1964	6,810	42.4	3,386	72.0	363	43.4	539	67.0
1965	6,418	39.5	3,432	71.5	298	36.8	541	64.1
1966	5,474	32.8	3,408	68.9	268	36.0	523	62.3
(Revised method[b]/)								
1966	5,164	31.2	3,215	64.6	317	42.4	524	62.7
1967	4,475	27.7	3,445	60.9	320	36.2	546	59.8
1968	3,710	22.9	3,439	58.7	320	34.8	525	56.7
1969	3,332	20.0	3,398	57.9	332	34.3	557	55.1

Year	Persons aged 65 years and over			
	Male		Female	
	Number (000)	Percent with no money income	Number (000)	Percent with no money income
	H243	H244	H245	H246
1956	6,577	5.6	7,716	28.6
1957	6,658	4.8	7,912	28.2
1958	6,770	3.8	8,137	26.9
1959	6,883	3.2	8,373	24.9
1960	6,970	3.6	8,601	23.6
1961	7,469	2.8	9,193	21.7
1962	7,525	1.7	9,401	79.7
1963	7,542	1.6	9,508	79.8
1964	7,635	1.9	9,727	18.0
1965	7,713	0.9	9,937	18.2
1966	7,785	0.7	10,152	16.7
1967	7,872	1.0	10,373	16.7
1968	7,954	0.7	10,595	17.0
1969				
1970				

Item	Series No.	1961	1964	1968	Average annual rate (percent) of increase or decrease (-)		
					1961-1964	1964-1968	1961-1968

Numbers in thousands

Item	Series No.	1961	1964	1968	1961-1964	1964-1968	1961-1968
FEMALE POPULATION (July 1)							
Total noninstitutional, 14 years & over	I001	65,873	69,097	74,080	1.6	1.8	1.7
Total noninstitutional, 18 years & over	I002	59,983	62,138	66,727	1.2	1.8	1.5
ORGANIZATIONS WITH FEMALE MEMBERS ONLY							
Estimated total membership	I003	45,623.6	48,887.7	52,656.6	2.3	1.9	2.1
Percent distribution by type of organization:	I004		Percent				
Girls' organizations	I004	9.7	9.8	9.6	2.5	1.4	1.9
Education	I005	2.9	2.8	2.6	1.1	0.0	0.5
Business, industry & professional (except education and sports)	I006	1.1	1.1	1.1	2.6	1.9	2.2
Women veterans	I007	0.2	0.2	0.2	1.9	-1.0	0.2
Public affairs	I008	1.4	1.3	1.2	0.3	0.5	0.4
Federated clubs (not classified elsewhere)	I009	2.0	1.9	1.7	-0.2	-0.1	-0.1
Social service	I010	0.6	0.6	0.6	1.5	2.1	1.9
Social welfare (non-professional)	I011	5.7	5.6	5.3	1.6	0.6	1.0
Rural life, farm, and garden	I012	15.1	13.8	12.6	-0.6	-0.4	-0.5
Sports and recreation	I013	3.3	5.1	5.4	18.5	3.1	9.4
Religious-affiliated	I014	45.5	46.2	48.9	2.8	3.3	3.1
Fraternal and ethnic	I015	8.7	8.1	7.5	0.1	-0.2	-0.1
Female relatives of members of armed forces	I016	3.2	3.0	2.8	-0.1	0.3	0.1
Hereditary (except ethnic)	I017	0.6	0.6	0.5	-0.6	0.0	-0.2

Numbers in thousands

Item	Series No.	1961	1964	1968	1961-1964	1964-1968	1961-1968
PRIMARILY OR LARGELY FEMALE MEMBERSHIP							
Estimated total membership	I018	15,267.2	13,549.8	14,804.1	0.6	-1.2	-0.4
Percent distribution by type of organization:			Percent				
Education	I019	89.2	89.5	88.9	0.7	-1.4	-0.5
Medical	I020	2.1	2.1	2.6	0.6	4.3	2.7
Occupations (except education and medical)	I021	0.7	0.8	1.1	4.7	6.7	5.8
Social welfare (non-professional)	I022	5.1	4.6	4.2	-2.3	-3.5	-3.0
Garden	I023	2.9	3.0	3.2	1.1	0.3	0.7

Membership in Girls' and Women's Voluntary Associations, and Women Members of Labor Unions, United States, 1940-1969 (numbers in thousands)

Calendar year	Girls' organizations — Girl Scouts of U.S.A. (girl members)	Education — American Association of University Women	Industry, business, professions — National Federation of Business and Professional Women's clubs	Industry, business, professions — National Secretaries Association	Industry, business, professions — National & international labor unions: estimated female membership in U. S.	Public affairs — League of Women Voters (yr. beginning April 1)	Social service — P.E.O. Sisterhood (yr. beginning April 1)
	I024	I025	I026	I027	I028	I029	I030
1940	509.0	69.7	74.4			50.5	71.7
1941	536.0	72.4	75.9			50.8	
1942	578.0	70.9	74.9			48.1	76.7
1943	683.0	70.2	76.4			49.2	
1944	831.0	75.6	85.2			52.1	84.0
1945	907.0	83.0	96.4			62.5	
1946	930.0	90.6	110.4			70.4	92.2
1947	1,092.0	96.1	128.4			83.1	
1948	973.0	103.1	142.7	9.7		88.9	100.8
1949	1,108.0	110.6	150.2	11.0		93.1	
1950	1,214.0	115.4	154.5	10.0		100.3	108.2
1951	1,337.0	119.0	158.1			105.8	
1952	1,476.0	122.7	160.1	12.0		121.9	116.0
1953	1,569.0	128.7	161.3	12.0		126.0	
1954	1,792.0	134.3	163.8	13.0	2,775.0	126.8	123.3
1955	1,944.0	138.6	167.5	15.0		125.7	
1956	2,193.0	141.2	170.5	16.5	3,205.0	127.9	130.1
1957	2,290.0	143.8	172.5	18.0		125.5	
1958	2,446.0	143.5	173.8	19.4	3,055.0	126.8	136.3
1959	2,492.0	143.3	174.4	20.8		127.3	139.2
1960	2,518.0	146.4	174.3	21.8	3,097.0	132.2	142.3
1961	2,535.0	149.7	171.4	22.2		131.9	145.4
1962	2,689.0	153.2	168.6	22.5	3,058.0	134.9	148.4
1963	2,778.0	156.5	168.7	23.2		135.6	151.8
1964	2,981.0	162.6	171.6	23.6	3,169.0	145.5	155.3
1965	3,021.0	169.3	175.5	24.3		146.3	159.0
1966	2,988.0	172.8	177.8	24.9	3,430.0	145.4	162.8
1967	3,121.0	175.0	178.4	25.8		149.3	165.8
1968	3,264.0	173.2	178.3	26.2	3,661.0	156.8	169.3
1969	3,298.0			26.3		155.6	172.9
1970							

(continued)

404

Calendar year	Social welfare	Rural life, farm, and garden	Religious-affiliated			Armed services	Hereditary
	Association of Junior Leagues of America	Federal Extension Home Economics Clubs	B'nai B'rith Women	Catholic Daughters of America	Wesleyan Service Guild	American Legion Auxiliary	National Society Daughters of the American Revolution
	I031	I032	I033	I034	I035	I036	I037
1940		1,140.7				501.4	143.2
1941		1,178.2					143.9
1942	35.0	1,258.9				535.3	144.3
1943		1,161.0	40.5				144.5
1944	39.0	1,106.9	40.7			569.4	146.7
1945	42.0	1,126.3	56.2			635.3	150.3
1946	44.0	1,162.3	75.9			775.0	154.1
1947	46.5	1,231.7	85.2			924.6	158.9
1948	49.0	1,313.5	107.9			949.8	163.6
1949	49.0	1,341.7	113.9		98.5	967.4	166.6
1950	53.4	1,408.7	121.2		98.5	963.8	168.7
1951		1,422.6	123.2	200.0		985.0	170.3
1952	59.0	1,432.8	123.7	200.0	110.5		172.3
1953	62.0	1,448.7	120.6	200.0	120.0	975.0	175.5
1954	63.0	1,520.9	121.4	200.0	124.1		179.0
1955	65.0	1,443.0	123.6	200.0	124.1		182.0
1956	69.0	1,403.3	127.9	200.0	127.7	999.1	183.9
1957	70.0	1,372.6	131.2	206.0	130.9		185.0
1958	71.0	1,335.7	131.4	208.0	130.1		185.9
1959	72.5	1,334.2	133.4	210.0	131.2		186.7
1960	78.0	1,304.4	133.2	210.0	131.2		186.7
1961	79.5	1,260.8	133.0	215.0	131.2	950.0	185.6
1962	83.7	1,181.9	131.1	215.0	131.6		184.5
1963	84.0	1,152.1	129.0	215.0	131.3		183.6
1964	87.0	1,114.4	128.9	215.0	131.0	915.0	183.2
1965	89.7		124.5	215.0	130.0		183.2
1966	90.0		125.8	215.0	130.0	908.6	184.0
1967	95.0		126.4	210.0	127.0	905.2	185.8
1968	98.0	1,079.6	129.2	205.0	112.8	910.2	187.6
1969	100.5		129.3	205.0	131.3	915.0	189.1
1970							

Approximate Number of Women Members Reported by National and International Labor Unions Biennially, 1954-1968[a]/ (Numbers in thousands)

Affiliation and union	Series No.	1968	1966	1964	1962	1960	1958	1956	1954
Estimated women members of national and international unions:									
United States, Canada and "other"	I040	3,940	3,689	3,413	3,272	3,304	3,274	3,400	2,950
Percent of all union members	I041	19.5	19.3	19.0	18.6	18.3	18.2	18.6	16.6
Estimated number in United States	I042	3,661	3,430	3,169	3,058	3,097	3,055	3,205	2,775

AFFILIATED WITH AFL-CIO

Affiliation and union	Series No.	1968	1966	1964	1962	1960	1958	1956	1954
Automobile Workers (disaffiliated 1968)		(See "Unaffiliated")	168.3	151.8	139.6	136.3	102.7	175.0	b/
Bakery	I043	32.8	20.8	28.0	24.1	25.5	21.4	53.3	53.3e/
Bookbinders	I044	32.1	37.1	36.2	33.8	38.4	35.4	35.0	32.6e/
Carpenters	I045	23.8	8.0	7.6	7.4	8.0	10.0	8.5	--
Chemical	I046	15.6	14.0	12.8	12.3	9.5	9.7	12.6	--
Clothing	I047	b/ c/	286.5	282.8	282.8	266.3	282.0	288.8	279.1f/
Communications Workers	I048	178.8	176.6	161.6	139.3	130.0	153.2	155.4	180.0f/
Distillery	I049	12.6	16.0	12.3	12.1	12.0	11.6	8.8	--
Electrical (IUE)	I050	113.5	112.0	90.2	98.2	115.2	111.3	159.0	--
Electrical (IBEW)	I051	269.1	262.5	241.8	237.9	231.3	225.0	202.5	189.0e/
Furniture	I052	11.2	11.2	11.3	b/ c/	b/ c/	7.5	6.5	6.3f/
Garment, United	I053	24.3	24.3	20.8	28.0	28.0	28.0	32.0	32.0e/
Garment, Ladies	I054	364.0	364.1	353.9	330.8	334.9	332.2	338.1	330.5e/
Glass Bottle	I055	b/ c/	20.4	17.5	18.0	b/ c/	17.7	18.1	12.8e/
Glass, Flint	I056	10.2	6.8	10.9	11.6	10.7	2.9	b/ c/	--
Government (AFGE)	I057	97.3	50.0	34.7	26.5	17.6	24.0	19.2	15.5e/
Hatters	I058	19.6	21.0	24.0	24.0	24.0	24.0	24.0	16.0e/
Hotel	I059	146.9	202.5	200.1	200.3	199.4	174.5	176.4	--
Industrial	I060	43.0	b/ c/	b/ c/	b/ c/	10.2	40.0	b/ c/	--
Laundry	I061	19.8	21.0	19.9	17.5	17.6	18.3	85.5	54.9e/
Leather Goods	I062	b/ c/	22.8	27.8	25.0	19.2	20.0	22.2	18.2e/
Machinists	I063	b/ c/	83.6	80.8	86.8	89.8	99.3	95.0	86.4
Meat Cutters	I064	75.0	45.9	44.4	46.6	50.0	48.8	62.0	39.8
Office	I065	49.3	49.0	42.3	40.0	37.1	b/ c/	b/ c/	40.0
Packinghouse	I066		28.3	30.0	17.6	15.4	28.4	27.0	--
Postal Clerks	I067	33.2	57.3	34.8	14.5				
Post Office Clerks	I068	(Merged into Postal Clerks, 1961)				13.3	b/ c/	14.6	--
Postal Transport	I069						0	0	d/
Printing, Pressmen	I070	b/ c/	b/ c/	b/ c/	34.8	b/ c/	49.5	33.0	37.5e/
Railway Clerks	I071	56.0	54.0	48.6	48.0	36.0	41.2	43.9	--
Retail Clerks	I072	b/ c/	250.2	213.8	182.0	198.4	176.9	150.0	132.5e/
Retail, Wholesale	I073	70.0	b/ c/	66.8	63.7	64.5	56.0	58.8	--
Rubber	I074	b/ c/	b/ c/	32.9	b/ c/	42.5	31.7	35.6	--
Service Employees	I075	128.4	97.6	96.0	82.4	76.2	52.0	69.0	--
Shoe, United	I076	26.7	27.0	28.1	30.8	31.9	29.0	30.0	--
Shoe, Boot	I077	26.0	24.0	24.0	20.0	16.0	b/ c/	16.0	24.0e/
Teachers	I078	99.0	b/ c/	60.0	42.5	33.7	33.0	30.0	27.1e/
Telegraph	I079	b/ c/	b/ c/	17.2	22.3	20.5	21.9	20.8	--
Textile, United	I080	20.8	18.8	17.6	16.4	16.0	27.6	52.0	36.0e/
Textile Workers	I081	73.2	72.8	70.8	73.2	76.8	78.8	81.0	117.0e/
Tobacco Workers	I082	17.9	17.8	18.5	17.9	16.5	19.2	26.0	--
Toys	I083	12.0	12.5	11.0	9.4	9.5	11.3	11.1	25.5e/
Transport Workers	I084	14.7	8.1	8.1	b/	2.7	1.4	b/	1.8f/
Upholsterers	I085	15.6	b/ c/	13.2	11.2	13.5	12.9	b/	12.7e/

UNAFFILIATED UNIONS

Affiliation and union	Series No.	1968	1966	1964	1962	1960	1958	1956	1954
Automobile Workers	I086	176.7	(Disaffiliated from AFL-CIO in 1968)						
Electrical (UE)	I087	41.8	41.8	41.3	40.8	b/ c/	48.0	25.0	--
Internal Revenue	I088	13.7	b/ c/	13.5	13.6	--	--	--	--
Mine Workers ("District 50")	I089	27.8	27.8	21.0	20.5	b/	b/	b/	--
Postal Alliance	I090	13.5	10.4	4.7	1.3	1.8	1.0	1.0	
Postmasters Assn.	I091	11.6	13.1	11.3	--	--	--	--	--
Teamsters	I092	b/ c/	b/ c/	b/ c/	b/ c/	b/ c/	156.0	150.5e/	49.2e/
Telephone	I093	51.5	56.2	50.4	b/ c/	54.0	54.0	60.0	66.0e/

Outdoor Summer Recreation Activity Days per Person, Persons 12 Years of Age and Over, By Type of Activity, Age Group, and Sex, United States, Summer 1960 and Summer 1965

Activity	Series No.	All persons 12 years of age and over				12-17 years of age			
		Male		Female		Male		Female	
		1960	1965	1960	1965	1960	1965	1960	1965
All outdoor summer activities	J01	36.23	52.14	30.02	42.45	89.23	21.22	65.05	92.39
Passive activities	J02	16.91	23.47	18.30	24.93	24.25	33.58	28.02	36.52
Driving for pleasure	J03	6.57	6.74	6.77	6.57	7.91	8.35	8.77	7.58
Walking for pleasure	J04	3.76	6.49	4.87	8.11	5.08	10.97	9.57	15.93
Picnics	J05	1.98	2.93	2.28	3.46	3.48	3.60	2.90	4.98
Sightseeing	J06	2.03	3.16	2.35	3.24	2.58	3.43	2.84	3.63
Attending outdoor sports events	J07	1.61	2.26	1.06	1.27	2.57	4.72	2.40	2.46
Nature walks, including nature photography and birdwatching	J08	0.76	1.58	0.74	1.92	2.10	2.04	1.16	1.37
Attending outdoor concerts, plays	J09	0.20	0.31	0.23	0.36	0.53	0.47	0.38	0.57
Water activities	J10	10.45	13.25	7.01	9.10	29.05	29.65	16.60	23.14
Swimming	J11	5.44	7.21	4.89	6.50	17.63	19.91	12.83	18.93
Fishing	J12	3.04	3.52	1.02	1.11	6.48	6.00	0.95	1.12
Boating (other than canoeing or sailing)	J13	1.55	1.98	0.91	1.18	3.74	2.86	2.17	2.23
Water skiing	J14	0.42	0.54	0.19	0.31	1.20	0.88	0.65	0.86
Other active recreation (except backwoods)	J15	7.59	13.87	4.14	7.48	32.33	54.11	19.16	30.68
Playing outdoor games or sports	J16	5.08	8.92	2.28	4.46	18.27	29.25	8.91	16.63
Bicycling	J17	2.04	4.32	1.48	2.57	11.68	23.18	8.29	12.00
Horseback riding	J18	0.47	0.63	0.38	0.45	2.38	1.68	1.96	2.05
Backwoods activities	J19	1.28	1.55	0.57	0.94	3.60	3.88	1.27	2.05
Camping	J20	0.57	0.77	0.36	0.56	1.31	1.54	0.83	1.03
Hiking	J21	0.33	0.34	0.20	0.34	1.40	1.18	0.41	0.85
Hunting	J22	0.38	0.44	0.01	0.04	0.89	1.16	0.03	0.17

(continued)

Outdoor Summer Recreation Activity Days per Person, Persons 12 Years of Age and Over, by Type of Activity, Age Group, and Sex, United States, Summer 1960 and Summer 1965 (cont.)

Activity	Series No.	18-24 years of age				25-44 years of age			
		Male		Female		Male		Female	
		1960	1965	1960	1965	1960	1965	1960	1965
All outdoor summer activities	J01	45.29	61.10	37.74	53.19	28.42	42.70	29.06	41.47
Passive activities	J02	23.17	28.07	26.41	33.41	14.82	22.47	17.56	25.40
Driving for pleasure	J03	12.24	12.18	12.40	11.70	6.04	6.76	6.17	6.64
Walking for pleasure	J04	3.31	5.22	6.14	9.53	2.36	4.23	4.02	6.89
Picnics	J05	2.31	3.59	3.10	4.50	2.37	3.76	2.92	4.44
Sightseeing	J06	2.06	3.25	2.53	4.04	1.85	3.84	2.31	3.33
Attending outdoor sports events	J07	2.07	2.26	1.25	1.72	1.73	2.27	1.21	1.45
Nature walks, including nature photography and birdwatching	J08	1.03	1.07	0.65	1.35	0.31	1.30	0.73	2.31
Attending outdoor concerts, plays	J09	0.15	0.50	0.34	0.57	0.16	0.31	0.20	0.34
Water activities	J10	12.53	17.95	7.50	11.28	8.88	11.33	8.11	9.38
Swimming	J11	6.55	10.87	5.06	7.81	4.23	5.49	5.74	6.47
Fishing	J12	3.89	3.03	1.19	1.28	2.66	3.42	1.17	1.29
Boating (other than canoeing or sailing)	J13	1.25	1.67	0.94	1.56	1.61	1.86	1.00	1.33
Water skiing	J14	0.84	1.38	0.31	0.63	0.38	0.56	0.20	0.29
Other active recreation (except backwoods)	J15	7.48	12.86	3.15	7.49	3.96	7.66	2.79	5.51
Playing outdoor games or sports	J16	6.41	10.12	2.32	5.20	3.42	6.33	1.93	3.58
Bicycling	J17	0.65	1.76	0.58	1.82	0.40	0.76	0.82	1.76
Horseback riding	J18	0.42	0.98	0.25	0.47	0.14	0.57	0.04	0.17
Backwoods activities	J19	2.11	2.22	0.68	1.01	0.76	1.24	0.60	1.18
Camping	J20	0.74	0.85	0.38	0.36	0.41	0.79	0.41	0.87
Hiking	J21	0.09	0.40	0.25	0.62	0.14	0.20	0.18	0.27
Hunting	J22	1.28	0.97	0.05	0.03	0.21	0.25	0.01	0.04

(continued)

Outdoor Summer Recreation Activity Days per Person, Persons 12 Years of Age and Over, by Type of Activity, Age Group, and Sex, United States, Summer 1960 and Summer 1965 (cont.)

Activity	Series No.	45-64 years of age				65 years of age and over			
		Male		Female		Male		Female	
		1960	1965	1960	1965	1960	1965	1960	1965
All outdoor summer activities	J01	20.76	31.43	19.41	24.83	17.98	20.75	10.97	15.72
Passive activities	J02	13.58	19.31	14.70	19.35	15.45	16.71	10.11	13.99
Driving for pleasure	J03	5.43	4.83	5.13	4.88	3.59	2.87	4.58	3.51
Walking for pleasure	J04	3.02	5.99	4.08	6.02	8.60	9.11	2.70	5.43
Picnics	J05	1.07	2.11	1.43	2.20	0.66·	0.88	0.91	0.94
Sightseeing	J06	2.08	].96	2.65	3.14	1.68	1.20	1.11	1.97
Attending outdoor sports events	J07	1.21	1.37	0.56	0.75	0.47	0.85	0.10	0.15
Nature walks, including nature photography and birdwatching	J08	0.64	1.86	0.69	2.06	0.33	1.65	0.53	1.90
Attending outdoor concerts, plays	J09	0.13	0.19	0.16	0.30	0.12	0.15	0.18	0.09
Water activities	J10	4.88	7.99	3.56	4.04	1.83	2.83	0.81	1.27
Swimming	J11	1.79	2.73	1.97	2.24	0.60	0.75	0.28	0.45
Fishing	J12	2.10	3.22	1.16	1.04	1.05	1.58	0.22	0.60
Boating (other than canoeing or sailing)	J13	0.96	1.88	0.43	0.73	0.18	0.50	0.31	0.22
Water skiing	J14	0.03	0.16	a/	0.03	a/	a/	a/	a/
Other active recreation (except backwoods)	J15	1.64	3.36	0.76	1.06	0.29	0.95	0.03	0.30
Playing outdoor games or sports	J16	1.36	2.80	0.49	0.72	0.28	0.83	0.02	0.29
Bicycling	J17	0.22	0.29	0.03	0.19	a/	0.07	0.01	0.01
Horseback riding	J18	0.06	0.17	0.24	0.15	0.01	0.05	a/	a/
Backwoods activities	J19	0.66	0.77	0.39	0.38	0.41	0.26	0.02	0.16
Camping	J20	0.49	0.48	0.22	0.26	0.11	0.18	0.02	0.08
Hiking	J21	0.08	0.12	0.17	0.12	0.26	0.05	a/	0.06
Hunting	J22	0.09	0.17	a/	a/	0.04	0.03	a/	0.02

Restricted Activity Days per Person per Year by Age and Sex, United States, 1958-1967

Sex and year ended June 30	All ages	Under 5 years	5-14 years	15-24 years	25-44 years	45-64 years	65-74 years	75 yrs. & over
MALE	K001	K002	K003	K004	K005	K006	K007	K008
1958	17.7	12.8	16.0	10.8	12.4	22.6	*	*
1959	13.6	11.3	12.1	6.9	8.9	17.4	33.9	40.0
1960	14.3	11.0	11.4	7.7	10.6	19.1	34.5	41.5
1961	14.6	11.2	10.8	8.6	10.4	20.1	35.2	45.7
1962	14.1	11.3	11.7	7.9	10.3	19.5	31.9	36.1
1963	14.5	11.3	11.5	8.3	10.0	20.6	*	*
1964	14.5	10.8	10.7	9.0	10.1	21.3	31.3	41.4
1965	14.7	11.7	11.2	7.7	10.8	21.0	32.8	41.2
1966	14.4	10.9	10.9	9.3	11.1	20.3	30.9	36.0
1967	14.1	10.7	9.5	8.6	11.2	21.2	28.8	37.0
1968								
1969								
1970								
FEMALE	K009	K010	K011	K012	K013	K014	K015	K016
1958	22.2	13.6	16.8	15.8	19.0	28.0	*	*
1959	17.9	10.3	12.0	11.5	17.0	22.8	33.4	51.3
1960	18.0	10.6	11.9	11.6	17.0	23.9	33.2	48.4
1961	18.3	11.4	10.5	12.0	18.1	23.6	36.4	49.9
1962	18.3	9.8	12.5	11.4	18.4	23.6	34.8	46.2
1963	17.8	9.7	10.9	12.0	17.4	23.1	*	*
1964	17.8	10.3	10.5	11.8	16.6	23.1	36.3	49.6
1965	18.0	9.9	10.7	11.8	17.0	23.7	35.8	49.6
1966	16.7	10.2	10.0	10.9	16.5	21.9	30.7	41.9
1967	16.5	8.9	9.7	10.2	16.1	21.5	33.2	45.6
1968								
1969								
1970								

* Available only for age-group "65 years and over":

Male
1958   45.2
1963   35.3

Female
1958   49.1
1963   38.6

410

Restricted Activity Days per Person per Year, by Family Income and Sex,
United States, 1958-1967

Sex and year ended June 30		Family income						
	Total	Under $2,000	$2,000-3,999	$4,000-6,999	$7,000 & over	$7,000-9,999	$10,000 & over	Unknown
MALE	K017	K018	K019	K020	K021	K022	K023	K024
1958	17.7	32.4	19.1	13.8	14.0	--	--	17.2
1959	13.6	24.8	14.3	11.0	10.5	--	--	12.0
1960	14.3	26.7	15.8	11.2	11.4	--	--	13.1
1961	14.6	27.5	17.3	12.0	11.0	--	--	10.9
1962	14.1	24.9	16.6	11.9	12.2	--	--	11.5
1963	14.5	28.4	16.5	11.9	11.7	--	--	13.8
1964	14.5	26.2	18.2	12.7	11.4	11.1	11.9	12.4
1965	14.7	27.6	19.2	12.7	11.6	11.5	11.6	13.2
1966*	14.4	28.8	19.7	13.1	11.2	11.4	10.9	11.5
1967*	14.1	29.2	19.7	13.6	11.0	10.9	11.2	11.2
1968								
1969								
1970								
FEMALE	K025	K026	K027	K028	K029	K030	K031	K032
1958	22.2	32.4	21.9	19.2	19.3	--	--	23.2
1959	17.9	28.9	15.6	16.1	16.6	--	--	19.8
1960	18.0	29.0	17.9	15.9	14.2	--	--	18.0
1961	18.3	31.7	18.0	15.5	15.0	--	--	18.2
1962	18.3	28.3	18.9	15.9	16.0	--	--	17.7
1963	17.8	29.7	18.9	15.5	14.5	--	--	16.3
1964	17.8	28.7	19.5	15.5	14.9	15.1	14.7	17.5
1965	18.0	32.3	20.2	15.0	15.0	15.3	14.7	16.5
1966*	16.7	29.6	19.3	14.2	14.2	13.7	14.6	15.0
1967*	16.5	30.5	21.9	14.6	13.1	13.7	12.6	15.3
1968								
1969								
1970								

* Rates also available, as follows:

	Under $3,000	$3,000-4,999	$5,000-6,999
Male			
1966	26.0	15.5	12.7
1967	26.2	15.9	13.1
Female			
1966	26.1	16.0	14.3
1967	28.6	16.7	14.3

411

Bed Disability Days, per Person per Year, by Age and Sex, United States, 1958-1967

Sex and year ended June 30	All ages	Under 5 years	5-14 years	15-24 years	25-44 years	45-64 years	65-74 years	75 yrs. & over
MALE	K033	K034	K035	K036	K037	K038	K039	K040
1958	6.9	5.2	7.6	4.9	4.4	7.7	*	*
1959	4.9	4.7	5.0	2.9	3.5	5.6	9.7	12.3
1960	5.3	4.9	4.7	2.9	3.8	6.7	11.0	17.6
1961	5.0	4.8	4.1	3.1	3.4	6.2	11.0	16.9
1962	5.4	5.0	5.2	3.0	3.9	6.3	11.4	14.6
1963	5.7	5.1	5.0	3.4	3.9	7.0	*	*
1964	5.3	5.3	4.3	3.4	3.6	6.5	10.8	17.6
1965	5.3	5.2	4.5	2.8	3.9	6.4	9.9	19.4
1966	5.5	5.1	4.8	3.8	4.3	6.1	11.5	14.5
1967	4.9	4.3	4.3	3.3	3.4	6.2	8.1	14.6
1968								
1969								
1970								
	K041	K042	K043	K044	K045	K046	K047	K048
FEMALE								
1958	8.7	6.4	8.0	7.6	7.0	9.8	*	*
1959	6.6	4.5	5.3	4.9	6.2	7.5	9.1	21.4
1960	6.7	4.6	5.2	5.1	5.8	8.2	10.9	19.3
1961	6.6	4.8	4.6	4.9	6.3	7.4	11.1	20.5
1962	7.4	4.5	6.0	5.4	6.9	8.2	12.5	23.6
1963	7.5	4.1	5.2	5.9	6.9	8.7	*	*
1964	6.8	4.8	4.6	5.6	6.3	7.5	11.3	20.0
1965	7.0	4.3	4.8	5.2	6.3	8.5	12.2	20.1
1966	7.0	5.1	4.9	5.6	7.1	8.3	11.0	16.0
1967	6.3	3.9	4.5	4.9	6.0	7.5	10.1	17.8
1968								
1969								
1970								

* Available only for age-group "65 years and over":

Male
1958   16.0
1963   14.3

Female
1958   16.6
1963   17.1

Bed Disability Days per Person per Year, by Family Income and Sex, United States, 1958-1967

Sex and year ended June 30	Family income							
	Total	Under $2,000	$2,000-3,999	$4,000-6,999	$7,000 & over	$7,000-9,999	$10,000 & over	Unknown
	K049	K050	K051	K052	K053	K054	K055	K056
MALE								
1958	6.9	12.0	7.2	5.7	5.0	--	--	7.0
1959	4.9	7.6	5.5	4.3	3.7	--	--	4.4
1960	5.3	9.4	5.8	4.2	4.4	--	--	5.6
1961	5.0	9.8	5.9	4.0	3.8	--	--	3.8
1962	5.4	8.7	6.6	4.6	4.3	--	--	4.8
1963	5.7	11.6	6.8	4.5	4.5	--	--	5.7
1964	5.3	9.1	6.4	4.7	4.2	4.0	4.5	5.3
1965	5.3	9.6	6.9	4.7	4.1	4.3	3.8	5.6
1966*	5.5	11.0	7.3	4.9	4.3	4.4	4.2	4.8
1967*	4.9	10.2	6.8	4.6	3.8	3.5	4.0	4.4
1968								
1969								
1970								
	K057	K058	K059	K060	K061	K062	K063	K064
FEMALE								
1958	8.7	12.3	8.3	8.1	7.1	--	--	9.0
1959	6.6	10.4	6.0	5.9	5.5	--	--	7.3
1960	6.7	10.1	6.7	6.2	5.1	--	--	6.6
1961	6.6	10.8	6.5	5.8	5.5	--	--	6.7
1962	7.4	11.5	8.1	6.5	6.2	--	--	6.6
1963	7.5	12.3	7.9	6.7	6.0	--	--	7.0
1964	6.8	9.7	7.7	6.2	5.7	5.8	5.6	6.8
1965	7.0	12.2	7.9	5.9	5.8	5.9	5.7	6.8
1966*	7.0	11.5	8.3	6.1	6.2	5.8	6.5	6.2
1967*	6.3	10.3	8.4	6.0	5.2	5.3	5.0	5.8
1968								
1969								
1970								

* Rates also available, as follows:		Under $3,000	$3,000-4,999	$5,000-6,999
	Male			
	1966	9.6	5.6	5.1
	1967	9.2	5.1	4.6
	Female			
	1966	16.6	6.7	6.2
	1967	10.1	6.7	5.9

Work-Loss Days per Currently Employed Person per Year, by Age and Sex
United States, 1960-1967

Sex and year ended June 30	Age in Years				
	All ages	17-24 years	25-44 years	45-64 years	65 yrs. & over
MALE	K065	K066	K067	K068	K069
1958	--	--	--	--	--
1959	--	--	--	--	--
1960	5.5	3.3	4.6	6.8	11.0
1961	5.3	3.4	4.3	6.8	9.8
1962	5.7	3.1	4.6	7.8	9.4
1963	5.9	3.7	4.6	7.6	10.9
1964	5.6	3.6	4.3	7.5	9.0
1965	5.7	3.4	4.4	7.8	9.8
1966	5.9	4.2	5.1	7.3	9.8
1967	5.3	3.5	4.4	7.0	7.0
1968					
1969					
1970					
FEMALE	K070	K071	K072	K073	K074
1958	--	--	--	--	--
1959	--	--	--	--	--
1960	5.6	4.4	5.5	6.2	7.4
1961	5.6	4.1	5.6	6.1	7.8
1962	5.8	4.4	6.0	6.4	4.6[a/]
1963	6.6	4.5	6.8	7.5	5.6
1964	5.3	4.3	5.4	6.0	3.5
1965	5.6	4.2	6.2	6.0	4.5
1966	5.6	4.1	6.2	5.9	5.1
1967	5.4	4.5	5.6	5.8	4.8
1968					
1969					
1970					

Work-Loss Days per Currently Employed Person per Year, by Family Income and Sex,
United States, 1960-1967

Sex and year ended June 30	Family income							
	Total	Under $2,000	$2,000-3,999	$4,000-6,999	$7,000 & over	$7,000-9,999	$10,000 & over	Unknown
MALE	K075	K076	K077	K078	K079	K080	K081	K082
1958	--	--	--	--	--	--	--	--
1959	--	--	--	--	--	--	--	--
1960	5.5	9.8	6.4	4.5	4.9	--	--	5.7
1961	5.3	8.8	6.2	4.9	4.4	--	--	5.6
1962	5.7	8.0	7.5	5.4	5.1	--	--	3.6
1963	5.9	10.2	7.6	5.4	4.9	--	--	5.0
1964	5.6	9.1	7.7	5.9	4.1	3.8	4.4	5.2
1965	5.7	10.2	7.3	5.9	4.6	4.8	4.4	4.8
1966*	5.9	9.2	8.4	6.5	4.8	5.1	4.6	4.4
1967*	5.3	9.7	7.8	6.1	4.3	4.1	4.4	3.9
1968								
1969								
1970								
FEMALE	K083	K084	K085	K086	K087	K088	K089	K090
1958	--	--	--	--	--	--	--	--
1959	--	--	--	--	--	--	--	--
1960	5.6	6.5	6.6	5.4	4.9	--	--	4.5
1961	5.6	7.0	5.5	5.6	5.3	--	--	4.6
1962	5.8	5.6	6.6	5.3	5.9	--	--	5.6
1963	6.6	7.5	6.8	6.6	6.5	--	--	4.6
1964	5.3	5.2	5.8	5.8	4.8	5.4	4.2	5.4
1965	5.6	7.4	6.3	5.1	5.4	5.2	5.6	5.0
1966*	5.6	6.2	6.3	6.1	4.9	4.9	4.9	4.2
1967*	5.4	6.4	6.8	5.6	4.9	4.9	4.9	4.2
1968								
1969								
1970								

*   Rates also available, as follows:

	Under $3,000	$3,000-4,999	$5,000-6,999
Male			
1966	8.2	7.9	6.4
1967	8.9	6.9	6.0
Female			
1966	6.4	5.8	6.2
1967	6.7	6.3	5.4

	Annual incidence of acute conditions per 100 persons		Percent with one or more chronic conditions		Annual number 17 years old and over injured per 100 persons		Discharges from short-stay hospitals			
	All Ages		All Ages		Total		Number of discharges per 100 persons per year		Average length of stay (days)	
	Male	Female	Male	Female	Male	Female	Male	Female	Male	Female
	K091	K092	K093	K094	K095	K096	K097	K098	K099	K100
1958	247.5	272.0	39.1	43.5	25.2	18.7	7.4	12.3	11.0	7.2
1959	204.6	224.4	38.9	42.0	29.2	18.7	7.6	13.0	10.0	7.4
1960	190.1	216.0	39.9	42.3	27.5	22.1	8.2	13.1	11.0	7.1
1961	193.5	209.8	41.2	44.0	28.5	19.8	8.2	13.2	10.4	6.9
1962	207.8	235.9	41.9	45.4	31.6	20.2	9.3	14.7	10.4	7.3
1963	203.7	233.1	43.2	45.7	30.1	20.7	10.1	14.7	10.5	7.1
1964	200.0	216.4	43.5	46.9	27.3	18.1	10.2	15.3	9.6	7.2
1965	202.9	222.0	44.6	48.0	29.6	20.2	10.3	15.3	10.3	7.3
1966	203.4	220.1	47.7	50.4	28.1	20.2	10.3	14.9	9.6	7.1
1967	185.4	194.7	48.7	51.0	29.6	20.2	10.5	14.5	10.4	7.4
1968	182.5	195.8					9.7	14.0	10.5	7.9
1969										
1970										

Age group and time period of survey	Survey a/	Percent of males of known cigarette-smoking status				Quit ratio of ever smokers b/
		Total known	Present smoker	Former smoker	Never smoked	
			K101	K102	K103	K104
Total, 17 years and older						
February 1955 (18 yrs. & older)	CPS	100.0	56.9	11.1	32.1	16
July 1964 - June 1965	HIS	100.0	51.1	19.3	29.6	27
July 1965 - June 1966	HIS	100.0	51.7	19.5	28.7	27
June 1966	CPS	100.0	50.0	17.7	32.3	26
August 1967	CPS	100.0	49.1	18.7	32.2	28
August 1968	CPS	100.0	47.0	19.7	33.4	30
			K105	K016	K107	K108
Age 17-24 years						
February 1955 (18-24 years)	CPS	100.0	56.6	3.6	39.8	6
July 1964 - June 1965	HIS	100.0	48.9	6.7	44.4	12
July 1965 - June 1966	HIS	100.0	49.4	5.4	45.2	10
June 1966	CPS	100.0	45.6	4.7	49.7	9
August 1967	CPS	100.0	45.0	5.3	49.7	11
August 1968	CPS	100.0	42.2	6.6	51.1	14
			K109	K110	K111	K112
Age 25-44 years						
February 1955	CPS	100.0	66.7	10.0	23.2	13
July 1964 - June 1965	HIS	100.0	59.4	17.8	22.8	23
July 1965 - June 1966	HIS	100.0	60.0	17.5	22.5	23
June 1966	CPS	100.0	59.2	16.4	24.4	22
August 1967	CPS	100.0	57.4	17.2	25.4	23
August 1968	CPS	100.0	55.6	18.1	26.2	25
			K113	K114	K115	K116
Age 45-64 years						
February 1955	CPS	100.0	55.7	14.0	30.3	20
July 1964 - June 1965	HIS	100.0	51.9	24.1	23.9	32
July 1965 - June 1966	HIS	100.0	53.0	25.1	21.9	32
June 1966	CPS	100.0	51.8	22.6	25.6	30
August 1967	CPS	100.0	51.1	23.8	25.1	32
August 1968	CPS	100.0	48.6	24.7	26.7	34
			K117	K118	K119	K120
Age 65 and over						
February 1955	CPS	100.0	26.8	13.5	59.7	33
July 1964 - June 1965	HIS	100.0	28.5	28.1	43.4	50
July 1965 - June 1966	HIS	100.0	28.3	30.8	40.9	52
June 1966	CPS	100.0	25.4	27.6	46.9	52
August 1967	CPS	100.0	26.4	28.7	44.9	52
August 1968	CPS	100.0	25.3	29.8	44.9	54

Age group and time period of survey	Survey a/	Percent of females of known cigarette-smoking status				Quit ratio of ever smokers b/
		Total known	Present smoker	Former smoker	Never smoked	
			K121	K122	K123	K124
Total, 17 years and older						
February 1955 (18 yrs. & older)	CPS	100.0	28.4	4.0	67.6	12
July 1964 - June 1965	HIS	100.0	33.3	7.9	58.8	19
July 1965 - June 1966	HIS	100.0	33.4	7.7	58.9	19
June 1966	CPS	100.0	32.3	6.6	61.0	17
August 1967	CPS	100.0	32.1	7.2	60.7	18
August 1968	CPS	100.0	31.2	8.1	60.7	21
Age 17-24 years			K125	K126	K127	K128
February 1955 (18-24 years)	CPS	100.0	34.8	3.5	61.7	9
July 1964 - June 1965	HIS	100.0	34.2	5.5	60.3	14
July 1965 - June 1966	HIS	100.0	33.2	5.0	61.9	13
June 1966	CPS	100.0	32.2	4.3	63.4	12
August 1967	CPS	100.0	31.8	4.8	63.3	13
August 1968	CPS	100.0	30.0	5.4	64.6	15
Age 25-44 years			K129	K130	K131	K132
February 1955	CPS	100.0	38.8	5.4	55.8	12
July 1964 - June 1965	HIS	100.0	43.7	9.7	46.6	18
July 1965- June 1966	HIS	100.0	43.5	9.8	46.6	18
June 1966	CPS	100.0	42.8	8.0	49.1	16
August 1967	CPS	100.0	42.1	9.0	48.9	18
August 1968	CPS	100.0	40.9	10.0	49.0	20
Age 45-64 years			K133	K134	K135	K136
February 1955	CPS	100.0	21.0	3.3	75.7	14
July 1964 - June 1965	HIS	100.0	32.0	8.6	59.4	21
July 1965 - June 1966	HIS	100.0	33.1	8.3	58.6	20
June 1966	CPS	100.0	31.9	7.8	60.3	20
August 1967	CPS	100.0	32.2	8.1	59.7	20
August 1968	CPS	100.0	31.4	9.0	59.5	22
Age 65 and over			K137	K138	K139	K140
February 1955	CPS	100.0	4.9	1.5	93.6	23
July 1964 - June 1965	HIS	100.0	9.5	4.5	85.9	32
July 1965 - June 1966	HIS	100.0	9.7	4.5	85.7	32
June 1966	CPS	100.0	8.3	3.9	87.8	32
August 1967	CPS	100.0	9.0	4.3	86.7	32
August 1968	CPS	100.0	9.8	5.0	85.2	34

Year	Expectation of life (years)							
	At birth				At age 15			
	White		Nonwhite		White		Nonwhite	
	Male L001	Female L002	Male L003	Female L004	Male L005	Female L006	Male L007	Female L008
1939	63.3	66.6	53.2	56.0				
1940	62.1	66.6	51.5	54.9	(52.3	56.1	44.0	46.2
1941	64.4	68.5	52.5	55.3				
1942	65.9	69.4	55.4	58.2				
1943	63.2	65.7	55.4	56.1				
1944	64.5	68.4	55.8	57.7				
1945	64.4	69.5	56.1	59.6	53.2	57.6	46.2	49.1
1946	65.1	70.3	57.5	61.0	53.6	58.1	47.2	50.1
1947	65.2	70.5	57.9	61.9	53.4	58.3	47.5	50.9
1948	65.5	71.0	58.1	62.5	53.6	58.6	47.4	51.3
1949	66.2	71.9	58.9	62.7	54.2	59.5	48.5	51.5
1950	66.5	72.2	59.1	62.9	54.4	59.7	48.5	51.9
1951	66.5	72.4	59.2	63.4	54.4	59.9	48.7	52.4
1952	66.6	72.6	59.1	63.8	54.4	59.9	48.5	52.5
1953	66.8	73.0	59.7	64.5	54.4	60.1	48.8	53.0
1954	67.5	73.7	61.1	65.9	55.0	60.7	50.0	54.2
1955	67.4	73.7	61.4	66.1	54.8	60.7	50.1	54.3
1956	67.5	73.9	61.3	66.1	54.8	60.7	50.0	54.2
1957	67.2	73.7	60.7	65.5	54.5	60.5	49.3	53.7
1958	67.4	73.9	61.0	65.8	54.7	60.7	49.7	54.1
1959	67.5	74.2	61.3	66.5	55.0	61.2	50.4	55.0
1960	67.4	61.1	66.3	54.8	61.1	50.1	54.7	45.5
1961	67.8	74.5	61.9	67.0	55.1	61.4	50.7	55.3
1962	67.6	74.4	61.5	66.8	54.9	61.3	50.2	55.0
1963	67.5	74.4	60.9	66.5	54.7	61.3	49.7	54.8
1964	67.7	74.6	61.1	67.2	54.9	61.5	49.9	55.4
1965	67.6	74.7	61.1	67.4	54.8	61.5	49.7	55.5
1966	67.6	74.7	60.7	67.4	54.7	61.5	49.2	55.5
1967	67.8	75.1	61.1	68.2	54.9	61.7	49.4	56.1
1968								
1969								
1970								

(continued)

Year	Expectation of life (years) (cont.)							
	At age 25				At age 35			
	White		Nonwhite		White		Nonwhite	
	Male L009	Female L010	Male L011	Female L012	Male L013	Female L014	Male L015	Female L016
1939								
1940	43.3	46.8	35.9	39.3	34.4	37.7	28.7	30.8
1941								
1942								
1943								
1944								
1945	44.0	48.2	37.8	40.6	34.9	38.9	30.0	32.6
1946	44.4	48.7	38.6	41.6	35.3	39.3	30.6	33.4
1947	44.2	48.7	38.9	42.3	35.0	39.4	30.8	34.0
1948	44.4	49.0	38.7	42.5	35.2	39.6	30.5	34.2
1949	45.0	49.9	39.8	42.6	35.8	40.4	31.6	34.2
1950	45.2	50.1	39.7	42.9	35.9	40.6	31.5	34.4
1951	45.1	50.3	40.0	43.3	35.9	40.8	31.7	34.7
1952	45.2	50.3	39.7	43.3	35.9	40.8	31.4	34.7
1953	45.2	50.5	39.9	43.7	35.9	40.9	31.6	35.0
1954	45.7	51.0	41.1	44.9	36.4	41.4	32.7	36.1
1955	45.6	51.0	41.2	45.0	36.3	41.4	32.6	36.1
1956	45.5	51.1	41.0	44.8	36.2	41.4	32.5	35.9
1957	45.3	50.9	40.3	44.3	35.9	41.3	31.8	35.4
1958	45.4	51.0	40.6	44.6	36.0	41.4	32.0	35.7
1959	45.7	51.5	41.4	45.6	36.4	41.9	32.9	36.6
1960	45.5	51.4	41.1	45.2	36.1	41.8	32.5	36.3
1961	45.8	51.7	41.6	45.8	36.4	42.1	33.0	36.8
1962	45.6	51.6	41.2	45.6	36.3	42.0	32.6	36.6
1963	45.5	51.6	40.7	45.3	36.1	42.0	32.2	36.3
1964	45.6	51.8	40.9	45.9	36.0	42.2	32.4	36.9
1965	45.6	51.8	40.7	46.1	36.3	42.2	32.3	37.1
1966	45.5	51.8	40.3	46.0	36.2	42.2	31.9	37.0
1967	45.7	52.1	40.5	46.6	36.4	42.5	32.2	37.7
1968								
1969								
1970								

(continued)

	Expectation of life (years)(cont.)											
	At age 45				At age 55				At age 65			
Year	White		Nonwhite		White		Nonwhite		White		Nonwhite	
	Male	Female	Male	Female	Male	Female	Male	Female	Male	Female	Male	Female
	L017	L018	L019	L020	L021	L022	L023	L024	L025	L026	L027	L028
1939												
1940	25.9	28.9	22.0	24.0	18.3	20.7	16.7	18.4	12.1	13.6	12.2	14.0
1941												
1942												
1943												
1944												
1945	26.3	30.0	22.9	25.3	18.7	21.7	17.2	19.1	12.4	14.3	12.2	14.1
1946	26.7	30.3	23.4	26.0	19.0	21.9	17.7	19.7	12.6	14.5	12.7	14.6
1947	26.3	30.3	23.6	26.6	18.7	21.9	17.9	20.5	12.3	14.4	13.3	15.9
1948	26.5	30.5	23.3	26.7	18.8	22.0	17.5	20.5	12.4	14.4	13.1	15.7
1949	27.0	31.3	24.0	26.5	19.2	22.8	18.0	20.3	13.0	15.2	13.7	15.7
1950	27.1	31.5	23.8	26.6	19.3	22.9	17.6	20.2	13.0	15.3	13.3	15.6
1951	27.1	31.6	24.0	26.9	19.3	23.0	17.8	20.4	13.0	15.4	13.5	15.8
1952	27.1	31.6	23.8	26.8	19.3	23.0	17.5	20.2	13.0	15.3	1 .8	14.8
1953	27.0	31.7	23.8	26.9	19.2	23.0	17.5	20.3	12.9	15.3	12.7	14.7
1954	27.5	32.2	24.8	28.0	19.6	23.5	18.4	21.3	13.1	15.7	13.5	15.7
1955	27.3	32.1	24.8	27.9	19.4	23.4	18.1	21.0	12.9	15.5	13.2	15.5
1956	27.3	32.1	24.6	27.8	19.3	23.4	17.8	20.7	12.9	15.5	12.9	15.3
1957	27.0	32.0	24.0	27.3	19.1	23.3	17.2	20.3	12.7	15.4	12.4	14.8
1958	27.1	32.1	24.1	27.5	19.2	23.3	17.3	20.3	12.7	15.4	12.1	14.8
1959	27.4	32.6	25.0	28.4	19.5	23.8	18.3	21.2	13.1	15.9	12.5	15.5
1960	27.2	32.5	24.6	28.0	19.3	23.8	17.8	20.9	12.9	15.9	12.7	15.2
1961	27.5	32.8	25.1	28.5	19.6	24.1	18.3	21.2	13.1	16.1	13.0	15.5
1962	27.3	32.7	24.7	28.3	19.4	24.0	18.0	20.9	12.9	16.0	12.7	15.2
1963	27.2	32.7	24.3	28.1	19.3	24.0	17.5	20.7	12.8	16.0	12.2	15.0
1964	27.4	32.9	24.7	28.7	19.4	24.2	18.0	21.4	13.0	16.3	12.8	15.6
1965	27.3	32.9	24.5	28.8	19.4	24.2	17.9	21.4	12.9	16.3	12.6	15.5
1966	27.2	32.9	24.2	28.8	19.3	24.2	17.6	21.3	12.9	16.3	12.4	15.2
1967	27.4	33.2	24.6	29.4	19.5	24.5	18.0	21.9	13.0	16.5	12.7	15.8
1968												
1969												
1970												

Deaths per 1,000 population, by age, color, and sex

Year	White		Nonwhite		White		Nonwhite		White		Nonwhite	
	Male	Female	Male	Female	Male	Female	Male	Female	Male	Female	Male	Female
	All ages[a/]				Under 1 year				1-4 years			
	L029	L030	L031	L032	L033	L034	L035	L036	L037	L038	L039	L040
1940	11.6	9.2	15.1	12.6	56.7	43.6	101.2	77.4	2.8	2.4	5.3	4.4
1941	11.4	8.9	14.8	12.2	53.3	41.7	98.7	79.4	2.7	2.3	5.2	4.8
1942	11.4	8.7	14.0	11.4	50.6	39.5	83.3	67.9	2.4	2.0	4.4	3.8
1943	12.2	9.2	14.0	11.6	45.5	35.2	80.3	64.6	2.5	2.1	4.5	3.9
1944	12.2	8.8	13.8	11.1	45.6	35.6	77.2	64.7	2.3	1.9	4.1	3.7
1945	12.5	8.6	13.5	10.5	44.1	34.3	73.8	58.1	2.0	1.7	3.5	3.0
1946	11.2	8.5	12.2	10.0	49.4	37.6	73.2	58.9	1.8	1.5	3.1	2.6
1947	11.4	8.5	12.5	10.3	36.1	27.5	62.5	50.5	1.6	1.3	2.7	2.4
1948	11.2	8.3	12.7	10.1	37.2	28.5	62.4	49.6	1.6	1.3	2.7	2.4
1949	11.0	8.1	12.5	10.0	36.4	27.8	62.2	49.2	1.5	1.2	2.7	2.3
1950	10.9	8.0	12.5	9.9	34.0	25.7	59.9	47.5	1.4	1.1	2.7	2.3
1951	11.0	8.0	12.5	9.8	33.3	25.1	58.9	45.4	1.3	1.1	2.7	2.3
1952	11.0	8.0	12.5	9.6	32.3	24.7	62.1	48.4	1.4	1.1	2.7	2.3
1953	11.0	8.0	12.3	9.4	31.4	23.4	57.1	46.8	1.3	1.1	2.4	2.0
1954	10.6	7.6	11.4	8.8	29.7	22.4	55.0	43.8	1.1	1.0	2.2	1.9
1955	10.7	7.8	11.3	8.8	28.8	21.7	53.5	42.8	1.1	0.9	2.1	1.9
1956	10.8	7.8	11.4	8.8	28.5	21.4	53.7	41.5	1.1	0.9	2.1	1.8
1957	11.0	8.0	11.9	9.1	28.0	21.1	53.4	42.9	1.1	0.9	2.1	1.8
1958	10.9	8.0	11.6	9.0	27.7	21.2	55.6	44.1	1.1	0.9	2.0	1.9
1959	10.8	7.9	11.3	8.6	27.4	20.5	52.6	42.2	1.0	0.8	2.1	1.7
1960	11.0	8.0	11.5	8.7	26.9	20.1	51.9	40.7	1.0	0.9	2.1	1.7
1961	10.7	7.8	10.9	8.4	25.6	19.3	45.2	36.4	1.0	0.8	1.8	1.6
1962[b/]	10.8	8.0	11.2	8.5	25.5	19.1	45.6	36.6	0.9	0.8	1.8	1.5
1963[b/]	11.0	8.1	11.5	8.7	25.2	19.0	46.0	36.5	0.9	0.8	1.9	1.6
1964	10.8	8.0	11.1	8.3	24.4	18.5	45.1	36.1	0.9	0.8	1.7	1.5
1965	10.8	8.0	11.1	8.2	23.7	17.9	44.5	35.9	0.9	0.7	1.6	1.4
1966	10.9	8.1	11.3	8.3	23.0	17.3	42.6	35.0	0.9	0.7	1.6	1.4
1967	10.8	8.0	10.9	7.9	22.4	16.7	38.8	32.0	0.8	0.7	1.5	1.2
1968					22.5*	16.5*	36.8*	29.3*				
1969												
1970												

Year	5-14 years				15-24 years				25-34 years			
	L041	L042	L043	L044	L045	L046	L047	L048	L049	L050	L051	L052
1940	1.1	0.8	1.6	1.4	2.0	1.4	5.0	5.0	2.8	2.2	8.5	7.4
1941	1.1	0.8	1.6	1.4	2.0	1.3	4.9	4.8	2.7	2.0	8.3	6.9
1942	1.0	0.7	1.5	1.2	2.0	1.2	4.6	4.3	2.7	1.9	7.8	6.3
1943	1.1	0.7	1.5	1.2	2.4	1.2	4.6	4.1	2.8	1.9	7.0	6.2
1944	1.1	0.7	1.5	1.2	2.6	1.1	4.4	3.8	2.8	1.8	6.9	5.9
1945	1.0	0.7	1.3	1.1	2.5	1.1	4.3	3.6	3.0	1.7	7.2	5.5
1946	0.9	0.6	1.3	1.0	1.9	1.0	3.6	3.2	2.3	1.5	5.7	5.0
1947	0.8	0.5	1.1	0.9	1.7	0.9	3.6	3.1	2.1	1.4	5.3	4.9
1948	0.8	0.5	1.0	0.9	1.6	0.8	3.3	2.7	2.0	1.3	5.2	4.4
1949*	0.8	0.5	1.0	0.8	1.5	0.7	3.1	2.4	1.9	1.2	5.0	4.1
1950	0.7	0.5	1.0	0.7	1.5	0.7	2.9	2.2	1.9	1.1	5.0	3.9
1951	0.7	0.4	1.0	0.7	1.6	0.7	2.9	2.0	1.9	1.1	4.8	3.6
1952	0.7	0.5	0.9	0.7	1.7	0.7	2.9	1.8	1.9	1.1	4.8	3.5
1953	0.6	0.4	0.9	0.6	1.6	0.6	2.8	1.6	1.8	1.0	4.6	3.1
1954	0.6	0.4	0.8	0.6	1.5	0.6	2.5	1.4	1.7	0.9	4.3	2.9
1955	0.6	0.4	0.8	0.6	1.6	0.6	2.4	1.3	1.7	0.9	4.1	2.8
1956	0.5	0.4	0.8	0.5	1.6	0.6	2.4	1.2	1.7	0.9	4.1	2.7
1957	0.6	0.4	0.8	0.6	1.6	0.6	2.3	1.3	1.7	0.9	4.3	2.8
1958	0.5	0.4	0.7	0.5	1.5	0.5	2.2	1.1	1.6	0.9	4.1	2.8
1959	0.6	0.3	0.8	0.5	1.5	0.5	2.2	1.2	1.6	0.9	4.1	2.6
1960	0.5	0.3	0.8	0.5	1.4	0.5	2.1	1.1	1.6	0.9	3.9	2.6
1961	0.5	0.3	0.7	0.5	1.4	0.5	2.1	1.1	1.6	0.8	3.8	2.5
1962[b/]	0.5	0.3	0.7	0.5	1.4	0.5	2.1	1.1	1.6	0.9	3.9	2.5
1963[b/]	0.5	0.3	0.7	0.5	1.4	0.6	2.2	1.0	1.7	0.9	4.0	2.6
1964	0.5	0.3	0.7	0.5	1.5	0.6	2.1	1.0	1.7	0.9	4.3	2.5
1965	0.5	0.3	0.7	0.5	1.5	0.6	2.2	1.0	1.7	0.9	4.4	2.5
1966	0.5	0.3	0.7	0.5	1.6	0.6	2.4	1.0	1.7	0.9	4.6	2.5
1967	0.5	0.3	0.7	0.4	1.6	0.6	2.5	1.0	1.7	0.8	4.8	2.5
1968												
1969												
1970												

* Provisional

(continued)

Year	White		Nonwhite		White		Nonwhite		White		Nonwhite	
	Male	Female	Male	Female	Male	Female	Male	Female	Male	Female	Male	Female
	35-44 years				45-54 years				55-64 years			
	L053	L054	L055	L056	L057	L058	L059	L060	L061	L062	L063	L064
1940	5.1	3.7	13.2	11.7	11.4	7.5	24.5	21.1	25.2	16.8	37.1	33.2
1941	5.0	3.4	12.7	11.3	11.2	7.2	23.6	20.1	24.5	16.0	35.3	31.4
1942	4.9	3.3	12.2	10.6	11.1	7.0	22.8	18.8	24.4	15.6	33.7	30.0
1943	4.9	3.3	11.7	10.4	11.2	7.1	22.3	18.9	25.0	16.1	34.4	31.1
1944	4.7	3.2	11.1	10.0	10.7	6.7	21.4	17.8	24.3	15.3	33.0	29.1
1945	4.9	3.1	10.9	9.4	10.7	6.5	20.8	17.2	24.4	14.9	32.3	28.1
1946	4.3	2.9	9.7	8.6	10.4	6.2	20.1	16.6	23.6	14.4	31.4	26.8
1947	4.3	2.7	9.4	8.2	10.5	6.1	20.2	17.1	24.3	14.2	32.7	27.8
1948	4.1	2.6	9.5	8.1	10.3	5.8	20.3	16.5	23.8	13.7	34.5	27.6
1949	3.9	2.4	8.9	7.8	10.0	5.6	19.3	16.1	23.4	13.2	33.7	27.4
1950	3.8	2.4	8.6	7.5	9.8	5.5	18.6	15.5	23.0	12.9	34.8	27.6
1951	3.8	2.3	8.4	7.2	9.8	5.4	18.3	15.3	22.9	12.7	35.9	28.6
1952	3.7	2.2	8.4	6.9	9.7	5.2	18.1	15.0	22.9	12.3	35.7	27.3
1953	3.6	2.1	8.0	6.5	9.6	5.1	18.0	14.5	22.8	12.1	35.1	26.3
1954	3.4	2.0	7.2	6.0	9.2	4.9	16.6	13.7	21.7	11.4	32.3	24.3
1955	3.4	2.0	7.2	5.8	9.1	4.6	15.9	12.9	21.8	11.2	31.9	24.4
1956	3.3	1.9	7.0	5.9	9.0	4.6	15.5	12.6	22.0	11.1	32.7	25.3
1957	3.4	2.0	7.3	5.9	9.2	4.7	16.2	12.9	22.5	11.3	33.8	25.6
1958	3.4	1.9	7.0	5.6	9.2	4.6	15.7	12.4	22.1	11.0	32.0	24.7
1959	3.3	1.9	7.2	5.4	9.1	4.5	15.3	11.4	22.0	10.7	31.0	23.4
1960	3.3	1.9	7.3	5.5	9.3	4.6	15.5	11.4	22.3	10.8	31.5	24.1
1961	3.3	1.9	7.2	5.3	9.0	4.5	14.7	10.8	21.6	10.3	30.0	23.4
1962 b/	3.3	1.9	7.4	5.4	9.1	4.6	15.3	10.7	21.8	10.4	30.5	23.7
1963 b/	3.3	1.9	7.6	5.5	9.2	4.6	15.7	11.0	22.3	10.5	31.8	24.2
1964	3.4	1.9	8.1	5.3	9.0	4.6	15.7	10.9	22.1	10.3	31.5	23.0
1965	3.4	1.9	8.1	5.4	9.0	4.6	15.9	10.4	22.2	10.2	31.3	22.2
1966	3.4	1.9	8.5	5.3	9.1	4.6	16.3	10.4	22.5	10.2	31.8	21.4
1967	3.4	1.9	8.5	5.1	9.0	4.6	16.1	10.1	22.2	10.1	30.9	20.6
1968												
1969												
1970												

Year	65-74 years				75-84 years				85 years & over			
	L065	L066	L067	L068	L069	L070	L071	L072	L073	L074	L075	L076
1940	54.0	41.5	62.8	52.3	122.0	104.8	108.8	84.1	251.4	235.0	199.7	159.7
1941	52.1	39.2	59.6	48.9	116.2	98.5	100.3	77.1	235.1	214.7	197.1	149.3
1942	50.8	38.1	56.5	46.9	112.4	94.8	89.6	70.5	225.6	209.2	181.9	136.7
1943	52.3	39.4	56.7	47.5	118.8	100.4	93.6	75.4	274.4	228.8	186.9	142.0
1944	50.0	37.3	53.5	44.5	112.5	95.2	85.7	68.8	229.0	214.3	183.1	137.7
1945	48.9	35.9	51.1	41.8	109.4	91.7	83.0	66.6	225.5	208.5	165.1	124.1
1946	47.4	34.7	48.7	40.9	105.9	88.9	76.9	63.4	227.5	211.0	157.6	117.0
1947	49.0	34.8	51.7	42.8	108.3	89.9	83.1	67.4	234.6	215.0	166.2	121.7
1948	48.4	33.6	54.0	44.2	106.4	87.5	86.0	67.9	232.0	210.3	161.6	127.8
1949	47.9	32.8	55.0	45.2	105.1	84.7	86.3	70.3	220.1	200.7	155.7	127.0
1950	48.6	32.4	57.9	46.1	105.3	84.8	90.3	70.6	221.2	196.8	160.2	133.7
1951	48.3	31.5	52.7	39.6	104.8	83.8	87.2	69.5	211.9	195.2	161.4	128.5
1952	47.5	31.0	52.2	39.3	103.4	81.8	87.8	65.8	199.9	191.1	156.6	126.0
1953	47.7	30.8	53.0	39.2	104.1	81.5	85.0	67.6	202.3	191.9	158.6	123.7
1954	46.5	29.2	50.1	37.0	99.4	77.2	79.9	62.2	190.8	182.8	143.8	110.5
1955	47.0	29.1	51.6	37.8	102.0	78.8	80.2	64.4	200.6	191.7	137.7	112.1
1956	47.3	28.8	51.8	38.3	102.3	78.4	81.2	64.3	205.1	192.7	144.5	113.3
1957	48.6	29.2	55.6	40.3	102.4	78.6	82.6	65.9	211.6	197.3	155.0	120.3
1958	47.9	28.5	56.1	40.1	102.7	78.1	84.4	66.1	213.5	196.5	156.1	121.7
1959	47.3	27.8	54.5	38.5	100.5	76.3	81.8	64.1	210.9	191.8	144.4	122.3
1960	48.5	27.8	56.6	39.8	103.0	77.0	86.6	67.1	217.5	194.8	152.4	128.7
1961	47.4	27.0	56.2	38.9	99.4	73.4	78.2	62.9	213.9	192.0	155.9	132.0
1962 b/	48.4	27.1	59.5	41.2	100.0	73.8	80.5	64.4	223.9	199.7	161.0	134.8
1963 b/	49.8	27.3	64.4	43.1	101.8	73.9	85.0	65.4	230.0	206.6	161.6	137.1
1964	48.9	26.7	61.4	41.4	98.6	71.1	79.2	61.3	218.2	200.0	134.3	123.3
1965	49.3	26.4	63.8	42.9	99.7	70.6	81.3	60.9	222.4	202.1	130.7	117.9
1966	49.8	26.7	66.9	45.2	99.9	70.2	82.1	62.2	218.6	202.7	127.0	114.6
1967	48.9	25.9	65.0	44.1	97.6	67.6	79.7	57.4	215.1	197.0	114.3	104.1
1968												
1969												
1970												

Age-adjusted[a] death rates (deaths per 100,000 population) for selected causes, by color and sex

Year	All causes				Major cardiovascular-renal[b] diseases (Code 330-334, 400-468, 592-594)				Arteriosclerotic heart disease, including coronary disease (Code 420)			
	White		Nonwhite		White		Nonwhite		White		Nonwhite	
	Male	Female	Male	Female	Male	Female	Male	Female	Male	Female	Male	Female
	L077	L078	L079	L080	L081	L082	L083	L084	L085	L086	L087	L088
1940	1155.1	879.0	1764.4	1504.7	535.3	402.6	691.3	647.1				
1941	1114.4	829.5	1691.3	1433.6	519.1	379.5	667.0	621.3				
1942	1088.2	798.1	1580.0	1327.8	516.5	373.8	643.7	593.8				
1943	1120.3	820.2	1563.6	1337.8	538.8	391.6	645.4	611.1				
1944	1082.4	779.2	1492.3	1265.0	516.0	368.2	604.6	572.7				
1945	1070.4	752.2	1446.2	1193.1	514.3	358.4	589.5	549.5				
1946	1022.8	730.6	1349.6	1135.1	492.8	344.9	554.4	527.1				
1947	1012.5	706.8	1356.4	1140.8	508.7	345.9	583.7	548.5				
1948	995.3	683.8	1378.0	1121.6	502.4	333.8	609.7	550.8				
1949	971.7	659.3	1346.6	1105.3	508.3	338.9	615.0	568.8	248.2	114.6	150.4	105.5
1950	963.1	645.0	1358.5	1095.7	514.1	339.0	633.7	570.8	259.5	120.6	164.0	112.6
1951	956.5	655.9	1327.9	1049.5	508.3	349.8	619.9	550.2	263.1	126.8	168.3	113.0
1952	944.4	619.1	1325.1	1021.7	501.9	325.1	621.4	538.6	266.7	124.4	175.2	116.2
1953	939.3	606.8	1297.1	989.1	501.5	321.5	611.2	520.9	275.1	127.7	186.6	123.9
1954	897.2	574.2	1202.2	918.2	480.4	303.2	567.4	489.4	272.7	125.8	181.0	117.6
1955	905.0	572.8	1187.5	909.9	487.0	303.8	567.3	486.1	281.6	130.6	188.8	126.8
1956	907.5	567.6	1193.1	912.1	488.8	301.9	568.2	490.8	288.6	133.8	198.2	134.6
1957	922.9	574.5	1239.8	938.1	496.8	305.3	589.7	503.6	296.4	138.0	213.2	141.7
1958	912.4	564.7	1216.2	917.5	495.1	301.6	582.1	492.4	297.8	136.1	212.0	139.5
1959	902.1	551.9	1186.9	877.5	487.3	292.6	562.2	465.4	298.4	136.0	215.0	137.1
1960	917.7	555.0	1211.0	893.3	493.2	291.5	564.0	467.1	305.3	137.8	219.5	145.8
1961	891.3	536.3	1158.6	856.1	480.8	281.4	548.1	455.1	301.9	135.5	220.6	145.7
1962	903.2	541.5	1196.2	873.4	484.8	283.4	569.4	462.5	307.5	138.7	234.7	152.0
1963	921.2	546.0	1248.6	894.2	490.8	283.5	584.3	466.0	313.4	140.8	244.4	156.8
1964	904.6	533.8	1222.8	859.0	479.6	275.5	565.6	449.2	308.9	138.9	242.8	156.0
1965	909.3	531.7	1238.2	851.9	479.3	272.9	569.8	440.8	310.9	138.7	247.7	156.0
1966	915.2	531.2	1271.2	856.4	480.2	272.0	575.6	437.8	312.7	139.1	255.0	158.5
1967	900.9	518.1	1243.3	820.7	469.0	263.0	551.0	417.3	307.0	136.1	247.0	152.8
1968												
1969												
1970												

(continued)

424

Age-adjusted[a]/ death rates (deaths per 100,000 population) for selected causes, by color and sex

Year	Hypertensive heart disease (Code 440-443)				Diabetes mellitus (Code 260)				All malignant neoplasms (Code 140-205)			
	White		Nonwhite		White		Nonwhite		White		Nonwhite	
	Male	Female	Male	Female	Male	Female	Male	Female	Male	Female	Male	Female
	L089	L090	L091	L092	L093	L094	L095	L096	L097	L098	L099	L100
1940					20.6	32.8	15.0	32.2	117.7	125.5	83.7	119.5
1941					19.1	31.2	13.6	29.1	116.2	122.6	82.7	115.9
1942					18.9	30.1	14.6	28.7	115.8	122.1	84.7	115.4
1943					19.7	31.5	14.4	30.3	116.0	122.0	82.4	114.4
1944					18.5	29.4	15.3	31.3	118.0	121.2	87.4	113.9
1945					18.3	29.1	13.7	27.9	120.7	121.1	92.1	116.6
1946					17.3	27.9	11.7	26.9	120.3	119.7	95.9	116.9
1947					18.4	28.8	14.0	29.3	123.4	119.8	101.1	122.1
1948					18.5	28.6	14.7	30.3	125.4	119.7	111.2	126.0
1949	42.2	43.4	113.8	123.4	11.7	17.6	11.0	23.0	130.1	120.6	117.7	126.7
1950	41.7	42.7	118.6	125.3	11.3	16.4	11.8	22.6	130.9	119.4	125.8	131.0
1951	40.2	42.6	113.7	120.5	11.2	16.6	11.8	21.3	131.1	119.1	125.3	126.4
1952	38.1	38.8	114.9	116.9	11.5	15.8	11.5	21.5	133.7	117.6	130.7	126.8
1953	35.7	36.5	106.5	109.9	11.2	15.6	11.3	22.9	135.5	116.4	133.2	125.1
1954	31.4	32.7	94.8	101.1	10.9	14.5	11.3	21.2	136.0	115.1	140.6	125.9
1955	29.7	30.9	93.8	96.7	10.9	14.1	11.2	21.6	137.4	114.3	138.7	124.7
1956	28.0	29.1	90.5	96.7	10.9	14.0	11.7	22.2	139.1	113.2	145.0	127.8
1957	27.1	28.0	89.7	97.7	10.9	14.3	12.5	23.6	139.9	112.6	149.2	125.2
1958	26.6	28.3	84.8	95.4	11.1	13.6	13.0	24.3	138.2	110.6	146.4	125.3
1959	23.9	24.9	78.7	85.1	11.0	13.5	14.1	24.2	139.4	109.4	152.5	121.3
1960	22.5	23.6	77.5	81.3	11.6	13.7	16.1	26.8	141.6	109.5	154.8	125.0
1961	20.7	21.6	72.3	77.6	11.4	13.3	14.9	26.7	142.0	108.5	157.8	124.3
1962	19.7	20.4	72.8	75.4	11.9	13.1	16.1	27.1	142.0	107.4	159.0	124.6
1963	19.0	19.4	72.2	74.6	11.9	13.3	16.6	29.1	143.8	107.3	168.5	124.3
1964	17.5	17.9	66.7	68.0	11.8	12.9	17.6	29.0	145.7	107.4	170.2	123.9
1965	16.7	16.5	64.2	63.2	11.9	12.9	18.1	28.6	148.0	108.1	173.3	125.2
1966	16.2	15.7	64.1	61.5	12.3	13.0	18.3	30.5	148.9	107.6	182.3	127.0
1967	14.7	14.2	58.1	55.0	12.4	12.8	18.5	29.7	150.3	107.9	186.6	126.6
1968												
1969												
1970												

(continued)

Age-adjusted[a]/ death rates (deaths per 100,000 population) for selected causes, by color and sex

Year	Malignant neoplasm of digestive organs and peritoneum, not secondary (150-156A,157-159)				Malignant neoplasm of respiratory system, not specified as secondary (Code 160-164)				Malignant neoplasm of breast[c]/ (Code 170)	
	White		Nonwhite		White		Nonwhite		Female	
	Male	Female	Male	Female	Male	Female	Male	Female	White	Nonwhite
	L101	L102	L103	L104	L105	L106	L107	L108	L109	L110
1940	61.6	50.7	46.8	36.4	11.5	3.4	6.3	2.3	23.6	18.4
1941	60.0	49.5	46.1	34.8	11.9	3.6	6.6[d]/	2.5	22.9	18.0
1942	60.0	49.1	46.6	35.8	12.5	3.7	7.9	2.4[d]/	23.0	17.3
1943	60.2	49.1	44.9	35.6	13.2	4.0	7.7[d]/	2.4[d]/	22.6	17.7
1944	60.1	48.7	48.3	35.2	14.2	4.0	7.7	2.7[d]/	22.5	17.1
1945	60.7	48.3	49.3	36.1	15.3	4.2	9.3	3.3[d]/	22.8	18.2
1946	59.3	47.0	50.5	36.6	16.4	4.2	11.2	3.4[d]/	22.8	18.0
1947	59.4	46.4	53.2	39.3	18.4	4.6	12.5	3.5	22.9	17.7
1948	59.2	45.8	57.1	40.8	19.8	4.8	13.9	3.9	23.7	19.0
1949	55.6	42.7	57.5	38.3	20.2	4.4	15.0	3.7	22.5	17.7
1950	54.0	41.1	59.5	40.2	21.6	4.6	17.0	4.1	22.5	19.0
1951	52.5	40.7	56.1	37.9	22.5	4.6	18.8	4.4	22.2	18.8
1952	52.0	39.2	59.0	37.1	24.0	4.6	20.2	4.3	22.4	18.9
1953	51.8	38.5	57.6	36.6	25.9	4.5	22.3	4.3	22.5	18.7
1954	50.8	37.8	60.7	36.8	26.6	4.5	23.2	4.2	22.2	19.8
1955	50.0	36.7	58.4	35.7	28.5	4.6	24.0	5.2	22.9	19.6
1956	50.0	36.5	59.6	36.2	30.1	4.8	26.9	4.8	22.6	20.4
1957	49.0	35.6	59.0	36.3	31.2	4.8	28.8	4.9[d]/	22.6	19.8
1958	48.0	34.7	57.6	37.2	32.0	5.0	29.8	5.2[d]/	22.2	19.2
1959	47.7	34.4	59.2	35.3	33.2	5.0	31.6	5.7	22.1	19.5
1960	47.5	33.9	59.8	37.2	34.6	5.1	35.6	5.6	22.4	20.7
1961	46.7	33.1	60.2	37.0	36.0	5.5	35.9	5.7	22.4	20.4
1962	45.6	32.4	57.8	36.8	37.3	5.7	37.3	6.0	22.2	20.2
1963	45.1	32.0	60.8	36.4	38.4	6.1	41.6	7.0	22.1	21.2
1964	45.4	31.5	61.9	37.0	40.2	6.3	41.7	6.8	22.8	21.1
1965	45.1	31.1	62.7	36.7	41.7	6.9	44.3	7.3	23.0	21.3
1966	44.3	31.0	64.7	37.5	43.0	7.2	50.0	8.1	23.1	21.2
1967	44.0	30.3	62.4	36.5	44.5	7.8	51.7	8.2	23.2	22.6
1968										
1969										
1970										

(continued)

426

Age-adjusted[a] death rates (deaths per 100,000 population) for selected causes, by color and sex

Year	Malignant neoplasm of genital organs (Code 171-179)				Influenza and pneumonia (except pneumonia of the newborn) (Code 480-493)				Tuberculosis of the respiratory system (Code 001-008)			
	White		Nonwhite		White		Nonwhite		White		Nonwhite	
	Male	Female	Male	Female	Male	Female	Male	Female	Male	Female	Male	Female
	L111	L112	L113	L114	L115	L116	L117	L118	L119	L120	L121	L122
1940	15.5	30.5	13.2	48.8	70.1	55.7	153.6	122.4	41.0	25.3	135.8	106.7
1941	15.6	29.9	12.6	46.0	62.9	47.5	142.5	113.1	39.3	24.4	129.1	104.1
1942	14.3	28.9	13.5	45.5	54.8	40.1	112.5	89.7	38.9	22.7	127.1	97.1
1943	14.2	29.2	13.1	44.7	65.0	46.0	129.7	98.0	39.4	21.8	123.3	91.4
1944	14.7	29.1	14.1	45.4	58.3	41.3	119.8	92.5	39.6	20.7	119.2	84.9
1945	15.3	28.7	15.1	44.9	48.1	33.7	98.9	77.7	39.3	19.2	116.8	79.6
1946	15.4	28.3	15.2	45.1	41.7	31.1	83.4	67.6	34.6	18.2	101.1	73.4
1947	15.4	28.4	15.9	45.7	38.9	27.1	76.1	61.5	32.4	15.8	98.1	71.6
1948	15.8	27.6	18.0	45.7	35.0	23.9	71.2	55.6	29.5	13.3	90.9	62.2
1949	14.5	25.8	17.4	46.1	26.5	18.0	60.4	46.5	25.2	11.3	86.9	56.0
1950	14.4	25.3	18.2	44.0	27.1	18.9	63.4	50.6	21.9	9.2	73.9	47.6
1951	14.1	24.3	18.2	41.3	26.6	19.7	62.3	47.2	19.9	8.3	66.6	38.1
1952	14.3	23.7	18.7	41.7	24.8	16.9	60.6	44.0	15.6	6.1	53.3	28.3
1953	14.3	23.7	19.0	41.6	27.5	18.2	68.6	49.1	12.5	4.5	40.9	20.6
1954	14.6	23.1	20.9	39.6	21.2	13.9	49.1	33.8	10.5	3.7	32.4	16.5
1955	14.5	22.8	20.6	39.5	22.3	14.9	50.8	33.9	9.4	3.2	28.5	14.0
1956	14.5	21.9	21.3	40.1	23.5	15.1	49.1	34.6	8.8	3.0	26.8	12.5
1957	14.3	22.1	22.2	38.1	30.5	19.3	65.0	46.4	8.5	2.7	25.0	11.3
1958	14.0	21.6	21.1	37.4	27.7	17.2	61.4	39.0	7.6	2.4	24.1	10.2
1959	13.4	20.9	22.5	35.0	25.8	16.2	53.6	35.2	6.9	2.2	20.5	9.4
1960	13.5	20.7	21.8	34.2	31.0	19.0	68.0	43.3	6.5	2.0	19.5	8.0
1961	13.6	20.2	22.3	34.6	24.8	15.5	49.7	30.6	5.7	1.7	18.2	7.1
1962	13.4	20.0	23.7	33.4	26.5	16.7	52.2	35.5	5.3	1.6	17.5	6.7
1963	13.6	19.6	22.7	32.8	30.8	19.0	66.7	45.1	5.2	1.5	17.1	6.1
1964	13.5	19.2	23.0	32.0	26.0	15.7	51.3	31.4	4.5	1.3	15.3	5.6
1965	13.5	19.0	22.5	31.6	26.9	16.1	52.3	32.3	4.2	1.2	14.6	5.4
1966	13.4	18.4	22.4	31.4	27.1	16.4	55.2	32.8	4.0	1.1	14.9	4.9
1967	13.2	17.8	24.3	29.5	24.2	14.3	47.6	26.6	3.4	1.0	13.7	4.5
1968												
1969												
1970												

(continued)

Age-adjusted[a] death rates (deaths per 100,000 population) for selected causes, by color and sex

Year	Syphilis and its sequelae (Code 020-029)				Motor vehicle accidents (Code E810-E835)				Suicide (Code E963, E970-E979)			
	White		Nonwhite		White		Nonwhite		White		Nonwhite	
	Male	Female	Male	Female	Male	Female	Male	Female	Male	Female	Male	Female
	L123	L124	L125	L126	L127	L128	L129	L130	L131	L132	L133	L134
1940	14.4	4.9	85.0	37.3	40.2	12.2	41.5	10.0	23.1	7.2	7.9	2.2
1941	13.5	4.4	74.2	33.9	45.8	13.7	51.6	11.7	20.3	6.7	7.3	1.8[d]
1942	12.3	4.1	66.4	29.5	33.4	8.6	35.5	7.7	19.0	6.1	6.5	2.0
1943	12.3	3.8	66.8	27.0	28.7	7.1	30.6	5.8	15.6	5.8	5.2	1.4
1944	11.0	3.5	61.2	25.1	30.0	7.5	31.7	6.8	15.1	5.7	5.3	1.5[d]
1945	10.3	3.1	57.6	22.4	36.2	8.9	33.5	7.4	17.3	6.0	6.3	1.5
1946	9.2	2.8	49.2	21.5	38.1	10.5	35.7	9.2	17.8	6.0	6.6	1.9
1947	8.8	2.8	45.7	20.2	36.2	10.2	34.6	8.1	18.0	5.7	7.1	1.7
1948	7.8	2.6	42.2	17.9	34.7	10.0	36.1	8.6	17.6	5.5	7.6	1.6
1949	5.7	1.7	30.4	13.0	33.2	9.7	37.2	9.3	18.2	5.2	7.8	1.7
1950	5.0	1.6	26.1	10.5	35.9	10.6	41.2	11.1	18.1	5.3	7.8	1.8
1951	4.1	1.2	21.9	8.7	37.8	11.2	45.2	12.5	16.5	4.8	7.3	1.9
1952	3.7	1.1	19.4	7.5	38.4	11.6	46.9	12.4	16.1	4.6	6.9	1.4[d]
1953	3.3	1.0	17.9	7.2	38.0	11.5	47.8	12.3	16.5	4.5	7.3	1.7
1954	2.9	0.9	15.3	6.2	35.4	10.6	42.6	11.8	16.8	4.3	7.8	1.7
1955	2.2	0.7	13.4[d]	4.9[d]	37.8	11.4	45.1	12.6	16.5	4.8	7.1	1.8
1956	2.3	0.7	11.8[d]	4.8	38.5	11.5	47.9	12.5	16.3	4.6	7.1	1.6
1957	2.1	0.7	11.4	4.7	36.8	11.2	43.5	12.5	16.0	4.5	8.1	2.1
1958	1.9	0.6	10.6[d]	4.4	34.3	10.8	40.4	10.2	17.6	5.0	8.4	2.3
1959	1.7	0.6	7.9	3.6	34.5	11.0	40.5	10.8	17.4	4.9	9.1	2.3
1960	1.6	0.5	7.6	3.0	34.0	11.1	39.5	10.6	17.5	5.3	8.7	2.3
1961	1.5	0.4	7.1	3.5	33.4	10.9	38.0	11.0	17.1	5.3	9.5	2.2
1962	1.5	0.5	6.5	2.7	35.0	12.0	40.3	11.4	17.9	6.0	9.0	2.7
1963	1.4	0.4	6.3	2.6	36.8	12.6	42.7	11.8	17.9	6.4	9.9	2.7
1964	1.3	0.4	5.3	2.4	38.1	13.6	44.2	12.4	17.4	6.2	9.1	2.6
1965	1.3	0.4	4.9	1.9	39.4	13.7	46.4	13.7	17.7	6.7	9.7	3.0
1966	1.2	0.3	3.5	1.7	41.9	14.7	50.1	15.0	17.4	6.5	9.9	2.9
1967	1.3	0.4	3.6	1.7	41.1	14.4	49.4	14.6	17.1	6.7	9.7	3.2
1968												
1969												
1970												

(continued)

Age-adjusted[a/] death rates (deaths per 100,000 population) for selected causes, by color and sex

Year	Homicide (Code E964, E980-E985)				Cirrhosis of the liver (Code 581)				Ulcer of stomach and duodenum (Code 540, 541)			
	White		Nonwhite		White		Nonwhite		White		Nonwhite	
	Male L135	Female L136	Male L137	Female L138	Male L139	Female L140	Male L141	Female L142	Male L143	Female L144	Male L145	Female L146
1940	5.0	1.3	57.1	12.6	11.7	5.6	9.2	5.0	11.1	2.2	11.2	4.0
1941	4.5	1.3	56.6	12.2	11.9	6.0	8.2	4.5	10.8	2.1	10.6	3.5
1942	4.4	1.2	55.2	11.8	12.4	6.2	8.6	4.6	11.2	2.0	10.7	3.9
1943	4.1	1.2	44.3	9.7	11.9	6.2	8.8	4.9	11.1	2.1	10.3	4.3
1944	4.1	1.1	47.4	9.5	10.7	5.6	8.3	4.9	10.4	2.0	9.2	3.2
1945	5.1	1.3	52.7	10.6	11.8	5.9	8.5	5.4	10.5	1.9	9.9	3.2
1946	4.9	1.5	56.4	12.4	12.3	6.1	8.2	4.6	9.0	1.8	7.6	3.0
1947	4.7	1.4	53.9	12.1	13.2	6.7	8.7	5.9	9.3	1.9	8.3	2.9
1948	4.5	1.5	53.9	11.9	14.5	7.0	10.1	6.5	9.3	1.8	7.7	2.6
1949	4.1	1.4	48.9	11.7	11.8	5.8	8.6	5.0	8.0	1.6	7.9	2.2
1950	3.9	1.4	49.1	11.5	11.6	5.8	9.0	5.9	8.2	1.7	8.0	2.2
1951	3.6	1.4	45.3	11.1	12.3	6.2	9.9	6.3	8.3	1.8	7.3	2.5
1952	3.8	1.3	50.4	11.3	13.0	6.2	10.6	5.7	8.4	1.8	7.2	1.9
1953	3.6	1.3	46.5	10.2	13.0	6.4	10.0	6.3	8.6	1.8	7.9	2.3
1954	3.6	1.4	46.2	10.3	12.8	6.0	9.8	6.5	8.5	1.9	7.4	2.5
1955	3.5	1.3	42.6	10.3	12.9	6.1	10.3	6.8	8.4	2.0	7.2	2.5
1956	3.5	1.3	43.2	11.3	13.4	6.5	11.8	7.8	8.5	2.1	6.8	2.5
1957	3.5	1.4	43.1	10.3	14.4	6.6	13.4	8.4	8.4	2.3	7.5	2.2
1958	3.6	1.4	41.6	10.5	13.7	6.3	12.5	7.4	8.5	2.3	7.4	2.9
1959	3.8	1.5	42.3	10.7	13.7	6.4	13.7	9.1	8.1	2.3	7.4	2.2
1960	3.9	1.5	41.9	11.2	14.4	6.6	14.9	9.1	8.5	2.4	7.8	2.4
1961	3.9	1.6	41.5	10.1	14.2	6.7	15.9	9.9	8.3	2.4	7.8	2.8
1962	4.1	1.7	44.4	10.3	14.6	6.8	16.8	11.0	8.4	2.6	8.3	2.6
1963	4.2	1.6	44.8	10.5	14.7	7.2	17.1	11.0	8.3	2.5	8.0	2.8
1964	4.3	1.7	47.1	10.6	15.0	7.3	19.5	11.3	7.3	2.3	7.4	2.8
1965	4.8	1.7	50.7	11.7	15.6	7.6	23.3	13.4	6.8	2.2	6.7	2.4
1966	4.9	1.9	54.8	12.4	16.8	7.9	26.6	15.0	6.4	2.2	7.3	2.5
1967	5.9	2.0	62.7	14.0	17.2	8.4	27.2	15.0	6.0	2.1	6.5	2.3
1968												
1969												
1970												

Year	Maternal mortality rates: deaths from maternal causes (Code 640-689) per 100,000 live births											
	Total	White	Non-white	Total	White	Non-white	Total	White	Non-white	Total	White	Non-white
	All ages			Under 20 years			20-24 years			25-29 years		
	L147	L148	L149	L150	L151	L152	L153	L154	L155	L156	L157	L158
1940	376.0	319.8	773.5	389.5	295.1	686.5	240.4	203.0	504.2	304.1	256.7	766.7
1941	316.5	266.0	678.1	292.7	211.0	546.5	210.9	173.6	483.3	245.1	205.3	646.4
1942	258.7	221.8	544.0	224.7	173.1	393.3	169.4	142.1	387.9	203.9	173.5	541.4
1943	245.2	210.5	509.9	225.7	175.2	386.8	158.4	137.2	320.3	193.3	163.9	513.5
1944	227.9	189.4	506.0	215.6	158.8	384.5	141.9	115.8	327.2	171.9	141.5	467.2
1945	207.2	172.1	454.8	186.9	145.5	302.8	131.9	105.7	308.8	153.4	128.4	389.6
1946	156.7	130.7	358.9	131.7	105.0	216.0	102.9	84.5	245.5	124.9	104.4	337.6
1947	134.5	108.6	334.6	118.3	86.1	232.6	83.3	67.6	204.5	107.5	87.5	314.1
1948	116.6	89.4	30.10	103.7	66.1	228.3	71.9	53.5	195.0	88.6	67.6	273.5
1949	90.3	68.1	234.8	83.1	53.6	177.7	51.2	37.7	137.1	70.4	53.0	217.0
1950	83.3	61.1	221.6	70.7	44.9	149.9	47.6	35.7	120.0	63.5	45.0	211.7
1951	75.0	54.9	201.3	62.1	42.6	124.8	44.2	32.6	117.3	61.0	43.9	195.1
1952	67.8	48.9	188.1	58.2	38.4	122.0	39.9	27.0	121.3	51.2	39.0	145.1
1953	61.1	44.1	166.1	51.4	30.6	119.1	33.8	24.4	91.9	42.1	29.8	132.6
1954	52.4	37.2	143.8	34.1	22.4	72.0	27.3	20.1	71.1	36.7	24.9	120.0
1955	47.0	32.8	130.3	33.5	20.3	76.4	25.2	18.5	65.0	36.6	26.1	109.4
1956	40.9	28.7	110.7	27.5	18.0	59.2	22.6	16.0	61.1	30.9	21.6	93.6
1957	41.0	27.5	118.3	30.0	17.8	71.7	19.6	13.2	56.9	30.3	19.4	103.4
1958	37.6	26.3	101.8	24.8	18.1	47.8	18.9	12.8	54.3	30.3	20.6	94.0
1959	37.4	25.8	102.1	27.2	17.0	62.4	20.6	14.0	60.0	29.7	20.4	88.7
1960	37.1	26.0	97.9	22.7	14.8	50.3	20.7	15.3	52.7	29.8	20.3	89.6
1961	36.9	24.9	101.3	20.4	12.6	47.5	18.9	12.6	55.5	29.5	20.6	83.1
1962	35.2	23.8	95.9	18.9	10.4	49.9	18.6	12.9	53.1	29.5	21.0	79.1
1963	35.8	24.0	96.9	23.1	14.6	51.0	18.9	13.6	50.1	28.2	17.2	90.4
1964	33.3	22.3	89.9	19.4	11.9	42.3	17.9	11.8	52.2	28.0	16.9	95.4
1965	31.6	21.0	83.7	19.9	11.7	43.9	17.5	13.4	39.9	26.5	15.4	91.5
1966	29.1	20.2	72.4	15.9	9.2	35.2	18.5	13.2	48.3	25.7	18.7	68.0
1967	28.0	19.5	69.5	22.1	15.1	40.7	16.6	11.0	48.5	20.4	14.9	55.4
1968												
1969												
1970												

Year	30-34 years			35-39 years			40-44 years		
	L159	L160	L161	L162	L163	L164	L165	L166	L167
1940	447.2	390.9	1103.8	744.8	656.4	1143.8	957.1	853.7	1765.0
1941	382.6	329.8	905.1	652.2	567.4	1312.3	976.4	894.4	1580.0
1942	325.5	282.5	773.2	564.7	498.4	1104.0	818.2	764.8	1212.5
1943	299.4	258.1	734.1	509.5	445.6	1051.2	742.4	673.8	1259.2
1944	280.1	235.6	719.2	454.0	387.0	1022.7	683.6	604.7	1290.2
1945	238.2	192.4	698.6	400.2	341.5	891.0	637.5	576.2	1100.4
1946	183.3	150.6	530.1	314.4	261.3	773.4	529.1	476.8	923.8
1947	168.7	135.0	519.2	285.5	232.8	723.9	484.1	407.4	1068.9
1948	145.4	110.7	465.2	266.7	217.0	643.7	422.7	358.3	899.7
1949	119.0	92.3	351.5	193.0	141.6	563.4	354.0	316.5	608.7
1950	107.7	75.9	370.7	191.2	144.0	522.7	318.2	270.8	631.2
1951	93.2	66.3	310.8	159.4	112.6	482.4	301.7	256.8	580.4
1952	87.6	59.8	310.5	150.8	109.1	451.2	224.9	173.6	556.3
1953	78.7	55.0	259.9	144.4	110.3	385.4	243.7	198.3	523.0
1954	71.7	44.3	274.3	125.8	98.3	313.3	234.0	180.1	576.4
1955	58.7	37.4	209.5	107.4	74.0	329.3	204.4	156.1	508.5
1956	53.6	35.0	178.7	94.9	67.7	268.9	172.7	132.2	421.4
1957	59.4	38.8	193.6	98.3	68.7	287.6	152.0	111.3	403.3
1958	54.0	36.2	167.3	90.7	64.1	256.2	143.2	107.5	361.9
1959	49.4	33.0	149.7	86.7	64.2	223.2	154.0	109.2	425.2
1960	50.3	34.3	145.0	92.8	64.1	261.0	138.7	107.7	316.5
1961	57.6	35.8	184.3	90.2	65.3	230.1	138.1	97.5	367.8
1962	58.4	38.6	169.7	81.6	54.9	228.9	131.2	91.0	356.4
1963	52.6	35.1	146.9	96.8	65.1	277.0	137.1	99.8	343.7
1964	46.5	32.9	120.7	95.5	62.9	268.4	117.5	90.0	259.3
1965	46.8	29.1	141.8	82.7	55.8	220.0	124.8	93.7	283.9
1966	41.9	28.0	115.7	70.9	46.0	196.1	127.6	97.6	269.5
1967	43.9	30.8	114.0	72.6	48.6	192.1	131.2	103.6	258.2
1968									
1969									
1970									

Year	Number of deaths, per 100,000 resident population, from motor vehicle traffic accidents (excluding accidents to pedestrians) within specified age-groups									
	Male	Female	Male	Female	Male	Female	Male	Female	Male	Female
	All ages		Under 5 years		5-9 years		10-14 years		15-19 years	
	L168	L169	L170	L171	L172	L173	L174	L175	L176	L177
1949	23.5	7.0	4.6	4.0	4.0	2.1	7.5	3.1	38.2	10.9
1950	26.0	7.9	4.8	4.2	4.0	2.2	7.4	3.3	42.3	12.0
1955	27.5	8.8	4.7	4.9	3.6	2.6	7.1	3.1	49.4	16.0
1960	25.0	8.5	4.5	4.1	3.7	2.5	6.9	3.1	48.5	15.1
1965	30.5	11.1	4.9	4.6	4.9	2.9	7.8	4.0	56.9	18.0
1967	32.4	11.7	4.8	5.0	4.8	3.4	8.2	4.3	62.1	20.6

Year	20-24 years		25-29 years		30-34 years		35-44 years		45-54 years	
	L178	L179	L180	L181	L182	L183	L184	L185	L186	L187
1949	55.8	9.1	35.5	7.0	29.4	6.7	23.6	6.2	21.9	7.4
1950	62.3	11.3	42.3	9.4	31.7	7.6	27.1	7.2	23.9	8.6
1955	78.9	12.9	47.4	10.0	34.5	8.7	30.1	8.5	26.5	9.8
1960	69.0	13.2	42.4	9.1	31.3	7.9	26.1	8.2	25.3	9.7
1965	76.0	18.0	50.5	11.8	37.2	11.1	32.4	11.4	30.6	12.4
1967	83.3	19.3	52.5	13.0	40.1	11.3	31.7	11.0	31.4	12.6

Year	55-64 years		65-74 years		75 years & over	
	L188	L189	L190	L191	L192	L193
1949	23.6	10.3	25.2	10.6	28.9	11.9
1950	25.7	10.6	27.8	11.7	28.3	11.9
1955	27.8	12.1	28.8	12.5	30.1	12.0
1960	25.7	11.7	28.3	12.9	31.5	13.3
1965	31.6	14.3	34.6	16.7	39.3	16.7
1967	31.3	14.2	36.0	17.4	39.7	16.4

Year	Number of deaths, per 100,000 resident population, from motor vehicle traffic accidents to pedestrians, within specified age groups									
	Male	Female	Male	Female	Male	Female	Male	Female	Male	Female
	All ages		Under 5 years		5-9 years		10-14 years		15-19 years	
	L194	L195	L196	L197	L198	L199	L200	L201	L202	L203
1949	8.5	2.7	5.3	3.4	8.7	4.2	3.2	1.4	3.0	1.1
1950	8.6	2.7	5.4	3.4	7.8	4.2	3.3	1.3	3.2	0.8
1955	6.9	2.4	4.4	2.7	6.9	3.2	2.7	1.1	2.9	0.8
1960	5.9	2.3	4.7	2.8	6.8	3.8	2.6	1.0	2.5	0.9
1965	6.1	2.4	4.9	2.6	7.0	3.8	2.9	1.3	3.4	0.9
1967	6.2	2.6	4.6	3.2	7.0	3.9	3.1	1.6	3.9	1.5

Year	20-24 years		25-29 years		30-34 years		35-44 years		45-54 years	
	L204	L205	L206	L207	L208	L209	L210	L211	L212	L213
1949	3.0	0.6	3.0	0.6	3.3	0.8	4.6	1.1	8.5	2.1
1950	3.0	0.9	2.7	0.6	3.2	0.8	4.7	1.3	8.9	2.3
1955	3.0	0.9	2.6	0.6	2.9	0.9	3.8	1.0	6.4	1.9
1960	3.3	0.7	2.9	0.5	2.2	0.8	3.2	0.9	5.5	1.8
1965	3.6	0.9	2.9	0.6	3.3	0.8	4.0	1.1	5.5	1.8
1967	4.0	0.9	3.0	0.7	3.6	0.9	4.2	1.2	5.5	1.7

Year	55-64 years		65-74 years		75 years & over	
	L214	L215	L216	L217	L218	L219
1949	16.0	4.0	31.4	8.7	54.4	13.1
1950	16.9	4.4	30.0	8.5	54.5	12.2
1955	11.6	3.5	22.8	7.2	41.3	12.0
1960	8.9	3.3	15.5	5.8	32.7	9.0
1965	8.6	3.1	15.0	6.1	30.7	8.6
1967	8.8	3.1	14.8	6.6	28.5	10.3

Bibliography

Bernard, Jessie

   1964   Academic Women. University Park, Pa.: Pennsylvania State University Press.

Blau, Peter M., and Otis Dudley Duncan

   1967   The American Population Structure. New York: John Wiley & Sons, Inc.

Bureau of Labor Statistics, U. S.

BLS 1955	Directory of National and International Labor Unions in the United States, 1955. Bulletin No. 1185. Washington, D.C.: U. S. Department of Labor.
BLS 1957	Directory of National and International Labor Unions in the United States, 1961. Bulletin No. 1320. Washington, D.C.: U. S. Department of Labor.
BLS 1959	Directory of National and International Labor Unions in the United States, 1959. Bulletin No. 1267. Washington, D.C.: U.S. Department of Labor.
BLS 1960	Educational Attainment of Workers, 1959. Special Labor Force Report No. 1. Reprinted from Monthly Labor Review (February). Reprint No. 2333.
BLS 1961	Directory of National and International Labor Unions in the United States, 1961. Bulletin No. 1320. Washington, D.C.: U.S. Department of Labor.
BLS 1963a	Educational Attainment of Workers, March 1962. Special Labor Force Report No. 30. Reprinted from Monthly Labor Review (May). Reprint No. 2416.
BLS 1963b	Directory of National and International Labor Unions in the United States, 1963. Bulletin No. 1395. Washington, D.C.: U. S. Department of Labor.
BLS 1965a	Educational Attainment of Workers, March 1964. Special Labor Force Report No. 53. Reprinted from Monthly Labor Review (May). Reprint No. 2463.
BLS 1965b	Directory of National and International Labor Unions in the United States, 1965. Bulletin No. 1493. Washington, D.C.: U.S. Department of Labor.
BLS 1966a	The Negroes in the United States: Their Economic and Social Situation. Bulletin No. 1511. Washington, D.C.: U. S. Department of Labor.
BLS 1966b	Educational Attainment of Workers, March 1965. Special Labor Force Report No. 65. Reprinted from Monthly Labor Review (March). Reprint No. 2488.
BLS 1967a	Educational Attainment of Workers, March 1966. Special Labor Force Report No. 83. Reprinted from Monthly Labor Review (June). Reprint No. 2528.
BLS 1967b	Directory of National and International Labor Unions in the United States, 1967. Bulletin No. 1596. Washington, D.C.: U.S. Department of Labor.
BLS 1968a	Women and the Labor Force. Special Labor Force Report No. 93. Reprinted from Monthly Labor Review (February). Reprint No. 2560.

Bureau of Labor Statistics, U. S.(cont'd)

    BLS   Educational Attainment of Workers, March 1967. Special Labor Force Report No. 92.
    1968b   Reprinted from Monthly Labor Review (February). Reprint No. 2559.

    BLS   Handbook of Labor Statistics, 1969. Bulletin No. 1630. Washington, D. C.: U. S.
    1969a   Department of Labor.

    BLS   Employment Status of School Age Youth, October 1968. Special Labor Force Report
    1969b   No. 111. Reprinted from Monthly Labor Review (August). Reprint No. 2634.

    BLS   Educational Attainment of Workers, March 1968. Special Labor Force Report No.
    1969c   103. Reprinted from Monthly Labor Review (February). Reprint No. 2600.

    BLS   The Social and Economic Status of Negroes in the United States, 1969. BLS Report
    1969d   No. 375; Census Current Population Reports, Series P-23, No. 29. Washington,
               D. C.: U. S. Department of Labor and U. S. Department of Commerce.

    BLS   Directory of National and International Labor Unions in the United States, 1969.
    1970a   Bulletin No. 1665. Washington, D. C.: U. S. Department of Labor.

    BLS   Monthly Labor Review, Vol. 93, No. 6 (June).
    1970b

Blood, Robert O., Jr.

    1963   "The husband-wife relationship." Pp. 282-304 in F. Ivan Nye and Lois W. Hoffman
              (eds.), The Employed Mother in America. Chicago: Rand McNally & Co.

Bogue, Donald J.

    1959   The Population of the United States. Glencoe, Ill.: The Free Press.

Bowen, William G., and T. A. Finegan

    1965   "Labor force participation and unemployment," in Arthur M. Ross (ed.), Employment
              Policy and the Labor Market. Berkeley: University of California Press. (Reprint
              published by Department of Economics, Princeton University).

Brady, Dorothy S.

    1965   Age and the Income Distribution. Social Security Administration Research Report
              No. 8. Washington, D. C.: U. S. Department of Health, Education and Welfare.

Burchinal, Lee G.

    1961   Maternal Employment, Family Relations and Selected Personality, School-Related
              and Social-Development Characteristics of Children. Bulletin 497. Ames, Iowa:
              Agricultural and Home Economics Experiment Station.

    1963   "Personality characteristics of children." Pp. 106-121 in F. Ivan Nye and Lois W.
              Hoffman (eds.), The Employed Mother in America. Chicago: Rand McNally & Co.

Cain, Glen G.

    1966   Married Women in the Labor Force. Chicago: University of Chicago Press.

Campbell, Angus and others

    1954   The Voter Decides. Evanston, Ill.: Row, Peterson.

Census, U. S. Bureau of the

    Census   "Educational attainment of the civilian population: April 1947." Current Popula-
    1948a   Reports, Population Characteristics, Series P-20, No. 15. Washington, D. C.:
              U. S. Department of Commerce.

    Census   "School enrollment of the civilian population: April 1947." Current Population
    1948b   Reports, Population Characteristics, Series P-20, No. 12. Washington, D. C.:
              U. S. Department of Commerce.

    Census   "Characteristics of single, widowed, and divorced persons in 1947." Current Popu-
    1948c   lation Reports, Population Characteristics, Series P-20, No. 10. Washington, D. C.:
              U. S. Department of Commerce.

Census, U. S. Bureau of the (cont'd)

Census   "Internal migration in the United States: April 1947 to April 1948." Current
1949a   Population Reports, Population Characteristics, Series P-20, No. 22. Washington,
              D. C.: U. S. Department of Commerce.

Census   "Marital status, number of times married, and duration of present marital status:
1949b   April 1948." Current Population Reports, Population Characteristics, Series P-20,
              No. 23. Washington, D. C.: U. S. Department of Commerce.

Census   "Internal migration in the United States: April 1948 to April 1949." Current
1950a   Population Reports, Population Characteristics, Series P-20, No. 28. Washington,
              D. C.: U. S. Department of Commerce.

Census   "Marital status and household characteristics: April 1949." Current Population
1950b   Reports, Population Characteristics, Series P-20, No. 26. Washington, D. C.:
              U. S. Department of Commerce.

Census   "Internal migration and mobility in the United States: March 1949 to March 1950."
1951a   Current Population Reports, Population Characteristics, Series P-20, No. 36.
              Washington, D. C.: U. S. Department of Commerce.

Census   "Marital status and household characteristics: March 1950." Current Population
1951b   Reports, Population Characteristics, Series P-20, No. 33. Washington, D. C.:
              U. S. Department of Commerce.

Census   "Mobility of the population for the United States: April 1950 to April 1951."
1952a   Current Population Reports, Population Characteristics, Series P-20, No. 39.
              Washington, D. C.: U. S. Department of Commerce.

Census   "Marital status and household characteristics: April 1951." Current Population
1952b   Reports, Population Characteristics, Series P-20, No. 38. Washington, D. C.:
              U. S. Department of Commerce.

Census   United States Census of Population: 1950. Characteristics of the Population,
1953a   Part 1, U. S. Summary, Chapter C. Washington, D. C.: U. S. Department of Commerce.

Census   "School enrollment, educational attainment, and illiteracy: October 1952."
1953b   Current Population Reports, Population Characteristics, Series P-20, No. 45.
              Washington, D. C.: U. S. Department of Commerce.

Census   "Mobility of the population of the United States: April 1952." Current Popula-
1953c   tion Characteristics, Series P-20, No. 47. Washington, D. C.: U. S. Department
              of Commerce.

Census   "Mobility of the population of the United States: April 1952 to April 1953."
1953d   Current Population Reports, Population Characteristics, Series P-20, No. 49.
              Washington, D. C.: U. S. Department of Commerce.

Census   "Marital status and household characteristics: April 1952." Current Population
1953e   Reports, Population Characteristics, Series P-20, No. 44. Washington, D. C.:
              U. S. Department of Commerce.

Census   "Marital status, year of marriage, and household relationship: April 1953."
1953f   Current Population Reports, Population Characteristics, Series P-20, No. 50.
              Washington, D. C.: U. S. Department of Commerce.

Census   Census of Population: 1950, Vol. II, Characteristics of the Population.
1953g   Washington, D. C.: U. S. Department of Commerce.

Census   "Educational attainment and literacy of workers: October 1952." Current Popula-
1953h   tion Reports, Labor Force, Series P-50, No. 49. Washington, D. C.: U. S.
              Department of Commerce.

Census   "School enrollment: October 1953." Current Population Reports, Population
1954   Characteristics, Series P-20, No. 52. Washington, D. C.: U. S. Department of
              Commerce.

Census   "School enrollment: October 1954." Current Population Reports, Population
1955a   Characteristics, Series P-20, No. 54. Washington, D. C.: U. S. Department of
              Commerce.

Census, U. S. Bureau of the (cont'd)

Census
1955b
"Mobility of the Population of the United States: April 1953 to April 1954." Current Population Reports, Population Characteristics, Series P-20, No. 57. Washington, D. C.: U. S. Department of Commerce.

Census
1955c
"Mobility of the population of the United States: April 1954 to April 1955." Current Population Reports, Population Characteristics, Series P-20, No. 61. Washington, D. C.: U. S. Department of Commerce.

Census
1955d
"Marital status and family status: April 1954." Current Population Reports, Population Characteristics, Series P-20, No. 56. Washington, D. C.: U. S. Department of Commerce.

Census
1955e
"Marital status and family status: April 1955." Current Population Reports, Population Characteristics, Series P-20, No. 62. Washington, D. C.: U. S. Department of Commerce.

Census
1956a
"School enrollment: October 1955." Current Population Reports, Population Characteristics, Series P-20, No. 66. Washington, D. C.: U. S. Department of Commerce.

Census
1956b
"Marital status and family status: March 1956." Current Population Reports, Population Characteristics, Series P-20, No. 72. Washington, D. C.: U. S. Department of Commerce.

Census
1956c
"Household and family characteristics: April 1955 and 1954." Current Population Reports, Population Characteristics, Series P-20, No. 67. Washington, D. C.: U. S. Department of Commerce.

Census
1957a
"Educational attainment: March 1957." Current Population Reports, Population Characteristics, Series P-20, No. 77. Washington, D. C.: U. S. Department of Commerce.

Census
1957b
"School enrollment: October 1956." Current Population Reports, Population Characteristics, Series P-20, No. 74. Washington, D. C.: U. S. Department of Commerce.

Census
1957c
"Mobility of the population of the United States: March 1955 to 1956." Current Population Reports, Population Characteristics, Series P-20, No. 73. Washington, D. C.: U. S. Department of Commerce.

Census
1957d
"Household and family characteristics: March 1956." Current Population Reports, Population Characteristics, Series P-20, No. 75. Washington, D. C.: U. S. Department of Commerce.

Census
1957e
"Educational attainment of workers: March 1957." Current Population Reports, Labor Force, Series P-50, No. 78. Washington, D. C.: U. S. Department of Commerce.

Census
1958a
"School enrollment: October 1957." Current Population Reports, Population Characteristics, Series P-20, No. 80. Washington, D. C.: U. S. Department of Commerce.

Census
1958b
"Mobility of the population of the United States: April 1956 to 1957." Current Population Reports, Population Characteristics, Series P-20, No. 82. Washington, D. C.: U. S. Department of Commerce.

Census
1958c
"Mobility of the population of the United States: March 1957 to 1958." Current Population Reports, Population Characteristics, Series P-20, No. 85. Washington, D. C.: U. S. Department of Commerce.

Census
1958d
"Marital status, economic status, and family status: March 1957." Current Population Reports, Population Characteristics, Series P-20, No. 81. Washington, D. C.: U. S. Department of Commerce.

Census
1958e
"Marital status and family status: March 1958." Current Population Reports, Population Characteristics, Series P-20, No. 87. Washington, D. C.: U. S. Department of Commerce.

Census, U. S. Bureau of the (cont'd)

Census
1958f
"Income of families and persons in the United States: 1956." Current Population Reports, Consumer Income, Series P-60, No. 27. Washington, D. C.: U. S. Department of Commerce.

Census
1958g
"Income of families and persons in the United States: 1957." Current Population Reports, Consumer Income, Series P-60, No. 30. Washington, D. C.: U. S. Department of Commerce.

Census
1958h
"Social and economic characteristics of households and families, March 1957." Current Population Reports, Population Characteristics, Series P-20, No. 83. Washington, D. C.: U. S. Department of Commerce.

Census
1958i
"Household and family characteristics: March 1958." Current Population Reports, Population Characteristics, Series P-20, No. 88. Washington, D. C.: U. S. Department of Commerce.

Census
1959a
"School enrollment: October 1958." Current Population Reports, Population Characteristics, Series P-20, No. 93. Washington, D. C.: U. S. Department of Commerce.

Census
1959b
"Marital status and family status: March 1959." Current Population Reports, Population Characteristics, Series P-20, No. 96. Washington, D. C.: U. S. Department of Commerce.

Census
1960a
"Literacy and educational attainment: March 1959." Current Population Reports, Population Characteristics, Series P-20, No.99. Washington, D. C.: U. S. Department of Commerce.

Census
1960b
"School enrollment: October 1959." Current Population Reports, Population Characteristics, Series P-20, No. 101. Washington, D. C.: U. S. Department of Commerce.

Census
1960c
"Mobility of the population of the United States: April 1958 to 1959." Current Population Reports, Population Characteristics, Series P-20, No. 104. Washington, D. C.: U. S. Department of Commerce.

Census
1960d
"Marital status and family status: March 1960." Current Population Reports, Population Characteristics, Series P-20, No. 105. Washington, D. C.: U. S. Department of Commerce.

Census
1960e
Historical Statistics of the United States: Colonial Times to 1957. Washington, D. C.: U. S. Department of Commerce.

Census
1960f
"Income of families and persons in the United States: 1958." Current Population Reports, Consumer Income, Series P-60, No. 33. Washington, D. C.: U. S. Department of Commerce.

Census
1960g
"Household and family characteristics: March 1959." Current Population Reports, Population Characteristics, Series P-20, No. 100. Washington: D. C.: U. S. Department of Commerce.

Census
1961a
"School enrollment and education of young adults and their fathers: October 1960." Current Population Reports, Population Characteristics, Series P-20, No. 110. Washington, D. C.: U. S. Department of Commerce.

Census
1961b
"Income of families and persons in the United States: 1959." Current Population Reports, Consumer Income, Series P-60, No. 35. Washington, D. C.: U. S. Department of Commerce.

Census
1961c
"Households and families by type: 1961." Current Population Reports, Population Characteristics, Series P-20, No. 109. Washington, D. C.: U. S. Department of Commerce.

Census
1961d
"Household and family characteristics: March 1960." Current Population Reports, Population Characteristics, Series P-20, No. 106. Washington, D. C.: U. S. Department of Commerce.

Census
1962a
"School enrollment: October 1961." Current Population Reports, Population Characteristics, Series P-20, No. 117. Washington, D. C.: U. S. Department of Commerce.

Census, U. S. Bureau of the (cont'd)

Census 1962b — "Mobility of the population of the United States: March 1959 to 1960." Current Population Reports, Population Characteristics, Series P-20, No. 113. Washington, D. C.: U. S. Department of Commerce.

Census 1962c — "Mobility of the population of the United States: March 1960 to March 1961." Current Population Reports, Population Characteristics, Series P-20, No. 118. Washington, D. C.: U. S. Department of Commerce.

Census 1962d — "Marital status and family status: March 1961." Current Population Reports, Population Characteristics, Series P-20, No. 114. Washington, D. C.: U. S. Department of Commerce.

Census 1962e — "Income of families and persons in the United States: 1960." Current Population Reports, Consumer Income, Series P-60, No. 37. Washington, D. C.: U. S. Department of Commerce.

Census 1962f — "Households and families by type: 1962." Current Population Reports, Population Characteristics, Series P-20, No. 119. Washington, D. C.: U. S. Department of Commerce.

Census 1962g — "Household and family characteristics: March 1961." Current Population Reports, Population Characteristics, Series P-20, No. 116. Washington, D. C.: U. S. Department of Commerce.

Census 1963a — United States Census of Population: 1960. Detailed Characteristics. United States Summary. Final Report, PC(1)-1D. Washington, D. C.: U. S. Department of Commerce.

Census 1963b — United States Census of Population: 1960. Subject Reports. Educational Attainment. Final Report PC(2)-5B. Washington, D. C.: U. S. Department of Commerce.

Census 1963c — "Educational attainment: March 1962." Current Population Reports, Population Characteristics, Series P-20, No. 121. Washington, D. C.: U. S. Department of Commerce.

Census 1963d — "School enrollment: October 1962." Current Population Reports, Population Characteristics, Series P-20, No. 126. Washington, D. C.: U. S. Department of Commerce.

Census 1963e — "Marital Status and family status: March 1962." Current Population Reports, Population Characteristics, Series P-20, No. 122. Washington, D. C.: U. S. Department of Commerce.

Census 1963f — "Income of families and persons in the United States: 1961." Current Population Reports, Consumer Income, Series P-60, No. 39. Washington, D. C.: U. S. Department of Commerce.

Census 1963g — "Income of families and persons in the United States: 1962." Current Population Reports, Consumer Income, Series P-60, No. 41. Washington, D. C.: U. S. Department of Commerce.

Census 1963h — "Households and families, by type: 1963." Current Population Reports, Population Characteristics, Series P-20, No. 124. Washington, D. C.: U. S. Department of Commerce.

Census 1963i — United States Census of Population: 1960. Subject Reports. Inmates of Institutions. Final Report PC(2)-8A. Washington, D. C.: U. S. Department of Commerce.

Census 1963j — "Household and family characteristics: March 1962." Current Population Reports, Population Characteristics, Series,P-20, No. 125. Washington, D. C.: U. S. Department of Commerce.

Census 1963k — The Current Population Survey, A Report on Methodology. Technical Paper No. 7, Washington, D. C.: U. S. Department of Commerce.

Census 1964a — "School enrollment: October 1963." Current Population Reports, Population Characteristics, Series P-20, No. 129. Washington, D. C.: U. S. Department of Commerce.

Census, U. S. Bureau of the (cont'd)

Census
1964b
"Mobility of the population of the United States: April 1961 to April 1962." Current Population Reports, Population Characteristics, Series P-20, No. 127. Washington, D. C.: U. S. Department of Commerce.

Census
1964c
"Income of families and persons in the United States: 1963." Current Population Reports, Consumer Income, Series P-60, No. 43. Washington, D. C.: U. S. Department of Commerce.

Census
1964d
"Households and families by type: 1964." Current Population Reports, Population Characteristics, Series P-20, No. 130. Washington, D. C.: U. S. Department of Commerce.

Census
1964e
"Concepts and methods used in manpower statistics from the Current Population Survey, June 1964." Bureau of Labor Statistics Report No. 279; Current Population Reports Series P-23, No. 13. Washington; D. C.: U. S. Department of Commerce and U. S. Department of Labor.

Census
1965a
"Educational attainment: March 1964." Current Population Reports, Population Characteristics, Series P-20, No. 138. Washington, D. C.: U. S. Department of Commerce.

Census
1965b
"Mobility of the population of the United States: March 1962 to March 1963." Current Population Reports, Population Characteristics, Series P-20, No. 134. Washington, D. C.: U. S. Department of Commerce.

Census
1965c
"Mobility of the population of the United States: March 1963 to March 1964." Current Population Reports, Population Characteristics, Series P-20, No. 141. Washington, D. C.: U. S. Department of Commerce.

Census
1965d
"Marital status and family status: March 1964 and 1963." Current Population Reports, Population Characteristics, Series P-20, No. 135. Washington, D. C.: U. S. Department of Commerce.

Census
1965e
"Marital status and family status: March 1965." Current Population Reports, Population Characteristics, Series P-20, No. 144. Washington, D. C.: U. S. Department of Commerce.

Census
1965f
"Income in 1964 of families and persons in the United States." Current Population Reports, Consumer Income, Series P-60, No. 47. Washington, D. C.: U. S. Department of Commerce.

Census
1965g
"Estimates of the population of the United States, by single years of age, color and sex: 1900 to 1959." Current Population Reports, Population Estimates, Series P-25, No. 311. Washington, D. C.: U. S. Department of Commerce.

Census
1965h
"Estimates of the population of the United States, by age, color and sex: July 1, 1960 to 1965." Current Population Reports, Population Estimates, Series P-25, No. 321. Washington, D. C.: U. S. Department of Commerce.

Census
1965i
Historical Statistics of the United States: Continuation to 1962 and Revisions. Washington, D. C.: U. S. Department of Commerce.

Census
1965j
"Households and families by type: 1965." Current Population Reports, Population Characteristics, Series P-20, No. 140. Washington, D. C.: U. S. Department of Commerce.

Census
1965k
"Household and family characteristics: March 1964 and 1963." Current Population Reports, Population Characteristics, Series P-20, No. 139. Washington, D. C.: U. S. Department of Commerce.

Census
1965L
"Estimates of the population of the United States, by single years of age, color and sex, 1960 to 1964." Current Population Reports, Population Estimates, Series P-25, No. 314. Washington, D. C.: U. S. Department of Commerce.

Census
1965m
"Voter participation in the national election, November 1964." Current Population Reports, Population Characteristics, Series P-20, No. 143. Washington, D. C.: U. S. Department of Commerce.

Census
1966a
"Educational attainment: March 1966 and 1965." Current Population Reports, Population Characteristics, Series P-20, No. 158. Washington, D. C.: U. S. Department of Commerce.

Census, U. S. Bureau of the (cont'd)

Census
1966b

"School enrollment: October 1964." Current Population Reports, Population Characteristics, Series P-20, No. 148. Washington, D. C.: U. S. Department of Commerce.

Census
1966c

"Mobility of the population of the United States: March 1964 to March 1965." Current Population Reports, Population Characteristics, Series P-20, No. 150. Washington, D. C.: U. S. Department of Commerce.

Census
1966d

"Mobility of the population of the United States: March 1965 to March 1966." Current Population Reports, Population Characteristics, Series P-20, No. 156. Washington, D. C.: U. S. Department of Commerce.

Census
1966e

Long Term Economic Growth: 1860-1965. ES4-No. 1. Washington, D. C.: U. S. Department of Commerce.

Census
1966f

"Households and families by type: 1966." Current Population Reports, Population Characteristics, Series P-20, No. 152. Washington, D. C.: U. S. Department of Commerce.

Census
1966g

"Household and family characteristics: March 1965." Current Population Reports, Population Characteristics, Series P-20, No. 153. Washington, D. C.: U. S. Department of Commerce.

Census
1967a

"School enrollment: October 1965." Current Population Reports, Population Characteristics, Series P-20, No. 162. Washington, D. C.: U. S. Department of Commerce.

Census
1967b

"School enrollment: October 1966." Current Population Reports, Population Characteristics, Series P-20, No. 167. Washington, D. C.: U. S. Department of Commerce.

Census
1967c

"Marital status and family status: March 1966." Current Population Reports, Population Characteristics, Series P-20, No. 159. Washington, D. C.: U. S. Department of Commerce.

Census
1967d

"Income in 1965 of families and persons in the United States." Current Population Reports, Consumer Income, Series P-60, No. 51. Washington, D. C.: U. S. Department of Commerce.

Census
1967e

"Income in 1966 of families and persons in the United States." Current Population Reports, Consumer Income, Series P-60, No. 53. Washington, D. C.: U. S. Department of Commerce.

Census
1967f

"Projections of the population of the United States, by age, sex and color to 1990, with extensions of population by age and sex to 2015." Current Population Reports, Population Estimates, Series P-25, No. 381. Washington, D. C.: U. S. Department of Commerce.

Census
1967g

"Households and families by type: 1967." Current Population Reports, Population Characteristics, Series P-20, No. 166. Washington, D. C.: U. S. Department of Commerce.

Census
1967h

"Household and family characteristics: March 1966." Current Population Reports, Population Characteristics, Series P-20, No. 164. Washington, D. C.: U. S. Department of Commerce.

Census
1967i

Trends in the Income of Families and Persons in the United States, 1947-1964 (by Mary F. Henson). Technical Paper 17. Washington, D. C.: U. S. Department of Commerce.

Census
1967j

United States Census of Population: 1960. Subject Reports. Socioeconomic Status. Final Report PC(2)-5C. Washington, D. C.: U. S. Department of Commerce.

Census
1967k

"Concepts and methods used in manpower statistics from the Current Population Survey, June 1967," Bureau of Labor Statistics Report No. 313; Current Population Reports, Series P-23, No. 22. Washington, D. C.: U. S. Department of Commerce and U. S. Department of Labor.

Census, U. S. Bureau of the (cont'd)

Census 1968a — "Educational attainment: March 1967". Current Population Reports, Population Characteristics, Series P-20, No. 169. Washington, D.C.: U. S. Department of Commerce.

Census 1968b — "Mobility of the population of the United States: March 1966 to March 1967". Current Population Reports, Population Characteristics, Series P-20, No. 171. Washington, D.C.: U.S. Department of Commerce.

Census 1968c — "Marital status and family status: March 1967". Current Population Reports, Population Characteristics, Series P-20, No. 170. Washington, D.C.: U. S. Department of Commerce.

Census 1968d — "Summary of demographic projections". Current Population Reports, Population Estimates, Series P-25, No. 388. Washington, D.C.: U. S. Department of Commerce.

Census 1968e — "Estimates of the population of the United States, by age, race and sex: July 1, 1964 to 1967". Current Population Reports, Population Estimates, Series P-25 No. 385. Washington, D.C.: U.S. Department of Commerce.

Census 1968f — "Households and families, by type: 1968". Current Population Reports, Population Characteristics, Series P-20, No. 176. Washington, D.C.: U. S. Department of Commerce.

Census 1968g — "Households and family characteristics: March 1967". Current Population Reports, Population Characteristics, Series P-20, No. 173. Washington, D.C.: U.S. Department of Commerce.

Census 1969a — "Educational Attainment: March 1968". Current Population Reports, Population Characteristics, Series P-20, No. 182. Washington, D.C.: U. S. Department of Commerce.

Census 1969b — "Income in 1967 of families in the United States". Current Population Reports, Consumer Income, Series P-60, No. 59. Washington, D.C.: U. S. Department of Commerce.

Census 1969c — "Income in 1967 of persons in the United States". Current Population Reports, Consumer Income, Series P-60, No. 60. Washington, D.C.: U.S. Department of Commerce.

Census 1969d — "Income in 1968 of families and persons in the United States". Current Population Reports, Consumer Income, Series P-60, No. 66. Washington, D.C.: U. S. Department of Commerce.

Census 1969e — "Supplementary Report on income in 1967 of families and persons in the United States". Current Population Reports, Consumer Income, Series P-60, No. 64. Washington, D.C.: U.S. Department of Commerce.

Census 1969f — "Mobility of the population of the United States, March 1967 to March 1968". Current Population Reports, Population Characteristics, Series P-20, No. 188. Washington, D.C.: U. S. Department of Commerce.

Census 1969g — "Mobility of the population of the United States, March 1968 to March 1969". Current Population Reports, Population Characteristics, Series P-20, No. 193. Washington, D.C.: U. S. Department of Commerce.

Census 1969h — "Marital status and family status: March 1968". Current Population Reports, Population Characteristics, Series P-20, No. 187. Washington, D.C.: U. S. Department of Commerce.

Census 1969i — "Household and family characteristics: March 1968". Current Population Reports, Population Characteristics, Series P-20, No. 191. Washington, D.C.: U. S. Department of Commerce.

Census 1969j — Statistical Abstract of the United States: 1969. Washington, D.C.: U. S. Department of Commerce.

Census 1969k — "Poverty in the United States: 1959 to 1968". Current Population Reports, Consumer Income, Series P-60, No. 68. Washington, D.C.: U.S. Department of Commerce.

Census, U. S. Bureau of the (cont'd)

Census   "Voting and registration in the election of November 1968." Current Popu-
1969L   lation Reports, Population Characteristics, Series P-20, No. 192, Washington,
             D. C.: U. S. Department of Commerce.

Census   "School enrollment: October 1968 and 1967." Current Population Reports, Popu-
1969m   lation Characteristics, Series P-20, No. 190. Washington, D. C.: U. S.
             Department of Commerce.

Census   "Educational attainment: March 1969." Current Population Reports, Population
1970a   Characteristics, Series P-20, No. 194. Washington, D. C.: U. S. Department of
             Commerce.

Census   "Estimates of the population of the United States, by age, race and sex: July 1,
1970b   1967 to July 1, 1969." Current Population Reports, Population Estimates and
             Projections, Series P-25, No. 441. Washington, D. C.: U. S. Department of
             Commerce.

Census   "Estimates of the population of the United States and components of change:
1970c   1940 to 1970." Current Population Reports, Population Estimates and Projections,
             Series P-25, No. 442. Washington, D. C.: U. S. Department of Commerce.

Census   "Marital status and family status: March 1969." Current Population Reports,
1970d   Population Characteristics, Series P-20, No. 198. Washington, D. C.: U. S.
             Department of Commerce.

Census   "Household and family characteristics: March 1969." Current Population Reports,
1970e   Population Characteristics, Series P-20, No. 200. Washington, D. C.: U. S.
             Department of Commerce.

Census   "Income growth rates in 1939 to 1968 for persons by occupation and industry
1970f   groups, for the United States." Current Population Reports, Consumer Income,
             Series P-60, No. 69. Washington, D. C.: U. S. Department of Commerce.

Census   "Labor union membership in 1966." Current Population Reports, Population
1970g   Characteristics, Series P-20, No. 202. Washington, D. C.: U. S. Department of
             Commerce.

Census   "Selected characteristics of persons and families: March 1970." Current Popu-
1970h   lation Reports, Population Characteristics, Series P-20, No. 204. Washington,
             D. C.: U. S. Department of Commerce.

Census   "Average family income up 9 percent in 1969: advance data from March 1970
1970i   sample survey." Current Population Reports, Consumer Income, Series P-60,
             No. 70. Washington, D. C.: U. S. Department of Co merce.

Cohen, Malcolm S.

1969   "Married women in the labor force: an analysis of participation rates." Monthly
             Labor Review 92 (October) 31-35.

Douglas, Jack D.

1968   "Suicide, I-social aspects," in David L. Sills (ed.), International Encyclo-
             pedia of the Social Sciences, Vol. 15, pp. 375-385. New York: Macmillan Co.
             and Free Press.

Duncan, Beverly

1968   "Trends in output and distribution of schooling." Pp. 601-674 in Eleanor
             Bernert Sheldon and Wilbert E. Moore, Indicators of Social Change, Concepts
             and Measurements. New York: Russell Sage Foundation.

Duncan, Otis Dudley and Beverly Duncan

1955   "Residential distribution and occupational stratification." American Journal
             of Sociology 60 (March) 493-503.

Dunham, Ralph E., and Patricia S. Wright

1966   Faculty and Other Professional Staff in Institutions of Higher Education, Fall
             Term, 1963-64. U. S. Office of Education, OE-53000-64. Washington, D. C.:
             U. S. Department of Health, Education and Welfare.

Education, U. S. Office of

Educ.   Biennial Survey of Education, 1938-40 and 1940-42, Vol. 2. Chapter 4,
1944   "Statistics of Higher Education, 1939-40 and 1941-42." Washington, D. C.:
         U. S. Department of Health, Education and Welfare.

Educ.   Biennial Survey of Education, 1942-44. Chapter 4, "Statistics of Higher
1946   Education, 1943-44." Washington, D. C.: U. S. Department of Health, Education
         and Welfare.

Educ.   Biennial Survey of Education, 1944-46. Chapter 4, "Statistics of Higher
1949   Education, 1945-46." Washington, D. C.: U. S. Department of Health, Education
         and Welfare.

Educ.   Biennial Survey of Education, 1946-48. Chapter 4, "Statistics of Higher
1950   Education, 1947-48." Washington, D. C.: U. S. Department of Health, Education
         and Welfare.

Educ.   Biennial Survey of Education, 1948-50. Chapter 1, "Statistical Summary of
1953   Education, 1949-50." Washington, D. C.: U. S. Department of Health, Education
         and Welfare.

Educ.   Biennial Survey of Education, 1952-54. Chapter 1, "Statistical Summary of
1957   Education, 1953-54." Washington, D. C.: U. S. Department of Health, Education
         and Welfare.

Educ.   Biennial Survey of Education, 1954-56. Chapter 1, "Statistical Summary of
1959   Education, 1955-56." Washington, D.C.: U. S. Department of Health, Education
         and Welfare.

Educ.   Biennial Survey of Education, 1956-58. Chapter 4, Section 1, "Statistic of
1962   Higher Education, 1957-58." Washington, D. C.: U. S. Department of Health,
         Education and Welfare.

Educ.   Digest of Educational Statistics, 1963 Edition. OE-10024.63, Bulletin 1963,
1963   No. 43. Washington, D. C.: U. S. Department of Health, Education and Welfare.

Educ.   Summary Report on Bachelor's and Higher Degrees Conferred During the Year
1966a   1964-65. OE-54016-65. Washington, D. C.: U. S. Department of Health, Educa-
         tion and Welfare.

Educ.   Earned Degrees Conferred, 1963-64, Bachelor's and Higher Degrees. OE-54013-64,
1966b   Misc. No. 54. Washington, D. C.: U. S. Department of Health, Education and
         Welfare.

Educ.   Summary Report on Bachelor's and Higher Degrees Conferred During the Year
1968a   1965-66. OE-54013A-66. Washington, D. C.: U. S. Department of Health,
         Education and Welfare.

Educ.   Earned Degrees Conferred: 1966-67. Part A, Summary Data, OE-54013-67.
1968b   Washington, D. C.: U. S. Department of Health, Education and Welfare.

Educ.   Projections of Educational Statistics to 1977-78. OE-10030-68. Washington,
1969a   D. C.: U. S. Department of Health, Education and Welfare.

Educ.   Earned Degrees Conferred: 1967-68. Part A, Summary Data, OE-54013-68-A.
1969b   Washington, D. C.: U. S. Department of Health, Education and Welfare.

Encyclopedia of Associations

1961   Encyclopedia of Associations. Volume I - National Organizations of the United
1964   States. Detroit, Mich.: Gale Research Co.
1968

Ennis, Philip H.

1968   "The definition and measurement of leisure." Pp. 525-572 in Eleanor Bernert
         Sheldon and Wilbert E. Moore, Indicators of Social Change: Concepts and
         Measurement. New York: Russell Sage Foundation.

Falkner, Frank (ed.)

1970   "Key Issues in Infant Mortality." Report of a conference, April 16-18, 1969,
            Bethesda, Md.: U. S. National Institute of Child Health and Human Development.

Federal Bureau of Investigation, U. S.

FBI   Crime in the United States. Uniform Crime Reports. Washington, D. C.: U. S.
1968   Department of Justice.

Federal Reserve Board, U. S.

FR   Federal Reserve Bulletin (March).
1970

Ferriss, Abbott L. and others

1962   National Recreation Survey. ORRRC Report No. 19. Washington, D. C.: The
            Outdoor Recreation Resources Review Commission.

Ferriss, Abbott L.

1969   Indicators of Trends in American Education. New York: Russell Sage Foundation.

1970   Indicators of Change in the American Family. New York: Russell Sage Foundation.

Folger, John K., and Charles B. Nam

1967   Education of the American Population. 1960 U. S. Bureau of the Census Monograph
            Washington, D.C.: U. S. Department of Commerce.

Gross, Edward

1968   "Plus ça change...? the sexual structure of occupations over time." Social
            Problems (Fall) 198-208.

Haenszel, William, Michael B. Shimkin, and Herman P. Miller

1956   Tobacco Smoking Patterns in the United States. U. S. Public Health Service
            Monograph 45. Washington, D. C.: U. S. Department of Health, Education and
            Welfare.

Hausknecht, Murray

1962   The Joiners. New York: Bedminster Press.

Health, Education and Welfare, U. S. Department of

HEW   Health, Education and Welfare Trends, 1966-67 Edition: Part 1, National Trends.
1967

Hedges, Janice Neipert

1970   "Women workers and manpower demands in the 1970's." Monthly Labor Review
            93 (June) 19-29.

Heer, David M.

1958   "Dominance and the working wife." Social Forces 36 (May), 341-347.

Hiestand, Dale L.

1964   Economic Growth and Employment Opportunities for Minorities. New York:
            Columbia University Press.

Hutchinson, Edward P. (ed.)

1966   "The new immigration." Annals of the American Academy of Political and Social
            Science. Volume 367 (September).

Immigration and Naturalization Service, U. S.

Immigra-   Annual Reports, 1950 through 1969. Washington, D.C.: U. S. Department of
tion   Justice.
1950-
1969

Knudsen, Dean D.

 1969 "The declining status of women: popular myths and the failure of functionalist thought". Social Forces 48 (Dec.) 183-193.

Labor, U.S. Department of

 Labor Manpower Report of the President: 1967. Washington, D. C.: U. S. Government
 1967 Printing Office.

 Labor Manpower Report of the President: 1969. Washington, D. C.: U. S. Government
 1969a Printing Office.

 Labor Statistics on Manpower: A Supplement to the Manpower Report of the President,
 1969b 1969. Washington, D. C.: U. S. Government Printing Office.

 Labor Manpower Report of the President: 1970. Washington, D. C.: U. S. Government
 1970 Printing Office.

Lerner, Monroe, and O.W. Anderson

 1963 Health Progress in the United States, 1900-1960. A report of Health Information Foundation. Chicago: University of Chicago Press.

Lopate, Carol

 1968 Women in Medicine. (Published for the Josiah Macy, Jr. Foundation). Baltimore, Md.: Johns Hopkins Press.

Merriam, Ida C.

 1968 "Welfare and its Measurement". Pp. 721-804 in Eleanor Bernert Sheldon and Wilbert E. Moore (eds.), Indicators of Social Change: Concepts and Measurement. New York, Russell Sage Foundation.

Miller, Herman P.

 1966 Income Distribution in the United States. A 1960 Census Monograph. Washington, D.C.: U. S. Department of Commerce.

Miller, S.M., Martin Rein, Pamela Roby, and Bertram M. Gross

 1967 "Poverty, inequality, and conflict". Annals of the American Academy of Political and Social Science, Vol. 373 (September) 16-52.

Mincer, Jacob

 1968 "Labor Force Participation", in International Encyclopedia of the Social Sciences, Vol. 8, pp. 474-481. New York: Macmillan Co. and Free Press.

Moriyama, Iwao M.

 1968 "Problems in the measurement of health status". Pp. 373-600 in Eleanor Bernert Sheldon and Wilbert E. Moore, Indicators of Social Change: Concepts and Measurement. New York: Russell Sage Foundation.

Moriyama, I. W., and S. Shapiro

 1963 "International trends in infant mortality and their implications for the United States". American Journal of Public Health 53 (May) 747-760.

Moss, Milton

 1968 "Consumption: a report on contemporary issues". Pp. 449-524 in Eleanor Bernert Sheldon and Wilbert E. Moore (eds.), Indicators of Social Change: Concepts and Measurement. New York: Russell Sage Foundation.

National Academy of Sciences, Office of Scientific Personnel

 NAS Doctorate Recipients from United States Universities, 1958-1966. Pub. No. 1489.
 1967 Washington, D.C.: National Academy of Sciences.

National Center for Health Statistics, U. S.

NCHS 1963a — Disability Days, United States, July 1961-June 1962. Public Health Service Publication 1000, Series 10, No. 4. Washington, D. C.: U. S. Department of Health, Education and Welfare.

NCHS 1963b — Infant, Fetal, and Maternal Mortality: United States, 1963. Public Health Service Publication 1000, Series 20, No. 3. Washington, D. C.: U. S. Department of Health, Education and Welfare.

NCHS 1964a — Vital Statistics of the United States, 1963. Vol. I - Natality. Washington, D. C.: U. S. Department of Health, Education and Welfare.

NCHS 1964b — Current Estimates from the Health Interview Survey, United States, July 1962-June 1963. Public Health Service Publication 1000, Series 10, No. 5. Washington, D. C.: U. S. Department of Health, Education and Welfare.

NCHS 1964c — Acute Conditions, Incidence and Associated Disability: United States, July 1962-June 1963. Public Health Service Publication 1000, Series 10, No. 10. Washington, D. C.: U. S. Department of Health, Education and Welfare.

NCHS 1964d — Current Estimates from the Health Interview Survey, United States, July 1963-June 1964. Public Health Service Publication 1000, Series 10, No. 13. Washington, D. C.: U. S. Department of Health, Education and Welfare.

NCHS 1964e — The Change in Mortality Trend in the United States. Public Health Service Publication 1000, Series 3, No. 1. Washington, D. C.: U. S. Department of Health, Education and Welfare.

NCHS 1965a — Vital Statistics of the United States, 1963. Vol. II - Mortality, Part A. Washington, D. C.: U. S. Department of Health, Education and Welfare.

NCHS 1965b — Vital Statistics of the United States, 1961. Vol. III - Marriage and Divorce. Washington, D. C.: U. S. Department of Health, Education and Welfare.

NCHS 1965c — Vital Statistics of the United States, 1962. Vol. III - Marriage and Divorce. Washington, D. C.: U. S. Department of Health, Education and Welfare.

NCHS 1965d — Chronic Conditions and Activity Limitation, United States, July 1961-June 1963. Public Health Service Publication 1000, Series 10, No. 17. Washington, D. C.: U. S. Department of Health, Education and Welfare.

NCHS 1965e — Current Estimates from the Health Interview Survey, United States, July 1964-June 1965. Public Health Service Publication 1000, Series 10, No. 25. Washington, D. C.: U. S. Department of Health, Education and Welfare.

NCHS 1965f — Fertility Measurement. A Report of the United States National Committee on Vital Health and Statistics. Public Health Service Publication 1000, Series 4, No. 1. Washington, D. C.: U. S. Department of Health, Education and Welfare.

NCHS 1965g — Acute Conditions, Incidence and Associated Disability, United States, July 1963-June 1964. Public Health Service Publication 1000, Series 10, No. 15. Washington, D. C.: U. S. Department of Health, Education and Welfare.

NCHS 1965h — Acute Conditions, Incidence and Associated Disability, United States, July 1964-June 1965. Public Health Service Publication 1000, Series 10, No. 26. Washington, D. C.: U. S. Department of Health, Education and Welfare.

NCHS 1965i — Disability Days, United States, July 1963-June 1964. Public Health Service Publication 1000, Series 10, No. 24. Washington, D. C.: U. S. Department of Health, Education and Welfare.

NCHS 1965j — Infant and Perinatal Mortality in the United States. Public Health Service Publication 1000, Series 3, No. 4. Washington, D. C.: U. S. Department of Health, Education and Welfare.

NCHS 1966a — Vital Statistics of the United States, 1964. Vol. I - Natality. Washington, D. C.: U. S. Department of Health, Education and Welfare.

NCHS 1966b — Vital Statistics of the United States, 1964. Vol. II - Mortality, Part A. Washington, D. C.: U. S. Department of Health, Education and Welfare.

National Center for Health Statistics, U. S. (cont'd)

NCHS
1966c
Age Patterns in Medical Care, Illness, and Disability, United States, July 1963-June 1965. Public Health Service Publication 1000, Series 10, No. 32. Washington, D. C.: U. S. Department of Health, Education and Welfare.

NCHS
1966d
Mortality Trends in the United States, 1954-1963. Public Health Service Publication 1000, Series 20, No. 2. Washington, D.C.: U. S. Department of Health, Education and Welfare.

NCHS
1967a
Homicide in the United States, 1950-1964. Public Health Service Publication 1000, Series 20, No. 6. Washington, D. C.: U. S. Department of Health, Education and Welfare.

NCHS
1967b
Vital Statistics of the United States, 1965. Vol. II - Mortality, Part A. Washington, D. C.: U. S. Department of Health, Education and Welfare.

NCHS
1967c
Vital Statistics of the United States, 1965. Vol. I - Natality. Washington, D. C.: U. S. Department of Health, Education and Welfare.

NCHS
1967d
Vital Statistics of the United States, 1963. Vol. III - Marriage and Divorce. Washington, D. C.: U. S. Department of Health, Education and Welfare.

NCHS
1967e
Current Estimates from the Health Interview Survey, United States, July 1965-June 1966. Public Health Service Publication 1000, Series 10, No. 37. Washington, D. C.: U. S. Department of Health, Education and Welfare.

NCHS
1967f
Cigarette Smoking and Health Characteristics, United States, July 1964-June 1965. Public Health Service Publication 1000, Series 10, No. 34. Washington, D. C.: U. S. Department of Health, Education and Welfare.

NCHS
1967g
Acute Conditions, Incidence and Associated Disability, United States, July 1965-June 1966. Public Health Service Publication 1000, Series 10, No. 38. Washington, D. C.: U. S. Department of Health, Education and Welfare.

NCHS
1967h
Suicide in the United States, 1950-1964. Public Health Service Publication 1000, Series 20, No. 5. Washington, D. C.: U. S. Department of Health, Education and Welfare.

NCHS
1967i
Natality Statistics Analysis: United States, 1964. Public Health Service Publication 1000, Series 21, No. 11. Washington, D. C.: U. S. Department of Health, Education and Welfare.

NCHS
1968a
Vital Statistics of the United States, 1966. Vol. I - Natality. Washington, D. C.: U. S. Department of Health, Education and Welfare.

NCHS
1968b
Trends in Illegitimacy, United States, 1940-1965. Public Health Service Publication 1000, Series 21, No. 15. Washington, D. C.: U. S. Department of Health, Education and Welfare.

NCHS
1968c
Vital Statistics of the United States, 1966. Vol. II - Mortality, Part A. Washington, D. C.: U. S. Department of Health, Education and Welfare.

NCHS
1968d
Vital Statistics of the United States, 1964. Vol. III - Marriage and Divorce. Washington, D. C.: U. S. Department of Health, Education and Welfare.

NCHS
1968e
Vital Statistics of the United States, 1965. Vol. III - Marriage and Divorce. Washington, D. C.: U. S. Department of Health, Education and Welfare.

NCHS
1968f
Current Estimates from the Health Interview Survey, United States, July 1966-June 1967. Public Health Service Publication 1000, Series 10, Number 43. Washington, D.C.: U. S. Department of Health, Education and Welfare.

NCHS
1968g
Limitation of Activity and Mobility Due to Chronic Conditions, United States, July 1965-June 1966. Public Health Service Publication 1000, Series 10, No. 45. Washington, D. C.: U. S. Department of Health, Education and Welfare.

NCHS
1968h
Vital Statistics Rates in the United States, 1940-1960. Public Health Service Publication 1677. Washington, D. C.: U. S. Department of Health, Education and Welfare.

NCHS
1968i
Acute Conditions, Incidence and Associated Disability, July 1966-June 1967. Public Health Service Publication 1000, Series 10, No. 44. Washington, D. C.: U. S. Department of Health, Education and Welfare.

National Center for Health Statistics, U. S.(cont'd)

NCHS 1968j
Marriage Statistics Analysis, United States, 1963. Public Health Service Publication 1000, Series 21, No. 16. Washington, D. C.: U. S. Department of Health, Education and Welfare.

NCHS 1968k
Disability Days, United States, July 1965-June 1966. Public Health Service Publication 1000, Series 10, No. 47. Washington, D. C.: U. S. Department of Health, Education and Welfare.

NCHS 1969a
Vital Statistics of the United States, 1967. Vol. I - Natality. Washington, D. C.: U. S. Department of Health, Education and Welfare.

NCHS 1969b
Chronic Conditions Causing Activity Limitation, United States, July 1963-June 1965. Public Health Service Publication 1000, Series 10, No. 51. Washington, D. C.: U. S. Department of Health, Education and Welfare.

NCHS 1969c
Current Estimates from the Health Interview Survey, United States, 1967. Public Health Service Publication 1000, Series 10, No. 52. Washington, D.C.: U. S. Department of Health, Education and Welfare.

NCHS 1969d
"Cigarette Smoking Status -- June 1966, August 1967, and August 1968." Monthly Vital Statistics Report, Vol. 18, No. 9, Supplement (December 5). Washington, D. C.: U. S. Department of Health, Education and Welfare.

NCHS 1969e
Vital Statistics of the United States, 1967. Vol. II - Mortality, Part A. Washington, D. C.: U. S. Department of Health, Education and Welfare.

NCHS 1969f
Acute Conditions, Incidence and Associated Disability, July 1967-June 1968. Public Health Service Publication 1000, Series 10, No. 54. Washington, D. C.: U. S. Department of Health, Education and Welfare.

NCHS 1969g
Vital Statistics of the United States, 1966. Vol. III - Marriage and Divorce. Washington, D. C.: U. S. Department of Health, Education and Welfare.

NCHS 1970a
"Advance report, final natality statistics, 1968." Monthly Vital Statistics Report, Vol. 18, No. 11, Supplement (January 30). Washington, D. C.: U. S. Department of Health, Education and Welfare.

NCHS 1970b
"Interval between first marriage and legitimate first birth, United States, 1964-66." Monthly Vital Statistics Report, Vol. 18, No. 12, Supplement (March 12). Washington, D.C.: U. S. Department of Health, Education and Welfare.

NCHS 1970c
"Births, marriages, divorces, and deaths for 1969." Monthly Vital Statistics Report, Vol. 18, No. 12 (March 12). Washington, D. C.: U. S. Department of Health, Education and Welfare.

NCHS 1970d
Persons Injured and Disability Days Due to Injury, United States, July 1965-June 1967. Public Health Service Publication 1000, Series 10, No. 58, Washington, D. C.: U. S. Department of Health, Education and Welfare.

NCHS 1970e
Changes in Cigarette Smoking Habits Between 1955 and 1966. Public Health Service Publication 1000, Series 10, No. 59. Washington, D. C.: U. S. Department of Health, Education and Welfare.

NCHS 1970f
"Annual estimates of persons injured in moving motor vehicle accidents in the United States, 1968." Monthly Vital Statistics Report, Vol. 19, No. 4, Supplement. Washington, D. C.: U. S. Department of Health, Education and Welfare.

National Clearinghouse for Smoking and Health, U. S.

1969
Use of Tobacco: Practices, Attitudes,Knowledge, and Beliefs, United States, Fall 1964 and Spring 1966. Washington, D. C.: U. S. Department of Health, Education and Welfare.

National Science Foundation

1965
Scientific and Technical Manpower Resources. NSF 64-28. Washington, D. C.: U. S. Government Printing Office.

Nolan, Francena L.

    1963   "Rural employment and husbands and wives." Pp. 241-250 in F. Ivan Nye and Lois W. Hoffman (eds.), The Employed Mother in America, Chicago: Rand McNally & Co.

National Vital Statistics Division, U. S. Public Health Service

    NVSD   Vital Statistics of the United States, 1960. Vol. I - Natality. Washington,
    1962   D. C.: U. S. Department of Health, Education and Welfare.

    NVSD   Vital Statistics of the United States, 1960. Vol. II - Mortality, Part A.
    1963a   Washington, D. C.: U. S. Department of Health, Education and Welfare.

    NVSD   Vital Statistics of the United States, 1961. Vol. I - Natality. Washington,
    1963b   D. C.: U. S. Department of Health, Education and Welfare.

    NVSD   Vital Statistics of the United States, 1961. Vol. II - Mortality, Part A.
    1964a   Washington, D. C.: U. S. Department of Health, Education and Welfare.

    NVSD   Vital Statistics of the United States, 1962. Vol. II - Mortality, Part A.
    1964b   Washington, D. C.: U. S. Department of Health, Education and Welfare.

    NVSD   Vital Statistics of the United States, 1960. Vol. III - Marriage and Divorce.
    1964c   Washington, D. C.: U. S. Department of Health, Education and Welfare.

    NVSD   Vital Statistics of the United States, 1962. Vol. I - Natality. Washington,
    1964d   D. C.: U. S. Department of Health, Education and Welfare.

Nye, F. Ivan

    1963a   "The adjustment of adolescent children." Pp. 133-141 in F. Ivan Nye and Lois W. Hoffman (eds.), The Employed Mother in America. Chicago: Rand McNally & Co.

    1963b   "Adjustment to children." Pp. 353-362 in F. Ivan Nye and Lois W. Hoffman (eds.), The Employed Mother in America. Chicago: Rand McNally & Co.

Oppenheimer, Valerie Kincade

    1970   The Female Labor Force in the United States: Demographic and Economic Factors Governing its Growth and Changing Composition. Berkeley, Calif.: Institute of International Studies, University of California.

Orcutt, Guy H., Martin Greenberger, John Korbel, and Alice M. Rivlin

    1961   Microanalysis of Socioeconomic Systems: A Simulation Study. New York: Harper and Row.

Orshansky, Mollie

    1965a   "Counting the poor: another look at the poverty profile." Social Security Bulletin (January) 3-29.

    1965b   "Who's who among the poor: a demographic view of poverty." Social Security Bulletin (July) 3-32.

Proctor, Charles

    1962   "Dependence of recreation participation on background characteristics of sample persons in the September 1960 National Recreation Survey." Pp. 77-94 in Abbott L. Ferriss, The National Recreation Survey. Washington: The Outdoor Recreation Resources Review Commission.

Public Health Service, U. S.

    PHS   Fertility Tables for Birth Cohorts of American Women, Part 1. Vital Statistics -
    1960   Special Reports, Vol. 51, No. 1. Washington, D. C.: U. S. Department of Health, Education and Welfare.

    PHS   Smoking and Health, Report of the Advisory Committee to the Surgeon General of
    1964   the Public Health Service. PHS Pub. No. 1103. Washington, D. C.: U. S. Department of Health, Education and Welfare.

Public Health Service, U. S. (cont'd)

PHS   The Health Consequences of Smoking, 1969 Supplement to the 1967 Public Health
1969   Review. Public Health Service Publ No. 1696-2. Washington, D. C.: U. S.
           Department of Health, Education and Welfare.

Public Roads, U. S. Bureau of

1969   Highway Statistics, 1968. Washington, D. C.: U. S. Department of Transportation.

Rossi, Alice S.

1964   "Equality between the sexes: an immodest proposal." Daedalus, 93, No. 2
           (Spring) 607-670.

Schmitt, George F.

1968   Diabetes for Diabetics. Miami, Fla.: Diabetes Press of America, Inc.

Sheldon, Eleanor Bernert, and Wilbert E. Moore (eds.)

1968   Indicators of Social Change: Concepts and Measurements. New York: Russell Sage
           Foundation.

Siegel, Alberta Engvall, Lois Meek Stolz, Ethel Alice Hitchcock, Jean Adamson

1963   "Dependence and independence in children." Pp. 67-81 in F. Ivan Nye and Lois W.
           Hoffman (eds.), The Employed Mother in America. Chicago: Rand McNally & Co.

Sills, David L.

1968   "Voluntary associations: sociological aspects," in David L. Sills (ed.)
           (ed.), International Encyclopedia of the Social Sciences, Vol. 16, pp. 362-
           379. New York, Macmillan Co. and Free Press.

Simon, Kenneth A., and W. Vance Grant

1967   Digest of Educational Statistics, 1967 Edition. OE-10024-67. Washington,
           D. C.: U. S. Office of Education.

Steinberg, Joseph

1953   "The current population survey," in Morris H. Hansen, William N. Hurwitz and
           William G. Madow (eds.), Sample Survey Methods and Theory, Methods and
           Application, Vol. 1, pp. 559-582. New York: John Wiley & Sons, Inc.

U. S. President

1970   Economic Report of the President. Transmitted to the Congress February 1970.
           Washington, D. C.: U. S. Government Printing Office.

Vincent, Clark E.

1968   "Illegitimacy," in David L. Sills (ed.), International Encyclopedia of the
           Social Sciences, Vol. 7, pp. 85-90. New York: Macmillan Co. and Free Press.

Vital Statistics, U. S. National Office of

VS   Vital Statistics of the United States, 1947, Part I. Washington, D. C.: U. S.
1949   Department of Health, Education and Welfare.

VS   Vital Statistics of the United States; 1949, Part I. Washington, D. C.: U. S.
1951   Department of Health, Education and Welfare.

VS   Vital Statistics of the United States, 1950, Vol. I. Washington, D. C.: U. S.
1954a   Department of Health, Education and Welfare.

VS   Vital Statistics of the United States, 1951, Vol. I. Washington, D. C.: U. S.
1954b   Department of Health, Education and Welfare.

VS   Vital Statistics of the United States, 1953, Vol. I. Washington, D. C.: U. S.
1955   Department of Health, Education and Welfare.

VS   Vital Statistics of the United States, 1955, Vol. I. Washington, D. C.: U. S.
1957   Department of Health, Education and Welfare.

Vital Statistics, U. S. National Office of (cont'd)

VS   Vital Statistics of the United States, 1957, Vol. I. Washington, D. C.: U. S.
1959   Department of Health, Education and Welfare.

VS   Vital Statistics of the United States, 1958, Vol. I. Washington, D. C.: U. S.
1960   Department of Health, Education and Welfare.

VS   Vital Statistics of the United States, 1959, Vol. I. Washington, D. C.: U. S.
1961   Department of Health, Education and Welfare.

Women's Bureau, U. S.

Women's   1948 Handbook of Facts on Women Workers. Bulletin 225. Washington, D. C.:
Bureau   U. S. Department of Labor.
1948

Women's   1950 Handbook of Facts on Women Workers. Bulletin 237. Washington, D. C.:
Bureau   U. S. Department of Labor.
1950

Women's   1952 Handbook of Facts on Women Workers. Bulletin 242. Washington, D. C.:
Bureau   U. S. Department of Labor.
1952

Women's   1954 Handbook on Women Workers. Bulletin 255. Washington, D. C.: U. S.
Bureau   Department of Labor.
1954

Women's   1956 Handbook on Women Workers. Bulletin 261. Washington, D. C.: U. S.
Bureau   Department of Labor.
1956

Women's   1960 Handbook on Women Workers. Bulletin 275. Washington, D. C.: U. S.
Bureau   Department of Labor.
1960

Women's   1965 Handbook on Women Workers. Bulletin 290. Washington, D. C.: U. S.
Bureau   Department of Labor.
1965

Women's   1969 Handbook on Women Workers. Bulletin 294. Washington, D. C.: U. S
Bureau   Department of Labor.
1969

World Almanac

1970   The World Almanac. (Annual issues 1961-1970). New York: World-Telegram
         and Sun (through 1966); Newspaper Enterprise Association (1967-1970).

Wright, Charles R., and Herbert H. Hyman

1958   "Voluntary association memberships of American adults: evidence from national
         sample surveys." American Sociological Review 23 (February) 284-294.